THE THEOLOGY OF THE BODY
Human Love in the Divine Plan

John Paul II

With a Foreword by
John S. Grabowski, Ph.D.

Pauline
BOOKS & MEDIA

BOSTON

Library of Congress Cataloging-in-Publication Data

John Paul II, Pope, 1920–

The theology of the body according to John Paul II : human love in the divine plan / John Paul II ; with a foreword by John S. Grabowski.

    p.   cm.

"Reprinted with permission from L'Osservatore Romano, English ed."—T.p. verso.

Includes index.

ISBN 0-8198-7394-2

1. Body, Human—Religious aspects—Catholic Church. 2. Catholic Church—Doctrines.   I. Title.

BT741.2.J64   1997

233'.5—dc21   97-15020
                                                    CIP

The material in this volume was originally published in four books: *Original Unity of Man and Woman, Blessed Are the Pure of Heart, The Theology of Marriage and Celibacy,* and *Reflections on* Humanae Vitae.

Reprinted with permission from *L'Osservatore Romano,* English Edition.

Printed in the U.S.A. by Pauline Books & Media, 50 St. Paul's Avenue, Boston, MA 02130.

www.pauline.org

Pauline Books & Media is the publishing house of the Daughters of St. Paul, an international congregation of women religious serving the Church with the communications media.

4 5 6 7 8 9 10 11   09 08 07 06 05 04 03 02

CONTENTS

Blessed Are the Pure of Heart

Catechesis on the Sermon on the Mount

PART TWO

Life according to the Spirit

St. Paul's Teaching on the Human Body

The Resurrection of the Body

Virginity for the Sake of the Kingdom

The Sacramentality of Marriage

Reflections on "Humanae Vitae"

Appendix

Index

FOREWORD

Karol Wojtyla, known to the world since 1978 as Pope John Paul II, has always been fascinated by the human person. As a university student in Poland during the dark days of its Nazi occupation, Wojtyla wrote plays which used biblical motifs to explore the suffering and identity of his people. Following the war, while Poland continued to suffer under a now Marxist form of totalitarianism, the newly ordained Fr. Wojtyla wrote still more plays wrestling with the meaning of human existence *(Our God's Brother)*. As his ministry grew and deepened, so did the range of subjects he treated in his plays. They extended from happiness and failure in marriage *(The Jewelers Shop),* to the situation of fallen humanity confronted by God's redemptive love *(The Radiation of Fatherhood).*

At the same time that his skill as a playwright matured, Karol Wojtyla was also honing his skills as a philosopher. His doctoral dissertation in philosophy attempted to explore the new philosophy of consciousness known as phenomenology as the basis for an exposition of Christian ethics. This subject would occupy much of his teaching career at the University of Lublin. It would also form the basis for his synthesis of St. Thomas' philosophy of being and a phenomenological account of human action and experience in the opus *The Acting Person.*

But Wojtyla's laboratory encompassed more than the library and the lectern. He also learned a great deal from his pastoral ministry as a priest, bishop, and finally cardinal. As cardinal of the huge diocese of Krakow, Wojtyla worked to establish programs which would help married couples live the Church's teaching on sexuality and marriage. The experience gained in his extensive pastoral work helped him develop a new philosophical account of Catholic sexual ethics in *Love and Responsibility.*

Especially important in his mind was the articulation of a cogent modern rationale for the Church's position on birth regulation. Whereas

Catholic moralists of preceding generations had treated contraception as a violation of chastity or a frustration of the natural law, Wojtyla developed a new personalist approach based on his philosophical work. In this view sexual intercourse in marriage has an inherent meaning of total bodily self-giving. Contraception overlays this meaning with a contradictory language of withholding and refusal. The fertility which is withheld or refused is not simply a superficial, biological component of the person which can be manipulated in the pursuit of other ends, but an aspect of the person as a whole. Contraception therefore violates the dignity of the person because it falsifies the total offering of self which intercourse is meant to express.

Wojtyla's pastoral and philosophical work earned him a spot on the Pontifical Study Commission on Family Population and Birth Problems called by John XXIII and repeatedly expanded by Paul VI during the first years of his pontificate. The Communist authorities in Poland prevented Wojtyla from attending the decisive final meetings of the commission. But his personal consultations with Paul VI and his published work were influential in *Humanae Vitae's* reiteration of the Church's traditional ban of artificial contraception (1968).

As a bishop in the diocese of Krakow with a budding scholarly career, Wojtyla was also an active participant in the Second Vatican Council. There he helped to draft important sections of the Council's Pastoral Constitution on the Church, *Gaudium et Spes*. At the same time he was deeply impressed by the document's understanding of the human person within the mystery of Christ:

> The truth is that only in the mystery of the incarnate Word does the mystery of man take on light.... Christ, the new Adam, in the very revelation of the mystery of the Father and of his love, fully reveals man to himself and brings to light his most high calling *(GS* 22 as cited in *Redemptor Hominis* 8).

Hence the central point of reference for any adequate understanding of the human person is the Incarnate Son of God. This theme would figure prominently in John Paul II's first encyclical, *Redemptor Hominis.*

Since his elevation to the papacy, John Paul II has continued to focus on the human person as revealed in the light of Christ. In this context we can locate his weekly general audiences which comprise the theology of the body. Given between September 1979 and November 1984, these audiences comprise a catechesis on the bodily dimension of human personhood, sexuality, and marriage in the light of biblical revelation.

The point of departure for this catechesis is found in Jesus' response to the Pharisees' question concerning the permissibility of divorce (cf. Mt

19:4-6). When confronted with such a fundamental question about the meaning of marriage and human sexuality, Jesus appealed to "the beginning" described in the opening chapters of Genesis. John Paul II proposes to do the same. While these chapters may be "mythic" in the sense that they are not history as we understand it, they nevertheless offer fundamental theological truths about the embodied human person and can shed light on our own present day experience.

Through this remarkable form of biblical analysis, the Pope locates and develops three such original experiences of humanity in the Garden of Eden: original solitude, original unity, and original nakedness. The first man depicted in Genesis, like all men and women, was aware of himself as a subject, an "I." Yet he also discovered the uniqueness of his existence because, unlike the animals whom he named (cf. Gn 2:19), his body was capable of expressing his subjectivity and freedom. This solitude provided an opportunity to respond in gratitude and obedience to the Creator. Yet it also produced a profound longing for another being like himself (cf. Gn 2:18).

This longing is answered in the creation of woman—another person, equal in dignity, another "I" revealed through the body. Yet this body was wonderfully different from that of the man, revealing a unique and "original" way of being a person. Far from dividing humanity, these differences were intended to summon them together in the unity of love. The body thus has a "nuptial" meaning which points toward the human need for community. The most fundamental and intense form of human community is the unity of man and woman in the covenant of marriage. When this communion is characterized by authentic self-giving love, marriage becomes a "communion of persons" which reflects God's own trinitarian life (cf. the general audience of January 16, 1980; and *Mulieris Dignitatem* 7).

The most intimate expression of this communion with marriage takes place through the bodies of husband and wife. In sexual self-donation the couple indeed speaks a "language of the body," expressing in a manner far more profound than words the totality of their gift to each other. In this embodied dialogue of mutual love the couple continually discovers each other and themselves more deeply. Hence the biblical expression for intercourse—"to know" (cf. Gn 4:la)—is especially apt since it expresses the knowledge gained in sexual self-giving.

As intended by God, this language spoken by husband and wife through their naked bodies was unattended by shame (cf. Gn 2:25). John Paul contrasts this shameless discovery of the nuptial character of the body with the experience of shame after the fall (cf. Gn 3:7). The experience of original nakedness given to us in the revealed text points to a time of integration within human persons when there was no "interior rupture and opposition between what is spiritual and what is sensible." It also points to a time of harmony between man and woman when there was no "rupture and opposition between...male and female" (cf. the general audience of January 2, 1980).

Sin shattered the original integrity of the person and the unity between male and female. The Pope describes the fall as "a constitutive break within the human person...almost a rupture of man's original spiritual and somatic unity" (cf. the general audience of May 28, 1980). In this fallen state, the body is no longer subordinated to the spirit and so its capacity to express the person is radically diminished. Now the experience of nakedness brings shame and fear (cf. Gn 3:7, 10). The unity between man and woman is also broken and replaced by suspicion and alienation. Rather than self-donation, masculine-feminine relationships are marked by domination and subservience. In the words of Yahweh to the woman following the sin of the first pair, "He shall rule over you" (Gn 3:16b), John Paul II sees a depiction of male "domination" of and discrimination against women (cf. *MD* 10). This domination diminishes the dignity of both sexes, but it has more serious consequences for the woman insofar as she is made the object of male control.

This also points to the heart of what the Pope means when he speaks of lust. It is the propensity of fallen humanity to regard others not as persons, but as objects to be controlled or means to be used for personal gratification. This lust limits both the nuptial character of the body and the ability of the individual to form a communion of persons with others. As fallen, humanity is faced with its own constant inclination to sin known as concupiscence. This inclination is continually played out in the relationship between the sexes (cf. *MD* 10).

But if the Pope's understanding of the person takes account of the ravages of sin, it is even more profoundly marked by hope in the power of the redemption. While it does not erase humanity's history as a fallen race or restore men and women to a state of original innocence, the grace of Christ makes it possible for them to live as God intended "from the beginning." This includes what John Paul calls the "redemption of the body," in which grace enables the body to once again express the person as it did at creation. Such an idea implies that the reality of creation already included humanity's election in Christ (cf. Eph 12:3-4). Hence marriage is a "primordial sacrament" (cf. the general audience of October 6, 1982).

Grace also overcomes the alienation between the sexes, making possible an appreciation of both their equal dignity and their irreducible "originality" as persons. This transformation is especially evident in marriage, where authority within marital communion comes to be understood and lived as "mutual subjection out of reverence for Christ" (Eph 5:21; cf. *MD* 24). When this communion is characterized by authentic self-giving love where each lives for the other, the Christian family becomes a manifestation of the eternal communion within the Trinity.

If the self-giving of marriage is a paradigm for all human community and indeed for the whole of reality, where does religious celibacy fit within the Pope's vision? For John Paul, consecrated virginity or celibacy is also a pre-eminent way of giving oneself to another in which the body expresses the person. Celibacy also points to the marital character of reality since it is a response of the person to the love of the Divine Spouse. Thus celibacy and marriage are two mutually illuminating realities through which human persons can realize their own humanity by being for another.

This catechesis also has practical moral implications, especially in regard to the crucial issue of birth regulation. In this regard, John Paul offers two distinct lines of argument for the Church's teaching. The first is a restatement of his personalist understanding which he developed as a professional philosopher. Contraception violates the language of the body as complete self-giving of the whole person (cf. the general audience of August 22, 1984; *EV* 13, 42). But here he adds a second line of argument. This teaching is not simply based on human reason (i.e., the natural law), but also "the moral order revealed by God" (cf. the general audience of July 18, 1984). The biblical text itself links the knowledge gained in sexual self-giving with motherhood and fatherhood (cf. Gn 4:1 a-b; the general audience of March 12, 1980; *EV* 43). In so doing he has provided a new source and a more authoritative foundation for the traditional Catholic understanding of this issue.

This present volume contains the whole of the magnificent vision presented in the Pope's catechesis on the body. Previously published as separate books *(Original Unity of Man and Woman; Blessed Are the Pure of Heart; The Theology of Marriage and Celibacy;* and *Reflections on "Humanae Vitae"),* these audiences are here brought together in a single source. Also included is Paul VI's landmark encyclical *Humanae Vitae.* As noted above, the elaboration and defense of the Church's position on birth regulation occupied much of Karol Wojtyla's work as professional philosopher and a pastor in Poland. It has also served as a stimulus for much of his continued reflection and teaching as Pope, including that offered within the catechesis on the body.

But this present volume offers more than simply John Paul II's theology of the body and its historical catalyst. It also contains two more authoritative developments and applications of the Pope's vision of the body-person. The first is his apostolic letter *Mulieris Dignitatem* promulgated within the Marian Year of 1988. This letter is a development and application of aspects of the theology of the body to the specific question of the dignity and vocation of women in relation to men. The second is his encyclical *Evangelium Vitae,* promulgated in 1995. This document is an authoritative defense of the value of human life at all stages in the light of the Gospel message.

The common thread which unites all of John Paul's teaching contained in this book is a focus on the human person in the light of the mystery of Christ. While much of the teaching of Paul VI in *Humanae Vitae* was based on an appeal to the natural law, John Paul II consistently bases his teaching, not only on the dignity of the person, but on biblical revelation. Thus it is primarily an exposition of various biblical texts which frames the teaching offered within the catechesis on the theology of the body, *Mulieris Dignitatem,* and *Evangelium Vitae.* This is consistent with the Pope's teaching as a whole. Whether grounding his understanding of morality within the invitation to discipleship which Jesus extended to the rich young man of Matthew 19 (cf. *Veritatis Splendor),* or his theology of work within the opening chapters of Genesis (cf. the social teaching in *Laborem Exercens),* John Paul II has attempted to make the human person revealed in the light of Christ the basis of the Church's teaching in sexual, social and medical morality.

The last thing which the reader of this volume should know is that the papal teaching contained here is not all of equal authority. In general, encyclical letters are more solemn than apostolic letters, and both of these genres are more weighty than catechesis offered in weekly papal audiences. This is most evident in the solemn condemnations of direct killing of the innocent (no. 57), direct abortion (no. 62), and euthanasia (no. 65) in *Evangelium Vitae.* But the whole of this encyclical is also authoritative, given the exposition of biblical thought which undergirds its presentation of the Church's life ethic. The teaching of Paul VI in *Humanae Vitae,* while based in natural law arguments, nevertheless represents a restatement of the Church's constant and authoritative tradition on the issue of artificial contraception. *Mulieris Dignitatem* addresses relatively new issues of sexual equality in the family and the Church, and therefore does not carry the same weight, but is still authentic magisterial teaching. The weekly general audiences on the body, even though they do not enjoy the same authority, form the indispensable backdrop for understanding these more weighty teachings. The understanding of the equal dignity and irreducible differences between the sexes, and the nuptial meaning of the body are integral to that authentic understanding of sexuality which is needed to build a new "culture of life" (cf. *EV* 95-100).

John S. Grabowski, Ph.D.

March 13, 1997

The Catholic University of America

PART ONE

ORIGINAL UNITY
OF MAN AND WOMAN

Catechesis on the Book of Genesis

The Unity and Indissolubility of Marriage

For some time now preparations have been going on for the next ordinary assembly of the Synod of Bishops, which will take place in Rome
in autumn of next year. The theme of the Synod, "The role of the Christian
family," concentrates our attention on this community of human and
Christian life, which has been fundamental from the beginning. The Lord
Jesus used precisely this expression "from the beginning" in the talk about
marriage, reported in the Gospels of St. Matthew and St. Mark. We wish to
raise the question what this word "beginning" means. We also wish
to clarify why Christ referred to the "beginning" on that occasion and,
therefore, we propose a more precise analysis of the relative text of Holy
Scripture.

During the talk with the Pharisees, who asked him the question about
the indissolubility of marriage, Jesus Christ referred twice to the "beginning." The talk took place in the following way:

"And Pharisees came up to him and tested him by asking, 'Is it lawful to divorce one's wife for any cause?' He answered, 'Have you not read
that he who made them from the beginning made them male and female,
and said, 'For this reason a man shall leave his father and mother and be
joined to his wife, and the two shall become one flesh'? So they are no
longer two but one flesh. What therefore God has joined together, let not
man put asunder.' They said to him, 'Why then did Moses command one
to give a certificate of divorce, and to put her away?' He said to them, 'For
your hardness of heart Moses allowed you to divorce your wives, but from
the beginning it was not so'" (Mt 19:3ff., cf. also Mk 10:2ff.).

Christ did not accept the discussion at the level at which his interlocutors tried to introduce it. In a certain sense he did not approve of

the dimension that they tried to give the problem. He avoided getting caught up in juridico-casuistical controversies. On the contrary, he referred twice to "the beginning." Acting in this way, he made a clear reference to the relative words in Genesis, which his interlocutors too knew by heart. From those words of the ancient revelation, Christ drew the conclusion and the talk ended.

Therefore, "the beginning" means that which Genesis speaks about. Christ quoted Genesis 1:27 in summary form: "In the beginning the Creator made them male and female." The original passage reads textually as follows: "God created man in his own image; in the image of God he created him; male and female he created them." Subsequently, the Master referred to Genesis 2:24: "Therefore, a man leaves his father and his mother and cleaves to his wife, and they become one flesh." Quoting these words almost in full, Christ gave them an even more explicit normative meaning (since it could be supported that in Genesis they express *de facto* statements: "leaves...cleaves...they become one flesh"). The normative meaning is plausible since Christ did not confine himself only to the quotation itself, but added: "So they are no longer two but one flesh. What therefore God has joined together, let not man put asunder." That "let not man put asunder" is decisive. In the light of these words of Christ, Genesis 2:24 sets forth the principle of the unity and indissolubility of marriage as the very content of the Word of God, expressed in the most ancient revelation.

It could be maintained at this point that the problem is exhausted, that Jesus Christ's words confirm the eternal law formulated and set up by God from "the beginning" as the creation of man. It might also seem that the Master, confirming this original law of the Creator, did nothing but establish exclusively his own normative meaning, referring to the authority itself of the first Legislator. However, that significant expression "from the beginning," repeated twice, clearly induced his interlocutors to reflect on the way in which man was formed in the mystery of creation, precisely as "male and female," in order to understand correctly the normative sense of the words of Genesis. This is no less valid for the people of today than for those of that time. Therefore, in the present study, considering all this, we must put ourselves precisely in the position of Christ's interlocutors today.

During the following Wednesday reflections at the general audiences, we will try, as Christ's interlocutors today, to dwell at greater length on St. Matthew's words (19:3ff.). To respond to the indication, inserted in them by Christ, we will try to penetrate toward that "beginning," to which he referred in such a significant way. Thus we will follow from a distance the great work which participants in the forthcoming Synod of Bishops are undertaking on this subject just now. Together with them, numerous groups of pastors and laymen are taking part in it, feeling especially responsible with regard to the role which Christ assigned to marriage and the Christian family, the role that he has always given, and still gives in our age, in the modern world.

The cycle of reflections we are beginning today, with the intention of continuing it during the following Wednesday meetings, also has the purpose, among other things, of accompanying from afar the work of preparation for the Synod. However, it will not touch its subject directly, but will turn our attention to the deep roots from which this subject springs.

General audience of September 5, 1979

Analysis of the Biblical Account of Creation

Last Wednesday we began this series of reflections on the reply Christ gave to his questioners on the subject of the unity and indissolubility of marriage. As we recall, the Pharisees who questioned him appealed to the Mosaic Law. However, Christ went back to the "beginning," quoting the words of Genesis.

The "beginning" in this case concerns what one of the first pages of Genesis treats. If we wish to analyze this reality, we must undoubtedly direct our attention first of all to the text. The words which Christ spoke in his talk with the Pharisees, found in Matthew 19 and Mark 10, constitute a passage which in its turn is set in a well-defined context, without reference to which they can neither be understood nor correctly interpreted.

This context is provided by the words, "Have you not read that the Creator from the beginning made them male and female...?" (Mt 19:4). It referred to the so-called first account of the creation of man inserted in the seven day cycle of the creation of the world (cf. Gn 1:1-2, 4). However, the context nearest to the other words of Christ, taken from Genesis 2:24, is the so-called second account of the creation of man (Gn 2:5-25). But indirectly it is the entire third chapter of Genesis.

The second account of the creation of man forms a conceptual and stylistic unity with the description of original innocence, man's happiness, and also his first fall. Granted the specific content of Christ's words taken from Genesis 2:24, one could also include in the context at least the first phrase of the fourth chapter of Genesis, which treats of the conception and birth of man from earthly parents. That is what we intend to do in the present analysis.

From the point of view of biblical criticism, it is necessary to mention immediately that the first account of man's creation is chronologically later than the second, whose origin is much more remote. This more ancient text is defined as "Yahwist" because the term "Yahweh" is used to name God. It is difficult not to be struck by the fact that the image of God presented there has quite considerable anthropomorphic traits. Among others, we read that "...the Lord God formed man of dust from the ground, and breathed into his nostrils the breath of life" (Gn 2:7).

In comparison with this description, the first account, that is, the one held to be chronologically later, is much more mature both as regards the image of God, and as regards the formulation of the essential truths about man. This account derives from the priestly and "Elohist" tradition, from "Elohim," the term used in that account for God.

In this narration man's creation as male and female—to which Jesus referred in his reply according to Matthew 19—is inserted into the seven day cycle of the creation of the world. A cosmological character could especially be attributed to it. Man is created on earth together with the visible world. But at the same time the Creator orders him to subdue and have dominion over the earth (cf. Gn 1:28); therefore he is placed over the world. Even though man is strictly bound to the visible world, the biblical narrative does not speak of his likeness to the rest of creatures, but only to God. "God created man in his own image; in the image of God he created him..." (Gn 1:27). In the seven day cycle of creation a precise graduated procedure is evident.[1] However, man is not created according to a natural succession. The Creator seems to halt before calling him into existence, as if he were pondering within himself to make a decision: "Let us make man in our image, after our likeness..." (Gn 1:26).

The level of that first account of man's creation, even though chronologically later, is especially of a theological character. An indication of that is especially the definition of man on the basis of his relationship with God. "In the image of God he created him." At the same time it affirms the absolute impossibility of reducing man to the world. Already in the light of the first phrases of the Bible, man cannot be either understood or explained completely in terms of categories taken from the "world," that is, from the visible complex of bodies. Notwithstanding this, man also is corporeal. Genesis 1:27 observes that this essential truth about man referred both to the male and the female: "God created man in his image...male and female he created them."[2] It must be recognized that the first account is concise, and free from any trace whatsoever of subjectivism. It contains only the objective facts and defines the objective reality, both when it speaks of man's creation, male and female, in the image of God, and when it adds a little later the words of the first blessing: "Be fruitful and multiply, and fill the earth; subdue it and have dominion over it" (Gn 1:28).

The first account of man's creation, which, as we observed, is of a theological nature, conceals within itself a powerful metaphysical content. Let it not be forgotten that this text of Genesis has become the source of the most profound inspirations for thinkers who have sought to understand "being" and "existence." (Perhaps only the third chapter of Exodus can bear comparison with this text.)[3] Notwithstanding certain detailed and plastic expressions of the passage, man is defined there, first of all, in the dimensions of being and of existence *("esse")*. He is defined in a way that is more metaphysical than physical.

To this mystery of his creation, ("In the image of God he created him"), corresponds the perspective of procreation, ("Be fruitful and multiply, fill the earth"), of that becoming in the world and in time, of that *fieri* which is necessarily bound up with the metaphysical situation of creation: of contingent being *(contingens)*. Precisely in this metaphysical context of the description of Genesis 1, it is necessary to understand the entity of the good, namely, the aspect of value. Indeed, this aspect appears in the cycle of nearly all the days of creation and reaches its culmination after the creation of man: "God saw everything that he had made, and behold, it was very good" (Gn 1:31). For this reason it can be said with certainty that the first chapter of Genesis has established an unassailable point of reference and a solid basis for a metaphysic and also for an anthropology and an ethic, according to which *ens et bonum convertuntur* (being and the good are convertible). Undoubtedly, all this also has a significance for theology, and especially for the theology of the body.

At this point let us interrupt our considerations. In a week's time we shall deal with the second account of creation. According to biblical scholars, it is chronologically more ancient. The expression "theology of the body" just now used deserves a more exact explanation, but we shall leave that for another occasion. First, we must seek to examine more closely that passage of Genesis which Christ had recourse to.

General audience of September 12, 1979

The Second Account of Creation:
The Subjective Definition of Man

With reference to Christ's words on the subject of marriage, in which he appealed to the "beginning," we directed our attention last week to the first account of man's creation in the first chapter of Genesis. Today we shall pass to the second account, which is frequently described as the "Yahwist," since it uses the name "Yahweh" for God.

The second account of man's creation (linked to the presentation both of original innocence and happiness and of the first fall) has by its nature a different character. While not wishing to anticipate the particulars of this narrative—because it will be better for us to recall them in later analyses—we should note that the entire text, in formulating the truth about man, amazes us with its typical profundity, different from that of the first chapter of Genesis.

This profundity has a especially subjective nature and is therefore, in a certain sense, psychological. The second chapter of Genesis constitutes, in a certain manner, the most ancient description and record of man's self-knowledge. Together with the third chapter it is the first testimony of human conscience. A reflection in depth on this text—through the whole archaic form of the narrative, which manifests its primitive mythical character[4]—provides us *in nucleo* with nearly all the elements of the analysis of man, to which modern, and especially contemporary philosophical anthropology is sensitive. It could be said that Genesis 2 presents the creation of man especially in its subjective aspect. Comparing both accounts, we conclude that this subjectivity corresponds to the objective reality of man created "in the image of God." This fact also is—in another way—important for the theology of the body, as we shall see in subsequent analyses.

It is significant that in his reply to the Pharisees, in which he appealed to the "beginning," Christ indicated first of all the creation of man by referring to Genesis 1:27: "The Creator from the beginning created them male and female." Only afterward did he quote the text of Genesis 2:24. The words which directly describe the unity and indissolubility of marriage are found in the immediate context of the second account of creation. Its characteristic feature is the separate creation of woman (cf. Gn 2:18-23), while the account of the creation of the first man is found in Genesis 2:5-7.

The Bible calls the first human being "man" *('adam),* but from the moment of the creation of the first woman, it begins to call him "man" *(ish),* in relation to *ishshah* ("woman," because she was taken from the man—*ish).*[5] It is also significant that in referring to Genesis 2:24, Christ not only linked the "beginning" with the mystery of creation, but also led us, one might say, to the limit of man's primitive innocence and of original sin. Genesis places the second description of man's creation precisely in this context. There we read first of all: "And the rib which the Lord God had taken from the man he made into a woman and brought her to the man; then the man said: 'This at last is bone of my bones and flesh of my flesh; she shall be called woman, because she was taken out of man'" (Gn 2:22-23). "Therefore a man leaves his father and his mother and cleaves to his wife, and they become one flesh" (Gn 2:24). "And the man and his wife were both naked, and they were not ashamed" (Gn 2:25).

Immediately after these verses, chapter 3 begins with its account of the first fall of the man and the woman, linked with the mysterious tree already called the "tree of the knowledge of good and evil" (Gn 2:17). Thus an entirely new situation emerges, essentially different from the preceding. The tree of knowledge of good and evil is the line of demarcation between the two original situations which Genesis speaks of.

The first situation was that of original innocence, in which man (male and female) was, as it were, outside the sphere of the knowledge of good and evil, until the moment when he transgressed the Creator's prohibition and ate the fruit of the tree of knowledge. The second situation, however, was that in which man, after having disobeyed the Creator's command at the prompting of the evil spirit, symbolized by the serpent, found himself, in a certain way, within the sphere of the knowledge of good and evil. This second situation determined the state of human sinfulness, in contrast to the state of primitive innocence.

Even though the "Yahwist" text is very concise, it suffices with clarity to differentiate and to set against each other those two original situations. We speak here of situations, having before our eyes the account which is a description of events. Nonetheless, by means of this description and all its particulars, the essential difference emerges between the state of man's sinfulness and that of his original innocence.[6]

Systematic theology will discern in these two antithetical situations two different states of human nature: the state of integral nature and the state of fallen nature. All this emerges from that "Yahwist" text of Genesis 2-3, which contains in itself the most ancient word of revelation. Evidently it has a fundamental significance for the theology of man and for the theology of the body.

When Christ, referring to the "beginning," directed his questioners to the words written in Genesis 2:24, he ordered them, in a certain sense, to go beyond the boundary which, in the Yahwist text of Genesis, runs between the first and second situation of man. He did not approve what Moses had permitted "for their hardness of heart." He appealed to the words of the first divine regulation, which in this text is expressly linked to man's state of original innocence. This means that this regulation has not lost its force, even though man has lost his primitive innocence.

Christ's reply is decisive and unequivocal. Therefore, we must draw from it the normative conclusions which have an essential significance not only for ethics, but especially for the theology of man and for the theology of the body. As a particular element of theological anthropology, it is

constituted on the basis of the Word of God which is revealed. During the
next meeting we shall seek to draw these conclusions.

General audience of September 19, 1979

The Boundary between Original Innocence and Redemption

Answering the question on the unity and indissolubility of marriage,
Christ referred to what was written about marriage in Genesis. In our two
preceding reflections we analyzed both the so-called Elohist text (Gn 1)
and the Yahwist one (Gn 2). Today we wish to draw some conclusions
from these analyses.

When Christ referred to the "beginning," he asked his questioners to
go beyond, in a certain sense, the boundary which in Genesis passes between the state of original innocence and that of sinfulness, which started
with the original fall.

Symbolically this boundary can be linked with the tree of the knowledge of good and evil, which in the Yahwist text delimits two diametrically opposed situations: the situation of original innocence and that of
original sin. These situations have a specific dimension in man, in his
inner self, in his knowledge, conscience, choice and decision. All this is in
relation to God the Creator who, in the Yahwist text (Gn 2 and 3), is at the
same time the God of the covenant, of the most ancient covenant of the
Creator with his creature—man.

As an expression and symbol of the covenant with God broken in
man's heart, the tree of the knowledge of good and evil delimits and contrasts two diametrically opposed situations and states: that of original innocence and that of original sin, and at the same time man's hereditary
sinfulness which derives from it. However, Christ's words, which refer to
the "beginning," enable us to find in man an essential continuity and a link
between these two different states or dimensions of the human being.

The state of sin is part of "historical man," both the one whom we
read about in Matthew 19, that is, Christ's questioner at that time, and also
of any other potential or actual questioner of all times of history, and
therefore, naturally, also of modern man. That state, however—the "historical" state—plunges its roots, in every man without exception, in his
own theological "prehistory," which is the state of original innocence.

It is not a question here of mere dialectic. The laws of knowing correspond to those of being. It is impossible to understand the state of historical sinfulness without referring or appealing (and Christ appealed to it)
to the state of original (in a certain sense, "prehistoric") and fundamental

innocence. Therefore, right from the beginning, the arising of sinfulness as a state, a dimension of human existence, is in relation to this real innocence of man as his original and fundamental state, as a dimension of his being created in the image of God.

It happens in this way not only for the first man, male and female, as *dramatis personae* and leading characters of the events described in the Yahwist text of chapters 2 and 3 of Genesis, but also for the whole historical course of human existence. Historical man is, so to speak, rooted in his revealed theological prehistory. So every point of his historical sinfulness is explained (both for the soul and for the body) with reference to original innocence. It can be said that this reference is a "co-inheritance" of sin, and precisely of original sin. If this sin signifies, in every historical man, a state of lost grace, then it also contains a reference to that grace, which was precisely the grace of original innocence.

According to chapter 19 of Matthew, when Christ referred to the "beginning," by this expression he did not indicate merely the state of original innocence as the lost horizon of human existence in history. To the words which he uttered with his own lips, we have the right to attribute at the same time the whole eloquence of the mystery of redemption. Already in the Yahwist texts of Genesis 2 and 3, we are witnesses of when man, male and female, after breaking the original covenant with the Creator, received the first promise of redemption in the words of the so-called *Proto-gospel* in Genesis 3:15[7] and began to live in the theological perspective of the redemption.

In the same way, therefore, historical man—both Christ's questioner at that time, of whom Matthew 19 speaks, and modern man—participates in this perspective. He participates not only in the history of human sinfulness, as a hereditary and at the same time personal and unique subject of this history; he also participates in the history of salvation, here, too, as its subject and co-creator. Therefore, he is not only closed, because of his sinfulness, with regard to original innocence, but is at the same time open to the mystery of redemption, which was accomplished in Christ and through Christ.

Paul, the author of the Letter to the Romans, expresses this perspective of redemption in which historical man lives, when he writes: "We ourselves, who have the first fruits of the Spirit, groan inwardly as we wait for...the redemption of our bodies" (Rom 8:23). We cannot lose sight of this perspective as we follow the words of Christ who, in his talk on the indissolubility of marriage, appealed to the "beginning."

If that beginning indicated only the creation of man as male and female, if—as we have already mentioned—it brought the questioners only over the boundary of man's state of sin to original innocence, and did not open at the same time the perspective of a "redemption of the body," Christ's answer would not at all be adequately understood. Precisely this perspective of the redemption of the body guarantees the continuity and unity between the hereditary state of man's sin and his original innocence, although this innocence was, historically, lost by him irremediably. It is clear, too, that Christ had every right to answer the question posed by the doctors of the law and of the covenant (as we read in Matthew 19 and in Mark 10), in the perspective of the redemption on which the covenant itself rests.

In the context of the theology of corporeal man, substantially outlined in this way, we can think of the method of further analyses about the revelation of the "beginning," in which it is essential to refer to the first chapters of Genesis. We must at once turn our attention to a factor which is especially important for theological interpretation, because it consists in the relationship between revelation and experience.[8]

In the interpretation of the revelation about man, and especially about the body, we must, for understandable reasons, refer to experience, since corporeal man is perceived by us mainly by experience. In the light of the above mentioned fundamental considerations, we have every right to the conviction that this "historical" experience of ours must, in a certain way, stop at the threshold of man's original innocence, since it is inadequate in relation to it. However, in the light of the same introductory considerations, we must arrive at the conviction that our human experience is, in this case, to some extent a legitimate means for the theological interpretation. In a certain sense, it is an indispensable point of reference, which we must keep in mind for interpreting the beginning. A more detailed analysis of the text will enable us to have a clearer view of it.

It seems that the words of Romans 8:23, just quoted, render in the best way the direction of our researches centered on the revelation of that "beginning" which Christ referred to in his talk on the indissolubility of marriage (cf. Mt 19 and Mk 10). All the subsequent analyses that will be made on the basis of the first chapters of Genesis will almost necessarily reflect the truth of Paul's words: "We who have the first fruit of the Spirit groan inwardly as we wait for...the redemption of our bodies." If we put ourselves in this position—so deeply in agreement with experience—the "beginning" must speak to us with the great richness of light that comes from revelation, to which above all theology wishes to be accountable. The continuation of the analyses will explain to us why and in what sense this must be a theology of the body.

General audience of September 26, 1979

The Meaning of Man's Original Solitude

In the last reflection of the present cycle we reached an introductory conclusion, taken from the words of Genesis on the creation of man as male and female. We reached these words, that is, the "beginning," to which the Lord Jesus referred in his talk on the indissolubility of marriage (cf. Mt 19:3-9; Mk 10:1-12). But the conclusion at which we arrived does not yet end the series of our analyses. We must reread the narrations of the first and second chapters of Genesis in a wider context, which will allow us to establish a series of meanings of the ancient text to which Christ referred. Therefore, today we will reflect on the meaning of man's original solitude.

The starting point of this reflection is provided for us directly by the following words of Genesis: "It is not good that man [male] should be alone; I will make him a helper fit for him" (Gn 2:18). God-Yahweh speaks these words. They belong to the second account of the creation of man, and so they come from the Yahwist tradition. As we have already recalled, it is significant that, as regards the Yahwist text, the account of the creation of the man is a separate passage (Gn 2:7). It precedes the account of the creation of the first woman (Gn 2:21-22). It is also significant that the first man *('adam),* created from "dust from the ground," is defined as a "male" *('is)* only after the creation of the first woman. So when God-Yahweh speaks the words about solitude, it is in reference to the solitude of "man" as such, and not just to that of the male.[9]

However, it is difficult to go very far in drawing conclusions merely on the basis of this fact. Nevertheless, the complete context of that solitude of which Genesis 2:18 speaks can convince us that it is a question here of the solitude of "man" (male and female) and not just of the solitude of man the male, caused by the lack of woman. Therefore, on the basis of the whole context, it seems that this solitude has two meanings: one derived from man's very nature, that is, from his humanity, and the other derived from the male-female relationship. The first meaning is evident in the account of Genesis 2, and the second is evident, in a certain way, on the basis of the first meaning. A detailed analysis of the description seems to confirm this.

The problem of solitude is manifested only in the context of the second account of the creation of man. The first account ignores this problem. There man is created in one act as male and female. "God created man in his own image...male and female he created them" (Gn 1:27). As we have already mentioned, the second account speaks first of the creation of the man and only afterward of the creation of the woman from the "rib" of the male. This account concentrates our attention on the fact that "man is alone." This appears as a fundamental anthropological problem, prior, in a certain sense, to the one raised by the fact that this man is male and female. This problem is prior not so much in the chronological sense, as in the existential sense. It is prior "by its very nature." The problem of man's solitude from the point of view of the theology of the body will also be revealed as such, if we succeed in making a thorough analysis of the second account of creation in Genesis 2.

The affirmation of God-Yahweh, "It is not good that man should be alone," appears not only in the immediate context of the decision to create woman, "I will make him a helper fit for him," but also in the wider context of reasons and circumstances. These explain more deeply the meaning of man's original solitude. The Yahwist text connects the creation of man first and foremost with the need to "till the ground" (Gn 2:5). That would correspond, in the first account, with the vocation to subdue and have dominion over the earth (cf. Gn 1:28). Then, the second account of creation speaks of man being put in the "garden in Eden," and in this way introduces us to the state of his original happiness. Up to this moment man is the object of the creative action of God-Yahweh, who at the same time, as legislator, establishes the conditions of the first covenant with man.

Man's subjectivity is already emphasized through this. It finds a further expression when the Lord God "formed out of the ground every beast of the field and every bird of the air, and brought them to man to see what he would call them" (Gn 2:19). In this way, therefore, the first meaning of man's original solitude is defined on the basis of a specific test or examination which man undergoes before God (and in a certain way also before himself). By means of this test, man becomes aware of his own superiority, that is, that he cannot be considered on the same footing as any other species of living beings on the earth.

As the text says, "Whatever the man called every living creature, that was its name" (Gn 2:19). "The man gave names to all cattle, and to the birds of the air, and to every beast of the field; but for the man [male] there was not found a helper fit for him" (Gn 2:20).

All this part of the text is unquestionably a preparation for the account of the creation of woman. However, it possesses a deep meaning even apart from this creation. Right from the first moment of his existence, created man finds himself before God as if in search of his own entity. It could be said he is in search of the definition of himself. A contemporary person would say he is in search of his own "identity." The fact that man "is alone" in the midst of the visible world and, in particular, among living beings, has a negative significance in this search, since it expresses what he "is not." Nevertheless, the fact of not being able to identify himself essentially with the visible world of other living beings *(animalia)* has, at the same time, a positive aspect for this primary search. Even if this fact is not yet a complete definition, it constitutes one of its elements. If we accept the Aristotelian tradition in logic and in anthropology, it would be necessary to define this element as the "proximate genus" *(genus proximum)*.[10]

However, the Yahwist text enables us to discover also further elements in that admirable passage. Man finds himself alone before God mainly to express, through a first self-definition, his own self-knowledge, as the original and fundamental manifestation of mankind. Self-knowledge develops at the same rate as knowledge of the world, of all the visible creatures, of all the living beings to which man has given a name to affirm his own dissimilarity with regard to them. In this way, consciousness reveals man as the one who possesses a cognitive faculty as regards the visible world. With this knowledge which, in a certain way, brings him out of his own being, man at the same time reveals himself to himself in all the peculiarity of his being. He is not only essentially and subjectively alone. Solitude also signifies man's subjectivity, which is constituted through self-knowledge. Man is alone because he is "different" from the visible world, from the world of living beings. Analyzing the text of Genesis we are, in a way, witnesses of how man "distinguishes himself" before God-Yahweh from the whole world of living beings *(animalia)* with his first act of self-consciousness, and of how he reveals himself to himself. At the same time he asserts himself as a "person" in the visible world. Sketched so incisively in Genesis 2:19-20, that process is a search for a definition of himself. Linking up with the Aristotelian tradition, it leads to indicating the *proximate genus*. Chapter 2 of Genesis expresses this with the words: "The man gave names...." There corresponds to this the specific differentia which is, according to Aristotle's definition, *nôus, zōón noētikón*. This process also leads to the first delineation of the human being as a human person with the specific subjectivity that characterizes him.

General audience of October 10, 1979

Man's Awareness of Being a Person

In the preceding talk we began to analyze the meaning of man's original solitude. The Yahwist text gave us the starting point, in particular by the following words: "It is not good that the man should be alone; I will make him a helper fit for him" (Gn 2:18). The analysis of the relative passages in the second chapter of Genesis has already brought us to surprising conclusions which concern the anthropology, that is, the fundamental science about man, contained in this book. In relatively few sentences, the ancient text portrays man as a person with the subjectivity that characterizes him.

God-Yahweh gave this first man, so formed, the order that concerned all the trees that grew in the garden of Eden, especially the tree of the knowledge of good and evil. This adds to the features of the man, described above, the moment of choice and self-determination, that is, of free will. In this way, the image of man, as a person endowed with a subjectivity of his own, appears before us, completed in his first outline.

The concept of original solitude includes both self-consciousness and self-determination. The fact that man is "alone" conceals within it this ontological structure and at the same time indicates true comprehension. Without that, we cannot understand correctly the subsequent words, which constitute the prelude to the creation of the first woman: "I will make a helper." But above all, without that deep significance of man's original solitude, it is not possible to understand and interpret correctly the whole situation of man, created in the image of God, which is the situation of the first, or rather original, covenant with God.

The narrative in the first chapter says that this man was created in the image of God. In the second narrative he is manifested as a subject of the covenant, that is, a subject constituted as a person, constituted in the dimension of "partner of the Absolute." He must consciously discern and choose between good and evil, between life and death. The words of the first order of God-Yahweh (Gn 2:16-17) speak directly of the submission and dependence of man the creature on his Creator. They indirectly reveal precisely this level of humanity as subject of the covenant and "partner of the Absolute." Man is "alone." That means that he, through his own humanity, through what he is, is constituted at the same time in a unique, exclusive and unrepeatable relationship with God himself. On its part, the anthropological definition contained in the Yahwist text approaches what is expressed in the theological definition of man, which we find in the first narrative of creation: "Let us make man in our image, after our likeness" (Gn 1:26).

Thus formed, man belongs to the visible world; he is a body among bodies. Taking up again and, in a way, reconstructing the meaning of original solitude, we apply it to man in his totality. His body, through which he participates in the visible created world, makes him at the same time conscious of being "alone." Otherwise, he would not have been able to arrive at that conviction which he reached (cf. Gn 2:20), if his body had not helped him to understand it, making the matter evident. Consciousness of solitude might have been shattered precisely because of his body itself. The man, *'adam,* might have reached the conclusion, on the basis of the experience of his own body, that he was substantially similar to other living beings *(animalia).* On the contrary, as we read, he did not arrive at this conclusion; he reached the conviction that he was "alone." The Yahwist text never speaks directly of the body. Even when it says that "The Lord God formed man of dust from the ground," it speaks of man and not of his body. Nevertheless, the narrative taken as a whole offers us a sufficient basis to perceive this man, created in the visible world, precisely as a body among bodies.

The analysis of the Yahwist text also enables us to link man's original solitude with consciousness of the body. Through it, man is distinguished from all the *animalia* and is separated from them, and also through it he is a person. It can be affirmed with certainty that man, thus formed, has at the same time consciousness and awareness of the meaning of his own body, on the basis of the experience of original solitude. All this can be considered as an implication of the second narrative of the creation of man, and the analysis of the text enables us to develop it amply.

At the beginning of the Yahwist text, even before it speaks of the creation of man from the "dust of the ground," we read that "there was no one to till the land or to make channels of water spring out of the earth to irrigate the whole land" (Gn 2:5-6). We rightly associate this passage with the one in the first narrative, in which God's command is expressed: "Fill the earth and subdue it, and have dominion..." (Gn 1:28). The second narrative alludes specifically to the work that man carries out to till the earth. The first fundamental means to dominate the earth lies in man himself. Man can dominate the earth because he alone—and no other of the living beings—is capable of "tilling it" and transforming it according to his own needs. ("He made channels of water spring out of the earth to irrigate the whole land.") This first outline of a specifically human activity seems to belong to the definition of man, as it emerges from the analysis of the Yahwist text. Consequently, it can be affirmed that this outline is intrinsic to the meaning of the original solitude and belongs to that dimension of solitude through which man, from the beginning, is in the visible world as a body among bodies and discovers the meaning of his own corporality.

General audience of October 24, 1979

The Alternative between Death and Immortality
Enters the Definition of Man

Today it is opportune to return to the meaning of man's original solitude, which emerges above all from the analysis of the so-called Yahwist
text of Genesis 2. As we have seen in the preceding reflections, the biblical text enables us to stress not only consciousness of the human body
(man is created in the visible world as a "body among bodies"), but also
that of its meaning.

In view of the great conciseness of the biblical text, it is admittedly
not possible to amplify this implication too much. It is certain, however,
that here we touch upon the central problem of anthropology. Consciousness of the body seems to be identified in this case with the discovery of
the complexity of one's own structure. On the basis of philosophical anthropology, this discovery consists, in short, in the relationship between
soul and body. The Yahwist narrative with its own language (that is, with
its own terminology), expresses it by saying: "The Lord God formed man
of dust from the ground and breathed into his nostrils the breath of life,
and man became a living being" (Gn 2:7).[11] Precisely this man, "a living
being," distinguishes himself continually from all other living beings in
the visible world.

The premise of man's distinguishing himself in this way is precisely
the fact that only he is capable of "tilling the earth" (cf. Gn 2:5) and "subduing it" (cf. Gn 1:28). It can be said that the consciousness of "superiority" contained in the definition of humanity is born right from the
beginning on the basis of a typically human praxis or behavior. This consciousness brings with it a particular perception of the meaning of one's
own body, emerging precisely from the fact that it falls to man to "till the
earth" and "subdue it." All that would be impossible without a typically
human intuition of the meaning of one's own body.

It seems necessary, then, to speak in the first place of this aspect,
rather than of the problem of anthropological complexity in the metaphysical sense. The original description of human consciousness, given by
the Yahwist text, comprises also the body in the narrative as a whole. It
contains the first testimony of the discovery of one's corporeality and
even, as has been said, the perception of the meaning of one's own body.
All this is revealed not on the basis of any primordial metaphysical analysis, but on the basis of a concrete subjectivity of man that is quite clear.

Man is a subject not only because of his self-awareness and self-
determination, but also on the basis of his own body. The structure of
this body permits him to be the author of a truly human activity. In this

self-reflection
will
body

activity the body expresses the person. Therefore, in all its materiality ("God formed man of dust from the ground"), it is almost penetrable and transparent, in such a way as to make it clear who man is (and who he should be), thanks to the structure of his consciousness and of his self-determination. On this rests the fundamental perception of the meaning of one's own body, which can be discovered when analyzing man's original solitude.

Here, with this fundamental understanding of the meaning of his own body, man, as subject of the ancient covenant with the Creator, is placed before the mystery of the tree of knowledge. "You may freely eat of every tree of the garden, but of the tree of the knowledge of good and evil you shall not eat, for in the day that you eat of it you shall die" (Gn 2:16-17). The original meaning of man's solitude is based on experience of the existence obtained from the Creator. This human existence is characterized precisely by subjectivity, which includes also the meaning of the body.

But could man—who in his original consciousness, knew exclusively the experience of existing and therefore of life—have understood the meaning of the words, "You shall die"? Would he have been able to arrive at understanding the meaning of these words through the complex structure of life, given to him when "the Lord God...breathed into his nostrils the breath of life"? It must be admitted that the word "die," a completely new one, appeared on the horizon of man's consciousness without his having ever experienced its reality. At the same time this word appeared before him as a radical antithesis of all that man had been endowed with.

For the first time, man heard the words "You shall die," without having any familiarity with them in his experience up to then. On the other hand, he could not but associate the meaning of death with that dimension of life which he had enjoyed up to then. The words of God-Yahweh addressed to man confirmed a dependence in existing, such as to make man a limited being and, by his very nature, liable to nonexistence.

These words raised the problem of death in a conditional way: "In the day that you eat of it you shall die." Man, who had heard these words, had to find their truth in the interior structure of his own solitude. In short, it depended on him, on his decision and free choice, if, with solitude, he was to enter also the circle of the antithesis revealed to him by the Creator, together with the tree of the knowledge of good and evil and thereby to make his own the experience of dying and death.

Listening to the words of God-Yahweh, man should have understood that the tree of knowledge had roots not only in the garden of Eden, but also in his humanity. Furthermore, he should have understood that that mysterious tree concealed within it a dimension of loneliness, hitherto unknown, with which the Creator had endowed him in the midst of the world of living beings. In the presence of the Creator himself, man had given names to them, in order to understand that none of them was similar to him.

The fundamental meaning of his body had already been established through its distinction from all other creatures. It had thereby become clear that the "invisible" determines man more than the "visible." Then, there was presented to him the alternative closely and directly connected by God with the tree of the knowledge of good and evil. The alternative between death and immortality, which emerges from Genesis 2:17, goes beyond the essential meaning of man's body. It grasps the eschatological meaning not only of the body, but of humanity itself, distinguished from all living beings, from "bodies." However, this alternative concerns in a quite particular way, the body created from "dust from the ground."

Not to prolong this analysis, we will merely note that right from the outset the alternative between death and immortality enters the definition of man. It belongs "from the beginning" to the meaning of his solitude before God himself. This original meaning of solitude, permeated by the alternative between death and immortality, also has a fundamental meaning for the whole theology of the body.

With this observation we conclude for the present our reflections on the meaning of man's original solitude. This observation, which emerges in a clear and penetrating way from the texts of Genesis, induces reflection both on the texts and on man. Perhaps he is too little conscious of the truth that concerns him, which is already contained in the first chapters of the Bible.

General audience of October 31, 1979

The Original Unity of Man and Woman

The words of Genesis, "It is not good that the man should be alone" (2:18) are a prelude to the narrative of the creation of woman. Together with this narrative, the sense of original solitude becomes part of the meaning of original unity, the key point of which seems to be precisely the words of Genesis 2:24. Christ referred to them in his talk with the Pharisees: "A man shall leave his father and mother and be joined to his wife, and the two shall become one flesh" (Mt 19:5). If Christ quoted these words referring to the "beginning," it is opportune for us to clarify the meaning of that original unity, which has its roots in the fact of the creation of man as male and female.

The narrative of the first chapter of Genesis does not know the problem of man's original solitude. Man is "male and female" right from the beginning. On the contrary, the Yahwist text of the second chapter authorizes us, in a way, to think first only of the man since, by means of the body, he belongs to the visible world but goes beyond it. Then, it makes us think of the same man, but through the dualism of sex.

Corporality and sexuality are not completely identified. In its normal constitution, the human body bears within it the signs of sex and is male or female by its nature. However, the fact that man is a "body" belongs to the structure of the personal subject more deeply than the fact that in his somatic constitution he is also male or female. Therefore, the meaning of "original solitude," which can be referred simply to "man," is substantially prior to the meaning of original unity. The latter is based on masculinity and femininity, as if on two different "incarnations," that is, on two ways of "being a body" of the same human being created "in the image of God" (Gn 1:27).

Following the Yahwist text, in which the creation of woman was described separately (Gn 2:21-22), we must have before our eyes, at the same time, that "image of God" of the first narrative of creation. In language and in style, the second narrative keeps all the characteristics of the Yahwist text. The way of narrating agrees with the way of thinking and expressing oneself of the period to which the text belongs.

Following the contemporary philosophy of religion and that of language, it can be said that the language in question is a mythical one. In this case, the term "myth" does not designate a fabulous content, but merely an archaic way of expressing a deeper content. Without any difficulty we discover that content, under the layer of the ancient narrative. It is really marvelous as regards the qualities and the condensation of the truths contained in it.

Let us add that up to a certain point, the second narrative of the creation of man keeps the form of a dialogue between man and God-Creator. That is manifested above all in that stage in which man *('adam)* is definitively created as male and female *('is—'issah)*.[12] The creation takes place almost simultaneously in two dimensions: the action of God-Yahweh who creates occurs in correlation with the process of human consciousness.

So, God-Yahweh says: "It is not good that the man should be alone; I will make him a helper fit for him" (Gn 2:18). At the same time the man confirms his own solitude (cf. Gn 2:20). Next we read: "So the Lord God caused a deep sleep to fall upon the man, and while he slept took one of his ribs and closed up its place with flesh. The rib which the Lord God had taken from the man he made into a woman" (Gn 2:21-22). Considering the specific language, first it must be recognized that in the Genesis account, that sleep in which the man is immersed—thanks to God-Yahweh—in preparation for the new creative act, gives us food for thought.

Against the background of contemporary mentality, accustomed—through analysis of the subconscious—to connecting sexual contents with the world of dreams, that sleep may bring forth a particular association.[13] However, the Bible narrative seems to go beyond the dimension of man's subconscious. If we admit, moreover, a significant difference of vocabulary, we can conclude that the man *('adam)* falls into that "sleep" in order to wake up "male" and "female." In Genesis 2:23, we come across the distinction *'is—'issah* for the first time. Perhaps, therefore, the analogy of sleep indicates here not so much a passing from consciousness to subconsciousness, as a specific return to non-being (sleep contains an element of annihilation of man's conscious existence). That is, it indicates a return to the moment preceding the creation, that through God's creative initiative, solitary "man" may emerge from it again in his double unity as male and female.[14]

In any case, in the light of the context of Genesis 2:18-20, there is no doubt that man falls into that "sleep" with the desire of finding a being like himself. If, by analogy with sleep, we can speak here also of a dream, we must say that the biblical archetype allows us to admit as the content of that dream a "second self." It is also personal and equally referred to the situation of original solitude, that is, to the whole process of the stabilization of human identity in relation to living beings *(animalia)* as a whole, since it is the process of man's "differentiation" from this environment. In this way, the circle of the solitude of the man-person is broken, because the first "man" awakens from his sleep as "male and female."

The woman is made "with the rib" that God-Yahweh had taken from the man. Considering the archaic, metaphorical and figurative way of expressing the thought, we can establish that it is a question here of homogeneity of the whole being of both. This homogeneity concerns above all the body, the somatic structure. It is also confirmed by the man's first words to the woman who has been created: "This at last is bone of my bones and flesh of my flesh" (Gn 2:23).[15] Yet the words quoted refer also to the humanity of the male. They must be read in the context of the affirmations made before the creation of the woman, in which, although the "incarnation" of the man does not yet exist, she is defined as "a helper fit for him" (cf. Gn 2:18 and 2:20).[16] In this way, therefore, the woman is created, in a sense, on the basis of the same humanity.

Somatic homogeneity, in spite of the difference in constitution bound up with the sexual difference, is so evident that the man, on waking up from the genetic sleep, expresses it at once, when he says: "This at last is bone of my bones and flesh of my flesh—she shall be called woman, because she was taken out of man" (Gn 2:23). In this way the man manifests for the first time joy and even exaltation, for which he had no reason before, owing to the lack of a being like himself. Joy in the other human being, in the second "self," dominates the words spoken by the man on seeing the woman. All this helps to establish the full meaning of original unity. The words here are few, but each one is of great weight. We must take into account—and we will do so also later—the fact that the first woman, "made with the rib...taken from the man," is at once accepted as a fit helper for him.

We shall return to this same subject, that is, the meaning of the original unity of man and of woman in humanity, in the next meditation.

General audience of November 7, 1979

By the Communion of Persons Man Becomes the Image of God

Following the narrative of Genesis, we have seen that the "definitive" creation of man consists in the creation of the unity of two beings. Their unity denotes above all the identity of human nature; their duality, on the other hand, manifests what, on the basis of this identity, constitutes the masculinity and femininity of created man. This ontological dimension of unity and duality has, at the same time, an axiological meaning. From the text of Genesis 2:23 and from the whole context, it is clearly seen that man was created as a particular value before God. "God saw everything that he had made, and behold, it was very good" (Gn 1:31). But man was also created as a particular value for himself—first, because he is man; second, because the woman is for the man, and vice versa, the man is for the woman.*

In this way the meaning of man's original unity, through masculinity and femininity, is expressed as an overcoming of the frontier of solitude. At the same time it is an affirmation—with regard to both human beings—of everything that constitutes man in solitude. In the Bible narrative, solitude is the way that leads to that unity which, following Vatican II, we can define as *communio personarum.*[17]

As we have already seen, in his original solitude man acquires a personal consciousness in the process of distinction from all living beings *(animalia).* At the same time, in this solitude, he opens up to a being akin to himself, defined in Genesis (2:18, 20) as "a helper fit for him." This opening is no less decisive for the person of man; in fact, it is perhaps even more decisive than the distinction itself. In the Yahwist narrative,

* *Please see page 102 for a corrigenda.*

man's solitude is presented to us not only as the first discovery of the characteristic transcendence peculiar to the person. It is also presented as the discovery of an adequate relationship "to" the person, and therefore as an opening and expectation of a "communion of persons."

The term "community" could also be used here, if it were not generic and did not have so many meanings. *Communio* expresses more, with greater precision, since it indicates precisely that "help" which is derived, in a sense, from the very fact of existing as a person "beside" a person. In the Bible narrative this fact becomes *eo ipso*—in itself—the existence of the person "for" the person, since man in his original solitude was, in a way, already in this relationship. That is confirmed, in a negative sense, precisely by this solitude.

Furthermore, the communion of persons could be formed only on the basis of a "double solitude" of man and of woman, that is, as their meeting in their distinction from the world of living beings *(animalia),* which gave them both the possibility of being and existing in a special reciprocity. The concept of "help" also expresses this reciprocity in existence, which no other living being could have ensured. All that constituted the foundation of the solitude of each of them was indispensable for this reciprocity. Self-knowledge and self-determination, that is, subjectivity and consciousness of the meaning of one's own body, was also indispensable.

In the first chapter, the narrative of the creation of man affirms directly, right from the beginning, that man was created in the image of God as male and female. The narrative of the second chapter, on the other hand, does not speak of the "image of God." But in its own way it reveals that the complete and definitive creation of "man" (subjected first to the experience of original solitude) is expressed in giving life to that *communio personarum* that man and woman form. In this way, the Yahwist narrative agrees with the content of the first narrative.

If, vice versa, we wish to draw also from the narrative of the Yahwist text the concept of "image of God," we can then deduce that man became the "image and likeness" of God not only through his own humanity, but also through the communion of persons which man and woman form right from the beginning. The function of the image is to reflect the one who is the model, to reproduce its own prototype. Man becomes the image of God not so much in the moment of solitude as in the moment of communion. Right "from the beginning," he is not only an image in which the solitude of a person who rules the world is reflected, but also, and essentially, an image of an inscrutable divine communion of persons.

In this way, the second narrative could also be a preparation for understanding the Trinitarian concept of the "image of God," even if the latter appears only in the first narrative. Obviously, that is not without significance for the theology of the body. Perhaps it even constitutes the deepest theological aspect of all that can be said about man. In the mystery of creation—on the basis of the original and constituent "solitude" of his being—man was endowed with a deep unity between what is, humanly and through the body, male in him and what is, equally humanly and through the body, female in him. On all this, right from the beginning, the blessing of fertility descended, linked with human procreation (cf. Gn 1:28).

In this way, we find ourselves almost at the heart of the anthropological reality that has the name "body." The words of Genesis 2:23 speak of it directly and for the first time in the following terms: "bone of my bones and flesh of my flesh." The man uttered these words, as if it were only at the sight of the woman that he was able to identify and call by name what makes them visibly similar to each other, and at the same time what manifests humanity.

In the light of the preceding analysis of all the "bodies" which man has come into contact with and which he has defined, conceptually giving them their name *(animalia),* the expression "flesh of my flesh" takes on precisely this meaning: the body reveals man. This concise formula already contains everything that human science could ever say about the structure of the body as organism, about its vitality, and its particular sexual physiology, etc. This first expression of the man, "flesh of my flesh," also contains a reference to what makes that body truly human. Therefore it referred to what determines man as a person, that is, as a being who, even in all his corporality, is similar to God.[18]

We find ourselves, therefore, almost at the very core of the anthropological reality, the name of which is "body," the human body. However, as can easily be seen, this core is not only anthropological, but also essentially theological. Right from the beginning, the theology of the body is bound up with the creation of man in the image of God. It becomes, in a way, also the theology of sex, or rather the theology of masculinity and femininity, which has its starting point here in Genesis.

The words of Genesis 2:24 bear witness to the original meaning of unity, which will have in the revelation of God an ample and distant perspective. This unity through the body—"and the two will be one flesh"—possesses a multiform dimension. It possesses an ethical dimension, as is confirmed by Christ's answer to the Pharisees in Matthew 19 (cf. Mk 10). It also has a sacramental dimension, a strictly theological one, as is proved by St. Paul's words to the Ephesians[19] which refer also to the tradition of the prophets (Hosea, Isaiah, Ezekiel). This is so because, right from the beginning, that unity which is realized through the body indicates not only the "body," but also the "incarnate" communion of persons—*communio personarum*—and calls for this communion.

Masculinity and femininity express the dual aspect of man's somatic constitution. "This at last is bone of my bones and flesh of my flesh." Furthermore, through the same words of Genesis 2:23, they indicate the new consciousness of the sense of one's own body. It can be said that this sense consists in a mutual enrichment. Precisely this consciousness, through which humanity is formed again as the communion of persons, seems to be the layer which in the narrative of the creation of man (and in the revelation of the body contained in it) is deeper than his somatic structure as male and female. In any case, this structure is presented right from the beginning with a deep consciousness of human corporality and sexuality, and that establishes an inalienable norm for the understanding of man on the theological plane.

General audience of November 14, 1979

In the First Chapters of Genesis, Marriage Is One and Indissoluble

Let us recall that when questioned about the unity and indissolubility of marriage, Christ referred to what was "in the beginning." He quoted the words written in the first chapters of Genesis. In the course of these reflections, we are trying to penetrate the specific meaning of these words and these chapters.

The meaning of the original unity of man, whom God created "male and female," is obtained (especially in the light of Genesis 2:23) by knowing man in the entire endowment of his being, that is, in all the riches of that mystery of creation, on which theological anthropology is based. This knowledge, that is, the study of the human identity of the one who, at the beginning, is "alone," must always pass through duality, "communion."

Let us recall the passage of Genesis 2:23: "Then the man said, 'This at last is bone of my bones and flesh of my flesh; she shall be called woman, because she was taken out of man.'" In the light of this text, we understand that knowledge of man passes through masculinity and femininity. These are, as it were, two "incarnations" of the same metaphysical solitude before God and the world. They are two ways of "being a body" and at the same time a man, which complete each other. They are two complementary dimensions of self-consciousness and self-determination and, at the same time, two complementary ways of being conscious of the meaning of the body.

As Genesis 2:23 already shows, femininity finds itself, in a sense, in the presence of masculinity, while masculinity is confirmed through femininity. Precisely the function of sex, which is in a sense, "a constituent part of the person" (not just "an attribute of the person"), proves how deeply man, with all his spiritual solitude, with the never to be repeated uniqueness of his person, is constituted by the body as "he" or "she." The presence of the feminine element, alongside the male element and together with it, signifies an enrichment for man in the whole perspective of his history, including the history of salvation. All this teaching on unity has already been expressed originally in Genesis 2:23.

The unity of which Genesis 2:24 speaks—"they become one flesh" —is undoubtedly expressed and realized in the conjugal act. The biblical formulation, extremely concise and simple, indicates sex, femininity and masculinity, as that characteristic of man—male and female—which permits them, when they become "one flesh," to submit their whole humanity to the blessing of fertility. However, the whole context of the lapidary formulation does not permit us to stop at the surface of human sexuality. It does not allow us to deal with the body and sex outside the full dimension of man and of the "communion of persons." Right from the beginning it obliges us to see the fullness and depth which are characteristic of this unity, which man and woman must constitute in the light of the revelation of the body.

The perspective expression which says, "a man cleaves to his wife" so intimately that "they become one flesh," always induces us to refer to what the biblical text expresses previously with regard to the union in humanity, which binds the woman and the man in the very mystery of creation. The words of Genesis 2:23, just analyzed, explain this concept in a particular way. Uniting with each other (in the conjugal act) so closely as to become "one flesh," man and woman, rediscover, so to speak, every time and in a special way, the mystery of creation. They return in this way to that union in humanity ("bone of my bones and flesh of my flesh") which allows them to recognize each other and, like the first time, to call each other by name.

This means reliving, in a sense, the original virginal value of man, which emerges from the mystery of his solitude before God and in the midst of the world. The fact that they become one flesh is a powerful bond established by the Creator. Through it they discover their own humanity, both in its original unity, and in the duality of a mysterious mutual attraction.

However, sex is something more than the mysterious power of human corporality, which acts almost by virtue of instinct. At the level of man and in the mutual relationship of persons, sex expresses an ever new surpassing of the limit of man's solitude that is inherent in the constitution of his body, and determines its original meaning. This surpassing always contains within it a certain assumption of the solitude of the body of the second "self" as one's own.

Therefore, it is bound up with choice. The formulation of Genesis 2:24 indicates that human beings, created as man and woman, were created for unity. It also indicates that precisely this unity, through which they become one flesh, has right from the beginning a character of union derived from a choice. We read: "A man leaves his father and mother and cleaves to his wife." If the man belongs "by nature" to his father and mother, by virtue of procreation, on the other hand, he cleaves by choice to his wife (or she to her husband).

The text of Genesis 2:24 defines this character of the conjugal bond with reference to the first man and the first woman. At the same time, it does so in the perspective of the whole earthly future of man. Therefore, in his time, Christ will appeal to that text, as equally relevant in his age. Formed in the image of God, also inasmuch as they form a true communion of persons, the first man and the first woman must constitute the beginning and the model of that communion for all men and women, who, in any period, are united so intimately as to be one flesh.

The body, which through its own masculinity or femininity right from the beginning helps both to find themselves in communion of persons, becomes, in a particular way, the constituent element of their union, when they become husband and wife. This takes place, however, through a mutual choice. This choice establishes the conjugal pact between persons,[20] who become one flesh only on this basis.

That corresponds to the structure of man's solitude, and in actual fact to the "twofold solitude." As the expression of self-determination, choice rests on the foundation of his self-consciousness. Only on the basis of the structure peculiar to man is he "a body" and, through the body, also male and female. When they both unite so closely as to become one flesh, their conjugal union presupposes a mature consciousness of the body. In fact, it bears within it a particular consciousness of the meaning of that body in the mutual self-giving of the persons.

In this sense too, Genesis 2:24 is a perspective text. It proves that in every conjugal union of man and woman, the same original consciousness of the unifying significance of the body in its masculinity and femininity is discovered again. At the same time, the biblical text indicates that each of these unions renews, in a way, the mystery of creation in all its original depth and vital power. "Taken out of man" as "flesh of his flesh," woman subsequently becomes, as wife and through her motherhood, mother of the living (cf. Gn 3:20), since her motherhood also has its origin in him. Procreation is rooted in creation, and every time, in a sense, reproduces its mystery.

A special reflection on "knowledge and procreation" will be devoted to this subject. In it, it will be necessary to refer further to other elements of the biblical text. The analysis made hitherto of the meaning of the original unity proves in what way that unity of man and woman, inherent in the mystery of creation, is "from the beginning" also given as a commitment in the perspective of all following times.

General audience of November 21, 1979

The Meaning of Original Human Experiences

The analysis of the first chapters of Genesis forces us, in a way, to reconstruct the elements that constitute man's original experience. In this sense, the character of the Yahwist text makes it a special source. Speaking of original human experiences, we have in mind not so much their distance in time, as rather their basic significance. The important thing is not that these experiences belong to man's prehistory (to his "theological prehistory"), but that they are always at the root of every human experience. That is true even if in the evolution of ordinary human existence, little attention is paid to these essential experiences. They are so intermingled with the ordinary things of life that we do not generally notice their extraordinary character.

On the basis of the analyses carried out up to now, we have already realized that what we called at the beginning the "revelation of the body," helps us somehow to discover the extraordinary side of what is ordinary. That is possible because the revelation (the original one, expressed first in the Yahwist account of Genesis 2:3, then in the text of Genesis 1) takes into consideration precisely these primordial experiences. In them, there appears almost completely the absolute originality of what the male-female human being is: as a man, that is, also through his body. As we discover it in the biblical text quoted, man's experience of his body is certainly on the threshold of his whole subsequent "historical" experience. However, it also seems to rest at such an ontological depth that man does not perceive it in his own everyday life. This is so even if at the same time, and in a certain way, he presupposes it and postulates it as part of the process of formation of his own image.

Without this introductory reflection, it would be impossible to define the meaning of original nakedness and tackle the analysis of Genesis 2:25, which runs as follows: "And the man and his wife were both naked, and were not ashamed." At first sight, the introduction of this detail, apparently a secondary one in the Yahwist account of man's creation, may seem something inadequate or misplaced. One would think that the passage quoted cannot bear comparison with what has been dealt with in the preceding verses and that, in a way, it goes beyond the context. However, this judgment does not stand up to a deeper analysis. Genesis 2:25 presents one of the key elements of the original revelation. It is as decisive as the other texts of Genesis 2:20 and 2:23, which have already enabled us to define the meaning of man's original solitude and original unity. To these is added, as the third element, the meaning of original nakedness, clearly stressed in the context. In the first biblical draft of anthropology, it is not something accidental. On the contrary, it is precisely the key for its full and complete understanding.

This element of the ancient biblical text makes a specific contribution to the theology of the body that absolutely cannot be ignored. Further analyses will confirm this. But before undertaking them, I take the liberty of pointing out that the text of Genesis 2:25 expressly requires that the reflections on the theology of the body should be connected with the dimension of man's personal subjectivity. It is within the latter that consciousness of the meaning of the body develops. Genesis 2:25 speaks about it far more directly than other parts of that Yahwist text, which we have already defined as the first recording of human consciousness.

The sentence, according to which the first human beings, man and woman, "were naked" and yet "were not ashamed," unquestionably describes their state of consciousness, in fact, their mutual experience of the body. It describes the experience on the part of the man of the femininity that is revealed in the nakedness of the body and, reciprocally, the similar experience of masculinity on the part of the woman. By saying that "they were not ashamed," the author tries to describe this mutual experience of the body with the greatest precision possible for him. It can be said that this type of precision reflects a basic experience of man in the "common" and pre-scientific sense. But it also corresponds to the requirements of anthropology and in particular of contemporary anthropology, which likes to refer to so-called fundamental experiences, such as the "experience of shame."[21]

Referring here to the precision of the account, such as was possible for the author of the Yahwist text, we are led to consider the degrees of experience of historical man, laden with the inheritance of sin. However, these degrees methodically start precisely from the state of original innocence. We have already seen that, referring to "the beginning" (which we have subjected here to successive contextual analyses), Christ indirectly established the idea of continuity and connection between those two states. This allows us to move back from the threshold of man's historical sinfulness to his original innocence. Genesis 2:25 makes it especially necessary to cross that threshold.

This passage, together with the meaning of original nakedness inherent in it, takes its place in the contextual setting of the Yahwist narrative. After some verses, the same author writes: "Then the eyes of both were opened, and they knew that they were naked, and they sewed fig leaves together and made themselves aprons" (Gn 3:7). The adverb "then" indicates a new moment and a new situation following the breaking of the first covenant. This situation follows the failure of the test connected with the tree of the knowledge of good and evil. At the same time that test constituted the first test of "obedience," that is, listening to the Word in all its truth and accepting love, according to the fullness of the demands of the creative Will. This new moment or new situation also implies a new content and a new quality of experience of the body, so that it can no longer be said: "They were naked, but were not ashamed." Here, shame is an experience that is not only original, but a "boundary" one.

The difference of formulations that divides Genesis 2:25 from Genesis 3:7 is significant—in the first case, "They were naked, but they were not ashamed"; in the second case, "They knew that they were naked." Does that mean that, to begin with, "They did not know that they were naked," or that they did not see the nakedness of each other's body? The significant change testified by the biblical text about the experience of shame (of which Genesis speaks again, especially in 3:10-12), takes place at a deeper level than the pure and simple use of the sense of sight.

A comparative analysis of Genesis 2:25 and Genesis 3 leads necessarily to the conclusion that it is not a question here of passing from "not knowing" to "knowing." Rather, it involves a radical change of the meaning of the original nakedness of the woman before the man and of the man before the woman. It emerges from their conscience, as a fruit of the tree of the knowledge of good and evil: "Who told you that you were naked? Have you eaten of the tree of which I commanded you not to eat?" (Gn 3:11).

This change directly concerns the experience of the meaning of one's body before the Creator and creatures. Subsequently, the man's words confirm this: "I heard the sound of you in the garden, and I was afraid, because I was naked, and I hid myself" (Gn 3:10). That change, which the

Yahwist text portrays so concisely and dramatically, concerns directly—perhaps in the most direct way possible—the man-woman, femininity-masculinity relationship.

We will have to return again to the analysis of this change in other parts of our further reflections. Now, having arrived at that border which crosses the sphere of the "beginning" to which Christ referred, we should ask ourselves if it is possible to reconstruct, in some way, the original meaning of nakedness. In Genesis, nakedness constitutes the immediate context of the doctrine about the unity of the human being as male and female. That seems possible, if we take as a reference point the experience of shame as it was clearly presented in the ancient biblical text as a "liminal" experience. We shall attempt this reconstruction in our following meditations.

General audience of December 12, 1979

The Fullness of Interpersonal Communication

What is shame and how can we explain its absence in the state of original innocence, in the depth of the mystery of the creation of man as male and female? From contemporary analyses of shame—and in particular of sexual modesty—we can deduce the complexity of this fundamental experience, in which man expresses himself as a person according to his own specific structure. In the experience of shame, the human being experiences fear with regard to his "second self," (for example, woman before man). This is substantially fear for one's own "self." With shame, the human being manifests almost instinctively the need of affirmation and acceptance of this "self," according to its rightful value. He experiences it at the same time both within himself, and externally, before the "other." Shame is a complex experience. Almost keeping one human being away from the other (woman from man), it seeks at the same time to draw them closer personally, creating a suitable basis and level to do so.

For the same reason, it has a fundamental significance as regards the formation of ethos in human society, and especially in the man-woman relationship. The analysis of shame clearly indicates how deeply it is rooted precisely in mutual relations, how exactly it expresses the essential rules for the "communion of persons," and likewise how deeply it touches the dimension of man's original "solitude." The appearance of shame in the subsequent biblical narration of chapter 3 of Genesis has a pluri-dimensional significance. It will be opportune to resume the analysis in due time.

On the other hand, what does its original absence mean in Genesis 2:25: "They were both naked and were not ashamed"?

In the first place, it is a question of a real non-presence of shame, and not a lack of its development. We cannot in any way sustain here a "primitivization" of its meaning. Therefore the text of Genesis 2:25 does not only exclude decisively the possibility of thinking of a "lack of shame" or immodesty. Even more, it excludes the possibility of explaining it by analogy with some positive human experiences, such as those of childhood or of the life of so-called primitive peoples. These analogies are insufficient and can even be misleading. The words of Genesis 2:25: "They were not ashamed," do not express a lack, but, on the contrary, serve to indicate a particular fullness of consciousness and experience. Above all they indicate a full understanding of the meaning of the body, bound up with the fact that they were naked.

The continuation of the Yahwist narrative testifies that this is how the text quoted is to be understood and interpreted. In it, the appearance of shame, and in particular of sexual modesty, is connected with the loss of that original fullness. Taking the experience of shame as a "borderline" experience, we must ask ourselves what does the meaning of the original nakedness which Genesis 2:25 speaks of, correspond to? To what fullness of conscience and experience, and in particular to what full understanding of the meaning of the body, does the meaning of original nakedness correspond to?

To answer this question, we must keep in mind the analytical process carried out so far, which has its basis in the Yahwist passage as a whole. In this context, man's original solitude was manifested as "non-identification" of his own humanity with the world of living beings *(animalia)* that surround him. A

This non-identification, following upon the creation of man as male and female, made way for the happy discovery of one's own humanity B with the help of the other human being. Thus the man recognized and found again his own humanity with the help of the woman (cf. Gn 2:25). At the same time, this act of theirs realized a perception of the world, which was carried out directly through the body ("flesh of my flesh"). It was the direct and visible source of the experience that arrived at establishing their unity in humanity. It is easy to understand that nakedness C corresponds to that fullness of consciousness of the meaning of the body, deriving from the typical perception of the senses.

One can think of this fullness in categories of truth of being or of reality, and it can be said that man and woman were originally given to each other precisely according to this truth, since they were naked. In analyzing the meaning of original nakedness, this dimension absolutely cannot be disregarded. This participating in perception of the world—in its "exterior" aspect—is a direct and almost spontaneous fact. It is prior to any "critical" complication of knowledge and of human experience and is seen as closely connected with the experience of the meaning of the human body. The original innocence of "knowledge" could already be perceived in this way.

However, it is not possible to determine the meaning of original nakedness considering only man's participation in exterior perception of the world. It is not possible to establish it without going into the depths of man. Genesis 2:25 introduces us specifically to this level and wants us to seek there the original innocence of knowing. The dimension of human interiority is necessary to explain and measure that particular fullness of interpersonal communication, thanks to which man and woman were naked and were not ashamed.

In our conventional language, the concept of communication has been practically alienated from its deepest, original semantic matrix. It is connected mainly with the sphere of the media, that is, for the most part, products that serve for understanding, exchange, and bringing closer together. On the other hand, it can be supposed that, in its original and deeper meaning, communication was and is directly connected with subjects. They communicate precisely on the basis of the common union that exists between them, both to reach and to express a reality that is peculiar and pertinent only to the sphere of person-subjects.

In this way, the human body acquires a completely new meaning, which cannot be placed on the plane of the remaining "external" perception of the world. It expresses the person in his ontological and existential concreteness, which is something more than the individual. Therefore the body expresses the personal human "self," which derives its exterior perception from within.

The whole biblical narrative, and in particular the Yahwist text, shows that the body through its own visibility manifests man. In manifesting him, it acts as intermediary, that is, it enables man and woman, right from the beginning, to communicate with each other according to that *communio personarum* willed by the Creator precisely for them. It seems that only this dimension enables us to rightly understand the meaning of original nakedness. In this connection, any "naturalistic" criterion is bound to fail, while, on the contrary, the "personalistic" criterion can be of great help. Genesis 2:25 certainly speaks of something extraordinary, which is outside the limits of the shame known through human experience. At the same time it decides the particular fullness of interpersonal communication, rooted at the very heart of that *communio,* which is thus revealed and developed. In this connection, the words "they were not ashamed" can mean *in sensu obliquo* only an original depth in affirming what is inherent in the person, what is "visibly" female and male, through which the personal intimacy of mutual communication in all its radical simplicity and purity is constituted. To this fullness of exterior perception, expressed by means of physical nakedness, there corresponds the interior fullness of man's vision in God, that is, according to the measure of the "image of God" (cf. Gn 1:17). According to this measure, man "is" really naked ("They were naked"—Gn 2:25),[22] even before realizing it (cf. Gn 3:7-10).

We shall still have to complete the analysis of this important text during the meditations that follow.

General audience of December 19, 1979

Creation As a Fundamental and Original Gift

Let us return to analyzing the text of Genesis 2:25: "And the man and his wife were both naked and were not ashamed" (Gn 2:25). According to this passage, the man and the woman saw themselves, as it were, through the mystery of creation. They saw themselves in this way, before knowing that they were naked. This seeing each other is not just a participation in exterior perception of the world. It also has an interior dimension of participation in the vision of the Creator himself—that vision of which the Elohist text speaks several times: "God saw everything that he had made, and behold, it was very good" (Gn 1:31).

Nakedness signifies the original good of God's vision. It signifies all the simplicity and fullness of the vision through which the "pure" value of humanity as male and female, the "pure" value of the body and of sex, is manifested. The situation that is indicated, in such a concise and at the same time inspiring way, by the original revelation of the body as seen especially by Genesis 2:25, does not know an interior rupture and opposition between what is spiritual and what is sensible. It does not know a rupture and opposition between what constitutes the person humanly and what in man is determined by sex—what is male and female.

Seeing each other, as if through the mystery of creation, man and woman see each other even more fully and distinctly than through the sense of sight itself, that is, through the eyes of the body. They see and know each other with all the peace of the interior gaze, which creates precisely the fullness of the intimacy of persons.

Shame brings with it a specific limitation in seeing with the eyes of the body. This takes place above all because personal intimacy is disturbed and almost threatened by this sight. According to Genesis 2:25, the man and the woman were not ashamed seeing and knowing each other in all the peace and tranquillity of the interior gaze. They communicate in the fullness of humanity, which is manifested in them as reciprocal complementarity precisely because they are "male" and "female." At the same time, they communicate on the basis of that communion of persons in which, through femininity and masculinity, they become a gift for each other. In this way they reach in reciprocity a special understanding of the meaning of their own body.

The original meaning of nakedness corresponds to that simplicity and fullness of vision in which understanding the meaning of the body comes about at the very heart of their community-communion. We will call it "nuptial." The man and the woman in Genesis 2:23-25 emerge, precisely at the "beginning," with this consciousness of the meaning of their body. This deserves a careful analysis.

The two narratives of the creation of man, the Elohist and the Yahwist, enable us to establish the original meaning of solitude, unity and nakedness. They thereby enable us also to find ourselves on the ground of an adequate anthropology, which tries to understand and interpret man in what is essentially human.[23]

The Bible texts contain the essential elements of this anthropology, which are manifested in the theological context of the "image of God." This concept conceals within it the root of the truth about man. This is revealed through that "beginning," which Christ referred to in the talk with the Pharisees (cf. Mt 19:3-9), when he treated of the creation of the human male and female. It must be recalled that all the analyses we make here are connected, at least indirectly, precisely with these words of his. Man, whom God created male and female, bears the divine image imprinted on his body "from the beginning." Man and woman constitute two different ways of the human "being a body" in the unity of that image.

Now, it is opportune to turn again to those fundamental words which Christ used, that is, the word "created" and the subject "Creator." They introduce in the considerations made so far a new dimension, a new criterion of understanding and interpretation, which we will call "hermeneutics of the gift." The dimension of the gift decides the essential truth and depth of meaning of the original solitude, unity and nakedness. It is also at the heart of the mystery of creation, which enables us to construct the theology of the body "from the beginning," but demands, at the same time, that we should construct it in this way.

On Christ's lips, the word "created" contains the same truth that we find in Genesis. The first account of creation repeats this word several times, from Genesis 1:1, "In the beginning God created the heavens and the earth," to Genesis 1:27, "So God created man in his own image."[24] God reveals himself above all as Creator. Christ referred to that fundamental revelation contained in Genesis. In it, the concept of creation has all its depth—not only metaphysical, but also fully theological.

The Creator is he who "calls to existence from nothingness," and who establishes the world in existence and man in the world, because he "is love" (1 Jn 4:8). Actually, we do not find this word in the narrative of creation. However, this narrative often repeats: "God saw what he had made, and behold, it was very good." Through these words we are led to glimpse in love the divine motive of creation, the source from which it springs. Only love gives a beginning to good and delights in good (cf. 1 Cor 13). As the action of God, the creation signifies not only calling from nothingness to existence and establishing the existence of the world and of man in the world. It also signifies, according to the first narrative, *beresit bara,* giving. It is a fundamental and "radical" giving, that is, a giving in which the gift comes into being precisely from nothingness.

The first chapters of Genesis introduce us to the mystery of creation, that is, the beginning of the world by the will of God, who is omnipotence and love. Consequently, every creature bears within it the sign of the original and fundamental gift.

At the same time, however, the concept of "giving" cannot refer to a nothingness. It indicates the one who gives and the one who receives the gift, and also the relationship that is established between them. Now, this relationship emerges in the account of creation at the moment of the creation of man. This relationship is manifested above all by the expression: "God created man in his own image; in the image of God he created him" (Gn 1:27).

In the narrative of the creation of the visible world, the giving has a meaning only with regard to man. In the whole work of creation, it can be said only of him that a gift was conferred on him; the visible world was created "for him." The biblical account of creation offers us sufficient reasons to understand and interpret in this way. Creation is a gift, because man appears in it. As the "image of God," man is capable of understanding the meaning of gift in the call from nothingness to existence. He is capable of answering the Creator with the language of this understanding. Interpreting the narrative of creation with this language, it can be deduced from it that creation constitutes the fundamental and original gift. Man appears in creation as the one who received the world as a gift, and it can also be said that the world received man as a gift.

At this point, we must interrupt our analysis. What we have said so far is in close relationship with all the anthropological problems of the "beginning." Man appears as created, that is, as the one who, in the midst of the "world," received the other man as a gift. Later we will have to make precisely this dimension of the gift the subject of a deep analysis in order to understand also the meaning of the human body in its rightful extent. That will be the subject of our following meditations.

General audience of January 2, 1980

The Nuptial Meaning of the Body

Rereading and analyzing the second narrative of creation, the Yahwist text, we must ask ourselves if the first "man" *('adam)*, in his original solitude, really "lived" the world as a gift, with an attitude in conformity with the actual condition of one who has received a gift, as is seen from the narrative in the first chapter. The second narrative shows us man in the garden of Eden (cf. Gn 2:8). Though man was in this situation of original happiness, the Creator himself (God-Yahweh) and then also "man," pointed out that man was alone—instead of stressing the aspect of the world as a subjectively beatifying gift created for man (cf. the first narrative and in particular Gn 26:29).

We have already analyzed the meaning of original solitude. Now we must note that a certain lack of good clearly appears for the first time: "It is not good that man should be alone"—God-Yahweh said—"I will make him a helper..." (Gn 2:18). The first man said the same thing. After having become thoroughly aware of his own solitude among all living beings on earth, waited for "a helper fit for him" (cf. Gn 2:20). None of these beings *(animalia)* offered man the basic conditions which make it possible to exist in a relationship of mutual giving.

In this way, these two expressions, namely, the adjective "alone" and the noun "helper," seem to be the key to understand the essence of the gift at the level of man, as existential content contained in the truth of the "image of God." The gift reveals, so to speak, a particular characteristic of personal existence, or rather, of the essence of the person. When God-Yahweh said, "It is not good that man should be alone," (Gn 2:18) he affirmed that "alone," man does not completely realize this essence. He realizes it only by existing "with someone"—and even more deeply and completely—by existing "for someone."

This norm of existence as a person is shown in Genesis as characteristic of creation, precisely by means of the meaning of these two words:

"alone" and "helper." These words indicate as fundamental and constitutive for man both the relationship and the communion of persons. The communion of persons means existing in a mutual "for," in a relationship of mutual gift. This relationship is precisely the fulfillment of "man's" original solitude.

In its origin, this fulfillment is beatifying. It is certainly implicit in man's original happiness, and constitutes that happiness which belongs to the mystery of creation effected by love, which belongs to the essence of creative giving. When man, the male, awakening from the sleep of Genesis, saw the female, drawn from him, he said: "This at last is bone of my bones and flesh of my flesh" (Gen 2:23). These words express, in a way, the subjectively beatifying beginning of human existence in the world. Since it took place at the "beginning," this confirms the process of individuation of man in the world. It springs from the depths of his human solitude, which he lives as a person in the presence of all other creatures and all living beings.

This "beginning" belongs to an adequate anthropology and can always be verified on the basis of the latter. This purely anthropological verification brings us, at the same time, to the subject of the "person" and to the subject of the "body-sex." This simultaneousness is essential. If we dealt with sex without the person, the whole adequacy of the anthropology which we find in Genesis would be destroyed. For our theological study the essential light of the revelation of the body, which appears so fully in these first affirmations, would then be veiled.

There is a deep connection between the mystery of creation, as a gift springing from love, and that beatifying "beginning" of the existence of man as male and female, in the whole truth of their body and their sex, which is the pure and simple truth of communion between persons. When the first man exclaimed, at the sight of the woman: "This is bone of my bones, and flesh of my flesh" (Gn 2:23), he merely affirmed the human identity of both. Exclaiming in this way, he seems to say that here is a body that expresses the person.

According to a preceding passage of the Yahwist text, it can also be said that this "body" reveals the "living soul," such as man became when God-Yahweh breathed life into him (cf. Gn 2:7). This resulted in his solitude before all other living beings. By traversing the depth of that original solitude, man now emerged in the dimension of the mutual gift. The expression of that gift—and for that reason the expression of his existence as a person—is the human body in all the original truth of its masculinity and femininity.

The body which expresses femininity manifests the reciprocity and communion of persons. It expresses it by means of the gift as the fundamental characteristic of personal existence. This is the body—a witness to creation as a fundamental gift, and so a witness to Love as the source from which this same giving springs. Masculinity and femininity—namely, sex—is the original sign of a creative donation and an awareness on the part of man, male-female, of a gift lived in an original way. Such is the meaning with which sex enters the theology of the body.

That beatifying "beginning" of man's being and existing, as male and female, is connected with the revelation and discovery of the meaning of the body, which can be called "nuptial." If we speak of revelation and at the same time of discovery, we do so in relation to the specificity of the Yahwist text. In it, the theological thread is also anthropological, appearing as a certain reality consciously lived by man.

We have already observed that the words which express the first joy of man's coming to existence as "male and female" (Gn 2:23) are followed by the verse which establishes their conjugal unity (cf. Gn 2:24). Then follows the verse which testifies to the nakedness of both, without mutual shame (Gn 2:25). This significant confrontation enables us to speak of the revelation and at the same time the discovery of the "nuptial" meaning of the body in the mystery of creation.

This meaning (inasmuch as it is revealed and also conscious, "lived" by man) confirms completely that the creative giving, which springs from Love, has reached the original consciousness of man. It becomes an experience of mutual giving, as can already be seen in the ancient text. That nakedness of both progenitors, free from shame, seems also to bear witness to that, perhaps even specifically.

Genesis 2:24 speaks of the finality of man's masculinity and femininity, in the life of the spouses-parents. Uniting with each other so closely as to become "one flesh," they will subject their humanity to the blessing of fertility, namely, "procreation," which the first narrative speaks of (cf. Gn 1:28). Man comes "into being" with consciousness of this finality of his own masculinity-femininity, that is, of his own sexuality. At the same time, the words of Genesis 2:25: "They were both naked, and were not ashamed," seem to add to this fundamental truth of the meaning of the human body, of its masculinity and femininity, another no less essential and fundamental truth. Aware of the procreative capacity of his body and of his sexuality, man is at the same time "free from the constraint" of his own body and sex.

That original nakedness, mutual and at the same time not weighed down by shame, expresses this interior freedom of man. Is this what freedom from the "sexual instinct" is? The concept of "instinct" already implies an interior constraint, similar to the instinct that stimulates fertility and procreation in the whole world of living beings *(animalia)*. It seems, however, that both texts of Genesis, the first and the second narrative of the creation of man, connected sufficiently the perspective of procreation with the fundamental characteristic of human existence in the personal sense. Consequently the analogy of the human body and of sex in relation to the world of animals—which we can call an analogy of nature—is also raised, in a way, in both narratives (though in a different way in each), to the level of "image of God," and to the level of the person and communion between persons.

Further analyses will be dedicated to this essential problem. For the conscience of man—also for modern man—it is important to know that the revelation of the "nuptial meaning of the body" is found in those biblical texts which speak of the "beginning" of man. But it is even more important to establish what this meaning expresses precisely.

General audience of January 9, 1980

The Human Person Becomes a Gift in the Freedom of Love

Let us continue today with the analysis of the texts of Genesis, which we have undertaken according to Christ's line of teaching. Let us recall that in the talk about marriage he referred to the "beginning."

The revelation, and at the same time the original discovery of the nuptial meaning of the body, consists in this: it presents man, male and female, in the whole reality and truth of his body and sex ("they were naked") and at the same time in full freedom from any constraint of the body and of sex. The nakedness of our progenitors, interiorly free from shame, seems to bear witness to this. It can be said that, created by Love, endowed in their being with masculinity and femininity, they are both "naked" because they are free with the freedom of the gift.

This freedom lies at the basis of the nuptial meaning of the body. The human body, with its sex, and its masculinity and femininity seen in the very mystery of creation, is not only a source of fruitfulness and procreation, as in the whole natural order. It includes right from the beginning the nuptial attribute, that is, the capacity of expressing love, that love in which the person becomes a gift and—by means of this gift—fulfills the meaning of his being and existence. Let us recall here the text of the last Council which declared that man is the only creature in the visible world that God willed "for its own sake." It then added that man "can fully discover his true self only in a sincere giving of himself" *(GS* 24).[25]

The root of that original nakedness free from shame, which Genesis 2:25 speaks of, must be sought in that complete truth about man. Man or woman, in the context of their beatifying beginning, are free with the freedom of the gift. To remain in the relationship of the "sincere gift of themselves" and to become such a gift for each other, through the whole of their humanity made of femininity and masculinity (also in relation to that perspective which Genesis 2:24 speaks of), they must be free precisely in this way.

We mean here freedom especially as mastery of oneself (self-control). From this aspect, it is indispensable that man may be able to "give himself," that he may become a gift, that he will be able to "fully discover his true self" in "a sincere giving of himself" (referring to the words of the Council). Thus the words, "They were naked and were not ashamed" can and must be understood as the revelation—and at the same time rediscovery—of freedom. This freedom makes possible and qualifies the nuptial sense of the body.

Genesis 2:25 says even more, however. It indicates the possibility and the characteristic of this mutual "experience of the body." It enables us also to identify that nuptial meaning of the body *in actu.* When we read: "They were naked and were not ashamed," we directly touch its fruits and indirectly touch almost the root of it. Free interiorly from the constraint of their own bodies and sex, free with the freedom of the gift, man and woman could enjoy the whole truth, the whole self-evidence of man, just as God-Yahweh had revealed these things to them in the mystery of creation.

This truth about man, which the conciliar text states precisely in the words quoted above, has two main emphases. The first affirms that man is the only creature in the world that the Creator willed "for its own sake." The second consists in saying that this same man, willed by the Creator in this way right from "the beginning," can find himself only in the disinterested giving of himself. Now, this truth about man, which seems in particular to grasp the original condition connected with the very beginning of man in the mystery of creation, can be reread in both directions, on the basis of the conciliar text. This rereading helps us to understand even more the nuptial meaning of the body. This meaning seems inscribed in the original condition of man and woman (according to Genesis 2:23-25) and in particular in the meaning of their original nakedness.

As we have noted, at the root of their nakedness is the interior freedom of the gift—the disinterested gift of oneself. This gift enables them both, man and woman, to find one another, since the Creator willed each of them "for his (her) own sake" (cf. *GS* 24). Thus man, in the first beatifying meeting, finds the woman, and she finds him. In this way he accepts her interiorly. He accepts her as she is willed "for her own sake" by the Creator, as she is constituted in the mystery of the image of God through her femininity. Reciprocally, she accepts him in the same way, as he is willed "for his own sake" by the Creator, and constituted by him by means of his masculinity. The revelation and the discovery of the nuptial meaning of the body consists in this. The Yahwist narrative, and in particular Genesis 2:25, enables us to deduce that man, as male and female, enters the world precisely with this awareness of the meaning of the body, of masculinity and femininity.

The human body, oriented interiorly by the sincere gift of the person, reveals not only its masculinity or femininity on the physical plane, but reveals also such a value and such a beauty as to go beyond the purely physical dimension of sexuality.[26] In this manner awareness of the nuptial meaning of the body, connected with man's masculinity-femininity, is in a way completed. On the one hand, this meaning indicates a particular capacity of expressing love, in which man becomes a gift. On the other hand, the capacity and deep availability for the affirmation of the person corresponds to it. This is, literally, the capacity of living the fact that the other—the woman for the man and the man for the woman—is, by means of the body, someone willed by the Creator for his or her own sake. The person is unique and unrepeatable, someone chosen by eternal Love.

The affirmation of the person is nothing but acceptance of the gift, which, by means of reciprocity, creates the communion of persons. This communion is constructed from within. It comprises also the whole "exteriority" of man, that is, everything that constitutes the pure and simple nakedness of the body in its masculinity and femininity. Then, as we read in Genesis 2:25, man and woman were not ashamed. The biblical expression "were not ashamed" directly indicates "the experience" as a subjective dimension.

Precisely in this subjective dimension, as two human "egos" determined by their masculinity and femininity, both of them, man and woman, appear in the mystery of their beatifying "beginning." (We are in the state of man's original innocence and at the same time, original happiness.) This is a short appearance, comprising only a few verses in Genesis. However it is full of a surprising content, theological and anthropological at the same time. The revelation and discovery of the nuptial meaning of the body explain man's original happiness. At the same time, it opens the perspective of his earthly history, in which he will never avoid this indispensable "theme" of his own existence.

The following verses of Genesis, according to the Yahwist text of chapter 3, show actually that this historical perspective will be constructed differently from the beatifying beginning (after original sin). It is all the more necessary, however, to penetrate deeply into the mysterious structure, theological and at the same time anthropological, of this beginning. In the whole perspective of his own history, man will not fail to confer a nuptial meaning on his own body. Even if this meaning will undergo many distortions, it will always remain the deepest level. It demands to be revealed in all its simplicity and purity, and to be shown in its whole truth, as a sign of the image of God. The way that goes from the mystery of creation to the "redemption of the body" also passes here (cf. Rom 8).

For the present we are remaining on the threshold of this historical perspective. On the basis of Genesis 2:23-25, we clearly realize the connection that exists between the revelation and the discovery of the nuptial meaning of the body, and man's original happiness. This nuptial meaning is also beatifying. As such, it manifests in a word the whole reality of that donation which the first pages of Genesis speak to us of. Reading them, we are convinced of the fact that the awareness of the meaning of the body that is derived from them—in particular of its nuptial meaning—is the fundamental element of human existence in the world.

This nuptial meaning of the human body can be understood only in the context of the person. The body has a nuptial meaning because the human person, as the Council says, is a creature that God willed for his own sake. At the same time, he can fully discover his true self only in a sincere giving of himself.

Christ revealed to man and woman, over and above the vocation to marriage, another vocation—namely, that of renouncing marriage, in view of the kingdom of heaven. With this vocation, he highlighted the same truth about the human person. If a man or a woman is capable of making a gift of himself for the kingdom of heaven, this proves in its turn (and perhaps even more) that there is the freedom of the gift in the human body. It means that this body possesses a full nuptial meaning.

General audience of January 16, 1980

The Mystery of Man's Original Innocence

The reality of the gift and the act of giving, outlined in the first chapters of Genesis as the content constituting the mystery of creation, confirms that the radiation of love is an integral part of this same mystery. Only love creates the good. Love alone can, in a word, be perceived in all its dimensions and its aspects in created things and especially in man. Its presence is almost the final result of that interpretation of the gift, which we are carrying out here. Original happiness, the beatifying beginning of man whom God created "male and female" (Gn 1:27), the nuptial significance of the body in its original nakedness—all this expresses its radication in love.

This consistent giving goes back to the deepest roots of consciousness and subconsciousness, to the ultimate levels of the subjective existence of both, man and woman. This giving is reflected in their mutual experience of the body and bears witness to its radication in love. The first verses of the Bible speak about it so much as to remove all doubt. They speak not only of the creation of the world and of man in the world. They also speak of grace, that is, of the communication of holiness, of the radiation of the Spirit, which produced a special state of "spiritualization" in that man, who in fact was the first. In biblical language, that is, in the language of revelation, the adjective "first" means precisely "of God": "Adam, the son of God" (cf. Lk 3:38).

Happiness is being rooted in love. Original happiness speaks to us of the beginning of man, who emerged from love and initiated love. That happened in an irrevocable way, despite the subsequent sin and death. In his time, Christ will be a witness to this irreversible love of the Creator and Father, which had already been expressed in the mystery of creation and in the grace of original innocence. The common beginning of man and woman, that is, the original truth of their body in masculinity and femininity, to which Genesis 2:25 draws our attention, does not know shame. This beginning can also be defined as the original and beatifying immunity from shame as the result of love.

This immunity directs us toward the mystery of man's original innocence. It is a mystery of his existence, prior to the knowledge of good and evil and almost "outside" it. The fact that man existed in this way, before breaking the first covenant with his Creator, belongs to the fullness of the mystery of creation. As we have already said, creation is a gift to man. His fullness and deepest dimension is determined by grace, that is, by participation in the interior life of God himself, in his holiness. This is also, in man, the interior foundation and source of his original innocence. With this concept, and more precisely with that of "original justice," theology defines the state of man before original sin.

In the present analysis of the beginning, which opens up for us the ways indispensable for understanding the theology of the body, we must dwell on the mystery of man's original state. That awareness of the body—rather, awareness of the meaning of the body—which we are trying to highlight through analysis of the beginning, reveals the peculiarity of original innocence.

Genesis 2:25 manifests in a direct way the mystery of this innocence which the original man and woman both bore, each in himself or herself. The body itself is, in a way, an "eyewitness" of this characteristic. Significantly, the affirmation contained in Genesis 2:25 about nakedness mutually free from shame is a statement unique in its kind in the whole Bible. It will never be repeated. On the contrary, we can quote many texts in which nakedness will be connected with shame or, in an even stronger sense, with ignominy.[27]

In this wide context the reasons are all the more visible for discovering in Genesis 2:25 a particular trace of the mystery of original innocence and a particular factor of its radiation in the human subject. This innocence belongs to the dimension of grace contained in the mystery of creation, that is, to that mysterious gift made to the inner man, to the human heart. It enables both of them, man and woman, to exist from the beginning in the mutual relationship of the disinterested gift of oneself.

This contains the revelation and at the same time the discovery of the nuptial meaning of the body in its masculinity and femininity. It can be understood why we speak, in this case, of revelation and at the same time of discovery. From the point of view of our analysis, it is essential that the discovery of the nuptial meaning of the body, which we read in the testimony of Genesis, takes place through original innocence. In fact, this discovery reveals and highlights the latter.

Original innocence belongs to the mystery of man's beginning, from which historical man was then separated by committing original sin. This does not mean, however, that he is not able to approach that mystery by means of his theological knowledge.

Historical man tries to understand the mystery of original innocence almost by means of a contrast, that is, going back also to the experience of his own sin and his own sinfulness.[28] He tries to understand original innocence as an essential characteristic for the theology of the body, starting from the experience of shame. In fact, the Bible text itself directs him in this way. Original innocence, therefore, is what "radically," that is, at its roots, excludes shame of the body in the man-woman relationship. It eliminates its necessity in man, in his heart, that is, in his conscience.

Original innocence speaks above all of the Creator's gift. It speaks of the grace that made it possible for man to experience the meaning of the primary donation of the world. In particular it concerns the meaning of the mutual donation of one to the other through masculinity and femininity in this world. However, this innocence seems to refer above all to the interior state of the human heart, of the human will. At least indirectly, it includes the revelation and discovery of human moral conscience, of the whole dimension of conscience. Obviously, this was before the knowledge of good and evil. In a certain sense, it must be understood as original righteousness.

In the prism of our historical *a posteriori,* we are trying to reconstruct, in a certain way, the characteristic of original innocence. This is understood as the content of the reciprocal experience of the body as experience of its nuptial meaning (according to Genesis 2:23-25). Happiness and innocence are part of the framework of the communion of persons, as if it were a question of two convergent threads of man's existence in the mystery of creation. So the beatifying awareness of the meaning of the body—that is, of the nuptial meaning of human masculinity and femininity—is conditioned by original innocence.

We can understand that original innocence as a particular "purity of heart," which preserves an interior faithfulness to the gift according to the nuptial meaning of the body. Consequently, original innocence, conceived in this way, is manifested as a tranquil testimony of conscience which (in this case) precedes any experience of good and evil. Yet this serene testimony of conscience is something all the more beatifying. It can be said that awareness of the nuptial meaning of the body, in its masculinity and femininity, becomes humanly beatifying only by means of this testimony.

We shall devote the next meditation to this subject—that is, to the link which, in the analysis of man's beginning, can be seen between his innocence (purity of heart) and his happiness.

General audience of January 30, 1980

Man and Woman: A Gift for Each Other

Let us continue the examination of that beginning, which Jesus referred to in his talk with the Pharisees on the subject of marriage. This reflection requires us to go beyond the threshold of man's history and arrive at the state of original innocence. To grasp the meaning of this innocence, we take as our basis, in a way, the experience of historical man, the testimony of his heart and conscience.

Following the historical *a posteriori* line, let us try to reconstruct the peculiarity of original innocence enclosed within the mutual experience of the body and its nuptial meaning, according to Genesis 2:23-25. The situation described here reveals the beatifying experience of the meaning of the body. Within the mystery of creation, man attains this in the complementarity of what is male and female in him. However, at the root of this experience there must be the interior freedom of the gift, united above all with innocence. The human will is originally innocent. In this way, the reciprocity and the exchange of the gift of the body, according to its masculinity and femininity, as the gift of the person, is facilitated. Consequently, the innocence to which Genesis 2:25 bears witness can be defined as innocence of the mutual experience of the body.

The sentence: "The man and his wife were both naked, and were not ashamed," expresses this innocence in the reciprocal experience of the body. This innocence inspires the interior exchange of the gift of the person. In the mutual relationship, this actualizes concretely the nuptial meaning of masculinity and femininity. To understand the innocence of the mutual experience of the body, we must try to clarify what the interior innocence in the exchange of the gift of the person consists of. This exchange constitutes the real source of the experience of innocence.

Interior innocence (that is, righteousness of intention) in the exchange of the gift consists in reciprocal "acceptance" of the other, such as to correspond to the essence of the gift. In this way, mutual donation creates the communion of persons. It is a question of "receiving" the other human being and "accepting" him. This is because in this mutual relationship, which Genesis 2:23-25 speaks of, the man and the woman become a gift for each other, through the whole truth and evidence of their own body in its masculinity and femininity. It is a question, then, of an "acceptance" or "welcome" that expresses and sustains, in mutual nakedness, the meaning of the gift. Therefore, it deepens the mutual dignity of it. This dignity corresponds profoundly to the fact that the Creator willed (and continually wills) man, male and female, "for his own sake." The innocence "of the heart," and consequently, the innocence of the experience, means a moral participation in the eternal and permanent act of God's will.

The opposite of this "welcoming" or "acceptance" of the other human being as a gift would be a privation of the gift itself. Therefore, it would be a changing and even a reduction of the other to an "object for myself" (an object of lust, of misappropriation, etc.).

We will not deal in detail now with this multiform, presumable antithesis of the gift. However, in the context of Genesis 2:23-25, we can note that this extorting of the gift from the other human being (from the woman by the man and vice versa) and reducing him or her interiorly to a mere "object for me," should mark the beginning of shame. The latter corresponds to a threat inflicted on the gift in its personal intimacy and bears witness to the interior collapse of innocence in the mutual experience.

According to Genesis 2:25, "The man and his wife were not ashamed." We can conclude that the exchange of the gift, in which the whole of their humanity participated, body and soul, femininity and masculinity, was actualized by preserving the interior characteristic (that is, precisely, innocence) of the donation of oneself and of the acceptance of the other as a gift. These two functions of mutual exchange are deeply connected in the whole process of the gift of oneself. The giving and the accepting of the gift interpenetrate, so that the giving itself becomes accepting, and the acceptance is transformed into giving.

Genesis 2:23-25 enables us to deduce that woman, who in the mystery of creation "is given" to man by the Creator, is "received," thanks to original innocence. That is, she is accepted by man as a gift. The Bible text is quite clear and limpid at this point. At the same time, the acceptance of the woman by the man and the very way of accepting her, become, as it were, a first donation. In giving herself (from the very first moment in which, in the mystery of creation, she was "given" to the man by the Creator), the woman "rediscovers herself" at the same time. This is because she has been accepted and welcomed, and because of the way in which she has been received by the man.

So she finds herself again in the very fact of giving herself "through a sincere gift of herself," (cf. *GS* 24), when she is accepted in the way in which the Creator wished her to be, that is, "for her own sake," through her humanity and femininity. When the whole dignity of the gift is ensured in this acceptance, through the offer of what she is in the whole truth of her humanity and in the whole reality of her body and sex, of her femininity, she reaches the inner depth of her person and full possession of herself.

Let us add that this finding of oneself in giving oneself becomes the source of a new giving of oneself. This grows by virtue of the interior disposition to the exchange of the gift and to the extent to which it meets with the same and even deeper acceptance and welcome as the fruit of a more and more intense awareness of the gift itself.

It seems that the second narrative of creation has assigned to man "from the beginning" the function of the one who, above all, receives the gift (cf. especially Gn 2:23). "From the beginning" the woman is entrusted to his eyes, to his consciousness, to his sensitivity, to his heart. On the other hand, he must, in a way, ensure the same process of the exchange of the gift, the mutual interpenetration of giving and receiving as a gift. Precisely through its reciprocity, it creates a real communion of persons.

In the mystery of creation, the woman was "given" to the man. On his part, in receiving her as a gift in the full truth of her person and femininity, man thereby enriches her. At the same time, he too is enriched in this mutual relationship. The man is enriched not only through her, who gives him her own person and femininity, but also through the gift of himself. The man's giving of himself, in response to that of the woman, enriches himself. It manifests the specific essence of his masculinity which, through the reality of the body and of sex, reaches the deep recesses of the "possession of self." Thanks to this he is capable both of giving himself and of receiving the other's gift.

Therefore, the man not only accepts the gift. At the same time he is received as a gift by the woman, in the revelation of the interior spiritual essence of his masculinity, together with the whole truth of his body and sex. Accepted in this way, he is enriched through this acceptance and welcoming of the gift of his own masculinity. Subsequently, this acceptance, in which the man finds himself again through the sincere gift of himself, becomes in him the source of a new and deeper enrichment of the woman. The exchange is mutual. In it the reciprocal effects of the sincere gift and of the finding oneself again are revealed and grow.

In this way, following the trail of the historical *a posteriori*—and above all, following the trail of human hearts—we can reproduce and, as it were, reconstruct that mutual exchange of the gift of the person, which was described in the ancient text of Genesis, so rich and deep.

General audience of February 6, 1980

Original Innocence and Man's Historical State

Today's meditation presupposes what has already been established by the various analyses made up to now. They sprang from the answer Jesus gave to his interlocutors (cf. Mt 19:3-9; Mk 10:1-12). They had asked him a question about the indissolubility and unity of marriage. The Master had urged them to consider carefully that which was "from the beginning." For this reason, so far in this series of meditations we have tried to reproduce somehow the reality of the union, or rather of the communion of persons, lived "from the beginning" by the man and the woman. Subsequently, we tried to penetrate the content of Genesis 2:25, which is so concise: "And the man and his wife were both naked, and were not ashamed."

These words refer to the gift of original innocence, revealing its character synthetically, so to speak. On this basis, theology has constructed the global image of man's original innocence and justice, prior to original sin, by applying the method of objectivization, proper to metaphysics and metaphysical anthropology. In this analysis we are trying rather to consider the aspect of human subjectivity. The latter, moreover, seems to be closer to the original texts, especially the second narrative of creation, the Yahwist text.

Apart from a certain diversity of interpretation, it seems quite clear that "the experience of the body," such as it can be inferred from the ancient text of Genesis 2:23 and even more from Genesis 2:25, indicates a degree of "spiritualization" of man. This is different from that which the same text speaks of after original sin (cf. Gn 3) and which we know from the experience of historical man. It is a different measure of "spiritualization." It involves another composition of the interior forces of man himself. It involves almost another body-soul relationship, and other inner proportions between sensitivity, spirituality and affectivity, that is, another degree of interior sensitiveness to the gifts of the Holy Spirit. All this conditions man's state of original innocence and at the same time determines it, permitting us also to understand the narrative of Genesis. Theology and also the Magisterium of the Church have given these fundamental truths a specific form.[29]

Undertaking the analysis of the beginning according to the dimension of the theology of the body, we do so on the basis of Christ's words in which he himself referred to that "beginning." When he said: "Have you not read that he who made them from the beginning made them male and female?" (Mt 19:4), he ordered us and he still orders us to return to the depths of the mystery of creation. We do so, fully aware of the gift of original innocence, characteristic of man before original sin. An insuperable barrier divides us from what man then was as male and female, by means of the gift of grace united with the mystery of creation, and from what they both were for each other, as a mutual gift. Yet we try to understand that state of original innocence in its connection with man's historical state after original sin: *"status naturae lapsae simul et redemptae."*

Through the category of the historical *a posteriori,* we try to arrive at the original meaning of the body. We try to grasp the connection existing between it and the nature of original innocence in the "experience of the body," as it is highlighted in such a significant way in the Genesis narrative. We conclude that it is important and essential to define this connection, not only with regard to man's "theological prehistory," in which the life of the couple was almost completely permeated by the grace of original innocence. We must also define this connection in relation to its possibility of revealing to us the permanent roots of the human and especially the theological aspect of the ethos of the body.

Man enters the world and enters the most intimate pattern of his future and his history with awareness of the nuptial meaning of his own body, of his own masculinity and femininity. Original innocence says that that meaning is conditioned "ethically," and furthermore, that on its part, it constitutes the future of the human ethos. This is very important for the theology of the body. It is the reason why we must construct this theology "from the beginning," carefully following the indication of Christ's words.

In the mystery of creation, man and woman were "given" in a special way to each other by the Creator. That was not only in the dimension of that first human couple and of that first communion of persons, but in the whole perspective of the existence of the human family. The fundamental fact of human existence at every stage of its history is that God "created them male and female." He always creates them in this way and they are always such. Understanding of the fundamental meanings contained in the mystery of creation, such as the nuptial meaning of the body (and of the fundamental conditionings of this meaning), is important. It is indispensable in order to know who man is and who he should be, and therefore how he should mold his own activity. It is an essential and important thing for the future of the human ethos.

Genesis 2:24 notes that the two, man and woman, were created for marriage: "Therefore, a man leaves his father and his mother and cleaves to his wife, and they become one flesh." In this way a great creative perspective is opened. It is precisely the perspective of man's existence, which is continually renewed by means of procreation, or, we could say, self-reproduction.

This perspective is deeply rooted in the consciousness of humanity (cf. Gn 2:23) and also in the particular consciousness of the nuptial meaning of the body (Gn 2:25). Before becoming husband and wife (later Genesis 4:1 speaks of this in the concrete), the man and the woman emerge from the mystery of creation in the first place as brother and sister in the same humanity. Understanding the nuptial meaning of the body in its masculinity and femininity reveals the depths of their freedom, which is freedom of giving.

From here that communion of persons begins, in which both meet and give themselves to each other in the fullness of their subjectivity. Thus both grow as persons-subjects. They grow mutually one for the other also through their body and through that nakedness free of shame. In this communion of persons the whole depth of the original solitude of man (of the first one and of all) is perfectly ensured. At the same time, this solitude becomes in a marvelous way permeated and broadened by the gift of the "other." If the man and the woman cease to be a disinterested gift for each other, as they were in the mystery of creation, then they recognize that "they are naked" (cf. Gn 3). Then the shame of that nakedness, which they had not felt in the state of original innocence, will spring up in their hearts.

Original innocence manifests and at the same time constitutes the perfect ethos of the gift.

General audience of February 13, 1980

Man Enters the World As a Subject of Truth and Love

Genesis points out that man and woman were created for marriage: "A man leaves his father and his mother and cleaves to his wife, and they become one flesh" (Gn 2:24). This opens the great creative perspective of human existence, which is always renewed by means of procreation, which is self-reproduction. This perspective is rooted in the consciousness of mankind and also in the particular understanding of the nuptial meaning of the body, with its masculinity and femininity. In the mystery of creation, man and woman are a mutual gift. Original innocence manifests and at the same time determines the perfect ethos of the gift.

We spoke about that at the preceding meeting. Through the ethos of the gift the problem of the "subjectivity" of man, who is a subject made in the image and likeness of God, is partly outlined. In the narrative of creation (especially in Genesis 2:23-25) the woman is certainly not merely an object for the man. They both remain in front of each other in all the fullness of their objectivity as creatures, as "bone of my bones and flesh of my flesh," as male and female, both naked. Only the nakedness that makes woman an object for man, or vice versa, is a source of shame. The fact that they were not ashamed means that the woman was not an "object" for the man nor he for her.

Interior innocence as purity of heart made it impossible somehow for one to be reduced by the other to the level of a mere object. The fact that they were not ashamed means that they were united by awareness of the gift. They were mutually conscious of the nuptial meaning of their bodies, in which the freedom of the gift is expressed and all the interior riches of the person as subject are manifested.

This mutual interpenetration of the "self" of the human persons, of the man and of the woman, seems to exclude subjectively any reduction to an object. This reveals the subjective profile of that love. It can be said that this love "is objective" to the depths, since it is nourished by the mutual "objectivity" of the gift.

After original sin, man and woman will lose the grace of original innocence. The discovery of the nuptial meaning of the body will cease to be for them a simple reality of revelation and grace. However, this meaning will remain as a commitment given to man by the ethos of the gift, inscribed in the depths of the human heart, as a distant echo of original innocence. From that nuptial meaning human love in its interior truth and its subjective authenticity will be formed. Through the veil of shame, man will continually rediscover himself as the guardian of the mystery of the subject, that is, of the freedom of the gift. This is so as to defend it from any reduction to the position of a mere object.

For the present, however, we are before the threshold of man's earthly history. The man and the woman have not yet crossed it toward knowledge of good and evil. They are immersed in the mystery of creation. The depth of this mystery hidden in their hearts is innocence, grace, love and justice: "And God saw everything that he had made, and behold, it was very good" (Gn 1:31).

Man appears in the visible world as the highest expression of the divine gift, because he bears within him the interior dimension of the gift. With it he brings into the world his particular likeness to God, with which he transcends and dominates also his "visibility" in the world, his corporality, his masculinity or femininity, his nakedness. A reflection of this likeness is also the primordial awareness of the nuptial meaning of the body, pervaded by the mystery of original innocence.

Thus, in this dimension, a primordial sacrament is constituted, understood as a sign that transmits effectively in the visible world the invisible mystery hidden in God from time immemorial. This is the mystery of truth and love, the mystery of divine life, in which man really participates. In the history of man, original innocence begins this participation and it is also a source of original happiness. The sacrament, as a visible sign, is constituted with man, as a body, by means of his visible masculinity and femininity. The body, and it alone, is capable of making visible what is invisible: the spiritual and the divine. It was created to transfer into the visible reality of the world the mystery hidden since time immemorial in God, and thus be a sign of it.

So the very sacramentality of creation, the sacramentality of the world was revealed in a way, in man created in the image of God. By means of his corporality, his masculinity and femininity, man becomes a visible sign of the economy of truth and love, which has its source in God himself and which was revealed already in the mystery of creation. Against this vast background we understand fully the words that constitute the sacrament of marriage, present in Genesis 2:24: "A man leaves his father and his mother and cleaves to his wife, and they become one flesh."

Against this vast background, we further understand that the words of Genesis 2:25, "They were both naked, and were not ashamed," through the whole depth of their anthropological meaning, express the fact that, together with man, holiness entered the visible world, created for him. The sacrament of the world, and the sacrament of man in the world, comes from the divine source of holiness, and at the same time is instituted for holiness. Connected with the experience of the nuptial meaning of the body, original innocence is the same holiness that enables man to express himself deeply with his own body. That happens precisely by means of the sincere gift of himself. In this case, awareness of the gift conditions "the sacrament of the body." In his body as male or female, man feels he is a subject of holiness.

With this consciousness of the meaning of his own body, man, as male and female, enters the world as a subject of truth and love. It can be said that Genesis 2:23-25 narrates the first feast of humanity in all the original fullness of the experience of the nuptial meaning of the body. It is a feast of humanity, which draws its origin from the divine sources of truth and love in the mystery of creation. Very soon, the horizon of sin and death will be extended over that original feast (cf. Gn 3). Yet right from the mystery of creation we already draw a first hope, that is, that the fruit of the divine economy of truth and love, which was revealed "at the beginning," is not death, but life. It is not so much the destruction of the body of the man created "in the image of God," as rather the "call to glory" (cf. Rom 8:30).

General audience of February 20, 1980

Analysis of Knowledge and of Procreation

To our analyses dedicated to the biblical beginning, we wish to add another short passage, taken from chapter 4 of Genesis. For this purpose, however, we must refer first of all to the words spoken by Jesus Christ in the talk with the Pharisees (cf. Mt 19 and Mk 10),[30] in the compass of which our reflections take place. They concern the context of human existence, according to which death and the destruction of the body connected with it have become the common fate of man (according to the words, "to dust you shall return" of Genesis 3:19). Christ referred to "the beginning," to the original dimension of the mystery of creation, when this dimension had already been shattered by the *mysterium iniquitatis,* that is, by sin and, together with it, by death, *mysterium mortis.*

Sin and death entered man's history, in a way, through the very heart of that unity which, from the beginning, was formed by man and woman, created and called to become "one flesh" (Gn 2:24). Already at the beginning of our meditations we saw that in referring to "the beginning," Christ leads us, in a certain way, beyond the limit of man's hereditary sinfulness to his original innocence. In this way he enables us to find the continuity and the connection existing between these two situations. By means of them, the drama of the origins was produced, as well as the revelation of the mystery of man to historical man.

This authorizes us to pass, after the analyses concerning the state of original innocence, to the last of them, that is, to the analysis of "knowledge and of procreation." Thematically, it is closely bound up with the blessing of fertility, which is inserted in the first narrative of man's creation as male and female (cf. Gn 1:27-28). Historically, on the other hand, it is already inserted in that horizon of sin and death. As Genesis teaches (cf. Gn 3), this has weighed on the consciousness of the meaning of the human body, together with the breaking of the first covenant with the Creator.

In Genesis 4, and therefore still within the scope of the Yahwist text, we read: "Adam knew Eve his wife, and she conceived and bore Cain, saying, 'I have begotten a man with the help of the Lord.' And again, she bore his brother Abel" (Gn 4:1-2). If we connect with knowledge that first fact of the birth of a man on earth, we do so on the basis of the literal translation of the text. According to it, the conjugal union is defined as knowledge. "Adam *knew* Eve his wife," which is a translation of the Semitic term *jadac*.[31]

We can see in this a sign of the poverty of the archaic language, which lacked varied expressions to define differentiated facts. Nevertheless, it is significant that the situation in which husband and wife unite so closely as to become one flesh has been defined as knowledge. In this way, from the very poverty of the language a specific depth of meaning seems to emerge. It derives precisely from all the meanings hitherto analyzed.

Evidently, this is also important as regards the "archetype" of our way of conceiving corporeal man, his masculinity and his femininity, and therefore his sex. In this way, through the term knowledge used in Genesis 4:1-2 and often in the Bible, the conjugal relationship of man and woman—that they become, through the duality of sex, "one flesh"—was raised and introduced into the specific dimension of persons. Genesis 4:1-2 speaks only of knowledge of the woman by the man, as if to stress above all the activity of the latter. It is also possible, however, to speak of the reciprocity of this knowledge, in which man and woman participate by means of their body and their sex. Let us add that a series of subsequent biblical texts, as, moreover, the same chapter of Genesis (cf. Gn 4:17, 4:25), speak with the same language. This goes up to the words Mary of Nazareth spoke in the annunciation: "How shall this be, since I know not man?" (Lk 1:34).

That biblical "knew" appears for the first time in Genesis 4:1-2. With it, we find ourselves in the presence of both the direct expression of human intentionality (because it is characteristic of knowledge), and of the whole reality of conjugal life and union. In it, man and woman become "one flesh."

Even though due to the poverty of the language, in speaking here of knowledge, the Bible indicates the deepest essence of the reality of married life. This essence appears as an element and at the same time a result of those meanings, the trace of which we have been trying to follow from the beginning of our study. It is part of the awareness of the meaning of one's own body. In Genesis 4:1, becoming "one flesh," the man and the woman experience in a particular way the meaning of their body. In this way, together they become almost the one subject of that act and that experience, while remaining, in this unity, two really different subjects. In a way, this authorizes the statement that "the husband knows his wife" or that both "know" each other. Then they reveal themselves to each other, with that specific depth of their own human self. Precisely this self is revealed also by means of their sex, their masculinity and femininity. Then, in a unique way, the woman "is given" to the man to be known, and he to her.

To maintain continuity with regard to the analyses made up to the present (especially the last ones, which interpret man in the dimension of a gift), it should be pointed out that, according to Genesis, *datum* [to give] and *donum* [gift] are equivalent.

However, Genesis 4:1-2 stresses *datum* above all. In conjugal knowledge, the woman is given to the man and he to her, since the body and sex directly enter the structure and the content of this knowledge. In this way, the reality of the conjugal union, in which the man and the woman become one flesh, contains a new and, in a way, definitive discovery of the meaning of the human body in its masculinity and femininity. But in connection with this discovery, is it right to speak only of "sexual life together"? We must consider that each of them, man and woman, is not just a passive object, defined by his or her own body and sex, and in this way determined "by nature." On the contrary, because they are a man and a woman, each of them is "given" to the other as a unique and unrepeatable subject, as "self," as a person.

Sex decides not only the somatic individuality of man, but defines at the same time his personal identity and concreteness. Precisely in this personal identity and concreteness, as an unrepeatable female-male "self," man is "known" when the words of Genesis 2:24 come true: "A man... cleaves to his wife, and they become one flesh." The knowledge which Genesis 4:1-2 and all the following biblical texts speak of, arrives at the deepest roots of this identity and concreteness, which man and woman owe to their sex. This concreteness means both the uniqueness and the unrepeatability of the person.

It was worthwhile, therefore, to reflect on the eloquence of the biblical text quoted and of the word "knew." In spite of the apparent lack of terminological precision, it allows us to dwell on the depth and dimension of a concept, which our contemporary language, precise though it is, often deprives us of.

General audience of March 5, 1980

The Mystery of Woman Is Revealed in Motherhood

In the preceding meditation, we analyzed the sentence of Genesis 4:1 and, in particular, the term "knew." The original text used this word to define conjugal union. We also pointed out that this biblical knowledge establishes a kind of personal archetype[32] of corporality and human sexuality. That seems absolutely fundamental in order to understand man, who, from the beginning, searches for the meaning of his own body. This meaning is at the basis of the theology of the body itself. The term "knew" (cf. Gn 4:1-2) synthesizes the whole density of the biblical text analyzed so far.

According to Genesis 4:1, the man "knows" the woman, his wife, for the first time in the act of conjugal union. He is that same man who, by imposing names, that is, also by "knowing," differentiated himself from the whole world of living beings or *animalia,* affirming himself as a person and subject. The knowledge of which Genesis 4:1 speaks does not and cannot take him away from the level of that original and fundamental self-awareness. Whatever a one-sidedly "naturalistic" mentality might say about it, in Genesis 4:1 it cannot be a question of passive acceptance of one's own determination by the body and by sex, precisely because it is a question of knowledge.

On the contrary, it is a further discovery of the meaning of one's own body. It is a common and reciprocal discovery, just as the existence of man, whom "God created male and female," is common and reciprocal from the beginning. Knowledge, which was at the basis of man's original solitude, is now at the basis of this unity of the man and the woman. The Creator enclosed the clear perspective of this in the mystery of creation (cf. Gn 1:27; 2:23). In this knowledge, man confirms the meaning of the name "Eve," given to his wife, "because she was the mother of all the living" (Gn 3:20).

According to Genesis 4:1, the one who knows is the man, and the one who is known is the woman-wife. It is as if the specific determination of the woman, through her own body and sex, hid what constitutes the depth of her femininity. On the other hand, after the sin, the man was the first to feel the shame of his nakedness. He was the first to say: "I was afraid, because I was naked, and I hid myself" (Gn 3:10). It will be necessary to return separately to the state of mind of them both after the loss of original innocence.

However, in the knowledge which Genesis 4:1 speaks of, the mystery of femininity is manifested and revealed completely by means of motherhood, as the text says: "She conceived and bore...." The woman stands before the man as a mother, the subject of the new human life that is conceived and develops in her, and from her is born into the world. Likewise, the mystery of man's masculinity, that is, the generative and fatherly meaning of his body, is also thoroughly revealed.[33]

The theology of the body contained in Genesis is concise and sparing of words. At the same time, fundamental contents, in a certain sense primary and definitive, find expression in it. Everyone finds himself again in his own way, in that biblical knowledge. The constitution of the woman is different, as compared with the man. We know today that it is different even in the deepest bio-physiological determinants. It is manifested externally only to a certain extent, in the construction and form of her body. Maternity manifests this constitution internally, as the particular potentiality of the female organism. With creative peculiarity it serves for the conception and begetting of the human being, with the help of man. Knowledge conditions begetting.

Begetting is a perspective, which man and woman insert in their mutual knowledge. The latter goes beyond the limits of subject-object, such as man and woman seem to be mutually. Knowledge indicates on the one side him who knows and on the other side her who is known or vice versa. The consummation of marriage, the specific *consummatum,* is also enclosed in this knowledge. In this way the reaching of the "objectivity" of the body, hidden in the somatic potentialities of the man and of the woman, is obtained, and at the same time the reaching of the objectivity of the man who "is" this body. By means of the body, the human person is husband and wife. At the same time, in this particular act of knowledge, mediated by personal femininity and masculinity, the discovery of the pure subjectivity of the gift—that is, mutual self-fulfillment in the gift—seems to be reached.

Procreation brings it about that the man and the woman (his wife) know each other reciprocally in the "third," sprung from them both. Therefore, this knowledge becomes a discovery. In a way it is a revelation of the new man, in whom both of them, man and woman, again recognize themselves, their humanity, their living image. In everything that is determined by both of them through the body and sex, knowledge inscribes a living and real content. So knowledge in the biblical sense means that the biological determination of man, by his body and sex, stops being something passive. It reaches the specific level and content of self-conscious and self-determinant persons. Therefore, it involves a particular consciousness of the meaning of the human body, bound up with fatherhood and motherhood.

The whole exterior constitution of woman's body, its particular aspect, the qualities which, with the power of perennial attractiveness, are at the beginning of the knowledge, which Genesis 4:1-2 speaks of ("Adam knew Eve his wife"), are in close union with motherhood. The Bible (and subsequently the liturgy), with its characteristic simplicity, honors and praises throughout the centuries "the womb that bore you and the breasts that you sucked" (Lk 11:27). These words constitute a eulogy of motherhood, of femininity, of the female body in its typical expression of creative love. In the Gospel these words are referred to the Mother of Christ, Mary, the second Eve. The first woman, on the other hand, at the moment when the maternal maturity of her body was revealed for the first time, when she conceived and bore, said: "I have begotten a man with the help of the Lord" (Gn 4:1).

These words express the whole theological depth of the function of begetting-procreating. The woman's body becomes the place of the conception of the new man.[34] In her womb, the conceived man assumes his specific human aspect before being born. The somatic homogeneousness of man and woman, which found its first expression in the words: "This is bone of my bones and flesh of my flesh" (Gn 2:23), is confirmed in turn by the words of the first woman-mother: "I have begotten a man!" In giving birth, the first woman is fully aware of the mystery of creation, which is renewed in human generation. She is also fully aware of the creative participation that God has in human generation, his work and that of her husband, since she says: "I have begotten a man with the help of the Lord."

There cannot be any confusion between the spheres of action of the causes. The first parents transmit to all human parents the fundamental truth about the birth of man in the image of God, according to natural laws. They transmit this even after sin, together with the fruit of the tree of knowledge of good and evil and almost at the threshold of all historical experiences. In this new man—born of the woman-parent thanks to the man-parent—there is reproduced every time the "image of God," of that God who constituted the humanity of the first man: "God created man in his own image; male and female he created them" (Gn 1:27).

There are deep differences between man's state of original innocence and his state of hereditary sinfulness. However, that "image of God" constitutes a basis of continuity and unity. The "knowledge" which Genesis

4:1 speaks of is the act which originates being. Rather, in union with the Creator, it establishes a new man in his existence. In his transcendental solitude, the first man took possession of the visible world, created for him, knowing and imposing names on living beings *(animalia)*. The same "man," as male and female, knowing each other in this specific community-communion of persons, in which they are united so closely with each other as to become "one flesh," constitutes humanity. That is, they confirm and renew the existence of man as the image of God. This happens every time both of them, man and woman, take up again, so to speak, this image from the mystery of creation and transmit it "with the help of the Lord God."

The words of Genesis are a testimony of the first birth of man on earth. They enclose within them at the same time everything that can and must be said of the dignity of human generation.

General audience of March 12, 1980

The Knowledge-Generation Cycle and the Perspective of Death

We are drawing to the end of the cycle of reflections wherein we have tried to follow Christ's appeal handed down to us by Matthew 19:3-9 and by Mark 10:1-12: "Have you not read that he who made them from the beginning made them male and female, and said, 'For this reason a man shall leave his father and mother and be joined to his wife, and the two shall become one flesh?'" (Mt 19:4-5). In Genesis, conjugal union is defined as knowledge. "Adam knew Eve his wife, and she conceived and bore...saying, 'I have begotten a man with the help of the Lord'" (Gn 4:1). In our preceding meditations, we have tried to throw light on the content of that biblical knowledge. With it man, male-female, not only gives his own name, as he did when he gave names to the other living beings *(animalia)*, thus taking possession of them, but he knows in the sense of Genesis 4:1 (and other passages of the Bible). That is, he realizes what the name "man" expresses. He realizes humanity in the new man generated. In a sense, therefore, he realizes himself, that is, the man-person.

In this way, the biblical cycle of "knowledge-generation" closes. This cycle of knowledge is constituted by the union of persons in love, which enables them to unite so closely that they become one flesh. Genesis reveals to us fully the truth of this cycle. By means of the knowledge of which the Bible speaks, man—male and female—conceives and generates a new being, like himself, to whom he can give the name of man ("I have begotten a man"). Thus man takes possession of his humanity, or rather retakes possession of it. However, that happens in a different way from the manner in which he had taken possession of all other living beings when he had given them their names. On that occasion, he had become their master. He had begun to carry out the content of the Creator's mandate: "Subdue the earth and have dominion over it" (cf. Gn 1:28).

However, the first part of the same command: "Be fruitful and multiply, and fill the earth" (Gn 1:28), conceals another content and indicates another element. In this knowledge, the man and the woman give rise to a being similar to them. They can say of it: "This is bone of my bones and flesh of my flesh" (Gn 2:24). In this knowledge they are almost "carried off" together. They are both taken possession of by the humanity which they, in union and in mutual knowledge, wish to express again. They wish to take possession of it again, deriving it from themselves, from their own humanity. They derive it from the marvelous male and female maturity of their bodies. Finally, through the whole sequence of human conceptions and generations right from the beginning, they derive it from the mystery of creation.

In this sense, biblical knowledge can be explained as "possession." Is it possible to see in it some biblical equivalent of *eros?* It is a question here of two conceptual spheres, of two languages, biblical and Platonic. Only with great caution can they be used to interpret each other.[35] However, it seems that in the original revelation the idea of man's possession of the woman, or vice versa, as of an object, is not present. On the other hand, it is well known that as a result of the sinfulness contracted after original sin, man and woman must reconstruct, with great effort, the meaning of the disinterested mutual gift. This will be the subject of our further analyses.

The revelation of the body, contained in Genesis, especially in chapter 3, shows with impressive clearness the cycle of "knowledge-generation." It shows that this cycle, so deeply rooted in the potentiality of the human body, was subjected, after sin, to the law of suffering and death. God-Yahweh says to the woman: "I will greatly multiply your pain in childbearing; in pain you shall bring forth children" (Gn 3:16). The horizon of death opens up before man, together with revelation of the generative meaning of the body in the spouses' act of mutual knowledge. The first man gives his wife the name Eve, "because she was the mother of all living" (Gn 3:20), when he had already heard the words of the sentence which determined the whole perspective of human existence "within" the knowledge of good and evil. This perspective is confirmed by the words: "You shall return to the ground, for out of it you were taken. You are dust, and to dust you shall return" (Gn 3:19).

The radical character of this sentence is confirmed by the evidence of the experiences of man's whole earthly history. The horizon of death extends over the whole perspective of human life on earth, life that was inserted in that original biblical cycle of "knowledge-generation." Man has broken the covenant with his Creator by picking the fruit of the tree of the knowledge of good and evil. He is detached by God-Yahweh from the tree of life: "Now, let him not put forth his hand and take also of the tree of life, and eat, and live forever" (Gn 3:21). In this way, the life given to man in the mystery of creation has not been taken away. But it is restricted by the limit of conceptions, births and deaths, and further aggravated by the perspective of hereditary sinfulness. But it is given to him again, in a way, as a task in the same ever-recurring cycle.

The sentence: "Adam knew his wife, and she conceived and bore..." (Gn 4:1) is like a seal impressed on the original revelation of the body at the very beginning of man's history on earth. This history is always formed anew in its most fundamental dimension as if from the beginning, by means of the same "knowledge-generation" which Genesis speaks of.

Thus, each person bears within him the mystery of his beginning, closely bound up with awareness of the generative meaning of the body. Genesis 4:1-2 seems to be silent on the subject of the relationship between the generative and the nuptial meaning of the body. Perhaps it is not yet the time or the place to clarify this relationship, even though it seems indispensable in the further analysis. It will be necessary, then, to raise again the questions connected with the appearance of shame in man, shame of his masculinity and femininity, not experienced before. However, for now this is in the background.

In the foreground there remains, however, the fact that "Adam knew Eve his wife, and she conceived and bore...." This is precisely the threshold of man's history. It is his beginning on the earth. On this threshold man, as male and female, stands with the awareness of the generative meaning of his own body. Masculinity conceals within it the meaning of fatherhood, and femininity that of motherhood. In the name of this meaning, Christ will one day give a categorical answer to the question that the Pharisees will ask him (cf. Mt 19; Mk 10). On the other hand, penetrating the simple content of this answer, we are trying at the same time to shed light on the context of that beginning to which Christ referred. The theology of the body has its roots in it.

Awareness of the meaning of the body and awareness of its generative meaning come into contact, in man, with awareness of death, the inevitable horizon of which they bear within them. Yet the "knowledge-generation" cycle always returns in human history. In it, life struggles ever anew with the inexorable perspective of death, and always overcomes it. It is as if the reason for this refusal of life to surrender, which is manifested in generation, were always the same knowledge. With that knowledge, man goes beyond the solitude of his own being, and decides again to affirm this being in an "other." Both of them, man and woman, affirm it in the new person generated.

In this affirmation, biblical knowledge seems to acquire an even greater dimension. It seems to take its place in that "vision" of God himself, which the first narrative of the creation of man ends with. The narrative is about the male and the female made in the image of God. "God saw everything that he had made and...it was very good" (Gn 1:31). In spite of all the experiences of his life, in spite of suffering, disappointment with himself, his sinfulness, and, finally, in spite of the inevitable prospect of death, man always continues to put knowledge at the beginning of generation. In this way, he seems to participate in that first "vision" of God himself: God the Creator "saw...and behold, it was very good." He confirms the truth of these words ever anew.

General audience of March 26, 1980

Marriage in the Integral Vision of Man

The Gospels according to Matthew and Mark report the answer Christ gave to the Pharisees when they questioned him about the indissolubility of marriage. They referred to the law of Moses, which in certain cases admitted the practice of the so-called certificate of divorce. Reminding them of the first chapters of Genesis, Christ answered: "Have you not read that he who made them from the beginning made them male and female, and said, 'For this reason a man shall leave his father and mother and be joined to his wife, and the two shall become one flesh'? So they are no longer two but one flesh. What, therefore, God has joined together, let not man put asunder." Then, referring to their question about the law of Moses, Christ added: "For your hardness of heart Moses allowed you to divorce your wives, but from the beginning it was not so" (Mt 19:3ff.; cf. Mk 12:2ff.). In his answer, Christ referred twice to the "beginning." Therefore we, too, in the course of our analyses, have tried to clarify in the deepest possible way the meaning of this "beginning." It is the first inheritance of every human being in the world, man and woman. It is the first attestation of human identity according to the revealed word, the first source of the certainty of man's vocation as a person created in the image of God himself.

Christ's reply has a historical meaning, but not only a historical one. People of all times raise the question on the same subject. Our contemporaries also do so. But in their questions they do not refer to the law of Moses, which admitted the certificate of divorce, but to other circumstances and other laws. These questions of theirs are charged with problems, unknown to Christ's interlocutors. We know what questions concerning marriage and the family were addressed to the last Council, to Pope Paul VI, and are continually formulated in the post-conciliar period, day after day, in the most varied circumstances. They are addressed by single persons, married couples, fiancés and young people. But they are also addressed by writers, journalists, politicians, economists and demographers, in a word, by contemporary culture and civilization.

I think that among the answers that Christ would give to the people of our time and to their questions, often so impatient, the one he gave to the Pharisees would still be fundamental. Answering those questions, Christ would refer above all to the "beginning." Perhaps he would do so all the more resolutely and essentially in that the interior and at the same time the cultural situation of modern man seems to be moving away from that beginning. It is assuming forms and dimensions which diverge from the biblical image of the beginning into points that are clearly more and more distant.

However, Christ would not be surprised by any of these situations, and I suppose that he would continue to refer mainly to the beginning.

For this reason, Christ's answer called for an especially thorough analysis. In that answer, fundamental and elementary truths about the human being, as man and woman, were recalled. It is the answer through which we catch a glimpse of the structure of human identity in the dimensions of the mystery of creation and, at the same time, in the perspective of the mystery of redemption. Without that there is no way of constructing a theological anthropology and, in its context, a theology of the body. From this the fully Christian view of marriage and the family takes its origin. Paul VI pointed this out when, in his encyclical dedicated to the problems of marriage and procreation in its responsible meaning on the human and Christian planes, he referred to the "total vision of man" *(Humanae Vitae* 7). In the answer to the Pharisees, Christ also put forward to his interlocutors this "total vision of man," without which no adequate answer can be given to questions connected with marriage and procreation. This total vision of man must be constructed from the beginning.

This applies also to the modern mentality, just as it did, though in a different way, to Christ's interlocutors. We are children of an age in which, owing to the development of various disciplines, this total vision of man may easily be rejected and replaced by multiple partial conceptions. Dwelling on one or other aspect of the *compositum humanum,* these do not reach man's *integrum,* or they leave it outside their own field of vision. Various cultural trends then take their place. On the basis of these partial truths, these trends formulate their proposals and practical indications on human behavior and, even more often, on how to behave with "man." Man then becomes more an object of determined techniques than the responsible subject of his own action. The answer Christ gave to the Pharisees also wishes man, male and female, to be this subject. This subject decides his own actions in the light of the complete truth about himself, since it is the original truth, or the foundation of genuinely human experiences. This is the truth that Christ makes us seek from the beginning. Thus we turn to the first chapters of Genesis.

The study of these chapters, perhaps more than of others, makes us aware of the meaning and the necessity of the theology of the body. The beginning tells us relatively little about the human body, in the naturalistic and modern sense of the word. From this point of view, in our study we are at a completely pre-scientific level. We know hardly anything about the interior structures and the regularities that reign in the human organism. However, at the same time, perhaps precisely because of the antiquity of the text, the truth that is important for the total vision of man is revealed in the most simple and full way. This truth concerns the meaning of the human body in the structure of the personal subject. Subsequently, reflection on those archaic texts enables us to extend this meaning of the whole sphere of human inter-subjectivity, especially in the perennial man-woman relationship. Thanks to that, we acquire with regard to this relationship a perspective which we must necessarily place at the basis of all modern science on human sexuality, in the bio-physiological sense. That does not mean that we must renounce this science or deprive ourselves of its results. On the contrary, it can teach us something about the education of man, in his masculinity and femininity, and about the sphere of marriage and procreation. If it is to do so, it is necessary—through all the single elements of contemporary science—always to arrive at what is fundamental and essentially personal, both in every individual, man or woman, and in their mutual relations.

It is precisely at this point that reflection on the ancient text of Genesis is irreplaceable. It is the beginning of the theology of the body. The fact that theology also considers the body should not astonish or surprise anyone who is aware of the mystery and reality of the Incarnation. Theology is that science whose subject is divinity. Through the fact that the Word of God became flesh, the body entered theology through the main door. The Incarnation and the redemption that springs from it became also the definitive source of the sacramentality of marriage, which we will deal with at greater length in due time.

The questions raised by modern man are also those of Christians—those who are preparing for the sacrament of marriage or those who are already living in marriage, which is the sacrament of the Church. These are not only the questions of science, but even more, the questions of human life. So many men and so many Christians seek the accomplishment of their vocation in marriage. So many people wish to find in it the way to salvation and holiness.

The answer Christ gave to the Pharisees, zealots of the Old Testament, is especially important for them. Those who seek the accomplishment of their own human and Christian vocation in marriage are called, first of all, to make this theology of the body, whose beginning we find in the first chapters of Genesis, the content of their life and behavior. How indispensable is a thorough knowledge of the meaning of the body, in its masculinity and femininity, along the way of this vocation! A precise awareness of the nuptial meaning of the body, of its generating meaning, is necessary. This is so since all that forms the content of the life of married couples must constantly find its full and personal dimension in life together, in behavior, in feelings! This is all the more so against the background of a civilization which remains under the pressure of a materialistic and utilitarian way of thinking and evaluating. Modern bio-physiology can supply a great deal of precise information about human sexuality. However, knowledge of the personal dignity of the human body and of sex must still be drawn from other sources. A special source is the Word of God himself, which contains the revelation of the body, going back to the beginning.

How significant it is that Christ, in the answer to all these questions, orders man to return, in a way, to the threshold of his theological history! He orders him to put himself at the border between original innocence, happiness and the inheritance of the first fall. Does he not perhaps mean to tell him that the path along which he leads man, male and female, in the sacrament of marriage, the path of the redemption of the body, must consist in regaining this dignity. In it there is simultaneously accomplished the real meaning of the human body, its personal meaning and its meaning of communion.

For the present, let us conclude the first part of our meditations dedicated to this important subject. To give an exhaustive answer to our questions, sometimes anxious ones, on marriage—or even more precisely, on the meaning of the body—we cannot dwell only on what Christ told the

Pharisees, referring to the beginning (cf. Mt 19:3ff.; Mk 10:2ff.). We must also consider all his other statements. Two of them, of an especially comprehensive character, emerge especially. The first one is from the Sermon on the Mount, on the possibilities of the human heart in relation to the lust of the body (cf. Mt 5:8). The second one is when Jesus referred to the future resurrection (cf. Mt 22:24-30; Mk 12:18-27; Lk 20:27-36).

We intend to make these two statements the subject of our following reflections.

General audience of April 2, 1980

NOTES

General audience of September 12, 1979

[1] Speaking of non-living matter, the biblical author used different predicates, such as "separated," "called," "made," "placed." However, speaking of beings endowed with life, he used the term "created" and "blessed." God ordered them: "Be fruitful and multiply." This order refers both to animals and to man, indicating that corporality is common to both (cf. Gn 1:22, 28).

However, in the biblical description, man's creation is essentially distinguished from God's preceding works. Not only is it preceded by a solemn introduction, as if it were a case of God deliberating before this important act, but above all, man's exceptional dignity is set out in relief by the "likeness" to God of whom he is the image.

Creating non-living matter, God "separated." He gave the order to the animals to be fruitful and multiply, but the difference of sex is underlined only in regard to man ("Male and female he created them") by blessing their fruitfulness at the same time, that is, the bond of the persons (cf. Gn 1:27, 28).

[2] The original text states: "God created man *(haadam*—a collective noun: 'humanity'?), in his own image; in the image of God he created him; male *(zakar* —masculine) and female *(uneqebah*—feminine) he created them" (Gn 1:27).

[3] *"Haec sublimis veritas":* "I am who I am" (Ex 3:14) constitutes an object of reflection for many philosophers, beginning from St. Augustine. He held that Plato must have known this text because it seemed very close to his ideas. Through St. Anselm, the Augustinian doctrine of the divine *essentialitas* exercised a profound influence on the theology of Richard of St. Victor, Alexander of Hales and St. Bonaventure.

"To pass from this philosophical interpretation of Exodus to that put forward by St. Thomas, one had necessarily to bridge the gap that separated 'the being of essence' from 'the being of existence.' The Thomistic proofs of the existence of God bridged it."

Meister Eckhart's position differs from this. On the basis of this text, he attributed to God the *puritas essendi: "est aliquid altius ente..."* ("the purity of being; he is something higher than *ens"); cf.* E. Gilson, *Le Thomisme* [Paris: Vrin, 1944], pp. 122-127; E. Gilson, *History of Christian Philosophy in the Middle Ages* [London: Sheed and Ward, 1955], p. 810).

General audience of September 19, 1979

[4] If in the language of the rationalism of the 19th century, the term "myth" indicated what was not contained in reality, the product of the imagination (Wundt), or what is irrational (Levy-Bruhl), the 20th century has modified the concept of myth.

L. Walk sees in myth natural philosophy, primitive and religious. R. Otto considers it as the instrument of religious knowledge. For C. G. Jung, however, myth is the manifestation of the archetypes and the expression of the "collective unconsciousness," the symbol of the interior processes.

M. Eliade discovers in myth the structure of the reality that is inaccessible to rational and empirical investigation. Myth transforms the event into a category, and makes us capable of perceiving the transcendental reality. It is not merely a symbol of the interior processes (as Jung states), but it is an autonomous and creative act of the human spirit by means of which revelation is realized (cf. *Traite d'histoire des religions* [Paris: 1949], p. 363; *Images et symboles* [Paris: 1952], pp. 199-235).

According to P. Tillich myth is a symbol, constituted by the elements of reality to present the absolute and the transcendence of being, to which the religious act tends.

H. Schlier emphasizes that the myth does not know historical facts and has no need of them, inasmuch as it describes man's cosmic destiny, which is always identical.

In short, the myth tends to know what is unknowable.

According to P. Ricoeur: "The myth is something other than an explanation of the world, of its history and its destiny. It expresses in terms of the world, indeed of what is beyond the world, or of a second world, the understanding that man has of himself through relation with the fundamental and the limit of his existence.... It expresses in an objective language the understanding that man has of his dependence in regard to what lies at the limit and the origin of his world" (P. Ricoeur, *Le conflit des interprétation* [Paris: Seuil, 1969], p. 383).

"The Adamic myth is *par excellence* the anthropological myth. Adam means Man. But not every myth of the 'primordial man' is an 'Adamic myth' which...alone is truly anthropological. By this three features are denoted:

"—the aetiological myth relates the origin of evil to an ancestor of present mankind, whose condition is homogeneous with ours....

"—the aetiological myth is the most extreme attempt to separate the origin of evil from that of good. The aim of this myth is to establish firmly that evil has a radical origin, distinct from the more primitive source of the goodness of things.... This distinction of what is radical and what is primitive is essential to the anthropological character of the Adamic myth. It is that which traces back to man the origin of evil placed in a creation which owes its absolute beginning to a creative act of God.

"—the Adamic myth subordinates to the central figure of primordial man other figures which tend to displace the center of the narrative, without, however, suppressing the primacy of the Adamic figure....

"The myth, in naming Adam, man, makes explicit the concrete universality of human evil; the spirit of penitence is given in the Adamic myth the symbol of this universality. Thus we find again...the universalizing function of the myth. But at the same time, we find the two other functions, equally called forth by the penitential experience.... The proto-historical myth thus serves not only to make general to mankind of all times and of all places the experience of Israel, but to extend to mankind the great tension of the condemnation and of mercy which the prophets had taught Israel to discern in its own destiny.

"Finally, the last function of the myth, which finds a motive in the faith of Israel: the myth prepares for speculation in exploring the point where the ontological and the historical part company" (P. Ricoeur, *Finitude et culpabilité: II Symbolique du mal* [Paris: Aubier, 1960], pp. 218-227).

[5] As regards etymology, it is not excluded that the Hebrew term *ish* is derived from a root which signifies "strength" *(ish* or *wsh)*, whereas *ishshah* is linked to a series of Semitic terms whose meaning varies between "woman" and "wife."

The etymology proposed by the biblical text is of a popular character and serves to underline the unity of the origin of man and woman. This seems to be confirmed by the assonance of both terms.

[6] "Religious language itself calls for the transposition from 'images' or rather 'symbolic modalities' to 'conceptual modalities' of expression.

"At first sight this transposition might appear to be a purely extrinsic change. Symbolic language seems inadequate to introduce the concept because of a reason that is peculiar to Western culture. In this culture religious language has always been conditioned by another language, the philosophical, which is the conceptual language *par excellence....* If it is true that a religious vocabulary is understood only in a community which interprets it and according to a tradition of interpretation, it is also true that there does not exist a tradition of interpretation that is not 'mediated' by some philosophical conception.

"So the word 'God,' which in the biblical texts receives its meaning from the *convergence* of different modes of discourse (narratives, prophecies, legislative texts and wisdom literature, proverbs and hymns)—viewing this convergence both as the point of intersection and as the horizon evasive of any and every form—had to be absorbed in the conceptual space, in order to be reinterpreted in terms of the philosophical Absolute, as the first Mover, first Cause, *Actus*

Essendi, perfect Being, etc. Our concept of God pertains therefore, to an onto-theology, in which there is organized the entire constellation of the key-words of theological semantics, but in a framework of meanings dictated by metaphysics" (P. Ricoeur, *Ermeneutica biblica* [Brescia: Morcelliana, 1978], pp. 140-141; original title, *Biblical Hermeneutics* [Montana: 1975]).

The question, whether the metaphysical reduction really expresses the content which the symbolical and metaphorical language conceals within itself, is another matter.

General audience of September 26, 1979

[7] Already the Greek translation of the Old Testament, the Septuagint, which goes back to about the 2nd century B.C., interprets Genesis 3:15 in the Messianic sense, applying the masculine pronoun *autós* in reference to the Greek neuter noun *sperma (semen* in the Vulgate). The Judaic tradition continues this interpretation.

Christian exegesis, beginning with St. Irenaeus *(Adv. Haer.* III, 23, 7), sees this text as "proto-gospel," which announces the victory won by Jesus Christ over Satan. In the last few centuries scripture scholars have interpreted this pericope differently, and some of them challenge the Messianic interpretation in recent times. However, there has been a return to it under a rather different aspect. The Yahwist author unites prehistory with the history of Israel, which reaches its peak in the Messianic dynasty of David, which will fulfill the promises of Genesis 3:15 (cf. 2 Sam 7:12).

The New Testament illustrated the fulfillment of the promise in the same Messianic perspective: Jesus is the Messiah, descendant of David (cf. Rom 1:3; 2 Tim 2:8), born of woman (cf. Gal 4:4), a new Adam-David (cf. 1 Cor 15), who must reign "until he has put all his enemies under his feet" (1 Cor 15:25). Finally Revelation 12:1-10 presents the final fulfillment of the prophecy of Genesis 3:15. While not being a clear and direct announcement of Jesus as Messiah of Israel, it leads to him, however, through the royal and Messianic tradition that unites the Old and the New Testament.

[8] Speaking here of the relationship between "experience" and "revelation," indeed of a surprising convergence between them, we wish merely to say that man in his present state of existing in the body, experiences numerous limitations, sufferings, passions, weaknesses and finally death itself, which, at the same time, refer this existence of his in the body to another and different state or dimension. When St. Paul writes of the "redemption of the body," he speaks with the language of revelation; experience, in fact, is not able to grasp this content or rather this reality. At the same time, in this content as a whole, the author of Romans 8:23 includes everything that is offered both to him and, in a certain way, to every man (independently of his relationship with revelation) through the experience of human existence, which is an existence in the body.

Therefore, we have the right to speak of the relationship between experience and revelation. In fact, we have the right to raise the problem of their mutual relation, even if for many people there passes between them a line of demarcation which is a line of complete antithesis and radical antinomy. In their opinion, this line must certainly be drawn between faith and science, between theology and philosophy. In the formulation of this point of view, abstract considerations rather than man as a living subject are considered.

General audience of October 10, 1979

[9] The Hebrew text constantly calls the first man *ha-'adam*, while the term *'is* ("male") is introduced only when contrasted with *'issa* ("female"). So "man" was solitary without reference to sex.

However, in the translation into some European languages it is difficult to express this concept of Genesis, because "man" and "male" are usually defined with one word: *homo, uomo, homme, man.*

[10] "An essential (quidditive) definition is a statement which explains the essence or nature of things. It will be essential when we can define a thing by its proximate genus and *specific differentia.*

"The *proximate genus* includes within its comprehension all the essential elements of the genera above it and, therefore, includes all the beings that are cognate or similar in nature to the thing that is being defined. The *specific differentia,* on the other hand, brings in the distinctive element which separates this thing from all others of a similar nature, by showing in what manner it is different from all others, with which it might be erroneously identified.

"Man is defined as a 'rational animal.' 'Animal' is his proximate genus; 'rational' is his *specific differentia.* The proximate genus 'animal' includes within its comprehension all the essential elements of the genera above it, because an animal is a 'sentient, living, material substance....'" The *specific differentia* 'rational' is the one distinctive essential element which distinguishes 'man' from every other 'animal.' It therefore makes him a species of his own and separates him from every other 'animal' and every other genus above animal, including plants, inanimate bodies and substance.

"Furthermore, since the *specific differentia* is the distinctive element in the essence of man, it includes all the characteristic 'properties' which lie in the nature of man as man, namely, power of speech, morality, etc., realities which are absent in all other beings in this physical world."

(C. N. Bittle, *The Science of Correct Thinking, Logic* [Milwaukee: 1947], pp. 73-74.)

General audience of October 31, 1979

[11] Biblical anthropology distinguishes in man not so much the body and the soul as body and life.

The biblical author presents here the conferring of the gift of life through "breath" which does not cease to belong to God. When God takes it away, man returns to dust, from which he was made (cf. Job 34:14-15; Ps 104:29f.).

General audience of November 7, 1979

[12] The Hebrew term *'adam* expresses the collective concept of the human species, that is, man who represents humanity. (The Bible defines the individual using the expression: "son of man," *ben-'adam.*) The contraposition: *'is-'issah* underlines the sexual difference (as in Greek *anergyne*).

After the creation of the woman, the Bible text continues to call the first man *'adam* (with the definite article) thus expressing his "corporate personality," since he has become "father of mankind," its progenitor and representative, just as Abraham was recognized as "father of believers" and Jacob was identified with Israel—the Chosen People.

[13] Adam's sleep, (in Hebrew, *tardemah)* is a deep one (in Latin, *sopor),* into which man falls without consciousness or dreams. (The Bible has another term to define a dream: *halom;* cf. Gn 15:12; 1 Sm 26:12.)

Freud examines on the other hand, the content of dreams (Latin: *somnium)* which, being formed with physical elements "pushed back into the subconscious" makes it possible, in his opinion, to allow the unconscious contents to emerge. The latter, he claims, are in the last analysis, always sexual. This idea is, of course, quite alien to the biblical author.

In the theology of the Yahwist author, the sleep into which God caused the first man to fall emphasizes the exclusivity of God's action in the work of the creation of the woman; the man had no conscious participation in it. God uses his "rib" only to stress the common nature of man and of woman.

[14] *Tardemah* (Italian *torpore,* English "sleep") is the term that appears in Sacred Scripture when, during sleep or immediately afterward, extraordinary events are to happen (cf. Gn 15:12; 1 Sm 26:12; Is 29:10; Job 4:13; 33:15). The Septuagint translates *tardemah* with *ekstasis* (ecstasy).

In the Pentateuch *tardemah* appears only once more in a mysterious context. On God's command, Abram has prepared a sacrifice of animals, driving away birds of prey from them. "As the sun was going down, a deep sleep fell on Abram, and lo, a dread fell upon him" (Gn 15:12). Just then God begins to speak and concludes a covenant with him, which is the summit of the revelation made to Abram.

This scene is similar in a way to the one in the garden of Gethsemane. Jesus "began to be greatly distressed and troubled" (Mk 14:33) and found the apostles "sleeping for sorrow" (Lk 22:45).

The biblical author admits in the first man a certain sense of privation and solitude, even if not of fear. ("It is not good that the man should be alone"; "For the man there was not found a helper fit for him.") Perhaps this state brings about "a sleep caused by sorrow," or perhaps, as in Abram, by "a dread" of non-being, as on the threshold of the work of creation: "The earth was without form and void, and darkness was upon the face of the deep" (Gn 1:2).

In any case, according to both texts, in which the Pentateuch or rather Genesis speaks of the deep sleep *tardemah,* a special divine action takes place, that is, a "covenant" pregnant with consequences for the whole history of salvation: Adam begins mankind, Abram the Chosen People.

[15] It is interesting to note that for the ancient Sumerians the cuneiform sign to indicate the noun "rib" coincided with the one used to indicate the word "life." As for the Yahwist narrative, according to a certain interpretation of Genesis 2:21, God, rather, covers the rib with flesh (instead of closing up its place with flesh) and in this way "makes" the woman, who comes from the "flesh and bones" of the first man (male).

In biblical language this is a definition of consanguinity or descent from the same lineage (cf. Gn 29:14). The woman belongs to the same species as the man, different from the other living beings created before.

In biblical anthropology, the term "bones" expresses a very important element of the body. Since for the Jews there was no precise distinction between "body" and "soul" (the body was considered an exterior manifestation of the personality), "bones" meant simply, by synecdoche, the human "being" (cf., for example, Psalm 139:15: "My frame was not hidden from you"; in Italian, *"Non ti erano nascoste le mie ossa"* [bones]).

"Bone of my bones" can therefore be understood in the relational sense, as "being of my being." "Flesh of my flesh" means that, though she has different physical characteristics, the woman has the same personality as the man possesses.

In the first man's "nuptial song," the expression "bone of my bones, flesh of my flesh" is a form of superlative, stressed, moreover, by the repetition of "this," "she." (In Italian there are three feminine forms: *questa, essa, la.)*

[16] It is difficult to translate exactly the Hebrew expression *cezer kenegdô,* which is translated in various ways in European languages, for example:

Latin: *adiutorium ei conveniens sicut oportebat iuxta eum;*
German: *eine Hilfe...die ihm entspricht;*
French: *égal vis-à-vis de lui;*
Italian: *un aiuto che gli sia simile;*
Spanish: *como él que le ayude;*
English: *a helper fit for him;*
Polish: *odopowicdnia alla niego pomoc.*

Since the term *aiuto* (help) seems to suggest the concept of "complementarity," or better, of "exact correspondence," the term "simile" is connected rather with that of "similarity," but in a different sense from man's likeness to God.

General audience of November 14, 1979

[17] "But God did not create man as a solitary being, for from the beginning 'male and female he created them' (Gn 1:27). Their companionship produces the primary form of interpersonal communion" *(GS 12).*

[18] The dualistic contraposition "soul-body" does not appear in the conception of the most ancient books of the Bible. As has already been stressed (cf.

L'Osservatore Romano, English edition, November 5, 1979, page 15, note 1),
we can speak rather of a complementary combination "body-life." The body is
the expression of man's personality, and if it does not fully exhaust this concept,
it must be understood in biblical language as *pars pro toto;* cf. for example:
"Flesh and blood has not revealed this to you, but my Father..." (Mt 16:17), that
is, it was not a man who revealed it to you.

[19] "For no man ever hates his own flesh, but nourishes it and cherishes it, as
Christ does the Church, because we are members of his body. For this reason a
man shall leave his father and mother and be joined to his wife, and the two
shall become one flesh. This mystery is a profound one, and I am saying that it
refers to Christ and the Church" (Eph 5:29-32).

This will be the subject of our reflections in the part entitled "The Sacrament."

General audience of November 21, 1979

[20] "The intimate partnership of married life and love has been established by
the Creator and qualified by his laws, and is rooted in the conjugal covenant of
irrevocable personal consent" *(GS* 48).

General audience of December 12, 1979

[21] Cf., for example: M. Scheler, *Über Scham und Schamgefühl* (Halle:
1914); Fr. Sawicki, *Fenomenologia wstydliwosci* (Phenomenology of shame)
(Krakow: 1949); and also K. Wojtyla, *Milosc i odpowiedzialnosc* (Krakow:
1962), pp. 165-185; (Love and Responsibilty [New York: 1981], chap. "The
Metaphysics of Shame."

General audience of December 19, 1979

[22] According to the words of Holy Scripture, God penetrates the creature, who
is completely "naked" before him. "And before him no creature is hidden, but
all are open *(páanta gymná)* and laid bare to the eyes of him with whom we
have to do" (Heb 4:13). This characteristic belongs in particular to divine Wisdom: "Wisdom...because of her pureness pervades and penetrates all things"
(Wis 7:24).

General audience of January 2, 1980

[23] The concept of an "adequate anthropology" has been explained in the text
itself as "understanding and interpretation of man in what is essentially human."
This concept determines the very principle of reduction, characteristic of the
philosophy of man, indicates the limit of this principle, and indirectly excludes
the possibility of going beyond this limit. An adequate anthropology rests on
essentially "human" experience, opposed to the reductionism of the "naturalistic" type, which often goes hand in hand with the evolutionistic theory about the
beginnings of man.

[24] The Hebrew term *bara*—created, used exclusively to determine the action of God—appears in the account of creation only in v. 1 (creation of the heavens and of the earth), in v. 21 (creation of animals), and in v. 27 (creation of man). However, it appears here as often as three times. This signifies the fullness and perfection of that act which is the creation of man, male and female. This repetition indicates that the world of creation reached its culminating point here.

General audience of January 16, 1980

[25] "Indeed, the Lord Jesus, when he prayed to the Father 'that all may be one...even as we are one' (Jn 17:21-22), opened up vistas closed to human reason, for he implied a certain likeness between the union of the divine Persons, and the unity of God's sons in truth and charity. This likeness reveals that man, who is the only creature on earth which God willed for itself, cannot fully find himself except through a sincere gift of himself" *(GS* 24).

The strictly theological analysis of Genesis, in particular Genesis 2:23-25, allows us to refer to this text. This constitutes another step between adequate anthropology and the theology of the body which is closely bound up with the discovery of the essential characteristics of personal existence in man's theological prehistory. Although this may meet with opposition on the part of the evolutionist mentality (even among theologians), it would be difficult, however, not to realize that the text of Genesis that we have analyzed, especially Genesis 2:23-25, proves not only the "original," but also the "exemplary" dimension of the existence of man, in particular of man as male and female.

[26] Biblical tradition reports a distant echo of the physical perfection of the first man. The prophet Ezekiel, implicitly comparing the king of Tyre with Adam in Eden, writes as follows:

"You were the signet of perfection, full of wisdom, and perfect in beauty; you were in Eden, the garden of God..." (Ez 28:12-13).

General audience of January 30, 1980

[27] In the ancient Middle East, "nakedness," in the sense of "lack of clothing," meant the state of abjection of men deprived of freedom: slaves, prisoners of war or condemned persons, those who did not enjoy the protection of the law. In women, nakedness was considered a dishonor (cf., e.g., the threats of the prophets: Hos 1:2 and Ez 23:26, 29).

A free man, concerned about his dignity, had to be dressed sumptuously. The longer the trains of his clothes, the higher was his dignity (cf., e.g., Joseph's coat, which made his brothers jealous, or that of the Pharisees, who lengthened their fringes).

The second meaning of "nakedness," in the euphemistic sense, concerned the sexual act. The Hebrew word *cerwat* means a spatial emptiness (for example of the landscape), lack of clothes, divesting, but there was in itself nothing disgraceful about it.

[28] "We know that the law is spiritual; but I am carnal, sold under sin. I do not understand my own actions. For I do not do what I want but I do the very thing I hate.... So then, it is no longer I that do it, but sin which dwells within me. For I know that nothing good dwells within me, that is in my flesh. I can will what is right, but I cannot do it. For I do not do the good I want, but the evil I do not want is what I do. Now if I do what I do not want, it is no longer I that do it, but sin which dwells within me. So I find it to be a law that when I want to do right, evil lies close at hand. For I delight in the law of God, in my inmost self, but I see in my members another law at war with the law of my mind and making me captive to the law of sin which dwells in my members. Wretched man that I am! Who will deliver me from this body of death?" (Rom 7:14-15, 17-24; cf. *"Video meliora proboque, deteriora sequor"* Ovid, *Metamorph.* VII, 20).

General audience of February 13, 1980

[29] "If one should not acknowledge that the first man Adam, on transgressing God's command in paradise, did not immediately lose the holiness and justice in which he had been constituted...let him be anathema" *(Council of Trent,* Sess. V, con. 1, 2: D.B. 788, 789).

"The first parents had been constituted in a state of holiness and justice.... The state of original justice conferred on the first parents was gratuitous and truly supernatural.... The first parents were constituted in a state of integral nature, i.e., immune from concupiscence, ignorance, pain and death...and they enjoyed a unique happiness.... The gifts of integrity granted to the first parents were gratuitous and preternatural" (A. Tanquerey, *Synopsis Theologiae Dogmaticae* [Paris: 1943], 24, pp. 545-549).

General audience of March 5, 1980

[30] The fact must be kept in mind that in the talk with the Pharisees (Mt 19:7-9; Mk 10:4-6), Christ took a position with regard to the practice of the Mosaic law concerning the so-called "certificate of divorce." The words, "for your hardness of heart," spoken by Christ, reflect not only "the history of hearts," but also the whole complexity of the positive law of the Old Testament, which always sought a "human compromise" in this delicate field.

[31] "To know" *(jadac)* in biblical language does not mean only a purely in-tellectual knowledge, but also concrete knowledge, such as the experience of suffering (cf. Is 53:3), of sin (Wis 3:13), of war and peace (Jgs 3:1; Is 59:8). From this experience moral judgment also springs: "knowledge of good and evil" (Gn 2:9-17).

"Knowledge" enters the field of interpersonal relations when it regards family solidarity (Dt 33:9) and especially conjugal relations. Precisely in reference to the conjugal act, the term stresses the paternity of illustrious characters and the origin of their offspring (cf. Gn 4:1, 25; 4:17; 1 Sm 1:19), as valid data for genealogy, to which the tradition of priests (hereditary in Israel) attached great importance.

However, "knowledge" could also mean all other sexual relations, even illicit ones (cf. Nm 31:17; Gn 19:5; Jgs 19:22).

In the negative form, the verb denotes abstention from sexual relations. especially if it is a question of virgins (cf. for example, 1 Kgs 2:4; Jgs 11:39). In this field, the New Testament uses two Hebraisms, speaking of Joseph (Mt 1:25) and of Mary (Lk 1:34).

The aspect of the existential relationship of "knowledge" takes on a special meaning when its subject or object is God himself (for example, Ps 139; Jer 31:34; Hos 2:22; and also Jn 14:7-9; 17:3).

General audience of March 12, 1980

[32] As for archetypes, C. G. Jung describes them as *a priori* forms of various functions of the soul: perception of relations, creative fantasy. The forms fill up with content by means of materials of experience. They are not inert, but are charged with sentiment and tendency (see especially: *Die psychologischen Aspekte des Mutterarchetypus,* Eranos 6, 1938, pp. 405-409).

According to this conception, an archetype can be met with in the mutual man-woman relationship, a relationship which is based on the dual and complementary realization of the human being in two sexes. The archetype will fill up with content by means of individual and collective experience, and can trigger off fantasy, the creator of images. It would be necessary to specify that the archetype: a) is not limited to, or exalted in, physical intercourse, but includes the relationship of "knowing"; b) it is charged with tendency: desire-fear, gift-possession; c) the archetype, as proto-image *(Urbild),* is a generator of images *(Bilder).*

The third aspect enables us to pass to hermeneutics, in the concrete, that of texts of Scripture and of Tradition. Primary religious language is symbolic (cf. W. Stählin, *Symbolon,* 1958; Macquarrie, *God Talk,* 1968; T. Fawcett, *The Symbolic Language of Religion,* 1970). Among the symbols, he prefers some radical or exemplary ones, which we can call archetypal. Among them the Bible uses the symbol of the conjugal relationship, concretely at the level of the "knowing" described.

One of the first poems of the Bible, which applies the conjugal archetype to God's relations with his people, culminates in the verb commented on: "You shall know the Lord" (Hos 2:22—*we yadacta 'et Yhwh;* weakened to "You will know that I am the Lord"—*wydct ky 'ny Yhwh:* Is 49:23; 60:16; Ez 16:62, which are the three "conjugal" poems). A literary tradition starts from here, which will culminate in the Pauline application of Ephesians 5 to Christ and to the Church; then it will pass to patristic tradition and to that of the great mystics (for example, *Llama de amor viva* of St. John of the Cross).

In the treatise *Grundzüge der Literatur-und Sprachwissenschaft,* vol. I. (Munchen: 1976), 4th ed., p. 462, archetypes are defined as follows: "Archaic images and motifs which, according to Jung, form the content of the collective unconscious common to all men; they present symbols, which, in all times and among all peoples, bring to life in a figurative way what is decisive for humanity as regards ideas, representations and instincts."

Freud, it seems, does not use the concept of archetype. He establishes a symbolism or code of fixed correspondences between present-patent images and latent thoughts. The meaning of the symbols is fixed, even if not just one; they may be reducible to an ultimate thought that is irreducible, which is usually some experience of childhood. These are primary and of sexual character (but he does not call them archetypes). See T. Todorov, *Théories du symbole* (Paris: 1977), pp. 317f.; also: J. Jacoby, Komplex, Archetyp, *Symbol in der Psychologie C .G. Jung* (Zurich: 1957).

[33] Fatherhood is one of the most important aspects of humanity in Sacred Scripture.

The text of Genesis 5:3: "Adam...became the father of a son *in his own likeness, after his image"* is explicitly linked with the narrative of the creation of man (Gn 1:27; 5:1) and seems to attribute to the earthly father participation in the divine work of transmitting life, and perhaps also in that joy present in the affirmation: God "saw everything that he had made, and behold, it was very good" (Gn 1:31).

[34] According to the text of Genesis 1:26, the "call" to existence is at the same time the transmission of the divine image and likeness. Man must proceed to transmit this image, thus continuing God's work. The narrative of the generation of Seth stresses this aspect: "When Adam had lived a hundred and thirty years, he became the father of a son in his own likeness, after his image" (Gn 5:3). Since Adam and Eve were the image of God, Seth inherited this likeness from his parents to transmit it to others.

In Sacred Scripture, however, every vocation is united with a mission. So the call to existence is already a predestination to God's work: "Before I formed you in the womb I knew you, and before you were born I consecrated you" (Jer 1:5; cf. also Is 44:1; 9:1-5). God is the One who not only calls to existence, but sustains and develops life from the first moment of conception: "Yet you are he who took me from the womb; you kept me safe upon my mother's breasts. Upon you was I cast from my birth, and since my mother bore me you have been my God" (Ps 22:10, 11; cf. Ps 139:13-15).

The attention of the biblical author is focused on the very fact of the gift of life. Interest in the way in which this takes place is rather secondary and appears only in the later books (cf. Jb 10:8, 11; 2 Mc 7:22-23; Wis 7:1-3).

General audience of March 26, 1980

[35] According to Plato, eros is love athirst for transcendent Beauty, and expresses insatiability straining toward its eternal object. Therefore, it always raises what is human toward the divine, which alone is able to satisfy the nostalgia of the soul imprisoned in matter. It is a love that does not draw back before the greatest effort, in order to reach the ecstasy of union. Therefore, it is an ego-

centric love. It is lust, although directed to sublime values (cf. A. Nygren, *Eros et Agapé* [Paris: 1951], vol. II, pp. 9-10).

Throughout the centuries, through many changes, the meaning of eros has been debased to merely sexual connotations. Characteristic, here, is the text of P. Chauchard, which even seems to deny eros the characteristics of human love:

"The cerebralization of sexuality does not lie in boring technical tricks, but in full recognition of its spirituality, since eros is human only when it is animated by agape and since agape demands to be incarnated in eros" (P. Chauchard, *Vices des vertus, vertus des vices* [Paris: 1963], p. 147).

The comparison of biblical knowledge with Platonic eros reveals the divergence of these two concepts. The Platonic concept is based on nostalgia for transcendent Beauty and on escape from matter. The biblical concept, on the contrary, is geared to concrete reality, and the dualism of spirit and matter is alien to it as also the specific hostility to matter ("And God saw that it was good"— Gn 1:10, 12, 18, 21, 25).

Whereas the Platonic concept of eros goes beyond the biblical scope of human knowledge, the modern concept seems too restricted. Biblical knowledge is not limited to satisfying instinct or hedonistic pleasure, but it is a fully human act, directed consciously toward procreation, and it is also the expression of interpersonal love (cf. Gn 29:20; 1 Sm 1:8; 2 Sm 12:24).

*The following paragraph was inadvertently omitted from page 45:

While the first chapter of Genesis expresses this value in a purely theological form (and indirectly a metaphysical one), the second chapter, on the other hand, reveals so to speak the first circle of the experience lived by man as value. This experience is already inscribed in the meaning of original solitude, and then in the whole narrative of the creation of man as male and female. The concise text of Genesis 2:23, which contains the words of the first man at the sight of the woman created, "taken out of him," can be considered the biblical prototype of the Canticle of Canticles. And if it is possible to read impressions and emotions through words so remote, one might also venture to say that the depth and force of this first and "original" emotion of the male-man in the presence of the humanity of the woman, and at the same time in the presence of the femininity of the other human being, seems something unique and unrepeatable.

BLESSED ARE THE PURE OF HEART

Catechesis on the Sermon on the Mount

Christ Appeals to Man's Heart

As the subject of our future reflections at the Wednesday meetings I wish to develop the following statement of Christ, which is part of the Sermon on the Mount: "You have heard that it was said, 'You shall not commit adultery.' But I say to you that everyone who looks at a woman lustfully has already committed adultery with her in his heart" (Mt 5:27-28).

This passage seems to have a key meaning for the theology of the body, like the one in which Christ referred to the "beginning," which served as the basis of the preceding analyses. We then realized how wide was the context of a sentence, or rather of a word, uttered by Christ. It was a question not only of the immediate context, which emerged in the course of the conversation with the Pharisees, but of the global context. We could not penetrate that without going back to the first chapters of Genesis (omitting what refers there to the other books of the Old Testament). The preceding analyses have shown what an extensive content Christ's reference to the "beginning" involves.

The statement to which we are now referring, Matthew 5:27-28, will certainly introduce us not only to the immediate context in which it appears. It will also introduce us to its wider context, the global context, through which the key meaning of the theology of the body will be revealed to us. This statement is one of the passages of the Sermon on the Mount in which Jesus Christ fundamentally revises the way of understanding and carrying out the moral law of the old covenant. It refers to the following commandments of the Decalogue, in order: the fifth, "You shall not kill" (cf. Mt 5:21-26); the sixth, "You shall not commit adultery" (cf. Mt 5:27-32); and the eighth, according to the text of Exodus (cf. Ex 20:7): "You shall not swear falsely, but shall perform to the Lord what you have sworn" (cf. Mt 5:33-37). It is significant that at the end of the passage about adultery the question of the certificate of divorce also appears (cf. Mt 5:31-32), already mentioned in the preceding chapter.

Above all, the words that precede these articles and the following ones of the Sermon on the Mount are significant. With these words Jesus declares: "Think not that I have come to abolish the law and the prophets; I have come not to abolish them but to fulfill them" (Mt 5:17). In the sentences that follow, Jesus explains the meaning of this opposition and the necessity of the fulfillment of the law in order to realize the kingdom of God: "Whoever...does them [these commandments] and teaches them shall be called great in the kingdom of heaven" (Mt 5:19). "The kingdom of heaven" means the kingdom of God in the eschatological dimension.

The fulfillment of the law fundamentally conditions this kingdom in the temporal dimension of human existence. However, it is a question of a fulfillment that fully corresponds to the meaning of the law, of the Decalogue, of the individual commandments. Only this fulfillment constructs that justice which God the legislator willed. Christ the Teacher urges us not to give such a human interpretation to the whole law and the individual commandments contained in it that it does not foster the justice willed by God the legislator: "Unless your righteousness exceeds that of the scribes and Pharisees, you will never enter the kingdom of heaven" (Mt 5:20).

Christ's statement in Matthew 5:27-28 appears in this context. We intend to take this text as the basis for the present analyses, considering it together with the other statement in Matthew 19:3-9 (and Mark 10) as the key to the theology of the body. Like the other one, this one has an explicitly normative character. It confirms the principle of human morality contained in the commandment, "You shall not commit adultery." At the same time, it determines an appropriate and full understanding of this principle, that is, an understanding of the foundation and at the same time of the condition for its adequate fulfillment. The latter is to be considered precisely in the light of the words of Matthew 5:17-20, already quoted, which we have just drawn attention to.

On the one hand, it is a question here of adhering to the meaning that God the legislator enclosed in the commandment, "You shall not commit adultery." On the other hand, it is a question of carrying out that "justice" on the part of man. This justice must superabound in man himself, that is, it must reach its specific fullness in him. These are the two aspects of fulfillment in the evangelical sense.

We find ourselves in this way at the heart of ethos, that is, in what can be defined as the interior form, almost the soul, of human morality.

Contemporary thinkers (e.g., Scheler) see in the Sermon on the Mount a great turning point in the field of ethos.[36] A living morality in the existential sense is not formed only by the norms that invest the form of the commandments, precepts and prohibitions, as in the case of "You shall not commit adultery." The morality in which there is realized the meaning of being a man is, at the same time, the fulfillment of the law by means of the "superabounding" of justice through subjective vitality. This morality is formed in the interior perception of values, from which duty springs as the expression of conscience, as the response of one's own personal "ego." At the same time ethos makes us enter the depth of the norm itself and descend within the human subject of morality. Moral value is connected with the dynamic process of man's intimacy. To reach it, it is not enough to stop at the surface of human actions. It is necessary to penetrate inside.

In addition to the commandment, "You shall not commit adultery," the Decalogue has also, "You shall not covet your neighbor's wife."[37] In the Sermon on the Mount, Christ connects them with each other, in a way: "Everyone who looks at a woman lustfully has already committed adultery with her in his heart." However, it is not so much a question of distinguishing the scope of those two commandments of the Decalogue as of pointing out the dimension of the interior action, referred to also in the words: "You shall not commit adultery."

This action finds its visible expression in the "act of the body," an act in which the man and the woman participate against the law of matrimonial exclusiveness. The casuistry of the books of the Old Testament aimed at investigating what constituted this "act of the body" according to exterior criteria. At the same time, it was directed at combating adultery, and opened to the latter various legal "loopholes."[38] In this way, on the basis of the multiple compromises "for hardness of heart" (Mt 19:8), the meaning of the commandment as willed by the legislator underwent a distortion. People kept to legalistic observance of the formula, which did not superabound in the interior justice of hearts.

Christ shifts the essence of the problem to another dimension when he says: "Everyone who looks at a woman lustfully has already committed adultery with her in his heart." (According to ancient translations, the text is: "...has already made her an adulteress in his heart," a formula which seems to be more exact.)[39]

In this way, therefore, Christ appeals to the interior man. He does so several times and under different circumstances. In this case it seems especially explicit and eloquent, not only with regard to the configuration of evangelical ethos, but also with regard to the way of viewing man. Not only the ethical reason, but also the anthropological one makes it advisable to dwell at greater length on the text of Matthew 5:27-28, which contains the words Christ spoke in the Sermon on the Mount.

General audience of April 16, 1980

The Ethical and Anthropological Content of the Commandment: "You Shall Not Commit Adultery"

Let us recall the words of the Sermon on the Mount, to which we are referring in this cycle of our Wednesday reflections. The Lord says: "You have heard that it was said, 'You shall not commit adultery.' But I say to you that everyone who looks at a woman lustfully has already committed adultery with her in his heart" (Mt 5:27-28).

The man to whom Jesus refers here is precisely historical man, the one whose beginning and theological prehistory we traced in the preceding series of analyses. Directly, it is the one who hears with his own ears the Sermon on the Mount. But together with him, there is also every other man, set before that moment of history, both in the immense space of the past, and in the equally vast one of the future. To this "future," confronted with the Sermon on the Mount, our present, our contemporary age also belongs.

This man is, in a way, "every" man, each of us. Both the man of the past and also the man of the future can be the one who knows the positive commandment, "You shall not commit adultery" as "contained in the Law" (cf. Rom 2:22-23). But he can equally be the one who, according to the Letter to the Romans, has this commandment only "written on his heart" (cf. Rom 2:15).[40] In the light of the previous reflections, he is the man who from his beginning has acquired a precise sense of the meaning of the body. He has acquired it even before crossing the threshold of his historical experiences, in the mystery of creation, since he emerged from it as "male and female" (cf. Gn 1:27). He is the historical man, who, at the beginning of his earthly vicissitudes, found himself "inside" the knowledge of good and evil, breaking the covenant with his Creator. He is the man who knew (the woman), his wife, and knew her several times. She "conceived and bore" (cf. Gn 4:1-2) according to the Creator's plan, which went back to the state of original innocence (cf. Gn 1:28; 2:24).

In his Sermon on the Mount, especially in the words of Matthew 5:27-28, Christ addresses precisely that man. He addresses the man of a given moment of history and, at the same time, all men belonging to the same human history. As we have already seen, he addresses the "interior" man. Christ's words have an explicit anthropological content. They concern those perennial meanings through which an "adequate" anthropology is constituted.

By means of their ethical content, these words simultaneously constitute such an anthropology. They demand that man should enter into his full image. The man who is "flesh," as a male remains in relationship with woman through his body and sex. (The expression "You shall not commit adultery" indicates this.) In the light of these words of Christ, this man must find himself again interiorly, in his heart.[41] The heart is this dimension of humanity with which the sense of the meaning of the human body, and the order of this sense, is directly linked. Here it is a question both of the meaning which, in the preceding analyses, we called nuptial, and of that which we called generative. What order are we treating of?

This part of our considerations must answer this question. Our answer must reach not only the ethical reasons, but also the anthropological, for they remain in a mutual relationship. For the time being, as a preliminary it is necessary to establish the meaning of Matthew 5:27-28, the meaning of the expressions used in it and their mutual relationship.

Adultery, to which the aforesaid commandment refers, means a breach of the unity by means of which man and woman, only as husband and wife, can unite so closely as to be "one flesh" (Gn 2:24). Man commits adultery if he unites in this way with a woman who is not his wife. The woman likewise commits adultery if she unites in this way with a man who is not her husband. It must be deduced from this that the "adultery in the heart," committed by the man when he "looks at a woman lustfully," means a quite definite interior act. It concerns a desire directed, in this case, by the man toward a woman who is not his wife, in order to unite with her as if she were his wife. Using the words of Genesis 2:24 again, it means uniting in such a way that "they become one flesh." This desire, as an interior act, is expressed by means of the sense of sight, that is, with looks. This was the case of David and Bathsheba, to use an example taken from the Bible (cf. 2 Sm 11:2).[42] The connection of lust with the sense of sight has been highlighted especially in Christ's words.

These words do not say clearly whether the woman—the object of lust—is the wife of another or whether simply she is not the wife of the man who looks at her in this way. She may be the wife of another, or even not bound by marriage. Rather, it is necessary to intuit it, especially on the basis of the expression which precisely defines as adultery what man has committed in his heart with his look. It must be correctly deduced that this lustful look, if addressed to his own wife, is not adultery "in his heart." This is precisely because the man's interior act refers to the woman who is his wife, with regard to whom adultery cannot take place. The conjugal act as an exterior act, in which "they become one flesh," is lawful in the relationship of the man in question with the woman who is his wife. In like manner, the interior act in the same relationship is in conformity with morality.

Nevertheless, that desire, indicated by the expression "everyone who looks at a woman lustfully," has a biblical and theological dimension of its own, which we must clarify here. Even if this dimension is not manifested directly in this one concrete expression of Matthew 5:27-28, it is deeply rooted in the global context, which refers to the revelation of the body. We must go back to this context, so that Christ's appeal to the heart, to the interior man, may ring out in all the fullness of its truth.

This statement of the Sermon on the Mount (Mt 5:27-28) fundamentally has an indicative character. The fact that Christ directly addresses man as the one "who looks at a woman lustfully," does not mean that his words, in their ethical meaning, do not refer also to woman. Christ expresses himself in this way to illustrate with a concrete example how the fulfillment of the law must be understood, according to the meaning that God the legislator gave to it. Furthermore, it is to show how that "superabounding of justice" in the man who observes the sixth commandment of the Decalogue must be understood.

Speaking in this way, Christ wants us not to dwell on the example in itself, but to penetrate the full ethical and anthropological meaning of the statement. If it has an indicative character, this means that, following its traces, we can arrive at understanding the general truth about historical man. This is valid also for the theology of the body. The further stages of our reflections will have the purpose of bringing us closer to understanding this truth.

General audience of April 23, 1980

Lust Is the Fruit of the Breach of the Covenant with God

During our last reflection, we said that the words of Christ in the Sermon on the Mount directly refer to the lust that arises immediately in the human heart. Indirectly, however, those words guide us to understanding a truth about man, which is of universal importance.

The words of Christ, taken from Matthew 5:27-28, direct us toward this truth about historical man, of universal importance. It seems to be expressed in the biblical doctrine on the three forms of lust. We are referring here to the concise statement in 1 John 2:16-17: "For all that is in the world, the lust of the flesh and the lust of the eyes and the pride of life, is not of the Father but is of the world. And the world passes away, and the lust of it, but he who does the will of God abides forever."

To understand these words, obviously it is necessary to carefully consider the context in which they appear, that is, the context of the whole Johannine theology.[43] However, the same words are inserted, at the same time, in the context of the whole Bible. They belong to the whole revealed truth about man, and are important for the theology of the body. They do not explain lust itself in its threefold form, since they seem to assume that "the lust of the flesh and the lust of the eyes and the pride of life," are, in some way, a clear and known concept. However, they explain the genesis of lust in its threefold form, indicating its origin which is "not of the Father," but "of the world."

The lust of the flesh and, together with it, the lust of the eyes and the pride of life, is "in the world." At the same time it "is of the world," not as the fruit of the mystery of creation, but as the fruit of the tree of knowledge of good and evil in man's heart (cf. Gn 2:17). What fructifies in the three forms of lust is not the "world" God created for man, the fundamental "goodness" of which we have read several times in Genesis 1: "God saw that it was good.... It was very good." On the contrary, in the three forms of lust there fructifies the breaking of the first covenant with the Creator, with God-Elohim, with God-Yahweh. This covenant was broken in man's heart. It would be necessary to make here a careful analysis of the events described in Genesis 3:1-6. However, we are referring only in general to the mystery of sin, to the beginnings of human history. The "world" of Genesis has become the "world" of the Johannine words (cf. 1 Jn 2:15-16), the place and source of lust, only as the consequence of sin, as the fruit of the breaking of the covenant with God in the human heart, in the inner recesses of man.

In this way, therefore, the statement that lust "is not of the Father but is of the world," seems to direct us once more to the biblical beginning. The genesis of lust in its three forms presented by John finds in this beginning its first and fundamental elucidation. This explanation is essential for the theology of the body. To understand that truth of universal importance about historical man, contained in Christ's words in the Sermon on the Mount (Mt 5:27-28), we must return once more to Genesis. We must linger once more at the threshold of the revelation of historical man. This is all the more necessary, since this threshold of the history of salvation proves to be at the same time the threshold of authentic human experiences, as we will see in the following analyses. The same fundamental meanings that we drew from the preceding analyses will come to life in them again, as essential elements of a fitting anthropology and the deep substratum of the theology of the body.

The question may arise again whether it is permissible to transport the content typical of the Johannine theology, contained in the entire First Letter (especially in 1 John 2:15-16), to the ground of the Sermon on the Mount according to Matthew, and precisely of Christ's statement in Matthew 5:27-28. ("You have heard that it was said, 'You shall not commit adultery.' But I say to you that everyone who looks at a woman lustfully has already committed adultery with her in his heart.") We will come back to this matter several times. Nevertheless, we are referring straightway to the general biblical context, to the whole truth about man revealed and expressed in it. Precisely in the name of this truth, we are trying to understand completely the man that Christ indicates in the text of Matthew 5:27-28, that is, the man who looks at a woman lustfully.

Is not this look to be explained by the fact that man is precisely a "man of lust," in the sense of the First Letter of John? Both the man who looks lustfully and the woman who is the object of this look are in the dimension of lust in its three forms, which "is not of the Father but is of the world." It is necessary to understand what that lust is, or rather who that "lustful man" of the Bible is. This is necessary in order to discover the depths of Christ's words according to Matthew 5:27-28, and to explain the significance of their reference to the human heart, so important for the theology of the body.

Let us return again to the Yahwist narrative. In it, the same man, male and female, appears at the beginning as a man of original innocence before original sin. Then he appears as the one who lost innocence, by breaking the original covenant with his Creator. We do not intend here to make a complete analysis of temptation and sin, according to the same text of Genesis 3:1-5, the doctrine of the Church in this connection and theology. It should merely be observed that the biblical description itself seems to highlight especially the key moment, in which the gift is questioned in man's heart. The man who gathers the fruit of the "tree of the knowledge of good and evil" makes, at the same time, a fundamental choice. He carries it out against the will of the Creator, God-Yahweh, accepting the motivation suggested by the tempter: "You will not die. For God knows that when you eat of it your eyes will be opened, and you will be like God, knowing good and evil." According to old translations: "You will be like gods, who know good and evil."[44]

This motivation clearly includes questioning the gift and the love from which creation has its origin as donation. As regards man, he receives the "world" as a gift and at the same time the image of God that is, humanity itself in all the truth of its male and female duality. It is enough to read carefully the whole passage of Genesis 3:1-5, to detect in it the mystery of man who turns his back on the Father (even if we do not find this name applied to God in the narrative). Questioning in his heart the deepest meaning of the donation, that is, love as the specific motive of the creation and of the original covenant (cf. Gn 3:5), man turns his back on God-Love, on the Father. In a way he casts God out of his heart. At the same time, he detaches his heart and almost cuts it off from what "is of the Father." Thus, there remains in him what "is of the world."

"Then the eyes of both were opened, and they knew that they were naked, and they sewed fig leaves together and made themselves aprons" (Gn 3:7). This is the first sentence of the Yahwist narrative, which refers to man's situation after sin and shows the new state of human nature. Does not this sentence also suggest the beginning of lust in man's heart? To answer this question more thoroughly, we cannot stop at that first sentence, but must read the whole text again. However, it is worth recalling here what was said in the first analyses on the subject of shame as the experience "of the limit."[45]

Genesis refers to this experience to show the "frontier" between the state of original innocence (cf. Gn 2:25, to which we devoted a great deal of attention in the preceding analyses) and man's sinfulness at the very "beginning." Genesis 2:25 emphasizes that they "were both naked, and were not ashamed." But Genesis 3:6 speaks explicitly of shame in connection with sin. That shame is almost the first source of the manifestation in both man and woman of what "is not of the Father, but of the world."

General audience of April 30, 1980

The Real Significance of Original Nakedness

We have already spoken of the shame which arose in the heart of the first man, male and female, together with sin. The first sentence of the biblical narrative concerning this runs as follows: "Then the eyes of both were opened, and they knew that they were naked, and they sewed fig leaves together and made themselves aprons" (Gn 3:7). This passage, which speaks of the mutual shame of the man and the woman as a symptom of the fall *(status naturae lapsae),* must be considered in its context. At that moment shame reaches its deepest level and seems to shake the foundations of their existence. "And they heard the sound of the Lord God walking in the garden in the cool of the day, and the man and his wife hid themselves from the presence of the Lord God among the trees of the garden" (Gn 3:8).

The necessity of hiding themselves indicates that in the depths of the shame they both feel before each other, as the immediate fruit of the tree of the knowledge of good and evil, a sense of fear before God has matured, a fear previously unknown. The "Lord God called to the man, and said to him, 'Where are you?' And he said, 'I heard the sound of you in the garden, and I was afraid, because I was naked, and I hid myself'" (Gn 3:9-10).

A certain fear always belongs to the essence of shame. Nevertheless, original shame reveals its character in a particular way: "I was afraid, because I was naked." We realize that something deeper than physical shame, bound up with a recent consciousness of his own nakedness, is in action here. Man tries to cover the real origin of fear with the shame of his own nakedness. Thus he indicates its effect, in order not to call its cause by name. Then God-Yahweh says in his turn: "Who told you that you were naked? Have you eaten of the tree of which I commanded you not to eat?" (Gn 3:11).

The precision of that dialogue is overwhelming; the precision of the whole narrative is overwhelming. It manifests the surface of man's emotions in living the events, in such a way as to reveal their depth at the same time. In all this, nakedness does not have solely a literal meaning. It does not refer only to the body; it is not the origin of a shame related only to the body. Actually, through nakedness, man deprived of participation in the gift is manifested, man alienated from that love which had been the source of the original gift, the source of the fullness of the good intended for the creature.

According to the formulas of the theological teaching of the Church,[46] this man was deprived of the supernatural and preternatural gifts which were part of his endowment before sin. Furthermore, he suffered a loss in what belongs to his nature itself, to humanity in the original fullness of the image of God. The three forms of lust do not correspond to the fullness of that image, but precisely to the loss, the deficiencies, the limitations that appeared with sin.

Lust is explained as a lack which has its roots in the original depth of the human spirit. If we wish to study this phenomenon in its origins, that is, at the threshold of the experiences of historical man, we must consider all the words that God-Yahweh addressed to the woman (Gn 3:16) and to the man (Gn 3:17-19). Furthermore, we must examine the state of their consciousness. The Yahwist text expressly enables us to do so. We have already called attention to the literary specificity of the text in this connection.

What state of consciousness can be manifested in the words: "I was afraid, because I was naked, and I hid myself"? What interior truth do they correspond to? What meaning of the body do they testify to? Certainly this new state differs a great deal from the original one. The words of Genesis 3:10 witness directly to a radical change of the meaning of original nakedness. As we pointed out previously, in the state of original innocence nakedness did not express a lack. Rather, it represented full acceptance of the body in all its human and therefore personal truth.

As the expression of the person, the body was the first sign of man's presence in the visible world. In that world, right from the beginning, man was able to distinguish himself, almost to be individualized—that is, confirm himself as a person—through his own body. It had been marked as a visible factor of the transcendence in virtue of which man, as a person, surpasses the visible world of living beings *(animalia)*. In this sense, the human body was from the beginning a faithful witness and a tangible verification of man's original solitude in the world. At the same time, by means of his masculinity and femininity, it became a limpid element of mutual donation in the communion of persons.

In this way, the human body bore in itself, in the mystery of creation, an unquestionable sign of the image of God. It also constituted the specific source of the certainty of that image, present in the whole human being. In a way, original acceptance of the body was the basis of the acceptance of the whole visible world. In its turn it was for man a guarantee of his dominion over the world, over the earth, which he was to subdue (cf. Gn 1:28).

The words "I was afraid, because I was naked, and I hid myself" (Gn 3:10), witness to a radical change in this relationship. In a way, man loses the original certainty of the image of God, expressed in his body. He also loses to some extent the sense of his right to participate in the perception of the world, which he enjoyed in the mystery of creation. This right had its foundation in man's inner self, in the fact that he himself participated in the divine vision of the world and of his own humanity. This gave him deep peace and joy in living the truth and value of his own body, in all its simplicity, transmitted to him by the Creator: "God saw [that] it was very good" (Gn 1:31).

The words of Genesis 3:10, "I was afraid, because I was naked, and I hid myself," confirm the collapse of the original acceptance of the body as a sign of the person in the visible world. At the same time, the acceptance of the material world in relation to man also seems to be shaken. The words of God-Yahweh forewarn the hostility of the world, the resistance of nature with regard to man and his tasks. They forewarn the fatigue that the human body was to feel in contact with the earth subdued by him: "Cursed is the ground because of you; in toil you shall eat of it all the days of your life; thorns and thistles it shall bring forth to you, and you shall eat the plants of the field. In the sweat of your face you shall eat bread till you return to the ground, for out of it you were taken" (Gn 3:17-19). Death is the end of this toil, of this struggle of man with the earth: "You are dust, and to dust you shall return" (Gn 3:19).

In this context, or rather in this perspective, Adam's words in Genesis 3:10, "I was afraid, because I was naked, and I hid myself," seem to express the awareness of being defenseless. They express the sense of insecurity of his bodily structure before the processes of nature, operating with inevitable determinism. Perhaps in this overwhelming statement a certain "cosmic shame" is implicit. In it, man's being created in the image of God and called to subdue the earth and dominate it (cf. Gn 1:28) expresses his own self. This happens precisely when, at the beginning of his historical experiences and in a manner so explicit, he is subjected to the earth, especially in the "part" of his transcendent constitution represented by the body.

General audience of May 14, 1980

A Fundamental Disquiet in All Human Existence

We are reading again the first chapters of Genesis, to understand how, with original sin, the "man of lust" took the place of the "man of original innocence." The words of Genesis 3:10, "I was afraid, because I was naked, and I hid myself," provide evidence of the first experience of man's shame with regard to his Creator—a shame that could also be called cosmic.

However, if it is possible to perceive its features in man's total situation after original sin, this cosmic shame makes way in the biblical text for another form of shame. It is the shame produced in humanity itself. It is caused by the deep disorder in that reality on account of which man, in the mystery of creation, was God's image. He was God's image both in his personal "ego" and in the interpersonal relationship, through the original communion of persons, constituted by the man and the woman together.

That shame, the cause of which is in humanity itself, is at once immanent and relative. It is manifested in the dimension of human interiority and at the same time refers to the "other." This is the woman's shame with regard to the man, and also the man's with regard to the woman. This mutual shame obliges them to cover their own nakedness, to hide their own bodies, to remove from the man's sight what is the visible sign of femininity, and from the woman's sight what is the visible sign of masculinity.

The shame of both was turned in this direction after original sin, when they realized that they were naked, as Genesis 3:7 bears witness.

The Yahwist text seems to indicate explicitly the sexual character of this shame. "They sewed fig leaves together and made themselves aprons." However, we may wonder if the sexual aspect has only a relative character, in other words, if it is a question of shame of one's own sexuality only in reference to a person of the other sex.

In the light of that one decisive sentence of Genesis 3:7, the answer to the question seems to support especially the relative character of original shame. Nevertheless, reflection on the whole immediate context makes it possible to discover its more immanent background. That shame, which is certainly manifested in the sexual order, reveals a specific difficulty in perceiving the human essentiality of one's own body. Man had not experienced this difficulty in the state of original innocence. The words, "I was afraid, because I was naked," can be understood in this way. They show clearly the consequences in the human heart of the fruit of the tree of the knowledge of good and evil.

Through these words a certain constitutive break within the human person is revealed, which is almost a rupture of man's original spiritual and somatic unity. He realizes for the first time that his body has ceased drawing upon the power of the spirit, which raised him to the level of the image of God. His original shame bears within it the signs of a specific humiliation mediated by the body. It conceals the germ of that contradiction, which will accompany historical man in his whole earthly path, as St. Paul writes: "For I delight in the law of God, in my inmost self, but I see in my members another law at war with the law of my mind" (Rom 7:22-23).

In this way, that shame is immanent. It contains such a cognitive acuteness as to create a fundamental disquiet in all human existence. This is not only in face of the prospect of death, but also before that on which the value and dignity of the person in his ethical significance depends. In this sense the original shame of the body ("I am naked") is already fear ("I was afraid"), and announces the uneasiness of conscience connected with lust.

The body is not subordinated to the spirit as in the state of original innocence. It bears within it a constant center of resistance to the spirit. It threatens, in a way, the unity of the person, that is, of the moral nature, which is firmly rooted in the constitution of the person. Lust, especially the lust of the body, is a specific threat to the structure of self-control and self-mastery, through which the human person is formed. It also constitutes a specific challenge for it. In any case, the man of lust does not control his own body in the same way, with equal simplicity and naturalness, as the man of original innocence did. The structure of self-mastery, essential for the person, is shaken to the very foundations in him. He again identifies himself with it in that he is continually ready to win it.

Immanent shame is connected with this interior imbalance. It has a sexual character, because the very sphere of human sexuality seems to highlight especially that imbalance, which springs from lust and especially from the lust of the body. From this point of view, that first impulse which Genesis 3:7 speaks of is very eloquent: "They knew that they were naked, and they sewed fig leaves together and made themselves aprons." It is as if the "man of lust" (man and woman "in the act of knowledge of good and evil") felt that he had just stopped, also through his own body and sex, being above the world of living beings or *animalia*. It is as if he felt a specific break of the personal integrity of his own body, especially in what determines its sexuality and is directly connected with the call to that unity in which man and woman "become one flesh" (Gn 2:24).

Therefore, that immanent and at the same time sexual shame is always, at least indirectly, relative. It is the shame of his own sexuality with regard to the other human being. Shame is manifested in this way in the narrative of Genesis 3. As a result of it we are, in a certain sense, witnesses of the birth of human lust. Also the motivation to go back from Christ's words about the man who "looks at a woman lustfully" (Mt 5:27-28), to that first moment in which shame is explained by means of lust, and lust by means of shame, is therefore sufficiently clear. In this way we understand better why and in what sense Christ speaks of desire as adultery committed in the heart, because he addresses the human heart.

The human heart keeps within it simultaneously desire and shame. The birth of shame directs us toward that moment in which the inner man, "the heart," closing himself to what "comes from the Father," opens to what "comes from the world." The birth of shame in the human heart keeps pace with the beginning of lust—of the threefold concupiscence according to Johannine theology (cf. 1 Jn 2:16), and in particular the concupiscence of the body.

Man is ashamed of his body because of lust. In fact, he is ashamed not so much of his body as precisely of lust. He is ashamed of his body owing to lust. He is ashamed of his body owing to that state of his spirit to which theology and psychology give the same name: desire or lust, although with a meaning that is not quite the same.

The biblical and theological meaning of desire and lust is different from that used in psychology. For the latter, desire comes from lack or necessity, which the value desired must satisfy. As we can deduce from 1 John 2:16, biblical lust indicates the state of the human spirit removed from the original simplicity and the fullness of values that man and the world possess in the dimensions of God. This simplicity and fullness of the value of the human body in the first experience of its masculinity-femininity, which Genesis 2:23-25 speaks of, has subsequently undergone, in the dimensions of the world, a radical transformation. Then, together with the lust of the body, shame was born.

Shame has a double meaning. It indicates the threat to the value and at the same time preserves this value interiorly.[47] The human heart, from the moment when the lust of the body was born in it, also keeps shame within itself. This fact indicates that it is possible and necessary to appeal to the heart when it is a question of guaranteeing those values from which lust takes away their original and full dimension. If we keep that in mind, we can understand better why Christ, speaking of lust, appeals to the human heart.

General audience of May 28, 1980

The Relationship of Lust to the Communion of Persons

Speaking of the birth of lust, on the basis of Genesis, we analyzed the original meaning of shame, which appeared with the first sin. In the light of the biblical narrative, the analysis of shame enables us to understand even more thoroughly the meaning it has for interpersonal man-woman relations as a whole. The third chapter of Genesis shows without any doubt that shame appeared in man's mutual relationship with woman. By reason of the shame itself, this relationship underwent a radical transformation. It was born in their hearts together with the lust of the body. Thus, the analysis of original shame enables us at the same time to examine what relationship this lust remains in with regard to the communion of persons. This communion was granted and assigned from the beginning as the task of the man and woman, owing to the fact that they had been created "in the image of God." Therefore, the further stage of the study of lust, which had been manifested "at the beginning" through the man and woman's shame, according to Genesis 3, is the analysis of the insatiability of the union, that is, of the communion of persons. This was to be expressed also by their bodies, according to their specific masculinity and femininity.

According to the biblical narrative, this shame induces man and woman to hide from each other their bodies and especially their sexual differentiation. This shame confirms that the original capacity of communicating themselves to each other, which Genesis 2:25 speaks of, has been shattered. The radical change of the meaning of original nakedness leads us to presume negative changes in the whole interpersonal man-woman relationship. That mutual communion in humanity itself by means of the body and by means of its masculinity and femininity, which resounded so strongly in the preceding passage of the Yahwist narrative (cf. Gn 2:23-25), is upset at this moment. It is as if the body, in its masculinity and femininity, no longer constituted the trustworthy substratum of the communion of persons, as if its original function were called in question in the consciousness of man and woman.

Having facilitated an extraordinary fullness in their mutual communication, the simplicity and purity of the original experience disappear. Obviously, our first progenitors did not stop communicating with each other through the body and its movements, gestures and expressions. But that simple and direct communion with each other, connected with the original experience of reciprocal nakedness, disappeared. Almost unexpectedly, an insuperable threshold appeared in their consciousness. It limited the original giving of oneself to the other, in full confidence in what constituted their own identity and, at the same time, their diversity, female on the one side, male on the other. The diversity, that is, the difference of the male sex and the female sex, was suddenly felt and understood as an element of mutual confrontation of persons. The concise expression of Genesis 3:7 and its immediate context testify to this: "They knew that they were naked." All that is also part of the analysis of the first shame. The Book of Genesis not only portrays its origin in the human being, but also makes it possible to reveal its degrees in both man and woman.

The ending of the capacity of a full mutual communion, which is manifested as sexual shame, enables us to understand better the original value of the unifying meaning of the body. It is not possible to understand otherwise that respective closure to each other, or shame, unless in relation to the meaning that the body, in its femininity and masculinity, previously had for man in the state of original innocence. That unifying meaning is understood with regard to the unity that man and woman, as spouses, were to constitute, becoming "one flesh" (Gn 2:24) through the conjugal act. It is also understood in reference to the communion of persons itself, which had been the specific dimension of man and woman's existence in the mystery of creation. The body in its masculinity and femininity constituted the peculiar "substratum" of this personal communion. Genesis 3:7 deals with this sexual shame. This shame bears witness to the loss of the original certainty that the human body, through its masculinity and femininity, is precisely that "substratum" of the communion of persons. The body expresses that communion simply, and it serves the purpose of realizing it (and thus also of completing the image of God in the visible world).

This state of consciousness in both has strong repercussions in the further context of Genesis 3, with which we shall deal shortly. If after original sin, man had lost the sense of the image of God in himself, that loss was manifested with shame of the body (cf. Gn 3:10-11). Encroaching upon the man-woman relationship in its totality, that shame was manifested with the imbalance of the original meaning of corporeal unity, that is, of the body as the peculiar "substratum" of the communion of persons. It is as if the personal profile of masculinity and femininity, which before had highlighted the meaning of the body for a full communion of persons, had made way only for the sensation of sexuality with regard to the other human being. It is as if sexuality became an obstacle in the personal relationship of man and woman. Concealing it from each other, according to Genesis 3:7, they both express it almost instinctively.

At the same time, this is the second discovery of sex, which in the biblical narrative differs radically from the first one. The whole context of the narrative confirms that this new discovery distinguishes historical man with his lust (with the three forms of lust) from the man of original innocence. What relationship does lust have, especially the lust of the flesh, with regard to the communion of persons mediated by the body, by its masculinity and femininity, that is, to the communion assigned "from the beginning" to man by the Creator? This question must be posed, precisely with regard to the beginning, about the experience of shame, which the biblical narrative refers to.

As we have already observed, shame is manifested in Genesis 3 as a symptom of man's detachment from the love in which he participated in the mystery of creation according to the Johannine expression, the love that "comes from the Father." "The love that is in the world," that is, lust, brings with it an almost constitutive difficulty of identification with one's own body. This is not only in the sphere of one's own subjectivity, but even more with regard to the subjectivity of the other human being, of woman for man, of man for woman.

Hence the necessity of hiding before the other with one's own body, with what determines one's own femininity-masculinity. This necessity proves the fundamental lack of trust, which in itself indicates the collapse of the original relationship of communion. Regard for the subjectivity of the other, and at the same time for one's own subjectivity, has aroused in this new situation, that is, in the context of lust, the necessity of hiding oneself, which Genesis 3:7 speaks of.

Here it seems to us that we can discover a deeper meaning of sexual shame and also the full meaning of that phenomenon, to which the biblical text refers, to point out the boundary between the man of original innocence and the historical man of lust. The complete text of Genesis 3 supplies us with elements to define the deepest dimension of shame, but that calls for a separate analysis. We will begin it in the next reflection.

General audience of June 4, 1980

Dominion over the Other in the Interpersonal Relation

With surprising precision, Genesis 3 describes the phenomenon of shame, which appeared in the first man together with original sin. Careful reflection on this text enables us to deduce from it that shame has a deeper dimension. This shame took the place of the absolute trust connected with the previous state of original innocence in the mutual relationship between man and woman. In this connection it is necessary to reread chapter 3 of Genesis to the end, and not limit ourselves to verse 7 or verses 10-11, which contain the testimony about the first experience of shame. After this narrative, the dialogue of God-Yahweh with the man and the woman breaks off and a monologue begins. Yahweh turns to the woman and speaks first of the pain of childbirth, which will accompany her from now on: "I will greatly multiply your pain in childbearing; in pain you shall bring forth children..." (Gn 3:16).

That is followed by the expression which characterizes the future relationship of both the man and the woman: "Your desire shall be for your husband, and he shall rule over you" (Gn 3:16).

These words, like those of Genesis 2:24, have a perspective character. The incisive formulation of 3:16 seems to regard the facts as a whole. They have already emerged, in a way, in the original experience of shame, and will subsequently be manifested in the entire interior experience of historical man. The history of consciences and of human hearts will continually confirm the words of Genesis 3:16. The words spoken at the beginning seem to refer to a particular "disability" of woman as compared with man. But there is no reason to understand it as a social disability or inequality. The expression: "Your desire shall be for your husband, and he shall rule over you" immediately indicates, on the other hand, another form of inequality. Woman will feel this as a lack of full unity precisely in the vast context of union with man, to which both were called according to Genesis 2:24.

The words of God-Yahweh: "Your desire shall be for your husband, and he shall rule over you" (Gn 3:16), do not concern exclusively the moment of man and woman's union, when both unite in such a way as to become one flesh (cf. Gn 2:24). They refer to the ample context of relations, including indirect ones, of conjugal union as a whole. For the first time the man is defined here as "husband." In the whole context of the Yahwist narrative these words mean above all, a violation, a fundamental loss, of the original community-communion of persons. The latter should have made man and woman mutually happy by the pursuit of a simple and pure union in humanity, by a reciprocal offering of themselves. That is the experience of the gift of the person expressed with the soul and with the body, with masculinity and femininity ("flesh of my flesh"—Gn 2:23). Finally, it should have made them happy by the subordination of this union to the blessing of fertility with procreation.

It seems that in the words which God-Yahweh addressed to the woman, there is a deeper echo of the shame which the man and woman began to experience after breaking the original covenant with God. We find, moreover, a fuller motivation of this shame. In a very discreet way, which is still decipherable and expressive, Genesis 3:16 testifies how that original beatifying conjugal union of persons will be distorted in man's heart by lust. These words are addressed directly to woman, but they refer to man, or rather to both together.

The previous analysis of Genesis 3:7 showed that in the new situation, after breaking the original covenant with God, the man and the woman found themselves more divided. Instead of being united, they were even opposed because of their masculinity and femininity. The biblical narrative stresses the instinctive impulse that had driven them both to cover their bodies. It describes at the same time the situation in which man, as male *or* female—before it was rather male *and* female—feels more estranged from the body, as from the source of the original union in humanity ("flesh of my flesh"). They were more opposed to the other precisely on the basis of the body and sex. This opposition does not destroy or exclude conjugal union, willed by the Creator (cf. Gn 2:24), or its procreative effects. But it confers on the realization of this union another direction, which will be that of the man of lust. Genesis 3:16 speaks precisely of this.

The woman, whose "desire shall be for her husband" (cf. Gn 3:16), and the man who responds to this desire, as we read: "He shall rule over you," unquestionably form the same human couple. It was the same marriage as in Genesis 2:24, the same community of persons. However, they are now something different. They are no longer called only to union and unity, but are also threatened by the insatiability of that union and unity. It does not cease to attract man and woman precisely because they are persons, called from eternity to exist in communion. In the light of the biblical narrative, sexual shame has its deep meaning. It is connected with the failure to satisfy the aspiration to realize in the conjugal union of the body (cf. Gn 2:24) the mutual communion of persons.

All this seems to confirm, from various aspects, that at the basis of shame, in which historical man has become a participant, there is the threefold lust spoken of in the First Letter of John. It is not only the lust of the flesh, but also "the lust of the eyes and the pride of life" (1 Jn 2:16). Does not the expression of Genesis 3:16 regarding "rule" ("He shall rule

over you") indicate this last form of lust? Does not the rule over the other
—of man over woman—change essentially the structure of communion in
the interpersonal relationship? Does it not transpose into the dimension of
this structure something that makes the human being an object, which can,
in a way, be desired by the lust of the eyes?

These questions spring from reflection on the words of God-Yahweh
according to Genesis 3:16. Delivered almost on the threshold of human
history after original sin, those words reveal to us not only the exterior
situation of man and woman, but enable us also to penetrate into the deep
mysteries of their hearts.

General audience of June 18, 1980

Lust Limits the Nuptial Meaning of the Body

The analysis we made during the preceding reflection was centered
on the words which God-Yahweh addressed to the first woman after original sin: "Your desire shall be for your husband, and he shall rule over you"
(Gn 3:16). We concluded that these words contain an adequate clarification and a deep interpretation of original shame (cf. Gn 3:7), which became part of man and of woman together with lust. The explanation of this
shame is not to be sought in the body itself, in the somatic sexuality of
both. It goes back to the deeper changes undergone by the human spirit.
This spirit is especially aware of how insatiable it is with regard to the mutual unity between man and woman.

This awareness blames the body, so to speak, and deprives it of the
simplicity and purity of the meaning connected with the original innocence of the human being. In relation to this awareness, shame is a secondary experience. If it reveals the moment of lust, at the same time it can
protect from the consequences of the three forms of lust. It can even be
said that man and woman, through shame, almost remain in the state of
original innocence. They continually become aware of the nuptial meaning of the body and aim at preserving it from lust. Similarly, they try to
maintain the value of communion, that is, of the union of persons in the
unity of the body.

Genesis 2:24 speaks with discretion but also with clarity of the union
of bodies in the sense of the authentic union of persons: "A man...cleaves
to his wife, and they become one flesh." From the context it is seen that
this union comes from a choice, since the man leaves his father and
mother to unite with his wife. Such a union of persons entails that they

should become one flesh. Starting from this "sacramental" expression, which corresponds to the communion of persons—of the man and the woman—in their original call to conjugal union, we can understand better the specific message of Genesis 3:16. We can establish and reconstruct what the imbalance consists of, the peculiar distortion of the original inter-personal relationship of communion, which the "sacramental" words of Genesis 2:24 refer to.

Studying Genesis 3:16, it can be said that the body, constituted in the unity of the personal subject, does not cease to stimulate the desires of personal union, precisely because of masculinity and femininity. ("Your desire shall be for your husband.") At the same time, lust directs these desires in its own way. The expression, "He shall rule over you," confirms this.

However, the lust of the flesh directs these desires to satisfy the body, often at the cost of a real and full communion of persons. In this sense, attention should be paid to the way in which semantic accentuations are distributed in the verses of Genesis 3. Although there are few of them, they reveal interior consistency. The man seems to feel ashamed of his own body with particular intensity: "I was afraid, because I was naked, and I hid myself" (Gn 3:10). These words emphasize the metaphysical character of shame. At the same time, for the man, shame united with lust will become an impulse to "dominate" the woman. ("He shall rule over you.")

Subsequently, the experience of this domination is manifested more directly in the woman as the insatiable desire for a different union. From the moment when the man "dominates" her, the communion of persons—made of the full spiritual union of the two subjects giving themselves to each other—is followed by a different mutual relationship. This is the relationship of possession of the other as the object of one's own desire. If this impulse prevails on the part of the man, the instincts that the woman directs to him, according to the expression of Genesis 3:16, can—and do—assume a similar character. Sometimes, perhaps, they precede the man's "desire," or even aim at arousing it and giving it impetus.

Genesis 3:16 seems to indicate the man especially as the one who "desires." This is similar to the text of Matthew 5:27-28, the starting point of these meditations. Nevertheless, both the man and the woman have become a human being subject to lust. Therefore the lot of both is shame. With its deep resonance, it touches the innermost recesses both of the male and of the female personality, even though in a different way. What we learn from Genesis 3 enables us barely to outline this duality, but even the mere references are very significant. Since it is a question of such an archaic text, it is surprisingly eloquent and acute.

An adequate analysis of Genesis 3 leads to the conclusion that the three forms of lust, including that of the body, bring with them a limitation of the nuptial meaning of the body itself, in which man and woman participated in the state of original innocence. When we speak of the meaning of the body, we refer first to the full awareness of the human being. But we also include all actual experience of the body in its masculinity and femininity, and, in any case, the constant predisposition to this experience.

The meaning of the body is not just something conceptual. We have already drawn attention to this sufficiently in the preceding analyses. The meaning of the body is at the same time what determines the attitude—it is the way of living the body. It is a measure which the interior man, that is, that heart which Christ referred to in the Sermon on the Mount, applies to the human body with regard to his masculinity/femininity (therefore with regard to his sexuality).

That meaning does not change the reality in itself, that which the human body is and does not cease to be in the sexuality that is characteristic of it, independently of the states of our conscience and our experiences. However, this purely objective significance of the body and of sex, outside the system of real and concrete interpersonal relations between man and woman, is, in a certain sense, "a-historical." On the contrary, in the present analysis, and in conformity with the biblical sources, we always take man's historicity into account (also because we start from his theological prehistory). Obviously it is a question here of an interior dimension, which eludes the external criteria of historicity, but which, however, can be considered historical. It is precisely at the basis of all the facts which constitute the history of man—also the history of sin and of salvation—and thus reveal the depth and very root of his historicity.

In this vast context, when we speak of lust as a limitation, infraction or even distortion of the nuptial meaning of the body, we are referring above all to the preceding analyses regarding the state of original innocence, that is, the theological prehistory of man. At the same time, we have in mind the measure that historical man, with his "heart," applies to his own body in relation to male/female sexuality. This measure is not something exclusively conceptual. It determines the attitudes and decides in general the way of living the body.

Certainly, Christ refers to that in his Sermon on the Mount. We are trying here to link the words taken from Matthew 5:27-28 to the threshold of man's theological history, considering them in the context of Genesis 3. Lust as a limitation, infraction or even distortion of the nuptial meaning of the body can be ascertained in an especially clear way in our first progenitors, Adam and Eve (despite the concise nature of the biblical narrative).

Thanks to them we have been able to find the nuptial meaning of the body and rediscover what it consists of as a measure of the human heart, such as to mold the original form of the communion of persons. In their personal experience (which the biblical text enables us to follow) that original form has undergone imbalance and distortion, as we have sought to prove through the analysis of shame. The nuptial meaning of the body, which in the situation of original innocence constituted the measure of the heart of both the man and the woman, also must have undergone a distortion. If we succeed in reconstructing what this distortion consists of, we shall also have the answer to our question. That is, what does lust of the flesh consist of, and what constitutes its theological and at the same time anthropological specific character? It seems that a theologically and anthropologically adequate answer—important as regards the meaning of Christ's words in the Sermon on the Mount (cf. Mt 5:27-28)—can already be obtained from the context of Genesis 3 and from the whole Yahwist narrative, which previously enabled us to clarify the nuptial meaning of the human body.

General audience of June 25, 1980

The Heart—A Battlefield between Love and Lust

We know from the analysis of Genesis 2:23-25 that the human body, in its original masculinity and femininity according to the mystery of creation, is not only a source of fertility, that is, of procreation. But right "from the beginning" it has a nuptial character. It is capable of expressing the love with which the man-person becomes a gift, thus fulfilling the deep meaning of his being and his existence. In this peculiarity, the body is the expression of the spirit and is called, in the mystery of creation, to exist in the communion of persons in the image of God. The concupiscence "that comes from the world"—here it is directly a question of the concupiscence of the body—limits and distorts the body's objective way of existing, of which man has become a participant.

The human heart experiences the degree of this limitation or distortion, especially in the sphere of man-woman mutual relations. Precisely in the experience of the heart, femininity and masculinity, in their mutual relations, no longer seem to express the spirit which aims at personal communion. They remain only an object of attraction, in a certain sense as happens in the world of living beings, which, like man, have received the blessing of fertility (cf. Gn 1).

This similarity is certainly contained in the work of creation. Genesis 2 and especially verse 24 confirm this. However, already in the mystery of creation, that which constituted the natural, somatic and sexual substratum of that attraction, fully expressed the call of man and woman to personal communion. After sin, on the contrary, in the new situation of which Genesis 3 speaks, this expression was weakened and dimmed. It is as if it were lacking in the shaping of mutual relations, or as if it were driven back to another plane.

The natural and somatic substratum of human sexuality was manifested as an almost autogenous force. It is marked by a certain "coercion of the body," operating according to its own dynamics, which limits the expression of the spirit and the experience of the exchange of the gift of the person. The words of Genesis 3:15 addressed to the first woman seem to indicate this quite clearly: "Your desire shall be for your husband, and he shall rule over you."

The human body in its masculinity and femininity has almost lost the capacity of expressing this love. In it, the man-person becomes a gift, in conformity with the deepest structure and finality of his personal existence, as we have already observed in preceding analyses. Here we do not formulate this judgment absolutely and we add the adverb "almost." We do so because the dimension of the gift—namely, the capacity of expressing love with which man, by means of femininity or masculinity, becomes a gift for the other—has continued to some extent to permeate and mold the love that is born in the human heart. The nuptial meaning of the body has not been completely suffocated by concupiscence, but only habitually threatened.

The heart has become a battlefield between love and lust. The more lust dominates the heart, the less the heart experiences the nuptial meaning of the body. It becomes less sensitive to the gift of the person, which expresses that meaning in the mutual relations of man and woman. Certainly, that lust which Christ speaks of in Matthew 5:27-28 appears in many forms in the human heart. It is not always plain and obvious. Sometimes it is concealed, so that it passes itself off as love, although it changes its true profile and dims the limpidity of the gift in the mutual relationship of persons. Does this mean that it is our duty to distrust the human heart? No! It only means that we must keep it under control.

The image of the concupiscence of the body, which emerges from the present analysis, has a clear reference to the image of the person, with which we connected our preceding reflections on the nuptial meaning of the body. Man as a person is "the only creature on earth that God has willed for its own sake" and, at the same time, he is the one who "can fully discover his true self only in a sincere giving of himself."[48] Lust in general

—and the lust of the body in particular—attacks this "sincere giving." It deprives man of the dignity of giving, which is expressed by his body through femininity and masculinity. In a way it depersonalizes man, making him an object "for the other." Instead of being "together with the other"—a subject in unity, in the sacramental unity of the body—man becomes an object for man, the female for the male and vice versa. Genesis 3:16 and Genesis 3:7 bear witness to this, with all the clearness of the contrast, as compared with Genesis 2:23-25.

Violating the dimension of the mutual giving of the man and the woman, concupiscence also calls in question the fact that each of them was willed by the Creator "for his own sake." In a certain sense, the subjectivity of the person gives way to the objectivity of the body. Owing to the body, man becomes an object for man—the female for the male and vice versa. Concupiscence means that the personal relations of man and of woman are unilaterally and reductively linked with the body and sex, in the sense that these relations become almost incapable of accepting the mutual gift of the person. They do not contain or deal with femininity/masculinity according to the full dimension of personal subjectivity. They do not express communion, but they remain unilaterally determined by sex.

Concupiscence entails the loss of the interior freedom of the gift. The nuptial meaning of the human body is connected precisely with this freedom. Man can become a gift—that is, the man and the woman can exist in the relationship of mutual self-giving—if each of them controls himself. Manifested as a "coercion *sui generis* of the body," concupiscence limits interiorly and reduces self-control. For that reason, in a certain sense it makes impossible the interior freedom of giving. Together with that, the beauty that the human body possesses in its male and female aspect, as an expression of the spirit, is obscured. The body remains as an object of lust and, therefore, as a "field of appropriation" of the other human being. In itself, concupiscence is not capable of promoting union as the communion of persons. By itself, it does not unite, but appropriates. The relationship of the gift is changed into the relationship of appropriation.

At this point, let us interrupt our reflections today. The last problem dealt with has such great importance, and is so subtle, from the point of view of the difference between authentic love (that is, between the "communion of persons") and lust, that we shall have to take it up again at our next meeting.

General audience of July 23, 1980

The Opposition in the Human Heart
between the Spirit and the Body

The reflections we are developing in the present cycle refer to the words which Christ uttered in the Sermon on the Mount on man's lust for woman. In the attempt to proceed with a thorough examination of what characterizes the man of lust, we went back again to Genesis. Here, the situation that came into being in the mutual relationship of man and woman is portrayed with great delicacy. The single sentences of Genesis 3 are very eloquent. In Genesis 3:16 God-Yahweh addressed the woman: "Your desire shall be for your husband, and he shall rule over you." Upon a careful analysis, these words seem to reveal in what way the relationship of mutual giving, which existed between them in the state of original innocence, changed after original sin to a relationship of mutual appropriation.

If man in his relationship with woman considers her only as an object to gain possession of and not as a gift, he condemns himself thereby to become also for her only an object of appropriation, and not a gift. It seems that the words of Genesis 3:16 deal with this bilateral relationship, although the only thing they say directly is: "He shall rule over you." Furthermore, in unilateral appropriation (which indirectly is bilateral) the structure of communion between persons disappears. Both human beings become almost incapable of attaining the interior measure of the heart, directed to the freedom of the giving of oneself and the nuptial meaning of the body, which is intrinsic to it. Genesis 3:16 seems to suggest that it is often at the expense of the woman that this happens, and that in any case she feels it more than man.

It is worth turning our attention now to this detail at least. It is possible to perceive a certain parallelism between the words of God-Yahweh according to Genesis 3:16, "Your desire shall be for your husband, and he shall rule over you," and those of Christ according to Matthew 5:27-28, "Everyone who looks at a woman lustfully...." Perhaps it is not a question here of the fact that the woman especially becomes the object of man's lust. But as we have already stressed, it is rather that "from the beginning" man was to have been the guardian of the reciprocity of donation and its true balance.

The analysis of that "beginning" (cf. Gn 2:23-25) shows precisely man's responsibility in accepting femininity as a gift and in borrowing it in a mutual, bilateral exchange. To take from woman her own gift by means of concupiscence is in open contrast with that. The maintenance of the balance of the gift seems to have been entrusted to both. But a special responsibility rests with man above all, as if it depended more on him whether the balance is maintained or broken or even—if already broken—re-established.

Certainly, the diversity of roles according to these statements, to which we are referring here as to key-texts, was also dictated by the social emargination of woman in the conditions of that time. (The Sacred Scripture of the Old and the New Testament gives us sufficient proofs of this.) Nevertheless, it contains a truth, which has its weight independently of specific conditionings due to the customs of that given historical situation.

As a consequence of lust, the body becomes almost a "ground" of appropriation of the other person. As is easy to understand, that entails the loss of the nuptial meaning of the body. Together with that, the mutual belonging of persons—who, uniting so as to "become one flesh" (Gn 2:24), are called at the same time to belong to each other—acquires another meaning. The particular dimension of the personal union of man and woman through love is expressed in the word "my." This pronoun, which has always belonged to the language of human love, often recurs in the verses of the Song of Songs and in other biblical texts.[49] In its "material" meaning, this pronoun denotes a relationship of possession. But in our case it indicates the personal analogy of this relationship.

The mutual belonging of man and woman, especially when they belong to each other as spouses "in the unity of the body," is formed according to this personal analogy. As is well known, an analogy indicates at the same time a similarity and also the lack of identity (namely, a substantial dissimilarity). We can speak of persons belonging to each other only if we consider such an analogy. In its original and specific meaning, belonging presupposes the relationship of the subject to the object, a relationship of possession and ownership. This relationship is not only objective, but above all "material"—the belonging of something, and therefore of an object to someone.

In the eternal language of human love, the term "my" certainly does not have this meaning. It indicates the reciprocity of the donation. It expresses the equal balance of the gift—perhaps precisely this, in the first place —namely, that in which the mutual *communio personarum* is established. If this is established by the mutual gift of masculinity and femininity, the nuptial meaning of the body is also preserved in it.

In the language of love, the word "my" seems a radical negation of belonging in the sense in which an object-thing belongs to the subject-person. The analogy preserves its functions until it falls into the meaning set forth above. Triple lust, and in particular the lust of the flesh, takes away from the mutual belonging of man and woman the specific dimension of the personal analogy, in which the term "my" preserves its essential meaning. This essential meaning lies outside the "law of ownership," outside the meaning of "object of possession." On the contrary, concupiscence is directed toward the latter meaning.

From possessing, a further step goes toward "enjoyment." The object I possess acquires a certain meaning for me since it is at my disposal and I avail myself of it, I use it. It is evident that the personal analogy of belonging is decidedly opposed to this meaning. This opposition is a sign that what "comes from the Father" in the mutual relationship of man and woman, still persists and continues in confrontation with what comes "from the world." However, concupiscence in itself drives man toward possession of the other as an object. It drives him to enjoyment, which brings with it the negation of the nuptial meaning of the body. In its essence, disinterested giving is excluded from selfish enjoyment. Do not the words of God-Yahweh addressed to woman in Genesis 3:16 already speak of this?

According to the First Letter of John (2:16), lust bears witness in the first place to the state of the human spirit. It will be opportune to devote a further analysis to this problem. We can apply Johannine theology to the field of the experiences described in Genesis 3, as well as to the words Christ spoke in the Sermon on the Mount (Mt 5:27-28). We find a concrete dimension of that opposition which, together with sin, was born in the human heart between the spirit and the body.

Its consequences are felt in the mutual relationship of persons, whose unity in humanity is determined right from the beginning by the fact that they are man and woman. "Another law at war with the law of my mind" (Rom 7:23) has been installed in man. So almost a constant danger exists of this way of seeing, evaluating, and loving, so that "the desire of the body" is more powerful than "the desire of the mind." We must always keep in mind this truth about man, this anthropological element, if we wish to understand completely the appeal Christ made to the human heart in the Sermon on the Mount.

General audience of July 30, 1980

The Sermon on the Mount to the Men of Our Day

Let us take up again today the Sermon on the Mount, and the statement: "Everyone who looks at a woman lustfully has already committed adultery with her in his heart" (Mt 5:28). Jesus appeals here to the heart.

In his talk with the Pharisees, referring to the "beginning" (cf. the preceding analyses), Jesus uttered the following words with regard to the certificate of divorce: "For your hardness of heart Moses allowed you to divorce your wives, but from the beginning it was not so" (Mt 19:8). This sentence undoubtedly contains an accusation. "Hardness of heart"[50] indicates what, according to the ethos of the people of the Old Testament, had brought about the situation contrary to the original plan of God-Yahweh in Genesis 2:24. There we must seek the key to interpret the whole legislation of Israel in the sphere of marriage and, in the wider sense, in relations between man and woman as a whole. Speaking of hardness of heart, Christ accuses the whole "interior subject" who is responsible for the distortion of the law. In the Sermon on the Mount (Mt 5:27-28), he also refers to the heart, but the words pronounced here do not seem only to accuse.

We must reflect on them again, placing them as far as possible in their historical dimension. The analysis made so far aimed at highlighting the man of lust in his genetic moment, almost at the initial point of his history interwoven with theology. This constitutes an ample introduction, especially an anthropological one, to the work that must still be undertaken. The following stage of our analysis will have an ethical character.

The Sermon on the Mount, and in particular that passage we have chosen as the center of our analyses, is part of the proclamation of the new ethos, the ethos of the Gospel. In the teaching of Christ, it is deeply connected with awareness of the "beginning," namely with the mystery of creation in its original simplicity and richness. At the same time, the ethos that Christ proclaims in the Sermon on the Mount is realistically addressed to historical man, who has become the man of lust. Lust in its three forms is the heritage of all humanity, and the human heart really participates in it.

Christ knows "what is in every man" (cf. Jn 2:25).[51] He cannot speak in any other way than with this awareness. From this point of view, in the words of Matthew 5:27-28 it is not the accusation that prevails but the judgment, a realistic judgment on the human heart. It is a judgment which has both an anthropological foundation and a directly ethical character. For the ethos of the Gospel it is a constitutive judgment.

In the Sermon on the Mount, Christ directly addresses the man who belongs to a well defined society. The Master, too, belongs to that society, to that people. So we must look in Christ's words for a reference to the facts, the situations and the institutions which he was familiar with in everyday life. These references must be analyzed at least in a summary way, so that the ethical meaning of the words of Matthew 5:27-28 may emerge more clearly.

However, with these words, Christ also addresses, in an indirect but real way, every historical man (understanding this adjective mainly in a theological sense). This man is precisely the man of lust, whose mystery and whose heart is known to Christ. "For he himself knew what was in man" (Jn 2:25). The Sermon on the Mount enables us to contact the interior experience of this man almost at every geographical latitude and longitude, in the various ages, in the different social and cultural conditionings. The man of our time feels called by name with this statement of Christ, no less than the man of that time, whom the Master was addressing directly.

The universality of the Gospel, which is not at all a generalization, lies in this. Perhaps precisely in this statement of Christ, which we are analyzing here, this is manifested with particular clarity. By virtue of this statement, the man of all times and all places feels called, in an adequate, concrete and unrepeatable way. This is because Christ appeals to the human heart, which cannot be subject to any generalization. With the category of the heart, everyone is characterized individually, even more than by name. Everyone is reached in what determines him in a unique and unrepeatable way, and is defined in his humanity from within.

The image of the man of lust concerns his inner being in the first place.[52] The history of the human heart after original sin is written under the pressure of lust in its three forms. Even the deepest image of ethos in its various historical documents is also connected with this lust. However, that inner being is also the force that decides exterior human behavior, and also the form of multiple structures and institutions at the level of social life. If we deduce the content of ethos, in its various historical formulations, from these structures and institutions, we always meet this inner aspect, characteristic of the interior image of man. This is the most essential element. Christ's words in the Sermon on the Mount, especially those of Matthew 5:27-28, indicate it unmistakably. No study on human ethos can regard it with indifference.

Therefore, in our subsequent reflections, we shall try to analyze in a more detailed way that statement of Christ which says: "You have heard that it was said, 'You shall not commit adultery.' But I say to you that everyone who looks at a woman lustfully has already committed adultery with her in his heart" (or "has already made her adulterous in his heart").

To understand this text better, we shall first analyze its single parts, so as to obtain afterward a deeper overall view. We shall consider not only those for whom it was intended at that time—those who actually heard the Sermon on the Mount—but also, as far as possible, modern man, the people of our time.

General audience of August 6, 1980

The Content of the Commandment:
"You Shall Not Commit Adultery"

The affirmation Christ made during the Sermon on the Mount regarding adultery and desire, which he called "adultery of the heart," must be analyzed from the very beginning. Christ said: "You have understood that it was said: 'You shall not commit adultery'" (Mt 5:27). He had in mind God's commandment, the sixth in the Decalogue, included in the so-called second Table of the Law which Moses received from God-Yahweh.

First of all, let's place ourselves in the situation of the audience present during the Sermon on the Mount, those who actually heard the words of Christ. They are sons and daughters of the chosen people—people who had received the law from God—Yahweh himself. These people had also received the prophets. Time and time again throughout the centuries, the prophets had reproved the people's behavior regarding this commandment, and the way in which it was continually broken. Christ also speaks of similar transgressions. But he speaks more precisely about a certain human interpretation of the law, which negates and does away with the correct meaning of right and wrong as specified by the will of the divine legislator. Above all, the law is a means—an indispensable means if "justice is to abound" (Mt 5:20). Christ desires such justice to be "superior to that of the scribes and Pharisees." He does not accept the interpretation they gave to the authentic content of the law through the centuries. In a certain way, this interpretation subjected this content, or rather the purpose and will of the legislator, to the varied weaknesses and limits of human willpower deriving precisely from the threefold concupiscence. This was a casuistic interpretation which was superimposed on the original version of right and wrong connected with the law of the Decalogue. If Christ tends to transform the ethos, he does so mainly to recover the fundamental clarity of the interpretation: "Do not think that I have come to abolish the law or the prophets; I have not come to abolish but to fulfill" (Mt 5:17). Fulfillment is conditioned by a correct understanding, and this is applied, among others, also to the commandment: "You shall not commit adultery."

Those who follow the history of the chosen people in the Old Testament from the time of Abraham will find many facts which witness to how this commandment was put into practice. As a result of such practice, the casuistic interpretation of the law developed. First, it is well known that the history of the Old Testament is the scene for the systematic defection from monogamy. This fact must have a fundamental significance in our understanding of the prohibition: "You shall not commit adultery." Especially at the time of the patriarchs, the abandonment of monogamy was dictated by the desire for offspring, a very numerous offspring. This desire was very profound, and procreation as the essential end of marriage was very evident. This was so much so that wives who loved their husbands but were not able to give them children, on their own initiative asked their husbands who loved them, if they could carry "on their own knees," or welcome, his children born of another woman, for example, those of the serving woman, the slave. Such was the case of Sarah regarding Abraham (cf. Gn 16:2) or the case of Rachel and Jacob (cf. Gn 30:3). These two narratives reflect the moral atmosphere in which the Decalogue was practiced. They illustrate the way in which the Israelite ethos was prepared to receive the commandment, "You shall not commit adultery," and how such a commandment was applied in the most ancient tradition of this people. The authority of the patriarchs was the highest in Israel and had a religious character. It was strictly bound to the covenant and to the promise.

The commandment, "You shall not commit adultery," did not change this tradition. Everything points to the fact that its further development was not limited by the motives (however exceptional) which had guided the behavior of Abraham and Sarah, or of Jacob and Rachel. For example, the lives of the most renowned Israelites after Moses, the kings of Israel, David and Solomon, show the establishing of real polygamy, which was undoubtedly for reasons of concupiscence.

In the history of David, who also had other wives, we are struck not only by the fact that he had taken the wife of one of his subjects, but also by the fact that he was clearly aware of having committed adultery. This fact, as well as the king's repentance, is described in a detailed and evocative way (cf. 2 Sm 11:2-27). Adultery is understood to mean only the possession of another man's wife, but it is not considered to be the possession of other women as wives together with the first one. All Old Testament tradition indicates that the real need for monogamy as an essential and indispensable implication of the commandment, "You shall not commit adultery," never reached the conscience and the ethos of the following generations of the chosen people.

Against this background one must also understand all the efforts which aim at putting the specific content of the commandment, "You shall not commit adultery," within the framework of the promulgated laws. It is confirmed by the books of the Bible in which we find the Old Testament legislation fully recorded as a whole. If we consider the letter of such legislation, we find that it takes a determined and open stand against adultery, using radical means, including the death penalty (cf. Lv 20:10; Dt 22:22).

It does so, however, by effectively supporting polygamy, even fully legalizing it, at least indirectly. Therefore, adultery was opposed only within special limits and within the sphere of definitive premises which make up the essential form of the Old Testament ethos. Adultery is understood above all (and perhaps exclusively) as the violation of man's right of possession regarding each woman who may be his own legal wife (usually, one among many). On the contrary, adultery is not understood as it appears from the point of view of monogamy as established by the Creator. We know now that Christ referred to the "beginning" precisely in regard to this argument (Mt 19:8).

Furthermore, the occasion in which Christ took the side of the woman caught in adultery and defended her from being stoned to death is most significant. He said to the accusers: "Whoever of you is without sin, let him throw the first stone" (Jn 3:7). When they put down the stones and went away, he said to the woman: "Go, and from now on, sin no more" (Jn 8:11). Therefore, Christ clearly identified adultery with sin. On the other hand, when he turned to those who wanted to stone the adulteress, he did not refer to the precepts of Israel's law but exclusively to conscience. The discernment between right and wrong engraved on the human conscience can show itself to be deeper and more correct than the content of a norm.

As we have seen, the history of God's people in the Old Testament (which we have tried to illustrate through only a few examples) took place mainly outside the normative content contained in God's commandment, "You shall not commit adultery." It went along, so to speak, side by side with it. Christ wanted to straighten out these errors, and thus we have his words spoken during the Sermon on the Mount.

General audience of August 13, 1980

Adultery according to the Law and the Prophets

In the Sermon on the Mount, Christ said: "You have heard that it was said: 'You shall not commit adultery'" (Mt 5:27). He referred to what each person present knew perfectly well, and by which everyone felt himself bound by virtue of the commandment of God-Yahweh. However, the history of the Old Testament shows us that both the life of the people bound to God-Yahweh by a special covenant, and the life of each person, often wanders away from this commandment. A brief look at the legislation which the Old Testament comprehensively documents also shows this.

The precepts of the law of the Old Testament were very severe. They were also very detailed and entered into the smallest details of the people's daily life.[53] One can presume that the more the legalizing of actual polygamy became evident in this law, the necessity to uphold its juridical dimension and protect its legal limits increased even more. Hence, we find the great number of precepts, and also the severity of the punishments the legislator provided for the violation of such norms. On the basis of the analysis which we have previously carried out regarding Christ's reference to the "beginning," in his discourse on the indissolubility of marriage and on the act of repudiation, the following is evident. He clearly saw the basic contradiction that the matrimonial law of the Old Testament had hidden within itself by accepting actual polygamy, namely the institution of the concubine, together with legal wives, or else the right of cohabitation with the slave.[54] Such a right, while it combated sin, at the same time contained within itself, or rather protected, the social dimension of sin, which it actually legalized. In these circumstances it became necessary for the fundamental ethical sense of the commandment, "You shall not commit adultery," to also undergo a basic reassessment. In the Sermon on the Mount, Christ revealed that sense again, namely by going beyond its traditional and legal restrictions.

It is worth adding that in the interpretation of the Old Testament, to the extent that the prohibition of adultery is balanced by the compromise with bodily concupiscence, the more the position regarding sexual deviations is clearly determined. This is confirmed by the relevant precepts which provide the death penalty for homosexuality and bestiality. Onanism had already been condemned in the tradition of the patriarchs (cf. Gn 38:8-10). The behavior of Onan, son of Judah (from where we have the origin of the word "onanism") "...was displeasing in the sight of the Lord, and he slew him also" (Gn 38:10).

In its widest and fullest meaning, the matrimonial law of the Old Testament puts in the foreground the procreative end of marriage. In certain cases it tries to be juridically equitable in the treatment of the woman and the man. For example, regarding the punishment for adultery, it says explicitly: "If a man commits adultery with his neighbor's wife, both the adulterer and the adulteress shall be put to death" (Lv 20:10). But on the whole, it judges the woman with greater severity.

Perhaps the terminology of this legislation should be emphasized. As always in such cases, the terminology tends to make objective the sexuality of that time. This terminology is important for the completeness of reflections on the theology of the body. We find the specific confirmation of the characteristic of shame which surrounds what pertains to sex in man. More than that, what is sexual is in a certain way considered as impure, especially when it regards physiological manifestations of human sexuality. The discovery of nudity (cf. Lv 20:11; 17:21) is branded as being the equivalent of an illicit and completed sexual act. The expression itself seems eloquent enough here. There is no doubt that the legislator has tried to use the terminology relating to the conscience and customs of contemporary society. Therefore, the terminology of the legislation of the Old Testament confirms our conviction that, not only are the physiology of sex and the bodily manifestations of sexual life known to the legislator, but also that these things are evaluated in a specific way. It is difficult to avoid the impression that such an evaluation was of a negative character. Certainly this in no way nullifies the truths which we know from Genesis. Nor does it lay the blame on the Old Testament and, among others, on the books of laws, as forerunners of a type of Manichaeism. The judgment expressed therein regarding the body and sex is not so much "negative" or severe, but rather marked by an objectivism, motivated by a desire to put this area of human life in order. This is not concerned directly with putting some order in the heart of man, but with putting order in the entire social life, at the base of which stands, as always, marriage and the family.

If we consider the sexual problem as a whole, perhaps we should briefly turn our attention again to another aspect. That is the existing bond among morality, law and medicine, emphasized in their respective books of the Old Testament. These contain many practical precepts regarding hygiene, or medicine, drawn rather from experience than from science, according to the level reached at that time.[55] Besides, the link between experience and science is distinctly still valid today. In this vast sphere of problems, medicine is always closely accompanied by ethics. As theology does, ethics seeks ways of collaborating with it.

When Christ said in the Sermon on the Mount: "You have heard that it was said: 'You shall not commit adultery,'" he immediately added: "But I say to you...." It is clear that he wanted to restore in the conscience of his audience the ethical significance of this commandment. He was disassociating himself from the interpretation of the "doctors of the law," official experts in it. But other than the interpretation derived from tradition, the Old Testament offers us still another tradition to understand the commandment, "Do not commit adultery." This is the tradition of the prophets. In reference to adultery, they wanted to remind Israel and Judah that their greatest sin was in abandoning the one true God in favor of the cult of various idols. In contact with other peoples, the chosen people had easily and thoughtlessly adopted such cults. Therefore, a precise characteristic of the language of the prophets is the analogy with adultery, rather than adultery itself. Such an analogy also helps to understand the commandment, "Do not commit adultery," and the relevant interpretation, the absence of which is noted in the legislative documents. In the pronouncements of the prophets, especially Isaiah, Hosea and Ezekiel, the God of the covenant—Yahweh—is often represented as a spouse. The love which united him to Israel can and must be identified with the nuptial love of a married couple. Because of its idolatry and abandonment of God-the-Spouse, in regard to him Israel commits a betrayal which can be compared to that of a woman in regard to her husband. Israel commits "adultery."

Using eloquent words, and often by means of images and extraordinarily flexible metaphors, the prophets show both the love of Yahweh-Spouse and the betrayal of Israel-spouse who gives itself over to adultery. This theme must be taken up again in our meditations when we will analyze the question of the "sacrament." However, we must already touch on the subject, inasmuch as it is necessary to understand the words of Christ in Matthew 5:27-28, to appreciate that renewal of the ethos, implied in these words: "But I say unto you...." On the one hand, Isaiah[56] in his texts emphasizes, above all, the love of Yahweh-Spouse who always takes the first step toward his spouse, passing over all her infidelities. On the other hand, Hosea and Ezekiel abound in comparisons which clarify primarily the ugliness and moral evil of the adultery by Israel-spouse.

In the next meditation we will try to penetrate still more profoundly the texts of the prophets, to further clarify the content which, in the conscience of those present during the Sermon on the Mount, corresponded to the commandment: "You shall not commit adultery."

General audience of August 20, 1980

Adultery Is a Breakdown of the Personal Covenant

In the Sermon on the Mount Christ said: "Think not that I have come to abolish the Law and the prophets; I have come not to abolish them but to fulfill them" (Mt 5:17). In order to understand clearly what such a fulfillment consists of, he then passes on to each single commandment. He also refers to the one which says: "You shall not commit adultery." Our previous meditation aimed at showing in what way the correct content of this commandment, desired by God, was obscured by the numerous compromises in the particular legislation of Israel. The prophets point out such content in a very true way. In their teachings they often denounce the abandonment of the true God-Yahweh by the people, comparing it to adultery.

Not only with words, but (as it seems) also in his behavior, Hosea is anxious to reveal to us (cf. Hos 1-3) that the people's betrayal is similar to that in marriage, or rather, even more, to adultery practiced as prostitution:

"Go, take to yourself a wife of harlotry, and have children of harlotry, for the land commits great harlotry by forsaking the Lord" (Hos 1:2). The prophet heeds this command within himself and accepts it as coming from God-Yahweh: "The Lord said to me, 'Go again, love a woman who is beloved of a paramour and is an adulteress'" (Hos 3:1). Although Israel may be so unfaithful with regard to its God, like the wife who "went after her lovers and forgot me" (Hos 2:13), Yahweh never ceases to search for his spouse. He does not tire of waiting for her conversion and her return, confirming this attitude with the words and actions of the prophet: "In that day, says the Lord, you will call me, 'My Husband,' and no longer will you call me, 'My Ba'al....' I will betroth you to me forever; I will betroth you to me in righteousness and in justice, in steadfast love and mercy. I will betroth you to me in faithfulness, and you shall know the Lord" (Hos 2:16, 19-20). This fervent call to conversion of the unfaithful wife-consort goes hand in hand with the following threat: "That she put away harlotry from her face, and her adultery from between her breasts, lest I strip her naked and make her as in the day she was born" (Hos 2:4-5).

Even within a wider sphere, the prophet Ezekiel reminded the unfaithful Israel-spouse of this image of the humiliating nudity of birth.

> But you were cast out on the open field, for you were abhorred, on the day that you were born. And when I passed by you, and saw you weltering in your blood, I said to you in your blood, "Live, and grow like a plant in the field." And you grew and became tall and arrived at full maidenhood. Your breasts were formed, and your hair had grown, yet you were naked and bare. When I passed by you again and looked upon you, behold, you were at the age for love, and I spread my skirt over you, and covered your nakedness. I plighted my troth to you and entered into a covenant with you, says the Lord God, and you became mine.... And I put a ring on your nose, and earrings in your ears, and a beautiful crown upon your head. Thus you were decked with gold and silver, and your raiment was of fine linen, and silk and embroidered cloth.... And your renown went forth among the nations because of your beauty, for it was perfect through the splendor which I had bestowed upon you.... But you trusted in your beauty, and played the harlot because of your renown, and lavished your harlotries on any passerby.... How lovesick is your heart, says the Lord God, seeing you did all these things, the deeds of a brazen harlot, making your lofty place in every square. Yet you were not like a harlot, because you scorned hire. Adulterous wife, who receives strangers instead of her husband (Ez 16:5-8, 12-15, 30-32).

The quotation is rather long. However, the text is so important that it was necessary to bring it up again. It expresses the analogy between adultery and idolatry in an especially strong and exhaustive way. The similarity between the two parts of the analogy consists in the covenant accompanied by love. Out of love, God-Yahweh settles the covenant with Israel, who is not worthy of it. For him Israel becomes the way a most affectionate, attentive, and generous spouse-consort is toward his own wife. In exchange for this love, which ever since the dawning of history accompanies the chosen people, Yahweh-Spouse receives numerous betrayals—"haughtiness." Here we have the cult of idols, in which "adultery" is committed by Israel-spouse. In the analysis we are carrying out here, the essential thing is the concept of adultery, as put forth by Ezekiel. However, it can be said that the situation as a whole, in which this concept is included (in the analogical sphere), is not typical. Here it is not so much a question of the mutual choice made by the husband and wife, which is born from mutual love, but of the choice of the wife (which was already made at the moment of her birth). This choice derives from the love of the husband, a love which on the part of the husband himself is an act of pure mercy. This choice is outlined in the following way. It corresponds to that part of the analogy which defines the covenant of Yahweh with Israel. But on the other hand, it corresponds to a lesser degree to the second part of it, which defines the nature of marriage.

Certainly, the mentality of that time was not very sensitive to this reality. According to the Israelites, marriage was rather the result of a unilateral choice, often made by the parents. Nevertheless, such a situation seldom forms part of our mentality.

Apart from this detail, we can note that the texts of the prophets have a different meaning of adultery from that given by the legislative tradition. Adultery is a sin because it constitutes the breakdown of the personal covenant between the man and the woman. In the legislative texts, the violation of and the right of ownership is pointed out, primarily the right of ownership of the man in regard to that woman who was his legal wife, one of many. In the text of the prophets, the background of real and legalized polygamy does not alter the ethical meaning of adultery. In many texts monogamy appears as the only correct analogy of monotheism as understood in the categories of the covenant, that is, of faithfulness and confidence toward the one true God-Yahweh, the Spouse of Israel. Adultery is the antithesis of that nuptial relationship. It is the antinomy of marriage (even as an institution) inasmuch as the monogamous marriage accomplishes within itself the interpersonal alliance of the man and the woman. It achieves the alliance born from love and received by both parties, precisely as marriage (and, as such, is recognized by society). This type of covenant between two people constitutes the foundation of that union when "man...cleaves to his wife and they become one flesh" (Gn 2:24). In the above-mentioned context, one can say that such bodily union is their "right" (bilateral). But above all, it is the regular sign of the communion of the two people, a union formed between the man and the woman in the capacity of husband and wife. Adultery committed by either one of them is not only the violation of this right, which is exclusive to the other marriage partner, but at the same time it is a radical falsification of this sign. It seems that in the pronouncements of the prophets, this aspect of adultery is expressed in a sufficiently clear manner.

Adultery is a falsification of that sign which does not have its "legality" so much as its simple interior truth in marriage—that is, in the cohabitation of the man and the woman who have become a married couple. In observing this, in a certain sense, we refer again to the basic statements made previously, considering them essential and important for the theology of the body, from both an ethical and anthropological point of view. Adultery is a "sin of the body." The whole tradition of the Old Testament bears witness to it, and Christ confirms it. The comparative analysis of his words in the Sermon on the Mount (Mt 5:27-28), like the several relevant enunciations contained in the Gospels and in other parts of the New Testament, allows us to establish the exact reason for the sinfulness of adultery. It is obvious that we determine the reason for sinfulness, or rather for moral evil, basing ourselves on the principle of contraposition, in regard to that moral goodness which is faithfulness in marriage. That goodness can be adequately achieved only in the exclusive relationship of both parties (that is, in the marriage relationship between a man and a woman). Such a relationship needs precisely nuptial love. As we have already pointed out, the interpersonal structure of this love is governed by the interior "normativity" of the communion of the two people concerned. Precisely this gives a fundamental significance to the covenant (either in the relationship of man-woman, or, analogously, in the relationship of Yahweh-Israel). One can judge on the basis of the contraposition of the marriage pact as it is understood, with adultery, its sinfulness, and the moral evil contained in it.

All this must be kept in mind when we say that adultery is a sin of the body. The body is considered here in the conceptual bond with the words of Genesis 2:24. This speaks of the man and the woman, who, as husband and wife, unite so closely as to form "one body only." Adultery indicates an act through which a man and a woman, who are not husband and wife, unite as "one body only" (that is, those who are not husband and wife in a monogamous sense, as was originally established, rather than in the legal casuistic sense of the Old Testament). The sin of the body can be identified only in regard to the relationship between the people concerned. One can speak of moral good and evil according to whether in this relationship there is a true "union of the body" and whether or not it has the character of the truthful sign. In this case, we can therefore judge adultery as a sin, according to the objective content of the act.

This is the content which Christ had in mind when, in the Sermon on the Mount, he reminded us: "You have understood that it was said: 'You shall not commit adultery.'" However Christ did not dwell on such an aspect of the problem.

General audience of August 27, 1980

The Meaning of Adultery
Is Transferred from the Body to the Heart

In the Sermon on the Mount Christ limited himself to recalling the commandment: "You shall not commit adultery," without evaluating the relative behavior of his listeners. What we previously said concerning this theme comes from other sources, especially from Christ's discussion with the Pharisees, in which he hearkened back to the "beginning" (cf. Mt 19:8; Mk 10:6). In the Sermon on the Mount Christ omitted such an evaluation, or rather, he implied it. What he will say in the second part of the statement, which begins with the words: "But I say to you..." will be something more than the dispute with the "doctors of the law" or with the moralists of the Torah. It will also be something more with respect to the evaluation of the Old Testament ethos. It will be a direct transition to the new ethos. Christ seemed to leave aside the whole dispute about the ethical significance of adultery on the plane of legislation and casuistry. In that plane the essential interpersonal relationship between husband and wife was considerably darkened by the objective relationship of property. Adultery acquires another dimension. Christ said: "But I say to you that everyone who looks at a woman lustfully has already committed adultery with her in his heart" (Mt 5:28). (When reading this passage there always comes to mind the ancient translation: "He has already made her an adulteress in his heart." Perhaps better than the present text, this version expresses the fact that here it deals with a purely interior and unilateral act.) Thus, adultery committed in the heart is in a certain sense counterposed with adultery committed in the body. We should ask ourselves why the point of gravity of sin is shifted, and what is the authentic significance of the analogy. If according to its fundamental meaning, adultery can only be a sin committed in the body, in what sense does that which man commits in his heart deserve to be called adultery also? Christ posed the foundation of the new ethos with words which for their part demand a thorough grounding in anthropology. Before answering these queries, let us pause for a while on the expression that, according to Matthew 5:27-28, in a certain way effects the transfer or rather the shifting of the significance of adultery of the body to the heart. These words concern desire.

Christ spoke of concupiscence: "Whoever looks lustfully." This expression requires a special analysis in order to understand the statement in its entirety. Here it is necessary to go back to the preceding analysis that aims, I would say, at reconstructing the image of the lustful man dating back to the beginning of history (cf. Gn 3). In the Sermon on the Mount Christ spoke about the man who "looks lustfully," who is without doubt the concupiscent man. For this reason, because it is part of bodily concupiscence, he desires and looks lustfully. The figure of the concupiscent man, reconstructed in the preceding aspect, will aid us now in interpreting desire, which Christ spoke about according to Matthew 5:27-28. This concerns here not only a psychological interpretation, but at the same time a theological interpretation. Christ spoke in the context of human experience and simultaneously in the context of the work of salvation. These two contexts in a certain way are superimposed upon and pervade one another. This has an essential and elemental significance for the entire ethos of the Gospel, and in particular for the content of the word lust or "looking lustfully."

Using such expressions, the Master first referred to the experience of his direct listeners. Then he also referred to the experience and conscience of the man of every time and place. Evangelical language may have a universal communicativeness. Yet for a direct listener, whose conscience was formed on the Bible, lust must be linked with many precepts and warnings. These are present in the first place in the Wisdom books, which contain repeated admonitions about concupiscence of the body and also advice on how to preserve oneself from it.

As we know, the Wisdom tradition had a special interest for the ethics and morality of Israelite society. A certain one-sidedness strikes us immediately in these admonitions and advice, appearing for example in Proverbs,[57] Sirach[58] or even Ecclesiastes.[59] The admonitions are above all directed to men. This can mean that for them they are especially necessary. As far as woman is concerned, it is true that in these warnings and advices she appears most often as an occasion of sin or as a downright seducer of whom to beware. Yet one must recognize that besides the warning to beware of woman and the seduction of her charm which lead man to sin (cf. Prv 5:1-6; 6:24-29; Sir 26:9-12), both Proverbs and Sirach also praise woman who is the "perfect life companion of her own husband" (cf. Prv 31:10ff.). They likewise praise the beauty and graciousness of a good wife who can make her husband happy.

"A modest wife adds charm to charm, and no balance can weigh the value of a chaste soul. Like the sun rising in the heights of the Lord, so is the beauty of a good wife in her well-ordered home. Like the shining lamp on the holy lampstand, so is a beautiful face on a stately figure. Like pillars of gold on a base of silver, so are beautiful feet with a steadfast heart.... A wife's charm delights her husband, and her skill puts fat on his bones" (Sir 26:15-18, 13).

In the Wisdom tradition a frequent admonition contrasts with the above praise of the woman-wife. The warning referred to the beauty and graciousness of the woman who is not one's own wife and is the cause of temptation and an occasion for adultery: "Do not desire her beauty in your heart..." (Prv 6:25). Sirach expresses the same warning in a more peremptory manner: "Turn away your eyes from a shapely woman, and do not look intently at beauty belonging to another. Many have been misled by a woman's beauty, and by it passion is kindled like a fire" (Sir 9:8-9).

The sense of the Wisdom texts has a prevalent pedagogical significance. They teach virtue and seek to protect the moral order, going back to God's law and to widely understood experience. Moreover, they are distinguished for their special knowledge of the human heart. We can say that they develop a specific moral psychology, yet without falling into psychologism. In a certain sense, they are close to that call of Christ to the heart that Matthew has handed down to us (cf. 5:27-28), even though it cannot be affirmed that they reveal any tendency to change ethos in a fundamental way. The authors of these books use the conscience of human inner life to teach morals somewhat in the sphere of ethos historically in action, and substantially confirmed by them. Sometimes one of them, such as Ecclesiastes, synthesizes this confirmation with its own "philosophy" of human existence. However, if it has an influence on the method with which warnings and advices are formulated, it does not change the fundamental structure of ethical evaluation.

For such a transformation it is necessary to wait until the Sermon on the Mount. Nonetheless, this wise knowledge of human psychology present in the Wisdom tradition was certainly not without significance for the circle of personal and immediate hearers of this sermon. If by virtue of the prophetic tradition these listeners were in a certain sense prepared for adequately understanding the concept of adultery, likewise by virtue of the Wisdom tradition they were prepared to understand the words that referred to the lustful look or alternatively to adultery committed in the heart.

It will be well for us to come back again to analyze the concept of concupiscence in the Sermon on the Mount.

General audience of September 3, 1980

Concupiscence Is a Separation
from the Nuptial Meaning of the Body

Let us reflect on the following words of Jesus from the Sermon on the Mount: "Everyone who looks at a woman lustfully has already committed adultery with her in his heart," or "has already made her an adulteress in his heart" (Mt 5:28). Christ said this before listeners who, on the basis of the books of the Old Testament, were in a certain sense prepared to understand the significance of the look that comes from concupiscence. Last Wednesday we referred to the texts taken from the so-called Wisdom books.

For example, here is another passage in which the biblical author analyzes the state of the soul of the man dominated by concupiscence of the flesh:

> The soul heated like a burning fire will not be quenched until it is consumed; a man who commits fornication...will never cease until the fire burns him up; to a fornicator all bread tastes sweet; he will never cease until he dies. A man who breaks his marriage vows says to himself: "Who sees me? Darkness surrounds me, and the walls hide me; no one sees me. Why should I fear? The Most High will not take notice of my sins." His fear is confined to the eyes of men; he does not realize that the eyes of the Lord are ten thousand times brighter than the sun. They look upon all the ways of men, and perceive even the hidden places. So it is with a woman who leaves her husband, and provides an heir by a stranger (Sir 23:17-22).

Analogous descriptions are not lacking in world literature.[60] Certainly, many of them are distinguished by a more penetrating discernment of psychological analysis and a more intense significance and expressive force. Yet, the biblical description from Sirach (23:17-22) includes some elements maintained to be "classic" in the analysis of carnal concupiscence. One element of this kind, for example, is a comparison between concupiscence of the flesh and fire. Flaring up in man, this invades his senses, excites his body, involves his feelings and in a certain sense takes possession of his heart. Such passion, originating in carnal concupiscence, suffocates in his heart the most profound voice of conscience, the sense of responsibility before God. That is especially evident in the biblical text just now quoted. On the other hand, external modesty with respect to men does persist, or rather an appearance of decency. It shows itself as fear of the consequences rather than of the evil in itself. In suffocating the voice of conscience, passion carries with itself a restlessness of the body and the senses. It is the restlessness of the external man. When the internal man has been reduced to silence, then passion, once it has been given freedom of action, exhibits itself as an insistent tendency to satisfy the senses and the body.

According to the criterion of the man dominated by passion, this gratification should put out the fire. But on the contrary, it does not reach the source of internal peace and it only touches the outermost level of the human person. Here the biblical author rightly observes that man, whose will is committed to satisfying the senses, finds neither peace nor himself, but, on the contrary, "is consumed." Passion aims at satisfaction. Therefore it blunts reflective activity and pays no attention to the voice of conscience. Thus, without itself having any principle of indestructibility, it "wears out." The dynamism of usage is natural for its continuity, but it tends to exhaust itself. Where passion enters into the whole of the most profound energies of the spirit, it can also become a creative force. In this case, however, it must undergo a radical transformation. If instead it suppresses the deepest forces of the heart and conscience (as occurs in the text of Sirach 23:17-22), it "wears out" and indirectly, man, who is its prey, is consumed.

When Christ in the Sermon on the Mount spoke of the man who lusts, who looks lustfully, it can be presumed that he had before his eyes also the images known to his listeners from the Wisdom tradition. Yet, at the same time he referred to every man who on the basis of his own internal experience knows the meaning of lust, looking at lustfully. The Master did not analyze this experience nor did he describe it, as Sirach had, for example (cf. 23:17-22). He seemed to presuppose, I would say, an adequate knowledge of that interior fact, to which he called the attention of his listeners, present and potential. Is it possible that some of them do not know what it is all about? If they really know nothing about it, the content of Christ's words would not apply to them, nor would any analysis or description be capable of explaining it to them. If instead they know—this deals with a knowledge completely internal, intrinsic to the heart and the conscience—they will immediately understand when the quoted words refer to them.

Christ did not describe or analyze what constitutes the experience of lust, the experience of concupiscence of the flesh. One even has the impression that he did not penetrate this experience in all the breadth of its interior dynamism, as occurs, for example, in the text quoted from Sirach, but rather he paused on its threshold. Lust has not yet been changed into an exterior action. It has still not become the act of the body, but is until now the interior act of the heart. It expresses itself in a look, in the way of looking at the woman. Nevertheless, it already lets itself be understood and reveals its content and its essential quality. It is now necessary for us to make this analysis. A look expresses what is in the heart. A look expresses, I would say, the man within. If in general it is maintained that man "acts according to his lights," *(operari sequitur esse),* Christ in this case wanted to bring out that the man looks in conformity with what he is: *intueri sequitur esse.* In a certain sense, man by his look reveals himself to the outside and to others. Above all he reveals what he perceives on the "inside."[61]

Christ, then, teaches us to consider a look almost like the threshold of inner truth. In a look, "in the way in which one looks," it is already possible to single out completely what concupiscence is. Let us try to explain it. Lust, looking at lustfully, indicates an experience of value to the body, in which its nuptial significance ceases to be that, just because of concupiscence. Its procreative meaning likewise ceases (we spoke about this in our previous considerations). When it concerns the conjugal union of man and woman, it is rooted in the nuptial meaning of the body and almost organically emerges from it. Now then, man, lusting, looking at lustfully (as we read in Matthew 5:27-28), attempts in a more or less explicit way the separation of that meaning of the body. As we have already observed in our reflections, this is at the basis of the communion of persons, whether outside of marriage, or, in a special way, when man and woman are called to build their union "in the body" (as the "gospel of the beginning" proclaims in the classic text of Genesis 2:24). The experience of the nuptial meaning of the body is subordinate in a special way to the sacramental call, but is not limited to this. This meaning qualifies the liberty of the gift that can be fulfilled not only in marriage but also in a different way, as we shall see more precisely in further analyses.

Christ said: "Everyone who looks at a woman lustfully has already committed adultery with her in his heart" (Mt 5:28). Did he not perhaps mean by this that concupiscence itself—like adultery—is an interior separation from the nuptial meaning of the body? Did he not want to refer his listeners to their internal experiences of such detachment? Is it not perhaps for this reason that he defines it as "adultery committed in the heart"?

General audience of September 10, 1980

Mutual Attraction Differs from Lust

During our last reflection, we asked ourselves what the lust was which Christ spoke of in the Sermon on the Mount (Mt 5:27-28). Let us recall that he spoke of it in relation to the commandment: "Do not commit adultery." Lust itself (more exactly: looking at lustfully), is defined as "adultery committed in the heart." That gives much food for thought. In the preceding reflections we said that by expressing himself in that way, Christ wanted to indicate to his listeners the separation from the matrimonial significance of the body felt by a human being (in this case the man) when concupiscence of the flesh is coupled with the inner act of lust. The separation of the matrimonial significance of the body causes at the same time a conflict with his personal dignity, a veritable conflict of conscience.

At this point it appears that the biblical (hence also theological) meaning of lust is different from the purely psychological. The latter describes lust as an intense inclination toward the object because of its particular value, and in the case considered here, its sexual value. As it seems, we will find such a definition in most of the works dealing with similar themes. Yet the biblical interpretation, while not underestimating the psychological aspect, places that ethic in relief above all, since a value is being impaired. I would say that lust is a deception of the human heart in the perennial call of man and woman—a call revealed in the mystery of creation—to communion by means of mutual giving. In the Sermon on the Mount (Mt 5:27-28) Christ referred to the heart or the internal man. His words do not cease being charged with that truth concerning the principle to which, in replying to the Pharisees (cf. Mt 19:8), he had reverted to the whole problem of man, woman and marriage.

The perennial call, which we have tried to analyze following Genesis (especially Genesis 2:23-25) and, in a certain sense, the perennial mutual attraction on man's part to femininity and on woman's part to masculinity, is an indirect invitation of the body. But it is not lust in the sense of the word in Matthew 5:27-28. That lust carries into effect the concupiscence of the flesh (also and especially in the purely internal act). It diminishes the significance of what that invitation and that reciprocal attraction were—and what in reality they do not cease being. The "eternal feminine" *(das ewig weibliche),* just like the "eternal masculine" for that matter, on the level of historicity, too, tends to free itself from pure concupiscence and seeks a position of achievement in the world of people. It testifies to that original sense of shame which Genesis 3 speaks of. The dimension of intentionality of thought and heart constitutes one of the main streams of universal human culture. Christ's words in the Sermon on the Mount confirm this dimension exactly.

Nonetheless, these words clearly assert that lust is a real part of the human heart. When compared with the original mutual attraction of masculinity and femininity, lust represents a reduction. In stating this, we have in mind an intentional reduction, almost a restriction or closing down of

the horizon of mind and heart. It is one thing to be conscious that the value
of sex is a part of all the rich storehouse of values with which the female
appears to the man. It is another to "reduce" all the personal riches of
femininity to that single value, that is, of sex, as a suitable object for the
gratification of sexuality itself. The same reasoning can be valid concerning what masculinity is for the woman, even though Matthew's words in
5:27-28 refer directly to the other relationship only. As can be seen, the
intentional reduction is primarily of an axiological nature. On one hand
the eternal attraction of man toward femininity (cf. Gn 2:23) frees in
him—or perhaps it should free—a gamut of spiritual-corporal desires of
an especially personal and "sharing" nature (cf. the analysis of the "beginning"), to which a proportionate pyramid of values corresponds. On the
other hand, lust limits this gamut, obscuring the pyramid of values that
marks the perennial attraction of male and female.

Lust has the internal effect, that is, in the heart, on the interior
horizon of man and woman, of obscuring the significance of the body, of
the person itself. Femininity thus ceases being above all else an object for
the man. It ceases being a specific language of the spirit. It loses its character of being a sign. I would say that it ceases bearing in itself the wonderful matrimonial significance of the body. It ceases its correlation to this
significance in the context of conscience and experience. Lust arising
from concupiscence of the flesh itself, from the first moment of its existence within the man—its existence in his heart—passes in a certain sense
close to such a context. (Using an image, one could say that it passes on
the ruins of the matrimonial significance of the body and all its subjective
parts.) By virtue of axiological intentionality itself, it aims directly at
an exclusive end—to satisfy only the sexual need of the body, as its precise object.

According to the words of Christ (Mt 5:27-28), such an intentional
and axiological reduction can take place in the sphere of the look (of looking), or rather, it takes place in the sphere of a purely interior act expressed by the look. A look (or rather looking) is in itself a cognitive act.
When concupiscence enters its inner structure, the look takes on the character of lustful knowledge. The biblical expression "to look at lustfully"
can indicate both a cognitive act, which the lusting man "makes use of,"
(that is, giving him the character of lust aiming at an object), and a cognitive act that arouses lust in the other object and above all in its will and in
its heart. As is seen, it is possible to place an intentional interpretation on
an interior act, being aware of one and the other pole of man's psychology:
knowledge or lust understood as *appetitus*. (This is something broader
than lust, since it indicates everything manifested in the object as aspira-

tion, and as such always tends to aim at something, that is, toward an object known under the aspect of value.) Yet, an adequate interpretation of Matthew 5:27-28 requires us, by means of the intentionality itself of knowledge or of the *appetitus* to discern something more—the intentionality of the very existence of man in relation to the other man. In our case, it is the man in relation to the woman and the woman in relation to the man.

It will be well for us to return to this subject. Concluding today's reflection, we add again that in that lust, in looking at lustfully, which the Sermon on the Mount deals with, for the man who looks in that way, the woman ceases to exist as an object of eternal attraction. She begins to be only an object of carnal concupiscence. To that is connected the profound inner separation of the matrimonial significance of the body, about which we spoke in the preceding reflection.

General audience of September 17, 1980

The Depersonalizing Effect of Concupiscence

In the Sermon on the Mount Christ said: "You have heard that it was said, 'You shall not commit adultery.' But I say to you that everyone who looks at a woman lustfully has already committed adultery with her in his heart" (Mt 5:27-28). We have been trying for some time to penetrate the meaning of this statement, analyzing the single elements in order to understand better the text as a whole.

When Christ spoke of a man who looks lustfully, he indicated not only the dimension of intentionality in looking, thus indicating lustful knowledge, the psychological dimension, but also the dimension of the intentionality of man's very existence. In the situation Christ described, that dimension passes unilaterally from the man, who is the subject, to the woman, who has become the object. (This does not mean, however, that such a dimension is only unilateral.) For the present we will not reverse the situation analyzed, or extend it to both parties, to both subjects. Let us dwell on the situation outlined by Christ, stressing that it is a question of a purely interior act, hidden in the heart and stopping on the threshold of the look.

It is enough to note that in this case the woman—who owing to her personal subjectivity exists perennially "for man," waiting for him, too, for the same reason, to exist "for her"—is deprived of the meaning of her attraction as a person. Though being characteristic of the "eternal feminine," she becomes at the same time only an object for the man. That is, she begins to exist intentionally as an object for the potential satisfaction of the sexual need inherent in his masculinity. Although the act is completely interior, hidden in the heart and expressed only by the look, there already occurs in him a change (subjectively unilateral) of the very intentionality of existence. If it were not so, if it were not a question of such a deep change, the following words of the same sentence: "...has already committed adultery with her in his heart" (Mt 5:28) would have no meaning.

That change of the intentionality of existence is carried out in the heart, since it is carried out in the will. By means of it, a certain woman begins to exist for a certain man not as a subject of call and personal attraction or as a subject of communion, but exclusively as an object for the potential satisfaction of the sexual need. Cognitive intentionality itself does not yet mean enslavement of the heart. It can be said that desire has also gained possession of the heart only when the intentional reduction, illustrated previously, sweeps the will along into its narrow horizon. It brings forth the decision of a relationship with another human being (in our case, with the woman) according to the specific scale of values of lust. Only when lust has gained possession of the will is it possible to say that it is dominant over the subjectivity of the person. Then it is at the basis of the will and of the possibility of choosing and deciding. Through that possibility—by virtue of self-decision or self-determination—the very way of existing with regard to another person is established. The intentionality of this existence then acquires a full subjective dimension.

Only then—that is from that subjective moment and on its subjective prolongation—is it possible to confirm what we read, for example, in Sirach (23:17-22), about the man dominated by lust, and what we read in even more eloquent descriptions in world literature. Then we can also speak of that more or less complete compulsion, which is called elsewhere compulsion of the body. This brings with it loss of the freedom of the gift, congenital in deep awareness of the matrimonial meaning of the body, of which we have also spoken in preceding analyses.

We can speak of desire as the transformation of the intentionality of a concrete existence, for example, of the man. For him (according to Mt 5:27-28), a certain woman becomes merely the object of the potential satisfaction of the sexual need inherent in his masculinity. Speaking of this desire is not at all a matter of questioning that need, as an objective dimension of human nature with the procreative finality that is characteristic of it. Christ's words in the Sermon on the Mount (in its whole context) are far from Manichaeism, as the true Christian tradition also is. In this case, therefore, objections of such kind cannot arise. On the contrary, it is a question of the man's and the woman's way of existing as persons. That is, it concerns their existing in a mutual "for," which can and must serve the building up of the unity of communion in their mutual relations. This happens also on the basis of what can be defined as the sexual need, according to the objective dimension of human nature. Such is the fundamental meaning characteristic of the perennial and reciprocal attraction of masculinity and femininity. This is contained in the very reality of the constitution of man as a person, body and sex together.

It can happen that one of the two persons exists only as the subject of the satisfaction of the sexual need, and the other becomes exclusively the object of this satisfaction. This does not correspond to the union or personal communion to which man and woman were mutually called from the beginning. On the contrary, it conflicts with it. Moreover, the case in which both the man and the woman exist reciprocally as the object of satisfaction of the sexual need, and each on his or her part is only the subject of that satisfaction, does not correspond to this unity of communion. On the contrary it clashes with it. This reduction of such a rich content of the reciprocal and perennial attraction of human persons in their masculinity or femininity does not at all correspond to the "nature" of the attraction in question. This reduction extinguishes the personal meaning of communion, characteristic of man and woman. According to Genesis 2:24, through it "a man...cleaves to his wife, and they become one flesh." Lust turns away the intentional dimension of the man's and woman's mutual existence. It turns away from the personal perspectives, "of communion," characteristic of their perennial and mutual attraction. It reduces it, and pushes it toward utilitarian dimensions, within which the human being uses the other human being, for the sake merely of satisfying his own needs.

In Christ's concise affirmation in the Sermon on the Mount, it seems possible to find this content again, charged with the human interior experience characteristic of different ages and environments. At the same time, we cannot in any case lose sight of the meaning that this affirmation attributes to man's interiority, to the integral dimension of the heart as the dimension of the inner man. Here lies the core of the transformation of ethos aimed at by Christ's words according to Matthew 5:27-28, expressed with powerful forcefulness and at the same time with admirable simplicity.

General audience of September 24, 1980

Establishing the Ethical Sense

We arrive in our analysis at the third part of Christ's enunciation in the Sermon on the Mount (Mt 5:27-28). The first part was: "You have heard that it was said, 'You shall not commit adultery.'" The second part was: "But I say to you that everyone who looks at a woman lustfully...."

This is grammatically connected with the third part: "...has already committed adultery with her in his heart."

The method applied here of dividing or splitting Christ's enunciation into three parts which follow one another may seem artificial. However, when we seek the ethical meaning of the enunciation in its totality, the division of the text used by us may be useful. This is provided that it is applied not only in a disjunctive, but in a conjunctive way. This is what we intend to do. Each of the distinct parts has its own specific content and connotations, and we wish to stress this by dividing the text. But it must be pointed out at the same time that each of the parts is explained in direct relationship with the others. That referred in the first place to the principal semantic elements by which the enunciation constitutes a whole. These elements are: to commit adultery, to desire to commit adultery in the body, to commit adultery in the heart. It would be especially difficult to establish the ethical sense of desiring without the element indicated here last, that is adultery in the heart. The preceding analysis has already considered this element to a certain extent. However, a fuller understanding of "to commit adultery in the heart" is possible only after a special analysis.

As we have already mentioned, it is a question here of establishing the ethical sense. Christ's enunciation in Matthew 5:27-28 starts from the commandment: "Do not commit adultery." This is in order to show how it must be understood and put into practice, so that the justice that God-Yahweh wished as legislator may abound in it. It is in order that it may abound to a greater extent than appeared from the interpretation and casuistry of the Old Testament doctors. If Christ's words in this sense aim at constructing the new ethos (and on the basis of the same commandment), the way to that passes through the rediscovery of the values which have been lost in the general Old Testament understanding and in the application of this commandment.

The formulation of the text of Matthew 5:27-28 is significant also from this point of view. The commandment "Do not commit adultery" is formulated as a prohibition which categorically excludes a given moral evil. It is well known that the same law (the Ten Commandments), as well as the prohibition "do not commit adultery," also include the prohibition, "Do not covet your neighbor's wife" (Ex 20:14, 17; Dt 5:18, 21). Christ did not nullify one prohibition with regard to the other. Although he spoke of desire, he aimed at a deeper clarification of adultery. It is significant that after mentioning the prohibition, "Do not commit adultery," as well known to his listeners, in the course of his enunciation he changed his style and the logical structure from the normative to the narrative-affirmative. When he said: "'Everyone who looks at a woman lustfully has already committed adultery with her in his heart," he described an interior fact, whose reality can easily be understood by his listeners. At the same time, through the fact thus described and qualified, he indicated how the commandment, "Do not commit adultery" must be understood and put into practice, so that it will lead to the justice willed by the legislator.

In this way we have reached the expression "has committed adultery in his heart." This is the key-expression, as it seems, for understanding its correct ethical meaning. This expression is at the same time the principal source for revealing the essential values of the new ethos, the ethos of the Sermon on the Mount. As often happens in the Gospel, here, too, we come up against a certain paradox. How can adultery take place without committing adultery, that is, without the exterior act which makes it possible to identify the act forbidden by the law? We have seen how much the casuistry of the doctors of the law devoted itself to defining this problem. But even apart from casuistry, it seems clear that adultery can be identified only in the flesh, that is, when the two, the man and the woman who unite with each other in such a way as to become one flesh (cf. Gn 2:24), are not legal spouses, husband and wife. What meaning, then, can adultery committed in the heart have? Is it not perhaps just a metaphorical expression the Master used to highlight the sinfulness of lust?

If we admitted this semantic reading of Christ's enunciation (Mt 5:27-28), it would be necessary to reflect deeply on the ethical consequences that would be derived from it, that is, on the conclusions about the ethical regularity of the behavior. Adultery takes place when the man and the woman who unite with each other so as to become one flesh (cf. Gn 2:24), that is, in the way characteristic of spouses, are not legal spouses. The detecting of adultery as a sin committed in the body is closely and exclusively united with the exterior act, with living together in a conjugal way. This referred also to the status of the acting persons, recognized by society. In the case in question, this status is improper and does not authorize such an act (hence the term "adultery").

Going on to the second part of Christ's enunciation (that is, the one in which the new ethos begins to take shape), it would be necessary to understand the expression, "Everyone who looks at a woman lustfully," in exclusive reference to persons according to their civil status. This is their status recognized by society, whether or not they are husband and wife. Here the questions begin to multiply. There can be no doubt about the fact that Christ indicated the sinfulness of the interior act of lust expressed through a way of looking at every woman who is not the wife of the one who so looks at her. Therefore we can and even must ask ourselves if, with the same expression, Christ admitted and approved such a look, such an interior act of lust, directed toward the woman who is the wife of the man who so looks at her.

The following logical premise seems to favor the affirmative answer to such a question. In the case in question, only the man who is the potential subject of adultery in the flesh can commit adultery in the heart. Since this subject cannot be the husband with regard to his own legitimate wife, therefore adultery in the heart cannot refer to him, but any other man can be considered guilty of it. If he is the husband, he cannot commit it with regard to his own wife. He alone has the exclusive right to desire, to look lustfully at the woman who is his wife. It can never be said that due to such an interior act he deserves to be accused of adultery committed in the heart. If by virtue of marriage he has the right to unite with his wife, so that the two become one flesh, this act can never be called adultery. Similarly the interior act of desire, dealt with in the Sermon on the Mount, cannot be defined as adultery committed in the heart.

This interpretation of Christ's words in Matthew 5:27-28 seems to correspond to the logic of the Ten Commandments. In addition to the commandment, "Do not commit adultery" they also contain the commandment, "Do not covet your neighbor's wife." Furthermore, the reasoning in support of this interpretation has all the characteristics of objective correctness and accuracy. Nevertheless, good grounds for doubt remain as to whether this reasoning takes into account all the aspects of revelation, as well as of the theology of the body. This must be considered, especially when we wish to understand Christ's words. We have already seen what the "specific weight" of this expression is, how rich the anthropological and theological implications are of the one sentence in which Christ referred "to the beginning" (cf. Mt 19:8). These implications of the enunciation in the Sermon on the Mount in which Christ referred to the human heart confer on the enunciation itself also a "specific weight" of its own. At the same time they determine its consistency with evangelical teaching as a whole. Therefore we must admit that the interpretation presented above, with all its objective correctness and logical precision, requires a certain amplification and, above all, a deepening. We must remember that the reference to the human heart, expressed perhaps in a paradoxical way (cf. Mt 5:27-28), comes from him who "knew what was in man" (Jn 2:25). If his words confirm the Decalogue (not only the sixth, but also the ninth commandment), at the same time they express that knowledge of man, which—as we have pointed out elsewhere—enables us to unite awareness of human sinfulness with the perspective of the redemption of the body (cf. Rom 8:23). This knowledge lies at the basis of the new ethos which emerges from the words of the Sermon on the Mount.

Considering all this, we conclude the following. In understanding adultery in the flesh, Christ criticized the erroneous and one-sided interpretation of adultery that is derived from the failure to observe monogamy (that is, marriage understood as the indefectible covenant of persons). So also in understanding adultery in the heart, Christ not only considered the real juridical status of the man and woman in question. He also made the moral evaluation of the desire depend above all on the personal dignity itself of the man and the woman. This has its importance both when it is a question of persons who are not married, and—perhaps even more— when they are spouses, wife and husband. From this point of view it will be useful for us to complete the analysis of the words of the Sermon on the Mount.

General audience of October 1, 1980

Interpreting the Concept of Concupiscence

Today I wish to conclude the analysis of the words Christ spoke in the Sermon on the Mount about adultery and lust, and especially the last element of this enunciation. In it, "lust of the eyes" is defined specifically as "adultery committed in the heart."

We have already seen that the above-mentioned words are usually understood as desire for another's wife (that is, according to the spirit of the ninth commandment of the Decalogue). However, it seems that this interpretation—a more restrictive one—can and must be widened in the light of the total context. The moral evaluation of lust (of looking lustfully), which Christ called adultery committed in the heart, seems to depend above all on the personal dignity itself of man and of woman. This holds true both for those who are not united in marriage, and—perhaps even more—for those who are husband and wife.

The analysis which we have made so far of Matthew 5:27-28 indicates the necessity of amplifying and above all deepening the interpretation presented previously, with regard to the ethical meaning that this enunciation contains. "You have heard that it was said, 'You shall not commit adultery.' But I say to you that everyone who looks at a woman lustfully has already committed adultery with her in his heart." Let us dwell on the situation described by the Master, a situation in which the one who commits adultery in his heart by means of an interior act of lust (expressed by the look) is the man. It is significant that in speaking of the object of this act, Christ did not stress that it is "another man's wife," or a woman who is not his own wife, but says generically, a woman. Adultery committed in the heart is not circumscribed in the limits of the interpersonal relationship which make it possible to determine adultery committed in the body. It is not these limits that decide exclusively and essentially about adultery committed in the heart, but the very nature of lust. It is expressed in this case by a look, that is, by the fact that that man—whom Christ speaks of for the sake of example—looks lustfully. Adultery in the heart is committed not only *because* man looks in this way at a woman who is not his wife, but *precisely* because he looks at a woman in this way. Even if he looked in this way at the woman who is his wife, he could likewise commit adultery in his heart.

This interpretation seems to consider more amply what has been said about lust in these analyses as a whole, and primarily about the lust of the flesh as a permanent element of man's sinfulness *(status naturae lapsae)*. The lust which, as an interior act, springs from this basis (as we tried to indicate in the preceding analyses) changes the very intentionality of the woman's existence "for" man. It reduces the riches of the perennial call to the communion of persons, the riches of the deep attractiveness of masculinity and femininity, to mere satisfaction of the sexual need of the body (the concept of "instinct" seems to be linked more closely with this). As a result of this reduction, the person (in this case, the woman) becomes for the other person (the man) mainly the object of the potential satisfaction of his own sexual need. In this way, that mutual "for" is distorted, losing its character of communion of persons in favor of the utilitarian function. A man who looks in this way, as Matthew 5:27-28 indicates, uses the woman, her femininity, to satisfy his own instinct. Although he does not do so with an exterior act, he has already assumed this attitude deep down, inwardly deciding in this way with regard to a given woman. This is what adultery committed in the heart consists of. Man can commit this adultery in the heart also with regard to his own wife, if he treats her only as an object to satisfy instinct.

It is impossible to arrive at the second interpretation of Matthew 5:27-28 if we confine ourselves to the purely psychological interpretation of lust without taking into account what constitutes its specific theological character, that is, the organic relationship between lust (as an act) and the lust of the flesh as a permanent disposition derived from man's sinfulness. The purely psychological (or "sexological") interpretation of lust does not seem to constitute a sufficient basis to understand the text of the Sermon on the Mount in question. On the other hand, if we refer to the theological interpretation—without underestimating what remains unchangeable in the first interpretation (the psychological one)—the second interpretation (the theological one) appears to us as more complete. Thanks to it, the ethical meaning of the key enunciation of the Sermon on the Mount, to which we owe the adequate dimension of the ethos of the Gospel, becomes clearer.

Sketching this dimension, Christ remained faithful to the law. "Do not think that I have come to abolish the law and the prophets; I have come not to abolish them but to fulfill them" (Mt 5:17). Consequently he showed how deep down it is necessary to go, how the recesses of the human heart must be thoroughly revealed, in order that this heart may become a place of "fulfillment" of the law. Matthew 5:27-28 is an extraordinary argument. It makes manifest the interior perspective of adultery committed in the heart, and in this perspective points out the right ways to fulfill the commandment: "Do not commit adultery." Matthew 5:27-28 referred to the sphere which especially concerns purity of heart (cf. Mt 5:8). (As is known, this expression has a wide meaning in the Bible.) Elsewhere, too, we will consider in what way the commandment "Do not commit adultery" is carried out precisely by means of purity of heart. As regards the way in which it is expressed and the content, this commandment is a univocal and severe prohibition (like the commandment, "You shall not covet your neighbor's wife"—Ex 20:17). The severity and strength of the prohibition are testified to directly by the following words of the Sermon on the Mount, in which Christ spoke figuratively of "plucking out one's eye" and "cutting off one's hand," if these members were the cause of sin (cf. Mt 5:29-30). We have already seen that the legislation of the Old Testament, though abounding in severe punishments, did not contribute to "fulfill the law," because its casuistry was marked by many compromises with the lust of the flesh. On the contrary, Christ taught that the commandment is carried out through purity of heart. This is not given to man except at the cost of firmness with regard to everything that springs from the lust of the flesh. Whoever is able to demand consistently from his heart and from his body, acquires purity of heart.

The commandment "Do not commit adultery" finds its rightful motivation in the indissolubility of marriage. In it, man and woman, by virtue of the original plan of the Creator, unite in such a way that "the two become one flesh" (cf. Gn 2:24). By its essence, adultery conflicts with this unity, in the sense in which this unity corresponds to the dignity of persons. Christ not only confirms this essential ethical meaning of the commandment, but aims at strengthening it in the depth of the human person. The new dimension of *ethos* is always connected with the revelation of that depth, which is called "heart," and with its liberation from lust. This is in order that man, male and female, in all the interior truth of the mutual "for," may shine forth more fully in that heart. Freed from the constraint and from the impairment of the spirit that the lust of the flesh brings with it, the human being, male and female, finds himself mutually in the freedom of the gift. This gift is the condition of all life together in truth, and, in particular, in the freedom of mutual giving. Both husband and wife must form the sacramental unity willed by the Creator himself, as Genesis 2:24 says.

As is plain, the necessity which, in the Sermon on the Mount, Christ placed on all his actual and potential listeners, belongs to the interior space in which man—precisely the one who is listening to him—must perceive anew the lost fullness of his humanity, and want to regain it. That fullness in the mutual relationship of persons, of the man and of the woman, was claimed by the Master in Matthew 5:27-28. He had in mind above all the indissolubility of marriage, but also every other form of the common life of men and women, that common life which constitutes the pure and simple fabric of existence. By its nature, human life is "coeducative." Its dignity and balance depend, at every moment of history and at every point of geographical longitude and latitude, on who she will be for him, and he for her.

The words Christ spoke in the Sermon on the Mount have certainly this universal and at the same time profound significance. Only in this way can they be understood in the mouth of him who knew thoroughly "what was in man," and who, at the same time, bore within him the mystery of the "redemption of the body," as St. Paul puts it. Are we to fear the severity of these words, or rather have confidence in their salvific content, in their power?

In any case, the analysis carried out of the words Christ spoke in the Sermon on the Mount opens the way to further indispensable reflections in order to reach full awareness of historical man, and above all of modern man.

General audience of October 8, 1980

Gospel Values and the Duties of the Human Heart

During our Wednesday meetings, we have analyzed in detail the words of the Sermon on the Mount, in which Christ referred to the human heart. As we now know, his words are exacting. Christ said: "You have heard that it was said, 'You shall not commit adultery.' But I say to you that everyone who looks at a woman lustfully has already committed adultery with her in his heart" (Mt 5:27-28). This reference to the heart throws light on the dimension of human interiority, the dimension of the inner man, characteristic of ethics, and even more of the theology of the body. Desire rises in the sphere of the lust of the flesh. It is at the same time an interior and theological reality, which is experienced, in a way, by every "historical" man. It is precisely this man—even if he does not know the words of Christ—who continually asks himself the question about his own heart. Christ's words make this question especially explicit: is the heart accused, or is it called to good? Toward the end of our reflections and analyses we now intend to consider this question, connected with the sentence of the Gospel, so concise and yet categorical at the same time, so pregnant with theological, anthropological, and ethical content.

A second question goes hand in hand with it, a more practical one: how can and must he act, the man who accepts Christ's words in the Sermon on the Mount, the man who accepts the ethos of the Gospel, and, in particular, accepts it in this field?

This man finds in the considerations made up to now the answer, at least an indirect one, to two questions. How *can* he act, that is, on what can he rely in his inner self, at the source of his interior or exterior acts? Furthermore, how *should* he act, that is, in what way do the values known according to the scale revealed in the Sermon on the Mount constitute a duty of his will and his heart, of his desires and his choices? In what way are they binding on him in action and behavior, if, accepted by means of knowledge, they already commit him in thinking and, in a certain way, in feeling? These questions are significant for human praxis, and indicate an organic connection of praxis with ethos. Lived morality is always the ethos of human practice.

It is possible to answer the aforesaid questions in various ways. In fact, various answers are given, both in the past and today. This is confirmed by an ample literature. In addition to the answers we find in it, it is necessary to consider the infinite number of answers that concrete man gives to these questions by himself, the ones that his conscience, his awareness and moral sensitivity give repeatedly, in the life of everyone. In this sphere an *interpenetration of ethos and praxis is carried out.* Here the individual principles live their own life (not exclusively "theoretical"). This not only concerns the norms of morality with their motivations which are worked out and made known by moralists. It also concerns the ones worked out—certainly not without a link with the work of moralists and scientists—by individual men, as authors and direct subjects of real morality, as co-authors of its history. On this the level of morality itself also depends, its progress or its decadence. All this reconfirms, everywhere and always, that historical man to whom Christ once spoke. He proclaimed the good news of the Gospel with the Sermon on the Mount, where he said among other things: "You have heard that it was said, 'You shall not commit adultery.' But I say to you that everyone who looks at a woman lustfully has already committed adultery with her in his heart" (Mt 5:27-28).

Matthew's enunciation is stupendously concise in comparison with everything that has been written on this subject in secular literature. Perhaps its power in the history of ethos consists precisely in this. At the same time it must be realized that the history of ethos flows in a multiform bed, in which the individual currents draw nearer to, or move further away from, one another in turn. Historical man always evaluates his own heart in his own way, just as he also judges his own body. So he passes from the pole of pessimism to the pole of optimism, from puritan severity to modern permissiveness. It is necessary to realize this, in order that the ethos of the Sermon on the Mount may always have due transparency with regard to human actions and behavior. For this purpose it is necessary to make some more analyses.

Our reflections on the meaning of the words of Christ according to Matthew 5:27-28 would not be complete if they did not dwell at least briefly on what can be called the echo of these words in the history of human thought and of the evaluation of ethos. The echo is always a transformation of the voice and of the words that the voice expresses. We know from experience that this transformation is sometimes full of mysterious fascination. In the case in question, the opposite happened. Christ's words have been stripped of their simplicity and depth. A meaning has been conferred far removed from the one expressed in them, a meaning that even contradicts them. We have in mind here all that happened outside Christianity under the name of Manichaeism,[62] and that also tried to enter the ground of Christianity as regards theology itself and the ethos of the body. Manichaeism arose in the East outside the biblical environment and sprang from Mazdeistic dualism. It is well known that, in its original form, Manichaeism saw the source of evil in matter, in the body, and therefore condemned everything that is corporeal in man. Since corporeity is manifested in man mainly through sex, the condemnation was extended to marriage and to conjugal life, as well as to other spheres of being and acting in which corporeity is expressed.

To an unaccustomed ear, the evident severity of that system might seem in harmony with the severe words of Matthew 5:29-30, in which Christ spoke of "plucking out one's eye" or "cutting off one's hand," if these members were the cause of scandal. Through the purely material interpretation of these expressions, it was also possible to obtain a Manichaean view of Christ's enunciation, in which he spoke of a man who has "committed adultery in his heart...by looking at a woman lustfully." In this case, too, the Manichaean interpretation aims at condemning the body, as the real source of evil, since the ontological principle of evil, according to Manichaeism, is concealed and at the same time manifested in it. The attempt was made, therefore, to see *this condemnation in the Gospel, and sometimes it was perceived, where actually only a particular requirement addressed to the human spirit had been expressed.*

Note that the condemnation might—and may always be—a loophole to avoid the requirements set in the Gospel by him who "knew what was in man" (Jn 2:25). History has no lack of proofs. We have already partially had the opportunity (and we will certainly have it again) to show to what extent such a requirement may arise solely from an affirmation—and not from a denial or a condemnation—if it has to lead to an affirmation that is even more mature and deep, objectively and subjectively. The words of Christ according to Matthew 5:27-28 must lead to such an affirmation of the femininity and masculinity of the human being, as the personal dimension of "being a body." This is the right ethical meaning of these words. They impress on the pages of the Gospel a peculiar dimension of ethos in order to impress it subsequently on human life.

General audience of October 15, 1980

The Value of the Body according to the Creator's Plan

Christ's words in the Sermon on the Mount have been at the center of our reflections for a long time now: "You have heard that it was said, 'You shall not commit adultery.' But I say to you that everyone who looks at a woman lustfully has already committed adultery with her in his heart" (Mt 5:27-28). These words have an essential meaning for the whole theology of the body contained in Christ's teaching. Therefore, we rightly attribute great importance to their correct understanding and interpretation. In our preceding reflection we noted that the Manichean doctrine, both in its primitive and in its later expressions, contradicts these words.

It is not possible to see in the sentence of the Sermon on the Mount, analyzed here, a "condemnation" or an accusation of the body. If anything, one could catch a glimpse of a condemnation of the human heart. However, the reflections we have made so far show that, if the words of Matthew 5:27-28 contain an accusation, it is directed above all at the man of lust. With those words the heart is not so much accused as subjected to a judgment. Or better, it is called to a critical, in fact a self-critical, examination: whether or not it succumbs to the lust of the flesh. Penetrating into the deep meaning of Matthew 5:27-28, we must note, however, that the judgment it contains about desire, as an act of lust of the flesh, brings with it not the negation, but rather the affirmation, of the body as an element which, together with the spirit, determines man's ontological subjectivity and shares in his dignity as a person. In this way, the judgment on the lust of the flesh has a meaning essentially different from the one which the Manichaean ontology presupposes and which necessarily springs from it.

In its masculinity and femininity, the body is called "from the beginning" to become the manifestation of the spirit. It does so also by means of the conjugal union of man and woman, when they unite in such a way as to form one flesh. Elsewhere (cf. Mt 19:5-6) Christ defended the inviolable rights of this unity, by means of which the body, in its masculinity and femininity, assumes the value of a sign—in a way, a sacramental sign. Furthermore, by warning against the lust of the flesh, he expressed the same truth about the ontological dimension of the body and confirmed its ethical meaning, consistent with his teaching as a whole. This ethical meaning has nothing in common with the Manichaean condemnation. On the contrary, it is deeply penetrated by the mystery of the redemption of the body, which St. Paul will write of in Romans (cf. Rom 8:23). The redemption of the body does not indicate, however, ontological evil as a constituent attribute of the human body. It only points out man's sinfulness, as a result of which he has, among other things, lost the clear sense of the nuptial meaning of the body, in which interior mastery and the freedom of the spirit is expressed. As we have already pointed out, it is a question here of a partial, potential loss, where the sense of the nuptial meaning of the body is confused, in a way, with lust, and easily lets itself be absorbed by it.

The appropriate interpretation of Christ's words according to Matthew 5:27-28, as well as the praxis in which the authentic ethos of the Sermon on the Mount will be subsequently expressed, must be absolutely free of Manichaean elements in thought and in attitude. A Manichaean attitude would lead to an "annihilation" of the body—if not real, at least intentional. It would lead to negation of the value of human sex, of the masculinity and femininity of the human person, or at least to their mere toleration in the limits of the need delimited by the necessity of procreation. On the basis of Christ's words in the Sermon on the Mount, Christian ethos is characterized by a transformation of the conscience and attitudes of the human person, both man and woman. This is such as to express and realize the value of the body and of sex, according to the Creator's original plan, placed as they are in the service of the communion of persons, which is the deepest substratum of human ethics and culture. For the Manichaean mentality, the body and sexuality constitute an "anti-value." For Christianity, on the contrary, they always remain a value not sufficiently appreciated, as I will explain better further on. The second attitude indicates the form of ethos in which the mystery of the redemption of the body takes root in the historical soil of human sinfulness. That is expressed by the theological formula, which defines the state of historical man as *status naturae lapsae simul ac redemptae* (the state of fallen, but at the same time redeemed, nature).

Christ's words in the Sermon on the Mount (cf. Mt 5:27-28) must be interpreted in the light of this complex truth about man. If they contain a certain "accusation" leveled at the human heart, all the more so they appeal to it. The accusation of the moral evil which desire, born of intemperate lust of the flesh, conceals within itself, is at the same time a call to overcome this evil. If victory over evil consists in detachment from it (hence the severe words in the context of Matthew 5:27-28), it is only a question of detaching oneself from the evil of the act (in the case in question, the interior act of lust), and never of transferring the negative character of this act to its object. Such a transfer would mean a certain acceptance—perhaps not fully conscious—of the Manichaean "anti-value." It would not constitute a real and deep victory over the evil of the act, which is evil by its moral essence, and so evil of a spiritual nature. On the contrary, it would conceal the great danger of justifying the act to the detriment of the object (the essential error of Manichaean ethos consists in this). It is clear that in Matthew 5:27-28, Christ demanded detachment from the evil of lust (or of the look of disorderly desire). But his enunciation does not let it be supposed in any way that the object of that desire, that is, the woman who is looked at lustfully, is an evil. (This clarification seems to be lacking sometimes in some Wisdom texts.)

Therefore we must specify the difference between the accusation and the appeal. The accusation leveled at the evil of lust is at the same time an appeal to overcome it. Consequently, this victory must be united with an effort to discover the true values of the object, in order that the Manichaean "anti-value" may not take root in man, in his conscience, and in his will. As a result of the evil of lust, that is, of the act of which Christ spoke in Matthew 5:27-28, the object to which it is addressed constitutes for the human subject a value not sufficiently appreciated. In the words of the Sermon on the Mount (Mt 5:27-28) which have been analyzed, the human heart is accused of lust (or is warned against that lust). At the same time, by means of the words themselves, it is called to discover the full sense of what, in the act of lust, constitutes for him a value that is not sufficiently appreciated. As we know, Christ said: "Everyone who looks at a woman lustfully has already committed adultery with her in his heart."

Adultery committed in the heart can and must be understood as "devaluation," or as the impoverishment of an authentic value. It is an intentional deprivation of that dignity to which the complete value of her femininity corresponds in the person in question. Matthew 5:27-28 contains a call to discover this value and this dignity, and to reassert them. It seems that only when the semantic significance of Matthew's words is respected they are understood in this way.

To conclude these concise considerations, it is necessary to note once more that the Manichaean way of understanding and evaluating man's body and sexuality is essentially alien to the Gospel. It is not in conformity with the exact meaning of the words Christ spoke in the Sermon on the Mount. The appeal to master the lust of the flesh springs precisely from the affirmation of the personal dignity of the body and of sex, and serves only this dignity. Anyone who wants to see in these words a Manichaean perspective would be committing an essential error.

General audience of October 22, 1980

The Power of Redeeming
Completes the Power of Creating

For a long time now, our Wednesday reflections have been centered on Christ's words in the Sermon on the Mount: "You have heard that it was said, 'You shall not commit adultery.' But I say to you that everyone who looks at a woman lustfully has already committed adultery with her in his heart" (Mt 5:27-28). We have recently explained that these words cannot be understood or interpreted in a Manichaean way. They do not in any way condemn the body and sexuality. They merely contain a call to overcome the three forms of lust, especially the lust of the flesh. This call springs precisely from the affirmation of the personal dignity of the body and of sexuality, and merely confirms this affirmation.

It is important to clarify this formulation, that is, to determine the specific meaning of the words of the Sermon on the Mount in which Christ appeals to the human heart (cf. Mt 5:27-28). This is important not only because of "inveterate habits," springing from Manichaeism, in the way of thinking and evaluating things, but also because of some contemporary positions which interpret the meaning of man and of morality. Ricoeur described Freud, Marx and Nietzsche as "masters of suspicion"[63] *("maîtres du soupçon")*. He had in mind the set of systems that each of them represents, and above all, perhaps, the hidden basis and the orientation of each of them in understanding and interpreting the *humanum* itself.

It seems necessary to refer, at least briefly, to this basis and to this orientation. It must be done to discover a significant convergence and also a fundamental divergence, which has its source in the Bible, and which we are trying to express in our analyses. What does the convergence consist of? It consists in the fact that the above-mentioned thinkers, who have and still do exercise a great influence on the way of thinking and evaluating of the men of our time, seem substantially also to judge and accuse man's heart. Even more, they seem to judge it and accuse it because of what biblical language, especially Johannine, calls lust, the three forms of lust.

Here a certain distribution of the parts could be made. In the Nietzschean interpretation, the judgment and accusation of the human heart correspond, in a way, to what is called in biblical language "the pride of life"; in the Marxist interpretation, to what is called "the lust of the eyes"; in the Freudian interpretation, to what is called "the lust of the flesh." The convergence of these conceptions with the interpretation of man founded on the Bible lies in the fact that, discovering the three forms of lust in the human heart, we, too, could have limited ourselves to putting that heart in a state of continual suspicion. However, the Bible does not allow us to stop here. The words of Christ according to Matthew 5:27-28 are such that, while manifesting the whole reality of desire and lust, they do not permit us to make this lust the absolute criterion of anthropology and ethics, that is, the very core of the hermeneutics of man. In the Bible, lust in its three forms does not constitute the fundamental and perhaps even unique and absolute criterion of anthropology and ethics, although it is certainly an important coefficient to understand man, his actions, and their moral value. The analysis we have carried out so far also shows this.

Though wishing to arrive at a complete interpretation of Christ's words on the man who "looks lustfully" (cf. Mt 5:27-28), we cannot be content with any conception of lust, even if the fullness of the psychological truth accessible to us were to be reached. On the contrary, we must draw on the First Letter of John 2:15-16 and the "theology of lust" that it contains. The man who looks lustfully is the man of the three forms of lust. He is the man of the lust of the flesh. Therefore he can look in this way and he must even be conscious that, leaving this interior act at the mercy of the forces of nature, he cannot avoid the influence of the lust of the flesh. In Matthew 5:27-28 Christ also dealt with this and drew attention to it. His words refer not only to the concrete act of lust, but, indirectly, also to the man of lust.

In spite of the convergence of what they say about the human heart (cf. also Mt 5:19-20) with what has been expressed in the interpretation of the "masters of suspicion," why cannot these words of the Sermon on the

Mount be considered as the foundation of the aforesaid interpretation or a similar one? Why do they constitute an expression, a configuration, of a completely different ethos, different not only from the Manichaean one, but also from the Freudian one? I think that the analyses and reflections made so far answer this question. Summing up, it can be said briefly that Christ's words according to Matthew 5:27-28 do not allow us to stop at the accusation of the human heart and to regard it continually with suspicion. But they must be understood and interpreted above all as an appeal to the heart. This derives from the nature of the ethos of redemption. On the basis of this mystery, which St. Paul defines as "the redemption of the body" (Rom 8:23), on the basis of the reality called "redemption" and, consequently, on the basis of the ethos of the redemption of the body, we cannot stop only at the accusation of the human heart on the basis of desire and lust of the flesh. Man cannot stop at putting the heart in a state of continual and irreversible suspicion due to the manifestations of the lust of the flesh and libido, which, among other things, a psychoanalyst perceives by analyzing the unconscious.[64] Redemption is a truth, a reality, in the name of which man must feel called, and "called with efficacy." He must realize this call also through Christ's words according to Matthew 5:27-28, reread in the full context of the revelation of the body. Man must feel called to rediscover, nay more, to realize the nuptial meaning of the body. He must feel called to express in this way the interior freedom of the gift, that is, of that spiritual state and that spiritual power which are derived from mastery of the lust of the flesh.

Man is called to this by the word of the Gospel, therefore from "outside," but at the same time he is also called from "inside." The words of Christ, who in the Sermon on the Mount appealed to the heart, induce the listener, in a way, to this interior call. If he lets them act in him, he will be able to hear within him at the same time almost the echo of that "beginning." Christ referred to that good beginning on another occasion, to remind his listeners who man is, who woman is, and who we are for each other in the work of creation. The words Christ uttered in the Sermon on the Mount are not a call hurled into emptiness. They are not addressed to the man who is completely absorbed in the lust of the flesh. This man is unable to seek another form of mutual relations in the sphere of the perennial attraction, which accompanies the history of man and woman precisely from the beginning. Christ's words bear witness that the original power (therefore also the grace) of the mystery of creation becomes for each of them power (that is, grace) of the mystery of redemption. That concerns the very nature, the very substratum of the humanity of the person, the deepest impulses of the heart. Does not man feel, at the same time as lust, a deep need to preserve the dignity of the mutual relations, which find their expression in the body, thanks to his masculinity and femininity? Does he not feel the need to impregnate them with everything that is noble and beautiful? Does he not feel the need to confer on them the supreme value which is love?

Rereading it, this appeal contained in Christ's words in the Sermon on the Mount cannot be an act detached from the context of concrete existence. It always means—though only in the dimension of the act to which it referred—the rediscovery of the meaning of the whole of existence, the meaning of life, which also contains that meaning of the body which here we call "nuptial." The meaning of the body is, in a sense, the antithesis of Freudian libido. The meaning of life is the antithesis of the interpretation "of suspicion." This interpretation is radically different from what we rediscover in Christ's words in the Sermon on the Mount. These words reveal not only another ethos, but also another vision of man's possibilities. It is important that he, precisely in his heart, should not only feel irrevocably accused and given as a prey to the lust of the flesh, but that he should feel forcefully called in this same heart. He is called precisely to that supreme value that is love. He is called as a person in the truth of his humanity, therefore also in the truth of his masculinity or femininity, in the truth of his body. He is called in that truth which has been his heritage from the beginning, the heritage of his heart, which is deeper than the sinfulness inherited, deeper than lust in its three forms. The words of Christ, set in the whole reality of creation and redemption, reactivate that deeper heritage and give it real power in human life.

General audience of October 29, 1980

Eros and Ethos Meet and Bear Fruit in the Human Heart

In our weekly reflections on Christ's words in the Sermon on the Mount, in which, referring to the commandment, "You shall not commit adultery," he compared lust (looking lustfully) with adultery committed in the heart, we are trying to answer the question: do these words only accuse the human heart, or are they first and foremost an appeal addressed to it? Of course, this concerns an appeal of ethical character, an important and essential appeal for the ethos of the Gospel. We answer that the above-mentioned words are above all an appeal.

At the same time, we are trying to bring our reflections nearer to the routes taken, in its sphere, by the conscience of contemporary men. In the preceding cycle of our considerations we mentioned "eros." This Greek term, which passed from mythology to philosophy, then to the literary language and finally to the spoken language, unlike the word "ethos," is alien and unknown to biblical language. In the present analyses of biblical texts, we use the term "ethos," known to the Septuagint and to the New Testament. We do so because of the general meaning it has acquired in philosophy and theology. It embraces in its content the complex spheres of good and evil, depending on human will and subject to the laws of conscience and the sensitivity of the human heart. Besides being the proper name of the mythological character, the term eros has a philosophical meaning in the writings of Plato.[65] This meaning seems to be different from the common meaning and also from what is usually attributed to it in literature. Obviously, we must consider here the vast range of meanings. They differ from one another in their finer shades, as regards both the mythological character and the philosophical content, and above all the somatic or sexual point of view. Taking into account such a vast range of meanings, it is opportune to evaluate, in an equally differentiated way, what is related to eros[66] and is defined as erotic.

According to Plato, eros represents the interior force that drags man toward everything good, true and beautiful. This attraction indicates, in this case, the intensity of a subjective act of the human spirit. In the common meaning, on the contrary—as also in literature—this attraction seems to be first and foremost of a sensual nature. It arouses the mutual tendency of both the man and the woman to draw closer to each other, to the union of bodies, to that union of which Genesis 2:24 spoke. It is a question here of answering the question whether eros connotes the same meaning in the biblical narrative (especially in Genesis 2:23-25). This narrative certainly bears witness to the mutual attraction and the perennial call of the human person—through masculinity and femininity—to that unity in the flesh which, at the same time, must realize the communion-union of persons. Precisely because of this interpretation of eros (as well as of its relationship with ethos), the way in which we understand the lust spoken about in the Sermon on the Mount takes on fundamental importance.

As it seems, common language considers above all that meaning of lust which we previously defined as psychological and which could also be called sexological. This is done on the basis of premises which are limited mainly to the naturalistic, somatic and sensualistic interpretation of human eroticism. (It is not a question here, in any way, of reducing the value of scientific researches in this field, but we wish to call attention to the danger of reductivism and exclusivism.) In the psychological and sexological sense, lust indicates the subjective intensity of straining toward the object because of its sexual character (sexual value). That straining has its subjective intensity due to the specific attraction which extends its dominion over man's emotional sphere and involves his corporeity (his somatic masculinity or femininity). In the Sermon on the Mount we hear of the concupiscence of the man who "looks at a woman lustfully." These words—understood in the psychological (sexological) sense—refer to the sphere of phenomena which in common language are described as erotic. Within the limits of Matthew 5:27-28, it is a question only of the interior act. It is mainly those ways of acting and of mutual behavior of the man and the woman, which are the external manifestation of these interior acts, that are defined "erotic." Nevertheless, reasoning in this way, there seems to be no doubt that it is almost necessary to put the sign of equality between erotic and what derives from desire (and serves to satisfy the lust of the flesh). If this were so, then the words of Christ according to Matthew 5:27-28 would express a negative judgment about what is erotic and, addressed to the human heart, would constitute at the same time a severe warning against eros.

However, we have already mentioned that the term eros has many semantic shades of meaning. Erotic phenomena are those mutual actions and ways of behaving through which man and woman approach each other and unite so as to be one flesh (cf. Gn 2:24). We wish to define the relationship of the enunciation of the Sermon on the Mount (Mt 5:27-28) with the wide sphere of erotic phenomena. It is necessary to take into account the multiplicity of the semantic shades of meaning of eros. It seems possible that in the sphere of the concept of eros—taking into account its Platonic meaning—there is room for that ethos. There is room for those ethical and indirectly even theological contents which, in our analyses, have been seen from Christ's appeal to the human heart in the Sermon on the Mount. Knowledge of the multiple semantic nuances of eros and of what—in the differentiated experience and description of man, at various periods and various points of geographical and cultural longitude and latitude—is defined as erotic, can help in understanding the specific and complex riches of the heart, to which Christ appealed in Matthew 5:27-28.

If we admit that eros means the interior force that attracts man toward what is true, good and beautiful, then, within the sphere of this concept, the way toward what Christ wished to express in the Sermon on the Mount, can also be seen to open. The words of Matthew 5:27-28, if they are an "accusation" of the human heart, are at the same time, even more, an appeal to it. This appeal is the specific category of the ethos of redemption. The call to what is true, good and beautiful means at the same time, in the ethos of redemption, the necessity of overcoming what is derived from lust in its three forms. It also means the possibility and the necessity of transforming what has been weighed down by the lust of the flesh. Furthermore, if the words of Matthew 5:27-28 represent this call, then they mean that, in the erotic sphere, eros and ethos do not differ from each other. They are not opposed to each other, but are called to meet in the human heart, and, in this meeting, to bear fruit. What is worthy of the human heart is that the form of what is erotic should be at the same time the form of ethos, that is, of what is ethical.

This affirmation is important for ethos and at the same time for ethics. A negative meaning is often connected with the latter concept, because ethics bears with it norms, commandments and prohibitions. We are commonly inclined to consider the words of the Sermon on the Mount on lust (on looking lustfully) exclusively as a prohibition—a prohibition in the sphere of eros (that is, in the erotic sphere). Often we are content merely with this understanding, without trying to reveal the deep and essential values that this prohibition covers, that is, ensures. Not only does it protect them, but it also makes them accessible and liberates them, if we learn to open our heart to them.

In the Sermon on the Mount Christ teaches us this and directs man's heart toward these values.

General audience of November 5, 1980

Spontaneity: The Mature Result of Conscience

Today we resume our analysis on the relationship between what is ethical and what is erotic. Our reflections follow the pattern of the words Christ spoke in the Sermon on the Mount, with which he referred to the commandment "You shall not commit adultery." At the same time he defined lust (looking lustfully) as "adultery committed in the heart." We see from these reflections that ethos is connected with the discovery of a new order of values. It is necessary to rediscover continually in what is erotic the nuptial meaning of the body and the true dignity of the gift. This is the role of the human spirit, a role of an ethical nature. If it does not assume this role, the attraction of the senses and the passion of the body may stop at mere lust devoid of ethical value. Then man, male and female, does not experience that fullness of eros, which means the aspiration of the human spirit toward what is true, good and beautiful, so that what is erotic also becomes true, good and beautiful. Therefore it is indispensable that ethos should become the constituent form of eros.

The above-mentioned reflections are closely connected with the problem of spontaneity. It is often thought that ethos itself takes away spontaneity from what is erotic in man's life and behavior. For this reason detachment from ethos is demanded "for the benefit" of eros. Also the words of the Sermon on the Mount would seem to hinder this "good." But this opinion is erroneous and, in any case, superficial. Obstinately accepting it and upholding it, we will never reach the full dimensions of eros. That inevitably has repercussions in the sphere of praxis, that is, in our behavior and also in the concrete experience of values. Whoever accepts the ethos of Matthew 5:27-28 must know that he is also called to full and mature spontaneity of the relations that spring from the perennial attraction of masculinity and femininity. This spontaneity is the gradual fruit of the discernment of the impulses of one's own heart.

Christ's words are severe. They demand from man that, in the sphere in which relations with persons of the other sex are formed, he should have full and deep consciousness of his own acts, and above all of interior acts. They demand that he should be aware of the internal impulses of his heart, so as to be able to distinguish them and qualify them maturely. Christ's words demand that in this sphere, which seems to belong exclusively to the body and to the senses, that is, to exterior man, he should succeed in being an interior man. He should be able to obey correct conscience, and to be the true master of his own deep impulses, like a guardian who watches over a hidden spring. Finally he should draw from all those impulses what is fitting for purity of heart, building with conscience and consistency that personal sense of the nuptial meaning of the body, which opens the interior space of the freedom of the gift.

If man wishes to respond to the call expressed by Matthew 5:27-28, he must learn, with perseverance and consistency, what the meaning of the body is, the meaning of femininity and masculinity. He must learn this not only through an objectivizing abstraction (although this, too, is necessary), but above all in the sphere of the interior reactions of his own heart. This is a "science," which cannot be learned only from books, because it is a question here in the first place of deep knowledge of human interiority. In the sphere of this knowledge, man learns to distinguish between what composes the multiform riches of masculinity and femininity in the signs that come from their perennial call and creative attraction, and what bears only the sign of lust. These variants and nuances of the internal movements of the heart can, within a certain limit, be confused with one another. However, it must be said that interior man has been called by Christ to acquire a mature and complete evaluation, leading him to discern and judge the various movements of his heart. It should be added that this task can be carried out and is worthy of man.

The discernment which we are speaking of has an essential relationship with spontaneity. The subjective structure of man shows, in this area, a specific richness and a clear distinction. Consequently, a noble gratification, for example, is one thing, while sexual desire is another. When sexual desire is linked with a noble gratification, it differs from desire pure and simple. Similarly, as regards the sphere of the immediate reactions of the heart, sexual excitement is very different from the deep emotion with which not only interior sensitivity, but sexuality itself reacts to the total expression of femininity and masculinity. It is not possible here to develop this subject further. But it is certain that, if we affirm that Christ's words according to Matthew 5:27-28 are severe, they are also severe in the sense that they contain within them the deep requirements concerning human spontaneity.

There cannot be such spontaneity in all the movements and impulses that arise from mere carnal lust, devoid as it is of a choice and of an adequate hierarchy. It is precisely at the price of self-control that man reaches that deeper and more mature spontaneity with which his heart, mastering his instincts, rediscovers the spiritual beauty of the sign constituted by the human body in its masculinity and femininity. Since this discovery is enhanced in the conscience as conviction, and in the will as guidance both of possible choices and of mere desires, the human heart becomes a participant in another spontaneity, of which "carnal man" knows nothing or very little. There is no doubt that through Christ's words according to Matthew 5:27-28, we are called precisely to such spontaneity. Perhaps the most important sphere of praxis—concerning the more interior acts—is precisely that which gradually prepares the way toward such spontaneity.

This is a vast subject which will be opportune for us to take up another time in the future, when we will dedicate ourselves to showing what the real nature of the evangelical purity of heart is. We conclude for the present, saying that the words of the Sermon on the Mount, with which Christ called the attention of his listeners—at that time and today—to lust (looking lustfully), indirectly indicate the way toward a mature spontaneity of the human heart. This does not suffocate its noble desires and aspirations, but on the contrary frees them and, in a way, facilitates them.

Let what we said about the mutual relationship between what is ethical and what is erotic, according to the ethos of the Sermon on the Mount, suffice for the present.

General audience of November 12, 1980

Christ Calls Us to Rediscover
the Living Forms of the New Man

At the beginning of our considerations on Christ's words in the Sermon on the Mount (Mt 5:27-28), we saw that they contain a deep ethical and anthropological meaning. It is a question here of the passage in which Christ recalled the commandment, "You shall not commit adultery," and added, "Everyone who looks at a woman lustfully has already committed adultery with her in his heart." We speak of the ethical and anthropological meaning of these words, because they allude to the two closely connected dimensions of ethos and historical man. In the course of the preceding analyses, we tried to follow these two dimensions, always keeping in mind that Christ's words are addressed to the heart, that is, to the interior man. Interior man is the specific subject of the ethos of the body, with which Christ wishes to imbue the conscience and will of his listeners and disciples. It is certainly a new ethos. It is new in comparison with the ethos of the Old Testament, as we have already tried to show in more detailed analyses. It is new also with regard to the state of historical man, subsequent to original sin, that is, with regard to the man of lust. It is, therefore, a new ethos in a universal sense and significance. It is new in relation to any man, independently of any geographical and historical longitude and latitude.

We have already called this new ethos, which emerges from the perspective of Christ's words in the Sermon on the Mount, the "ethos of redemption" and, more precisely, the ethos of the redemption of the body. Here we followed St. Paul. In the Letter to the Romans he contrasts "bondage to decay" (Rom 8:21) and submission "to futility" (Rom 8:20)—in which the whole of creation has become participant owing to sin—with the desire for "the redemption of our bodies" (Rom 8:23). In this context, the Apostle spoke of the groans "of the whole creation," which "waits with eager longing..." to "be set free from its bondage to decay and obtain the glorious liberty of the children of God" (Rom 8:20-21). In this way, St. Paul reveals the situation of all creation, especially that of man after sin. The aspiration which—together with the new "adoption as sons" (Rom 8:23)—strives precisely toward "the redemption of the body," is significant for this situation. The redemption of the body is presented as the end, the eschatological and mature fruit of the mystery of the redemption of man and of the world, carried out by Christ.

Therefore, in what sense can we speak of the ethos of redemption and especially of the ethos of the redemption of the body? We must recognize that in the context of the words of the Sermon on the Mount

(Mt 5:27-28), which we have analyzed, this meaning does not yet appear in all its fullness. It will be manifested more completely when we examine other words of Christ, the ones, that is, in which he referred to the resurrection (cf. Mt 22:30; Mk 12:25; Lk 20:35-36). However, there is no doubt that also in the Sermon on the Mount, Christ spoke in the perspective of the redemption of man and of the world (and, therefore, precisely of the redemption of the body). This is the perspective of the whole Gospel, of the whole teaching, of the whole mission of Christ. The immediate context of the Sermon on the Mount indicates the law and the prophets as the historical reference point, characteristic of the People of God of the old covenant. Yet we can never forget that in Christ's teaching the fundamental reference to the question of marriage and the problem of the relations between man and woman referred to the beginning. Such a reference can be justified only by the reality of the redemption. Outside it, there would remain only the three forms of lust or that "bondage to decay," which Paul writes of (Rom 8:21). Only the perspective of the redemption justifies the reference to the "beginning," that is, the perspective of the mystery of creation in the totality of Christ's teaching on the problems of marriage, man and woman and their mutual relationship. The words of Matthew 5:27-28 are set, in a word, in the same theological perspective.

In the Sermon on the Mount Christ did not invite man to return to the state of original innocence, because humanity has irrevocably left it behind. But he called him to rediscover—on the foundation of the perennial and indestructible meanings of what is human—the living forms of the new man. In this way a link, or rather a continuity is established between the beginning and the perspective of redemption. In the ethos of the redemption of the body, the original ethos of creation will have to be taken up again. Christ did not change the law, but confirmed the commandment, "You shall not commit adultery." At the same time, he led the intellect and the heart of listeners toward that "fullness of justice," willed by God the Creator and legislator, that this commandment contains. This fullness is discovered, first with an interior view of the heart, and then with an adequate way of being and acting. The form of the new man can emerge from this way of being and acting, to the extent to which the ethos of the redemption of the body dominates the lust of the flesh and the whole man of lust. Christ clearly indicated that the way to attain this must be the way of temperance and mastery of desires, that is, at the very root, already in the purely interior sphere ("Everyone who looks at a woman lustfully..."). The ethos of redemption contains in every area—and directly in the sphere of the lust of the flesh—the imperative of self-control, the necessity of immediate continence and of habitual temperance.

However, if it may be put in this way, temperance and continence do not mean suspension in emptiness, neither in the emptiness of values nor in the emptiness of the subject. The ethos of redemption is realized in self-mastery, by means of temperance, that is, continence of desires. In this behavior the human heart remains bound to the value from which, through desire, it would otherwise have moved away, turning toward pure lust deprived of ethical value (as we said in the preceding analysis). In the field of the ethos of redemption, union with that value by means of an act of mastery is confirmed or re-established with an even deeper power and firmness. It is a question here of the value of the nuptial meaning of the body, of the value of a transparent sign. By means of this the Creator—together with the perennial mutual attraction of man and woman through masculinity and femininity—has written in the heart of them both the gift of communion, that is, the mysterious reality of his image and likeness. It is a question of this value in the act of self-mastery and temperance, to which Christ referred in the Sermon on the Mount (Mt 5:27-28).

This act may give the impression of suspension "in the emptiness of the subject." It may give this impression especially when it is necessary to make up one's mind to carry it out for the first time, or, even more, when the opposite habit has been formed, when man is accustomed to yield to the lust of the flesh. However, even the first time, and all the more so if he then acquires the capacity, man already gradually experiences his own dignity. By means of temperance, he bears witness to his own self-mastery and shows that he is carrying out what is essentially personal in him. Furthermore, he gradually experiences the freedom of the gift, which in one way is the condition, and in another way is the response of the subject to the nuptial value of the human body, in its femininity and masculinity. In this way, the ethos of the redemption of the body is realized through self-mastery, through the temperance of "desires." This happens when the human heart enters an alliance with this ethos, or rather confirms it by means of its own integral subjectivity; when the deepest and yet most real possibilities and dispositions of the person are manifested; when the innermost layers of his potentiality acquire a voice, layers which the lust of the flesh would not permit to show themselves. Nor can these layers emerge when the human heart is bound in permanent suspicion, as is the case in Freudian hermeneutics. Nor can they be manifested when the Manichaean anti-value is dominant in consciousness. The ethos of redemption, on the other hand, is based on a close alliance with those layers.

Further reflections will give us other proofs. Concluding our analyses on Christ's significant enunciation according to Matthew 5:27-28, we see that in it the human heart is above all the object of a call and not of an accusation. At the same time, we must admit that the consciousness of sinfulness is, in historical man, not only a necessary starting point. It is also an indispensable condition of his aspiration to virtue, to purity of heart, to perfection. The ethos of the redemption of the body remains deeply rooted in the anthropological and axiological realism of revelation. Referring in this case to the heart, Christ formulated his words in the most concrete way. Man is unique and unrepeatable above all because of his heart, which decides his being from within. The category of the heart is, in a way, the equivalent of personal subjectivity. The way of appeal to purity of heart, as it was expressed in the Sermon on the Mount, is in any case a reminiscence of the original solitude, from which the man was liberated through opening to the other human being, woman. Purity of heart is explained, finally, with regard for the other subject, who is originally and perennially co-called.

Purity is a requirement of love. It is the dimension of its interior truth in man's heart.

General audience of December 3, 1980

Purity of Heart

The analysis of purity is an indispensable completion of the words Christ spoke in the Sermon on the Mount, which our present reflections are centered on. When explaining the correct meaning of the commandment, "You shall not commit adultery," Christ appealed to the interior man. At the same time he specified the fundamental dimension of purity that marks the relations between man and woman both in marriage and outside it. The words, "But I say to you that everyone who looks at a woman lustfully has already committed adultery with her in his heart" (Mt 5:27-28), express what is opposed to purity. At the same time, these words demand the purity which, in the Sermon on the Mount, is included in the list of the beatitudes: "Blessed are the pure in heart, for they shall see God" (Mt 5:8). In this way Christ appealed to the human heart. He called upon it and did not accuse it, as we have already clarified.

Christ sees in the heart, in man's inner self, the source of purity—but also of moral impurity—in the fundamental and most generic sense of the word. That is confirmed, for example, by the answer he gave to the Pharisees, who were scandalized by the fact that his disciples "transgress the tradition of the elders. For they do not wash their hands when they eat" (Mt 15:2). Jesus then said to those present: "Not what goes into the mouth defiles a man, but what comes out of the mouth defiles a man" (Mt 15:11).

Answering Peter's question, he explained these words to his disciples as follows: "What comes out of the mouth proceeds from the heart, and this defiles a man. For out of the heart come evil thoughts, murder, adultery, fornication, theft, false witness, slander. These are what defile a man, but to eat with unwashed hands does not defile a man" (cf. Mt 15:18-20; also Mk 7:20-23).

When we say "purity" or "pure," in the first meaning of these words, we indicate what contrasts with what is dirty. "To dirty" means "to make filthy," "to pollute." That referred to the various spheres of the physical world. For example, we talk of a dirty road or a dirty room; we also talk of polluted air. In the same way man can be filthy, when his body is not clean. The body must be washed to remove dirt.

The Old Testament tradition attributed great importance to ritual ablutions, for example, to wash one's hands before eating, which the above-mentioned text spoke of. Many detailed prescriptions concerned the ablutions of the body in relation to sexual impurity, understood in the exclusively physiological sense, to which we have referred previously (cf. Lv 15). According to the medical science of the time, the various ablutions may have corresponded to hygienic prescriptions. Since they were imposed in God's name and contained in the sacred books of the Old Testament legislation, their observance indirectly acquired a religious meaning. They were ritual ablutions and, in the life of the people of the old covenant, they served ritual "purity."

In relation to the aforesaid juridico-religious tradition of the old covenant, an erroneous way of understanding moral purity developed.[67] It was often taken in the exclusively exterior and material sense. In any case, an explicit tendency to this interpretation spread. Christ opposed it radically. Nothing from outside makes one filthy, no "material" dirt makes one impure in the moral, that is, interior sense. No ablution, not even of a ritual nature, is capable in itself of producing moral purity. This has its exclusive source within man. It comes from the heart.

Probably the respective prescriptions in the Old Testament (for example, those found in Leviticus 15:16-24; 18:1ff.; or 12:1-5) served, in addition to hygienic purposes, to attribute a certain dimension of interiority to what is corporeal and sexual in the human person. In any case, Christ took good care not to connect purity in the moral (ethical) sense with physiology and its organic processes. In the light of the words of Matthew 15:18-20, quoted above, none of the aspects of sexual "dirtiness," in the strictly bodily, biophysiological sense, falls by itself into the definition of purity or impurity in the moral (ethical) sense.

The aforesaid assertion (Mt 15:18-20) is important above all for semantic reasons. Speaking of purity in the moral sense, that is, of the virtue of purity, we use an analogy, according to which moral evil is compared precisely to uncleanness. Certainly this analogy has been a part of the sphere of ethical concepts from the most remote times. Christ took it up again and confirmed it in all its extension: "What comes out of the mouth proceeds from the heart, and this defiles a man." Here Christ spoke of all moral evil, of all sin, that is, of transgressions of the various commandments. He enumerates "evil thoughts, murder, adultery, fornication, theft, false witness, slander," without confining himself to a specific kind of sin. It follows that the concept of purity and impurity in the moral sense is in the first place a general concept, not a specific one. All moral good is a manifestation of purity, and all moral evil is a manifestation of impurity.

Matthew 15:18-20 does not limit purity to one area of morality, namely, to the one connected with the commandment, "You shall not commit adultery" and "Do not covet your neighbor's wife," that is, to the one that concerns the relations between man and woman, linked to the body and to the relative concupiscence. Similarly we can understand the beatitude of the Sermon on the Mount, addressed to "the pure in heart," both in the general and in the more specific sense. Only the actual context will make it possible to delimit and clarify this meaning.

The wider and more general meaning of purity is present also in St. Paul's letters. In them we shall gradually pick out the contexts which explicitly limit the meaning of purity to the bodily and sexual sphere, that is, to that meaning which we can grasp from Christ's words in the Sermon on the Mount on lust. This is already expressed in "looking at a woman," and is regarded as equivalent to "committing adultery in one's heart" (cf. Mt 5:27-28).

St. Paul is not the author of the words about the three forms of lust. As we know, they occur in the First Letter of John. John spoke of the opposition within man between God and the world, between what comes "from the Father" and what comes "from the world" (cf. 1 Jn 2:16-17). This opposition is born in the heart and penetrates into man's actions as "the lust of the flesh and the lust of the eyes and the pride of life." Similarly, St. Paul points out another contradiction in the Christian. It is the opposition and at the same time the tension between the "flesh" and the "Spirit" (written with a capital letter, that is, the Holy Spirit). "But I say, walk by the Spirit, and do not gratify the desires of the flesh. For the desires of the flesh are against the Spirit, and the desires of the Spirit are against the flesh. For these are opposed to each other, to prevent you from doing what you would" (Gal 5:16-17). It follows that life "according to the flesh" is in opposition to life "according to the Spirit." "For those who live according to the flesh set their minds on the things of the flesh, but those who live according to the Spirit set their minds on the things of the Spirit" (Rom 8:5).

In subsequent analyses we shall seek to show that purity—the purity of heart which Christ spoke of in the Sermon on the Mount—is realized precisely in life according to the Spirit.

General audience of December 10, 1980

NOTES

General audience of April 16, 1980

[36] Ich kenne kein grandioseres Zeugnis für eine solche Neuerschliessung eines ganzen Werbereiches, die das ältere Ethos relativiert, als die Bergpredigt, die auch in ihrer Form als Zeugnis solcher Neuerschliessung und Relativierung der älteren "Gesetzes"-werte sich überall kundgibt: "Ich aber sage euch" (Max Scheler, *Der Formalismus in der Ethik und die materiale Wertethik* [Halle a.d.s., Verlag M. Niemeyer, 1921], p. 316, no. 1).

[37] Cf. Ex 20:17; Dt 5:21.

[38] On this point, see the continuation of the present meditations.

[39] The text of the Vulgate offers a faithful translation of the original: *iam moechatus est eam in corde suo.* In fact, the Greek verb *moicheúo* is transitive. In modern European languages, on the other hand, "to commit adultery" is an intransitive verb; so we get the translation: "...has committed adultery *with* her." And thus,

—in Italian: *"...ha già commesso adulterio con lei nel suo cuore"* (Version of the Italian Episcopal Conference, 1971; similarly the version of the Pontifical Biblical Institute, 1961, and the one prepared by S. Garofalo, 1966).

—In French: *"...a déjà commis, dans son coeur, l'adultère avec elle"* (*Bible de Jérusalem* [Paris: 1973]; Traduction Oecuménique [Paris: 1972]; Crampon); only Fillion translates: *"A déjà commis l'adultere dans son coeur."*

—in English: *"...has already committed adultery with her in his heart"* (*Douay* Version, 1582, similarly *Revised Standard Version,* from 1611 to 1966, R. Knox, *New English Bible, Jeruşalem Bible,* 1966).

—in German: *"...hat in seinem Herzen schon Ehebruch mit ihr begangen"* (Einheitsübersetzung der Heiligen Schrift, im Auftrag der Bischöfe des deutschen Sprachbereiches, 1979).

—in Spanish: *"...ya cometió adulterio con ella en su corazón"* (Bibl. Societ., 1966).

—in Portuguese: *"...já cometeu adulterio com ela no seu coraçaõ"* (M. Soares, Sao Paolo, 1933).

—in Polish: ancient translations: *"...juz ja scudzolozyl w sercu swoim";* last translation: *"...juz sie w swoim ser cu dopuscil z nia cudzolostwa"* (Biblia Tysiaclecia).

General audience of April 23, 1980

[40] In this way, the content of our reflections shifts, in a way, to the field of natural law. The words quoted from the Letter to the Romans (2:15) have always been considered, in revelation, as a source of confirmation for the existence of natural law. Thus the concept of natural law also acquires a theological meaning.

Cf. among others, D. Composta, *Teologia del diritto naturale, status quaestionis* (Brescia: Ed. Civilta, 1972), pp. 7-22, 41-53; J. Fuchs, S.J., *Lex naturae. Zur Theologie des Naturrechts* (Dusseldorf: 1955), pp. 22-30; E. Hamel, S.J., *Loi naturelle et loi du Christ* (Bruges-Paris: Desclée de Brouwer, 1964), p. 18; A. Sacchi, "La legge naturale nella Bibbia," *La legge naturale. Le relazioni del Convegno dei teologi moralisti dell'Italia settentrionale,* September 11-13, 1969 (Bologna: Ed. Dehoniane, 1970), p. 53; F. Böckle, "La legge naturale e la legge cristiana," *ibid.,* pp. 214-215; A. Feuillet, "Le fondement de la morale ancienne et chrétienne d'apres l'Epitre aux Romains," *Revue Thomiste* 78 (1970), pp. 357-386; Th. Herr, *Naturrecht aus der kritischen Sicht des Neuen Testaments* (München: Schönig, 1976), pp. 155-164.

[41] "The typically Hebraic usage reflected in the New Testament implies an understanding of man as unity of thought, will and feeling.... It depicts man as a whole, viewed from his intentionality; *the heart as the center of man is thought of as source of will, emotion, thoughts and affections.*

"Paul related this traditional Judaic conception to Hellenistic categories, such as mind, attitude, thoughts and desires. Such a coordination between the Judaic and Hellenistic categories is found in Phillipians 1:7, 4:7; Romans 1:21-24, where 'heart' is thought of as the center from which these things flow" (R. Jewett, *Paul's Anthropological Terms, A Study of Their Use in Conflict Settings* [Leiden: Brill, 1971], p. 448).

"Das Herz...ist die verborgene, inwendige Mitte und Wurzel des Menschen und damit seiner Welt...der unergründliche Grund und die lebendige Kraft aller Daseinserfahrung und—entscheidung" (H. Schlier, "Das Menschenherz nach dem Apostel Paulus," *Lebendiges Zeugnis,* 1965, p. 123).

Cf. also F. Baumgärtel and J. Behm, "Kardia," *Theologisches Wörterbuch zum Neuen Testament,* II [Stuttgart: Kohlhammer, 1933], pp. 609-616.

[42] This is perhaps the best-known one, but other similar examples can be found in the Bible (cf. Gn 34:2; Jgs 14:1, 16:1).

General audience of April 30, 1980

[43] Cf. e.g.; J. Bonsirven, *Epitres de Saint Jean* (Paris: Beauchesne, 1954), pp. 113-119; E. Brooke, *Critical and Exegetical Commentary on the Johannine Epistles,* International Critical Commentary (Edinburgh: Clark, 1912), pp. 47-49; P. De Ambroggi, *Le Epistole Cattoliche* (Torino: Marietti, 1947), pp. 216-217; C. H. Dodd, *The Johannine Epistles,* Moffatt New Testament Commentary (London: 1946), pp. 41-42; J. Houlden, *A Commentary on the Johannine Epistles* (London: Black, 1973), pp. 73-74; B. Prete, *Lettere di Giovanni* (Roma: Ed. Paoline, 1970), p. 61; R. Schnackenburg, *Die Johan-nesbriefe,* Herders Theologischer Kommentar zum Neuen Testament (Freiburg: 1953), pp. 112-115; J. R. W. Stott, *Epistles of John,* Tyndale New Testament Commentaries (London: 1969), pp. 99-101.

On the subject of John's theology, see in particular A. Feuillet, *Le mystère de l'amour divin dans la théologie johannique* (Paris: Gabalda, 1972).

[44] The Hebrew text can have both meanings, because it runs: "ELOHIM knows that when you eat of it [the fruit of the tree of the knowledge of good and evil] your eyes will be opened, and you will be like ELOHIM, knowing good and evil." The term *elohim* is the plural of eloah *(pluralis excellentiae).*

In relation to Yahweh, it has a singular meaning, but it may indicate the plural of other heavenly beings or pagan divinities (e.g. Ps 8:6; Ex 12:12; Jgs 10:16; Hos 31:1 and others).

Here are some translations:

—English: "you will be *like God,* knowing good and evil" *(Revised Standard Version,* 1966).

—French: "vous serez *comme des dieux,* qui connaissent le bien et le mal" *(Bible de Jérusalem,* 1973).

—Italian: "diverreste *come Dio,* conoscendo il bene e il male" *(Pont. Istit. Biblico,* 1961).

—Spanish: "seréis *como dioses,* conocedores del bien y del mal" (S. Ausejo Barcelona, 1964).

"seréis *como Dios* en el conocimiento del bien y del mal" (A. Alonso-Schökel, Madrid, 1970).

[45] Cf. general audience of December 12, 1979 *(L'Osservatore Romano,* English edition, December 17, 1979).

General audience of May 14, 1980

[46] The Magisterium of the Church dealt more closely with these problems, in three periods, according to the needs of the age.

The declarations of the period of the controversies with the Pelagians (5th-6th centuries) affirm that the first man, by virtue of divine grace, possessed *"naturalem possibilitatem et innocentiam" (DS* 239), also called "freedom" *("libertas," "libertas arbitrii"), (DS* 371, 242, 383, 622). He remained in a state which the Synod of Orange (in the year 529) calls *"integritas"*: *"Natura huma-*

na, etiamsi in illa integritate, in qua condita est, permaneret, nullo modo se ipsam, Creatore suo non adiuvante, servaret..." (DS 389).

The concepts of *integritas* and, in particular, that of *libertas*, presuppose freedom from concupiscence, although the ecclesiastical documents of this age do not mention it explicitly.

The first man was furthermore free from the necessity of death (cf. *DS* 222, 372, 1511).

The Council of Trent defines the state of the first man, prior to sin, as "holiness and justice" *("sanctitas et iustitia"—DS* 1511, 1512) or as "innocence" *("innocentia"—DS* 1521).

Further declarations on this matter defend the absolute gratuitousness of the original gift of grace, against the affirmations of the Jansenists. The *"integritas primae creationis"* was an unmerited elevation of human nature *("indebita humanae naturae exaltatio")* and not "the state due to him by nature" *("naturalis eius condicio"—DS* 1926). God, therefore, could have created man without these graces and gifts (cf. *DS* 1955); that would not have shattered the essence of human nature and would not have deprived it of its fundamental privileges (cf. *DS* 1903-1907, 1909, 1921, 1923, 1924, 1926, 1955, 2434, 2437, 2616, 2617).

In analogy with the anti-Pelagian Synod, the Council of Trent deals above all with the dogma of original sin, integrating in its teaching preceding declarations in this connection. Here, however, a certain clarification was introduced, which partly changed the content comprised in the concept of *liberum arbitrium.* The "freedom" or "free will" of the anti-Pelagian documents did not mean the possibility of choice, connected with human nature, and therefore constant, but referred only to the possibility of carrying out meritorious acts, the freedom that springs from grace and that man may lose.

Because of sin, Adam lost what did not belong to human nature in the strict sense of the word, that is *integritas, sanctitas, innocentia, iustitia. Liberum arbitrium,* free will, was not taken away, but became weaker:

"...liberum arbitrium minime exstinctum...viribus licet attenuatum et inclinatum..." (DS 1521—Trid. Sess. VI, Decr. de Justificatione, C. 1).

Concupiscence and the inevitability of death appear together with sin:

"...primum hominem...cum mandatum Dei...fuisset transgressus, statim sanctitatem et iustitiam, in qua constitutus fuerat, amisisse incurrisseque per offensam praevaricationis huismodi iram et indignationem Dei atque ideo mortem...et cum morte captivitatem sub eius potestate, qui 'mortis' deinde 'habuit imperium'...'totumque Adam per illam praevaricationis offensam secundum corpus et animam in deterius commutatum fuisse...'" (DS 1511, Trid. Sess. V, Decr. de Pecc. Orig. 1).

Cf. *Mysterium Salutis, II,* Einsiedeln-Zurich-Köln 1967, pp. 827-828; W. Seibel, "Der Mensch als Gottes übernatürliches Ebenbild und der Urstand des Menschen."

General audience of May 28, 1980

[47] Cf. Karol Wojtyla, *Love and Responsibility* (New York: 1981), chap. "The Metaphysics of Shame."

General audience of July 23, 1980

[48] *Gaudium et Spes,* no. 24: "Indeed, the Lord Jesus, when he prayed to the Father 'that all may be one...even as we are one' (Jn 17:21-22), opened up vistas closed to human reason, for he implied a certain likeness between the union of the divine Persons, and the unity of God's sons in truth and charity. This likeness reveals that man, who is the only creature on earth which God willed for itself, cannot fully find himself except through a sincere gift of himself."

General audience of July 30, 1980

[49] Cf., for example, Sgs, 1:9, 13, 14, 15, 16; 2:2, 3, 8, 9, 10, 13, 14, 16, 17; 3:2, 4, 5; 4:1, 10; 5:1, 2, 4; 6:2, 3, 4, 9; 7:11; 8:12, 14.
Cf. also, for example, Ez 16:8; Hos 2:18; Tb 8:7.

General audience of August 6, 1980

[50] The Greek term *sklerokardía* was formed by the authors of the Septuagint to express what in the Hebrew meant: "non-circumcision of the heart" (cf. e.g., Dt 10:16; Jer 4:4; Sir 3:26f.) and which, in the literal translation of the New Testament, appears only once (cf. Acts 7:51).

"Non-circumcision" meant "paganism," "immodesty," "distance from the covenant with God"; "non-circumcision of the heart" expressed unyielding obstinacy in opposing God. This is confirmed by the exclamation of the deacon Stephen: "You stiff-necked people, uncircumcised in heart and ears, you always resist the Holy Spirit. As your fathers did, so do you" (Acts 7:51).

So "hardness of heart" must be understood in this philological context.

[51] Cf. Rv 2:23: "....he who searches mind and heart..."; Acts 1:24: "Lord, who knows the hearts of all men..." *(kardiognostes).*

[52] "For out of the heart come evil thoughts, murder, adultery, fornication, theft, false witness, slander. These are what defile a man..." (Mt 15:19-20).

General audience of August 20, 1980

[53] Cf., for example, Dt 21:10-13; Nm 30:7-16; Dt 24:1-4; Dt 22:13-21; Lv 20:10-21 and others.

[54] Although Genesis may present the monogamous marriages of Adam, Seth and Noah as models to be imitated, and seems to condemn bigamy, which only appeared among Cain's descendants, (cf. Gn 4:19), the lives of the patriarchs provide other examples to the contrary. Abraham observed the precepts of the law of Hammurabi, which allowed the taking of a second wife in marriage if the first wife was sterile, and Jacob had two wives and two concubines (cf. Gn 30:1-19).

Deuteronomy admits the legal existence of bigamy (cf. Dt 21:15-17) and even of polygamy, warning the king not to have too many wives (cf. Dt 17:17); it also confirms the institution of concubines—prisoners of war (cf. Dt 21:10-14) or even slaves (cf. Est 21:7-11). Cf. R. De Vaux, *Ancient Israel, Its Life and Institutions* (London: Darton, Longman, Todd, 1976), pp. 24-25, 83. In the Old Testament there is no explicit mention of the obligation of monogamy, although the picture given in the following books shows that it prevailed in the social practice (cf., for example, the Wisdom books, except Sirach 37:11; Tobit).

55 Cf., for example, Lv 12:1-6; 15:1-28; Dt 21:12-13.

56 Cf., for example, Is 54; 62:1-5.

General audience of September 3, 1980

57 Cf., e.g., Prv 5:3-6, 15-20; 6:24-7:27; 21:9, 19; 22:14; 30:20.

58 Cf., e.g., Sir 7:19, 24-26; 9:1-9; 23:22-27; 25:13-26, 18; 36:21-25; 42:6, 9-14.

59 Cf., e.g., Eccl 7:26-28; 9:9.

General audience of September 10, 1980

60 Cf. *Confessions of St. Augustine,* VI, 12, 21, 22; VII, 17; VIII, 11; Dante, *The Divine Comedy,* "Inferno" V. 37-43; C. S. Lewis, *The Four Loves* (New York: Harcourt, Brace, 1960), p. 28.

61 A philological analysis confirms the significance of the expression *ho blépon* ("one who looks"; Mt 5:28).

"If *blépo* of Matthew 5:28 has the value of internal perception, equivalent to 'I think, I pay attention to, I look'—a more precise and more sublime evangelical teaching may result regarding the interpersonal relationship among the disciples of Christ.

"According to Jesus not just a lustful glance makes a person adulterous, but a thought in the heart suffices" (M. Adinolfi, "The Desire of a Woman in Matthew 5:28," *Fondamenti biblici della teologia moral,* Proceedings of 22nd Italian Biblical Week [Brescia: Paideia, 1973], p. 279).

General audience of October 15, 1980

62 Manichaeism contains and brings to maturation the characteristic elements of all *gnosis,* that is, the *dualism* of two coeternal and radically opposed principles and the concept of a *salvation* which is realized only through *knowledge (gnosis)* or self-understanding. In the whole Manichaean myth there is only one hero and only one situation which is always repeated: the fallen soul is imprisoned in matter and is liberated by knowledge.

The present historical situation is negative for man, because it is a provisional and abnormal mixture of spirit and matter, good and evil, which presupposes a prior, original state, in which the two substances were separate and independent. There are, therefore, three "Times": *initium,* or the original separation; the *medium*, that is, the present mixture; and the *finis*, which consists in return to the original division, in salvation, implying a complete break between Spirit and Matter.

Matter is, fundamentally, concupiscence, an evil instinct for pleasure, the instinct of death, comparable, if not identical, with sexual desire, libido. It is a force that tries to attack Light; it is disorderly movement, bestial, brutal and semiconscious desire.

Adam and Eve were begotten by two demons; our species was born from a series of repelling acts of cannibalism and sexuality and keeps signs of this diabolical origin, which are the body, which is the animal form of the "Archons of hell" and libido, which drives man to copulate and reproduce himself, that is, to keep his luminous soul always in prison.

If he wants to be saved, man must try to liberate his "living self" *(nous)* from the flesh and from the body. Since Matter has its supreme expression in concupiscence, the capital sin lies in sexual union (fornication), which is brutality and bestiality, and makes men instruments and accomplices of Evil for procreation.

The elect constitute the group of the perfect, whose virtue has an ascetic characteristic, practicing the abstinence commanded by the three "seals": the "seal of the mouth" forbids all blasphemy and also commands fasting, and abstention from meat, blood, wine and all alcoholic drinks; the "seal of the hands" commands respect of the life (the "Light") enclosed in bodies, in seeds, in trees, and forbids the gathering of fruit, the tearing up of plants, the taking of the life of men and of animals; the "seal of the womb" prescribes total continence. Cf. H. Ch. Puech: *Le Manicheisme; son fondateur—sa doctrine* (Paris: Musée Guimet, LVI, 1949), pp. 73-88; H. Ch. Puech, *Le Manicheisme,* "Histoire des Religions," *Encyclopedie de la Pleiade II* (Gallimard: 1972), pp. 522-645; J. Ties, "Manicheisme," *Catholicisme hier, aujourd'hui, demain,* Vol. 34 (Lille: Letouzey-Ane, 1977), pp. 314-320.

General audience of October 29, 1980

[63] Cf. Paul Ricoeur, *Le conflit des interpretations* (Paris: Seuil, 1969), pp. 149-150.

[64] Cf., for example, the characteristic affirmation of Freud's last work: S. Freud, *Abriss der Psychoanalyse, Das Unbehagen der Kultur* (Frankfurt-M. Hamburg: Fisher, 1955), pp. 74-75.

Then that "core" or "heart" of man would be dominated by the union between the erotic instinct and the destructive one, and life would consist in satisfying them.

General audience of November 5, 1980

[65] According to Plato, man, placed between the world of the senses and the world of Ideas, has the destiny of passing from the first to the second. The world of Ideas, however, is not able by itself to overcome the world of the senses. Only

eros, congenital in man, can do that. When man begins to have a presentiment of Ideas, thanks to contemplation of the objects existing in the world of the senses, he receives the impulse from eros, that is, from the desire for pure Ideas. Eros, in fact, is the guiding of the "sensual" or "sensitive" man toward what is transcendent: the force that directs the soul toward the world of Ideas. In the *Symposium,* Plato describes the stages of this influence of eros: the latter raises man's soul from the beauty of a single body to that of all bodies, and so to the beauty of knowledge and finally to the very idea of Beauty (cf. *Symposio* 211; *Repubblica* 514).

Eros is neither purely human nor divine: it is something intermediate *(daimonion)* and intermediary. Its principal characteristic is permanent aspiration and desire. Even when it seems to give freely, eros persists as the "desire of possessing." Yet it is different from purely sensual love, being the love that strives toward the sublime.

According to Plato, the gods do not love because they do not feel desires, since their desires are all satisfied. Therefore, they can only be the object, but not the subject of love (cf. *Symposio* 200-201). So they do not have a direct relationship with man. Only the mediation of eros makes it possible for a relationship to be established (cf. *Symposio* 203). Therefore, eros is the way that leads man to divinity, but not vice-versa.

The aspiration to transcendence is, therefore, a constituent element of the Platonic concept of eros, a concept that overcomes the radical dualism of the world of Ideas and the world of the senses. Eros makes it possible to pass from one to the other. It is therefore a form of escape beyond the material world, which the soul must renounce, because the beauty of the sensible subject has a value only insofar as it leads higher.

However, eros always remains, for Plato, egocentric love. It aims at winning and possessing the object which, for man, represents a value. To love good means desiring to possess it forever. Love is, therefore, always a desire for immortality, and that, too, shows the egocentric character of eros (cf. A. Nygren, *Eros et Agapé. La notion chrétienne de l'amour et ses transformations,* I [Paris: Aubier, 1962], pp. 180-200).

For Plato, eros is a passing from the most elementary knowledge to deeper knowledge; at the same time it is the aspiration to pass from "that which is not," and is evil, to what "exists in fullness," and is good (cf. M. Scheler, "Amour et connaissance," *Le sens de la souffrance, suivi de deux autres essais* [Paris: Aubier], p. 145).

[66] Cf., e.g., C. S. Lewis, "Eros," *The Four Loves* (New York: Harcourt, Brace, 1960), pp. 131-133, 152, 159-160; P. Chauchard, *Vices des vertus, vertus des vices* (Paris: Mame, 1965), p. 147.

General audience of December 10, 1980

[67] Alongside a complex system of prescriptions concerning ritual purity, on which legal casuistry was based, the concept of moral purity also existed in the Old Testament. It was handed down by means of two channels.

The *prophets* demanded behavior in conformity with God's will, which presupposes conversion of heart, interior obedience and complete uprightness before him (cf. for example, Is 1:10-20; Jer 4:14; 24:7; Ez 36:25ff.). A similar attitude is required also by the Psalmist:

"Who shall ascend the hill of the Lord... / He who has clean hands and a pure heart... / will receive blessing from the Lord" (Ps 24:3-5).

According to the *priestly* tradition, man is aware of his deep sinfulness and, not being able to purify himself by his own power, he beseeches God to bring about this change of heart, which can only be the work of a creative act of his:

"Create in me a clean heart, O God... / wash me, and I shall be whiter than snow... / a broken and contrite heart, O God, you will not despise" (Ps 51:10, 7, 17).

Both Old Testament channels meet in the beatitude of the "pure in heart" (Mt 5:8), even if its verbal formulation seems to be closer to Psalm 24 (cf. J. Dupont, *Les Béatitudes,* vol. III; *Les Evangélistes* [Paris: Gabalda, 1973], pp. 603-604).

PART TWO

LIFE ACCORDING TO THE SPIRIT

St. Paul's Teaching on the Human Body

Justification in Christ

"The desires of the flesh are against the Spirit, and the desires of the Spirit are against the flesh." Today we wish to study further these words of St. Paul in Galatians (5:17), with which we ended our reflections last week on the correct meaning of purity. Paul has in mind the tension existing within man, precisely in his heart. It is not a question here only of the body (matter) and of the spirit (the soul), as of two essentially different anthropological elements which constitute from the beginning the essence of man. But it presupposes that disposition of forces formed in man with original sin, in which every historical man participates. In this disposition, formed within man, the body opposes the spirit and easily prevails over it.[68] The Pauline terminology, however, means something more. Here the prevalence of the flesh seems almost to coincide with the threefold lust "of the world," according to Johannine terminology. In the language of St. Paul's letters,[69] the flesh indicates not only the "exterior" man, but also the man who is "interiorly" subjected to the "world."[70] He is closed, in a way, in the area of those values that belong only to the world and of those ends that it is capable of imposing on man—values, therefore, to which man as flesh is sensitive. Thus Paul's language seems to link with the essential contents of John. The language of both denotes what is defined by various terms of modern ethics and anthropology, such as humanistic autarchy, secularism or also, in a general sense, sensualism. The man who lives according to the flesh is ready only for what is of the world. He is the man of the senses, the man of the threefold lust. His actions confirm this, as we shall say shortly.

This man lives almost at the opposite pole as compared with what the Spirit wants. The Spirit of God wants a different reality from the one desired by the flesh. He aspires to a reality different from the one which the flesh aspires to, and that already within man, already at the interior source of man's aspirations and actions—"to prevent you from doing what you would" (Gal 5:17).

Paul expresses that in an even more explicit way. Elsewhere he writes of the evil he did, though he did not want to do it, and of the impossibility—or rather the limited possibility—of carrying out the good he wants (cf. Rom 7:19). Without going into the problems of a detailed exegesis of this text, it could be said that the tension between the flesh and the spirit is immanent, even if it is not reduced to this level. It is manifested in his heart as a fight between good and evil. Although it is an interior act, that desire which Christ spoke of in the Sermon on the Mount (cf. Mt 5:27-28) is certainly—according to Pauline language—a manifestation of life according to the flesh. At the same time, that desire enables us to see how, within man, life according to the flesh is opposed to life according to the Spirit. We see how the latter, in man's present state, in view of his hereditary sinfulness, is constantly exposed to the weakness and insufficiency of the former, to which it often yields, if it is not strengthened interiorly to do precisely what "the Spirit wants." We can deduce from this that Paul's words, which deal with life according to the flesh and according to the Spirit, are at the same time a synthesis and a program. It is necessary to understand them in this key.

We find the same opposition of life according to the flesh and life according to the Spirit in Romans. Here too, as in Galatians, it is placed in the context of the Pauline doctrine on justification by means of faith, that is, by the power of Christ himself operating within man by the Holy Spirit. In this context Paul takes that opposition to its extreme consequences when he writes: "Those who live according to the flesh set their minds on the things of the flesh, but those who live according to the Spirit set their minds on the things of the Spirit. To set the mind on the flesh is death, but to set the mind on the Spirit is life and peace. For the mind that is set on the flesh is hostile to God; it does not submit to God's law, indeed it cannot. Those who are in the flesh cannot please God. But you are not in the flesh. You are in the Spirit, if in fact the Spirit of God dwells in you. Anyone who does not have the Spirit of Christ does not belong to him. But if Christ is in you, although your bodies are dead because of sin, your spirits are alive because of righteousness" (Rom 8:5-10).

The horizons that Paul delineates in this text can clearly be seen. He goes back to the "beginning"—that is, in this case, to the first sin from which life according to the flesh originated. It created in man the heritage of a predisposition to live only such a life, together with the legacy of death. At the same time Paul anticipates the final victory over sin and death. The resurrection of Christ is a sign and announcement of this: "He who raised Christ Jesus from the dead will give life to your mortal bodies also through his Spirit who dwells in you" (Rom 8:11). In this eschatological perspective, St. Paul stresses justification in Christ. This is already intended for historical man, for every man of "yesterday, today and tomorrow" in the history of the world and also in the history of salvation. This justification is essential for the interior man. It is destined precisely for that heart to which Christ appealed, when speaking of purity and impurity in the moral sense. This justification by faith is not just a dimension of the divine plan for our salvation and sanctification, but according to St. Paul, is a real power that operates in man and is revealed and asserts itself in his actions.

Here again are the words of Galatians: "Now the works of the flesh are plain: fornication, impurity, licentiousness, idolatry, sorcery, enmity, strife, jealousy, anger, selfishness, dissension, party spirit, envy, drunkenness, carousing, and the like..." (5:19-21). "But the fruit of the Spirit is love, joy, peace, patience, kindness, goodness, faithfulness, gentleness, self-control..." (5:22-23). In the Pauline doctrine, life according to the flesh is opposed to life according to the Spirit. This is not only within man, in his heart, but, as can be seen, it finds an ample and differentiated field to express itself in works. Paul speaks of the works which spring from the flesh—it could be said, from the works in which the man who lives according to the flesh is manifested. He also speaks of the fruit of the Spirit, that is of the actions,[71] of the ways of behaving, of the virtues, in which the man who lives according to the Spirit is manifested. In the first case we are dealing with man abandoned to the threefold lust, which John said is "of the world." In the second case we have before us what we have already called the ethos of redemption. Only now are we able to clarify fully the nature and structure of that ethos. It is expressed and affirmed through what in man, in all his "operating," in actions and in behavior, is the fruit of dominion over the threefold lust—of the flesh, of the eyes, and of the pride of life (of all that the human heart can rightly be "accused" of, and which man and his interiority can continually be suspected of).

As we read in Galatians, mastery in the sphere of ethos is manifested and realized as "love, joy, peace, patience, kindness, goodness, faithfulness, gentleness, self-control." Behind each of these realizations, these ways of behaving, these moral virtues, there is a specific choice. That is, there is an effort of the will, the fruit of the human spirit permeated by the Spirit of God, which is manifested in choosing good. Speaking with the language of Paul, "The desires of the Spirit are against the flesh" (Gal

5:17). In these desires the Spirit shows himself to be stronger than the flesh and the desires brought forth by the threefold lust. In this struggle between good and evil, man proves himself stronger, thanks to the power of the Holy Spirit, who, operating within man's spirit, causes his desires to bear fruit in good. Therefore, these are not only—and not so much—"works" of man, as "fruit," that is, the effect of the action of the Spirit in man. Therefore Paul speaks of the fruit of the Spirit, intending this word with a capital letter.

Without penetrating the structures of human interiority by means of the subtle differentiations furnished to us by systematic theology (especially from Thomas Aquinas), we limit ourselves to a summary exposition of the biblical doctrine. This enables us to understand, in an essential and sufficient way, the distinction and the opposition of the flesh and the Spirit.

We have pointed out that among the fruits of the Spirit the Apostle also puts self-control. This must not be forgotten, because in our further reflections we will take up this subject again to deal with it in a more detailed way.

General audience of December 17, 1980

Opposition between the Flesh and the Spirit

What does the statement mean: "The desires of the flesh are against the Spirit, and the desires of the Spirit are against the flesh" (Gal 5:17)? This question seems important, even fundamental, in the context of our reflections on purity of heart, which the Gospel speaks of. However, in this regard the author of Galatians opens before us even wider horizons. This contrast between the flesh and the Spirit (Spirit of God), and between life according to the flesh and life according to the Spirit, contains the Pauline theology about justification. This is the expression of faith in the anthropological and ethical realism of the redemption carried out by Christ, which Paul, in the context already known to us, also calls the redemption of the body. According to Romans 8:23, the "redemption of the body" also has a "cosmic" dimension (referred to the whole of creation). But man is at its center—man constituted in the personal unity of spirit and body. Precisely in this man, in his heart, and consequently in all his behavior, Christ's redemption bears fruit. This is thanks to those powers of the Spirit which bring about justification, that is, which enable justice to abound in man. This is inculcated in the Sermon on the Mount (cf. Mt 5:20), to abound to the extent that God himself willed and which he expects.

It is significant that speaking of the "works of the flesh" (cf. Gal 5:19-21), Paul mentions not only "fornication, impurity, licentiousness... drunkenness, carousing." This is everything that, according to an objective way of understanding, takes on the character of carnal sins and of the sensual enjoyment connected with the flesh. He names other sins too, to which we would not be inclined to also attribute a carnal and sensual character: "idolatry, sorcery, enmity, strife, jealousy, anger, selfishness, dissension, party spirit, envy..." (Gal 5:20-21). According to our anthropological (and ethical) categories, we would rather be inclined to call all the works listed here sins of the spirit, rather than sins of the flesh. Not without reason we might have glimpsed in them the effects of the lust of the eyes or of the pride of life, rather than the effects of the lust of the flesh. However, Paul describes them all as works of the flesh. That is intended exclusively against the background of that wider meaning (in a way a metonymical one), which the term flesh assumes in the Pauline letters. It is opposed not only and not so much to the human spirit as to the Holy Spirit who works in man's soul (spirit).

Therefore, a significant analogy exists between what Paul defines as works of the flesh and the words Christ used to explain to his disciples what he had previously said to the Pharisees about ritual purity and impurity (cf. Mt 15:2-20). According to Christ's words, real purity (as also impurity) in the moral sense is in the heart and comes from the heart of man. Impure works in the same sense are defined not only as adultery and fornication, and so the sins of the flesh in the strict sense, but also "evil thoughts...theft, false witness, slander." As we have already noted, Christ uses here both the general and the specific meaning of impurity (and, indirectly also of purity). St. Paul expresses himself in a similar way. The works of the flesh are understood in the Pauline text both in the general and in the specific sense. All sins are an expression of life according to the flesh, which contrasts with life according to the Spirit. In conformity with our linguistic convention (which is partially justified), what is considered as a sin of the flesh is, in Paul's list, one of the many manifestations (or species) of what he calls works of the flesh. In this sense, it is one of the symptoms, that is, actualizations of life according to the flesh, and not according to the Spirit.

Paul writes to the Romans: "So then, brothers, we are debtors, not to the flesh, to live according to the flesh; for if you live according to the flesh you will die, but if by the Spirit you put to death the deeds of the body you will live" (Rom 8:12-13). These words introduce us again into the rich and differentiated sphere of the meanings which the terms "body" and Spirit have for him. However, the definitive meaning of that enunciation is advisory, exhortative, and so valid for the evangelical ethos. When he speaks of the necessity of putting to death the deeds of the body with the help of the Spirit, Paul expresses precisely what Christ spoke about in the Sermon on the Mount—appealing to the human heart and exhorting it to control desires, even those expressed in a man's look at a woman for the purpose of satisfying the lust of the flesh. This mastery, or as Paul writes, "putting to death the works of the body with the help of the Spirit," is an indispensable condition of life according to the Spirit, that is, of the life which is an antithesis of the death spoken about in the same context. Life according to the flesh has death as its fruit. That is, it involves as its effect the "death" of the spirit.

So the term "death" does not mean only the death of the body, but also sin, which moral theology will call "mortal." In Romans and Galatians, the Apostle continually widens the horizon of "sin-death," both toward the beginning of human history, and toward its end. Therefore, after listing the multiform works of the flesh, he affirms that "those who do such things shall not inherit the kingdom of God" (Gal 5:21). Elsewhere he will write with similar firmness: "Be sure of this, that no fornicator or impure man, or one who is covetous (that is, an idolater), has any inheritance in the kingdom of God" (Eph 5:5). In this case, too, the works that exclude inheritance in the kingdom of Christ and of God—that is, the works of the flesh—are listed as an example and with general value, although sins against purity in the specific sense are at the top of the list here (cf. Eph 5:3-7).

To complete the picture of the opposition between the body and the fruit of the Spirit, it should be observed that in everything that manifests life and behavior according to the Spirit, Paul sees at once the manifestation of that freedom for which Christ "has set us free" (Gal 5:1). He writes: "For you were called to freedom, brethren; only do not use your freedom as an opportunity for the flesh, but through love be servants of one another. For the whole law is fulfilled in one word, 'You shall love your neighbor as yourself'" (Gal 5:13-14). As we have already pointed out, the opposition between body and Spirit, and between life according to the flesh and life according to the Spirit, deeply permeates the whole Pauline doctrine on justification. With exceptional force of conviction, the Apostle of the Gentiles proclaims that justification is carried out in Christ and through Christ. Man obtains justification in "faith working through love" (Gal 5:6), and not only by means of the observance of the individual prescriptions of Old Testament law (in particular, that of circumcision). Justification comes therefore "from the Spirit" (of God) and not "from the flesh." Paul exhorts the recipients of his letter to free themselves from the erroneous carnal concept of justification, to follow the true one, that is, the spiritual one. In this sense he exhorts them to consider themselves free from the law, and even more to be free with the freedom for which Christ "has set us free."

In this way, following the Apostle's thought, we should consider and above all realize evangelical purity, that is, the purity of the heart, according to the measure of that freedom for which Christ "has set us free."

General audience of January 7, 1981

Life in the Spirit Is Based on True Freedom

St. Paul writes in Galatians: "For you were called to freedom, brethren; only do not use your freedom as an opportunity for the flesh, but through love be servants of one another. For the whole law is fulfilled in one word, 'You shall love your neighbor as yourself'" (Gal 5:13-14). We have already dwelled on this enunciation. However, we are taking it up again today, in connection with the main argument of our reflections.

The passage quoted refers above all to the subject of justification. However, here the Apostle aims explicitly at driving home the ethical dimension of the "body-Spirit" opposition, that is, the opposition between life according to the flesh and life according to the Spirit. Here he touches the essential point, revealing the anthropological roots of the Gospel ethos. If the whole law (the moral law of the Old Testament) is fulfilled in the commandment of charity, the dimension of the new Gospel ethos is nothing but an appeal to human freedom. It is an appeal to its fuller implementation and, in a way, to fuller "utilization" of the potential of the human spirit.

It might seem that Paul was only contrasting freedom with the law and the law with freedom. However, a deeper analysis of the text shows that in Galatians St. Paul emphasizes above all the ethical subordination of freedom to that element in which the whole law is fulfilled, that is, to love, which is the content of the greatest commandment of the Gospel. "Christ set us free in order that we might remain free," precisely in the sense that he manifested to us the ethical (and theological) subordination of freedom to charity, and that he linked freedom with the commandment of love. To understand the vocation to freedom in this way ("You were called to freedom, brethren"—Gal 5:13), means giving a form to the ethos in which life "according to the Spirit" is realized. The danger of wrongly understanding freedom also exists. Paul clearly points this out, writing in the same context: "Only do not use your freedom as an opportunity for the flesh, but through love be servants of one another" (Gal 5:13).

In other words, Paul warns us of the possibility of making a bad use of freedom. Such a use is in opposition to the liberation of the human spirit carried out by Christ and contradicts that freedom with which "Christ set us free." Christ realized and manifested the freedom that finds its fullness in charity, the freedom thanks to which we are servants of one another. In other words, that freedom becomes a source of new works and life according to the Spirit. The antithesis and, in a way, the negation of this use of freedom takes place when it becomes a pretext to live according to the flesh. Freedom then becomes a source of works and of life according to the flesh. It stops being the true freedom for which "Christ set us free," and becomes "an opportunity for the flesh," a source (or instrument) of a specific yoke on the part of pride of life, the lust of the eyes, and the lust of the flesh. Anyone who lives in this way according to the flesh, that is, submits —although in a way that is not quite conscious, but nevertheless actual—to the three forms of lust, especially to the lust of the flesh, ceases to be capable of that freedom for which "Christ set us free." He also ceases to be suitable for the real gift of himself, which is the fruit and expression of this freedom. Moreover, he ceases to be capable of that gift which is organically connected with the nuptial meaning of the human body, with which we dealt in the preceding analyses of Genesis (cf. Gn 2:23-25).

In the Pauline doctrine on purity we find the faithful and true echo of the Sermon on the Mount. This doctrine permits us to see evangelical and Christian purity of heart in a wider perspective, and above all permits us to link it with the charity in which the law is fulfilled. In a way similar to Christ, Paul knows a double meaning of purity (and of impurity)—a generic meaning and a specific meaning. In the first case, everything that is morally good is pure, and on the contrary, everything that is morally bad is impure. Christ's words according to Matthew 15:18-20, quoted previously, clearly affirm this. In Paul's enunciations about the works of the flesh, which he contrasts with the fruit of the Spirit, we find the basis for a similar way of understanding this problem. Among the works of the flesh Paul puts what is morally bad, while every moral good is linked with life according to the Spirit. In this way, one of the manifestations of life according to the Spirit is behavior in conformity with that virtue which Paul in Galatians seems to define rather indirectly, but which he speaks directly of in First Thessalonians.

In the passages of Galatians, which we have already submitted to detailed analysis, the Apostle lists fornication, impurity and licentiousness in the first place among the works of the flesh. Subsequently, however, when he contrasts these works with the fruit of the Spirit, he does not speak directly of purity, but names only self-control, *enkrateia*. This control can be recognized as a virtue which concerns continence in the area of all the desires of the senses, especially in the sexual sphere. It is in opposition to fornication, impurity and licentiousness, and also to drunkenness and carousing. It could be admitted that Pauline self-control contains what is expressed in the term "continence" or "temperance," which corresponds to the Latin term *temperantia*. In this case, we would find ourselves in the presence of the well-known system of virtues which later theology, especially Scholasticism, will borrow from the ethics of Aristotle. However, Paul certainly does not use this system in his text. Since purity must be understood as the correct way of treating the sexual sphere according to one's personal state (and not necessarily absolute abstention from sexual life), then undoubtedly this purity is included in the Pauline concept of self-control or *enkrateia*. Therefore, within the Pauline text we find only a generic and indirect mention of purity. Now and again the author contrasts these works of the flesh, such as fornication, impurity and licentiousness, with the fruit of the Spirit—that is, the new works which manifest life according to the Spirit. It can be deduced that one of these new works is precisely purity—that is the one that is opposed to impurity and also to fornication and licentiousness.

But already in First Thessalonians, Paul writes on this subject in an explicit and unambiguous way. We read: "For this is the will of God, your sanctification: that you abstain from unchastity; that each one of you know how to control his own body[72] in holiness and honor, not in the passion of lust like heathens who do not know God" (1 Th 4:3-5). Then: "God has not called us for uncleanness, but in holiness. Therefore whoever disregards this, disregards not man but God, who gives his Holy Spirit to you" (1 Th 4:7-8). In this text we also have before us the generic meaning of purity, identified in this case with holiness (since uncleanness is named as the antithesis of holiness). Nevertheless, the whole context indicates clearly what purity or impurity it is a question of, that is, the content of what Paul calls here uncleanness, and in what way purity contributes to the holiness of man.

Therefore, in the following reflections, it will be useful to take up again the text of First Thessalonians, which has just been quoted.

General audience of January 14, 1981

St. Paul's Teaching on the Human Body

St. Paul writes in First Thessalonians: "This is the will of God, your sanctification: that you abstain from unchastity, that each one of you know how to control his own body in holiness and honor, not in the passion of lust like heathens who do not know God" (1 Th 4:3-5). After some verses, he continues: "God has not called us for uncleanness, but in holiness. Therefore whoever disregards this, disregards not man but God, who gives his Holy Spirit to you" (1 Th 4:7-8). We referred to these sentences of the Apostle during our last meeting. We take them up again today because they are especially important for the subject of our meditations.

The purity which Paul speaks of in First Thessalonians (4:3-5, 7-8) is manifested in the fact that man "knows how to control his own body in holiness and honor, not in the passion of lust." In this formulation every word has a particular meaning and therefore deserves an adequate comment.

In the first place, purity is a "capacity," that is, in the traditional language of anthropology and ethics, an aptitude. In this sense it is a virtue. If this ability, that is, virtue, leads to abstaining from unchastity, that happens because the man who possesses it "knows how to control his own body in holiness and honor, not in the passion of lust." It is a question here of a practical capacity which makes man capable of acting in a given way, and at the same time of not acting in the opposite way. For purity to be such a capacity or aptitude, it must obviously be rooted in the will, in the foundation of man's willing and conscious acting. In his teaching on virtues, Thomas Aquinas sees in an even more direct way the object of purity in the faculty of sensitive desire, which he calls *appetitus concupiscibilis*. This faculty must be mastered, subordinated and made capable of acting in a way that is in conformity with virtue, in order that purity may be attributed to man. According to this concept, purity consists in the first place in containing the impulse of sensitive desire, which has as its object what is corporeal and sexual in man. Purity is a different form of the virtue of temperance.

The text of First Thessalonians (4:3-5) shows that in Paul's concept, the virtue of purity consists also in the mastery and overcoming of the passion of lust. That means that the capacity for controlling the impulses of sensitive desire, that is, the virtue of temperance, belongs necessarily to its nature. At the same time, however, this Pauline text turns our attention to another role of the virtue of purity. It could be said that this other dimension is more positive than negative. The task of purity, which the author of the letter seems to stress above all, is not only (and not so much) abstention from unchastity and from what leads to it, and thus abstention from the passion of lust. But at the same time, it is the control of one's own body in holiness and honor, and indirectly also that of others.

These two functions, abstention and control, are closely connected and dependent on each other. It is not possible to "control one's body in holiness and honor" if that abstention from unchastity and from what leads to it is lacking. Consequently it can be admitted that control of one's body (and indirectly that of others) in holiness and honor confers adequate meaning and value on that abstention. This in itself calls for overcoming something that is in man and that arises spontaneously in him as an inclination, an attraction, and also as a value. This acts above all in the sphere of the senses, but often not without repercussions on the other dimensions of human subjectivity, and particularly on the affective-emotional dimension.

The Pauline image of the virtue of purity emerges from the eloquent comparison of the function of abstention (that is, of temperance) with that of "control of one's body in holiness and honor." Considering all this, it seems that this image is deeply right, complete and adequate. Perhaps we owe this completeness to nothing else than the fact that Paul considers purity not only as a capacity (that is, an aptitude) of man's subjective faculties, but at the same time, as a concrete manifestation of life according to the Spirit. In this life, human capacity is interiorly made fruitful and enriched by what Paul calls in Galatians 5:22 the "fruit of the Spirit." The honor that arises in man for everything that is corporeal and sexual, both in himself and in any other person, male and female, is seen to be the most essential power to control the body in holiness. To understand the Pauline teaching on purity, it is necessary to penetrate fully the meaning of the term "honor," which is obviously understood here as a power of the spiritual order. Precisely this interior power confers its full dimension on purity as a virtue, that is, as the capacity of acting in that whole field in which man discovers within himself the multiple impulses of the passion of lust and for various reasons, sometimes surrenders to them.

To grasp better the thought of the author of First Thessalonians, it will be a good thing to keep in mind also another text, which we find in First Corinthians. Paul sets forth in it his great ecclesiological doctrine, according to which the Church is the Body of Christ. Paul takes the opportunity to formulate the following argumentation about the human body: "God arranged the organs in the body, each one of them, as he chose" (1 Cor 12:18). Further on he said: "On the contrary, the parts of the body which seem to be weaker are indispensable, and those parts of the body which we think less honorable we invest with the greater honor, and our unpresentable parts are treated with greater modesty, which our more presentable parts do not require. But God has so composed the body, giving the greater honor to the inferior part, that there may be no discord in the body, but that the members may have the same care for one another" (1 Cor 12:22-25).

The specific subject of the text in question is the theology of the Church as the Body of Christ. However, in connection with this passage it can be said that Paul, by means of his great ecclesiological analogy (which recurs in other letters, and which we will take up again in due time), contributes, at the same time, to deepening the theology of the body. While in First Thessalonians he writes about control of the body in holiness and honor, in the passage now quoted from First Corinthians he wishes to show this human body as worthy of honor. It could also be said that he wishes to teach the receivers of his letter the correct concept of the human body.

Therefore, this Pauline description of the human body in First Corinthians seems to be closely connected with the recommendations of First Thessalonians: "...that each one of you know how to control his own body in holiness and honor" (1 Th 4:4). This is an important thread, perhaps the essential one, of the Pauline doctrine on purity.

General audience of January 28, 1981

St. Paul's Description of the Body and His Teaching on Purity

In our last considerations on purity according to the teaching of St. Paul, we called attention to the text of First Corinthians. In it the Apostle presents the Church as the Body of Christ. That offers him the opportunity to reason as follows about the human body: "God arranged the organs in the body, each one of them, as he chose.... On the contrary, the parts of the body which seem to be weaker are indispensable, and those parts of the body which we think less honorable we invest with the greater honor, and our unpresentable parts are treated with greater modesty, which our more presentable parts do not require. But God has so composed the body, giving the greater honor to the inferior part, that there may be no discord in the body, but that the members may have the same care for one another" (1 Cor 12:18, 22-25).

The Pauline description of the human body corresponds to the reality which constitutes it, so it is a realistic description. At the same time, a very fine thread of evaluation is intermingled with the realism of this description, conferring on it a deeply evangelical, Christian value. Certainly, it is possible to describe the human body, to express its truth with the objectivity characteristic of the natural sciences. But such a description—with all its precision—cannot be adequate (that is, commensurable with its object). It is not just a question of the body (intended as an organism, in the somatic sense) but of man, who expresses himself through that body and in this sense is, I would say, that body. So that thread of evaluation, seeing that it is a question of man as a person, is indispensable in describing the human body. Furthermore, it is necessary to say how right this evaluation is. This is one of the tasks and one of the perennial themes of all culture—of literature, sculpture, painting, and also of dancing, of theatrical works, and finally of the culture of everyday life, private or social. This is a subject that would be worth dealing with separately.

The Pauline description in First Corinthians 12:18-25 certainly does not have a scientific meaning. It does not present a biological study on the human organism or on human somatics. From this point of view it is a simple pre-scientific description, a concise one made up of barely a few sentences. It has all the characteristics of common realism and is unquestionably sufficiently realistic. However, what determines its specific character, what especially justifies its presence in Holy Scripture, is precisely that evaluation intermingled with the description expressed in its narrative-realistic tissue. It can be said with certainty that this description would not be possible without the whole truth of creation and also without the whole truth of the redemption of the body, which Paul professes and proclaims. It can also be affirmed that the Pauline description of the body corresponds precisely to the spiritual attitude of respect for the human body, due because of the holiness (cf. 1 Th 4:3-5, 7-8) which springs from the mysteries of creation and redemption. The Pauline description is equally far from Manichaean contempt for the body and from the various manifestations of a naturalistic cult of the body.

The author of First Corinthians 12:18-25 has before his eyes the human body in all its truth, and so the body permeated in the first place (if it can be expressed in this way) by the whole reality of the person and of his dignity. At the same time, it is the body of historical man, male and female, that is, of that man who, after sin, was conceived, so to speak, within and by the reality of the man who had had the experience of original innocence. In Paul's expressions about the unpresentable parts of the human body, as also about the ones which seem to be weaker or the ones which we think less honorable, we seem to find again the testimony of the same shame that the first human beings, male and female, had experienced after original sin. This shame was imprinted on them and on all the generations of historical man as the fruit of the three forms of lust (with particular reference to the lust of the flesh). As the preceding analyses

have highlighted, at the same time a certain "echo" of man's original innocence is imprinted on this shame —a "negative," as it were, of the image
whose "positive" had been precisely original innocence.

The Pauline description of the human body seems to confirm
perfectly our previous analyses. The human body has "unpresentable
parts," not because of their somatic nature (since a scientific and physiological description deals with all the parts and organs of the human body
in a neutral way, with the same objectivity). But it is only and exclusively
because that shame exists in man himself—that shame which perceives
some parts of the body as unpresentable and causes them to be considered
such. At the same time, that shame seems to be at the basis of what the
Apostle writes in First Corinthians: "Those parts of the body which we think
less honorable we invest with the greater honor, and our unpresentable
parts are treated with greater modesty" (1 Cor 12:23). Hence it can be said
that from shame springs respect for one's own body, respect which Paul,
in First Thessalonians (4:4), urges us to keep. This control of the body in
holiness and honor is considered essential for the virtue of purity.

Returning again to the Pauline description of the body in First Corinthians 12:18-25, we wish to draw attention to the following fact. According to Paul, that particular effort which aims at respecting the human body,
and especially its weaker or unpresentable parts, corresponds to the
Creator's original plan, that is, to that vision which Genesis speaks of,
"God saw everything that he had made, and behold, it was very good" (Gn
1:31). Paul writes: "God has so composed the body, giving the greater
honor to the inferior parts, that there may be no discord in the body, but
that the members may have the same care for one another" (1 Cor 12:24-
25). As a result of discord in the body, some parts are considered weaker,
less honorable, and so unpresentable. This discord is a further expression
of the vision of man's interior state after original sin, that is, of historical
man. The man of original innocence, male and female, did not even feel
that discord in the body. In Genesis 2:25 we read that they "were naked,
and were not ashamed." The Creator endowed the body with an objective
harmony, which Paul specifies as mutual care of the members for one another (cf. 1 Cor 12:25). This harmony corresponded to a similar harmony
within man, the harmony of the heart. This harmony, that is precisely purity of heart, enabled man and woman in the state of original innocence to
experience simply (and in a way that originally made them both happy)
the uniting power of their bodies, which was, so to speak, the unsuspected
substratum of their personal union or *communio personarum.*

As can be seen in First Corinthians 12:18-25, the Apostle links his
description of the human body with the state of historical man. At the

threshold of this man's history there is the experience of shame connected with "discord in the body," with the sense of modesty regarding that body (especially those parts of it that somatically determine masculinity and femininity). However, in the same description, Paul also indicates the way which (precisely on the basis of the sense of shame) leads to the transformation of this state to the point of gradual victory over that discord in the body. This victory can and must take place in man's heart. This is the way to purity, that is, "to control one's own body in holiness and honor." Paul connects First Corinthians 12:18-25 with the honor which First Thessalonians 4:3-5 deals with. He uses some equivalent expressions when he speaks of honor, that is, esteem for the less honorable, weaker parts of the body, and when he recommends greater modesty with regard to what is considered unpresentable in man. These expressions more precisely characterize that honor, especially in the sphere of human relations and behavior with regard to the body. This is important both as regards one's own body, and of course also in mutual relations (especially between man and woman, although not limited to them).

We have no doubt that the description of the human body in First Corinthians has a fundamental meaning for the Pauline doctrine on purity as a whole.

General audience of February 4, 1981

The Virtue of Purity Is the Expression and Fruit of Life according to the Spirit

During our recent Wednesday meetings we have analyzed two passages taken from First Thessalonians 4:3-5 and First Corinthians 12:18-25. This was with a view to showing what seems to be essential in St. Paul's doctrine on purity, understood in the moral sense, that is, as a virtue. In this text of First Thessalonians we can see that purity consists in temperance. However, as in First Corinthians, the text highlights the element of respect. (Let us add that, according to First Corinthians, respect is seen precisely in relation to its element of modesty.) By means of such respect due to the human body, purity as a Christian virtue is revealed in the Pauline letters as an effective way to become detached from what, in the human heart, is the fruit of the lust of the flesh.

Abstention from unchastity implies controlling one's body in holiness and honor. This abstention makes it possible to deduce that, according to the Apostle's doctrine, purity is a capacity centered on the dignity of the body. That is, it is centered on the dignity of the person in relation to his own body, to the femininity or masculinity which is manifested in this body. Understood as capacity, purity is precisely the expression and fruit of life according to the Spirit in the full meaning of the expression. It is a new capacity of the human being, in which the gift of the Holy Spirit bears fruit.

These two dimensions of purity—the moral dimension, or virtue, and the charismatic dimension, namely the gift of the Holy Spirit—are present and closely connected in Paul's message. He emphasizes this especially in First Corinthians, in which he calls the body "a temple [therefore, a dwelling and shrine] of the Holy Spirit."

"Do you not know that your body is a temple of the Holy Spirit within you, which you have from God? You are not your own" (1 Cor 6:19). Paul said this to the Corinthians after having first instructed them with great severity about the moral requirements of purity. "Shun immorality. Every other sin which a man commits is outside the body, but the immoral man sins against his own body" (1 Cor 6:18). The peculiar characteristic of the sin that the Apostle stigmatizes here lies in the fact that this sin, unlike all others, is against the body (while other sins are outside the body). In this way, we find in the Pauline terminology the motivation for expressions such as "the sins of the body" or "carnal sins." These sins are in opposition precisely to that virtue by force of which man keeps his body in holiness and honor (cf. 1 Th 4:3-5).

Such sins profane the body. They deprive the man's or woman's body of the honor due to it because of the dignity of the person. However, the Apostle goes further. According to him, sin against the body is also "profanation of the temple." In Paul's eyes, it is not only the human spirit, thanks to which man is constituted as a personal subject, that decides the dignity of the human body. But even more so it is the supernatural reality constituted by the indwelling and the continual presence of the Holy Spirit in man—in his soul and in his body—as fruit of the redemption carried out by Christ.

It follows that man's body is no longer just his own. It deserves that respect whose manifestation in the mutual conduct of man, male and female, constitutes the virtue of purity. This is not only because it is the body of the person. When the Apostle writes: "Your body is a temple of the Holy Spirit within you, which you have from God" (1 Cor 6:19), he intends to indicate yet another source of the dignity of the body, precisely the Holy Spirit, who is also the source of the moral duty deriving from this dignity.

The reality of redemption, which is also redemption of the body, constitutes this source. For Paul, this mystery of faith is a living reality, geared directly to every person. Through redemption, every man has received from God again, as it were, himself and his own body. Christ has imprinted new dignity on the human body—on the body of every man and every woman, since in Christ the human body has been admitted, together with the soul, to union with the Person of the Son-Word. With this new dignity, through the redemption of the body, a new obligation arose at the same time. Paul writes of this concisely, but in an extremely moving way: "You were bought with a price" (1 Cor 6:20). The fruit of redemption is the Holy Spirit, who dwells in man and in his body as in a temple. In this Gift, which sanctifies every man, the Christian receives himself again as a gift from God. This new, double gift is binding. The Apostle refers to this binding dimension when he writes to believers, aware of the Gift, to convince them that one must not commit unchastity. One must not sin "against one's own body" (1 Cor 6:18). He writes: "The body is not meant for immorality, but for the Lord, and the Lord for the body" (1 Cor 6:13).

It is difficult to express more concisely what the mystery of the Incarnation brings with it for every believer. The fact that the human body becomes in Jesus Christ the body of God-Man obtains for this reason, in every man, a new supernatural elevation. Every Christian must take this into account in his behavior with regard to his own body and, of course, with regard to the other's body—man with regard to woman and woman with regard to man. The redemption of the body involves the institution, in Christ and through Christ, of a new measure of the holiness of the body. Paul refers precisely to this holiness in First Thessalonians 4:3-5 when he writes of "controlling one's own body in holiness and honor."

In chapter six of First Corinthians, Paul specifies the truth about the holiness of the body. He stigmatizes unchastity, that is, the sin against the holiness of the body, the sin of impurity, with words that are even drastic: "Do you not know that your bodies are members of Christ? Shall I therefore take the members of Christ and make them members of a prostitute? Never! Do you not know that he who joins himself to a prostitute becomes one body with her? For, as it is written, 'The two shall become one flesh.' But he who is united to the Lord becomes one spirit with him" (1 Cor 6:15-17). According to the Pauline teaching, purity is an aspect of life according to the Spirit. That means that the mystery of the redemption of the body as part of the mystery of Christ, started in the Incarnation and already addressed to every man through it, bears fruit in it.

This mystery bears fruit also in purity understood as a particular commitment based on ethics. The fact that we were "bought with a price" (1 Cor 6:20), that is, at the price of Christ's redemption, gives rise to a special commitment, that is, the duty of controlling one's body in holiness and honor. Awareness of the redemption of the body operates in the human will in favor of abstention from unchastity. It operates in acts for the purpose of causing man to acquire an appropriate ability or capacity, called the virtue of purity.

What can be seen from the words of First Corinthians 6:15-17 about Paul's teaching on the Christian virtue of purity as the implementation of life according to the Spirit is of special depth and has the power of the supernatural realism of faith. We will have to come back to reflection on this subject more than once.

General audience of February 11, 1981

The Pauline Doctrine of Purity as Life according to the Spirit

At our meeting some weeks ago, we concentrated our attention on the passage in First Corinthians in which St. Paul calls the human body "a temple of the Holy Spirit." He writes: "Do you not know that your body is a temple of the Holy Spirit within you, which you have from God? You are not your own; you were bought with a price" (1 Cor 6:19-20). "Do you not know that your bodies are members of Christ?" (1 Cor 6:15). The Apostle points out the mystery of the redemption of the body, carried out by Christ, as a source of a special moral duty which commits the Christian to purity. This is what Paul himself defines elsewhere as the necessity of "controlling his own body in holiness and honor" (1 Th 4:4).

However, we would not completely discover the riches of the thought contained in the Pauline texts, if we did not note that the mystery of redemption bears fruit in man also in a charismatic way. According to the Apostle's words, the Holy Spirit enters the human body as his own "temple," dwells there and operates together with his spiritual gifts. Among these gifts, known in the history of spirituality as the seven gifts of the Holy Spirit (cf. Is 11:2, according to the Septuagint and the Vulgate), the one most congenial to the virtue of purity seems to be the gift of piety *(eusebeia, donum pietatis).*[73] If purity prepares man to "control his own body in holiness and honor" (1 Th 4:3-5), piety, which is a gift of the Holy Spirit, seems to serve purity in a particular way. It makes the human subject sensitive to that dignity which is characteristic of the human body by virtue of the mystery of creation and redemption. "Do you not know that your body is a temple of the Holy Spirit within you.... You are not your own" (1 Cor 6:19). Thanks to the gift of piety, Paul's words acquire the eloquence of an experience of the nuptial meaning of the body and of the freedom of the gift connected with it, in which the profound aspect of purity and its organic link with love is revealed.

Control of one's body in holiness and honor is acquired through abstention from immorality, and this way is indispensable. Yet it always bears fruit in deeper experience of that love, which was inscribed from the beginning, according to the image and likeness of God himself, in the whole human being and so also in his body. Therefore, St. Paul ends his argumentation in chapter six of First Corinthians with a significant exhortation: "So glorify God in your body" (v. 20). Purity as the virtue is the capacity of controlling one's body in holiness and honor. Together with the gift of piety, as the fruit of the dwelling of the Holy Spirit in the temple of the body, purity brings about in the body such a fullness of dignity in interpersonal relations that God himself is thereby glorified. Purity is the glory of the human body before God. It is God's glory in the human body, through which masculinity and femininity are manifested. From purity springs that extraordinary beauty which permeates every sphere of men's common life and makes it possible to express in it simplicity and depth, cordiality and the unrepeatable authenticity of personal trust. (There will perhaps be an opportunity later to deal with this subject more fully. The connection of purity with love and also the connection of purity in love with that gift of the Holy Spirit, piety, is a part of the theology of the body which is little known, but which deserves particular study. That will be possible in the course of the analysis concerning the sacramentality of marriage.)

And now a brief reference to the Old Testament. The Pauline doctrine about purity, understood as life according to the Spirit, seems to indicate a certain continuity with regard to the Wisdom books of the Old Testament. For example, we find there the following prayer to obtain purity in thought, word and deed: "O Lord, Father and God of my life...remove from me evil desire, let neither gluttony nor lust overcome me" (Sir 23:4-6). Purity is the condition for finding wisdom and following it, as we read in the same book: "I directed my soul to her [that is, to Wisdom], and through purification I found her" (Sir 51:20). We could also consider the text of the Book of Wisdom (8:21), known by the liturgy in the Vulgate version: *"Scivi quoniam aliter non possum esse continens, nisi Deus det; et hoc ipsum erat sapientiae, scire, cuius esset hoc donum."*[74]

According to this concept, it is not so much purity that is a condition for wisdom, but wisdom that is a condition for purity, as for a special gift of God. It seems that already in the above-mentioned Wisdom texts the double meaning of purity takes shape—as a virtue and as a gift. The virtue is in the service of wisdom, and wisdom is a preparation to receive the gift that comes from God. This gift strengthens the virtue and makes it possible to enjoy, in wisdom, the fruits of a behavior and life that are pure.

In his beatitude in the Sermon on the Mount which referred to the "pure in heart," Christ highlights the "sight of God," the fruit of purity, in an eschatological perspective. Just so, Paul in his turn sheds light on its diffusion in the dimensions of temporality, when he writes: "To the pure all things are pure, but to the corrupt and unbelieving nothing is pure; their very minds and consciences are corrupted. They profess to know God, but they deny him by their deeds..." (Ti 1:15f.). These words can also refer both to the general and to the specific meaning of purity, as to the characteristic note of all moral good. For the Pauline concept of purity, in the sense spoken of in First Thessalonians 4:3-5 and First Corinthians 6:13-20, that is, in the sense of life according to the Spirit, the anthropology of rebirth in the Holy Spirit (cf. also Jn 3:5ff.) seems to be fundamental. This can be seen from these considerations of ours as a whole. It grows from roots set in the reality of the redemption of the body, carried out by Christ—redemption whose ultimate expression is the resurrection. There are profound reasons for connecting the whole theme of purity with the words of the Gospel, in which Christ referred to the resurrection (and that will be the subject of the further stage of our considerations). Here we have mainly linked it with the ethos of the redemption of the body.

The way of understanding and presenting purity—inherited from the tradition of the Old Testament and characteristic of the Wisdom Books— was certainly an indirect, but nonetheless real, preparation for the Pauline doctrine about purity understood as life according to the Spirit. That way unquestionably helped many listeners of the Sermon on the Mount to understand Christ's words when, explaining the commandment, "You shall not commit adultery," he appealed to the human heart. In this way our reflections as a whole have been able to show, at least to a certain extent, how rich and profound the doctrine on purity is in its biblical and evangelical sources.

General audience of March 18, 1981

The Positive Function of Purity of Heart

Before concluding the series of considerations concerning the words Jesus Christ uttered in the Sermon on the Mount, it is necessary to recall these words once more and briefly retrace the thread of ideas whose basis they constitute. Here is the tenor of Jesus' words: "You have heard that it was said, 'You shall not commit adultery.' But I say to you that everyone who looks at a woman lustfully has already committed adultery with her in his heart" (Mt 5:27-28). These concise words call for deep reflection, in the same way as the words in which Christ referred to the beginning. The Pharisees had asked him, referring to the law of Moses which admitted the so-called act of repudiation: "Is it lawful to divorce one's wife for any cause?" He replied: "Have you not read that he who made them from the beginning made them male and female?... For this reason a man shall leave his father and mother and be joined to his wife, and the two shall become one flesh.... What therefore God has joined together, let not man put asunder" (Mt 19:3-6). These words, too, called for a deep reflection, to derive all the riches contained in them. A reflection of this kind enabled us to outline the true theology of the body.

Following the reference Christ made to the beginning, we dedicated a series of reflections to the relative texts in Genesis, which deal precisely with that beginning. An image of the situation of man—male and female—in the state of original innocence emerged from that analysis, as well as the theological basis of the truth about man and about his particular vocation. This springs from the eternal mystery of the person—the image of God, incarnate in the visible and corporeal fact of the masculinity or femininity of the human person. This truth is at the basis of the answer Christ gave about the nature of marriage, and especially its indissolubility. It is truth about man, truth rooted in the state of original innocence, truth which must therefore be understood in the context of that situation prior to sin, as we tried to do in the preceding series of reflections.

At the same time, however, it is necessary to consider, understand and interpret the same fundamental truth about man, his being male and female, in the prism of another situation—that is, of the one that was formed through breaking the first covenant with the Creator, that is, through original sin. Such truth about man—male and female—should be seen in the context of his hereditary sinfulness. It is precisely here that we find Christ's enunciation in the Sermon on the Mount. It is obvious that in the Scriptures of the old and new covenant there are many narratives, phrases and words which confirm the same truth, that is, that historical man bears within him the inheritance of original sin. Nevertheless, with all their concise enunciation, Christ's words in the Sermon on the Mount seem to have an especially rich eloquence. This is shown also by the previous analyses, which gradually revealed what those words contain. To clarify the statements concerning lust, it is necessary to grasp the biblical meaning of lust itself—of the three forms of lust—and principally that of the flesh. Then, little by little, we arrive at understanding why Jesus defined that lust (looking at lustfully) as adultery committed in the heart. Making the relative analyses, we tried at the same time to understand what meaning Christ's words had for his immediate listeners. They had been brought up in the tradition of the Old Testament, that is, in the tradition of the legislative texts, as well as the prophetic and sapiential ones. Furthermore, we tried to understand what meaning Christ's words can have for the person of every other era, especially for modern man, considering his various cultural conditionings. We are convinced that these words, in their essential content, refer to the man of every time and every place. Their comprehensive value consists also in this: they proclaim to each one the truth that is valid and substantial for him.

What is this truth? Unquestionably, it is a truth of an ethical nature and therefore a truth of a normative nature, just as the truth contained in the commandment: "You shall not commit adultery," is normative. The interpretation of this commandment, made by Christ, indicates the evil that must be avoided and overcome—precisely the evil of lust of the flesh. At the same time it points out the good for which the way is opened by overcoming desire. This good is purity of heart, which Christ spoke of in the same context of the Sermon on the Mount. From the biblical point of view, purity of heart means freedom from every kind of sin or guilt, not just from sins that concern the lust of the flesh. However, we are dealing here especially with one of the aspects of that purity, which constitutes the opposite of adultery committed in the heart. If that purity of heart, about which we are concerned, is understood according to St. Paul's thought as life according to the Spirit, then the Pauline context offers us a complete image of the content present in the words Christ spoke in the Sermon on the Mount. They contain a truth of an ethical nature. They warn us against evil and indicate the moral good of human conduct. In fact, they direct listeners to avoid the evil of lust and acquire purity of heart. Therefore these words have a meaning that is both normative and indicative. Directing toward the good of purity of heart, at the same time they indicate the values toward which the human heart can and must aspire.

Hence the question: what truth, valid for every man, is contained in Christ's words? We must answer that not only an ethical truth, but also the essential truth, the anthropological truth about man is contained in them. Precisely for this reason we go back to these words in formulating here the theology of the body. It is closely related to and is in the perspective of the preceding words in which Christ had referred to the beginning. It can be affirmed that, with their expressive evangelical eloquence, the man of original innocence is, in a way, recalled to the consciousness of the man of lust.

But Christ's words are realistic. They do not try to make the human heart return to the state of original innocence, which man left behind him at the moment when he committed original sin. On the contrary, they indicate to him the way to a purity of heart which is possible and accessible to him even in the state of hereditary sinfulness. This is the purity of the man of lust. However, he is inspired by the word of the Gospel and open to life according to the Spirit (in conformity with St. Paul's words), that is, the purity of the man of lust who is entirely enveloped by the redemption of the body Christ carried out. For this reason we find in the words of the Sermon on the Mount the reference to the heart, that is, to the interior man. The interior man must open himself to life according to the Spirit, in order to participate in evangelical purity of heart, to rediscover and realize the value of the body, freed through redemption from the bonds of lust. The normative meaning of Christ's words is deeply rooted in their anthropological meaning, in the dimension of human interiority.

According to the evangelical doctrine, developed in such a stupendous way in Paul's letters, purity is not just temperance or abstention from unchastity (cf. 1 Th 4:3). At the same time, it also opens the way to a more and more perfect discovery of the dignity of the human body. The body is organically connected with the freedom of the gift of the person in the complete authenticity of his personal subjectivity, male or female. In this way, purity in the sense of temperance matures in the heart of the person who cultivates it and tends to reveal and strengthen the nuptial meaning of the body in its integral truth. This truth must be known interiorly. In a way, it must be felt with the heart, in order that the mutual relations of man and of woman—even mere looks—may reacquire that authentically nuptial content of their meanings. In the Gospel, purity of heart indicates precisely this content.

If in the interior experience of man (that is, the man of lust), temperance takes shape as a negative function, the analysis of Christ's words in the Sermon on the Mount and connected with the texts of St. Paul enables us to shift this meaning toward the positive function of purity of heart. In mature purity man enjoys the fruits of the victory won over lust, a victory which St. Paul writes of, exhorting man to "control his own body in holiness and honor" (1 Th 4:4). The efficacy of the gift of the Holy Spirit, whose "temple" the human body is (cf. 1 Cor 6:19), is partly manifested precisely in such mature purity. This gift is above all that of piety *(donum pietatis)*, which restores to the experience of the body—especially when it is a question of the sphere of the mutual relations of man and woman—all its simplicity, its explicitness and also its interior joy. As can be seen, this is a spiritual climate which is very different from the "passion of lust" of which Paul writes (and which we know, moreover, from the preceding analyses; cf. Sir 26:13, 15-18). The satisfaction of the passions is one thing, and the joy that man finds in mastering himself more fully is another thing. In this way he can also become more fully a real gift for another person.

The words Christ spoke in the Sermon on the Mount direct the human heart toward this joy. We must entrust ourselves, our thoughts and our actions to them, in order to find joy and give it to others.

General audience of April 1, 1981

The Pronouncements of the Magisterium
Apply Christ's Words Today

The time has now come to conclude the reflections and analyses based on the words Christ spoke in the Sermon on the Mount, with which he appealed to the human heart, exhorting it to purity: "You have heard that it was said, 'You shall not commit adultery.' But I say to you that everyone who looks at a woman lustfully has already committed adultery with her in his heart" (Mt 5:27-28). We have said several times that these words, spoken once to the limited number of listeners to that Sermon, refer to people of all times and places. They appeal to the human heart, in which the most interior and, in a way, the most essential design of history is inscribed. It is the history of good and evil (whose beginning is connected, in Genesis, with the mysterious tree of the knowledge of good and evil). At the same time, it is the history of salvation, whose word is the Gospel, and whose power is the Holy Spirit, given to those who accept the Gospel with a sincere heart.

Christ's appeal to the human heart and, still earlier, his reference to the beginning, enable us to construct or at least to outline an anthropology which we can call the theology of the body. At the same time, such a theology is a pedagogy. Pedagogy aims at educating, setting before man the requirements, motivating them, and pointing out the ways that lead to their fulfillment. Christ's pronouncements also have this purpose—they are pedagogical enunciations. They contain a pedagogy of the body, expressed in a concise and at the same time extremely complete way. Both the answer given to the Pharisees with regard to the indissolubility of marriage, and the words of the Sermon on the Mount concerning the mastery of lust, prove the following, at least indirectly: the Creator has assigned as a task to man his body, his masculinity and femininity. In masculinity and femininity he, in a way, assigned to him as a task his humanity, the dignity of the person, and also the clear sign of the interpersonal communion in which man fulfills himself through the authentic gift of himself. Setting before man the requirements conforming to the tasks entrusted to him, at the same time the Creator points out to man, male and female, the ways that lead to assuming and discharging them.

Analyzing these key texts of the Bible to their very roots, we discover that anthropology which can be called the theology of the body. This theology of the body is the basis of the most suitable method of the pedagogy of the body, that is, the education (the self-education) of man. This takes on particular relevance for modern man, whose science in the field of biophysiology and biomedicine has made great progress. However, this science deals with man under a determined aspect and so is partial rather than global. We know well the functions of the body as an organism, the functions connected with the masculinity and femininity of the human person. But in itself, this science does not yet develop the awareness of the body as a sign of the person, as a manifestation of the spirit.

The whole development of modern science, regarding the body as an organism, has rather the character of biological knowledge. This is because it is based on the separation of that which is corporeal in man from that which is spiritual. Using such a one-sided knowledge of the functions of the body as an organism, it is not difficult to arrive at treating the body, in a more or less systematic way, as an object of manipulations. In this case man ceases to identify himself subjectively with his own body, because it is deprived of the meaning and the dignity deriving from the fact that this body is proper to the person. We here touch upon problems often demanding fundamental solutions, which are impossible without an integral view of man.

Here it clearly appears that the theology of the body, which we derive from those key texts of Christ's words, becomes the fundamental method of pedagogy, that is, of man's education from the point of view of the body, in full consideration of his masculinity and femininity. That pedagogy can be understood under the aspect of a specific "spirituality of the body." In its masculinity or femininity the body is given as a task to the human spirit (this was expressed in a stupendous way by St. Paul in his own characteristic language). By means of an adequate maturity of the spirit it too becomes a sign of the person, which the person is conscious of, and authentic "matter" in the communion of persons. In other words, through his spiritual maturity, man discovers the nuptial meaning proper to the body.

Christ's words in the Sermon on the Mount indicate that lust in itself does not reveal that meaning to man, but on the contrary dims and obscures it. Purely biological knowledge of the functions of the body as an organism, connected with the masculinity and femininity of the human person, is capable of helping to discover the true nuptial meaning of the body only if it is accompanied by an adequate spiritual maturity of the human person. Otherwise, such knowledge can have quite the opposite effect. This is confirmed by many experiences of our time.

From this point of view it is necessary to consider prudently the pronouncements of the modern Church. Their adequate understanding and interpretation, as well as their practical application (that is, pedagogy) demand that deep theology of the body which we derive mainly from the key words of Christ. As for the pronouncements of the Church in modern times, it is necessary to study the chapter entitled, "The Dignity of Marriage and the Family," of *Gaudium et Spes (GS,* part II, chap. 1) and, subsequently, Paul VI's Encyclical *Humanae Vitae.* Without any doubt, the words of Christ, which we have analyzed at great length, had no other purpose than to emphasize the dignity of marriage and the family. Hence there is a fundamental convergence between them and the content of both the above-mentioned statements of the modern Church. Christ was speaking to the man of all times and places. The pronouncements of the Church aim at applying Christ's words to the here and now. Therefore they must be reread according to the key of that theology and that pedagogy which find roots and support in Christ's words.

It is difficult here to make a total analysis of the cited pronouncements of the supreme Magisterium of the Church. We will confine ourselves to quoting some passages. Here is how the Second Vatican Council —placing among the most urgent problems of the Church in the modern world the dignity of marriage and the family—characterizes the situation that exists in this area: "The excellence of this institution is not everywhere reflected with equal brilliance, since polygamy, the plague of divorce, so-called free love and other disfigurements have an obscuring effect. In addition, married love is too often profaned by excessive self-love, the worship of pleasure and illicit practices against human generation" *(GS* 47). Setting forth this last problem in *Humanae Vitae,* Paul VI writes, among other things: "Another thing that gives cause for alarm is that a man who grows accustomed to the use of contraceptive methods may forget the reverence due to a woman, and, disregarding her physical and emotional equilibrium, reduce her to being a mere instrument for the satisfaction of his own desires, no longer considering her as his partner whom he should surround with care and affection" *(HV* 17).

Are we not here in the sphere of the same concern which once dictated Christ's words on the unity and indissolubility of marriage, as well as those of the Sermon on the Mount, concerning purity of heart and mastery of the lust of the flesh, words that were later developed with so much acuteness by the Apostle Paul?

In the same spirit, speaking of the demands of Christian morality, the author of *Humanae Vitae* presents at the same time the possibility of fulfilling them when he writes: "The mastery of instinct by one's reason and free will undoubtedly demands an asceticism"—Paul VI uses this term— "so that the affective manifestations of conjugal life may be in keeping with right order, in particular with regard to the observance of periodic continence. Yet this discipline which is proper to the purity of married couples, far from harming conjugal love, rather confers on it a higher human value. It demands a continual effort [this effort was called above 'asceticism'], yet, thanks to its beneficent influence, husband and wife fully develop their personalities, [and] enrich each other with spiritual values.... It favors attention for one's partner, helps both parties to drive out selfishness, the enemy of true love, and deepens their sense of responsibility..." *(HV 21)*.

Let us pause on these few passages. Especially the last one, they clearly show how indispensable the theology of the body is for an adequate understanding of the pronouncements of the Magisterium of the modern Church. We sought the foundations of this theology especially in the words of Christ himself. As we have already said, that theology becomes the fundamental method of the whole Christian pedagogy of the body. Referring to the words quoted, it can be affirmed that the purpose of the pedagogy of the body lies in ensuring that the "affective manifestations," particularly those "proper to conjugal life," be in conformity with the moral order, or, in a word, with the dignity of the person. In these words the problem returns of the mutual relationship between eros and ethos, which we have already dealt with. Theology, understood as a method of the pedagogy of the body, prepares us also for further reflections on the sacramentality of human life and especially married life.

The Gospel of purity of heart, yesterday and today—with this phrase we conclude this cycle of our considerations before going on to the next one. The basis of the next series of analyses will be Christ's words on the resurrection of the body. But we still wish to devote some attention to "the need of creating an atmosphere favorable to education in chastity," which Paul VI's encyclical deals with (cf. *HV* 22). We wish to focus these observations on the problem of the ethos of the body in works of artistic culture, referring especially to the situations we encounter in modern life.

General audience of April 8, 1981

The Human Body: Subject of Works of Art

In our preceding reflections we have analyzed both Christ's words, in which he referred to the beginning, and those of the Sermon on the Mount when he referred to the human heart. In these reflections we have systematically tried to show how the dimension of man's personal subjectivity is an indispensable element present in theological hermeneutics, which we must discover and presuppose at the basis of the problem of the human body. Therefore, not only the objective reality of the body, but far more, as it seems, subjective consciousness and also the subjective experience of the body, enter at every step into the structure of the biblical texts. Therefore they must be considered and find their reflection in theology. Consequently theological hermeneutics must always take these two aspects into account. We cannot consider the body an objective reality outside the personal subjectivity of man, of human beings, male and female. Nearly all the problems of the ethos of the body are bound up at the same time with its ontological identification as the body of the person. They are also bound up with the content and quality of the subjective experience, that is, of the "life" both of one's own body and in its interpersonal relations, especially in the perennial man-woman relationship. Without any doubt, the words of First Thessalonians—in which the author exhorts us to "control our own body in holiness and honor" (that is, the whole problem of "purity of heart")—indicate these two dimensions.

These dimensions directly concern concrete, living men, their attitudes and behavior. Works of culture, especially of art, enable those dimensions of "being a body" and "experiencing the body" to extend, in a way, outside these living men. Man meets the "reality of the body" and "experiences the body" even when it becomes a subject of creative activity, a work of art, a content of culture. Generally speaking, it must be recognized that this contact takes place on the plane of aesthetic experience. In this plane, it is a question of viewing the work of art (in Greek *aisthá nomai:* I look, I observe). Therefore, in the given case, it is a question of the objectivized body, outside its ontological identity, in a different way and according to the criteria characteristic of artistic activity. Yet the man who is admitted to viewing in this way is a priori deeply bound up with the meaning of the prototype, or model. In this case the prototype is himself— the living man and the living human body. He is too deeply bound up with it to be able to detach and separate completely that act, substantially an aesthetic one, of the work in itself and of its contemplation from those dynamisms or reactions of behavior and from the evaluations which direct that first experience and that first way of living. By its very nature, this looking is aesthetic. It cannot be completely isolated, in man's subjective conscience, from that looking of which Christ spoke in the Sermon on the Mount, warning against lust.

Therefore, in this way the whole sphere of aesthetic experiences is, at the same time, in the area of the ethos of the body. Rightly we must think here too of the necessity of creating a climate favorable to purity. This climate can be threatened not only in the way in which the relations and society of living men take place, but also in the area of the objectivizations characteristic of works of culture; in the area of social communications, when it is a question of the spoken or written word; in the area of the image, that is, of representation and vision, both in the traditional meaning of this term and in the modern one. In this way we reach the various fields and products of artistic, plastic and dramatic culture, as also that based on modern audio-visual techniques. In this field, a vast and very differentiated one, we must ask ourselves a question in the light of the ethos of the body, outlined in the analyses made so far on the human body as an object of culture.

First of all it must be noted that the human body is a perennial object of culture, in the widest meaning of the term. This is for the simple reason that man himself is a subject of culture, and in his cultural and creative activity he involves his humanity, including his body. In these reflections, however, we must restrict the concept of object of culture, limiting ourselves to the concept understood as the subject of works of culture and in particular of works of art. It is a question, in a word, of the thematic nature, that is, of the "objectivation" of the body in these works. However, some distinctions must be made here at once, even if by way of example. One thing is the living human body, of man and of woman, which creates in itself the object of art and the work of art (for example, in the theater, in the ballet and, to a certain point, also in the course of a concert). Another thing is the body as the model of the work of art, as in the plastic arts, sculpture or painting. Is it possible to also put films or the photographic art in a wide sense on the same level? It seems so, although from the point of view of the body as object-theme, a quite essential difference takes place in this case. In painting or sculpture the human body always remains a model, undergoing specific elaboration on the part of the artist. In the film, and even more in the photographic art, it is not the model that is transfigured, but the living man is reproduced. In this case man, the human body, is not a model for the work of art, but the object of a reproduction obtained by means of suitable techniques.

It should be pointed out right away that the above-mentioned distinction is important from the point of view of the ethos of the body in works of culture. It should be added at once that when artistic reproduction becomes the content of representation and transmission (on television or in films), it loses, in a way, its fundamental contact with the human body, of which it is a reproduction. It often becomes an anonymous object, just like an anonymous photographic document published in illustrated magazines, or an image diffused on the screens of the whole world. This anonymity is the effect of the "propagation" of the image-reproduction of the human body, objectivized first with the help of the techniques of reproduction. As has been recalled above, this seems to be essentially differentiated from the transfiguration of the model typical of the work of art, especially in the plastic arts. This anonymity (which, moreover, is a way of veiling or hiding the identity of the person reproduced) also constitutes a specific problem from the point of view of the ethos of the human body in works of culture, especially in the modern works of mass culture, as it is called.

Let us confine ourselves today to these preliminary considerations, which have a fundamental meaning for the ethos of the human body in works of artistic culture. Subsequently these considerations will make us aware of how closely bound they are to the words which Christ spoke in the Sermon on the Mount, comparing "looking lustfully" with "adultery committed in the heart." The extension of these words to the area of artistic culture is especially important, insofar as it is a question of "creating an atmosphere favorable to chastity," which Paul VI spoke of in *Humanae Vitae*. Let us try to understand this subject in a deep and fundamental way.

General audience of April 15, 1981

Reflections on the Ethos of the Human Body in Works of Artistic Culture

With regard to Christ's words in the Sermon on the Mount, let us now reflect on the problem of the ethos of the human body in works of artistic culture. This problem has very deep roots. It is opportune to recall here the series of analyses carried out in connection with Christ's reference to the beginning, and subsequently to the reference he made to the human heart, in the Sermon on the Mount. The human body—the naked human body in the whole truth of its masculinity and femininity—has the meaning of a gift of the person to the person. The ethos of the body, that is, the ethical norms that govern its nakedness, because of the dignity of the personal subject, is closely connected with that system of reference. This is understood as the nuptial system, in which the giving of one party meets the appropriate and adequate response of the other party to the gift. This response decides the reciprocity of the gift.

The artistic objectivization of the human body in its male and female nakedness, in order to make it first of all a model and then the subject of the work of art, is always to a certain extent a going outside of this original and, for the body, its specific configuration of interpersonal donation. In a way, that constitutes an uprooting of the human body from this configuration and its transfer to the dimension of artistic objectivation—the specific dimension of the work of art or of the reproduction typical of the film and photographic techniques of our time.

In each of these dimensions—and in a different way in each one—the human body loses that deeply subjective meaning of the gift. It becomes an object destined for the knowledge of many. This happens in such a way that those who look at the body, assimilate or even, in a way, take possession of what evidently exists, of what in fact should exist essentially at the level of a gift, made by the person to the person, not just in the image but in the living man. Actually, that "taking possession" already happens at another level—that is, at the level of the object of the transfiguration or artistic reproduction. However it is impossible not to perceive that from the point of view of the ethos of the body, deeply understood, a problem arises here. This is a very delicate problem, which has its levels of intensity according to various motives and circumstances both as regards artistic activity and as regards knowledge of the work of art or of its reproduction. The fact that this problem is raised does not mean that the human body, in its nakedness, cannot become a subject of works of art, but only that this problem is not purely aesthetic, nor morally indifferent.

In our preceding analyses (especially with regard to Christ's reference to the "beginning"), we devoted a great deal of space to the meaning of shame. We tried to understand the difference between the situation and the state of original innocence, in which "they were both naked, and were not ashamed" (Gn 2:25), and, subsequently, between the situation and the state of sinfulness. In that state there arose between man and woman, together with shame, the specific necessity of privacy with regard to their own bodies.

In the heart of man, subject to lust, this necessity serves, even indirectly, to ensure the gift and the possibility of mutual donation. This necessity also forms man's way of acting as "an object of culture," in the widest meaning of the term. If culture shows an explicit tendency to cover the nakedness of the human body, it certainly does so not only for climatic reasons, but also in relation to the process of growth of man's personal sensitivity. The anonymous nakedness of the man-object contrasts with the progress of the truly human culture of morals. It is probably possible to confirm this also in the life of so-called primitive populations. The process of refining personal human sensitivity is certainly a factor and fruit of culture.

Beyond the need of shame, that is, of the privacy of one's own body (on which the biblical sources give such precise information in Genesis 3), there is a deeper norm. This norm is the gift, directed toward the very depths of the personal subject or toward the other person—especially in the man-woman relationship according to the perennial norms regulating the mutual donation. In this way, in the processes of human culture understood in the wide sense, we note—even in man's state of hereditary sinfulness—quite an explicit continuity of the nuptial meaning of the body in its masculinity and femininity. That original shame, known already from the first chapters of the Bible, is a permanent element of culture and morals. It belongs to the genesis of the ethos of the human body.

The person of developed sensitivity overcomes the limit of that shame with difficulty and interior resistance. This is seen clearly even in situations which justify the necessity of undressing the body, such as in the case of medical examinations or operations. Mention should also be made especially of other circumstances, such as those of concentration camps or places of extermination, where the violation of bodily shame is a method used deliberately to destroy personal sensitivity and the sense of human dignity. The same rule is confirmed everywhere, though in different ways. Following personal sensitivity, man does not wish to become an object for others through his own anonymous nakedness. Nor does he wish the other to become an object for him in a similar way. Evidently he does not wish this to the extent to which he lets himself be guided by the sense of the dignity of the human body. Various motives can induce, incite and even press man to act in a way contrary to the requirements of the dignity of the human body, a dignity connected with personal sensitivity. It cannot be forgotten that the fundamental interior situation of historical man is the state of threefold lust (cf. 1 Jn 2:16). This state, especially the lust of the flesh, makes itself felt in various ways, both in the interior impulses of the human heart and in the whole climate of interhuman relations and social morals.

We cannot forget this, not even when it is a question of the broad sphere of artistic culture, particularly that of visual and spectacular character, as also when it is a question of mass culture. This is so significant for our times and connected with the use of the media of audiovisual communication. A question arises: when and in what case is this sphere of man's activity—from the point of view of the ethos of the body—regarded as pornovision, just as in literature some writings were and are often regarded as pornography (this second term is an older one).

Both take place when the limit of shame is overstepped, that is, of personal sensitivity with regard to what is connected with the human body with its nakedness. They take place when in the work of art or by means of the media of audiovisual reproduction the right to the privacy of the body in its masculinity or femininity is violated. In the last analysis, they take place when those deep governing rules of the gift and of mutual donation, which are inscribed in this femininity and masculinity through the whole structure of the human being, are violated. This deep inscription—or rather incision—decides the nuptial meaning of the human body, that is, of the fundamental call it receives to form the "communion of persons" and take part in it.

At this point we will break off our consideration, which we intend to continue next Wednesday. It should be noted that observance or non-observance of these norms, so deeply connected with man's personal sensitivity, cannot be a matter of indifference for the problem of creating a climate favorable to chastity in life and social education.

General audience of April 22, 1981

Art Must Not Violate the Right to Privacy

We have already dedicated a series of reflections to the meaning of the words Christ spoke in the Sermon on the Mount, in which he exhorts to purity of heart, calling attention even to the "lustful look." We cannot forget these words of Christ even when it is a question of the vast sphere of artistic culture, especially that of a visual and spectacular character, and when it is a question of the sphere of "mass" culture. Connected with the use of the audiovisual communications media, this culture is so significant for our times. We said recently that the above-mentioned sphere of activity is sometimes accused of pornovision, just as the accusation of pornography is made with regard to literature. Both facts take place by going beyond the limit of shame, that is, of personal sensitivity with regard to what is connected with the human body and its nakedness. It happens when in the artistic work by means of the media of audiovisual production the right to the privacy of the body in its masculinity or femininity is violated. In the last analysis, it happens when that intimate and constant destination to the gift and to mutual donation, which is inscribed in that femininity and masculinity through the whole structure of the being-man, is violated. That deep inscription, or rather incision, decides the nuptial meaning of the body, that is, the fundamental call it receives to form a communion of persons and to participate in it.

It is obvious that in works of art, or in the products of audiovisual artistic reproduction, the above-mentioned constant destination to the gift, that is, that deep inscription of the meaning of the human body, can be violated only in the intentional order of the reproduction and the representation. As has already been said, it is a question of the human body as model or subject. However, if the sense of shame and personal sensitivity is offended in these cases, that happens because of their transfer to the dimension of social communication. Therefore, it is owing to the fact that what, in man's rightful feeling, belongs and must belong strictly to the interpersonal relationship becomes, so to speak, public property. As has already been pointed out, the interpersonal relationship is linked with the communion of persons itself. In its sphere, it corresponds to the interior truth of man, and so also to the complete truth about man.

At this point it is not possible to agree with the representatives of so-called naturalism. They demand the right to "everything that is human" in works of art and in the products of artistic reproduction. They affirm that they act in this way in the name of the realistic truth about man. It is precisely this truth about man—the whole truth about man—that makes it necessary to consider both the sense of the privacy of the body and the consistency of the gift connected with the masculinity and femininity of the body itself, in which the mystery of man, peculiar to the interior structure of the person, is reflected. This truth about man must also be considered in the artistic order, if we want to speak of a full realism.

In this case, it is evident that the deep governing rule related to the communion of persons is in profound agreement with the vast and differentiated area of communication. As we stated in the preceding analyses (in which we referred to Genesis 2:25), the human body in its nakedness becomes the source of a particular interpersonal communication. This happens when the body is understood as a manifestation of the person and as his gift, that is, a sign of trust and donation to the other person. The other person is conscious of the gift, and is chosen and resolved to respond to it in an equally personal way.

As has already been said, this is a particular communication in humanity itself. That interpersonal communication penetrates deeply into the system of communion *(communio personarum)*. At the same time it grows from it and develops correctly within it. The body in its nakedness expresses precisely "the element" of the gift. Precisely because of the great value of the body in this system of interpersonal communion, to make the body in its nakedness an object-subject of the work of art or of the audiovisual reproduction, is a problem which is not only aesthetic, but also ethical. That "element of the gift" is, so to speak, suspended in the dimension of an unknown reception and an unforeseen response. Thereby it is in a way threatened in the order of intention, in the sense that it may become an anonymous object of appropriation, an object of abuse. Precisely for this reason the integral truth about man constitutes in this case the foundation of the norm according to which the good or evil of determined actions, of behavior, of morals and situations, is modeled. The truth about man, about what is particularly personal and interior in him—precisely because of his body and his sex (femininity-masculinity)—creates here precise limits which it is unlawful to exceed.

These limits must be recognized and observed by the artist who makes the human body the object, model or subject of the work of art or of the audiovisual reproduction. Neither he nor others who are responsible in this field have the right to demand, propose or bring it about that other people, invited, exhorted or admitted to see, to contemplate the image, should violate those limits together with them, or because of them. It is a question of the image, in which that which in itself constitutes the content and the deeply personal value, that which belongs to the order of the gift and of the mutual donation of person to person, is, as a subject, uprooted from its own authentic substratum. It becomes, through social communication, an object and what is more, in a way, an anonymous object.

As can be seen from what is said above, the whole problem of pornovision and pornography is not the effect of a puritanical mentality or of a narrow moralism, just as it is not the product of a thought imbued with Manichaeism. It is a question of an extremely important, fundamental sphere of values. Before it, man cannot remain indifferent because of the dignity of humanity, the personal character and the eloquence of the human body. By means of works of art and the activity of the audiovisual media, all those contents and values can be modeled and studied. But they can also be distorted and destroyed in the heart of man. As can be seen, we find ourselves continually within the orbit of the words Christ spoke in the Sermon on the Mount. Also the problems which we are dealing with here must be examined in the light of those words, which consider a look that springs from lust as "adultery committed in the heart."

It seems, therefore, that reflection on these problems, which is important to create a climate favorable to education to chastity, constitutes an indispensable appendage to all the preceding analyses which we have dedicated to this subject in the course of these Wednesday meetings.

General audience of April 29, 1981

Ethical Responsibilities in Art

In the Sermon on the Mount Christ spoke the words to which we have devoted a series of reflections for almost a year. Explaining to his listeners the specific meaning of the commandment, "You shall not commit adultery," Christ expressed himself as follows: "But I say to you that everyone who looks at a woman lustfully has already committed adultery with her in his heart" (Mt 5:28). The above-mentioned words seem to refer also to the vast spheres of human culture, especially those of artistic activity, which we have recently dealt with in the course of some of the Wednesday meetings. Today it is opportune for us to dedicate the final part of these reflections to the problem of the relationship between the ethos of the image—or of the description—and the ethos of the viewing and listening, reading or other forms of cognitive reception with which one meets the content of the work of art or of audiovision understood in the broad sense.

Here we return once more to the problem already mentioned: whether and to what extent can the human body, in the whole visible truth of its masculinity and femininity, be a subject of works of art and thereby a subject of that specific social communication for which these works are intended? This question referred even more to modern mass culture, connected with the audiovisual media. Can the human body be such a model-subject? We know that this is connected with that objectivity "without choice" which we first called anonymity. This seems to bring with it a serious potential threat to the whole sphere of meanings, peculiar to the body of man and woman because of the personal character of the human subject and the character of communion of interpersonal relations.

One can add at this point that the expressions pornography and pornovision appeared in language relatively late, despite their ancient etymology. The traditional Latin terminology used the word *obscaena,* indicating in this way everything that should not appear before the eyes of spectators, what should be surrounded with opportune discretion, what cannot be presented to human view without any choice.

Asking the preceding question, we realize that, *de facto,* during whole periods of human culture and artistic activity, the human body has been and is such a model-subject of visual works of art. Similarly, the whole sphere of love between man and woman, and, connected with it, also the mutual donation of masculinity and femininity in their corporeal expression, has been, is and will be a subject of literary narrative. Such narration found its place even in the Bible, especially in the text of the Song of Songs, which it will be opportune to take up again on another occasion. It should be noted that in the history of literature or art, in the history of human culture, this subject seems quite frequent and is especially important. In fact, it concerns a problem which in itself is great and important. We showed this right from the beginning of our reflections, following the scriptural texts. These reveal to us the proper dimension of this problem, that is, the dignity of man in his masculine and feminine corporeity, and the nuptial meaning of femininity and masculinity, inscribed in the whole interior—and at the same time visible—structure of the human person.

Our preceding reflections did not intend to question the right to this subject. They aim merely at proving that its treatment is connected with a special responsibility which is not only artistic, but also ethical in nature. The artist who undertakes that theme in any sphere of art or through audiovisual media, must be aware of the full truth of the object, of the whole scale of values connected with it. He must not only take them into account in *abstracto,* but also live them correctly himself. This corresponds also to that principle of purity of heart, which in determined cases must be transferred from the existential sphere of attitudes and ways of behavior to the intentional sphere of creation or artistic reproduction.

It seems that the process of this creation aims not only at making the model concrete (and in a way at a new "materializing"), but at the same time, at expressing in such concretizing what can be called the creative idea of the artist. This manifests his interior world of values, and so also his living the truth of his object. In this process a characteristic transfiguration of the model or of the material takes place and, in particular, of what is man, the human body in the whole truth of its masculinity or femininity. (From this point of view, as we have already mentioned, there is a very important difference, for example, between the painting or sculpture and the photograph or film.) Invited by the artist to look at his work, the viewer communicates not only with the concretizing, and so, in a sense, with a new "materializing" of the model or of the material. But at the same time he communicates with the truth of the object which the author, in his artistic "materializing," has succeeded in expressing with his own specific media.

In the course of the various eras, beginning from antiquity—and above all in the great period of Greek classical art—there are works of art whose subject is the human body in its nakedness. The contemplation of this makes it possible to concentrate, in a way, on the whole truth of man, on the dignity and the beauty—also the "suprasensual" beauty—of his masculinity and femininity. These works bear within them, almost hidden, an element of sublimation. This leads the viewer, through the body, to the whole personal mystery of man. In contact with these works, where we do not feel drawn by their content to "looking lustfully," which the Sermon on the Mount speaks about, we learn in a way that nuptial meaning of the body which corresponds to, and is the measure of, "purity of heart." But there are also works of art, and perhaps even more often reproductions, which arouse objection in the sphere of man's personal sensitivity. This is not because of their object, since the human body in itself always has its inalienable dignity. But it is because of the quality or way of its reproduction, portrayal or artistic representation. The various coefficients of the work or the reproduction can be decisive with regard to that way and that quality, as well as multiple circumstances, often more of a technical nature than an artistic one.

It is well known that through all these elements the fundamental intentionality of the work of art or of the product of the respective media becomes, in a way, accessible to the viewer, as to the listener or the reader. If our personal sensitivity reacts with objection and disapproval, it is because in that fundamental intentionality, together with the concretizing of man and his body, we discover as indispensable for the work of art or its reproduction, his simultaneous reduction to the level of an object. He becomes an object of "enjoyment," intended for the satisfaction of concupiscence itself. This is contrary to the dignity of man also in the intentional order of art and reproduction. By analogy, the same thing must be applied to the various fields of artistic activity—according to the respective specific character—as also to the various audiovisual media.

Paul VI's Encyclical *Humanae Vitae* emphasizes the "need to create an atmosphere favorable to education in chastity" (n. 22). With this he intends to affirm that the way of living the human body in the whole truth of its masculinity and femininity must correspond to the dignity of this body and to its significance in building the communion of persons. It can be said that this is one of the fundamental dimensions of human culture, understood as an affirmation which ennobles everything that is human. Therefore we have dedicated this brief sketch to the problem which, in synthesis, could be called that of the ethos of the image. It is a question of the image which serves as an extraordinary "visualization" of man, and which must be understood more or less directly. The sculpted or painted image expresses man visually; the play or the ballet expresses him visually in another way, and the film in another way. Even literary work, in its own way, aims at arousing interior images, using the riches of the imagination or of human memory. So what we have called the ethos of the image cannot be considered apart from the correlative element, which we would have to call the ethos of seeing. Between the two elements the whole process of communication is contained, independently of the vastness of the circles described by this communication, which, in this case, is always social.

The creation of the atmosphere favorable to education in chastity contains these two elements. It concerns a reciprocal circuit which takes place between the image and the seeing, between the ethos of the image and the ethos of seeing. The creation of the image, in the broad and differentiated sense of the term, imposes on the author, artist or reproducer, obligations not only of an aesthetic, but also of an ethical nature. In the same way, "looking," understood according to the same broad analogy, imposes obligations on the one who is the recipient of the work.

True and responsible artistic activity aims at overcoming the anonymity of the human body as an object "without choice." As has already been said, it seeks through creative effort such an artistic expression of the truth about man in his feminine and masculine corporeity, which is, so to speak, assigned as a task to the viewer and, in the wider range, to every recipient of the work. It depends on him, in his turn, to decide whether to make his own effort to approach this truth, or to remain merely a superficial consumer of impressions, that is, one who exploits the meeting with the anonymous body-subject only at the level of sensuality which, by itself, reacts to its object precisely without choice.

We conclude here this important chapter of our reflections on the theology of the body, whose starting point was the words Christ spoke in the Sermon on the Mount. These words are valid for the man of all times, for the historical man, and for each one of us.

The reflections on the theology of the body would not be complete, however, if we did not consider other words of Christ, namely, those when he referred to the future resurrection. So we propose to devote the next cycle of our considerations to them.

General audience of May 6, 1981

NOTES

General audience of December 17, 1980

[68] "Paul never, like the Greeks, identified 'sinful flesh' with the physical body....

"Flesh, then, in Paul is not to be identified with sex or with the physical body. It is closer to the Hebrew thought of the physical personality—the self including physical and psychical elements as vehicles of the outward life and the lower levels of experience.

"It is man in his humanness with all the limitations, moral weakness, vulnerability, creatureliness and morality, which being human implies....

"Man is vulnerable both to evil and to God; he is a vehicle, a channel, a dwelling place, a temple, a battlefield (Paul uses each metaphor) for good and evil.

"Which shall possess, indwell, master him—whether sin, evil, the spirit that now works in the children of disobedience, or Christ, the Holy Spirit, faith, grace—it is for each man to choose.

"That he *can* so choose brings to view the other side of Paul's conception of human nature, man's *conscience* and the human *spirit*" (R. E. O. White, *Biblical Ethics* [Exeter: Paternoster Press, 1979], pp. 135-138).

⁶⁹ The interpretation of the Greek word *sarx* (flesh) in Paul's letters depends on the context of the letter. In Galatians, for example, at least two distinct meanings of *sarx* can be specified.

Writing to the Galatians, Paul was fighting two dangers which threatened the young Christian community.

On the one hand, converts from Judaism were trying to convince converts from paganism to accept circumcision, which was obligatory in Judaism. Paul reproaches them with "wanting to make a good showing in the flesh," that is, of restoring hope in the circumcision of the flesh. So "flesh" in this context (Gal 3:1-5, 12; 6:12-18) means "circumcision," as the symbol of a new submission to the laws of Judaism.

The second danger in the young Galatian Church came from the influence of the "Pneumatics" who understood the work of the Holy Spirit as the divinization of man rather than as a power operating in an ethical sense. That led them to underestimate moral principles. Writing to them, Paul calls "flesh" everything that brings man closer to the object of his lust and entices him with the tempting promise of a life that is apparently fuller (cf. Gal 5:13; 6:10).

Sarx, therefore, "makes a good showing" of the "Law" as well as of its infraction, and in both cases promises what it cannot fulfill.

Paul distinguishes explicitly between the object of the action and *sarx*. The center of the decision is not in the flesh: "Walk by the Spirit, and do not gratify the desires of the flesh" (Gal 5:16).

Man falls into the slavery of the flesh when he trusts in the flesh and in what it promises (in the sense of the "Law" or of infraction of the law). (Cf. F. Mussner, *Der Galaterbrief, Herders Theolog. Kommentar zum NT,* IX [Freiburg: Herder, 1974), p. 367; R. Jewett, *Paul's Anthropological Terms, A Study of Their Use in Conflict Settings, Arbeiten zur Geschichte des antiken Judentums und des Urchistentums,* X [Leiden: Brill, 1971], pp. 95-106).

⁷⁰ In his letters Paul stresses the dramatic character of what is going on in the world. Since men, through their fault, have forgotten God, "therefore God gave them up in the lusts of their hearts to impurity" (Rom 1:24), from which there

also comes all moral disorder, which distorts both sexual life (cf. Rom 1:24-27), the operation of social and economic life (cf. Rom 1:29-32) and even cultural life; in fact, "though they know God's decree that those who do such things deserve to die, they not only do them but approve those who practice them" (Rom 1:32).

From the moment that, through one man, sin came into the world (cf. Rom 5:12), "the god of this world has blinded the minds of the unbelievers, to keep them from seeing the light of the Gospel of the glory of Christ" (2 Cor 4:4). Therefore too "the wrath of God is revealed from heaven against all ungodliness and wickedness of men who by their wickedness suppress the truth" (Rom 1:1).

Therefore "the creation waits with eager longing for the revealing of the sons of God...because the creation itself will be set free from its bondage to decay and obtain the glorious liberty of the children of God" (Rom 8:19-21), that liberty for which "Christ has set us free" (Gal 5:1).

The concept of "world" in St. John has various meanings: in his first letter, the world is the place in which the threefold lust is manifested (cf. 1 Jn 2:15-16) and in which the false prophets and adversaries of Christ try to seduce the faithful. But Christians defeat the world thanks to their faith (cf. 1 Jn 5:4). The world, in fact, passes away with its lust, and he who does the will of God lives forever (cf. 1 Jn 2:17).

(Cf. P. Grelot, "Monde," *Dictionnaire de Spiritualité, Ascétique et mystique, doctrine et histoire,* fascicules 68-69, Beauchesne, p. 1628ff. Furthermore, J. Mateos J. Barreto, *Vocabulario teologico del Evangelio de Juan* [Madrid: Edic. Cristianidad, 1980], pp. 211-215).

[71] Exegetes point out that, although for Paul the concept of "fruit" is sometimes applied also to the "works of the flesh" (e.g., Rom 6:21; 7:5), yet "the fruit of the Spirit" is never called "work."

For Paul, "works" are the specific acts of man (or that in which Israel lays hope, without a reason), for which he will be answerable before God.

Paul also avoids the term "virtue," *arete;* it is found only once, in a very general sense, in Phillipians 4:8. In the Greek world this word had a too anthropocentric meaning; the Stoics especially stressed the self-sufficiency or *autarchy* of virtue.

On the other hand, the term "fruit of the Spirit" emphasizes God's action in man. This "fruit" grows in him like the gift of a life whose only Author is God. Man can, at most, promote suitable conditions, in order that the fruit may grow and ripen.

The fruit of the Spirit, in the singular form, corresponds in some way to the "justice" of the Old Testament, which embraces the whole of life in conformity with God's will; it also corresponds, in a certain sense, to the "virtue" of the Stoics, which was indivisible. We see this, for example, in Ephesians 5:9-11: "The fruit of light is found in all that is good and right and true.... Take no part in the unfruitful works of darkness...."

However, "the fruit of the Spirit" is different both from "justice" and from "virtue," because "in all its manifestations and differentiations which are seen in the lists of virtues" it contains the effect of the action of the Spirit, which, in the Church, is the foundation and fulfillment of the Christian's life.

Cf. H. Schlier, "Der Brief an die Galater," *Meyer's Kommentar* (Göttingen: Vandenhoeck-Ruprecht, 1971-5), pp. 255-264; O. Bauernfeind, "Arete," *Theological Dictionary of the New Testament,* Vol. 1, ed. G. Kittel, G. Bromley (Grand Rapids: Eerdmans, 1978-9), p. 460; W. Tatarkiewicz, *Historia Filozofii* (Warszawa: PWN, 1970), p. 121; E. Kamlah, "Die Form der katalogischen Paränese im Neuen Testament," *Wissenschaftliche Untersuchungen zum Neuen Testament,* 7 (Tübingen: Mhr, 1964), p. 14.

General audience of January 14, 1981

[72] Without going into the detailed discussions of the exegetes, it should, however, be pointed out that the Greek expression *to heautou skeuos* can refer also to the wife (cf. 1 Pt 3:7).

General audience of March 18, 1981

[73] In the Greco-Roman period *eusebeia* or *pietas* generally referred to the veneration of the gods (as "devotion"), but it still kept its broader original meaning of respect for vital structures.

Eusebeia defined the mutual behavior of relatives, relations between husband and wife, and also the attitude due by the legions toward Caesar or by slaves to their masters.

In the New Testament, only the later writings apply *eusebeia* to Christians; in the older writings this term characterizes "good pagans" (Acts 10:2, 7; 17:23).

And so the Greek *eusebeia,* as also the *donum pietatis,* while they certainly refer to divine veneration, have a wide basis in the connotation of interpersonal relations (cf. W. Foerster, "Eusebeia," *Theological Dictionary of the New Testament,* Vol. 7, ed. G. Kittel, G. Bromley [Grand Rapids: Eerdmans, 1971], pp. 177-182).

[74] This version of the Vulgate, retained by the Neo-Vulgate and by the liturgy, quoted several times by Augustine *(De S. Virg.,* par. 43; *Confess.* VI, 11; X, 29; *Serm.* CLX, 7), changes, however, the meaning of the original Greek, which can be translated as follows: "Knowing that I would not have obtained it [Wisdom] otherwise, if God had not granted it to me...."

The Resurrection of the Body

Marriage and Celibacy in the Light
of the Resurrection of the Body

After a rather long pause, today we will resume the meditations which have been going on for some time, which we have called reflections on the theology of the body. In continuing, it is opportune to go back to the words of the Gospel in which Christ referred to the resurrection. These words are of fundamental importance for understanding marriage in the Christian sense and also the renunciation of conjugal life for the kingdom of heaven.

The complex casuistry of the Old Testament in the field of marriage not only drove the Pharisees to go to Christ to pose to him the problem of the indissolubility of marriage (cf. Mt 19:3-9; Mk 10:2-12). Another time, it also drove the Sadducees to question him about the so-called levirate law.[75] This conversation is harmoniously reported by the synoptic Gospels (cf. Mt 22:24-30; Mk 12:18-27; Lk 20:27-40). Although all three accounts are almost identical, we note some slight yet significant differences. Since the conversation contains elements which have an essential significance for the theology of the body and since it is reported in three versions, those of Matthew, Mark and Luke, a deeper analysis is necessary.

There are two other important conversations, namely, the one in which Christ referred to the "beginning" (cf. Mt 19:3-9; Mk 10:2-12), and the other in which an appeal was made to man's inner self (to the heart), indicating desire and the lust of the flesh as a source of sin (cf. Mt 5:27-32). Alongside these two conversations, the one which we now propose to analyze constitutes, I would say, the third element of the triptych of the enunciations of Christ himself. It is a triptych of words that are essential and constitutive for the theology of the body. In this conversation Jesus referred to the resurrection, thus revealing a completely new dimension of the mystery of man.

The revelation of this dimension of the body, stupendous in its content—and yet connected with the Gospel reread as a whole and in depth—emerges in the conversation with the Sadducees, "who say that there is no resurrection" (Mt 22:23).[76] They had come to Christ to set before him an argument which in their judgment confirmed the soundness of their position. This argument was to contradict "the hypothesis of the resurrection." The Sadducees' argument is the following: "Teacher, Moses wrote for us that if a man's brother dies and leaves a wife, but leaves no child, the man must take the wife, and raise up children for his brother" (Mk 12:19). The Sadducees were referring here to the so-called levirate law (cf. Dt 25:5-10). Drawing upon the prescription of this ancient law, they presented the following case: "There were seven brothers. The first took a wife, and when he died, he left no children. The second took her, and died, leaving no children, and the third likewise, and the seven left no children. Last of all the woman also died. In the resurrection whose wife will she be? For the seven had her as wife" (Mk 12:20-23).[77]

Christ's reply is one of the answer-keys of the Gospel. Starting from purely human arguments and in contrast with them, it reveals another dimension of the question, that is, the one that corresponds to the wisdom and power of God himself. Similarly, the case had arisen of the tax coin with Caesar's image and of the correct relationship between what is divine and what is human (Caesar's) in the sphere of authority (cf. Mt 22:15-22). This time Jesus replied as follows: "Is not this why you are wrong, that you know neither the Scriptures nor the power of God? For when they rise from the dead, they neither marry nor are given in marriage, but are like angels in heaven" (Mk 12:24-25). This is the fundamental reply to the case, that is, to the problem it contains. Knowing the thoughts of the Sadducees, and realizing their real intentions, Christ subsequently took up again the problem of the possibility of resurrection, denied by the Sadducees themselves: "As for the dead being raised, have you not read in the book of Moses, in the passage about the bush, how God said to him, 'I am the God of Abraham, and the God of Isaac, and the God of Jacob'? He is not a God of the dead, but of the living" (Mk 12:26-27). As we can see, Christ quoted the same Moses to whom the Sadducees had referred, and ended with the affirmation: "You are quite wrong" (Mk 12:27).

Christ repeated this conclusive affirmation even a second time. In fact, he said it the first time at the beginning of his explanation. Then he said: "You are wrong, because you know neither the Scriptures nor the power of God" (Mt 22:29). We read in Mark: "Is not this why you are wrong, that you know neither the Scriptures nor the power of God?" (12:24). In Luke's version (20:27-36), on the contrary, Christ's same answer is without polemical tones, without that, "You are quite wrong." On the other hand, he proclaimed the same thing since in his answer he introduced some elements which are not found either in Matthew or in Mark. Here is the text: "Jesus said to them, 'The sons of this age marry and are given in marriage. But those who are accounted worthy to attain to that age and to the resurrection from the dead neither marry nor are given in marriage, for they cannot die any more, because they are equal to angels and are sons of God, being sons of the resurrection'" (Lk 20:34-36). With regard to the possibility of resurrection, Luke, like the other two synoptics, referred to.Moses, that is, to the passage in Exodus 3:2-6. This passage narrates that the great legislator of the old covenant had heard from the bush, which "was burning, yet not consumed," the following words: "I am the God of your father, the God of Abraham, the God of Isaac, and the God of Jacob" (Ex 3:6). In the same place, when Moses had asked God's name, he had heard the answer: "I am who am" (Ex 3:14).

In this way, therefore, speaking of the future resurrection of the body, Christ referred to the power of the living God.

General audience of November 11, 1981

The Living God Continually Renews the Reality of Life

Christ said to the Sadducees, "You are wrong, because you know neither the Scriptures nor the power of God" (Mt 22:29). Rejecting faith in the future resurrection of the body, they had proposed to him the following case: "Now there were seven brothers among us. The first married and died, and having no children left his wife to his brother" (according to the Mosaic levirate law). "So too the second and third, down to the seventh. After them all, the woman died. In the resurrection, therefore, to which of the seven will she be wife?" (Mt 22:25-28)

Christ answered the Sadducees by stating, at the beginning and at the end of his reply, that they were greatly mistaken, not knowing either the Scriptures or the power of God (cf. Mk 12:24; Mt 22:29). Since the conversation with the Sadducees is reported by all three synoptic Gospels, let us briefly compare the texts in question.

Although it does not refer to the burning bush, Matthew's version (22:24-30) agrees almost completely with Mark's (12:18-25). Both versions contain two essential elements: 1) the enunciation about the future resurrection of the body; 2) the enunciation about the state of the body of risen man.[78] These two elements are also found in Luke (20:27-36).[79] Especially in Matthew and Mark, the first element, concerning the future resurrection of the body, is combined with the words addressed to the Sadducees, according to which they "know neither the Scriptures nor the power of God." This statement deserves particular attention, because in it Christ defined the foundations of faith in the resurrection, to which he had referred in answering the question posed by the Sadducees with the concrete example of the Mosaic levirate law.

Unquestionably, the Sadducees treated the question of resurrection as a type of theory or hypothesis which can be disproved.[80] Jesus first showed them an error of method, that they did not know the Scriptures. Then he showed them an error of substance, that they did not accept what is revealed by the Scriptures. They did not know the power of God, and they did not believe in him who revealed himself to Moses in the burning bush. It is a significant and very precise answer. Here Christ encountered men who considered themselves experts and competent interpreters of the Scriptures. To these men, that is, to the Sadducees, Jesus replied that mere literal knowledge of Scripture is not sufficient. The Scriptures are above all a means to know the power of the living God who reveals himself in them, just as he revealed himself to Moses in the bush. In this revelation he called himself "the God of Abraham, the God of Isaac and the God of Jacob"[81]—of those, therefore, who had been Moses' ancestors in the faith that from the revelation of the living God. They had all been dead for a long time. However, Christ completed the reference to them with the statement that God "is not God of the dead, but of the living." This statement, in which Christ interpreted the words addressed to Moses from the burning bush, can be understood only if one admits the reality of a life which death did not end. Moses' fathers in faith, Abraham, Isaac and Jacob, were living persons for God (cf. Lk 20:38, "for all live for him"), although according to human criteria, they must be numbered among the dead. To reread the Scriptures correctly, and in particular the aforementioned words of God, means to know and accept with faith the power of the Giver of life, who is not bound by the law of death which rules man's earthly history.

It seems that Christ's answer to the Sadducees about the possibility of resurrection,[82] according to the version of all three synoptics, is to be interpreted in this way. The moment would come in which Christ would give the answer on this matter with his own resurrection. However, for now he referred to the testimony of the Old Testament, showing how to discover there the truth about immortality and resurrection. It is necessary to do so not by dwelling only on the sound of the words, but by going back to the power of God which is revealed by those words. The reference to Abraham, Isaac and Jacob in that theophany granted to Moses, of which we read in the Book of Exodus (3:2-6), constitutes a testimony that the living God gives to those who live "for him"—to those who, thanks to his power, have life, even if according to the dimensions of history, it would be necessary to include them among those who have been dead for a long time.

The full significance of this testimony, which Jesus referred to in his conversation with the Sadducees, could be grasped (still only in the light of the Old Testament) in the following way. He who is—he who lives and is Life—is the inexhaustible source of existence and of life, as is revealed at the "beginning," in Genesis (cf. Gn 1:3). Due to sin, physical death has become man's lot (cf. Gn 3:19),[83] and he has been forbidden (cf. Gn 3:22) access to the Tree of Life (the great symbol of the book of Genesis). Yet the living God, making his covenant with man (Abraham, the patriarchs, Moses, Israel), continually renews, in this covenant, the reality of life. He reveals its perspective again and in a certain sense opens access again to the Tree of Life. Along with the covenant, this life, whose source is God himself, is communicated to those men who, as a result of breaking the first covenant, had lost access to the Tree of Life, and, in the dimensions of their earthly history, had been subject to death.

Christ is God's ultimate word on this subject. The covenant, which with him and for him is established between God and mankind, opens an infinite perspective of life. Access to the Tree of Life—according to the original plan of the God of the covenant—is revealed to every man in its definitive fullness. This will be the meaning of the death and resurrection of Christ. This will be the testimony of the paschal mystery. However, the conversation with the Sadducees took place in the pre-paschal phase of Christ's messianic mission. The course of the conversation according to Matthew (22:24-30), Mark (12:18-27), and Luke (20:27-36) manifests that Christ—who had spoken several times, especially in talks with his disciples, of the future resurrection of the Son of Man (cf., e.g., Mt 17:9, 23; 20:19 and parallels)—did not refer to this matter in the conversation with the Sadducees. The reasons are obvious and clear. The discussion was with the Sadducees, "who say that there is no resurrection" (as the evangelist stresses). That is, they questioned its very possibility. At the same time they considered themselves experts on the Old Testament Scriptures, and qualified interpreters of them. That is why Jesus referred to the Old Testament and showed, on its basis, that they did "not know the power of God."[84]

Regarding the possibility of resurrection, Christ referred precisely to that power which goes hand in hand with the testimony of the living God, who is the God of Abraham, of Isaac, of Jacob—and the God of Moses. God, whom the Sadducees "deprived" of this power, was no longer the true God of their fathers, but the God of their hypotheses and interpretations. Christ, on the contrary, had come to bear witness to the God of life in the whole truth of his power which is unfolded upon human life.

General audience of November 18, 1981

The Resurrection and Theological Anthropology

"When they rise from the dead, they neither marry nor are given in marriage" (Mk 12:25). These words have a key meaning for the theology of the body. Christ uttered them after having affirmed, in the conversation with the Sadducees, that the resurrection is in conformity with the power of the living God. All three synoptic Gospels report the same statement, except that Luke's version is different in some details from that of Matthew and Mark. Essential for them all is the fact that, in the future resurrection, human beings, after having reacquired their bodies in the fullness of the perfection characteristic of the image and likeness of God—after having reacquired them in their masculinity and femininity—"neither marry nor are given in marriage." Luke expresses the same idea in chapter 20:34-35, in the following words: "The children of this age marry and are given in marriage, but those who are accounted worthy to attain to that age and to the resurrection from the dead neither marry nor are given in marriage."

As can be seen from these words, marriage, that union in which, according to Genesis, "A man cleaves to his wife, and they become one flesh" (2:24)—the union characteristic of man right from the beginning—belongs exclusively to this age. Marriage and procreation do not constitute, on the other hand, the eschatological future of man. In the resurrection they lose, so to speak, their *raison d'être*. "That age," of which Luke spoke (20:35), means the definitive fulfillment of mankind. It is the quantitative closing of that circle of beings, who were created in the image and likeness of God, in order that, multiplying through the conjugal "unity in the body" of men and women, they might subdue the earth. "That age" is not the world of the earth, but the world of God, who, as we know from the First Letter of Paul to the Corinthians, will fill it entirely, becoming "everything to everyone" (1 Cor 15:28).

At the same time "that age," which according to revelation is "the kingdom of God," is also the definitive and eternal "homeland" of man (cf. Phil 3:20). It is the "Father's house" (Jn 14:2). As man's new homeland, that age emerges definitively from the present world, which is temporal—subjected to death, that is, to the destruction of the body (cf. Gen 3:19, "to dust you shall return")—through the resurrection. According to Christ's words reported by the synoptic Gospels, the resurrection means not only the recovery of corporeity and the re-establishment of human life in its integrity by means of the union of the body with the soul, but also a completely new state of human life itself.

We find the confirmation of this new state of the body in the resurrection of Christ (cf. Rom 6:5-11). The words reported by the synoptic Gospels (Mt 22:30; Mk 12:25; Lk 20:34-35) will ring out then (that is, after Christ's resurrection) to those who had heard them—I would say almost with a new probative force, and at the same time they will acquire the character of a convincing promise. For the present, however, we will dwell on these words in their pre-paschal phase, referring only to the situation in which they were spoken. There is no doubt that already in the answer given to the Sadducees, Christ revealed the new condition of the human body in the resurrection. He did so precisely by proposing a reference and a comparison with the condition in which man had participated since the "beginning."

The words, "They neither marry nor are given in marriage" seem to affirm at the same time that human bodies, recovered and at the same time renewed in the resurrection, will keep their masculine or feminine peculiarity. The sense of being a male or a female in the body will be constituted and understood in that age in a different way from what it had been from the beginning, and then in the whole dimension of earthly existence. The words of Genesis: "A man leaves his father and mother and cleaves to his wife, and they become one flesh" (2:24), constituted right from the beginning that condition and relationship of masculinity and femininity, extended also to the body, which must rightly be defined as conjugal and at the same time as procreative and generative. It is connected with the blessing of fertility, pronounced by God *(Elohim)* when he created man "male and female" (Gn 1:27). The words Christ spoke about the resurrection enable us to deduce that the dimension of masculinity and femininity—that is, being male and female in the body—will again be constituted together with the resurrection of the body in "that age."

Is it possible to say something more detailed on this subject? Beyond all doubt, Christ's words reported by the synoptic Gospels (especially in the version of Luke 20:27-40) authorize us to do so. We read there that "Those who are accounted worthy to attain to that age and to the resurrection from the dead...cannot die any more, because they are equal to angels and are sons of God" (Matthew and Mark report only that "They are like angels in heaven"). This statement made it possible above all to deduce a spiritualization of man according to a different dimension from that of earthly life (and even different from that of the beginning itself). It is obvious that it is not a question here of transforming man's nature into that of the angels, that is, a purely spiritual one. The context indicates clearly that in that age man will keep his own human psychosomatic nature. If it were otherwise, it would be meaningless to speak of the resurrection.

The resurrection means the restoring to the real life of human corporeity, which was subjected to death in its temporal phase. In the expression of Luke (20:36) just quoted (and in that of Mathew 22:30 and Mark 12:25), it is certainly a question of human, that is, psychosomatic nature. The comparison with heavenly beings, used in the context, is no novelty in the Bible. Among others, it is said in a psalm, exalting man as the work of the Creator, "You have made him little less than the angels" (Ps 8:5). It must be supposed that in the resurrection this similarity will become greater. It will not be through a disincarnation of man, but by means of another kind (we could also say another degree) of spiritualization of his somatic nature—that is, by means of another "system of forces" within man. The resurrection means a new submission of the body to the spirit.

Before beginning to develop this subject, it should be recalled that the truth about the resurrection had a key meaning for the formation of all theological anthropology, which could be considered simply as an anthropology of the resurrection. As a result of reflection on the resurrection, Thomas Aquinas neglected in his metaphysical (and at the same time theological) anthropology Plato's philosophical conception on the relationship between the soul and the body and drew closer to the conception of Aristotle.[85] The resurrection bears witness, at least indirectly, that the body, in the composite being of man as a whole, is not only connected temporarily with the soul (as its earthly "prison," as Plato believed).[86] But together with the soul it constitutes the unity and integrity of the human being. Aristotle taught precisely that,[87] unlike Plato. If St. Thomas accepted Aristotle's conception in his anthropology, he did so considering the truth about the resurrection. The truth about the resurrection clearly affirmed, in fact, that the eschatological perfection and happiness of man cannot be understood as a state of the soul alone, separated (according to Plato: liberated) from the body. But it must be understood as the state of man definitively and perfectly "integrated" through such a union of the soul and the body, which qualifies and definitively ensures this perfect integrity.

At this point let us interrupt our reflection on the words Christ spoke about the resurrection. The great wealth of content enclosed in these words induces us to take them up again in further considerations.

General audience of December 2, 1981

The Resurrection Perfects the Person

"At the resurrection they neither marry nor are given in marriage, but are like angels in heaven" (Mt 22:30; cf. Mk 12:25). "They are equal to angels and are sons of God, being sons of the resurrection" (Lk 20:36).

Let us try to understand these words of Christ about the future resurrection in order to draw a conclusion with regard to the spiritualization of man, different from that of earthly life. We could speak here also of a perfect system of forces in mutual relations between what is spiritual in man and what is physical. As a result of original sin, historical man experiences a multiple imperfection in this system of forces, which is expressed in St. Paul's well-known words: "I see in my members another law at war with the law of my mind" (Rom 7:23).

Eschatological man will be free from that opposition. In the resurrection the body will return to perfect unity and harmony with the spirit. Man will no longer experience the opposition between what is spiritual and what is physical in him. Spiritualization means not only that the spirit will dominate the body, but, I would say, that it will fully permeate the body, and that the forces of the spirit will permeate the energies of the body.

In earthly life, the dominion of the spirit over the body—and the simultaneous subordination of the body to the spirit—can, as the result of persevering work on themselves, express a personality that is spiritually mature. However, the fact that the energies of the spirit succeed in dominating the forces of the body does not remove the possibility of their mutual opposition. The spiritualization to which the synoptic Gospels refer in the texts analyzed here (cf. Mt 22:30; Mk 12:25; Lk 20:34-35), already lies beyond this possibility. It is therefore a perfect spiritualization, in which the possibility that "another law is at war with the law of...the mind" (cf. Rom 7:23) is completely eliminated. This state which, as is evident, is differentiated essentially (and not only with regard to degree) from what we experience in earthly life, does not signify any disincarnation of the body nor, consequently, a dehumanization of man. On the contrary, it signifies his perfect realization. In fact, in the composite, psychosomatic being which man is, perfection cannot consist in a mutual opposition of spirit and body. But it consists in a deep harmony between them, in safeguarding the primacy of the spirit. In the "other world," this primacy will be realized and will be manifested in a perfect spontaneity, without any opposition on the part of the body. However, that must not be understood as a definitive victory of the spirit over the body. The resurrection will consist in the perfect participation of all that is physical in man in what is spiritual in him. At the same time it will consist in the perfect realization of what is personal in man.

The words of the synoptic Gospels testify that the state of man in the other world will not only be a state of perfect spiritualization, but also of fundamental divinization of his humanity. As we read in Luke 20:36, the "sons of the resurrection" are not only equal to angels, but are also sons of

God. The conclusion can be drawn that the degree of spiritualization characteristic of eschatological man will have its source in the degree of his divinization, incomparably superior to the one that can be attained in earthly life. It must be added that here it is a question not only of a different degree, but in a way, of another kind of divinization. Participation in divine nature, participation in the interior life of God himself, penetration and permeation of what is essentially human by what is essentially divine, will then reach its peak, so that the life of the human spirit will arrive at such fullness which previously had been absolutely inaccessible to it. This new spiritualization will therefore be the fruit of grace, that is, of the communication of God in his very divinity, not only to man's soul, but to his whole psychosomatic subjectivity. We speak here of subjectivity (and not only of "nature"). This is because that divinization is to be understood not only as an interior state of man (that is, of the subject) capable of seeing God face to face, but also as a new formation of the whole personal subjectivity of man in accordance with union with God in his Trinitarian mystery and of intimacy with him in the perfect communion of persons. This intimacy—with all its subjective intensity—will not absorb man's personal subjectivity, but rather will make it stand out to an incomparably greater and fuller extent.

As indicated by Christ's words, divinization in the other world will bring the human spirit such a range of experience of truth and love such as man would never have been able to attain in earthly life. When Christ spoke of the resurrection, he proved at the same time that the human body will also take part, in its way, in this eschatological experience of truth and love, united with the vision of God face to face. When Christ said that those who take part in the future resurrection "neither marry nor are given in marriage" (Mk 12:25), his words—as has already been pointed out— not only affirmed the end of earthly history, bound up with marriage and procreation, but they also seemed to reveal the new meaning of the body. Is it possible, in this case, at the level of biblical eschatology, to think of the discovery of the nuptial meaning of the body, above all as the virginal meaning of being male and female, as regards the body? To answer this question, which emerges from the words reported by the synoptic Gospels, we should penetrate more deeply into the essence of what will be the beatific vision of the divine Being, a vision of God face to face in the future life. It is also necessary to let oneself be guided by that range of experience of truth and love which goes beyond the limits of the cognitive and spiritual possibilities of man in temporality, and in which he will become a participant in the other world.

This eschatological experience of the living God will not only concentrate in itself all man's spiritual energies. But at the same time, it will reveal to him, in a deep and experiential way, the self-communication of God to the whole of creation and, in particular, to man. This is the most personal self-giving by God, in his very divinity, to man, to that being who, from the beginning, bears within himself the image and likeness of God. In this way, in the other world the object of the vision will be that mystery hidden in the Father from eternity, a mystery which in time was revealed in Christ, in order to be accomplished incessantly through the Holy Spirit. That mystery will become, if we may use the expression, the content of the eschatological experience and the form of the entire human existence in the dimension of the other world. Eternal life must be understood in the eschatological sense, that is, as the full and perfect experience of that grace *(charis)* of God, in which man becomes a participant through faith during earthly life, and which, on the contrary, will not only have to reveal itself in all its penetrating depth to those who take part in the other world, but also will have to be experienced in its beatifying reality.

We suspend here our reflection centered on Christ's words about the future resurrection of the body. In this spiritualization and divinization in which man will participate in the resurrection, we discover—in an eschatological dimension—the same characteristics that qualified the nuptial meaning of the body. We discover them in the meeting with the mystery of the living God, which is revealed through the vision of him face to face.

General audience of December 9, 1981

Christ's Words on the Resurrection Complete the Revelation of the Body

"In the resurrection they neither marry nor are given in marriage, but are like angels in heaven" (Mt 22:30, cf. Mk 12:25). "They are equal to angels and are sons of God, being sons of the resurrection" (Lk 20:36).

The eschatological communion *(communio)* of man with God, constituted thanks to the love of a perfect union, will be nourished by the vision, face to face, of contemplation of that more perfect communion—because it is purely divine—which is the trinitarian communion of the divine Persons in the unity of the same divinity.

Christ's words, reported by the synoptic Gospels, enable us to deduce that participants in the "other world"—in this union with the living God which springs from the beatific vision of his unity and trinitarian communion—will not only keep their authentic subjectivity, but will acquire it to a far more perfect extent than in earthly life. Furthermore, this will confirm the law of the integral order of the person, according to which the perfection of communion is not only conditioned by the perfection or spiritual maturity of the subject, but also in turn determines it. Those who participate in the future world, that is, in perfect communion with the living God, will enjoy a perfectly mature subjectivity. In this perfect subjectivity, while keeping masculinity and femininity in their risen, glorious body, "They neither marry nor are given in marriage." This is explained not only with the end of history, but also, and above all, with the eschatological authenticity of the response to that self-communication of the divine subject. This will constitute the beatifying experience of the gift of himself on God's part, which is absolutely superior to any experience proper to earthly life.

The reciprocal gift of oneself to God—a gift in which man will concentrate and express all the energies of his own personal and at the same time psychosomatic subjectivity—will be the response to God's gift of himself to man.[88] In this mutual gift of himself by man, a gift which will become completely and definitively beatifying, as a response worthy of a personal subject to God's gift of Himself, virginity, or rather the virginal state of the body, will be totally manifested as the eschatological fulfillment of the nuptial meaning of the body, as the specific sign and the authentic expression of all personal subjectivity. In this way, therefore, that eschatological situation in which "They neither marry nor are given in marriage" has its solid foundation in the future state of the personal subject. This will happen when, as a result of the vision of God face to face, there will be born in him a love of such depth and power of concentration on God himself, as to completely absorb his whole psychosomatic subjectivity.

This concentration of knowledge (vision) and love on God himself—a concentration that cannot be other than full participation in the interior life of God, that is, in the very trinitarian reality—will be at the same time the discovery, in God, of the whole "world" of relations, constitutive of his perennial order *(cosmos)*. This concentration will be above all man's rediscovery of himself, not only in the depth of his own person, but also in that union which is proper to the world of persons in their psychosomatic constitution. This is certainly a union of communion. The concentration of knowledge and love on God himself in the trinitarian communion of Persons can find a beatifying response in those who become participants in the other world, only through realizing mutual communion adapted to created persons. For this reason we profess faith in the "communion of saints" *(communio sanctorum),* and we profess it in organic connection with faith in the resurrection of the dead. Christ's words which affirm that in the other world, "They neither marry nor are given in marriage" are at the basis of these contents of our faith. At the same time they require an adequate interpretation in its light. We must think of the reality of the other world in the categories of the rediscovery of a new, perfect subjectivity of everyone and at the same time of the rediscovery of a new, perfect intersubjectivity of all. In this way, this reality signifies the real and definitive fulfillment of human subjectivity, and on this basis, the definitive fulfillment of the nuptial meaning of the body. The complete concentration of created subjectivity, redeemed and glorified, on God himself will not take man away from this fulfillment. On the contrary, it will introduce him into it and consolidate him in it. One can say, finally, that in this way eschatological reality will become the source of the perfect realization of the trinitarian order in the created world of persons.

The words with which Christ referred to the future resurrection—words confirmed in a singular way by his own resurrection—complete what in the present reflections we are accustomed to call the revelation of the body. This revelation penetrates in a way into the heart of the reality which we are experiencing. This reality is above all man, his body, the body of historical man. At the same time, this revelation enables us to go beyond the sphere of this experience in two directions—in the first place, in the direction of that beginning which Christ referred to in his conversation with the Pharisees regarding the indissolubility of marriage (cf. Mt 19:3-9); in the second place, in the direction of the other world, to which the Master drew the attention of his listeners in the presence of the Sadducees, who "say that there is no resurrection" (Mt 22:23). These two extensions of the sphere of the experience of the body (if we may say so) are not completely beyond the reach of our (obviously theological) understanding of the body. What the human body is in the sphere of man's historical experience is not completely cut off from those two dimensions of his existence, which are revealed through Christ's words.

It is clear that here it is a question not so much of the body in abstract, but of man who is at once spiritual and physical. Continuing in the two directions indicated by Christ's words, and linking up again with the experience of the body in the dimension of our earthly existence (therefore in the historical dimension), we can make a certain theological reconstruction. This is a reconstruction of what might have been the experience of the body on the basis of man's revealed beginning, and also of what it will be in the dimension of the other world. The possibility of this reconstruction, which extends our experience of man-body, indicates, at least indirectly, the consistency of man's theological image in these three dimensions, which together contribute to the constitution of the theology of the body.

General audience of December 16, 1981

The New Threshold of the Complete Truth about Man

"When they rise from the dead, they neither marry nor are given in marriage, but are like angels in heaven" (Mk 12:25; cf. Mt 22:30). "They are equal to angels and are sons of God, being sons of the resurrection" (Lk 20:36).

The words in which Christ referred to the future resurrection—words confirmed in an extraordinary way by his own resurrection—complete what we are accustomed to call in these reflections the revelation of the body. This revelation penetrates the heart of the reality that we experience, and this reality is above all man, his body, the body of historical man. At the same time, this revelation permits us to go beyond the sphere of this experience in two directions—first, in the direction of that beginning which Christ referred to in his conversation with the Pharisees concerning the indissolubility of marriage (cf. Mt 19:3-8); then, in the direction of the future world, to which the Master addressed the hearts of his listeners in the presence of the Sadducees, who "say that there is no resurrection" (Mt 22:23).

Neither the truth about that beginning of which Christ spoke, nor the eschatological truth can be reached by man with empirical and rationalistic methods alone. However, is it not possible to affirm that man bears, in a way, these two dimensions in the depth of the experience of his own being, or rather that he is somehow on his way to them as to dimensions that fully justify the meaning of his being a body, that is, of his being a carnal man? As regards the eschatological dimension, is it not true that death itself and the destruction of the body can confer on man an eloquent significance about the experience in which the personal meaning of existence is realized? When Christ spoke of the future resurrection, his words did not fall in a void. The experience of mankind, and especially the experience of the body, enable the listener to unite with those words the image of his new existence in the "future world," for which earthly experience supplies the substratum and the base. An adequate theological reconstruction is possible.

As regards content, this image corresponds to the article of our profession of faith: "I believe in the resurrection of the dead." The awareness that a connection exists between earthly experience and the whole dimension of the biblical beginning of man in the world greatly contributes to the construction of this image. If at the beginning God "created them male and female" (cf. Gn 1:27); if in this duality concerning the body he envisaged also such a unity that "they become one flesh" (Gn 2:24); if he linked this unity with the blessing of fertility, that is, of procreation (cf. Gn 1:29);

if speaking before the Sadducees about the future resurrection, Christ explained that "In the resurrection they neither marry nor are given in marriage," then it is clear that it is a question here of a development of the truth about man himself. Christ indicated his identity, although this identity is realized in eschatological experience in a different way from the experience of the beginning itself and of all history. Yet man will always be the same, such as he came from the hands of his Creator and Father. Christ said: "They neither marry nor are given in marriage." But he did not state that this man of the future world will no longer be male and female as he was from the beginning. It is clear therefore that, as regards the body, the meaning of being male or female in the future world must be sought outside marriage and procreation. But there is no reason to seek it outside that which (independently of the blessing of procreation) derives from the mystery of creation and which subsequently forms also the deepest structure of man's history on earth, since the mystery of redemption has deeply penetrated this history.

Therefore, in his original situation man is alone and at the same time he becomes male and female—unity of the two. In his solitude he is revealed to himself as a person, in order to reveal, at the same time, the communion of persons in the unity of the two. In both states the human being is constituted as an image and likeness of God. From the beginning man is also a body among bodies. In the unity of the couple he becomes male and female, discovering the nuptial meaning of his body as a personal subject. Subsequently, the meaning of being a body and, in particular, being male and female in the body, is connected with marriage and procreation (that is, with fatherhood and motherhood). However, the original and fundamental significance of being a body, as well as being, by reason of the body, male and female—that is precisely that nuptial significance—is united with the fact that man is created as a person and called to a life in *communione personarum.* Marriage and procreation in itself do not determine definitively the original and fundamental meaning of being a body or of being, as a body, male and female. Marriage and procreation merely give a concrete reality to that meaning in the dimensions of history.

The resurrection indicates the end of the historical dimension. The words, "When they rise from the dead, they neither marry nor are given in marriage" (Mk 12:25), express univocally not only the meaning which the human body will not have in the future world. But they enable us also to deduce that the nuptial meaning of the body in the resurrection to the future life will correspond perfectly both to the fact that man, as a male-female, is a person created in the "image and likeness of God," and to the fact that this image is realized in the communion of persons. That nuptial meaning of being a body will be realized, therefore, as a meaning that is perfectly personal and communitarian at the same time.

Speaking of the body glorified through the resurrection to the future life, we have in mind man, male-female, in all the truth of his humanity—man who, together with the eschatological experience of the living God (the face to face vision), will experience precisely this meaning of his own body. This will be a completely new experience. At the same time it will not be alienated in any way from what man took part in from the beginning nor from what, in the historical dimension of his existence, constituted in him the source of the tension between spirit and body, concerning mainly the procreative meaning of the body and sex. The man of the future world will find again in this new experience of his own body precisely the completion of what he bore within himself perennially and historically, in a certain sense, as a heritage and even more as a duty and objective, as the content of the ethical norm.

The glorification of the body, as the eschatological fruit of its divinizing spiritualization, will reveal the definitive value of what was to be from the beginning a distinctive sign of the created person in the visible world, as well as a means of mutual communication between persons and a genuine expression of truth and love, for which the *communio personarum* is constituted. That perennial meaning of the human body—to which the existence of every man, weighed down by the heritage of concupiscence, has necessarily brought a series of limitations, struggles and sufferings—will then be revealed again. It will be revealed in such simplicity and splendor when every participant in the other world will find again in his glorified body the source of the freedom of the gift. The perfect freedom of the children of God (cf. Rom 8:14) will nourish also with that gift each of the communions which will make up the great community of the communion of saints.

On the basis of man's experiences and knowledge in his temporal life, that is, in this world, it is all too clear that it is difficult to construct a fully adequate image of the future world. However, at the same time there is no doubt that, with the help of Christ's words, at least a certain approximation to this image is possible and attainable. We use this theological approximation, professing our faith in the resurrection of the dead and in eternal life, as well as faith in the communion of saints, which belongs to the reality of the future world.

Concluding this part of our reflections, it is opportune to state once more that Christ's words reported by the synoptic Gospels (cf. Mt 22:30; Mk 12:25; Lk 20:34-35) have a decisive meaning not only as regards the words of Genesis (which Christ referred to on another occasion), but also in what concerns the entire Bible. These words enable us, in a certain sense, to read again, that is, in depth, the whole revealed meaning of the body, the meaning of being a man, that is, a person incarnated, of being male or female as regards the body. These words permit us to understand the meaning, in the eschatological dimension of the other world, of that unity in humanity. This unity was constituted in the beginning. The words of Genesis 2:24, "A man cleaves to his wife, and they become one flesh" —uttered in the act of man's creation as male and female—seemed to direct it, if not completely, at least especially toward this world. The words of Genesis are almost the threshold of the whole theology of the body— the threshold which Christ took as his foundation in his teaching on marriage and its indissolubility. It must be admitted that the words reported by the synoptics are, as it were, a new threshold of this complete truth about man, which we find in God's revealed Word. It is indispensable to dwell upon this threshold, if we wish our theology of the body and also our Christian spirituality of the body—to be able to use it as a complete image.

General audience of January 13, 1982

The Doctrine of the Resurrection according to St. Paul

During the preceding audiences we reflected on Christ's words about the other world, which will emerge together with the resurrection of bodies. Those words had an extraordinarily intense resonance in the teaching of St. Paul. Between the answer given to the Sadducees, transmitted by the synoptic Gospels (cf. Mt 22:30; Mk 12:25; Lk 20:35-36), and Paul's apostolate there took place first of all the fact of the resurrection of Christ himself and a series of meetings with the risen Christ. Among these must be included, as the last link, the event that occurred in the neighborhood of Damascus. Saul or Paul of Tarsus who, on his conversion, became the Apostle of the Gentiles, also had his own post-paschal experience, similar to that of the other apostles. At the basis of his faith in the resurrection, which he expresses above all in First Corinthians (ch. 15), there is certainly that meeting with the risen Christ, which became the beginning and foundation of his apostolate.

It is difficult to sum up here and comment adequately on the stupendous and ample argumentation of the fifteenth chapter of First Corinthians in all its details. It is significant that, while Christ replied to the Sadducees, who "say that there is no resurrection" (Lk 20:27), with the words reported by the synoptic Gospels, Paul, on his part, replied or rather engaged in polemics (in conformity with his temperament) with those who contested it.[89] In his (pre-paschal) answer, Christ did not refer to his own resurrection, but appealed to the fundamental reality of the Old Testament covenant, to the reality of the living God. The conviction of the possibility of the resurrection is based on this: the living God "is not God of the dead, but of the living" (Mk 12:27). Paul's post-paschal argumentation on the future resurrection referred above all to the reality and the truth of the resurrection of Christ. In fact, he defends this truth even as the foundation of the faith in its integrity: "If Christ has not been raised, then our preaching is in vain and your faith is in vain.... But, in fact, Christ has been raised from the dead" (1 Cor 15:14, 20).

Here we are on the same line as revelation. The resurrection of Christ is the last and the fullest word of the self-revelation of the living God as "not God of the dead, but of the living" (Mk 12:27). It is the last and fullest confirmation of the truth about God which is expressed right from the beginning through this revelation. Furthermore, the resurrection is the reply of the God of life to the historical inevitability of death, to which man was subjected from the moment of breaking the first covenant and which, together with sin, entered his history. This answer about the victory won over death is illustrated by First Corinthians (ch. 15) with extraordinary perspicacity. It presents the resurrection of Christ as the beginning of that eschatological fulfillment, in which, through him and in him, everything will return to the Father, everything will be subjected to him, that is, handed back definitively, "that God may be everything to everyone" (1 Cor 15:28). Then, in this definitive victory over sin, over what opposed the creature to the Creator, death also will be vanquished: "The last enemy to be destroyed is death" (1 Cor 15:26).

The words that can be considered the synthesis of Pauline anthropology concerning the resurrection take their place in this context. It will be opportune to dwell longer here on these words. We read in First Corinthians 15:42-46 about the resurrection of the dead: "What is sown is perishable; what is raised is imperishable. It is sown in dishonor; it is raised in glory. It is sown in weakness; it is raised in power. It is sown a physical body; it is raised a spiritual body. If there is a physical body, there is also a spiritual body. Thus it is written, 'The first man Adam became a living being'; the last Adam became a life-giving spirit. But it is not the spiritual which is first but the physical, and then the spiritual."

An essential consistency exists between this Pauline anthropology of the resurrection and the one that emerges from the text of the synoptic Gospels (cf. Mt 22:30; Mk 12:25; Lk 20:35-36). But the text of First Corinthians is more developed. Paul studies in depth what Christ had proclaimed. At the same time, he penetrates the various aspects of that truth which had been expressed concisely and substantially in the words written in the synoptic Gospels. It is also significant for the Pauline text that man's eschatological perspective, based on faith in the resurrection of the dead, is united with reference to the beginning as well as with deep awareness of man's historical situation. The man whom Paul addressed in First Corinthians and who (like the Sadducees) is contrary to the possibility of the resurrection, has also his (historical) experience of the body. From this experience it emerges quite clearly that the body is perishable, weak, physical, in dishonor.

Paul confronts such a man, to whom his words are addressed—either in the community of Corinth or also, I would say, in all times—with the risen Christ, the last Adam. Doing so, Paul invites him, in a way, to follow in the footsteps of his own post-paschal experience. At the same time he recalls to him the first Adam. That is, he induces him to turn to the beginning, to that first truth about man and the world which is at the basis of the revelation of the mystery of the living God. In this way, Paul reproduces in his synthesis all that Christ had announced when he had referred, at three different moments, to the beginning in the conversation with the Pharisees (cf. Mt 19:3-8; Mk 10:2-9); to the human heart, as the place of struggle with lusts within man, during the Sermon on the Mount (cf. Mt 5:27); and to the resurrection as the reality of the "other world," in the conversation with the Sadducees (cf. Mt 22:30; Mk 12:25; Lk 20:35-36).

It belongs to the style of Paul's synthesis that it plunges its roots into the revealed mystery of creation and redemption as a whole, from which it is developed and in the light of which alone it can be explained. According to the biblical narrative, the creation of man is an enlivening of matter by means of the spirit, thanks to which "the first man Adam became a living being" (1 Cor 15:45). The Pauline text repeats here the words of Genesis (2:7), that is, of the second narrative of the creation of man (the so-called Yahwist narrative). From the same source it is known that this original "animation of the body" underwent corruption because of sin.

At this point of First Corinthians the author does not speak directly of original sin. Yet the series of definitions which he attributes to the body of historical man, writing that it is "perishable...weak...physical...in dishonor..." indicates sufficiently what the consequence of sin is, according to revelation. Paul himself will call it elsewhere "bondage to decay" (Rom 8:21). The whole of creation is subjected indirectly to this "bondage to decay" owing to the sin of man, who was placed by the Creator in the midst of the visible world in order to subdue it (cf. Gn 1:28). So man's sin has a dimension that is not only interior, but also cosmic. According to this dimension, the body—which Paul (in conformity with his experience) characterizes as "perishable...weak...physical...in dishonor..."—expresses in itself the state of creation after sin. This creation "has been groaning in travail together until now" (Rom 8:22).

However, just as labor pains are united with the desire for birth, with the hope of a new child, so, too, the whole of creation "waits with eager longing for the revealing of the sons of God..." and cherishes the hope to "be set free from its bondage to decay, and obtain the glorious liberty of the children of God" (Rom 8:19-21).

Through this cosmic context of the affirmation contained in Romans —in a way, through the "body of all creatures"—let us try to understand completely the Pauline interpretation of the resurrection. According to Paul, this image of the body of historical man, so deeply realistic and adapted to the universal experience of men, conceals within itself not only the "bondage of decay," but also hope, like the hope that accompanies labor pains. That happens because the Apostle grasps in this image also the presence of the mystery of redemption. Awareness of that mystery comes precisely from all man's experiences which can be defined as the "bondage of decay." It comes because redemption operates in man's soul by means of the gifts of the Spirit: "We ourselves, who have the first fruits of the Spirit, groan inwardly as we wait for adoption as sons, the redemption of our bodies" (Rom 8:23). Redemption is the way to the resurrection. The resurrection constitutes the definitive accomplishment of the redemption of the body.

We will come back to the analysis of the Pauline text in First Corinthians in our further reflections.

General audience of January 27, 1982

The Risen Body Will Be Incorruptible, Glorious, Full of Dynamism, and Spiritual

From the words of Christ on the future resurrection of the body, reported by all three synoptic Gospels, we have passed to the Pauline anthropology of the resurrection. We are analyzing First Corinthians 15:42-49.

According to the words of the Apostle, in the resurrection the human body is seen "incorruptible, glorious, full of dynamism, spiritual." The resurrection is not only a manifestation of the life that conquers death— almost a final return to the tree of life, from which man had been separated at the moment of original sin. It is also a revelation of the ultimate destiny of man in all the fullness of his psychosomatic nature and his personal subjectivity. Following in the footsteps of the other apostles, Paul of

Tarsus had experienced in his meeting with the risen Christ the state of his glorified body. Basing himself on this experience, Paul announces in his Letter to the Romans "the redemption of the body" (Rom 8:23) and in his First Letter to the Corinthians (1 Cor 15:42-49) the completion of this redemption in the future resurrection.

The literary method Paul applies here perfectly corresponds to his style, which uses antitheses that simultaneously bring together those things which they contrast. In this way they are useful in having us understand Pauline thought about the resurrection. It concerns both its "cosmic" dimension and also the characteristic of the internal structure of the "earthly" and the "heavenly" man. In contrasting Adam and the risen Christ—that is, the first Adam with the second Adam—the Apostle in a certain way shows two poles between which, in the mystery of creation and redemption, man has been placed in the cosmos. One could say that man has been put in tension between these two poles in the perspective of his eternal destiny regarding, from beginning to end, his human nature itself. When Paul writes: "The first man was from the earth, a man of dust; the second man is from heaven" (1 Cor 15:47), he has in mind both Adam-man and also Christ as man. Between these two poles—between the first and the second Adam—the process takes place that he expresses in the following words: "As we have borne the image of the man of earth, so we will bear the image of the man of heaven" (1 Cor 15:49).

This "man of heaven"—the man of the resurrection whose prototype is the risen Christ—is not so much an antithesis and negation of the "man of earth" (whose prototype is the first Adam), but is above all his completion and confirmation. It is the completion and confirmation of what corresponds to the psychosomatic makeup of humanity, in the sphere of his eternal destiny, that is, in the thought and the plan of him who from the beginning created man in his own image and likeness. The humanity of the first Adam, the "man of earth," bears in itself a particular potential (which is a capacity and readiness) to receive all that became the second Adam, the man of heaven, namely, Christ—what he became in his resurrection. All men, children of the first Adam, share that humanity, along with the heritage of sin. Being carnal, it is corruptible at the same time, and bears in itself the potentiality of incorruptibility.

In all its psychosomatic makeup that humanity appears ignoble. Yet it bears within itself the interior desire for glory, that is, the tendency and the capacity to become "glorious" in the image of the risen Christ. In conformity with the experience of all men, the Apostle said that this same humanity is "weak" and has an "animal body," yet it bears in itself the aspiration to become full of dynamism and spiritual.

We are speaking here of human nature in its integrity, that is, of human nature in its psychosomatic makeup. However, Paul speaks of the body. Nevertheless we can admit, on the basis of the immediate context and the remote one, that for him it is not a question only of the body, but of the entire man in his corporeity, therefore also of his ontological complexity. There is no doubt here that precisely in the whole visible world (cosmos) that one body which is the human body bears in itself the potentiality for resurrection, that is, the aspiration and capacity to become definitively incorruptible, glorious, full of dynamism, spiritual. This happens because, persisting from the beginning in the psychosomatic unity of the personal being, he can receive and reproduce in this earthly image and likeness of God also the heavenly image of the second Adam, Christ.

The Pauline anthropology of the resurrection is cosmic and universal at the same time. Every man bears in himself the image of Adam and every man is also called to bear in himself the image of Christ, the image of the risen one. This image is the reality of the "other world," the eschatological reality (St. Paul writes, "We *will* bear"). But in the meantime it is already in a certain way a reality of this world, since it was revealed in this world through the resurrection of Christ. It is a reality ingrafted in the man of this world, a reality that is developing in him toward final completion.

All the antitheses that are suggested in Paul's text help to construct a valid sketch of the anthropology of the resurrection. This sketch is at the same time more detailed than the one which comes from the text of the synoptic Gospels (cf. Mt 22:30; Mk 12:25; Lk 20:34-35). But on the other hand it is in a certain sense more unilateral. The words of Christ which the synoptics report open before us the perspective of the eschatological perfection of the body, fully subject to the divinizing profundity of the vision of God face to face. In that vision it will find its inexhaustible source of perpetual virginity (united to the nuptial meaning of the body), and of the perpetual intersubjectivity of all men, who will become (as males and females) sharers in the resurrection. The Pauline sketch of the eschatological perfection of the glorified body seems to remain rather in the sphere of the interior structure of the man-person. His interpretation of the future resurrection would seem to link up again with body-spirit dualism which constitutes the source of the interior system of forces in man.

This system of forces will undergo a radical change in the resurrection. Paul's words, which explicitly suggest this, cannot however be understood or interpreted in the spirit of dualistic anthropology,[90] which we will try to show in the continuation of our analysis. In fact, it will be suitable to dedicate yet another reflection to the anthropology of the resurrection in the light of First Corinthians.

General audience of February 3, 1982

The Body's Spiritualization Will Be
the Source of Its Power and Incorruptibility

From Christ's words on the future resurrection of the body, recorded by all three synoptic Gospels, our reflections have brought us to what St. Paul wrote on the subject in First Corinthians (ch. 15). Our analysis is centered above all on what might be called the anthropology of the resurrection according to St. Paul. He contrasts the state of the "earthly" man (i.e., historical) with the state of the risen man, characterizing in a lapidary and at the same time penetrating manner, the interior system of forces specific to each of these states.

That this interior system of forces should undergo a radical transformation would seem to be indicated, first of all, by the contrast between the weak body and the body full of power. Paul writes: "What is sown is perishable; what is raised is imperishable. It is sown in dishonor; it is raised in glory. It is sown in weakness; it is raised in power" (1 Cor 15:42-45). "Weak," therefore, is the description of the body which—in metaphysical terms—rises from the temporal soil of humanity. The Pauline metaphor corresponds likewise to the scientific terminology which defines man's beginning as a body by the use of the same term *(semen,* seed).

If, in the Apostle's view, the human body which arises from earthly seed is weak, this means not only that it is perishable, subject to death, and to all that leads to it, but also that it is an animal body.[91] The body full of power, however, which man will inherit from the second Adam, Christ, in virtue of the future resurrection, will be a spiritual body. It will be imperishable, no longer subject to the threat of death. Thus the antinomy, weak—full of power, refers explicitly not only to the body considered separately, but also to the whole constitution of man considered in his corporeal nature. Only within the framework of such a constitution can the body become spiritual. This spiritualization of the body will be the source of its power and incorruptibility (or immortality).

This theme has its origin already in the first chapter of Genesis. It can be said that St. Paul sees the reality of the future resurrection as a certain *restitutio in integrum,* that is, as the reintegration and at the same time as the attaining of the fullness of humanity. It is not truly a restitution, because in that case the resurrection would be, in a certain sense, a return to the state which the soul enjoyed before sin, apart from the knowledge of good and evil (cf. Gn 1-2). But such a return does not correspond to the internal logic of the whole economy of salvation, to the most profound meaning of the mystery of the redemption. *Restitutio in integrum,* linked with the resurrection and the reality of the other world, can only be an introduction to a new fullness. This will be a fullness that presupposes the whole of human history, formed by the drama of the tree of the knowledge of good and evil (cf. Gn 3) and at the same time permeated by the text of First Corinthians.

According to the text of First Corinthians, in man, concupiscence—that is, the "animal body" (1 Cor 15:44)—prevails over the spiritual. Man is condemned to death. He should rise, however, as a spiritual body, man in whom the Spirit will achieve a just supremacy over the body, spirituality over sensuality. It is easy to understand that Paul is here thinking of sensuality as the sum total of the factors limiting human spirituality, that is, as a force that "ties down" the spirit (not necessarily in the Platonic sense) by restricting its own faculty of knowing (seeing) the truth and also the faculty to will freely and to love in truth. However, here it cannot be a question of that fundamental function of the senses which serves to liberate spirituality, that is to say, of the simple faculty of knowing and willing proper to the psychosomatic *compositum* of the human subject.

Just as one speaks of the resurrection of the body, that is, of man in his true corporeal nature, consequently the spiritual body should mean precisely the perfect sensitivity of the senses, their perfect harmonization with the activity of the human spirit in truth and liberty. The animal body, which is the earthly antithesis of the spiritual body, indicates sensuality as a force prejudicial to man. This is precisely because while living "in the knowledge of good and evil," he is often attracted and impelled toward evil.

It cannot be forgotten that here it is not so much a question of anthropological dualism, but of a basic antinomy. Constituting it is not only the body (as the Aristotelian *hyle),* but also the soul, or man as a "living being" (cf. Gn 2:7). Its constituents are the whole man, the sum total of his psychosomatic subjectivity, inasmuch as he remains under the influence of the vivifying Spirit of Christ, and on the other hand, the same man inasmuch as he resists and opposes this Spirit. In the second case man is an animal body (and his works are works of the flesh). However, if he remains under the influence of the Holy Spirit, man is spiritual (and produces the "fruit of the Spirit"—Gal 5:22).

Consequently, it can be said that we are dealing with the anthropology of the resurrection not only in First Corinthians 15, but that the whole of St. Paul's anthropology (and ethics) are permeated with the mystery of the resurrection through which we have definitively received the Holy Spirit. Chapter 15 of First Corinthians constitutes the Pauline interpretation of the other world and of man's state in that world. In it each one, together with the resurrection of the body, will fully participate in the gift of the vivifying Spirit, that is, in the fruit of Christ's resurrection.

Concluding the analysis of the anthropology of the resurrection according to First Corinthians, it is fitting to turn our minds again to Christ's words on the resurrection and on the other world which the evangelists Matthew, Mark and Luke quote. We recall that in his reply to the Sadducees, Christ linked faith in the resurrection with the entire revelation of the God of Abraham, of Isaac, of Jacob and of Moses (Mt 22:32). At the same time, while rejecting the objection proposed by those who questioned him, he uttered these significant words: "When they rise from the dead, they neither marry nor are given in marriage" (Mk 12:25). We devoted our previous reflections to these words in their immediate context, passing on then to the analysis of First Corinthians (1 Cor 15).

These reflections have a fundamental significance for the whole theology of the body, for an understanding both of marriage and of celibacy for the kingdom of heaven. Our further analyses will be devoted to this latter subject.

General audience of February 10, 1982

NOTES

General audience of November 11, 1981

[75] This law, contained in Dt 25:7-10, concerns brothers who lived under the same roof. If one of them died without leaving children, the dead man's brother had to marry his brother's widow. The child born of this marriage was recognized as the son of the deceased, so that his stock would not be extinguished and the inheritance would be kept in the family (cf. 3:9-4:12).

[76] In the time of Christ, the Sadducees formed, within Judaism, a sect bound to the circle of the priestly aristocracy. In opposition to the oral tradition and theology elaborated by the Pharisees, they proposed the literal interpretation of the Pentateuch, which they considered the main source of the Yahwist religion. Since there was no mention of life after death in the most ancient books of the Bible, the Sadducees rejected the eschatology proclaimed by the Pharisees, affirming that "souls die together with the body" (cf. Joseph, *Antiquitates Judaicae*, XVII, 1.4, 16).

The conceptions of the Sadducees are not directly known to us, however, since all their writings were lost after the destruction of Jerusalem in the year 70, when the sect itself disappeared. We get what little information there is about the Sadducees from the writings of their ideological opponents.

[77] The Sadducees, turning to Jesus for a purely theoretical "case," at the same time attacked the primitive conception of the Pharisees on life after the resurrection of the body. They insinuated, in fact, that faith in the resurrection of the body leads to admitting polyandry, which is contrary to God's law.

General audience of November 18, 1981

[78] The expression "the resurrection of the body" is not known in the New Testament. (It will appear for the first time in St. Clement—*2 Clem* 9:1, and in Justin—*Dialogue* 80:5.) The New Testament uses the expression "resurrection of the dead," intending thereby man in his integrity. However, it is possible to find in many New Testament texts faith in the immortality of the soul and its existence also outside the body (cf. for example, Lk 23:43; Phil 1:23-24; 2 Cor 5:6-8).

[79] Luke's text contains some new elements which are an object of discussion among exegetes.

[80] As is known, in the Judaism of that period there was no clearly formulated doctrine concerning the resurrection. There existed only the various theories launched by the individual schools.

The Pharisees, who cultivated theological speculation, greatly developed the doctrine on the resurrection, seeing allusions to it in all the Old Testament books. They understood the future resurrection, however, in an earthly and primitive way, announcing, for example, an enormous increase of crops and of fertility in life after the resurrection.

On the other hand, the Sadducees polemicized with such a conception, starting from the premise that the Pentateuch does not speak of eschatology. It must also be kept in mind that in the first century the canon of the Old Testament books had not yet been established.

The case presented by the Sadducees directly attacks the Pharisaic concept of the resurrection. In fact, the Sadducees were of the opinion that Christ was one of their followers. Christ's answer equally corrects the conceptions of the Pharisees and those of the Sadducees.

[81] This expression does not mean, "God who was honored by Abraham, Isaac and Jacob," but, "God who took care of the patriarchs and liberated them."

This formula returns in Ex 3:6; 3:15, 16; 4:5, always in the context of the promised liberation of Israel. The name of the God of Abraham, Isaac and Jacob is a token and guarantee of this liberation.

"The God of X is synonymous with help, support and shelter for Israel." A similar sense is found in Gn 49:24: "God of Jacob—the Shepherd and Rock of Israel, the God of your Fathers who will help you" (cf. Gn 49:24-25; cf. also Gn 24:27; 26:24; 28:13; 32:10; 46:3).

Cf. F. Dreyfus, O.P., "L'argument scripturaire de Jesus en faveur de la résurrection des morts (Mk 12:26-27)," *Revue Biblique,* Vol. 66 (1959), p. 218.

In Judaic exegesis in Jesus' time, the formula: "God of Abraham, Isaac and

Jacob," in which all three names of the patriarchs are mentioned, indicated God's relationship with the people of the covenant as a community.

Cf. E. Ellis, "Jesus, the Sadducees and Qumran," *New Testament Studies,* Vol. 10 (1963-64), p. 275.

[82] In our modern way of understanding this Gospel text, the reasoning of Jesus concerns only immortality; if in fact the patriarchs still now live after their death, before the eschatological resurrection of the body, then the statement of Jesus concerns the immortality of the soul and does not speak of the resurrection of the body.

But the reasoning of Jesus was addressed to the Sadducees who did not know the dualism of body and soul, accepting only the biblical psycho-physical unity of man who is "the body and the breath of life." Therefore, according to them the soul dies with the body. The affirmation of Jesus, according to which the patriarchs are alive, could mean for the Sadducees only resurrection with the body.

[83] We will not dwell here on the concept of death in the purely Old Testament sense, but consider theological anthropology as a whole.

[84] This is the determinant argument that proves the authenticity of the discussion with the Sadducees.

If the passage were "a post-paschal addition of the Christian community" (as R. Bultmann thought, for example), faith in the resurrection of the body would be supported by the fact of the resurrection of Christ, which imposed itself as an irresistible force, as St. Paul, for example, has us understand (cf. 1 Cor 15:12).

Cf. J. Jeremias, *Neutestamentliche Theologie,* I Teil (Gutersloh: Mohn, 1971); cf. besides I. H. Marshall, *The Gospel of Luke* (Exeter: The Paternoster Press, 1978), p. 738.

The reference to the Pentateuch—while in the Old Testament there were texts which dealt directly with resurrection (as, for example, Is 26:19 or Dt 12:2)—bears witness that the conversation really took place with the Sadducees, who considered the Pentateuch the only decisive authority.

The structure of the controversy shows that this was a rabbinic discussion, according to the classical models in use in the academies of that time.

Cf. J. Le Moyne, OSB, *Les Sadducéens* (Paris: Gabalda, 1972), pp. 124f.; E. Lohmeyer, *Das Evangelium des Markus* (Göttingen: 1959), p. 257; D. Daube, *New Testament and Rabbinic Judaism* (London: 1956), pp. 158-163; J. Radamakers, SJ, *La bonne nouvelle de Jésus silon St. Marc* (Bruxelles: Institut d'Etudes Théologiques, 1974), p. 313.

General audience of December 2, 1981

[85] Cf., e.g.: "Now the soul has one mode of being when in the body, and another when apart from it, its nature remaining always the same; but this does not mean that its union with the body is an accidental thing, for, on the contrary, such union belongs to its very nature...

"The soul united to the body can understand only by turning to the phantasms, as experience shows. Did this not proceed from the soul's very nature, but accidentally through its being bound up with the body, as the Platonists said, the difficulty would vanish; for in that case when the body was once removed, the soul would at once return to its own nature, and would understand intelligible things simply, without turning to the phantasms, as is exemplified in the case of other separate substances. In that case, however, the union of soul and body would not be for the soul's good, for evidently it would understand worse in the body than out of it; but for the good of the body, which would be unreasonable, since matter exists on account of the form, and not the form for the sake of matter" (St. Thomas, *Summa Theol.*, I, q. 89, a. 1 [New York: Benziger, 1947]).

"To be united to the body belongs to the soul by reason of itself, as it belongs to a light body by reason of itself to be raised up.... So the human soul retains its proper existence when separated from the body, having an aptitude and a natural inclination to be united to the body" (St. Thomas, *Summa Theol.*, I, q. 76, a. 1, ad 6 [New York: Benziger, 1947]).

[86] *To men soma estin hemin sema* (Platone, *Gorgias* 493 A; cf. also *Phaedo* 66B; *Cratylus* 400C).

[87] Aristotle, *De anima,* II, 412a, 19-22; cf. also *Metaph.* 1029, b 11; 1030, b 14.

General audience of December 16, 1981

[88] "In the biblical conception...it is a question of a 'dialogic' immortality (resuscitation!), that is, that immortality does not derive merely from the obvious truth that the indivisible cannot die, but from the saving act of him who loves, who has the power to do so; therefore man cannot completely disappear, because he is known and loved by God. If all love postulates eternity, love of God not only wishes it, but actuates it and is it.

"...Since the immortality presented by the Bible does not derive from the power of what is in itself indestructible, but from being accepted in the dialogue with the Creator, for this reason it must be called resuscitation..." J. Ratzinger, "Risurrezione della carne—aspetto teologico," *Sacramentum Mundi,* Vol. 7 (Brescia: Morcelliana, 1977, pp. 160-161).

General audience of January 27, 1982

[89] Among the Corinthians there were probably movements of thought marked by Platonic dualism and neo-Pythagoreanism of a religious shade, Stoicism and Epicureanism. All Greek philosophies, moreover, denied the resurrection of the body. Paul had already experienced in Athens the reaction of the Greeks to the doctrine of the resurrection, during his address at the Areopagus (cf. Acts 17:32).

General audience of February 3, 1982

[90] "Paul takes absolutely no account of the Greek dichotomy between 'soul and body'.... The Apostle resorts to a kind of trichotomy in which the totality of man is body, soul and spirit.... All these terms are alive and the division itself has no fixed limit. He insists on the fact that body and soul are capable of being 'pneumatic,' spiritual" (B. Rigaux, *Dieu l'a ressuscité. Exégèse et Théologie biblique* [Gembloux: Duculot, 1973], pp. 406–408).

General audience of February 10, 1982

[91] The original Greek uses the term *psychikon*. In St. Paul it is found only in First Corinthians (2:14; 15:44; 15:46) *and not elsewhere,* probably because of the pre-gnostic tendencies of the Corinthians, and it has a pejorative connotation. As regards its meaning, it corresponds to the term "carnal" (cf. 2 Cor 1:12; 10:4).

However, in the other Pauline letters, "psyche" and its derivatives signify man in his manifestations, the individual's way of living, and even the human person *in a positive sense* (e.g., to indicate the ideal of life of the ecclesial community: *miâ-i psychê-i* = "in one spirit"—Phil 1:27; *sympsychoi* = "by being of the same mind"—Phil 2:2; *isópsychon* "like him"—Phil 2:20; cf. R. Jewett, *Paul's Anthropological Terms. A Study of Their Use in Conflict Settings* [Leiden: Brill, 1971], pp. 2, 448–449).

Virginity for the Sake of the Kingdom

Virginity or Celibacy for the Sake of the Kingdom

Today we begin to reflect on virginity or celibacy for the kingdom of heaven. The question of the call to an exclusive donation of self to God in virginity and in celibacy thrusts its roots deep in the Gospel soil of the theology of the body. To indicate the dimensions proper to it, one must bear in mind Christ's words about the beginning, and also what he said about the resurrection of the body. The observation, "When they rise from the dead they neither marry nor are given in marriage" (Mk 12:25), indicates that there is a condition of life without marriage. In that condition, man, male and female, finds at the same time the fullness of personal donation and of the intersubjective communion of persons, thanks to the glorification of his entire psychosomatic being in the eternal union with God. When the call to continence for the kingdom of heaven finds an echo in the human soul, in the conditions of this temporal life, that is, in the conditions in which persons usually "marry and are given in marriage" (Lk 20:34), it is not difficult to perceive there a particular sensitiveness of the human spirit. Already in the conditions of the present temporal life this seems to anticipate what man will share in, in the future resurrection.

However, Christ did not speak of this problem, of this particular vocation, in the immediate context of his conversation with the Sadducees (cf. Mt 22:23-30; Mk 12:18-25; Lk 20:27-36), when there was reference to the resurrection of the body. Instead he had already spoken of it in the context of his conversation with the Pharisees on marriage and on the grounds of indissolubility, as if it were a continuation of that conversation (cf. Mt 19:3-9). His concluding words concern the so-called certificate of divorce permitted by Moses in some cases. Christ said, "For your hardness of heart Moses allowed you to divorce your wives, but from the beginning it was not so. And I say to you, whoever divorces his wife, except in the case of concubinage, and marries another, commits adultery" (Mt 19:8-9). Then the disciples who—as can be deduced from the context—were listening attentively to the conversation and especially to the final words spoken by Jesus, said to him: "If such is the case of a man with his wife, it is not expedient to marry" (Mt 19:10). Christ gave the following reply: "Not all men can receive the precept, but only those to whom it is given. For there are eunuchs who have been so from birth, and there are eunuchs who have been made eunuchs by men, and there are eunuchs who have made themselves eunuchs for the sake of the kingdom of heaven. He who is able to receive this, let him receive it" (Mt 19:11-12).

In regard to this conversation recorded by Matthew one could ask the question: what did the disciples think when, after hearing Jesus' reply to the Pharisees, they remarked: "If such is the case of a man with his wife, it is not expedient to marry"? Christ considered it an opportune occasion to speak to them about voluntary continence for the kingdom of heaven. In saying this, he did not directly take a position in regard to what the disciples said, nor did he remain in the line of their reasoning.[92] Hence he did not reply: "It is expedient to marry" or "It is not expedient to marry." The question of continence for the kingdom of heaven is not set in opposition to marriage, nor is it based on a negative judgment in regard to its importance. After all, speaking previously about the indissolubility of marriage, Christ had referred to the beginning, that is, to the mystery of creation, thereby indicating the first and fundamental source of its value. Consequently, to reply to the disciples' question, or rather, to clarify the problem placed by them, Christ recurred to another principle. Those who in life choose continence for the kingdom of heaven do so, not because it is inexpedient to marry or because of a supposed negative value of marriage, but in view of the particular value connected with this choice and which must be discovered and welcomed personally as one's own vocation. For that reason Christ said: "He who is able to receive this, let him receive it" (Mt 19:12). But immediately beforehand he said: "Not all men can receive this precept, but only those to whom it is given" (Mt 19:11).

As can be seen, in his reply to the disciples' problem, Christ stated clearly a rule for the understanding of his words. In the Church's doctrine the conviction exists that these words do not express a command by which all are bound, but a counsel which concerns only some persons[93]—precisely those who are able "to receive it." Those able "to receive it" are those "to whom it has been given." The words quoted clearly indicate the importance of the personal choice and also the importance of the particular grace, that is, of the gift which man receives to make such a choice. It may be said that the choice of continence for the kingdom of heaven is a charismatic orientation toward that eschatological state in which men "neither marry nor are given in marriage." However, there is an essential difference between man's state in the resurrection of the body and the voluntary choice of continence for the kingdom of heaven in the earthly life and in the historical state of man fallen and redeemed. The eschatological absence of marriage will be a state, that is, the proper and fundamental mode of existence of human beings, men and women, in their glorified bodies. Continence for the kingdom of heaven, as the fruit of a charismatic choice, is an exception in respect to the other stage, namely, that state in which man "from the beginning" became and remains a participant during the course of his whole earthly existence.

It is very significant that Christ did not directly link his words on continence for the kingdom of heaven with his foretelling of the "other world" in which "they will neither marry nor be given in marriage" (Mk 12:25). However, as we already said, his words are found in the prolongation of the conversation with the Pharisees in which Jesus referred to the beginning. He was indicating the institution of marriage on the part of the Creator, and recalling its indissoluble character which, in God's plan, corresponds to the conjugal unity of man and woman.

The counsel and therefore the charismatic choice of continence for the kingdom of heaven are linked, in Christ's words, with the highest recognition of the historical order of human existence relative to the soul and body. On the basis of the immediate context of the words on continence for the kingdom of heaven in man's earthly life, one must see in the vocation to such continence a kind of exception to what is rather a general rule of this life. Christ indicates this especially. That such an exception contains within itself the anticipation of the eschatological life without marriage and proper to the "other world" (that is, of the final stage of the "kingdom of heaven"), is not directly spoken of here by Christ. It is a question indeed, not of continence *in* the kingdom of heaven, but of continence *for* the kingdom of heaven. The idea of virginity or of celibacy as an anticipation and eschatological sign[94] derives from the association of the words spoken here with those which Jesus uttered on another occasion, in the conversation with the Sadducees, when he proclaimed the future resurrection of the body.

We shall resume this theme in the course of the following Wednesday reflections.

General audience of March 10, 1982

The Vocation to Continence in This Earthly Life

We continue the reflection on virginity or celibacy for the kingdom of heaven—a theme that is important also for a complete theology of the body. In the immediate context of the words on continence for the kingdom of heaven, Christ made a very significant comparison. This confirms us still more in the conviction that he wished to root the vocation to such continence deep in the reality of the earthly life, thereby gaining an entrance into the mentality of his hearers. He listed three categories of eunuchs.

This term concerns the physical defects which render procreation in marriage impossible. These defects explain the first two categories, when

Jesus spoke of both congenital defects: "eunuchs who have been so from birth" (Mt 19:11), and of acquired defects caused by human intervention: "There are eunuchs who have been made eunuchs by men" (Mt 19:12). In both cases it is a state of compulsion, and therefore not voluntary. If Christ in his comparison then spoke of those "who have made themselves eunuchs for the sake of the kingdom of heaven" (Mt 19:12), as of a third category, undoubtedly he made this distinction to indicate still further its voluntary and supernatural character. It is voluntary, because those pertaining to this category "have made themselves eunuchs," and it is supernatural, because they have done so "for the kingdom of heaven."

The distinction is clear and forceful. Nevertheless, the comparison also is strong and eloquent. Christ spoke to men to whom the tradition of the old covenant had not handed down the ideal of celibacy or of virginity. Marriage was so common that only physical impotence could constitute an exception. The reply given to the disciples in Matthew (15:10-12) is at the same time directed, in a certain sense, at the whole tradition of the Old Testament. This is confirmed by a single example taken from the Book of Judges. We refer to this here not merely because of the event that took place, but also because of the significant words that accompanied it. "Let it be granted to me...to bewail my virginity" (Jgs 11:37) the daughter of Jephthah said to her father after learning from him that she was destined to be sacrificed in fulfillment of a vow made to the Lord. (The biblical text explains how such a situation came about.) "Go," the text continues, "and he let her go.... She went with her companions and bewailed her virginity on the mountains. At the end of two months she returned to her father who did with her according to his vow which he had made. She had never known a man" (Jgs 11:38-39).

As far as we know, in the Old Testament tradition there is no place for this significance of the body, which Christ, in speaking of continence for the kingdom of God, wished to present and reveal to his own disciples. Among the personages known to us as spiritual *condottieri* of the people of the old covenant, there is not one who would have proclaimed such continence by word or example.[95] At that time, marriage was not only a common state, but still more, in that tradition it had acquired a consecrated significance because of the promise the Lord made to Abraham: "Behold, my covenant is with you, and you shall be the father of a multitude of nations.... I will make you exceedingly fruitful, and I will make nations of you, and kings shall come forth from you. And I will establish my covenant between me and you and your descendants after you throughout their generations for an everlasting covenant, to be God to you and to your descendants after you" (Gn 17:4, 6-7). Hence in the Old Testament

tradition, marriage, as a source of fruitfulness and of procreation in regard
to descendants, was a religiously privileged state, and privileged by revelation itself. Against the background of this tradition, according to which
the Messiah should be the "son of David" (Mt 20:30), it was difficult
to understand the ideal of continence. Marriage had everything going in its
favor, not only reasons of human nature, but also those of the kingdom
of God.[96]

In this environment Christ's words determine a decisive turning
point. When he spoke to his disciples for the first time about continence
for the kingdom of heaven, one clearly realizes that as children of the Old
Law tradition, they must have associated celibacy and virginity with the
situation of individuals, especially of the male sex, who because of defects
of a physical nature cannot marry ("the eunuchs"). For that reason he referred directly to them. This reference has a multiple background, both
historical and psychological, as well as ethical and religious. In a certain
sense, with this reference Jesus touched all these backgrounds, as if he
wished to say: I know that what I am going to say to you now will cause
great difficulty in your conscience, in your way of understanding the significance of the body. In fact, I shall speak to you of continence. Undoubtedly, you will associate this with the state of physical deficiency, whether
congenital or brought about by human cause. But I wish to tell you that
continence can also be voluntary and chosen by man for the kingdom of
heaven.

In chapter 19, Matthew does not record any immediate reaction of
the disciples to these words. We find it later only in the writings of the
apostles, especially in Paul (cf. 1 Cor 7:25-40; see also Rv 14:4). This
confirms that these words were impressed in the conscience of the first
generation of Christ's disciples and they repeatedly bore fruit in a manifold way in the generations of his confessors in the Church (and perhaps
also outside it). So, from the viewpoint of theology—that is, of the revelation of the significance of the body, completely new in respect to the Old
Testament tradition—these words mark a turning point. Their analysis
shows how precise and substantial they are, notwithstanding their conciseness. (We will observe it still better when we analyze the Pauline text
of First Corinthians, chapter 7.) Christ spoke of continence "for" the
kingdom of heaven. In this way he wished to emphasize that this state,
consciously chosen by man in this temporal life, in which people usually
"marry or are given in marriage," has a singular supernatural finality. Continence, even if consciously chosen or personally decided upon, but without that finality, does not come within the scope of the above-mentioned
statement of Christ. Speaking of those who have consciously chosen celibacy

or virginity for the kingdom of heaven (that is, "They have made themselves eunuchs"), Christ pointed out—at least in an indirect way—that this choice during the earthly life is joined to renunciation and also to a determined spiritual effort.

The same supernatural finality—for the kingdom of heaven—admits of a series of more detailed interpretations which Christ did not enumerate in this passage. However, it can be said that by means of the lapidary formula which he used, he indicated indirectly all that is said on the subject in revelation, in the Bible and in Tradition—all that has become the spiritual riches of the Church's experience in which celibacy and virginity for the kingdom of heaven have borne fruit in a manifold way in the various generations of the Lord's disciples and followers.

General audience of March 17, 1982

Continence for the Sake of the Kingdom— and Its Spiritual Fulfillment

We continue our reflections on celibacy and virginity for the kingdom of heaven. Continence for the kingdom of heaven is certainly linked to the revelation of the fact that in the kingdom of heaven people "will no longer marry" (Mt 22:30). It is a charismatic sign. The human being, male and female, who, in the earthly situation where people usually marry (Lk 20:34), freely chooses continence for the kingdom of heaven, indicates that in that kingdom, which is the other world of the resurrection, people will no longer marry (Mk 12:25). This is because God will be "everything to everyone" (1 Cor 15:28).

Such a human being, man and woman, indicates the eschatological virginity of the risen man. In him there will be revealed, I would say, the absolute and eternal nuptial meaning of the glorified body in union with God himself through the "face to face" vision of him, and glorified also through the union of a perfect intersubjectivity. This will unite all who participate in the other world, men and women, in the mystery of the communion of saints.

Earthly continence for the kingdom of heaven is undoubtedly a sign that indicates this truth and this reality. It is a sign that the body, whose end is not the grave, is directed to glorification. Already by this very fact, continence for the kingdom of heaven is a witness among men that anticipates the future resurrection. However, this charismatic sign of the other world expresses the force and the most authentic dynamics of the mystery of the redemption of the body. Christ has inscribed this mystery in man's earthly history and it has been deeply rooted by him in this history. So, then, continence for the kingdom of heaven bears, above all, the imprint of the likeness to Christ. In the work of redemption, he himself made this choice for the kingdom of heaven.

Indeed, Christ's whole life, right from the beginning, was a discreet but clear distancing of himself from that which in the Old Testament had so profoundly determined the meaning of the body. As if against the expectations of the whole Old Testament tradition, Christ was born of Mary. At the moment of the annunciation, she clearly said of herself: "How can this be, since I know not man" (Lk 1:34), and thereby professed her virginity. Though he was born of her like every other man, as a son of his mother, even though his coming into the world was accompanied by the presence of a man who was Mary's spouse and, in the eyes of the law and of men, her husband, nonetheless Mary's maternity was virginal. The virginal mystery of Joseph corresponds to this virginal maternity of Mary. Following the voice from on high, Joseph did not hesitate to "take Mary...for that which is conceived in her is of the Holy Spirit" (Mt 1:20).

Even though Jesus Christ's virginal conception and birth were hidden from men, even though in the eyes of his contemporaries of Nazareth he was regarded as "the carpenter's son" (Mt 13:55) *(ut putabatur filius Joseph*—Lk 3:23), the reality and essential truth of his conception and birth was in itself far removed from what in the Old Testament tradition was exclusively in favor of marriage, and which rendered continence incomprehensible and out of favor. Therefore, how could continence for the kingdom of heaven be understood, if the expected Messiah was to be David's descendant, and as was held, was to be a son of the royal stock according to the flesh? Only Mary and Joseph, who had lived the mystery of his conception and birth, became the first witnesses of a fruitfulness different from that of the flesh, that is, of a fruitfulness of the Spirit: "That which is conceived in her is of the Holy Spirit" (Mt 1:20).

The story of Jesus' birth is certainly in line with that "continence for the kingdom of heaven" of which Christ will speak one day to his disciples. However, this event remained hidden to the men of that time and also to the disciples. Only gradually would it be revealed to the eyes of the Church on the basis of the witness and texts of the Gospels of Matthew and Luke. The marriage of Mary and Joseph (in which the Church honors Joseph as Mary's spouse, and Mary as his spouse), conceals within itself, at the same time, the mystery of the perfect communion of the persons, of the man and the woman in the conjugal pact, and also the mystery of that singular continence for the kingdom of heaven. This continence served, in the history of salvation, the most perfect fruitfulness of the Holy Spirit.

Indeed, in a certain sense it was the absolute fullness of that spiritual fruitfulness, since precisely in the Nazareth conditions of the pact of Mary and Joseph in marriage and in continence, the gift of the Incarnation of the Eternal Word was realized. The Son of God, consubstantial with the Father, was conceived and born as man from the Virgin Mary.

The grace of the hypostatic union is connected precisely with this absolute fullness of supernatural fruitfulness, fruitfulness in the Holy Spirit, participated by a human creature, Mary, in the order of continence for the kingdom of heaven. Mary's divine maternity is also, in a certain sense, a superabundant revelation of that fruitfulness in the Holy Spirit to which man submits his spirit, when he freely chooses continence in the body, namely, continence for the kingdom of heaven.

This image had to be gradually revealed to the Church's awareness in the ever new generations of confessors of Christ. This happened when— together with the infancy Gospel—there was consolidated in them the certainty of the divine maternity of the Virgin, who had conceived by the Holy Spirit. Even though only indirectly—yet essentially and fundamentally—this certainly should help one to understand, on the one hand, the sanctity of marriage, and on the other, the disinterestedness in view of the kingdom of heaven, of which Christ had spoken to his disciples. Nonetheless, when he spoke to them about it for the first time (as attested by the evangelist Matthew in chapter 19:10-12), that great mystery of his conception and birth was completely unknown to them. It was hidden from them as it was from all the hearers and interlocutors of Jesus of Nazareth. When Christ spoke of those who "had made themselves eunuchs for the kingdom of heaven" (Mt 19:12), the disciples could understand it only on the basis of his personal example. Such a continence must have impressed itself on their consciousness as a particular trait of likeness to Christ, who had himself remained celibate "for the kingdom of heaven." In the tradition of the old covenant, marriage and procreative fruitfulness in the body were a religiously privileged condition. The departure from this tradition had to be effected especially on the basis of the example of Christ himself. Only little by little did it come to be realized that "for the sake of the kingdom of heaven" attaches a particular meaning to that spiritual and supernatural fruitfulness of man which comes from the Holy Spirit (Spirit of God), and that fruitfulness, in a specific sense and in determined cases, is served precisely by continence for the kingdom of heaven.

More or less all these elements of Gospel awareness (that is, of an exact consciousness of the new covenant in Christ) concerning continence are found in Paul. We shall seek to show that at a suitable time.

To sum up, we can say that the principal theme of today's reflection has been the relationship between continence for the kingdom of heaven, proclaimed by Christ, and the supernatural fruitfulness of the human spirit which comes from the Holy Spirit.

General audience of March 24, 1982

The Effective and Privileged Way of Continence

We continue our reflections on celibacy and on virginity for the kingdom of heaven, on the basis of Matthew's Gospel (Mt 19:10-12). Speaking of continence for the kingdom of heaven and basing it on the example of his own life, Christ undoubtedly wished that his disciples should understand it especially in relation to the kingdom which he had come to announce and for which he indicated the correct ways. The continence he spoke of is precisely one of these ways. As appears from the context of Matthew's Gospel, it is an especially effective and privileged way. Indeed, that preference given to celibacy and virginity for the kingdom was an absolute novelty in comparison with the old covenant tradition, and had a decisive significance both for the ethos and the theology of the body.

In his statement, Christ especially pointed out its finality. He said that the way of continence, to which his own life bore witness, not only exists and is possible, but it is especially efficacious and important for the kingdom of heaven. So should it be, seeing that Christ chose it for himself. If this way is so efficacious and important, then continence for the kingdom of heaven must have a special value. As we have already noted, Christ did not approach the problem on the same level and according to the same line of reasoning in which it was posed by the disciples when they said: "If such is the case...it is not expedient to marry" (Mt 19:10). Their words implied a certain utilitarianism. However, in his reply Christ indicated indirectly that marriage, true to its original institution by the Creator (we recall that the Master at this point spoke of the beginning), is fully appropriate and of a value that is fundamental, universal and ordinary. If this is so, then continence, on its part, possesses a particular and exceptional value for this kingdom. It is obviously a question of continence consciously chosen for supernatural motives.

If Christ in his statement pointed out, before all else, the supernatural finality of that continence, he did so not only in an objective sense, but also in an explicitly subjective sense. That is, he indicated the necessity of a motivation that corresponds adequately and fully to the objective finality implied by the expression "for the kingdom." To achieve the end in question—that is, to rediscover in continence that particular spiritual fruitfulness which comes from the Holy Spirit—then continence must be willed and chosen by virtue of a deep faith. This faith does not merely show us the kingdom of God in its future fulfillment. It permits us and makes it possible for us to identify ourselves in a special way with the truth and reality of that kingdom, such as it is revealed by Christ in his Gospel message and especially by the personal example of his life and manner of behavior. Hence, it was said above that continence for the kingdom of heaven—as an unquestionable sign of the other world—bears in itself especially the interior dynamism of the mystery of the redemption of the body (cf. Lk 20:35). In this sense it possesses also the characteristic of a particular likeness to Christ. Whoever consciously chooses such continence, chooses, in a certain sense, a special participation in the mystery of the redemption (of the body). He wishes in a particular way to complete it, so to say, in his own flesh (cf. Col 1:24), finding thereby also the imprint of a likeness to Christ.

All this refers to the motivation of the choice (or to its finality in the subjective sense). In choosing continence for the kingdom of heaven, man should let himself be guided precisely by this motivation. In the case in question, Christ did not say that man is obliged to it (in any event it is certainly not a question of a duty deriving from a commandment). However, without any doubt, his concise words on continence "for the kingdom of heaven" place in bold relief its precise motivation. They point that out (that is, they indicate the finality of which the subject is well aware), both in the first part of the entire statement, and also in the second part. They indicate that here it is a question of a particular choice—a choice that is proper to a rather exceptional vocation, and not one that is universal and ordinary.

At the beginning, in the first part of his statement, Christ spoke of an understanding: "Not all men can understand it, but only those to whom it is given" (Mt 19:11). It is not a question of an understanding in the abstract, but such as to influence the decision, the personal choice, in which the gift, that is, the grace should find an adequate response in the human will. Such an understanding involves the motivation. Subsequently, the motivation influences the choice of continence, accepted after having understood its significance for the kingdom of heaven. In the second part of his statement, Christ declared then that a man makes himself a eunuch when he chooses continence for the kingdom of heaven and makes it the fundamental situation or state of his whole earthly life. In such a firm decision a supernatural motivation exists, from which the decision itself originated. It subsists by renewing itself continually.

We have already turned our attention to the particular significance of the final assertion. In the case quoted, Christ spoke of making oneself a eunuch. He not only placed in relief the specific importance of this decision which is explained by the motivation born of a deep faith, but he did not even seek to conceal the anguish that such a decision and its enduring consequences can have for a man for the normal (and on the other hand noble) inclinations of his nature.

The reference to "the beginning" in the problem of marriage enabled us to discover all the original beauty of that vocation of man, male and female. This vocation comes from God and corresponds to the twofold constitution of man, as well as to the call to the communion of persons. In preaching continence for the kingdom of God, Christ not only took a stand against the whole tradition of the old covenant, according to which marriage and procreation were religiously privileged, as we have said. But in a certain sense he expressed himself even in opposition to that beginning to which he himself had appealed. Perhaps also for this reason he nuanced his words with that particular rule of understanding to which we referred above. The analysis of the beginning (especially on the basis of the Yahwist text) had demonstrated that, even though it be possible to conceive man as solitary before God, God himself drew him from this solitude when he said: "It is not good that the man should be alone; I will make him a helper fit for him" (Gn 2:18).

So then, the double aspect, male and female, proper to the constitution of humanity, and the unity of the two which is based on it, remain the work of God "from the beginning," that is, to their ontological depth. Speaking of continence for the kingdom of heaven, Christ had before him this reality. Not without reason did he speak of it (according to Matthew) in the most immediate context in which he referred precisely to the beginning, that is, to the divine beginning of marriage in the constitution of man.

On the strength of Christ's words it can be asserted that marriage helps us to understand continence for the kingdom of heaven. Not only that, but also continence itself sheds a particular light on marriage viewed in the mystery of creation and redemption.

General audience of March 31, 1982

The "Superiority" of Continence
Does Not Devalue Marriage

In proclaiming continence for the kingdom of heaven, Christ fully accepted all that the Creator wrought and instituted from the beginning. Consequently, on the one hand, continence must demonstrate that in his deepest being, man is not only "dual," but also (in this duality) "alone" before God, with God. Nevertheless, on the other hand, what is an invitation to solitude for God in the call to continence for the kingdom of heaven at the same time respects both the "dual nature of mankind" (that is, his masculinity and femininity), and the dimension of communion of existence that is proper to the person. Whoever, in compliance with Christ's words, correctly comprehends the call to continence for the kingdom of heaven and responds to it, thereby preserves the integral truth of his own humanity. He does this without losing along the way any of the essential elements of the vocation of the person created in God's image and likeness. This is important to the idea itself, or rather, to the idea of continence, that is, for its objective content, which appears in Christ's teachings as radically new. It is equally important to the accomplishment of that ideal, in order for the actual decision made by man or woman to live in celibacy or virginity for the kingdom of heaven (he who "makes himself" a eunuch, to use Christ's words) to be fully sincere in its motivation.

From the context of the Gospel according to Matthew (Mt 19:10-12), it can be seen sufficiently clearly that here it is not a question of diminishing the value of matrimony in favor of continence, nor of lessening the value of one in comparison with the other. Instead, it is a question of breaking away from, with full awareness, that which in man, by the Creator's will, causes him to marry, and to move toward continence. This reveals itself to the concrete man, masculine or feminine, as a call and gift of particular eloquence and meaning for the kingdom of heaven. Christ's words (cf. Mt 19:11-12) arise from the reality of man's condition. With the same realism, they lead him out toward the call in which, in a new way— even though remaining "dual" by nature (that is, directed as man toward woman, and as woman toward man)—he is capable of discovering in his solitude, which never ceases to be a personal dimension of everyone's dual nature, a new and even fuller form of intersubjective communion with others. This guidance of the call explains explicitly the expression "for the kingdom of heaven." Indeed, the achievement of this kingdom must be found along the line of the authentic development of the image and likeness of God in its trinitarian meaning, that is, precisely of communion. By choosing continence for the kingdom of heaven, man has the knowledge of being able in that way to fulfill himself differently and, in a certain way, more than through matrimony, becoming a "true gift to others" (cf. *GS* 24).

Through the words recorded in Matthew (Mt 19:11-12), Christ makes us understand clearly that that going toward continence for the sake of the kingdom of heaven is linked with a voluntary giving up of matrimony. In that state, man and woman (according to the meaning the Creator gave to their union "in the beginning") become gifts to one another through their masculinity and femininity, also through their physical union. Continence means a conscious and voluntary renouncement of that union and all that is connected to it in the full meaning of life and human society. The man who renounces matrimony also gives up procreation as the foundation of the family, concessive renouncements and voluntary children. The words of Christ to which we refer indicate without doubt this kind of renunciation, although they do not go into detail. The way in which these words were stated leads us to assume that Christ understood the importance of such a sacrifice, and that he understood it not only in view of the opinions on the subject prevailing in Jewish society at that time. He understood the importance of this sacrifice also in relationship to the good which matrimony and the family in themselves constitute due to their divine institution. Therefore, through the way in which he stated the words he made it understood that breaking away from the circle of the good that he himself called "for the sake of the kingdom of heaven," is connected with a certain self-sacrifice. That break also becomes the beginning of successive self-sacrifices that are indispensable if the first and fundamental choice must be consistent in the breadth of one's entire earthly life. Thanks only to such consistency, that choice is internally reasonable and not contradictory.

In this way, in the call to continence as Christ stated it—concisely but at the same time precisely—the outline and dynamism of the mystery of the redemption emerge, as has previously been stated. It is the same profile under which Jesus, in his Sermon on the Mount, pronounced the words about the need to guard against concupiscence, against the desire that begins with "looking at" and becomes at that very moment "adultery in the heart." Behind Matthew's words, both in chapter 19 (verses 11-12) and in chapter 5 (verses 27-28), the same anthropology and the same ethos are found. In the invitation to voluntary continence for the kingdom of heaven, the prospects of this ethos are enlarged upon. The anthropology of historical man is found in the overall view of the words of the Sermon on the Mount. In the overall view of the words on voluntary continence, essentially the same anthropology remains. But it is illumined by the prospect of the kingdom of heaven, in other words, of the future anthropology of the resurrection. Nonetheless, along the path of this voluntary continence during earthly life, the anthropology of the resurrection does not replace the anthropology of historical man. In him the heritage of the threefold concupiscence remains at the same time, the heritage of sin together with the heritage of redemption. It remains in the one who must make the decision about continence for the kingdom of heaven. He must put this decision into effect, subjugating the sinfulness of his human nature to the forces that spring from the mystery of the redemption of the body. He must do so just as any other man does who has not made a similar decision and whose way remains that of matrimony. The only difference is the type of responsibility for the good chosen, just as the type of good chosen is different.

In his pronouncement, did Christ perhaps suggest the superiority of continence for the kingdom of heaven to matrimony? Certainly, he said that this is an exceptional vocation, not a common one. In addition he affirmed that it is especially important and necessary to the kingdom of heaven. If we understand superiority to matrimony in this sense, we must admit that Christ set it out implicitly. However, he did not express it directly. Only Paul will say of those who choose matrimony that they do "well." About those who are willing to live in voluntary continence, he will say that they do "better" (1 Cor 7:38).

That is also the opinion of the whole of Tradition, both doctrinal and pastoral. The "superiority" of continence to matrimony in the authentic Tradition of the Church never means disparagement of matrimony or belittlement of its essential value. It does not even mean a shift, even implicit, on the Manichean positions, or a support of ways of evaluating or acting based on the Manichean understanding of the body and sexuality, matrimony and procreation. The evangelical and authentically Christian superiority of virginity and continence is dictated by the motive of the kingdom of heaven. In Christ's words recorded in Matthew (Mt 19:11-12) we find a solid basis for admitting only this superiority, while we do not find any basis whatever for any disparagement of matrimony which, however, could have been present in the recognition of that superiority.

General audience of April 7, 1982

Marriage and Continence Complement Each Other

Let us now continue our reflections of the previous weeks on the words about continence for the sake of the kingdom of heaven which Christ addressed to his disciples, according to the Gospel of Matthew (cf. 19:10-12).

Let us say once more that these words, as concise as they are, are admirably rich and precise. They are rich with a number of implications both of a doctrinal and pastoral nature. At the same time they establish a proper limit on the subject. Therefore, any kind of Manichaean interpretation decidedly goes beyond that limit, so that, according to what Christ said in the Sermon on the Mount, there is lustful desire "in the heart" (Mt 5:27-28).

In Christ's words on continence for the kingdom of heaven there is no reference to the inferiority of marriage with regard to the body, or in other words with regard to the essence of marriage, consisting in the fact that man and woman join together in marriage, thus becoming one flesh. "The two will become one flesh" (Gn 2:24). Christ's words recorded in Matthew 19:11-12 (as also the words of Paul in 1 Corinthians 7) give no reason to assert the inferiority of marriage, nor the superiority of virginity or celibacy inasmuch as by their nature virginity and celibacy consist in abstinence from the conjugal union in the body. Christ's words on this point are quite clear. He proposes to his disciples the ideal of continence and the call to it, not by reason of inferiority, nor with prejudice against conjugal union of the body, but only for the sake of the kingdom of heaven.

In this light a deeper clarification of the expression "for the sake of the kingdom. of heaven" is especially useful. This is what we shall try to do in the following, at least briefly. However, with regard to the correct understanding of the relationship between marriage and continence that Christ speaks about, and the understanding of that relationship as all Tradition has understood it, it is worthwhile to add that superiority and inferiority fall within the limits of the same complementarity of marriage and continence for the kingdom of God.

Marriage and continence are neither opposed to each other, nor do they divide the human (and Christian) community into two camps (let us say, those who are "perfect" because of continence and those who are "imperfect" or "less perfect" because of the reality of married life). But as it is often said, these two basic situations, these two "states," in a certain sense explain and complete each other as regards the existence and Christian life of this community. In its entirety and in each of its members this is fulfilled in the dimension of the kingdom of God and has an eschatological orientation, which is precisely of that kingdom. So, with regard to this dimension and this orientation—in which the entire community, that is, all of those who belong to it, must share in the faith—continence for the kingdom of heaven has a particular importance and a special eloquence for those who live a married life. Besides, these constitute the majority.

It therefore seems that a complementarity understood in this way finds its foundation in the words of Christ according to Matthew 19:11-12 (and also 1 Cor 7). On the other hand there is no basis for a presumed counterposition according to which celibates (or unmarried persons), only by reason of their continence, would make up the class of those who are "perfect," and, to the contrary, married persons would make up a class of those who are "imperfect" (or "less perfect"). If, according to a certain theological tradition, one speaks of a state of perfection *(status perfectionis)*, it is done not by reason of continence in itself. But it is in regard to the entirety of a life based on the evangelical counsels (poverty, chastity and obedience), since this life corresponds to Christ's call to perfection: "If you would be perfect..." (Mt 19:21). Perfection of the Christian life, instead, is measured with the rule of charity. It follows that a person who does not live in the state of perfection (that is, in an institute that bases its life plan on vows of poverty, chastity and obedience), or in other words, who does not live in a religious institute but in the "world," can *de facto* reach a superior degree of perfection—whose measure is charity—in comparison to the person who lives in the state of perfection with a lesser degree of charity. In any case, the evangelical counsels undoubtedly help us to achieve a fuller charity. Therefore, whoever achieves it, even if he does not live in an institutionalized state of perfection, reaches that perfection which flows from charity, through fidelity to the spirit of those counsels. Such perfection is possible and accessible to every person, both in a religious institute and in the "world."

It seems then that the complementarity of marriage and continence for the kingdom of heaven, in their significance and manifold importance, adequately corresponds to Christ's words recorded in Matthew (19:11-12). In the life of an authentically Christian community the attitudes and values proper to the one and the other state—that is, to one or the other essential and conscious choice as a vocation for one's entire earthly life and in the perspective of the "heavenly Church"—complete and in a certain sense interpenetrate each other. Perfect conjugal love must be marked by that fidelity and that donation to the only Spouse (and also of the fidelity and donation of the Spouse to the only Bride), on which religious profession and priestly celibacy are founded. Finally, the nature of one and the other love is "conjugal," that is, expressed through the total gift of oneself. Both types of love tend to express that conjugal meaning of the body which from the beginning has been inscribed in the personal makeup of man and woman. We shall return to this point at a later date.

On the other hand, conjugal love which finds its expression in continence for the kingdom of heaven must lead in its normal development to paternity or maternity in a spiritual sense (in other words, precisely to that fruitfulness of the Holy Spirit that we have already spoken about), in a way analogous to conjugal love, which matures in physical paternity and maternity, and in this way confirms itself as conjugal love. For its part, physical procreation also fully responds to its meaning only if it is completed by paternity and maternity in the spirit, whose expression and fruit is all the educative work of the parents in regard to the children born of their conjugal corporeal union.

As can be seen, there are many aspects and spheres of the complementarity between the vocation, in an evangelical sense, of those who "marry and are given in marriage" (Lk 20:34), and of those who knowingly and voluntarily choose continence "for the kingdom of heaven" (Mt 19:12).

In First Corinthians (which we will analyze later in our considerations), St. Paul will write on this subject: "Each has his special gift from God, one of one kind and one of another" (1 Cor 7:7).

General audience of April 14, 1982

The Value of Continence Is Found in Love

Let us continue our reflections on Christ's words about continence for the sake of the kingdom of heaven. It is impossible to understand fully the significance and the nature of continence if the last phrase of Christ's statement, "for the sake of the kingdom of heaven," is not complete in its adequate, concrete and objective content. We have previously said that this phrase expresses the motive, or in a certain sense places in relief, the subjective purpose of Christ's call to continence. However, the expression in itself has an objective character. It indicates an objective reality for which individual persons, men and women, can "make themselves" eunuchs (as Christ says). The reality of the kingdom in Christ's statement according to Matthew (19:11-12) is defined in a precise, but at the same time general way, so as to be able to include all the determinations and particular meanings that are proper to it.

The kingdom of heaven means the kingdom of God, which Christ preached in its final, that is, eschatological, completion. Christ preached this kingdom in its temporal realization or establishment, and at the same time he foretold it in its eschatological completion. The temporal establishment of the kingdom of God is at the same time its beginning and its preparation for definitive fulfillment. Christ calls to this kingdom and in a certain sense invites everyone to it (cf. the parable of the wedding banquet in Mathew 22:1-14). If he calls some to continence "for the sake of the kingdom of heaven," it follows from the content of that expression that he calls them to participate in a singular way in the establishment of the kingdom of God on earth, through which the definitive phase of the kingdom of heaven is begun and prepared.

In this sense we have said that this call bears in itself the particular sign of the dynamism of the mystery of the redemption of the body. Therefore, as we have already mentioned, continence for the sake of the kingdom of God manifests the renunciation of one's self, taking up one's cross every day, and following Christ (cf. Lk 9:23). This can reach the point of implying the renunciation of marriage and a family of one's own. All this arises from the conviction that in this way it is possible to contribute more greatly to the realization of the kingdom of God in its earthly dimension with the prospect of eschatological completion. In his statement according to Matthew (19:11-12), Christ said generically that the voluntary renunciation of marriage has this purpose, but he did not say so specifically. In his first statement on this subject, he still did not specify through what concrete obligation this voluntary continence is necessary and even indispensable for the realization of the kingdom of God on earth and for its preparation for future fulfillment. We will hear something further on this point from Paul of Tarsus (1 Cor) and the rest will be completed by the life of the Church in her historical development, borne by the current of authentic Tradition.

In Christ's statement on continence for the sake of the kingdom of heaven, we do not find any more detailed indication about how to understand that kingdom—with regard to its earthly realization and its definitive completion—in its specific and exceptional relation with those who voluntarily "make themselves eunuchs" for it.

Neither is it said through which particular aspect of the reality that constitutes the kingdom are those associated to it who freely are made "eunuchs." In fact, we know that the kingdom of heaven is for everybody. Those who "marry and are given in marriage" also are in a relation with it on earth (and in heaven). For everybody it is the Lord's vineyard in which they must work here on earth, and subsequently it is the Father's house in which they must be in eternity. Therefore, what is that kingdom for those who choose voluntary continence in view of it?

For now, we do not find any answer to this question in Christ's statement as reported by Matthew (19:11-12). It seems that this is in keeping with the character of the whole statement. Christ answered his disciples in such a way as not to keep in line with their thought and their evaluation, which contained, at least indirectly, a utilitarian attitude regarding marriage ("If this is the case...it is better not to marry"—Mt 19:10). The Master explicitly evaded these general lines of the problem. Therefore, speaking about continence for the sake of the kingdom of heaven, he did not indicate in this way why the renunciation of marriage is worthwhile, so that the "it is better" would not be understood by his disciples in any utilitarian sense. He said only that this continence is at times required, if not indispensable, for the kingdom of God. With this he pointed out that continence, in the kingdom which Christ preached and to which he calls, constitutes a particular value in itself. Those who voluntarily choose it must do so with regard to that value it has, and not as a result of any other calculation whatever.

This essential tone of Christ's answer, which refers directly to continence itself "for the sake of the kingdom of heaven," can also be referred indirectly to the previous problem of marriage (cf. Mt 19:3-9). Therefore, considering his statement as a whole, according to Christ's basic intention, the answer would be as follows. If anyone chooses marriage, he must choose it just as it was instituted by the Creator "from the beginning." He must seek in it those values that correspond to God's plan. If on the other hand anyone decides to pursue continence for the kingdom of heaven, he must seek in it the values proper to such a vocation. In other words, one must act in conformity with his chosen vocation.

The kingdom of heaven is certainly the definitive fulfillment of the aspirations of all men, to whom Christ addressed his message. It is the fullness of the good that the human heart desires beyond the limits of all that can be his lot in this earthly life. It is the maximum fullness of God's bounty toward man. In his conversation with the Sadducees (cf. Mt 22:24-30; Mk 12:18-27; Lk 20:27-40), which we have previously analyzed, we find other details about that kingdom, or rather about that other world. There are still more in the whole New Testament. Therefore, it seems that to clarify what the kingdom of heaven is for those who choose voluntary continence for its sake, the revelation of the nuptial relationship of Christ with the Church has a particular significance. Among the other texts, however, a decisive one is that from Ephesians 5:25ff. It will be especially well to rely on this when we consider the question of the sacramentality of marriage.

That text is equally valid both for the theology of marriage and for the theology of continence for the sake of the kingdom, that is, the theology of virginity or celibacy. It seems that in that text we find almost concretized what Christ had said to his disciples, inviting them to voluntary continence for the sake of the kingdom of heaven.

In this analysis it has already been sufficiently emphasized that Christ's words—with all their great conciseness—are fundamental, full of essential content and also characterized by a certain severity. There is no doubt that Christ put out his call to continence in the perspective of the other world. But in this call he put the emphasis on everything which expresses the temporal realism of the decision for such continence, a decision bound with the will to share in the redeeming work of Christ.

So in the light of Christ's respective words reported by Matthew (19:11-12), the depth and the gravity of the decision to live in continence for the sake of the kingdom emerge above all, and the importance of the renunciation that such a decision implies finds its expression. Undoubtedly, throughout all this, through the gravity and depth of the decision, through the severity and the responsibility that it bears with it, love appears and shines through—love as the readiness to give the exclusive gift of oneself for the sake of the kingdom of God. However, in Christ's words this love seems to be veiled by what is put in the foreground instead. Christ did not conceal from his disciples the fact that the choice of continence for the sake of the kingdom of heaven, viewed in the light of temporal categories, is a renunciation. That way of speaking to his disciples, which clearly expresses the truth of his teaching and of the demands contained in it, is significant through the whole Gospel. It is precisely this that confers on it, among other things, so convincing a mark and power.

General audience of April 21, 1982

Celibacy Is a Particular Response to the Love of the Divine Spouse

"There are others who have made themselves eunuchs for the sake of the kingdom of heaven." This is how Christ expressed himself in St. Matthew's Gospel (Mt 19:12).

It is natural for the human heart to accept demands, even difficult ones, in the name of love for an ideal, and above all in the name of love for a person. (By its very nature, love is directed toward a person.) Therefore in that call to continence for the sake of the kingdom of heaven, first the disciples themselves, and then the whole living Tradition of the Church, will soon discover the love that is referred to Christ himself as the Spouse of the Church, the Spouse of souls. He has given himself to them to the very limit, in the paschal and Eucharistic mystery.

In this way, continence for the sake of the kingdom of heaven, the choice of virginity or celibacy for one's whole life, has become in the experience of Christ's disciples and followers the act of a particular response of love for the divine Spouse. Therefore it has acquired the significance of an act of nuptial love, that is, a nuptial giving of oneself for the purpose of reciprocating in a particular way the nuptial love of the Redeemer. It is a giving of oneself understood as renunciation, but made above all out of love.

In this way we obtained all the wealth of the meaning contained in the very concise, but at the same time very profound, statement of Christ about continence for the sake of the kingdom of heaven. But now it is fitting that we direct our attention to the significance that these words have for the theology of the body, just as we tried to present and reconstruct the biblical foundations for it "from the beginning." Christ referred to that biblical "beginning" in his conversation with the Pharisees on the subject of marriage, its unity and indissolubility (cf. Mt 19:3-9). He did this shortly before addressing to his disciples the words about continence for the sake of the kingdom of heaven (cf. Mt 19:10-12). This analysis of that "beginning" allows us to recall the profound truth about the nuptial meaning of the human body in its masculinity and femininity, as we deduced at that time from the analysis of the first chapters of Genesis (especially from 2:23-25). It was in just this way that it was necessary to formulate and specify what we find in those ancient texts.

The modern mentality is accustomed to thinking and speaking about the sexual instinct, transferring onto the level of human reality what is proper to the world of living beings, of animals. Now deep reflection on the concise text of the first and second chapters of Genesis permits us to establish with certainty and conviction that right from the beginning a very clear and univocal boundary is laid down in the Bible between the world of animals *(animalia)* and the man created in the image and likeness of God. In that text, though relatively brief, there is nevertheless enough to demonstrate that man has a clear awareness of what essentially distinguishes him from all other living beings *(animalia)*.

Therefore, it is not at all appropriate and adequate to apply to man this substantially naturalistic category that is contained in the concept and in the expression of sexual instinct. It is obvious that such application can become the basis for a certain analogy. In fact, the particular characteristic of man compared with the whole world of living beings *(animalia)* is such that man, understood from the viewpoint of species, can not even basically qualify as an *animal,* but a *rational animal.* Therefore, despite this analogy, applying the concept of sexual instinct to man—given the dual nature in which he exists as male or female—nevertheless greatly limits, and in a certain sense diminishes what is the very masculinity-femininity in the personal dimension of human subjectivity. It limits and diminishes even what for both of them, man and woman, unite to become one flesh (cf. Gn 2:24). In order to express this in an appropriate and adequate way, we must use also an analysis different from the naturalistic one. It is precisely the study of the biblical beginning that obliges us to do this convincingly. The truth about the nuptial meaning of the human body in its masculinity and femininity seems to be a key concept in this area. It is deduced from the first chapters of Genesis (especially from 2:23-25), that is, the discovery at the time of the nuptial meaning of the body in the personal makeup of the subjectivity of man and woman. At the same time it is the only appropriate and adequate concept.

It is necessary to reread and understand Christ's words about continence for the sake of the kingdom of heaven precisely in relation to this concept, to this truth about the nuptial meaning of the human body. His words were spoken in the immediate context of that reference to the beginning, on which he based his teaching about the unity and indissolubility of marriage. At the basis of Christ's call to continence there is not only the sexual instinct, which is in the category, I would say, of a naturalistic necessity. But there is also the consciousness of the freedom of the gift. This is organically connected with the profound and mature knowledge of the nuptial meaning of the body, in the total makeup of the personal subjectivity of man and woman. Only in relation to such a meaning of the masculinity and femininity of the human person does the call to voluntary continence for the sake of the kingdom of heaven find full warranty and motivation. Only and exclusively in this perspective did Christ say, "He who is able to receive this, let him receive it" (Mt 19:12). With this, he indicated that such continence—although in each case it is above all a gift—can be also received. That is, it can be drawn and deduced from the concept that man has his own psychosomatic "I" in its entirety, and especially the masculinity and femininity of this "I" in the reciprocal relationship which is as though by nature inscribed in every human subjectivity.

As we recall from the previous analyses, developed on the basis of Genesis (cf. Gn 2:23-25), that reciprocal relationship of masculinity and femininity, that reciprocal "for" of man and woman, can be understood in an appropriate and adequate way only in the overall dynamics of the personal subject. Christ's words in Matthew (cf. 19:11-12) consequently show that this "for," present from the beginning at the basis of marriage, can also be at the basis of continence "for" the kingdom of heaven! Based on the same disposition of the personal subject, thanks to which man fully rediscovers himself through a sincere gift of himself (cf. *GS* 24), man (male and female) is capable of choosing the personal gift of his very self. This is made to another person in a conjugal pact in which they become "one flesh." He is also capable of freely renouncing such a giving of himself to another person, so that, choosing continence for the sake of the kingdom of heaven, he can give himself totally to Christ. On the basis of the same disposition of the personal subject and on the basis of the same nuptial meaning of the being as a body, male or female, there can be formed the love that commits man to marriage for the whole duration of his life (cf. Mt 19:3-10). But there can also be formed the love that commits man to a life of continence for the sake of the kingdom of heaven (cf. Mt 19:11-12). Christ is speaking precisely about this in his overall statement addressed to the Pharisees (cf. Mt 19:3-10) and then to the disciples (cf. Mt 19:11-12).

It is evident that the choice of marriage, just as it was instituted by the Creator from the beginning, supposes the learning and the interior acceptance of the nuptial meaning of the body, bound up with the masculinity and femininity of the human person. In fact, this very thing is expressed concisely in the verses of Genesis. In listening to Christ's words addressed to the disciples about continence for the sake of the kingdom of heaven (cf. Mt 19:11-12), we cannot think that this second kind of choice can be made consciously and freely without reference to one's masculinity or femininity and to that nuptial meaning which is proper to man precisely in the masculinity or femininity of his being as a personal subject. Furthermore, in the light of Christ's words, we must admit that this second kind of choice, namely, continence for the sake of the kingdom of God, comes about also in relation to the masculinity or femininity proper to the person who makes such a choice. It comes about on the basis of full consciousness of that nuptial meaning which masculinity and femininity contain in themselves. If this choice should come about by way of some artificial "prescinding" from this real wealth of every human subject, it would not appropriately and adequately correspond to the content of Christ's words in Matthew 19:11-12.

Here Christ explicitly required full understanding when he said, "He who is able to receive this, let him receive it" (Mt 19:12).

General audience of April 28, 1982

Celibacy for the Kingdom Affirms Marriage

In answering the Pharisees' questions about marriage and its indissolubility, Christ referred to the beginning, that is, to its original institution on the part of the Creator. Since those with whom he was speaking recalled the law of Moses, which provided for the possibility of the so-called "decree of divorce," he answered, "Because of the hardness of your hearts Moses permitted you to divorce your wives, but it was not so from the beginning" (Mt 19:8).

After the conversation with the Pharisees, Christ's disciples addressed the following words to him: "'If this is the case of a man with his wife, it is not expedient to marry.' He answered them, 'Not all men can receive this precept, but only those to whom it is given. For there are eunuchs who have been so from birth, and there are eunuchs who have been made eunuchs by men, and there are eunuchs who have made themselves eunuchs for the sake of the kingdom of heaven. He who is able to receive this, let him receive it'" (Mt 19:10-12).

Christ's words undoubtedly allude to a conscious and voluntary renunciation of marriage. This renunciation is possible only when one admits an authentic knowledge of that value that is constituted by the nuptial disposition of masculinity and femininity to marriage. In order for man to be fully aware of what he is choosing (continence for the sake of the kingdom), he must also be fully aware of what he is renouncing. (It is a question here of the knowledge of the value in an ideal sense; nevertheless this knowledge is after all realistic.) In this way, Christ certainly demands a mature choice. The form in which the call to continence for the sake of the kingdom of heaven is expressed proves this without a doubt.

But a renunciation made with full awareness of the above-mentioned value is not enough. In the light of Christ's words, and also in the light of the whole authentic Christian Tradition, it is possible to deduce that this renunciation is at the same time a particular form of affirming that value from which the unmarried person consistently abstains, following the evangelical counsel. This can seem paradoxical. Nevertheless, it is known that many statements in the Gospel are paradoxical, and those are often the most eloquent and profound. Accepting such a meaning of the call to continence for the sake of the kingdom of heaven, we draw a correct conclusion. The realization of this call serves also in a particular way to confirm the nuptial meaning of the human body in its masculinity and femininity. The renunciation of marriage for the kingdom of God at the same time highlights that meaning in all its interior truth and personal beauty. We can say that this renunciation on the part of individual persons, men and women, in a certain sense is indispensable. This is so that the nuptial meaning of the body can be more easily recognized in all the ethos of human life and above all in the ethos of conjugal and family life.

So continence for the sake of the kingdom of heaven (virginity, celibacy) orients the life of persons who freely choose it toward the exclusion of the common way of conjugal and family life. Nevertheless it is not without significance for this life, for its style, its value and its evangelical authenticity. Let us not forget that the only key to understanding the sacramentality of marriage is the spousal love of Christ for the Church (cf. Eph 5:22-23)—Christ, the Son of the Virgin, who was himself a virgin, that is, a "eunuch for the sake of the kingdom of heaven," in the most perfect meaning of the term. It will be convenient for us to take up this point again at a later time.

At the end of these reflections a concrete problem still remains. In what way is this call formed in man—to whom the call to continence for the sake of the kingdom has been given—on the basis of the knowledge of the nuptial meaning of the body in its masculinity and femininity, and further, as the fruit of such knowledge? In what way is it formed, or rather transformed? This question is equally important, both from the viewpoint of the theology of the body, and from the viewpoint of the development of the human personality, which has a personalistic and charismatic character at the same time. If we should want to answer this question exhaustively—in the measure of all the aspects and all the concrete problems that it includes—it would be necessary to make a study based on the relationship between marriage and virginity and between marriage and celibacy. However this would go beyond the limits of the present considerations.

Remaining within the sphere of Christ's words according to Matthew (19:11-12), we must conclude our reflections with the following affirmation. First, if continence for the sake of the kingdom of heaven undoubtedly signifies a renunciation, this renunciation is at the same time an affirmation. It is an affirmation that arises from the discovery of the gift, that is, at the same time from the discovery of a new perspective of the personal realization of oneself "through a sincere gift of oneself" (GS 24). This discovery still lies in a profound interior harmony with the significance of the nuptial meaning of the body, bound "from the beginning" to the masculinity or femininity of man as a personal subject. Second, although continence for the sake of the kingdom of heaven is identified with the renunciation of marriage, which in the life of a man and woman gives rise to the family, in no way can one see in this a denial of the essential value of marriage. On the contrary, continence serves indirectly to highlight what is most lasting and most profoundly personal in the vocation to marriage. It highlights that which in the dimensions of temporality (and at the same time in the perspective of the other world) corresponds to the dignity of the personal gift, bound to the nuptial meaning of the body in its masculinity or femininity.

In this way, Christ's call to continence "for the sake of the kingdom of heaven," rightly associated to the reference to the future resurrection (cf. Mt 21:24-30; Mk 12:18-27; Lk 20:27-40), has a capital significance not only for Christian ethos and spirituality, but also for anthropology and for the whole theology of the body, which we discover at its foundation. We remember that Christ, referring to the resurrection of the body in the other world, said, according to the version of the three synoptic Gospels, "When they rise from the dead...they will neither marry nor be given in marriage..." (Mk 12:25). These words, already analyzed, form part of our overall considerations on the theology of the body and contribute to building this theology.

General audience of May 5, 1982

Voluntary Continence Derives from a Counsel, Not from a Command

Having analyzed Christ's words reported in Matthew's Gospel (Mt 19:10-12), it is now fitting to pass on to Paul's treatment of virginity and marriage.

Christ's statement about continence for the sake of the kingdom of heaven is concise and fundamental. In Paul's teaching, as we will soon be convinced, we can distinguish a correlating of the words of the Master. However, the significance of his statement (1 Cor 7) taken as a whole is assessed in a different way. The greatness of Paul's teaching consists in the fact that in presenting the truth proclaimed by Christ in all its authenticity and identity, he gives it a stamp of his own. In a certain sense it is his own personal interpretation, but it is drawn primarily from the experiences of his apostolic missionary activity, and perhaps directly from the necessity to answer the concrete questions of those to whom this activity was directed. So in Paul we encounter the question of the mutual relationship between marriage and celibacy or virginity. This subject troubled the minds of the first generation of Christ's confessors, the generation of disciples, of apostles, of the first Christian communities. This happened through the converts from hellenism, therefore from paganism, more than through the converts from Judaism. This can explain the fact that the subject appears precisely in a letter addressed to the community in Corinth.

The tone of the whole statement is without doubt a magisterial one. However, the tone as well as the language is also pastoral. Paul teaches the doctrine handed down by the Master to the apostles. At the same time he engages in a continuous conversation on the subject in question with the recipients of his letter. He speaks as a classical teacher of morality, facing and resolving problems of conscience. Therefore moralists love to turn preferably to the explanations and resolutions of this First Letter to the Corinthians (chapter 7). However it is necessary to remember that the ultimate basis for those resolutions is sought in the life and teaching of Christ himself.

The Apostle emphasizes with great clarity that virginity, or voluntary continence, derives exclusively from a counsel and not from a commandment: "With regard to virgins, I have no command from the Lord, but I give my opinion." Paul gives this opinion "as one who has obtained mercy from the Lord and merits your trust" (1 Cor 7:25). As is seen from the words quoted, the Apostle, just as the Gospel (cf. Mt 19:11-12), distinguishes between counsel and commandment. On the basis of the doctrinal rule of understanding proclaimed teaching, he wants to counsel. He wishes to give his personal opinions to those who turned to him. So in First Corinthians (chapter 7), the counsel clearly has two different meanings. The author states that virginity is a counsel and not a commandment. At the same time he gives his opinions to persons already married and also to those who still must make a decision in this regard, and finally to those who have been widowed. The problem is substantially the same as the one which we meet in the whole statement of Christ reported by Matthew (19:2-12)—first on marriage and its indissolubility, and then on voluntary continence for the sake of the kingdom of heaven. Nevertheless, the style of this problem is totally his own. It is Paul's.

"If however someone thinks he is not behaving properly with regard to his betrothed, if his passions are strong, and it has to be, let him do as he wishes; he does not sin. Let them marry! But whoever is firmly established in his heart, being under no necessity but having his desire under control, and has determined this in his heart, to keep her as his betrothed, he will do well. So then, he who marries his betrothed does well, and he who refrains from marriage does better" (1 Cor 7:36-38).

The one who had sought advice could have been a young man who found himself faced with the decision to take a wife, or perhaps a newly-wed who in the face of the current asceticism existing in Corinth was reflecting on the direction to give to his marriage. It could have even been a father, or the guardian of a girl, who had posed the question of her marriage. In any case, it would deal directly with the decision that derives from their rights as guardians. Paul is writing at a time when decisions in general belonged more to parents and guardians than to the young people themselves. Therefore, in answering in this way the question that was addressed to him, he tried to explain very precisely that the decision about continence, that is, about the life of virginity, must be voluntary, and that only such continence is better than marriage. The expressions, "he does well," "he does better," are completely univocal in this context.

So then the Apostle teaches that virginity, or voluntary continence, the young woman's abstention from marriage, derives exclusively from a counsel, and given the appropriate circumstances, it is better than marriage. The question of sin does not enter in any way. "Are you bound to a wife? Do not seek to be free. Are you free from a wife? Do not seek marriage. But if you marry, you do not sin, and if a girl marries, she does not sin" (1 Cor 7:27-28). Solely on the basis of these words, we certainly cannot make judgments on what the Apostle was thinking or teaching about marriage. This subject will indeed be partially explained in the context of First Corinthians (chapter 7) and more fully in Ephesians (Eph 5:21-33). In our case, he is probably dealing with the answer to the question of whether marriage is a sin. One could also think that in such a question there might be some influence from dualistic pro-gnostic currents, which later become encratism and Manichaeism. Paul answers that the question of sin absolutely does not enter into play here. It is not a question of the difference between good and evil, but only between good and better. He later goes on to justify why one who chooses marriage will do well and one who chooses virginity, or voluntary continence, will do better.

We will treat of Paul's argumentation in our next reflection.

General audience of June 23, 1982

"The Unmarried Person Is Anxious to Please the Lord"

In explaining in the seventh chapter of First Corinthians the question of marriage and virginity (or continence for the sake of the kingdom of God), St. Paul tries to give the reason why one who chooses marriage does well, while one who decides on a life of continence or virginity does better. He writes: "I tell you this, brothers, the time is already short. From now on, let those who have wives live as though they had none...." And then: "...those who buy, as though they had no goods; those who deal with the world, as though they had no dealings with it, for the form of this world is passing away. I want you to be free from anxieties..." (1 Cor 7:29 -32).

The last words of the text just quoted show that in his argumentation, Paul is also referring to his own experience, which makes his reasoning more personal. He not only formulates the principle and seeks to justify it as such, but he ties it in with personal reflections and convictions arising from his practice of the evangelical counsel of celibacy. The individual expressions and phrases testify to their persuasive power. The Apostle not only writes to his Corinthians: "I wish that all were as I myself am" (1 Cor 7:7), but he goes further when, referring to men who contract marriage, he writes: "Yet they will have troubles in the flesh, and I would want to spare you that" (1 Cor 7:28). However, this personal conviction of his was already expressed in the first words of the seventh chapter of the same letter, referring to this opinion of the Corinthians, in order to modify it as well: "Now concerning the matters about which you wrote, it is well for a man not to touch a woman..." (1 Cor 7:1).

We can ask here, what "troubles in the flesh" did Paul have in mind? Christ spoke only of suffering (or "afflictions"), which a woman experiences when she is to deliver a child. However, he emphasized the joy that fills her as a reward for these sufferings after the birth of her child, the joy of motherhood (cf. Jn 16:21). Paul, rather, writes of the "tribulations of the body" which spouses expect. Would this be an expression of the Apostle's personal aversion with regard to marriage? In this realistic observation we must see a just warning for those who—as at times young people do—hold that conjugal union and living together must bring them only happiness and joy. The experience of life shows that spouses are not rarely disappointed in what they were greatly expecting. The joy of the union brings with it also those "troubles in the flesh" that the Apostle writes about in his letter to the Corinthians. These are often troubles of a moral nature. If by this he intends to say that true conjugal love—precisely that love by virtue of which "a man...cleaves to his wife and the two become one flesh" (Gn 2:24)—is also a difficult love, he certainly remains on the grounds of evangelical truth. There is no reason here to see symptoms of the attitude that later was to characterize Manichaeism.

In his words about continence for the sake of the kingdom of God, Christ did not in any way try to direct his listeners to celibacy or virginity by pointing out to them the troubles of marriage. We see rather that he tried to highlight various aspects, humanly painful, of deciding on continence. Both the social reason and reasons of a subjective nature led Christ to say about the man who makes such a decision, that he makes himself a eunuch, that is, he voluntarily embraces continence. But precisely thanks to this, the whole subjective significance, the greatness and exceptional character of such a decision clearly springs forth. It is the significance of a mature response to a particular gift of the Spirit.

In the First Letter to the Corinthians, St. Paul does not understand the counsel of continence differently, but he expresses it in a different way. He writes: "I tell you this, brothers, the time is already short..." (1 Cor 7:29), and a little later on, "the form of this world is passing away..." (1 Cor 7:31). This observation about the perishability of human existence and the transience of the temporal world, in a certain sense about the accidental nature of all that is created, should cause "those who have wives to live as though they had none" (1 Cor 7:29; cf. 7:31). At the same time it should prepare the ground for the teaching on continence. At the center of his reasoning, Paul places the key phrase that can be joined to Christ's statement, one of its own kind, on the subject of continence for the sake of the kingdom of God (cf. Mt 19:12).

While Christ emphasized the greatness of the renunciation, inseparable from such a decision, Paul demonstrates above all what the kingdom of God must mean in the life of the person who has renounced marriage in view of it. While the triple parallelism of Christ's statement reaches its climax in the word that signifies the greatness of the renunciation voluntarily made ("...and there are others who have become eunuchs for the sake of the kingdom of heaven"—Mt 19:12), Paul describes the situation with only one word: the "unmarried" *(agamos)*. Further on, however, he expresses the whole content of the expression "kingdom of heaven" in a splendid synthesis. He says: "The unmarried person is anxious about the affairs of the Lord, how to please the Lord" (1 Cor 7:32). Each word of this statement deserves a special analysis.

The context of the word "to be anxious" or "to try" in the Gospel of Luke, Paul's disciple, indicates that one must truly seek only the kingdom of God (cf. Lk 12:31), that which constitutes the better part, the *unum necessarium,* the one thing necessary (cf. Lk 10:41). Paul himself speaks directly about his "anxiety for all the churches" (2 Cor 11:28), about his search for Christ through his concern for the problems of the brethren, for the members of the Body of Christ (cf. Phil 2:20-21; 1 Cor 12:25). Already from this context the whole vast field of the "anxiety" emerges, to which the unmarried can totally dedicate his mind, his toil, his heart. Man can "be anxious" only about what is truly in his heart.

In Paul's statement, the unmarried person is anxious about the affairs of the Lord *(ta tou kyriou).* With this concise expression, Paul embraces the entire objective reality of the kingdom of God. "The earth is the Lord's and everything in it," he himself will say a little further on in this letter (1 Cor 10:26; cf. Ps 24:1).

The object of the Christian's concern is the whole world! But Paul, with the name "Lord," describes first of all Jesus Christ (cf. Phil 2:11). Therefore the "affairs of the Lord" signify in the first place the kingdom of

Christ, his Body which is the Church (cf. Col 1:18) and all that contributes to its growth. The unmarried person is anxious about all this. Therefore Paul, being in the full sense of the term the "Apostle of Jesus Christ" (1 Cor 1:1) and minister of the Gospel (cf. Col. 1:23), writes to the Corinthians: "I wish that all of you were as I myself am" (1 Cor 7:7).

Nevertheless, apostolic zeal and most fruitful activity do not yet exhaust what is contained in the Pauline motivation for continence. We could even say that their root or source is found in the second part of the sentence, which demonstrates the subjective reality of the kingdom of God: "The unmarried person is anxious...how to please the Lord." This observation embraces the whole field of man's personal relationship with God. "To please God"—the expression is found in ancient books of the Bible (cf. Dt 13:19)—is synonymous with life in God's grace and expresses the attitude of one who seeks God, of one who behaves according to his will so as to please him. In one of the last books of Sacred Scripture this expression becomes a theological synthesis of sanctity. St. John applies it only once to Christ: "I always do what is pleasing to him [the Father]" (Jn 8:29). St. Paul observes in his Letter to the Romans that Christ "did not please himself" (Rom 15:3).

Between these two observations all that makes up the content of "pleasing God" is contained, understood in the New Testament as following in the footsteps of Christ.

It seems that both parts of the Pauline expression overlap. In fact, to be anxious about what "pertains to the Lord," about the "affairs of the Lord," one must "please the Lord." On the other hand, one who pleases God cannot be closed in upon himself, but is open to the world, to everything that is to be led to Christ. These evidently are only two aspects of the same reality of God and his kingdom. Paul nevertheless had to distinguish them in order to show more clearly the nature and the possibility of continence "for the sake of the kingdom of heaven."

General audience of June 30, 1982

Everyone Has His Own Gift from God, Suited to His Vocation

During last Wednesday's meeting, we tried to investigate the reasoning St. Paul uses in First Corinthians to convince them that whoever chooses marriage does well, while whoever chooses virginity (or continence according to the spirit of the evangelical counsel) does better (cf. 1 Cor 7:38). Continuing this meditation today, let us remember that according to Paul, "the unmarried person is anxious...how to please the Lord" (1 Cor 7:32).

"To please the Lord" has love as its foundation. This foundation arises from a further comparison. The unmarried person is anxious about how to please God, while the married man is anxious also about how to please his wife. In a certain sense, the spousal character of "continence for the sake of the kingdom of God" is apparent here. Man always tries to please the person he loves. Therefore, "to please God" is not without this character that distinguishes the interpersonal relationship between spouses. On the one hand, it is an effort of the man who is inclined toward God and seeks the way to please him, that is, to actively express his love. On the other hand, an approval by God corresponds to this aspiration. By accepting man's efforts, God crowns his own work by giving a new grace. Right from the beginning, this aspiration has been his gift. "Being anxious how to please God" is therefore a contribution of man in the continual dialogue of salvation that God has begun. Evidently, every Christian who lives his faith takes part in this dialogue.

However, Paul observes that the man who is bound by the marriage bond "is divided" (1 Cor 7:34) by reason of his family obligations (cf. 1 Cor 7:34). From this remark it apparently follows that the unmarried person would be characterized by an interior integration, by a unification that would allow him to dedicate himself completely to the service of the kingdom of God in all its dimensions. This attitude presupposes abstention from marriage, exclusively for the sake of the kingdom of God, and a life uniquely directed to this goal. In a different way the "division" can also sneak into the life of an unmarried person. Being deprived of married life on the one hand, and on the other, of a clear goal for which he should renounce marriage, he could find himself faced with a certain emptiness.

The Apostle seems to know all this very well. He takes pains to specify that he does not want to lay any restraint on one whom he advises not to marry, but he gives this advice to direct him to what is worthy and keeps him united to the Lord without any distractions (cf. 1 Cor 7:35). These words bring to mind what Christ said to his apostles during the Last Supper, according to the Gospel of Luke: "You are those who have continued with me in my trials [literally, 'in temptations'], and I prepare a kingdom for you, as the Father has prepared for me" (Lk 22:28-29). The unmarried person, "being united to the Lord," can be certain that his difficulties will be met with understanding: "For we do not have a high priest who is unable to sympathize with our weaknesses, but one who in every respect has been tempted as we are, yet without sinning" (Heb 4:15). This allows the unmarried person not so much to immerse himself exclusively in possible personal problems, but rather to include them in the great stream of the sufferings of Christ and of his Body, the Church.

The Apostle shows how one can be "united to the Lord"—what can be attained by aspiring to a constant remaining with him, to a rejoicing in his presence *(eupáredron),* without letting oneself be distracted by nonessential things *(aperispástos)* (cf. 1 Cor 7:35).

Paul explains this thought even more clearly when he speaks of the situation of the married woman and of one who has chosen virginity or is widowed. While the married woman must be anxious about "how to please her husband," the unmarried woman "is anxious about the affairs of the Lord, in order to be holy in body and spirit" (1 Cor 7:34).

In order to grasp adequately the whole depth of Paul's thought, we must note that according to the biblical concept, holiness is a state rather than an action. It has first of all an ontological character and then also a moral one. Especially in the Old Testament it is a separation from what is not subject to God's influence, from what is profane, in order to belong exclusively to God. Holiness in body and spirit, therefore, signifies also the sacredness of virginity or celibacy accepted for the sake of the kingdom of God. At the same time, what is offered to God must be distinguished by moral purity and therefore presupposes behavior "without spot or wrinkle," "holy and immaculate," according to the virginal example of the Church in the presence of Christ (Eph 5:27).

In this chapter of First Corinthians, the Apostle touches upon the problems of marriage and celibacy or virginity in a way that is deeply human and realistic, keeping in mind the mentality of his audience. Paul's reasoning is to a certain extent *ad hominem.* In the ambiance of his audience in Corinth, the new world, the new order of values that he proclaims must encounter another "world" and another order of values, different even from the one that the words addressed by Christ reached.

If Paul, with his teaching about marriage and continence, refers also to the transience of the world and human life in it, he certainly does so in reference to the ambiance which in a certain sense was programmed for the "use of the world." From this viewpoint, his appeal to "those who make use of the world" is significant, that they do it "as though they had no dealings with it" (1 Cor 7:31). From the immediate context it follows that in this ambiance, even marriage was understood as a way of "making use of the world"—differently from how it had been in the whole Jewish tradition (despite some perversions, which Jesus pointed out in his conversation with the Pharisees and in his Sermon on the Mount). Undoubtedly, all this explains the style of Paul's answer. The Apostle is well aware that by encouraging abstinence from marriage, at the same time he had to stress a way of understanding marriage that would be in conformity with the whole evangelical order of values. He had to do it with the greatest realism—that is, keeping before his eyes the ambiance to which he was addressing himself, the ideas and the ways of evaluating things that were predominant in it.

To men who lived in an ambiance where marriage was considered above all one of the ways of "making use of the world," Paul therefore expresses himself with significant words about virginity or celibacy (as we have seen), and also about marriage itself: "To unmarried persons and to widows I say, 'It is good for them to remain as I am. But if they cannot live in continence, let them marry. It is better to marry than to burn'" (1 Cor 7:8-9). Paul had already expressed almost the same idea: "Now concerning the matters about which you wrote, it is well for a man not to touch a woman. But because of the danger of incontinence, each man should have his own wife and each woman her own husband" (1 Cor 7:1-2).

Does the Apostle in First Corinthians perhaps look upon marriage exclusively from the viewpoint of a remedy for concupiscence, as used to be said in traditional theological language? The statements mentioned a little while ago would seem to verify this. However, right next to the statements quoted, we read a passage in the seventh chapter of First Corinthians that leads us to see differently Paul's teaching as a whole: "I wish that all were as I myself am, [he repeats his favorite argument for abstaining from marriage]—but each has his own special gift from God, one of one kind, and one of another" (1 Cor 7:7). Therefore even those who choose marriage and live in it receive a gift from God, his own gift, that is, the grace proper to this choice, to this way of living, to this state. The gift received by persons who live in marriage is different from the one received by persons who live in virginity and choose continence for the sake of the kingdom of God. All the same, it is a true gift from God, one's own gift, intended for concrete persons. It is specific, that is, suited to their vocation in life.

We can therefore say that while the Apostle, in his characterization of marriage on the human side (and perhaps still more in view of the local situation that prevailed in Corinth) strongly emphasizes the reason concerning concupiscence of the flesh, at the same time, with no less strength of conviction, he stresses also its sacramental and charismatic character. With the same clarity with which he sees man's situation in relation to concupiscence of the flesh, he sees also the action of grace in every person—in one who lives in marriage no less than in one who willingly chooses continence, keeping in mind that "the form of this world is passing away."

General audience of July 7, 1982

Man's Eternal Destiny—The Kingdom of God, Not the World

During our previous considerations in analyzing the seventh chapter of First Corinthians, we have been striving to gather together and understand the teachings and advice that St. Paul gives to the recipients of his letter about the questions concerning marriage and voluntary continence (or abstention from marriage). Declaring that one who chooses marriage does well and one who chooses virginity does better, the Apostle refers to the passing away of the world—that is, of everything that is temporal.

It is easy to see that the argument from the perishable and transient nature of what is temporal speaks with much greater force in this case than reference to the reality of the other world. The Apostle here expresses himself with some difficulty. Nevertheless, we can agree that at the basis of the Pauline interpretation of the subject of marriage-virginity, there is found not so much the very metaphysics of accidental being (therefore fleeting), but rather the theology of a great expectation, of which Paul was a fervent champion. The world is not man's eternal destiny, but the kingdom of God. Man cannot become too attached to the goods that are linked to a perishable world.

Marriage also is tied in with the form of this world which is passing away. In a certain sense, here we are very close to the perspective Christ opened in his statement about the future resurrection (cf. Mt 22:23-32; Mk 12:18-27; Lk 20:27-40). Therefore according to Paul's teaching, the Christian must live marriage from the point of view of his definitive vocation. Marriage is tied in with the form of this world which is passing away and therefore in a certain sense imposes the necessity of being locked in this transiency. On the other hand, abstention from marriage could be said to be free of this necessity. For this reason the Apostle declares that one who chooses continence does better. Although his argumentation follows this course, nevertheless he decidedly stresses above all (as we have already seen) the question of "pleasing the Lord" and "being anxious about the affairs of the Lord."

It can be admitted that the same reasons speak in favor of what the Apostle advises women who are widowed: "A wife is bound to her husband as long as he lives. If the husband dies, she is free to be married to whom she wishes, only in the Lord. But in my judgment she is happier if she remains as she is. And I think that I have the Spirit of God" (1 Cor 7:39-40). Therefore, she should remain a widow rather than contract a new marriage.

Through what we discover from a thoughtful reading of First Corinthians, especially chapter seven, the whole realism of the Pauline theology of the body is revealed. In the letter the Apostle proclaims: "Your body is a temple of the Holy Spirit who is in you" (1 Cor 6:19). Yet at the same time he is fully aware of the weakness and sinfulness to which man is subjected, precisely by reason of the concupiscence of the flesh.

However, this awareness in no way obscures for him the reality of God's gift. This is shared by those who abstain from marriage and also by those who take a wife or husband. In the seventh chapter of First Corinthians we find clear encouragement for abstention from marriage, the conviction that whoever decides on this abstention, does better. But we do not find any foundation for considering those who live in marriage as carnal and those who instead choose continence for religious motives as spiritual. In both the one and the other way of living—today we would say in one and the other vocation—the "gift" that each one receives from God is operative, that is, the grace that makes the body a "temple of the Holy Spirit." This gift remains, in virginity (in continence) as well as in marriage, if the person remains faithful to his gift and, according to his state, does not dishonor this temple of the Holy Spirit, which is his body.

In Paul's teaching, contained above all in the seventh chapter of First Corinthians, we find no introduction to what will later be called Manichaeism. The Apostle is fully aware that—insofar as continence for the sake of the kingdom of God is always worthy of recommendation—at the same time grace, that is, "one's own gift from God," also helps married couples. It helps them in that common life in which (according to the words of Genesis 2:24) they are so closely united that they become one body. This carnal common life is therefore subject to the power of their own gift from God. The Apostle writes about it with the same realism that marks his whole reasoning in the seventh chapter of this letter: "The husband should give to his wife her conjugal rights, and likewise the wife to her husband. For the wife does not rule over her own body, but the husband does; likewise, the husband does not rule over his own body, but the wife does" (verses 3-4).

It can be said that these statements are a clear comment in the New Testament on the words scarcely recorded in Genesis (cf. Gn 2:24). Nevertheless, the words used here, especially the expressions "rights" and "does not rule," cannot be explained apart from the proper context of the marriage covenant, as we have tried to clarify in analyzing the Genesis texts. We will attempt to do it even more fully when we speak about the sacramentality of marriage, drawing on the Letter to the Ephesians (cf. Eph 5:22-33). At the proper time it will be necessary to return to these significant expressions, which have passed from Paul's vocabulary into the whole theology of marriage.

For now we will continue to direct our attention to the other sentences in the same passage of the seventh chapter of First Corinthians, in which the Apostle addresses these words to married couples: "Do not refuse one another except perhaps by agreement for a season, that you may devote yourselves to prayer. But then come together again, lest Satan tempt you through lack of self-control. I say this by way of concession, not of command" (1 Cor 7:5-6). This is a very significant text, and it will perhaps be necessary to refer to it again in the context of our meditations on the other subjects.

In all of his argumentation about marriage and continence, the Apostle makes a clear distinction, as Christ does, between the commandment and the evangelical counsel. It is very significant that St. Paul feels the need to refer also to a "concession," as to an additional rule, above all precisely in reference to married couples and their mutual common life. St. Paul clearly says that conjugal common life and the voluntary and periodic abstinence by the couple must be the fruit of this gift of God which is their own. He says that the couple themselves, by knowingly cooperating with it, can maintain and strengthen that mutual personal bond and also that dignity conferred on the body by the fact that it is a "temple of the Holy Spirit who is in them" (1 Cor 6:19).

It seems that the Pauline rule of "concession" indicates the need to consider all that in some way corresponds to the very different subjectivity of the man and the woman. Everything in this subjectivity that is not only of a spiritual but also of a psychosomatic nature, all the subjective richness of man which, between his spiritual being and his corporeal, is expressed in the sensitivity whether for the man or for the woman—all this must remain under the influence of the gift that each one receives from God, a gift that is one's own.

As is evident, in the seventh chapter of First Corinthians, St. Paul interprets Christ's teaching about continence for the sake of the kingdom of heaven in that very pastoral way that is proper to him, not sparing on this occasion entirely personal accents. He interprets the teaching on continence and virginity along parallel lines with the doctrine on marriage. He keeps the realism that is proper to a pastor, and at the same time the proportions that we find in the Gospel, in the words of Christ himself.

In Paul's statement we can find again that fundamental structure containing the revealed doctrine about man, that even with his body he is destined for future life. This supporting structure is at the basis of all the Gospel teaching about continence for the sake of the kingdom of God (cf. Mt 19:12). But at the same time there also rests on it the definitive (eschatological) fulfillment of the Gospel doctrine on marriage (cf. Mt

22:30; Mk 12:25; Lk 20:36). These two dimensions of the human vocation are not opposed to each other, but are complementary. Both furnish a full answer to one of man's fundamental questions, the question about the significance of "being a body," that is, about the significance of masculinity and femininity, of being "in the body" a man or a woman.

What we usually define here as the theology of the body is shown to be something truly fundamental and constitutive for all anthropological hermeneutics. At the same time it is equally fundamental for ethics and for the theology of the human ethos. In each one of these fields we must listen attentively to the words of Christ, in which he recalled the beginning (cf. Mt 19:4) or the heart as the interior, and at the same time historical place of meeting with the concupiscence of the flesh. But we must also listen attentively to the words through which Christ recalled the resurrection in order to implant in the same restless heart of man the first seeds of the answer to the question about the significance of being flesh in the perspective of the other world.

General audience of July 14, 1982

The Mystery of the Body's Redemption

"We ourselves, who have the first fruits of the Spirit, groan inwardly as we await...the redemption of our body" (Rom 8:23). In his Letter to the Romans, St. Paul sees this redemption of the body in both an anthropological and a cosmic dimension. Creation "in fact was subjected to futility" (Rom 8:20). All visible creation, all the universe, bears the effects of man's sin. "The whole creation has been groaning in travail together until now" (Rom 8:22). At the same time, the whole "creation awaits with eager longing the revelation of the sons of God" and "nourishes the hope of also being freed from the slavery of corruption, to obtain the glorious liberty of the children of God" (Rom 8:19, 20-21).

According to Paul, the redemption of the body is the object of hope. This hope was implanted in the heart of man in a certain sense immediately after the first sin. Suffice it to recall the words of Genesis, which are traditionally called the *proto-evangelium* (cf. Gn 3:15). We could therefore also call them the beginning of the Good News, the first announcement of salvation. According to Romans, the redemption of the body is connected precisely with this hope in which, as we read, "we have been saved" (Rom 8:24). Through the hope that arises at man's very origin, the redemption of the body has its anthropological dimension. It is the redemption of man. At the same time it radiates, in a certain sense, on all creation, which from the beginning has been bound in a particular way to man and subordinated to him (cf. Gn 1:28-30). The redemption of the body is therefore the redemption of the world. It has a cosmic dimension.

Presenting in Romans the cosmic image of redemption, Paul of Tarsus places man at its very center, just as "in the beginning" he had been placed at the very center of the image of creation. It is precisely man who has "the first fruits of the Spirit," who groans inwardly, awaiting the redemption of his body (cf. Rom 8:23). Christ came to reveal man to man fully by making him aware of his sublime vocation (cf. *GS* 22). Christ speaks in the Gospel from the divine depths of the mystery of redemption, which finds its specific historical subject precisely in Christ himself. Christ therefore speaks in the name of that hope that had already been implanted in the heart of man in the *proto-evangelium.* Christ gives fulfillment to this hope, not only with the words of his teaching, but above all with the testimony of his death and resurrection. So the redemption of the body has already been accomplished in Christ. That hope in which "we have been saved" has been confirmed in him. At the same time, that hope has been opened anew to its definitive eschatological fulfillment. "The revelation of the sons of God" in Christ has been definitively directed toward that glorious liberty that is to be definitively shared by the children of God.

To understand all that the redemption of the body implies according to Paul's Letter to the Romans, an authentic theology of the body is necessary. We have tried to construct this theology by referring first of all to the words of Christ. The constitutive elements of the theology of the body are contained in what Christ says: in recalling "the beginning," concerning the question about the indissolubility of marriage (cf. Mt 19:8); in what he says about concupiscence, referring to the human heart in his Sermon on the Mount (cf. Mt 5:28); and also in what he says in reference to the resurrection (cf. Mt 22:30). Each one of these statements contains a rich content of an anthropological and ethical nature. Christ is speaking to man, and he is speaking about man: about man who is "body" and who has been created male and female in the image and likeness of God. He is speaking about man whose heart is subject to concupiscence, and finally, about man before whom the eschatological prospect of the resurrection of the body is opened.

According to Genesis, "body" means the visible aspect of man and his belonging to the visible world. For St. Paul it means not only this belonging, but sometimes also the alienation of man by the influence of the Spirit of God. Both the one meaning and the other are in relation to the resurrection of the body.

Since in the previously analyzed texts Christ is speaking from the divine depths of the mystery of redemption, his words serve that hope which Paul speaks of in Romans. According to the Apostle, ultimately we await the redemption of the body. So we await precisely the eschatological victory over death, to which Christ gave testimony above all by his resurrection. In the light of the paschal mystery, his words about the resurrection of the body and about the reality of the other world, recorded by the synoptic Gospels, have acquired their full eloquence. Christ, and then Paul of Tarsus, proclaimed the call for abstention from marriage for the sake of the kingdom of heaven, precisely in the name of this eschatological reality.

However, the redemption of the body is expressed not only in the resurrection as victory over death. It is present also in Christ's words addressed to historical man, when they confirm the principle of the indissolubility of marriage as a principle coming from the Creator himself, and also when, in the Sermon on the Mount, Christ called man to overcome concupiscence, even in the uniquely interior movements of the human heart. The key to both the one and the other of these statements must be to say that they refer to human morality, that they have an ethical meaning. Here it is a question not of the eschatological hope of the resurrection, but of the hope of victory over sin, which can be called the hope of every day.

In his daily life man must draw from the mystery of the redemption of the body the inspiration and the strength to overcome the evil that is dormant in him under the form of the threefold concupiscence. Man and woman, bound in marriage, must daily undertake the task of the indissoluble union of that covenant which they have made between them. But also a man or a woman who has voluntarily chosen continence for the sake of the kingdom of heaven must daily give a living witness of fidelity to that choice, heeding the directives of Christ in the Gospel and those of Paul the Apostle in First Corinthians. In each case it is a question of the hope of every day, which in proportion to the normal duties and difficulties of human life helps to overcome "evil with good" (Rom 12:21). In fact, "in hope we have been saved." The hope of every day manifests its power in human works and even in the very movements of the human heart, clearing a path, in a certain sense, for the great eschatological hope bound with the redemption of the body.

Penetrating daily life with the dimension of human morality, the redemption of the body helps first of all to discover all this good in which man achieves the victory over sin and concupiscence. Christ's words spring from the divine depths of the mystery of redemption. They permit us to discover and strengthen that bond that exists between the dignity of the human being (man or woman) and the nuptial meaning of the body.

They permit us to understand and put into practice, on the basis of that meaning, the mature freedom of the gift. It is expressed in one way in indissoluble marriage and in another way through abstention from marriage for the sake of the kingdom of God. In these different ways Christ fully reveals man to man, making him aware of his sublime vocation. This vocation is inscribed in man according to all his psycho-physical makeup, precisely through the mystery of the redemption of the body.

Everything we have tried to do in the course of our meditations in order to understand Christ's words has its ultimate foundation in the mystery of the redemption of the body.

General audience of July 21, 1982

NOTES

General audience of March 10, 1982

[92] On the more detailed problems of the exegesis of this passage, see for example: L. Sabourin, *Il Vangelo di Matteo, Teologia e Esegesi,* Vol. II (Roma: Ed. Paoline, 1977), pp. 834-836; "The Positive Values of Consecrated Celibacy," *The Way,* Supplement 10, summer 1970, p. 51; J. Blinzler, "Eisin eunuchoi, Zur Auslegung von Mt 19:12," *Zeitschrift für die Neutestamentliche Wissenschaft,* 48 (1957) 268ff.

[93] "Likewise, the holiness of the Church is fostered in a special way by the observance of the counsels proposed in the Gospel by Our Lord to his disciples. An eminent position among these is held by virginity or the celibate state. This is a precious gift of divine grace given by the Father to certain souls (cf. Mt 19:11; 1 Cor 7:7), whereby they may devote themselves to God alone the more easily, due to an undivided heart" *(LG 42).*

[94] Cf. *LG* 44; *PC* 12.

General audience of March 17, 1982

[95] It is true that Jeremiah, by explicit command of the Lord, had to observe celibacy (cf. Jer 16:1-2). But this was a "prophetic sign," which symbolized the future abandonment and destruction of the country and of the people.

[96] It is true, as we know from sources outside the Bible, that in the period between the two Testaments, celibacy was maintained in the circles of Judaism by some members of the sect of the Essenes (cf. Josephus Flavius, *Bell. Jud.,* II 8, 2:120-121; Philo Al., *Hypothel,* 11, 14). But this happened on the margin of

official Judaism and probably did not continue beyond the beginning of the second century.

In the Qumran community celibacy did not oblige everyone, but some members observed it until death, transferring to the sphere of life during peacetime, the prescription of Dt 23:10-14 on the ritual purity which was of obligation during the holy war. According to the beliefs of the Qumran community, this war lasted always "between the children of light and the children of darkness"; so celibacy was for them the expression of their being ready for the battle (cf. 1 QM 7, 5-7).

The Sacramentality of Marriage

Marital Love Reflects God's Love for His People

Today we begin a new chapter on the subject of marriage, reading the words of St. Paul to the Ephesians:

> Wives, be subject to your husbands as to the Lord. For the husband is the head of the wife as Christ is the head of the Church, his body, and is himself its savior. As the Church is subject to Christ, so let wives also be subject in everything to their husbands.

> Husbands, love your wives, as Christ loved the Church and gave himself up for her, that he might sanctify her, having cleansed her by the washing of water with the word, that he might present the Church to himself in splendor, without spot or wrinkle or any such thing, that she might be holy and without blemish. Even so husbands should love their wives as their own bodies. He who loves his wife loves himself. For no man ever hates his own flesh, but nourishes and cherishes it, as Christ does the Church, because we are members of his body. "For this reason a man shall leave his father and mother and be joined to his wife, and the two shall become one." This is a great mystery, and I mean in reference to Christ and the Church. However, let each one of you love his wife as himself, and let the wife see that she respects her husband (Eph 5:21-33).

We should now subject to deep analysis the quoted text contained in this fifth chapter of Ephesians, just as we have previously analyzed the individual words of Christ that seem to have a key significance for the theology of the body. The analysis dealt with the words with which Christ recalled the beginning (cf. Mt 19:4; Mk 10:6), the human heart, in the Sermon on the Mount (cf. Mt 5:28), and the future resurrection (cf. Mt 22:30; Mk 12:25; Lk 20:35). This passage of Ephesians constitutes almost a crowning of those other concise key words. The theology of the body has emerged from them along its evangelical lines, simple and at the same time fundamental. In a certain sense it is necessary to presuppose that theology in interpreting the above-mentioned passage of Ephesians. Therefore if we want to interpret that passage, we must do so in the light of what Christ told us about the human body. He spoke not only to remind historical man, and therefore man himself, who is always contemporary, about concupiscence (in his heart). But he also spoke to reveal, on the one hand, the prospectives of the beginning or original innocence or justice, and on the other hand, the eschatological prospectives of the resurrection of the body, when "They will neither marry nor be given in marriage" (cf. Lk 20:35). All of this is part of the theological viewpoint of the "redemption of our body" (Rom 8:23).

Even the words of the author of Ephesians[97] are centered on the body, both its metaphorical meaning, namely the Body of Christ which is the Church, and its concrete meaning, namely the human body in its perennial masculinity and femininity, in its perennial destiny for union in marriage, as Genesis says: "The man will leave his father and his mother and will cling to his wife and the two will be one flesh" (Gn 2:24).

In what way do these two meanings of the body appear together and converge in the passage of Ephesians? Why do they appear together and converge there? We must ask these questions, expecting not so much immediate and direct answers, but possibly studied and long-term answers for which our previous analyses have prepared. In fact, that passage from Ephesians cannot be correctly understood except in the full biblical context, considering it as the crowning of the themes and truths which, through the Word of God revealed in Sacred Scripture, ebb and flow like long waves. They are central themes and essential truths. Therefore the quoted text from Ephesians is also a key and classic text.

This text is well known in the liturgy, in which it always appears in relation to the sacrament of marriage. The Church's *lex orandi* sees in it an explicit reference to this sacrament, and the *lex orandi* presupposes and at the same time always expresses the *lex credendi*. Admitting this premise, we must immediately ask ourselves: in this classic text of Ephesians, how does the truth about the sacramentality of marriage emerge? In what way is it expressed and confirmed there? It will become clear that the answers to these questions cannot be immediate and direct, but gradual and long-term. This is proved even at a first glance at this text, which brings us back to Genesis and therefore to "the beginning." In the description of the relationship between Christ and the Church, this text takes from the writings of the Old Testament prophets the well-known analogy of the spousal love between God and his chosen people. Without examining these relationships it would be difficult to answer the question about how the sacramentality of marriage is dealt with in Ephesians. We will also see how the answer we are seeking must pass through the whole sphere of the questions previously analyzed, that is, through the theology of the body.

The sacrament or the sacramentality—in the more general sense of this term—meets with the body and presupposes the theology of the body. According to the generally known meaning, the sacrament is a visible sign. The body also signifies that which is visible. It signifies the visibility of the world and of man. Therefore, in some way, even if in the most general way, the body enters the definition of sacrament, being "a visible sign of an invisible reality," that is, of the spiritual, transcendent, divine reality.

In this sign and through this sign, God gives himself to man in his transcendent truth and in his love. The sacrament is a sign of grace, and it is an efficacious sign. Not only does the sacrament indicate grace and express it in a visible way, but it also produces it. The sacrament effectively contributes to having grace become part of man, and to realizing and fulfilling in him the work of salvation, the work begun by God from all eternity and fully revealed in Jesus Christ.

I would say that already this first glance at the classic text of Ephesians points out the direction in which our further analyses must be developed. It is necessary that these analyses begin with the preliminary understanding of the text itself. However, they must subsequently lead us, so to say, beyond their limits, in order to understand possibly to the very depths how much richness of the truth revealed by God is contained in the scope of that wonderful page. Using the well-known expression from *Gaudium et Spes,* we can say that the passage we have selected from Ephesians, "reveals—in a particular way—man to man, and makes him aware of his lofty vocation" *(GS 22),* inasmuch as he shares in the experience of the incarnate person. In fact, creating man in his image, from the very beginning God created him "male and female" (Gn 1:27).

During the subsequent analyses we will try—above all in the light of the quoted text from Ephesians—to more deeply understand the sacrament (especially marriage as a sacrament), first in the dimension of the covenant and grace, and afterward in the dimension of the sacramental sign.

General audience of July 28, 1982

The Call to Be Imitators of God and to Walk in Love

After an introductory glance at this classic text (Eph 5:21-33), one should examine the way in which this passage—so important both for the mystery of the Church and of the sacramental character of marriage—is situated in the immediate context of the whole letter.

While realizing that there are a number of problems discussed among biblical scholars as regards the authorship, the date of composition, and those to whom the letter was addressed, one must note that Ephesians has a very significant structure. The author begins this letter by presenting the eternal plan of the salvation of man in Jesus Christ.

"God the Father of our Lord Jesus Christ...has chosen us in him that we should be holy and blameless before him. He destined us in love to be his sons through Jesus Christ according to the purpose of his will, to the praise of his glorious grace which he freely bestowed on us in the Beloved. In him we have redemption through his blood, the forgiveness of our trespasses, according to the riches of his grace...as a plan for the fullness of time to unite all things in him..." (Eph 1:3, 4-7, 10).

After having presented in words full of gratitude the plan which, from eternity, is in God, and at a certain time is already fulfilled in the life of humanity, the author of Ephesians beseeches the Lord that men (and directly those to whom the letter is addressed) may fully know Christ as head: "He has made him the head over all things for the Church, which is his body, the fullness of him who fills all in all" (1:22-23).

Sinful humanity is called to a new life in Christ, in which the pagans and the Hebrews should join together as in a temple (cf. 2:11-21). The Apostle preaches the mystery of Christ among the pagans, to whom he especially addresses himself in his letter, bending "the knee before the Father" and asking him to grant them "according to the riches of his glory to be strengthened with might through his Spirit in the inner man" (3:14, 16).

After this profound and moving revelation of Christ in the Church, in the second part of the letter the author passes to more detailed instructions. These are aimed at defining the Christian life as a vocation flowing from the divine plan, which we have previously spoken of, namely, from the mystery of Christ in the Church. Here also the author touches various questions which are always valid for the Christian life. He makes an exhortation for the preservation of unity, underlining at the same time that this unity is constructed on the multiplicity and diversity of Christ's gifts. To each one is given a different gift, but all, as Christians, must "put on the new nature created after the likeness of God in true righteousness and holiness" (4:24). To this is linked the categorical summons to overcome vices and to acquire the virtues corresponding to the vocation which all have obtained through Christ (cf. 4:25-32). The author writes: "Therefore be imitators of God, as beloved children. And walk in love, as Christ loved us and gave himself up for us...in sacrifice" (5:1-2).

In the fifth chapter of Ephesians these directives become more detailed. The author severely condemns pagan abuses, writing: "For once you were darkness, but now you are light in the Lord; walk as children of light" (5:8). And then: "Therefore do not be foolish but understand what the will of the Lord is. Do not get drunk with wine [referring to the book of Proverbs 23:31]...but be filled with the Spirit, addressing one another in psalms and hymns and spiritual songs, singing and making melody to the Lord with all your heart" (5:17-19). The author of the letter wishes to illustrate in these words the climate of spiritual life which should animate every Christian community. At this point he then goes on to consider the domestic community, namely, the family. He writes: "Be filled with the

Spirit...always and for everything giving thanks in the name of our Lord Jesus Christ, to God the Father. Be subject to one another out of reverence for Christ" (5:20-21). Thus we enter precisely into that passage of the letter which will be the theme of our special analysis. We might easily observe that the essential content of this classic text appears at the meeting of the two principal guidelines of the entire Letter to the Ephesians: the first, that of the mystery of Christ which, as the expression of the divine plan for the salvation of man, is realized in the Church; the second, that of the Christian vocation as the model of life of the baptized individual, and of the single communities, corresponding to the mystery of Christ, or to the divine plan for the salvation of man.

In the immediate context of the passage quoted, the author of the letter seeks to explain in what way the Christian vocation thus understood should be realized and manifested in the relations between all members of the family; therefore, not merely between the husband and wife (treated of precisely in the passage of 5:21-33 which we have chosen), but also between parents and children. The author writes: "Children, obey your parents in the Lord, for this is right. Honor your father and mother—this is the first commandment with a promise—that it may be well with you and that you may live long on the earth. Fathers, do not provoke your children to anger but bring them up in the discipline and instruction of the Lord" (6:1-4). Following that, he speaks of the duty of servants in regard to their masters and, vice versa, of masters in regard to servants, that is, in regard to the slaves (cf. 6: 5-9). This is to be referred also to the directives concerning the family in the broad sense. The family, indeed, comprised not only the parents and children (according to the succession of generations), but included also in the wide sense, the servants or slaves of both sexes.

Thus, then, the text of Ephesians which we proposed as the object of a deeper analysis is found in the immediate context of the teaching on the moral obligations of the family society (the so-called *Haustaflen* or domestic codes according to Luther's definition). We find similar instructions also in other letters (e.g., in Colossians 3:18-24, and in First Peter 2:13; 3:7). Moreover, this immediate context forms part of our passage, inasmuch as the classic text which we have chosen treats of the reciprocal duties of husbands and wives. However, one must note that *per se* the passage of Ephesians 5:21-33 deals exclusively with married couples and marriage, and what regards the family also in the broad sense is already found in the context. First, however, before undertaking a more detailed analysis of the text, it should be added that the whole letter ends with a stupendous encouragement to the spiritual battle (cf. 6:10-20), with brief recommendations (cf. 6:21-22) and with a final farewell (cf. 6:23-24).

That call to the spiritual battle seems to be based logically on the line of argument of the entire letter. It is the explicit fulfillment of its principal guidelines.

Having thus before our eyes the overall structure of the entire Letter to the Ephesians, we shall seek in the first analysis to clarify the meaning of the words: "Be subject to one another out of reverence for Christ" (5:21), addressed to husbands and to wives.

General audience of August 4, 1982

Reverence for Christ Is the Basis of the Relationship between Spouses

Today we begin a more detailed analysis of the passage of Ephesians 5:21-33. Addressing husbands and wives, the author recommends them to be "subject to one another out of reverence for Christ" (5:21).

Here it is a question of a relationship of a double dimension or degree: reciprocal and communitarian. One clarifies and characterizes the other. The mutual relations of husband and wife should flow from their common relationship with Christ. The author of the letter speaks of "reverence for Christ" in a sense analogous to that when he speaks of the "fear of God." In this case it is not a question of fear which is a defensive attitude before the threat of evil. But it is above all a case of respect for holiness, for the *sacrum*. It is a question of *pietas,* which, in the language of the Old Testament, was expressed by the term "fear of God" (cf., e.g., Ps 103:11; Prv 1:7; 23:17; Sir 1:11-16). Arising from a profound awareness of the mystery of Christ, this *pietas* should constitute the basis of the reciprocal relations between husbands and wives.

The text chosen by us, as likewise the immediate context, has a parenetic character, that is, of moral instruction. The author of the letter wishes to indicate to husbands and wives the basis of their mutual relationship and their entire conduct. He deduces the relative indications and directives from the mystery of Christ presented at the beginning of the letter. This mystery should be spiritually present in the mutual relationship of spouses. The mystery of Christ, penetrating their hearts, engendering in them that holy "reverence for Christ" (namely *pietas),* should lead them to "be subject to one another"—the mystery of Christ, that is, the mystery of the choice from eternity of each of them in Christ to be the adoptive sons of God.

The opening expression of our passage of Ephesians 5:21-33, which we have approached by an analysis of the remote and immediate context, has quite a special eloquence. The author speaks of the mutual subjection of the spouses, husband and wife, and in this way he explains the words which he will write afterward on the subjection of the wife to the husband. In fact we read: "Wives, be subject to your husbands, as to the Lord" (5:22). In saying this, the author does not intend to say that the husband is the lord of the wife and that the interpersonal pact proper to marriage is a pact of domination of the husband over the wife. Instead, he expresses a different concept—that the wife can and should find in her relationship with Christ, who is the one Lord of both the spouses, the motivation of that relationship with her husband which flows from the very essence of marriage and of the family. Such a relationship, however, is not one of one-sided domination. According to Ephesians, marriage excludes that element of the pact which was a burden and, at times, does not cease to be a burden on this institution. The husband and the wife are in fact "subject to one another," and are mutually subordinated to one another. The source of this mutual subjection is to be found in Christian pietas, and its expression is love.

The author of the letter underlines this love in a special way, in addressing himself to husbands. He writes: "Husbands, love your wives...." By expressing himself in this way, he removes any fear that might have arisen (given the modern sensitivity) from the previous phrase: "Wives, be subject to your husbands." Love excludes every kind of subjection whereby the wife might become a servant or a slave of the husband, an object of unilateral domination. Love makes the husband simultaneously subject to the wife, and thereby subject to the Lord himself, just as the wife to the husband. The community or unity which they should establish through marriage is constituted by a reciprocal donation of self, which is also a mutual subjection. Christ is the source and at the same time the model of that subjection, which, being reciprocal "out of reverence for Christ," confers on the conjugal union a profound and mature character. In this source and before this model many elements of a psychological or moral nature are so transformed as to give rise, I would say, to a new and precious fusion of the bilateral relations and conduct.

The author of Ephesians does not fear to accept those concepts which were characteristic of the mentality and customs of the times. He does not fear to speak of the subjection of the wife to the husband. He does not fear (also in the last verse of the text quoted by us) to recommend to the wife that "she respect her husband" (5:33). It is certain that when the husband and wife are subject to one another "out of reverence for Christ," a just balance will be established, such as to correspond to their Christian vocation in the mystery of Christ.

Nowadays our contemporary sensitivity is certainly different. Our mentality and customs are quite different, too, as is the social position of women in regard to men. Nevertheless, the fundamental moral principle which we find in Ephesians remains the same and produces the same results. The mutual subjection "out of reverence for Christ"—a subjection arising from the basis of Christian *pietas*—always produces that profound and solid structure of the community of the spouses in which the true "communion" of the person is constituted.

The author of Ephesians, who began his letter with a magnificent vision of God's eternal plan in regard to humanity, does not limit himself to emphasizing merely the traditional aspects of morality or the ethical aspects of marriage. He goes beyond the scope of teaching and writing on the reciprocal relationship of the spouses. He discovers therein the dimension of the mystery of Christ of which he is the herald and the apostle: "Wives, be subject to your husbands as to the Lord. For the husband is the head of the wife as Christ is the head of the Church, his Body, and is himself its Savior. As the Church is subject to Christ, so let wives also be subject in everything to their husbands. Husbands, love your wives, as Christ loved the Church and gave himself up for her..." (5:22-25). In this way, the teaching of this parenetic part of the letter is inserted, in a certain sense, into the reality of the mystery hidden from eternity in God and revealed to mankind in Jesus Christ. In Ephesians we are, I would say, witnesses of a particular meeting of that mystery with the essence of the vocation to marriage. How are we to understand this meeting? The text of Ephesians presents it above all as a great analogy. There we read: "Wives, be subject to your husbands as to the Lord...." Here we have the first component of the analogy. "For the husband is the head of the wife as Christ is the head of the Church...." Here we have the second component which clarifies and motivates the first. "As the Church is subject to Christ, so let wives also be subject to their husbands...." The relationship of Christ to the Church, presented previously, is now expressed as a relationship of the Church to Christ, and this contains the successive component of the analogy. Finally: "Husbands, love your wives, as Christ loved the Church and gave himself up for her...." This is the ultimate component of the analogy. The remainder of the text of the letter develops the fundamental thought contained in the passage just now quoted. The entire text of Ephesians in 5:21-33 is completely permeated with the same analogy. That is to say, the mutual relationship between the spouses, husband and wife, is to be understood by Christians in the light of the relationship between Christ and the Church.

General audience of August 11, 1982

A Deeper Understanding of the Church and Marriage

Analyzing the respective components of Ephesians, we established that the reciprocal relationship between husband and wife is to be understood by Christians as an image of the relationship between Christ and the Church.

This relationship is a revelation and a realization in time of the mystery of salvation, of the election of love, hidden from eternity in God. In this revelation and realization the mystery of salvation includes the particular aspect of conjugal love in the relationship of Christ to the Church. Thus one can express it most adequately by applying the analogy of the relationship which exists—which should exist—between husband and wife in marriage. Such an analogy clarifies the mystery, at least to a certain degree. Indeed, according to the author of Ephesians, it seems that this analogy serves as a complement to that of the Mystical Body (cf. Eph 1:22-23) when we attempt to express the mystery of the relationship of Christ to the Church—and going back even further, the mystery of the eternal love of God for man and for humanity, that mystery which is expressed and is realized in time through the relationship of Christ to the Church.

If, as has been said, this analogy illuminates the mystery, it in its turn is illuminated by that mystery. According to the author of Ephesians, the conjugal relationship which unites husband and wife should help us to understand the love which unites Christ to the Church, that reciprocal love between Christ and the Church in which the divine eternal plan for the salvation of man is realized. Yet the content of meaning of the analogy does not end here. The analogy used in Ephesians, illuminating the mystery of the relationship between Christ and the Church, contemporaneously unveils the essential truth about marriage. Marriage corresponds to the vocation of Christians only when it reflects the love which Christ the Bridegroom gives to the Church his Bride, and which the Church (resembling the "subject" wife, that is, completely given) attempts to return to Christ. This is redeeming love, love as salvation, the love with which man from eternity has been loved by God in Christ: "...even as he chose us in him before the foundation of the world, that we should be holy and blameless before him..." (Eph 1:4).

Marriage corresponds to the vocation of Christians as spouses only if that love is reflected and effected therein. This will become clear if we attempt to reread the Pauline analogy inversely, that is, beginning with the relationship of Christ to the Church and turning next to the relationship of husband and wife in marriage. In the text, an exhortative tone is used: "As the Church is subject to Christ, so let wives also be subject in everything to their husbands." On the other hand: "Husbands, love your wives, as Christ loved the Church...." These expressions make it clear that a moral obligation is involved. Yet, in order to recommend such an obligation one must admit that in the essence of marriage a particle of the same mystery is captured. Otherwise, the entire analogy would hang suspended in a void. The call which the author of Ephesians directed to the spouses, that they model their reciprocal relationship on the relationship of Christ to the Church *("as—so"),* would be without a real basis, as if it had no ground beneath its feet. Such is the logic of the analogy used in the cited text of Ephesians.

As we can see, the analogy operates in two directions. On the one hand, it helps us to understand better the essence of the relationship between Christ and the Church. On the other, at the same time, it helps us to see more deeply into the essence of marriage to which Christians are called. In a certain sense, the analogy shows the way in which this marriage, in its deepest essence, emerges from the mystery of God's eternal love for man and for humanity. It emerges from that salvific mystery which is fulfilled in time through the spousal love of Christ for the Church. Beginning with the words of Ephesians (5:21-33), we can move on to develop the thought contained in the great Pauline analogy in two directions: either in the direction of a deeper understanding of the Church, or in the direction of a deeper understanding of marriage. In our considerations, we will pursue the latter first of all, mindful that the spousal relationship of Christ to the Church is at the basis of an understanding of marriage in its essence. That relationship will be analyzed even more precisely in order to establish—presupposing the analogy with marriage—in what way the latter becomes a visible sign of the divine eternal mystery, as an image of the Church united with Christ. In this way Ephesians leads us to the foundations of the sacramentality of marriage.

Let us undertake, then, a detailed analysis of the text. We read in Ephesians that "the husband is the head of the wife as Christ is the head of the Church, his body, and is himself its Savior" (Eph 5:23). The author has already explained that the submission of the wife to the husband as head is intended as reciprocal submission "out of reverence for Christ." We can presume that the author goes back to the concept rooted in the mentality of the time, to express first of all the truth concerning the relationship of Christ to the Church, that is, that Christ is the head of the Church. He is head as "Savior of his Body." The Church is exactly that Body which—being submissive in everything to Christ as its head—receives from him all that through which it becomes and is his Body. It receives the fullness of salvation as the gift of Christ, who "gave himself up for her" to the last.

Christ's "giving himself up" to the Father by obedience unto death on the cross acquired here a strictly ecclesiological sense: "Christ loved the Church and gave himself up for her" (Eph 5:25). Through a total giving up of himself because of his love, he formed the Church as his Body and continually builds her up, becoming her head. As head he is the Savior of his Body, and, at the same time, as Savior he is head. As head and Savior of the Church, he is also Bridegroom of his Bride.

Inasmuch as the Church is herself, so, as Body, she receives from Christ her head the entire gift of salvation as the fruit of Christ's love and of his giving himself up for the Church, the fruit of his giving himself up to the last. That gift of himself to the Father by obedience unto death (cf. Phil 2:8) is contemporaneously, according to Ephesians, a "giving himself up for the Church." In this expression, redeeming love is transformed, I would say, into spousal love. Giving himself up for the Church, through the same redeeming act Christ is united once and for all with her, as bridegroom with the bride, as husband with his wife. Christ gives himself through all that which is once and for all contained in his "giving himself up" for the Church. In this way, the mystery of the redemption of the body conceals within itself, in a certain sense, the mystery "of the marriage of the Lamb" (cf. Rv 19:7). Because Christ is the head of the Body, the entire salvific gift of the redemption penetrates the Church as the Body of that head, and continually forms the most profound, essential substance of her life. It is the spousal form, given that in the cited text the analogy of body-head becomes an analogy of groom-bride, or rather of husband-wife. This is demonstrated by the subsequent passages of the text, which will be considered next.

General audience of August 18, 1982

St. Paul's Analogy of the Union of Head and Body

In the preceding reflections on Ephesians 5:21-33, we drew attention especially to the analogy of the relationship which exists between Christ and the Church, and of that which exists between husband and wife united by the bond of marriage. Before undertaking the analysis of the further passages of the text in question, we must note that within the range of the fundamental Pauline analogy—Christ and the Church, on the one hand, and man and woman as spouses on the other—there is a supplementary analogy: the analogy of the head and of the body. This analogy confers a chiefly ecclesiological significance on the statement we analyzed: the Church as such is formed by Christ; it is constituted by him in its essential part, as the body is by the head. The union of the body with the head is above all of an organic nature. To put it simply, it is the somatic union of the human organism. The biological union is founded directly on this organic union, inasmuch as it can be said that the body lives by the head (even if at the same time, though in a different way, the head lives by the body). Besides, in the case of man, the psychic union, understood in its integrity, and the integral unity of the human person is also founded on this organic union.

As already stated (at least in the passage analyzed), the author of Ephesians has introduced the supplementary analogy of the head and the body within the limits of the analogy of marriage. He even seems to have conceived the first analogy, "head-body," in a more central manner from the point of view of the truth about Christ and the Church proclaimed by him. However, one must equally affirm that he has not placed it alongside or outside of the analogy of marriage as a conjugal bond—quite the contrary. In the whole text of Ephesians (5:21-33), especially in the first part with which we are dealing (5:22-23), the author speaks as if in marriage also the husband is "head of the wife," and the wife "the body of the husband," as if the married couple formed one organic union. This can find its basis in the text of Genesis which speaks of one flesh (Gn 2:24), or in that same text to which the author of Ephesians will shortly refer in the context of this great analogy. Nevertheless, the text of Genesis makes clear that the man and the woman are two distinct personal subjects who knowingly decide on their conjugal union, defined by that ancient text with the words "one flesh." This is equally clear also in Ephesians. The author uses a twofold analogy: head-body, husband-wife, for the purpose of illustrating clearly the nature of the union between Christ and the Church. In a certain sense, especially in the first part of Ephesians 5:22-23, the ecclesiological dimension seems decisive and dominant.

"Wives, be subject to your husbands, as to the Lord. For the husband is the head of the wife as Christ is the head of the Church, his body, and is himself its Savior. As the Church is subject to Christ, so let wives also be subject in everything to their husbands. Husbands, love your wives, as Christ loved the Church, and gave himself up for her..." (Eph 5:22-25). This supplementary analogy "head-body" indicates that within the limits of the entire passage of Ephesians 5:21-33, we are dealing with two distinct subjects. In virtue of a particular reciprocal relationship, in a certain sense they become a single subject. The head, together with the body, constitutes a subject (in the physical and metaphysical sense), an organism, a human person, a being. There is no doubt that Christ is a subject different from the Church. However, in virtue of a particular relationship, he is united with her, as in an organic union of head and body. The Church is so strongly, so essentially herself in virtue of a mystical union with Christ. Is it possible to say the same thing of the spouses, of the man and the woman united by the marriage bond? If the author of Ephesians sees also in marriage the analogy of the union of head and body, this analogy in a certain sense seems to apply to marriage in consideration of the union which Christ constitutes with the Church, and the Church with Christ. Therefore, the analogy regards, above all, marriage itself as that union through which "the two become one flesh" (Eph 5:31; cf. Gn 2:24).

However, this analogy does not blur the individuality of the subjects: that of the husband and that of the wife, that is, the essential bi-subjectivity which is at the basis of the image of "one single body." Rather, the essential bi-subjectivity of the husband and wife in marriage, which makes of them in a certain sense "one single body," passes within the limits of the whole text we are examining (Eph 5:21-33) to the image of Church-Body united with Christ as head. This is seen especially in this text where the author describes the relationship of Christ to the Church precisely by means of the image of the relationship of the husband to the wife. In this description the Church-Body of Christ appears clearly as the second subject of the spousal union to which the first subject, Christ, manifests the love with which he has loved her by giving himself for her. That love is an image and above all a model of the love which the husband should show to his wife in marriage, when the two are subject to each other "out of reverence for Christ."

We read: "Husbands, love your wives, as Christ loved the Church and gave himself up for her, that he might sanctify her, having cleansed her by the washing of water with the word, that he might present the Church to himself in splendor, without spot or wrinkle or any such thing, that she might be holy and without blemish. Even so husbands should love their wives as their own bodies. He who loves his wife loves himself. For no man ever hates his own flesh, but nourishes and cherishes it, as Christ does the Church, because we are members of his body. 'For this reason a man should leave his father and mother and be joined to his wife, and the two shall become one flesh'" (Eph 5:25-31).

It is easy to perceive that in this part of the text of Ephesians (5:21-33), bi-subjectivity clearly dominates. It is manifested both in the relationship Christ-Church, and also in the relationship husband-wife. This does not mean to say that the image of a single subject disappears—the image of "a single body." It is preserved also in the passage of our text, and in a certain sense it is better explained there. This will be seen more clearly when we submit the above-quoted passage to a detailed analysis. Thus the author of Ephesians speaks of the love of Christ for the Church by explaining the way in which that love is expressed, and by presenting at the same time both that love and its expressions as a model which the husband should follow in regard to his wife. The love of Christ for the Church has essentially her sanctification as its scope. "Christ loved the Church and gave himself up for her that he might sanctify her" (5:25-26). Baptism is a principle of this sanctification. Baptism is the first and essential fruit of Christ's giving himself for the Church. In this text baptism is not called by its own proper name, but is defined as purification "by the washing of water with the word" (5:26). This washing, with the power that derives from the redemptive giving of himself by Christ for the Church, brings about the fundamental purification through which Christ's love for the Church acquires a spousal character, in the eyes of the author of the letter.

It is known that the sacrament of baptism is received by an individual subject in the Church. However, beyond the individual subject of baptism the author of the letter sees the whole Church. The spousal love of Christ is applied to her, the Church, every time that a single person receives in her the fundamental purification by means of baptism. Whoever receives baptism becomes at the same time—by the virtue of the redemptive love of Christ—a participant in his spousal love for the Church. In our text "the washing of water with the word" is an expression of the spousal love in the sense that it prepares the Bride (Church) for the Bridegroom. It makes the Church the spouse of Christ, I would say, in *actu primo*. Some biblical scholars observe that in this text, the washing with water recalls the ritual ablution which preceded the wedding—something which constituted an important religious rite also among the Greeks.

As the sacrament of baptism, "the washing of water with the word" (Eph 5:26) renders the Church a spouse not only in *actu primo* but also in the more distant perspective, in the eschatological perspective. This opens up before us when we read in Ephesians that "the washing of water" serves, on the part of the groom "to present the Church to himself in splendor without spot or wrinkle or any such thing, that she might be holy and without blemish" (Eph 5:27). The expression "to present to himself" seems to indicate that moment of the wedding in which the bride is led to the groom, already clothed in the bridal dress and adorned for the wedding. The text quoted indicates that the Christ-spouse himself takes care to adorn the spouse-Church. He is concerned that she should be beautiful with the beauty of grace, beautiful by virtue of the gift of salvation in its fullness, already granted from the moment of the sacrament of baptism. But baptism is only the beginning from which the figure of the glorious Church will emerge (as we read in the text), as a definitive fruit of the redemptive and spousal love, only with the final coming of Christ *(parousia).*

We see how profoundly the author of Ephesians examines the sacramental reality, proclaiming its grand analogy. Both the union of Christ with the Church, and the conjugal union of man and woman in marriage are illumined in this way by a particular supernatural light.

General audience of August 25, 1982

The Sacredness of the Human Body and Marriage

Proclaiming the analogy between the spousal bond which unites Christ and the Church, and that which unites the husband and wife in marriage, the author of Ephesians writes as follows: "Husbands, love your wives, as Christ loved the Church and gave himself up for her, that he might sanctify her, having cleansed her by the washing of water with the word, that he might present the Church to himself in splendor, without spot or wrinkle or any such thing, that she might be holy and without blemish" (Eph 5:25-27).

It is significant that the image of the Church in splendor is presented in the text quoted as a bride all beautiful in her body. Certainly this is a metaphor. But it is very eloquent, and it shows how deeply important the body is in the analogy of spousal love. The Church in splendor is "without spot or wrinkle." "Spot" can be understood as a sign of ugliness, and "wrinkle" as a sign of old age or senility. In the metaphorical sense, both terms indicate moral defects, sin. It may be added that in St. Paul the "old man" signifies sinful man (cf. Rom 6:6). Therefore Christ with his redemptive and spousal love ensures that the Church not only becomes sinless, but remains "eternally young."

As may be seen, the scope of the metaphor is quite vast. The expressions which refer directly and immediately to the human body, characterizing it in the reciprocal relationships between husband and wife, indicate at the same time attributes and qualities of the moral, spiritual and supernatural order. This is essential for such an analogy. Therefore the author of the letter can define the state of the Church in splendor in relation to the state of the body of the bride, free from signs of ugliness or old age ("or any such thing"), simply as holiness and absence of sin. Such is the Church "holy and without blemish." It is obvious then what kind of beauty of the bride is in question, in what sense the Church is the Body of Christ, and in what sense that Body-Bride welcomes the gift of the Bridegroom who "has loved the Church and has given himself for her." Nevertheless it is significant that St. Paul explains all this reality, which is essentially spiritual and supernatural, by means of the resemblance of the body and of the love whereby husband and wife become "one flesh."

In the entire passage of the text cited, the principle of bi-subjectivity is clearly preserved: Christ-Church, Bridegroom-Bride (husband-wife). The author presents the love of Christ for the Church—that love which makes the Church the Body of Christ of which he is the head—as the model of the love of the spouses and as the model of the marriage of the bridegroom and the bride. Love obliges the bridegroom-husband to be so-licitous for the welfare of the bride-wife. It commits him to desire her beauty and at the same time to appreciate this beauty and to care for it. Here it is a case of visible beauty, of physical beauty. The bridegroom ex-amines his bride with attention as though in a creative, loving anxiety to find everything that is good and beautiful in her and which he desires for her. That good which he who loves creates, through his love, in the one that is loved, is like a test of that same love and its measure. Giving him-self in the most disinterested way, he who loves does so only within the limits of this measure and of this control.

In the succeeding verses of the text (5:28-29) the author of Ephesians turns his mind exclusively to the spouses themselves. Then the analogy of the relationship of Christ to the Church is still more profound and impels him to express himself thus: "Husbands should love their wives as their own bodies" (Eph 5:28). Here the motive of "one flesh" returns again. In the above-mentioned phrase and in the subsequent phrases it is not only taken up again, but also clarified. If husbands should love their wives as their own bodies, this means that uni-subjectivity is based on bi-subjectivity and does not have a real character but only an intentional one. The wife's body is not the husband's own body, but it must be loved like his own body. It is therefore a question of unity, not in the ontological sense, but in the moral sense—unity through love.

"He who loves his wife loves himself" (Eph 5:28). This phrase con-firms that character of unity still more. In a certain sense, love makes the "I" of the other person his own "I": the "I" of the wife, I would say, be-comes through love the "I" of the husband. The body is the expression of that "I" and the foundation of its identity. The union of husband and wife in love is expressed also by means of the body.

It is expressed in the reciprocal relationship, even though the author of the letter indicates it especially from the part of the husband. This re-sults from the structure of the total image. The spouses should be "subject to one another out of reverence for Christ" (this was already made evident in the first verses of the text quoted: Ephesians 5:21-23). However, later on, the husband is above all, *he who loves* and the wife, on the other hand, is *she who is loved.* One could even hazard the idea that the wife's submission to her husband, understood in the context of the entire passage of Ephesians (5:21-33), signifies above all the "experiencing of love." This is all the more so since this submission is related to the image of the submission of the Church to Christ, which certainly consists in experiencing his love. The Church, as bride, being the object of the redemptive love of Christ-Bridegroom, becomes his Body. Being the object of the spousal love of the husband, the wife becomes "one flesh" with him, in a certain sense, his own flesh. The author will repeat this idea once again in the last phrase of the passage analyzed here: "However, let each one of you love his wife as himself" (Eph 5:33).

This is a moral unity, conditioned and constituted by love. Love not only unites the two subjects, but allows them to be mutually interpenetrated, spiritually belonging to one another to such a degree that the author of the letter can affirm: "He who loves his wife loves himself" (Eph 5:28). The "I" becomes in a certain sense the "you" and the "you" the "I" (in a moral sense, that is). Therefore the continuation of the text analyzed by us reads as follows: "For no man ever hates his own flesh, but nourishes and cherishes it, as Christ does the Church, because we are members of his body" (Eph 5:29-30). The phrase, which initially still referred to the relationships of the married couple, returns successively in an explicit manner to the relationship Christ-Church. So, in the light of that relationship, it leads us to define the sense of the entire phrase. After explaining the character of the relationship of the husband to his own wife by forming "one flesh," the author wishes to reinforce still more his previous statement ("He who loves his wife loves himself"). In a certain sense, he wishes to maintain it by the negation and exclusion of the opposite possibility ("No man ever hates his own flesh"—Eph 5:29). In the union through love the body of the other becomes one's own in the sense that one cares for the welfare of the other's body as he does for his own. It may be said that the above-mentioned words, characterizing the "carnal" love which should unite the spouses, express the most general and at the same time, the most essential content. They seem to speak of this love above all in the language of *agape.*

The expression according to which man "nourishes and cherishes his own flesh"—that is, that the husband "nourishes and cherishes" the flesh of his wife as his own—seems rather to indicate the solicitude of the parents, the protective relationship, instead of the conjugal tenderness. The motivation of this character should be sought in the fact that the author here passes distinctly from the relationship which unites the spouses to the relationship between Christ and the Church. The expressions which refer to the care of the body, and in the first place to its nourishment, to its sustenance, suggest to many Scripture scholars a reference to the Eucharist with which Christ in his spousal love nourishes the Church. These expressions, even though in a minor key, indicate the specific character of conjugal love, especially of that love whereby the spouses become "one flesh." At the same time they help us to understand, at least in a general way, the dignity of the body and the moral imperative to care for its good, for that good which corresponds to its dignity. The comparison with the Church as the Body of Christ, the Body of his redemptive and at the same time spousal love, should leave in the minds of those to whom Ephesians was destined a profound sense of the "sacredness" of the human body in general, and especially in marriage, as the "situation" in which this sense of the sacred determines in an especially profound way, the reciprocal relationships of the persons and, above all, those of the man with the woman, inasmuch as she is wife and mother of their children.

General audience of September 1, 1982

Christ's Redemptive Love Has a Spousal Nature

The author of Ephesians writes: "No man ever hates his own flesh, but nourishes and cherishes it, as Christ does the Church, because we are members of his body" (Eph 5:29-30). After this verse the author deems it opportune to cite what can be considered the fundamental text on marriage in the entire Bible, the text contained in Genesis 2:24: "For this reason a man shall leave his father and mother and be joined to his wife, and the two shall become one flesh" (cf. Eph 5:31). It is possible to deduce from the immediate context of Ephesians that the citation from Genesis (2:24) is necessary here not so much to recall the unity of the spouses, determined from the beginning in the work of creation. But it is necessary to present the mystery of Christ with the Church from which the author deduces the truth about the unity of the spouses. This is the most important point of the whole text, in a certain sense, the keystone. The author of Ephesians sums up in these words all that he had said previously, tracing the analogy and presenting the similarity between the unity of the spouses and the unity of Christ with the Church. Citing the words of Genesis 2:24, the author points out where the bases of this analogy are to be sought. They are to be sought in the line which, in God's salvific plan, unites marriage, as the most ancient revelation (manifestation) of the plan in the created world, with the definitive revelation and manifestation—the revelation that "Christ loved the Church and gave himself up for her" (Eph 5:25), conferring on his redemptive love a spousal character and meaning.

So then this analogy which permeates the text of Ephesians (5:21-33) has its ultimate basis in God's salvific plan. This will become still more clear and evident when we place the passage of this text analyzed by us in the overall context of Ephesians. Then one will more easily understand why the author, after citing the words of Genesis 2:24, writes: "This is a great mystery, and I mean in reference to Christ and the Church" (Eph 5:32).

In the overall context of Ephesians and likewise in the wider context of the words of the Sacred Scriptures, which reveal God's salvific plan "from the beginning," one must admit that here the term *mystérion* signifies the mystery, first of all hidden in God's mind, and later revealed in the history of man. Indeed, it is a question of a "great" mystery, given its importance. That mystery, as God's salvific plan in regard to humanity, is in a certain sense the central theme of all revelation, its central reality. God, as Creator and Father, wishes above all to transmit this to mankind in his Word.

It is a question not only of transmitting the Good News of salvation, but of initiating at the same time the work of salvation, as a fruit of grace which sanctifies man for eternal life in union with God. Precisely along the line of this revelation and accomplishment, St. Paul sets in relief the continuity between the most ancient covenant which God established by constituting marriage in the work of creation, and the definitive covenant. After having loved the Church and given himself up for her, in that covenant Christ is united to her in a spousal way, corresponding to the image of spouses. This continuity of God's salvific initiative constitutes the essential basis of the great analogy contained in Ephesians. The continuity of God's salvific initiative signifies the continuity and even the identity of the mystery—of the great mystery in the different phases of its revelation and therefore, in a certain sense, of its manifestation—and at the same time of its accomplishment: in its "most ancient" phase from the point of view of the history of man and salvation, and in the phase "of the fullness of time" (Gal 4:4).

Is it possible to understand that great mystery as a sacrament? In the text quoted by us, is the author of Ephesians speaking perchance of the sacrament of marriage? If he is not speaking of it directly, in the strict sense—here one must agree with the sufficiently widespread opinion of Biblical scholars and theologians—however it seems that in this text he is speaking of the bases of the sacramentality of the whole of Christian life and in particular of the bases of the sacramentality of marriage. He speaks then of the sacramentality of the whole of Christian existence in the Church and in particular of marriage in an indirect way, but in the most fundamental way possible.

Is not "sacrament" synonymous with "mystery"?[98] The mystery indeed remains "obscure"—hidden in God himself—in such wise that even after its proclamation (or its revelation) it does not cease to be called "mystery," and it is also preached as a mystery. The sacrament presupposes the revelation of the mystery and presupposes also its acceptance by means of faith on the part of man. However, at the same time, it is something more than the proclamation of the mystery and its acceptance by faith. The sacrament consists in the "manifesting" of that mystery in a sign which serves not only to proclaim the mystery, but also to accomplish it in man. The sacrament is a visible and efficacious sign of grace. Through it, that mystery hidden from eternity in God is accomplished in man, that mystery which Ephesians speaks of at the very beginning (cf. Eph 1:9). It is the mystery of God's call of man in Christ to holiness, and the mystery of his predestination to become his adopted son. This becomes a reality in a mysterious way, under the veil of a sign. Nonetheless that sign is always a "making visible" of the supernatural mystery which it works in man under its veil.

Considering the passage of Ephesians analyzed here, especially the words: "This is a great mystery, and I mean in reference to Christ and the Church," one must note the following. The author of the letter writes not only of the great mystery hidden in God, but also, and above all, of the mystery which is accomplished by Christ. With an act of redemptive love, Christ loved the Church and gave himself up for her. By the same act he is united with the Church in a spousal manner, as the husband and wife are reciprocally united in marriage instituted by the Creator. It seems that the words of Ephesians provide sufficient motivation for what is stated at the very beginning of *Lumen Gentium:* "The Church is in Christ in the nature of a sacrament—a sign and instrument, that is, of communion with God and of unity among all men" *(LG* 1). This text of Vatican II does not say: "The Church is a sacrament," but "It is in the nature of a sacrament." Thereby it indicates that one must speak of the sacramentality of the Church in a manner which is analogical and not identical in regard to what we mean when we speak of the seven sacraments administered by the Church by Christ's institution. If there are bases for speaking of the Church as in the nature of a sacrament, such bases for the greater part have been indicated precisely in Ephesians.

It may be said that this sacramentality of the Church is constituted by all the sacraments by means of which she carries out her mission of sanctification. It can also be said that the sacramentality of the Church is the source of the sacraments and in particular of Baptism and the Eucharist. This can be seen from the passage of Ephesians which we have already analyzed (cf. Eph 5:25-30). Finally it must be said that the sacramentality of the Church remains in a particular relationship with marriage, the most ancient sacrament.

General audience of September 8, 1982

Moral Aspects of the Christian's Vocation

We have before us the text of Ephesians 5:21-33, which we have already been analyzing for some time because of its importance in regard to marriage and the sacrament. In its whole content, beginning from the first chapter, the letter treats above all of the mystery for ages hidden in God as a gift eternally destined for mankind. "Blessed be the God and Father of our Lord Jesus Christ, who has blessed us in Christ with every spiritual blessing in the heavenly places, even as he chose us in him before the foundation of the world, that we should be holy and blameless before him. He destined us in love to be his sons through Jesus Christ, according to the purpose of his will, to the praise of his glorious grace which he freely bestowed on us in the Beloved" (Eph 1:3-6).

Until now the letter speaks of the mystery hidden for ages in God (cf. Eph 3:9). The subsequent phrases introduce the reader to the phase of fulfillment of this mystery in the history of man. The gift, destined for him for ages in Christ, becomes a real part of man in the same Christ: "...in him we have redemption through his blood, the forgiveness of our trespasses, according to the riches of his grace, which he lavished upon us. For he has made known to us in all wisdom and insight the mystery of his will, according to his purpose which he set forth in Christ, as a plan for the fullness of time, to unite all things in him, things in heaven and things on earth" (Eph 1:7-10).

So the eternal mystery passed from the mystery of "being hidden in God" to the phase of revelation and actualization. In Christ, humanity was for ages chosen and blessed "with every spiritual blessing of the Father." Christ was destined according to the eternal "plan" of God, so that in him, as in a head "all things might be united, things in heaven and things on earth" in the eschatological perspective. Christ reveals the eternal mystery and accomplishes it among men. Therefore the author of Ephesians, in the remainder of the letter, exhorts those who have received this revelation, and those who have accepted it in faith, to model their lives in the spirit of the truth they have learned. To the same end, in a particular way he exhorts Christian couples, husbands and wives.

For the greater part of the context the letter becomes instruction or *parenesis.* The author seems to speak above all of the moral aspects of the vocation of Christians. However, he continually refers to the mystery which is already at work in them, by virtue of the redemption of Christ, and efficaciously works in them especially by virtue of Baptism. He writes: "In him you also, who have heard the word of truth, the gospel of your salvation, and have believed in him, were sealed with the promised Holy Spirit" (Eph 1:13). Thus the moral aspects of the Christian vocation remain linked not only with the revelation of the eternal divine mystery in Christ and with its acceptance through faith, but also with the sacramental order. Although it is not placed in the forefront in the whole letter, it seems to be present in a discreet manner. It could not be otherwise seeing that the Apostle is writing to Christians who, through Baptism, had become members of the ecclesial community. From this point of view, the passage of Ephesians 5:21-33, analyzed up to the present, seems to have a special importance. Indeed, it throws a special light on the essential relationship of the mystery with the sacrament and especially on the sacramentality of matrimony.

Christ is at the heart of the mystery. In him—precisely in him—humanity has been eternally blessed "with every spiritual blessing." In him, in Christ, humanity has been chosen "before the creation of the world," chosen in love and predestined to the adoption of sons. When later, in the fullness of time this eternal mystery is accomplished in time, this is brought about also in him and through him—in Christ and through Christ. The mystery of divine love is revealed through Christ. Through him and in him it is accomplished. In him, "We have redemption through his blood, the forgiveness of our trespasses..." (Eph 1:7). In this manner men who through faith accept the gift offered to them in Christ, really become participants in the eternal mystery, even though it works in them under the veil of faith. According to Ephesians 5:21-33, this supernatural conferring of the fruits of redemption accomplished by Christ acquires the character of a spousal donation of Christ himself to the Church, similar to the spousal relationship between husband and wife. Therefore, not only the fruits of redemption are a gift, but above all, Christ himself is a gift. He gives himself to the Church as to his spouse.

We should ask whether in this matter such an analogy does not permit us to penetrate the essential content of the mystery more profoundly and with greater exactitude. We should ask ourselves this question with all the greater reason because this classic passage of Ephesians (5:21-33) does not appear in the abstract and isolated. But it constitutes a continuity. In a certain sense it is a continuation of the statements of the Old Testament, which presented the love of God-Yahweh for his chosen people Israel according to the same analogy. We are dealing in the first place with the texts of the prophets who, in their discourses, introduced the similarity of spousal love in order to characterize in a particular way the love which Yahweh has for Israel. On the part of the chosen people, this love was not understood and reciprocated. Rather it encountered infidelity and betrayal. That infidelity and betrayal was expressed especially in idolatry, a worship given to strange gods.

Truth to tell, in the greater part of the cases, the prophets were pointing out in a dramatic manner that very betrayal and infidelity which were called the "adultery" of Israel. However, the explicit conviction that the love of Yahweh for the chosen people can and should be compared to the love which unites husband and wife is at the basis of all these statements of the prophets. Here one could quote many passages from Isaiah, Hosea and Ezekiel. (Some of these were already quoted when we were analyzing the concept of adultery against the background of Christ's words in the Sermon on the Mount.) One cannot forget that the Song of Solomon also belongs to the patrimony of the Old Testament. It is true that in the Song of Solomon the image of spousal love is traced without the typical analogy of the prophetic texts, which presented in that love the image of the love of Yahweh for Israel. But the Song is also without that negative element which, in the other texts, constitutes the motive of "adultery" or infidelity. Thus, the analogy of the spouses, which enabled the author of Ephesians to define the relationship of Christ to the Church, possesses an abundant tradition in the books of the Old Testament. In analyzing this analogy in the classic text of Ephesians, we cannot but refer to that tradition.

To illustrate this tradition we will limit ourselves for the moment to citing a passage of Isaiah.

The prophet says: "Fear not, for you will not be ashamed; be not confounded, for you will not be put to shame; for you will forget the shame of your youth and the reproach of your widowhood you will remember no more. For your Maker is your husband, the Lord of hosts is his name, and the Holy One of Israel is your Redeemer; the God of the whole earth he is called. For the Lord has called you like a wife forsaken and grieved in spirit, like a wife of youth when she is cast off, says your God. For a brief moment I forsook you, but with great compassion I will gather you...but my steadfast love shall not depart from you, and my covenant of peace shall not be removed, says the Lord, who has compassion on you" (Is 54:4-7,10).

During our next meeting we shall begin the analysis of the text cited from Isaiah.

General audience of September 15, 1982

The Relationship of Christ to the Church Is Connected with the Tradition of the Prophets

By comparing the relation between Christ and the Church with the spousal relationship of husband and wife, Ephesians refers to the tradition of the prophets of the Old Testament. To illustrate it we recall again the following passage of Isaiah:

> Fear not, for you will not be ashamed; be not confounded, for you will not be put to shame; for you will forget the shame of your youth, and the reproach of your widowhood you will remember no more. For your Maker is your husband, the Lord of hosts is his name, and the Holy One of Israel is your Redeemer; the God of the whole earth he is called. For the Lord has called you like a wife forsaken and grieved in spirit, like a wife of youth when she is cast off, says your God. For a brief moment I forsook you, but with great compassion I will gather you. In overflowing wrath for a moment I hid my face from you, but with everlasting love, I will have compassion on you, says the Lord, your Redeemer. For this is like the days of Noah to me: as I swore that the waters of Noah should no more go over the earth, so I have sworn that I will not be angry with you and will not rebuke you. For the mountains may depart and the hills be removed, but my steadfast love shall not depart from you, and my covenant of peace shall not be removed, says the Lord, who has compassion on you (Is 54:4-10).

Isaiah in this case does not contain the reproaches made to Israel as an unfaithful spouse, which echo so strongly in the other texts, especially of Hosea and Ezekiel. Thanks to this, the essential content of the biblical analogy becomes more evident. The love of God-Yahweh for the chosen people-Israel is expressed as the love of the man-spouse for the woman chosen to be his wife by means of the marriage alliance. In this way Isaiah explains the events which make up the course of Israel's history, going back to the mystery hidden in the heart of God. In a certain sense, he leads us in the same direction in which, after many centuries, the author of Ephesians will lead us. Basing himself on the redemption already accomplished in Christ, he will reveal much more fully the depth of the mystery itself.

The text of the prophet has all the coloring of the tradition and the mentality of the people of the Old Testament. Speaking in the name of

God and, as it were, with his words, the prophet addresses Israel as a husband would address the wife he chose. These words brim over with an authentic ardor of love. At the same time they place in relief the whole specific character both of the situation and of the outlook proper to that age. They underline that the choice on the part of the man takes away the woman's "dishonor." According to the opinion of society, this "dishonor" seems connected with the marriageable state, whether original (virginity), or secondary (widowhood), or finally that deriving from repudiation of a wife who is not loved (cf. Dt 24:1) or in the case of an unfaithful wife. However, the text quoted does not mention infidelity, but it indicates the motive of the "love of compassion."[99] Thereby it indicates not merely the social nature of marriage in the Old Testament, but also the very character of the gift, which is the love of God for the spouse-Israel—a gift which derives entirely from God's initiative. In other words, it indicates the dimension of grace, which from the beginning is contained in that love. This is perhaps the strongest declaration of love on God's part, linked with the solemn oath of faithfulness forever.

The analogy of the love which unites spouses is brought out strongly in this passage. Isaiah says: "...for your Maker is your husband, the Lord of hosts is his name, and the Holy One of Israel is your Redeemer; the God of the whole earth he is called" (Is 54:5). So then, in that text God himself, in all his majesty as Creator and Lord of creation, is explicitly called "spouse" of the chosen people. This spouse speaks of his great compassion, which will not depart from Israel-spouse, but will constitute a stable foundation of the alliance of peace with him. Thus the motif of spousal love and of marriage is linked with the motif of alliance. Besides, the Lord of hosts calls himself not only "Creator," but also "Redeemer." The text has a theological content of extraordinary richness.

Comparing the text of Isaiah with Ephesians and noting the continuity regarding the analogy of spousal love and of marriage, we should point out at the same time a certain diversity of theological viewpoint. Already in the first chapter the author of the letter speaks of the mystery of love and of election, whereby "God the Father of our Lord Jesus Christ" embraces mankind in his Son, especially as a mystery "hidden in the mind of God." This is a mystery of eternal love, the mystery of election to holiness ("...to be holy and blameless before him"—Eph 1:4) and of adoption as sons in Christ ("He destined us to be his adopted sons through Jesus Christ"—Eph 1:5). In this context, the deduction of the analogy concerning marriage which we have found in Isaiah ("For your Maker is your husband, the Lord of hosts is his name"—Is 54:5), seems to be a foreshortened view constituting a part of the theological perspective. The first dimension of love and of election, as a mystery hidden for ages in God, is a paternal and not a "conjugal" dimension. According to Ephesians the first characteristic note of that mystery remains connected with the paternity of God, set out in relief especially by the prophets (cf. Hos 11:1-4; Is 63:8-9; 64:7; Mal 1:6).

The analogy of spousal love and of marriage appears only when the Creator and the Holy One of Israel of the text of Isaiah is manifested as Redeemer. Isaiah says: "For your Maker is your husband, the Lord of hosts is his name, and the Holy One of Israel is your Redeemer" (Is 54:5). Already in this text it is possible, in a certain sense, to read the parallelism between the spouse and the Redeemer. Passing to Ephesians we should observe that this thought is fully developed there. The figure of the Redeemer[100] is already delineated in the first chapter as proper to him who is the first "beloved Son" of the Father (Eph 1:6), beloved from eternity, of him, in whom all of us have been loved by the Father "for ages." It is the Son of the same substance of the Father, "in whom we have redemption through his blood, the forgiveness of our trespasses according to the riches of his grace" (Eph 1:7). The same Son, as Christ (or as the Messiah) "has loved the Church and has given himself up for her" (Eph 5:25).

This splendid formulation of Ephesians summarizes in itself and at the same time sets in relief the elements of the Canticle on the Servant of Yahweh and of the Canticle of Sion (cf. e.g., Is 42:1; 53:8-12; 54:8).

Thus the giving of himself up for the Church is equivalent to carrying out the work of redemption. In this way the "Creator Lord of hosts" of Isaiah becomes the "Holy One of Israel," of the new Israel, as Redeemer.

In Ephesians the theological perspective of the prophetic text is preserved and at the same time deepened and transformed. New revealed moments enter: the trinitarian, Christological[101] and finally the eschatological moment.

Thus St. Paul, writing the letter to the People of God of the new covenant and precisely to the church of Ephesus, will no longer repeat: "Your Maker is your husband." But he will show in what way the Redeemer, who is the firstborn Son and for ages "beloved of the Father," reveals contemporaneously his salvific love. This love consists in giving himself up for the Church, as spousal love whereby he espouses the Church and makes it his own Body. Thus the analogy of the prophetic texts of the Old Testament (in this case especially of Isaiah) remains preserved in Ephesians and at the same time obviously transformed. A mystery corresponds to the analogy, a mystery which is expressed and, in a certain sense, explained by means of it. In the text of Isaiah this mystery is scarcely outlined, "half-open" as it were; however, in Ephesians it is fully revealed (but of course without ceasing to be a mystery). In Ephesians both dimensions are explicitly clear: the eternal dimension of the mystery inasmuch as it is hidden in God ("the Father of our Lord Jesus Christ"), and the dimension of its historical fulfillment, according to its Christological and at the same ecclesiological dimension. The analogy of marriage referred especially to the second dimension. Also in the prophets (in Isaiah) the analogy of marriage referred directly to a historical dimension. It was linked with the history of the chosen people of the old covenant, with the history of Israel. On the other hand the Christological and the ecclesiological dimension was found only as an embryo in the Old Testament fulfillment of the mystery; it was only foretold.

Nonetheless it is clear that the text of Isaiah helps us to understand better the Letter to the Ephesians and the great analogy of the spousal love of Christ and the Church.

General audience of September 22, 1982

The Analogy of Spousal Love
Indicates the Radical Character of Grace

In Ephesians (5:21-33)—as in the prophets of the Old Testament (e.g., in Isaiah)—we find the great analogy of marriage or of the spousal love between Christ and the Church.

What function does this analogy fulfill in regard to the mystery revealed in the old and the new covenants? The answer to this question must be gradual. First of all, the analogy of spousal or conjugal love helps to penetrate the essence of the mystery. It helps to understand it up to a certain point, naturally, in an analogical way. It is obvious that the analogy of earthly human love of the husband for his wife, of human spousal love, cannot provide an adequate and complete understanding of that absolutely transcendent Reality which is the divine mystery, both as hidden for ages in God, and in its historical fulfillment in time, when "Christ so loved the Church and gave himself up for her" (Eph 5:25). The mystery remains transcendent in regard to this analogy as in regard to any other analogy, whereby we seek to express it in human language. At the same time, however, this analogy offers the possibility of a certain cognoscitive penetration into the essence of the mystery.

The analogy of spousal love permits us to understand in a certain way the mystery which for ages was hidden in God, and which in turn was realized by Christ, as a love proper to a total and irrevocable gift of self on the part of God to man in Christ. It is a question of "man" in the personal and at the same time communitarian dimension. (This communitarian dimension is expressed in the Book of Isaiah and in the prophets as "Israel," and in Ephesians as the "Church"—one could say: the People of God of the old and of the new covenant.) We may add that in both conceptions, in a certain sense the communitarian dimension is placed in the forefront. But it is not to such an extent as completely to hide the personal dimension, which, on the other hand, pertains simply to the essence of conjugal love. In both cases we are dealing rather with a significant "reduction of the community to the person":[102] Israel and the Church are considered as bride-person in relation to the bridegroom-person (Yahweh and Christ). Every concrete "I" should find itself in that biblical "we."

So then, the analogy which we are speaking of permits us to understand in a certain degree the revealed mystery of the living God who is Creator and Redeemer. (And as such he is, at the same time, God of the covenant.) It permits us to understand this mystery in the manner of a spousal love, just as it allows us to understand it also in the manner of a love of "compassion" (according to the text of Isaiah), or in the manner of a "paternal" love (according to Ephesians, especially in the first chapter). The above-mentioned ways of understanding the mystery are also without doubt analogical. The analogy of spousal love contains in itself a characteristic of the mystery, which is not directly emphasized either by the analogy of the love of compassion or by the analogy of paternal love (or by any other analogy used in the Bible to which we would have referred).

The analogy of spousal love seems to emphasize especially the aspect of the gift of self on the part of God to man, "for ages" chosen in Christ (literally: to "Israel," to the "Church"). It is a total (or rather radical) and irrevocable gift in its essential character, that is, as a gift. This gift is certainly radical and therefore total. We cannot speak of that totality in a metaphysical sense. Indeed, as a creature man is not capable of receiving the gift of God in the transcendental fullness of his divinity. Such a total gift (uncreated) is shared only by God himself in the triune communion of the Persons. On the contrary, God's gift of himself to man, which the analogy of spousal love speaks of, can only have the form of a participation in the divine nature (cf. 2 Pt 1:4), as theology makes clear with very great precision. Nevertheless, according to this measure, the gift made to man on the part of God in Christ is a total, that is, a radical gift, as the analogy of spousal love indicates. In a certain sense, it is all that God could give of himself to man, considering the limited faculties of man, a creature. In this way, the analogy of spousal love indicates the radical character of grace, of the whole order of created grace.

The foregoing seems to be what can be said in reference to the primary function of our great analogy, which has passed from the writings of the prophets of the Old Testament to the Letter to the Ephesians, where, as has already been noted, it underwent a significant transformation. The analogy of marriage, as a human reality in which spousal love is incarnated, helps to a certain degree and in a certain way to understand the mystery of grace as an eternal reality in God and as a historical fruit of mankind's redemption in Christ. However, we said before that this biblical analogy not only "explains" the mystery. On the other hand the mystery defines and determines the adequate manner of understanding the analogy, and precisely this element, in which the biblical authors see "the image and likeness" of the divine mystery. So then, the comparison of marriage (because of spousal love) to the relationship of Yahweh-Israel in the old covenant and of Christ-Church in the new covenant decides, at the same time, the manner of understanding marriage itself and determines this manner.

This is the second function of our great analogy. In the perspective of this function we approach the problem of sacrament and mystery, that is, in the general and fundamental sense, the problem of the sacramentality of marriage. This seems especially justified in the light of the analysis of Ephesians (5:21-33). Indeed, in presenting the relationship of Christ to the Church in the image of the conjugal union of husband and wife, the author of this letter speaks in the most general and at the same time fundamental way. He speaks not only of the fulfillment of the eternal divine mystery, but also of the way in which that mystery is expressed in the visible order, of the way in which it has become visible, and therefore has entered into the sphere of sign.

By the term "sign" we mean here simply the "visibility of the Invisible." The mystery for ages hidden in God—that is, invisible—has become visible first of all in the historical event of Christ. The relationship of Christ to the Church, which is defined in Ephesians as "a great mystery," constitutes the fulfillment and the concretization of the visibility of the mystery itself. The author of Ephesians compares the indissoluble relationship of Christ and the Church to the relationship between husband and wife, that is, to marriage. At the same time he refers to the words of Genesis (2:24), which by God's creative act originally instituted marriage. Thus the author of Ephesians turns our attention to what was already presented—in the context of the mystery of creation—as the "visibility of the Invisible," to the very "origin" of the theological history of man.

It can be said that the visible sign of marriage "in the beginning," inasmuch as it is linked to the visible sign of Christ and of the Church, to the summit of the salvific economy of God, transfers the eternal plan of love into the historical dimension and makes it the foundation of the whole sacramental order. It is a special merit of the author of Ephesians that he brought these two signs together, and made of them one great sign—that is, a great sacrament *(sacramentum magnum)*.

General audience of September 29, 1982

Marriage Is the Central Point of the "Sacrament of Creation"

We continue the analysis of the classic text of Ephesians 5:21-33. For this purpose it is necessary to quote some phrases contained in one of the preceding analyses devoted to this theme: "Man appears in the visible world as the highest expression of the divine gift, because he bears within himself the interior dimension of the gift. With it he brings into the world his particular likeness to God, whereby he transcends and dominates also his 'visibility' in the world, his corporality, his masculinity or femininity, his nakedness. Resulting from this likeness there is also the primordial awareness of the conjugal significance of the body, pervaded by the mystery of original innocence" *(L'amore umano nel piano divino,* Città del Vaticano, 1980, p. 90). These phrases sum up in a few words the result of the analyses devoted to the first chapters of Genesis, in relation to the words with which Christ, in his conversation with the Pharisees on the subject of marriage and its indissolubility, referred to the "beginning." Other phrases of the same analysis pose the problem of the primordial sacrament: "Thus, in this dimension, there is constituted a primordial sacrament, understood as a sign which effectively transmits in the visible world the invisible mystery hidden from eternity in God. This is the mystery of truth and love, the mystery of the divine life in which man really shares.... It is the original innocence which initiates this participation..." *(Ibid.,* p. 90).

It is necessary to look again at the content of these statements in the light of the Pauline doctrine expressed in Ephesians, bearing in mind especially the passage of chapter 5, verses 21-33, situated in the overall context of the entire letter. In any event, the letter authorizes us to do this, because the author himself referred to the "beginning," and precisely to the words of the institution of marriage in Genesis (Eph 5:31; cf. Gn 2:24). In what sense can we see in these words a statement about the sacrament, about the primordial sacrament? The previous analyses of the biblical "beginning" have led us gradually to this, in consideration of the state of the original endowment of man in existence and in grace, which was the state of innocence and original justice. Ephesians leads us to approach this situation—that is, the state of man before original sin—from the point of view of the mystery hidden in God from eternity. In fact, we read in the first phrases of the letter that "God, Father of our Lord Jesus Christ...has blessed us in Christ with every spiritual blessing in the heavenly places. He chose us in him before the foundation of the world, that we should be holy and blameless before him" (Eph 1:3-4).

Ephesians opens up before us the supernatural world of the eternal mystery, of the eternal plans of God the Father concerning man. These plans precede the creation of the world, and therefore also the creation of man. At the same time those divine plans begin to be put into effect already in the entire reality of creation. If also the state of original innocence of man, created as male and female in the likeness of God, pertains to the mystery of creation, this implies that the primordial gift conferred on man by God already includes within itself the fruit of having been chosen, which we read of in Ephesians: "He chose us...that we should be holy and blameless before him" (Eph 1:4). This indeed seems to be indicated by the words of Genesis, when the Creator-Elohim finds in man—male and female—who appeared before him, a good worthy of gratification: "God saw everything that he had made, and behold, it was very good" (Gn 1:31). Only after sin, after breaking the original covenant with the Creator, man feels the need to hide himself "from the Lord God." "I heard the sound of you in the garden, and I was afraid, because I was naked, and I hid myself" (Gn 3:10).

On the contrary, before sin, man bore in his soul the fruit of eternal election in Christ, the eternal Son of the Father. By means of the grace of this election man, male and female, was "holy and blameless" before God. That primordial (or original) holiness and purity were expressed also in the fact that, although both were "naked, they were not ashamed" (Gn 2:25), as we have sought to make evident in the previous analyses. Comparing the testimony of the "beginning" found in the first chapters of Genesis, with the testimony of Ephesians, one must deduce that the reality of man's creation was already imbued by the perennial election of man in Christ. Man is called to sanctity through the grace of the adoption as sons. "He destined us to be his sons through Jesus Christ, according to the purpose of his will, to the praise of his glorious grace which he freely bestowed on us in the Beloved" (Eph 1:5-6).

Man, male and female, shared from the beginning in this supernatural gift. This bounty was granted in consideration of him, who from eternity was beloved as Son, even though—according to the dimensions of time and history—it had preceded the Incarnation of this beloved Son and also the redemption which we have in him through his blood (cf. Eph 1:7).

The redemption was to become the source of man's supernatural endowment after sin and, in a certain sense, in spite of sin. This supernatural endowment, which took place before original sin, that is, the grace of justice
and original innocence—an endowment which was the fruit of man's election in Christ before the ages—was accomplished precisely in reference to
him, to the beloved One, while anticipating chronologically his coming in
the body. In the dimensions of the mystery of creation the election to the
dignity of adopted sonship was proper only to the first Adam, that is, to
the man created in the image and likeness of God, male and female.

In what way is the reality of the sacrament, of the primordial sacrament, verified in this context? In the analysis of the beginning, from which
we quoted a passage a short time ago, we said that "the sacrament, as a
visible sign, is constituted by man inasmuch as he is a 'body,' through his
visible masculinity and femininity. The body, in fact, and only it, is capable of making visible what is invisible: the spiritual and the divine. It
was created to transfer into the visible reality of the world the mystery hidden from eternity in God, and thus to be its sign" *(loc. cit.,* p. 90).

This sign has besides an efficacy of its own, as I also said: "Original
innocence linked to the experience of the conjugal significance of the
body" has as its effect "that man feels himself, in his body as male and
female, the subject of holiness" *(Ibid.,* p. 91). He feels himself such and he
is such from the beginning. That holiness which the Creator conferred
originally on man pertains to the reality of the "sacrament of creation."
The words of Genesis 2:24, "A man...cleaves to his wife and they become
one flesh," spoken in the context of this original reality in a theological
sense, constitute marriage as an integral part and, in a certain sense, a central part of the "sacrament of creation." They constitute, or perhaps rather
they simply confirm the character of its origin. According to these words,
marriage is a sacrament inasmuch as it is an integral part and, I would say,
the central point of "the sacrament of creation." In this sense it is the primordial sacrament.

According to Genesis 2:24, the institution of marriage expresses the
beginning of the fundamental human community which through the "procreative" power that is proper to it serves to continue the work of creation.
"Be fruitful and multiply" (Gn 1:28). Not only this, it expresses at the
same time the salvific initiative of the Creator, corresponding to the eternal election of man, which Ephesians speaks of. That salvific initiative
comes from God-Creator and its supernatural efficacy is identified with
the very act of man's creation in the state of original innocence. In this
state, already in the act of man's creation, his eternal election in Christ
fructified. In this way one must recognize that the original sacrament of

creation draws its efficacy from the beloved Son (cf. Eph 1:6 where it speaks of the "grace which he gave us in his beloved Son"). If then it treats of marriage, one can deduce that—instituted in the context of the sacrament of creation in its globality, that is, in the state of original innocence—it should serve not only to prolong the work of creation, that is, of procreation. It should also serve to extend to further generations of men the same sacrament of creation, that is, the supernatural fruits of man's eternal election on the part of the Father in the eternal Son—those fruits which man was endowed with by God in the very act of creation.

Ephesians seems to authorize us to interpret Genesis in this way, and the truth about the "beginning" of man and of marriage contained therein.

General audience of October 6, 1982

The Loss of the Original Sacrament Is Restored with Redemption in the Marriage-Sacrament

In our previous consideration we have tried to study in depth—in the light of Ephesians—the sacramental "beginning" of man and marriage in the state of original justice (or innocence).

We know, however, that the heritage of grace was driven out of the human heart when the first covenant with the Creator was broken. The perspective of procreation, instead of being illumined by the heritage of original grace, given by God as soon as he infused a rational soul, became dimmed by the heritage of original sin. We can say that marriage, as a primordial sacrament, was deprived of that supernatural efficacy which at the moment of its institution belonged to the sacrament of creation in its totality. Nonetheless, even in this state, that is, in the state of man's hereditary sinfulness, marriage never ceased being the figure of that sacrament we read about in Ephesians (Eph 5:21-33) and which the author of that letter does not hesitate to call a "great mystery." Can we not perhaps deduce that marriage has remained the platform for the actuation of God's eternal designs, according to which the sacrament of creation had drawn near to men and had prepared them for the sacrament of redemption, introducing them to the dimension of the work of salvation? The analysis of Ephesians, especially the classic text (5:21-33), seems to lean toward such a conclusion.

In verse 31 the author refers to the words of the institution of marriage contained in Genesis: "For this reason a man will leave his father and mother and will cling to his wife, and the two shall become one body" (Gn 2:24). Then he immediately states: "This is a great mystery; I mean that it refers to Christ and the Church" (Eph 5:32). He seems to indicate not only the identity of the mystery hidden in God from all eternity, but also that continuity of its actuation. This exists between the primordial sacrament connected with the supernatural gracing of man in creation itself and the new gracing, which occurred when "Christ loved the Church and gave himself up for her to make her holy..." (Eph 5:25-26). This gracing can be defined in its entirety as the sacrament of redemption. This redemptive gift of himself "for" the Church also contains—according to Pauline thought—Christ's gift of himself to the Church, in the image of the nuptial relationship that unites husband and wife in marriage. In this way, the sacrament of redemption again takes on, in a certain sense, the figure and form of the primordial sacrament. To the marriage of the first husband and wife, as a sign of the supernatural gracing of man in the sacrament of creation, there corresponds the marriage, or rather the analogy of the marriage, of Christ with the Church, as the fundamental great sign of the supernatural gracing of man in the sacrament of redemption. It is a sign of the gracing in which the covenant of the grace of election is renewed in a definitive way, the covenant which was broken in the beginning by sin.

The image contained in the quoted passage from Ephesians seems to speak above all of the sacrament of redemption as that definitive fulfillment of the mystery hidden from eternity in God. Everything that Ephesians had treated in the first chapter is actuated in this *mysterium magnum* (great mystery). As we recall, it says not only "In him [that is, in Christ] God chose us before the world began, to be holy and blameless in his sight..." (Eph 1:4), but also "in whom [Christ] we have redemption through his blood, the remission of sins, so immeasurably generous is God's favor to us..." (Eph 1:7-8). The new supernatural gracing of man in the sacrament of redemption is also a new actuation of the mystery hidden in God from all eternity—new in relation to the sacrament of creation. At this moment, gracing is in a certain sense a new creation. However, it differs from the sacrament of creation insofar as the original gracing, united to man's creation, constituted that man in the beginning, through grace, in the state of original innocence and justice. The new gracing of man in the sacrament of redemption, instead, gives him above all the remission of sins. Yet even here grace can "abound even more," as St. Paul expresses elsewhere: "Where sin increased, grace has abounded even more" (Rom 5:20).

The sacrament of redemption—the fruit of Christ's redemptive love—becomes, on the basis of his spousal love for the Church, a permanent dimension of the life of the Church herself, a fundamental and life-giving dimension. It is the *mysterium magnum* (great mystery) of Christ and the Church. It is the eternal mystery actuated by Christ, who "gave himself up for her" (Eph 5:25). It is the mystery that is continually actuated in the Church, because Christ "loved the Church" (Eph 5:25), uniting himself with her in an indissoluble love, just as spouses, husband and wife, unite themselves in marriage. In this way the Church lives on the sacrament of redemption. In her turn she completes this sacrament just as the wife, in virtue of spousal love, completes her husband. In a certain way this had already been pointed out "in the beginning" when the first man found in the first woman "a helper fit for him" (Gn 2:20). Although the analogy in Ephesians does not state it precisely, we can add also that the Church united to Christ, as the wife to her husband, draws from the sacrament of redemption all her fruitfulness and spiritual motherhood. The words of the letter of St. Peter testify to this in some way when he writes that we have been "reborn not from a corruptible, but from an incorruptible seed, through the living and enduring word of God" (1 Pt 1:23). So the mystery hidden in God from all eternity—the mystery that in the beginning, in the sacrament of creation, became a visible reality through the union of the first man and woman in the perspective of marriage—becomes in the sacrament of redemption a visible reality of the indissoluble union of Christ with the Church, which the author of Ephesians presents as the nuptial union of spouses, husband and wife.

The *sacramentum magnum* (the Greek text reads: *tò mystérion toûto méga estín*) of Ephesians speaks of the new actuation of the mystery hidden in God from all eternity. It is the definitive actuation from the point of view of the earthly history of salvation. It also speaks of "making the mystery visible"—the visibility of the Invisible. This visibility is not had unless the mystery ceases to be a mystery. This refers to the marriage constituted in the beginning, in the state of original innocence, in the context of the sacrament of creation. It refers also to the union of Christ with the Church, as the great mystery of the sacrament of redemption. The visibility of the Invisible does not mean a total clearing of the mystery, if it can be said this way. As an object of faith, the mystery remains veiled even through what is precisely expressed and fulfilled. The visibility of the Invisible therefore belongs to the order of signs, and the sign indicates only the reality of the mystery, but not the unveiling. The "first Adam"—man, male and female—created in the state of original innocence and called in this state to conjugal union (in this sense we are speaking of the sacrament of creation) was a sign of the eternal mystery. So the "second Adam," Christ, united with the Church through the sacrament of redemption by an indissoluble bond, analogous to the indissoluble covenant of spouses, is a definitive sign of the same eternal mystery. Therefore, in speaking about the eternal mystery being actuated, we are speaking also about the fact that it becomes visible with the visibility of the sign. Therefore we are speaking also about the sacramentality of the whole heritage of the sacrament of redemption, in reference to the entire work of creation and redemption, and more so in reference to marriage instituted within the context of the sacrament of creation, as also in reference to the Church as the spouse of Christ, endowed by a quasi-conjugal covenant with him.

General audience of October 13, 1982

Marriage Is an Integral Part of the New Sacramental Economy

Last Wednesday we spoke of the integral heritage of the covenant with God, and of the grace originally united to the divine work of creation. Marriage was also a part of this integral heritage, as can be deduced from Ephesians 5:21-33—marriage, that is, as a primordial sacrament instituted from the beginning and linked with the sacrament of creation in its globality. The sacramentality of marriage is not merely a model and figure of the sacrament of the Church (of Christ and of the Church). It also constitutes an essential part of the new heritage, that of the sacrament of redemption, with which the Church is endowed in Christ.

Here it is necessary yet again to refer to Christ's words in Matthew 19:3-9 (cf. also Mk 10:5-9). In replying to the question of the Pharisees concerning marriage, Christ referred only and exclusively to its original institution on the part of the Creator at the beginning. Reflecting on the significance of this reply in the light of Ephesians, and in particular of Ephesians 5:21-33, we end up with a relationship—in a certain sense twofold—of marriage with the whole sacramental order which, in the new covenant, emerges from the same sacrament of redemption.

Marriage as a primordial sacrament constitutes, on the one hand, the figure (the likeness, the analogy), according to which there is constructed the basic main structure of the new economy of salvation and of the sacramental order. This order draws its origin from the spousal gracing which the Church received from Christ, together with all the benefits of redemption (one could say, using the opening words of Ephesians, "with every spiritual blessing"—1:3). In this way marriage, as a primordial sacrament, is assumed and inserted into the integral structure of the new sacramental economy, arising from redemption in the form, I would say, of a "prototype." It is assumed and inserted as it were from its very bases. In conversation with the Pharisees, Christ himself first of all reconfirmed its existence (Mt 19:3-9). Reflecting deeply on this dimension, one would have to conclude that in a certain sense all the sacraments of the new covenant find their prototype in marriage as the primordial sacrament. This seems to be indicated in the classic passage quoted from Ephesians, as we shall say again soon.

However, the relationship of marriage with the whole sacramental order, deriving from the endowment of the Church with the benefits of the redemption, is not limited merely to the dimension of model. In his conversation with the Pharisees (cf. Mt 19), Christ confirms the existence of marriage instituted from the beginning by the Creator. Not only that, he declared it also an integral part of the new sacramental economy, of the new order of salvific signs which derives its origin from the sacrament of redemption, just as the original economy emerged from the sacrament of creation. In fact, Christ limited himself to the unique sacrament which was marriage instituted in the state of innocence and of original justice of man, created male and female "in the image and likeness of God."

The new sacramental economy which is constituted on the basis of the sacrament of redemption, deriving from the spousal gracing of the Church on the part of Christ, differs from the original economy. Indeed, it is directed not to the man of justice and original innocence, but to the man burdened with the heritage of original sin and with the state of sinfulness *(status naturae lapsae)*. It is directed to the man of the threefold concupiscence, according to the classic words of First John 2:16, to the man in whom "the desires of the flesh are against the Spirit, and the desires of the Spirit are against the flesh" (Gal 5:17), according to the Pauline theology (and anthropology), to which we have devoted much space in our previous reflections.

Following upon a deeper analysis of the significance of Christ's statement in the Sermon on the Mount concerning the lustful look as adultery of the heart, these considerations prepare for an understanding of marriage as an integral part of the new sacramental order. This order has its origin in the sacrament of redemption, that is to say, in that great mystery which, as the mystery of Christ and of the Church, determines the sacramentality of the Church itself. These considerations also prepare for an understanding of marriage as a sacrament of the new covenant, whose salvific work is organically linked with the ensemble of that ethos which was defined in the previous analyses as the ethos of redemption. Ephesians expresses the same truth in its own way. It speaks of marriage as a great sacrament in a wide parenetic context, that is, in the context of exhortations of a moral nature. It concerns precisely the ethos which should characterize the life of Christians, that is, of people aware of the election which is realized in Christ and in the Church.

Against this vast background of reflections which emerge from reading Ephesians (especially 5:21-33), one can and should eventually touch again the problem of the sacraments of the Church. The text cited from Ephesians speaks of it in an indirect and, I would say, secondary way, though sufficient to bring this problem within the scope of our considerations. However, it is fitting to clarify here, at least briefly, the sense in which we use the term "sacrament," which is significant for our considerations.

Until now we have used the term "sacrament" (in conformity with the whole of biblical-patristic tradition)[103] in a sense wider than that proper to traditional and contemporary theological terminology. By the word "sacrament" this terminology means the signs instituted by Christ and administered by the Church, which signify and confer divine grace on the person who receives the relative sacrament. In this sense each of the seven sacraments of the Church is characterized by a determinate liturgical action, made up of words (the form) and the specific sacramental "matter." This is according to the widespread hylomorphic theory deriving from Thomas Aquinas and the whole scholastic tradition.

In relationship to this rather restricted meaning, we have used in our considerations a wider and perhaps also more ancient and fundamental meaning of the term "sacrament."[104] Ephesians, especially 5:21-33, seems in a particular way to authorize us to do so. Here sacrament signifies the very mystery of God, which is hidden from eternity; however, not in an eternal concealment, but above all, in its very revelation and actuation (furthermore, in its revelation through its actuation). In this sense we spoke also of the sacrament of creation and of the sacrament of redemption. On the basis of the sacrament of creation, one must understand the original sacramentality of marriage (the primordial sacrament). Following upon this, on the basis of the sacrament of redemption one can understand the sacramentality of the Church, or rather the sacramentality of the union of Christ with the Church. The author of Ephesians presents this under the simile of marriage, of the conjugal union of husband and wife. A careful analysis of the text shows that in this case, it is not merely a comparison in a metaphorical sense, but of a real renewal (or of a "re-creation," that is, of a new creation) of that which constituted the salvific content (in a certain sense, the "salvific substance") of the primordial sacrament. This observation has an essential significance both for the clarification of the sacramentality of the Church (the very significant words of the first chapter of *Lumen Gentium* refer to this), and also for the understanding of the sacramentality of marriage, understood precisely as one of the sacraments of the Church.

General audience of October 20, 1982

The Indissolubility of the Sacrament of Marriage
in the Mystery of the Redemption of the Body

The text of Ephesians (5:21-33) speaks of the sacraments of the Church—and in particular of Baptism and the Eucharist. But it does so only in an indirect and, in a certain sense, allusive manner, developing the analogy of marriage in reference to Christ and the Church. So we read at first that Christ who "loved the Church and gave himself up for her" (5:25), did so "that he might sanctify her, having cleansed her by the washing of water with the word" (5:26). Doubtlessly this treats of the sacrament of Baptism, which by Christ's institution was from the beginning conferred on those who were converted. The words quoted show very graphically in what way Baptism draws its essential significance and its sacramental power from that spousal love of the Redeemer, by means of which the sacramentality of the Church itself is constituted above all *(sacramentum magnum)*. The same can also be said perhaps of the Eucharist. This would seem to be indicated by the following words about nourishing one's own body, which indeed every man nourishes and cherishes "as Christ does the Church, because we are members of his body" (5:29-30). In fact Christ nourishes the Church with his body precisely in the Eucharist.

However, one sees that neither in the first nor second case can we speak of a well-developed sacramental theology. One cannot speak about it even when treating of the sacrament of marriage as one of the sacraments of the Church. Expressing the spousal relationship of Christ to the Church, Ephesians lets it be understood that on the basis of this relationship the Church itself is the "great sacrament." It is the new sign of the covenant and of grace, which draws its roots from the depths of the sacrament of redemption, just as from the depths of the sacrament of creation marriage has emerged, a primordial sign of the covenant and of grace. The author of Ephesians proclaims that that primordial sacrament is realized in a new way in the sacrament of Christ and of the Church. For this reason also, in the same classic text of Ephesians 5:21-33, the Apostle urges spouses to be "subject to one another out of reverence for Christ" (5:21) and model their conjugal life by basing it on the sacrament instituted at the beginning by the Creator. This sacrament found its definitive greatness and holiness in the spousal covenant of grace between Christ and the Church.

Even though Ephesians does not speak directly and immediately of marriage as one of the sacraments of the Church, the sacramentality of marriage is especially confirmed and closely examined in it. In the great sacrament of Christ and of the Church, Christian spouses are called upon to model their life and their vocation on the sacramental foundation.

In the classic text of Ephesians 5:21-33, addressed to Christian spouses, Paul announces to them the great mystery *(sacramentum magnum)* of the spousal love of Christ and of the Church. After the analysis of this text, it is opportune to return to those significant words of the Gospel which we have analyzed previously, seeing in them the key statements for the theology of the body. Christ spoke these words, one might say, from the divine depth of the redemption of the body (cf. Rom 8:23). All these words have a fundamental significance for man inasmuch as he is a body—inasmuch as he is male or female. They have a significance for marriage in which man and woman unite so that the two become "one flesh," according to the expression of Genesis (2:24). However, at the same time, Christ's words also indicate the vocation to continence "for the sake of the kingdom of heaven" (Mt 19:12).

In each of these ways the redemption of the body is a great expectation of those who possess "the first fruits of the spirit" (Rom 8:23). Not only that, it is also a permanent source of hope that creation will be "set free from its bondage to decay and obtain the glorious liberty of the children of God" (Rom 8:21). Spoken from the divine depth of the mystery of redemption and of the redemption of the body, Christ's words bear within them the leaven of this hope. They open to it a perspective both in the eschatological dimension and also in the dimension of daily life. In fact, the words addressed to his immediate hearers are simultaneously addressed to historical man of various times and places. That man indeed who possesses "the first fruits of the spirit...groans...waiting for the redemption...of the body" (Rom 8:23). There is also concentrated in him the "cosmic" hope of the whole of creation, which in him, in man, "waits with eager longing for the revealing of the sons of God" (Rom 8:19).

Christ spoke with the Pharisees, who asked him: "Is it lawful to divorce one's wife for any cause?" (Mt 19:3) They questioned him in this way precisely because the law attributed to Moses permitted the so-called "bill of divorce" (Dt 24:1). Christ replied: "Have you not read that he who made them from the beginning made them male and female, and said, 'For this reason a man shall leave his father and mother and be joined to his wife, and the two shall become one'? So they are no longer two but one. What therefore God has joined together, let no man put asunder" (Mt 19:2-6). They then went on to speak about the "bill of divorce" and Christ said to them: "For your hardness of heart Moses allowed you to divorce your wives, but from the beginning it was not so. And I say to you: Whoever divorces his wife, except for unchastity, and marries another, commits adultery" (Mt 19:8-9). "He who marries a woman divorced from her husband, commits adultery" (Lk 16:18).

The horizon of the redemption of the body is opened up with these words, which constitute the reply to a concrete question of a juridical-moral nature. It is opened up especially by the fact that Christ took his stand on the plane of that primordial sacrament which his questioners inherited in a singular manner, given that they also inherited the revelation of the mystery of creation, contained in the first chapters of Genesis.

These words contain at the same time a universal reply addressed to historical man of all times and places, since they are decisive for marriage and for its indissolubility. In fact they refer to that which man is, male and female, such as he has become in an irreversible way by the fact of having been created in the image and likeness of God. Man does not cease to be such even after original sin, even though this has deprived him of original innocence and justice. In replying to the query of the Pharisees, Christ referred to the "beginning." He seemed in this way to stress especially the fact that he was speaking from the depth of the mystery of redemption, and of the redemption of the body. Redemption signifies, as it were, a "new creation." It signifies the assuming of all that is created to express in creation the fullness of justice, of equity and of sanctity designated by God, and to express that fullness especially in man, created as male and female in the image of God.

In the perspective of Christ's words to the Pharisees on that which marriage was from the beginning, we reread also the classic text of Ephesians (5:21-33) as a testimony of the sacramentality of marriage based on the great mystery of Christ and of the Church.

General audience of October 27, 1982

Christ Opened Marriage to the Saving Action of God

We have analyzed Ephesians, especially the passage of 5:21-33, from the point of view of the sacramentality of marriage. Now we shall examine the same text in the perspective of the words of the Gospel.

Christ's words to the Pharisees (cf. Mt 19) refer to marriage as a sacrament, that is, to the primordial revelation of God's salvific will and deed at the beginning, in the very mystery of creation. In virtue of that salvific will and deed of God, man and woman, joining together in such a way as to become "one flesh" (Gn 2:24), were at the same time destined to be united "in truth and love" as children of God (cf. *GS* 24), adopted children in the only-begotten Son, beloved from all eternity. The words of Christ are directed to this unity and toward this communion of persons, in the likeness of the union of the divine persons (cf. *GS* 24). His words refer to marriage as the primordial sacrament and at the same time confirm that sacrament on the basis of the mystery of redemption. In fact, the original "unity in the body" of man and woman does not cease to mold the history of man on earth, even though it has lost the clarity of the sacrament, of the sign of salvation, which it possessed at the beginning.

In the presence of those with whom he was conversing, in the Gospels of Matthew and Mark (cf. Mt 19; Mk 10), Christ confirmed marriage as a sacrament instituted by the Creator at the beginning. If in conformity with this he insisted on its indissolubility, he thereby opened marriage to the salvific action of God, to the forces which flow from the redemption of the body. These help to overcome the consequences of sin and to constitute the unity of man and woman according to the eternal plan of the Creator. The salvific action which derives from the mystery of redemption assumes in itself the original sanctifying action of God in the mystery of creation.

The words of the Gospel of Matthew (cf. Mt 19:3-9; Mk 10:2-12), have at the same time a very expressive ethical eloquence. On the basis of the mystery of redemption, these words confirm the primordial sacrament. At the same time, they establish an adequate ethos which in our previous reflections we have called the ethos of redemption. The evangelical and Christian ethos, in its theological essence, is the ethos of redemption. Certainly, for that ethos we can find a rational interpretation, a philosophical interpretation of a personalistic character. However, in its theological essence, it is an ethos of redemption, rather, an ethos of the redemption of the body. Redemption becomes at the same time the basis for understanding the particular dignity of the human body, rooted in the personal dignity of the man and the woman. The reason for this dignity lies at the root of the indissolubility of the conjugal covenant.

Christ referred to the indissoluble character of marriage as a primordial sacrament. Confirming this sacrament on the basis of the mystery of redemption, he simultaneously drew conclusions of an ethical nature: "Whoever divorces his wife and marries another commits adultery against her, and if she divorces her husband and marries another, she commits adultery" (Mk 10:11-12; cf. Mt 19:9). It can be said that in this way redemption is given to man as a grace of the new covenant with God in Christ. At the same time it is assigned to him as an ethos, as the form of the morality corresponding to God's action in the mystery of redemption. Marriage as a sacrament is an effective sign of God's salvific action "from the beginning." At the same time—in the light of Christ's words which are being considered here—this sacrament constitutes also an exhortation addressed to man, male and female, so that they may participate consciously in the redemption of the body.

The ethical dimension of the redemption of the body is delineated in an especially profound way when we meditate on Christ's words in the Sermon on the Mount in regard to the commandment, "You shall not commit adultery." "You have heard that it was said, 'You shall not commit adultery.' But I say to you that everyone who looks at a woman lustfully has already committed adultery with her in his heart" (Mt 5:27-28). We have previously given an ample commentary on this statement of Christ in the conviction that it has a fundamental significance for the whole theology of the body, especially in the dimension of historical man. Although these words do not refer directly and immediately to marriage as a sacrament, it is impossible to separate them from the whole sacramental substratum. As far as concerns the conjugal pact, the existence of man as male and female is placed in that substratum, both in the original context of the mystery of creation and then, later, in the context of the mystery of redemption. This sacramental substratum always regards individual persons. It penetrates into that which man and woman are (or rather, into *who* man and woman are) in their original dignity of image and likeness of God by reason of creation, and at the same time, in the same dignity inherited in spite of sin and again continually "assigned" to man as a duty through the reality of the redemption.

In the Sermon on the Mount, Christ gave his own interpretation of the commandment, "You shall not commit adultery." This interpretation constitutes a new ethos. With the same lapidary words he assigned as a duty to every man the dignity of every woman. Simultaneously (even though this can be deduced from the text only in an indirect way), he also assigned to every woman the dignity of every man.[105] Finally he assigned to everyone—both to man and woman—their own dignity, in a certain sense, the *sacrum* of the person. This is in consideration of their femininity or masculinity, in consideration of the body. It is not difficult to see that Christ's words in the Sermon on the Mount regard the ethos. At the same time, it is not difficult to affirm after deeper reflection that these words flow from the very profundity of the redemption of the body. Although they do not refer directly to marriage as a sacrament, it is not difficult to observe that they achieve their proper and full significance in relationship with the sacrament—whether that primordial sacrament which is united with the mystery of creation, or that in which historical man, after sin and because of his hereditary sinfulness, should find again the dignity and holiness of the conjugal union in the body, on the basis of the mystery of redemption.

In the Sermon on the Mount—as also in the conversation with the Pharisees on the indissolubility of marriage—Christ spoke from the depths of that divine mystery. At the same time he entered into the depths of the human mystery. For that reason he mentioned the heart, that intimate place where good and evil struggle in man—sin and justice, concupiscence and holiness. Speaking of concupiscence (of the lustful look: cf. Mt 5:28), Christ made his hearers aware that everyone bears within himself, together with the mystery of sin, the interior dimension "of the man of concupiscence." This is three-fold: "the concupiscence of the flesh, the concupiscence of the eyes and the pride of life" (1 Jn 2:16).

Precisely to this man of concupiscence there is given in marriage the sacrament of redemption as a grace and a sign of the covenant with God, and it is assigned to him as an ethos. Simultaneously, in regard to marriage as a sacrament, it is assigned as an ethos to every man, male and female. It is assigned to his heart, to his conscience, to his looks, and to his behavior. According to Christ's words (cf. Mt 19:4), marriage is a sacrament from the very beginning. At the same time, on the basis of man's historic sinfulness, it is a sacrament arising from the mystery of the redemption of the body.

General audience of November 24, 1982

The Marriage Sacrament
Is an Effective Sign of God's Saving Power

We have analyzed Ephesians, especially 5:21-33, in the perspective of the sacramentality of marriage. Now we shall seek once again to consider the same text in the light of the words of the Gospel and of St. Paul's Letters to the Corinthians and the Romans.

As a sacrament born of the mystery of the redemption and reborn, in a certain sense, in the spousal love of Christ and of the Church, marriage is an efficacious expression of the saving power of God. He accomplishes his eternal plan even after sin and in spite of the threefold concupiscence hidden in the heart of every man, male and female. As a sacramental expression of that saving power, marriage is also an exhortation to dominate concupiscence (as Christ spoke of it in the Sermon on the Mount). The unity and indissolubility of marriage are the fruit of this dominion, as is a deepened sense of the dignity of woman in the heart of a man (and also the dignity of man in the heart of a woman), both in conjugal life together, and in every other circle of mutual relations.

The truth according to which marriage as a sacrament of redemption is given to the "man of concupiscence" as a grace and at the same time as an ethos, has also found particular expression in the teaching of St. Paul, especially in the seventh chapter of First Corinthians. Comparing marriage with virginity (or with "celibacy for the sake of the kingdom of heaven") and deciding for the "superiority" of virginity, the Apostle observes at the same time that "each has his own special gift from God, one of one kind and one of another" (1 Cor 7:7). On the basis of the mystery of redemption, a special "gift," that is, a grace, corresponds to marriage. In the same text, giving advice to those to whom he is writing, the Apostle recommends marriage "because of the temptation to immorality" (1 Cor 7:2). Later he recommends to the married couple that "the husband should give to his wife her conjugal rights, and likewise the wife to her husband" (1 Cor 7:3). He continues thus: "It is better to marry than to be aflame with passion" (1 Cor 7:9).

These statements of St. Paul have given rise to the opinion that marriage constitutes a specific remedy for concupiscence. However, as we have already observed, St. Paul teaches explicitly that marriage has a corresponding special "gift," and that in the mystery of redemption marriage is given to a man and a woman as a grace. In his striking and at the same time paradoxical words, St. Paul simply expresses the thought that marriage is assigned to the spouses as an ethos. In the Pauline words, "It is better to marry than to be aflame with passion," the verb *ardere* signifies a disorder of the passions, deriving from the concupiscence of the flesh. (Concupiscence is presented in a similar way in the Old Testament by Sirach; cf. Sir 23:17.) However, marriage signifies the ethical order, which is consciously introduced in this context. It can be said that marriage is the meeting place of eros with ethos and of their mutual compenetration in the heart of man and of woman, as also in all their mutual relationships.

This truth—namely, that marriage as a sacrament derived from the mystery of redemption is given to historical man as a grace and at the same time as an ethos—determines moreover the character of marriage as one of the sacraments of the Church. As a sacrament of the Church, marriage has the nature of indissolubility. As a sacrament of the Church, it is also a word of the Spirit which exhorts man and woman to model their whole life together by drawing power from the mystery of the "redemption of the body." In this way they are called to chastity as to a state of life "according to the Spirit" which is proper to them (cf. Rom 8:4-5; Gal 5:25). The redemption of the body also signifies in this case that hope which, in the dimension of marriage, can be defined as the hope of daily life, the hope of temporal life. On the basis of such a hope the concupiscence of the flesh as the source of the tendency toward an egoistic gratification is dominated. In the sacramental alliance of masculinity and femininity, the same flesh becomes the specific "substratum" of an enduring and indissoluble communion of the persons *(communio personarum)* in a manner worthy of the persons.

Those who, as spouses, according to the eternal divine plan, join together so as to become in a certain sense one flesh, are also in their turn called, through the sacrament, to a life according to the Spirit. This corresponds to the gift received in the sacrament. In virtue of that gift, by leading a life according to the Spirit, the spouses are capable of rediscovering the particular gratification which they have become sharers of. As much as concupiscence darkens the horizon of the inward vision and deprives the heart of the clarity of desires and aspirations, so much does "life according to the Spirit" (that is, the grace of the sacrament of marriage) permit man and woman to find again the true liberty of the gift, united to the awareness of the spousal meaning of the body in its masculinity and femininity.

The life according to the Spirit is also expressed in the mutual union (cf. Gn 4:1), whereby the spouses, becoming one flesh, submit their femininity and masculinity to the blessing of procreation: "Adam knew Eve his wife, and she conceived and gave birth...saying: 'I have begotten a man with the help of the Lord'" (Gn 4:1).

The life according to the Spirit is also expressed here in the consciousness of the gratification, to which there corresponds the dignity of the spouses themselves as parents. That is to say, it is expressed in the profound awareness of the sanctity of the life *(sacrum)* to which the two give origin, participating as progenitors in the forces of the mystery of creation. In the light of that hope, which is connected with the mystery of the redemption of the body (cf. Rom 8:19-23), this new human life, a new man conceived and born of the conjugal union of his father and mother, opens to "the first fruits of the Spirit" (Rom 8:23), "to enter into the liberty of the glory of the children of God" (Rom 8:21). If "the whole creation has been groaning in travail together until now" (Rom 8:22), a particular hope accompanies the pains of the mother in labor, that is, the hope of the "revelation of the sons of God" (Rom 8:22), a hope of which every newborn babe who comes into the world bears a spark within himself.

This hope which is in the world, penetrating the whole of creation, as St. Paul teaches, is not at the same time from the world. Still further, it must struggle in the human heart with that which is from the world, with that which is in the world. "Because everything that is in the world, the lust of the flesh and the lust of the eyes and the pride of life, is not of the Father, but is of the world" (1 Jn 2:16). As the primordial sacrament, and at the same time as the sacrament born in the mystery of the redemption of the body from the spousal love of Christ and of the Church, marriage "comes from the Father." It is not from the world but from the Father. Consequently, marriage also as a sacrament constitutes the basis of hope for the person, that is, for man and woman, for parents and children, for the human generations. On the one hand, "The world passes away and the lust thereof," while on the other, "He who does the will of God abides forever" (1 Jn 2:17). The origin of man in the world is united with marriage as a sacrament, and its future is also inscribed in it. This is not merely in the historical dimensions, but also in the eschatological.

Christ's words referred to this when he spoke of the resurrection of the body. His words are reported by the three synoptics (cf. Mt 22:23-32; Mk 12:18-27; Lk 20:34-39). "In the resurrection they neither marry nor are given in marriage, but are like angels in heaven," states Matthew, and in like manner Mark. In Luke we read: "The sons of this age marry and are given in marriage; but those who are accounted worthy to attain to that age and to the resurrection of the dead neither marry nor are given in marriage, for they cannot die any more, because they are equal to angels and are sons of God" (Lk 20:34-36). These texts were previously subjected to a detailed analysis.

Christ stated that marriage—the sacrament of the origin of man in the temporal visible world—does not pertain to the eschatological reality of the future world. However, called to participate in this eschatological future by means of the resurrection of the body, man is the same man, male and female, whose origin in the temporal visible world is linked with marriage as the primordial sacrament of the mystery of creation. Rather, every man, called to share in the reality of the future resurrection, brings this vocation into the world by the fact that in the temporal visible world he has his origin by means of the marriage of his parents. Thus, then, Christ's words which exclude marriage from the reality of the future world, reveal indirectly at the same time the significance of this sacrament for the participation of men, sons and daughters, in the future resurrection.

Marriage is the primordial sacrament, reborn in a certain sense in the spousal love of Christ and of the Church. Marriage does not pertain to the redemption of the body in the dimension of the eschatological hope (cf. Rom 8:23). Marriage is given to man as a grace, as a gift destined by God precisely for the spouses, and at the same time assigned to them by Christ's words as an ethos. That sacramental marriage is accomplished and realized in the perspective of the eschatological hope. It has an essential significance for the redemption of the body in the dimension of this hope. It comes indeed from the Father and to him it owes its origin in the world. If this "world passes," and if with it the lust of the flesh, the lust of the eyes and the pride of life which come from the world also passes, marriage as a sacrament immutably ensures that man, male and female, by dominating concupiscence, does the will of the Father. And he "who does the will of God remains forever" (1 Jn 2:17).

In this sense marriage as a sacrament also bears within itself the germ of man's eschatological future, that is, the perspective of the "redemption of the body" in the dimension of the eschatological hope which corresponds to Christ's words about the resurrection: "In the resurrection they neither marry nor are given in marriage" (Mt 22:30). However, also those who, "being sons of the resurrection...are equal to angels and are sons of God" (Lk 20:36), owe their origin in the temporal visible world to the marriage and procreation of man and woman. As the sacrament of the human beginning, as the sacrament of the temporality of the historical man, marriage fulfills in this way an irreplaceable service in regard to his extra-temporal future, in regard to the mystery of the redemption of the body in the dimension of the eschatological hope.

General audience of December 1, 1982

The Redemptive and Spousal Dimension of Love

As we have already seen, the author of Ephesians speaks of a "great mystery," linked to the primordial sacrament through the continuity of God's saving plan. He also referred to the "beginning," as Christ did in his conversation with the Pharisees (cf. Mt 19:8), quoting the same words: "Therefore a man leaves his father and his mother and cleaves to his wife, and they become one flesh" (Gn 2:24). This "great mystery" is above all the mystery of the union of Christ with the Church, which the Apostle presents under the similitude of the unity of the spouses: "I mean it in reference to Christ and the Church" (Eph 5:32). We find ourselves in the domain of the great analogy in which marriage as a sacrament is presupposed on the one hand, and on the other hand, rediscovered. It is presupposed as the sacrament of the "beginning" of mankind united to the mystery of the creation. However, it is rediscovered as the fruit of the spousal love of Christ and of the Church linked with the mystery of the redemption.

Addressing spouses directly, the author of Ephesians exhorts them to mold their reciprocal relationship on the model of the spousal union of Christ and the Church. It can be said that—presupposing the sacramentality of marriage in its primordial significance—he orders them to learn anew this sacrament of the spousal unity of Christ and the Church: "Husbands, love your wives, as Christ loved the Church and gave himself up for her, that he might sanctify her..." (cf. Eph 5:25-26). This invitation which the Apostle addressed to Christian spouses is fully motivated by the fact that through marriage as a sacrament, they participate in Christ's saving love, which is expressed at the same time as his spousal love for the Church. In the light of Ephesians—precisely through participation in this saving love of Christ—marriage as a sacrament of the human "beginning" is confirmed and at the same time renewed. It is the sacrament in which man and woman, called to become "one flesh," participate in God's own creative love. They participate in it both by the fact that, created in the image of God, they are called by reason of this image to a particular union *(communio personarum)*, and because this same union has from the beginning been blessed with the blessing of fruitfulness (cf. Gn 1:28).

All this original and stable structure of marriage as a sacrament of the mystery of creation, according to the classic text of Ephesians (Eph 5:21-33), is renewed in the mystery of the redemption, when that mystery assumes the aspect of the spousal love of the Church on the part of Christ. That original and stable form of marriage is renewed when the spouses receive it as a sacrament of the Church, drawing from the new depths of God's love for man. This love is revealed and opened with the mystery of the redemption, "when Christ loved the Church and gave himself up for her to make her holy..." (Eph 5:25-26). That original and stable image of marriage as a sacrament is renewed when Christian spouses, conscious of the authentic profundity of the redemption of the body, are united "out of reverence for Christ" (Eph 5:21).

The Pauline image of marriage, inscribed in the "great mystery" of Christ and of the Church, brings together the redemptive dimension and the spousal dimension of love. In a certain sense it fuses these two dimensions into one. Christ has become the spouse of the Church. He has married the Church as a bride, because "He has given himself up for her" (Eph 5:25). Through marriage as a sacrament (as one of the sacraments of the Church) both these dimensions of love, the spousal and the redemptive, together with the grace of the sacrament, permeate the life of the spouses. The spousal significance of the body in its masculinity and femininity was manifested for the first time in the mystery of creation against the background of man's original innocence. This significance is linked in the image of Ephesians with the redemptive significance, and in this way it is confirmed and in a certain sense, "newly created."

This is important in regard to marriage and to the Christian vocation of husbands and wives. The text of Ephesians (5:21-33) is directly addressed to them and speaks especially to them. However, that linking of the spousal significance of the body with its redemptive significance is equally essential and valid for the understanding of man in general, for the fundamental problem of understanding him and for the self-comprehension of his being in the world. It is obvious that we cannot exclude from this problem the question on the meaning of being a body, on the sense of being, as a body, man and woman. These questions were posed for the first time in relation to the analysis of the human beginning, in the context of Genesis. In a certain sense, that very context demanded that they should be posed. It is equally demanded by the classic text of Ephesians. The great mystery of the union of Christ to the Church obliges us to link the spousal significance of the body with its redemptive significance. In this link the spouses find the answer to the question concerning the meaning of "being a body," and not only they, although this text of the Apostle's letter is addressed especially to them.

The Pauline image of the great mystery of Christ and of the Church also spoke indirectly of celibacy for the sake of the kingdom of heaven. In this celibacy, both dimensions of love, the spousal and redemptive, are reciprocally united in a way different from that of marriage, according to diverse proportions. Is not perhaps that spousal love wherewith Christ "loved the Church"—his bride—"and gave himself up for her," at the same time the fullest incarnation of the ideal of celibacy for the kingdom of heaven (cf. Mt 19:12)? Is not support found precisely in this by all those—men and women—who, choosing the same ideal, desire to link the spousal dimension of love with the redemptive dimension according to the model of Christ himself? They wish to confirm with their life that the spousal significance of the body—of its masculinity and femininity—profoundly inscribed in the essential structure of the human person, has been opened in a new way on the part of Christ and with the example of his life, to the hope united to the redemption of the body. Thus, the grace of the mystery of the redemption bears fruit also—rather bears fruit in a special way—with the vocation to celibacy for the kingdom of heaven.

The text of Ephesians (5:21-33) does not speak of it explicitly. It is addressed to spouses and constructed according to the image of marriage, which by analogy explains the union of Christ with the Church—a union in both redemptive and spousal love together. Is it not perhaps precisely this love which, as the living and vivifying expression of the mystery of the redemption, goes beyond the circle of the recipients of the letter circumscribed by the analogy of marriage? Does it not embrace every man and, in a certain sense, the whole of creation as indicated by the Pauline text on the redemption of the body in Romans (cf. Rom 8:23)? The great sacrament in this sense is a new sacrament of man in Christ and in the Church. It is the sacrament "of man and of the world," just as the creation of man, male and female, in the image of God, was the original sacrament of man and of the world. In this new sacrament of redemption marriage is organically inscribed, just as it was inscribed in the original sacrament of creation.

Man, who "from the beginning" is male and female, should seek the meaning of his existence and the meaning of his humanity by reaching out to the mystery of creation through the reality of redemption. There one finds also the essential answer to the question on the significance of the human body, and the significance of the masculinity and femininity of the human person. The union of Christ with the Church permits us to understand in what way the spousal significance of the body is completed with the redemptive significance, and this in the diverse ways of life and in diverse situations. It is not only in marriage or in continency (that is, virginity and celibacy), but also, for example, in the many forms of human suffering, indeed, in the very birth and death of man. By means of the great mystery which Ephesians treats of, by means of the new covenant of Christ with the Church, marriage is again inscribed in that "sacrament of man" which embraces the universe, in the sacrament of man and of the world which, thanks to the forces of the redemption of the body is modeled on the spousal love of Christ for the Church, to the measure of the definitive fulfillment of the kingdom of the Father.

Marriage as a sacrament remains a living and vivifying part of this saving process.

General audience of December 15, 1982

The Language of the Body Is the Substratum and Content of the Sacramental Sign of Spousal Communion

"I take you as my wife"; "I take you as my husband." These words are at the center of the liturgy of marriage as a sacrament of the Church. These words spoken by the engaged couple are inserted in the following formula of consent: "I promise to be faithful to you always, in joy and in sorrow, in sickness and in health, and to love and honor you all the days of my life." With these words the engaged couple enter the marriage contract and at the same time receive the sacrament of which both are the ministers. Both of them, the man and the woman, administer the sacrament. They do it before witnesses. The priest is a qualified witness, and at the same time he blesses the marriage and presides over the whole sacramental liturgy. Moreover, all those participating in the marriage rite are in a certain sense witnesses, and some of them (usually two) are called specifically to act as witnesses in an official way. They must testify that the marriage was contracted before God and confirmed by the Church. In the ordinary course of events sacramental marriage is a public act by means of which two persons, a man and a woman, become husband and wife before the ecclesial society, that is, they become the actual subject of the marriage vocation and life.

Marriage is a sacrament which is contracted by means of the word which is a sacramental sign by reason of its content: "I take you as my wife—as my husband—and I promise to be always faithful to you, in joy and sorrow, in sickness and in health, and to love you and honor you all the days of my life." However, this sacramental word is, *per se,* merely the sign of the coming into being of marriage. The coming into being of marriage is distinguished from its consummation, to the extent that without this consummation the marriage is not yet constituted in its full reality. The fact that a marriage is juridically contracted but not consummated *(ratum—non consummatum)* corresponds to the fact that it has not been fully constituted as a marriage. Indeed the very words "I take you as my wife—my husband" refer not only to a determinate reality, but they can be fulfilled only by means of conjugal intercourse. This reality (conjugal intercourse) has moreover been determined from the very beginning by institution of the Creator: "Therefore a man leaves his father and his mother and cleaves to his wife, and they become one flesh" (cf. Gn 2:24).

Thus then, from the words whereby the man and the woman express their willingness to become "one flesh" according to the eternal truth established in the mystery of creation, we pass to the reality which corresponds to these words. Both the one and the other element are important in regard to the structure of the sacramental sign, to which it is fitting to devote the remainder of the present reflections. Granted that the sacrament is a sign which expresses and at the same time effects the saving reality of grace and of the covenant, one must now consider it under the aspect of sign, whereas the previous reflections were dedicated to the reality of grace and of the covenant.

As a sacrament of the Church, marriage is contracted by means of the words of the ministers, that is, of the newlyweds. These words signify and indicate, in the order of intention, that which (or rather, who) both have decided to be from now on, the one for the other and the one with the other. The words of the newlyweds form a part of the integral structure of the sacramental sign, not merely *for what* they signify but also, in a certain sense, *with what* they signify and determine. The sacramental sign is constituted in the order of intention insofar as it is simultaneously constituted in the real order.

Consequently, the sacramental sign of marriage is constituted by the words of the newlyweds inasmuch as the "reality" which they themselves constitute corresponds to those words. Both of them, as man and woman, being the ministers of the sacrament in the moment of contracting marriage, constitute at the same time the full and real visible sign of the sacrament itself. The words spoken by them would not, *per se,* constitute the sacramental sign of marriage unless there corresponded to them the human subjectivity of the engaged couple and at the same time the awareness of the body, linked to the masculinity and femininity of the husband and wife. Here it is necessary to recall to mind the whole series of our previous analyses in regard to Genesis (cf. Gn 1:2). The structure of the sacramental sign remains essentially the same as "in the beginning." In a certain sense, it is determined by the language of the body. This is inasmuch as the man and the woman, who through marriage should become one flesh, express in this sign the reciprocal gift of masculinity and femininity as the basis of the conjugal union of the persons.

The sacramental sign of marriage is constituted by the fact that the words spoken by the newlyweds use again the same language of the body as at the "beginning," and in any case they give a concrete and unique expression to it. They give it an intentional expression on the level of intellect and will, of consciousness and of the heart. The words "I take you as my wife/as my husband" imply precisely that perennial, unique and unrepeatable language of the body. At the same time they situate it in the context of the communion of the persons: "I promise to be always faithful to you, in joy and in sadness, in sickness and in health, and to love you and honor you all the days of my life." In this way the enduring and ever new language of the body is not only the "substratum," but in a certain sense, it is the constitutive element of the communion of the persons. The persons —man and woman—become for each other a mutual gift. They become that gift in their masculinity and femininity, discovering the spousal significance of the body and referring it reciprocally to themselves in an irreversible manner—in a life-long dimension.

Thus the sacrament of marriage as a sign enables us to understand the words of the newlyweds. These words confer a new aspect on their life in a dimension strictly personal (and interpersonal: *communio personarum),* on the basis of the language of the body. The administration of the sacrament consists in this: that in the moment of contracting marriage the man and the woman, by means of suitable words and recalling the perennial language of the body, form a sign, an unrepeatable sign, which has also a significance for the future: "all the days of my life," that is to say, until death. This is a visible and efficacious sign of the covenant with God in Christ, that is, of grace which in this sign should become a part of them as "their own special gift" (according to the expression of 1 Corinthians 7:7).

Expressing this matter in socio-juridical terms, one can say that between the newlyweds there is a stipulated, well-defined conjugal pact. It can also be said that following upon this pact, they have become spouses in a manner socially recognized, and that in this way the family as the fundamental social cell is also constituted in germ. This manner of understanding it is obviously in agreement with the human reality of marriage. Indeed, it is also fundamental in the religious and religious-moral sense. However, from the point of view of the theology of the sacrament, the key for the understanding of marriage is always the reality of the sign whereby marriage is constituted on the basis of the covenant of man with God in Christ and in the Church. It is constituted in the supernatural order of the sacred bond requiring grace. In this order marriage is a visible and efficacious sign. Having its origin in the mystery of creation, it derives its new origin from the mystery of redemption at the service of the "union of the sons of God in truth and in love" *(GS* 24). The liturgy of the sacrament of marriage gave a form to that sign: directly, during the sacramental rite, on the basis of the *ensemble* of its eloquent expressions; indirectly, throughout the whole of life. As spouses, the man and woman bear this sign throughout the whole of their lives and they remain as that sign until death.

General audience of January 5, 1983

The Language of the Body in the Structure of Marriage

We now analyze the sacramentality of marriage under the aspect of sign. When we say that the language of the body also enters essentially into the structure of marriage as a sacramental sign, we refer to a long biblical tradition. This has its origin in Genesis (especially 2:23-25) and it finds its definitive culmination in Ephesians (cf. Eph 5:21-33). The prophets of the Old Testament had an essential role in forming this tradition. Analyzing the texts of Hosea, Ezekiel, Deutero-Isaiah, and of the other prophets, we find ourselves face to face with the great analogy whose final expression is the proclamation of the new covenant under the form of a marriage between Christ and the Church (cf. Eph 5:21-33). On the basis of this long tradition it is possible to speak of a specific "prophetism of the body," both because of the fact that we find this analogy especially in the prophets, and also in regard to its content. Here, the "prophetism of the body" signifies precisely the language of the body.

The analogy seems to have two levels. On the first and fundamental level the prophets present the covenant between God and Israel as a marriage. This also permits us to understand marriage itself as a covenant

between husband and wife (cf. Prv 2:17; Mal 2:14). In this case the covenant derives from the initiative of God, the Lord of Israel. The fact that
he, as Creator and Lord, makes a covenant first of all with Abraham and
then with Moses, already bears witness to a special choice. Therefore the
pro-phets, presupposing the entire juridical-moral content of the covenant,
go much deeper and reveal a dimension incomparably more profound
than that of a mere "pact." In choosing Israel, God is united with his
people through love and grace. He is bound with a special bond, profoundly personal. Therefore Israel, even though a people, is presented in this
prophetic vision of the covenant as a spouse or wife, and therefore, in a
certain sense, as a person:

> For your Maker is your husband,
> the Lord of Hosts is his name;
> and the Holy One of Israel is your Redeemer,
> the God of the whole earth he is called....
> But my steadfast love shall not depart from you
> and my covenant of peace shall not be removed,
> says the Lord (Is 54:5, 10).

Yahweh is the Lord of Israel, but he also becomes her Spouse. The
books of the Old Testament bear witness to the absolute original character
of the dominion of Yahweh over his people. To the other aspects of the
dominion of Yahweh, Lord of the covenant and Father of Israel, a new
aspect revealed by the prophets is added, that is to say, the stupendous
dimension of this dominion, which is the spousal dimension. In this way,
the absolute of dominion is the absolute of love. In regard to this absolute,
the breach of the covenant signifies not only an infraction of the "pact"
linked with the authority of the supreme Legislator, but also infidelity and
betrayal. It is a blow which even pierces his heart as Father, as Spouse and
as Lord.

If, in the analogy employed by the prophets, one can speak of levels,
this is in a certain sense the first and fundamental level. Given that the
covenant of Yahweh with Israel has the character of a spousal bond like to
the conjugal pact, that first level of the analogy reveals a second which is
precisely the language of the body. Here we have in mind, in the first
place, the language in an objective sense. The prophets compare the covenant to marriage. They refer to the primordial sacrament spoken of in
Genesis 2:24, in which the man and the woman, by free choice, become
"one flesh." However, it is characteristic of the prophets' manner of expressing themselves that, presupposing the language of the body in the
objective sense, they pass at the same time to its subjective meaning. That
is to say, after a manner of speaking, they allow the body itself to speak. In

the prophetic texts of the covenant, on the basis of the analogy of the spousal union of the married couple, the body itself "speaks." It speaks by means of its masculinity and femininity. It speaks in the mysterious language of the personal gift. It speaks ultimately—and this happens more frequently—both in the language of fidelity, that is, of love, and also in the language of conjugal infidelity, that is, of adultery.

It is well known that the different sins of the Chosen People—and especially their frequent infidelities in regard to the worship of the one God, that is, various forms of idolatry—offered the prophets the occasion to denounce the aforesaid sins. In a special way, Hosea was the prophet of the "adultery" of Israel. He condemned it not only in words, but also, in a certain sense, in actions of a symbolic significance: "Go, take to yourself a wife of harlotry and have children of harlotry, for the land commits great harlotry by forsaking the Lord" (Hos 1:2). Hosea sets out in relief all the splendor of the covenant—of that marriage in which Yahweh manifests himself as a sensitive, affectionate Spouse disposed to forgiveness, and at the same time, exigent and severe. The adultery and the harlotry of Israel evidently contrast with the marriage bond, on which the covenant is based, as likewise, analogically, the marriage of man and woman.

In a similar way, Ezekiel condemned idolatry. He used the symbol of the adultery of Jerusalem (cf. Ez 16) and, in another passage, of Jerusalem and of Samaria (cf. Ez 23). "When I passed by you again and looked upon you, behold, you were at the age for love.... I plighted my troth to you and entered into a covenant with you, says the Lord God, and you became mine" (Ez 16:8). "But you trusted in your beauty and played the harlot because of your renown, and lavished your harlotry on any passerby" (Ez 16:15).

In the texts of the prophets the human body speaks a "language" which it is not the author of. Its author is man as male or female, as husband or wife—man with his everlasting vocation to the communion of persons. However, man cannot, in a certain sense, express this singular language of his personal existence and of his vocation without the body. He has already been constituted in such a way from the beginning, in such wise that the most profound words of the spirit—words of love, of giving, of fidelity—demand an adequate language of the body. Without that they cannot be fully expressed. We know from the Gospel that this refers both to marriage and also to celibacy for the sake of the kingdom.

As the inspired mouthpieces of the covenant of Yahweh with Israel, the prophets seek precisely through this language of the body to express both the spousal profundity of the aforesaid covenant and all that is opposed to it. They praise fidelity and they condemn infidelity as adultery.

They speak therefore according to ethical categories, setting moral good and evil in mutual opposition. The opposition between good and evil is essential for morality. The texts of the prophets have an essential significance in this sphere, as we have shown in our previous reflections. However, it seems that the language of the body according to the prophets is not merely a language of morality, a praise of fidelity and of purity, and a condemnation of adultery and of harlotry. In fact, for every language as an expression of knowledge, the categories of truth and of non-truth (that is, of falsity) are essential. In the writings of the prophets, who catch a fleeting glimpse of the analogy of the covenant of Yahweh with Israel in marriage, the body speaks the truth through fidelity and conjugal love. When it commits adultery it speaks lies; it is guilty of falsity.

It is not a case of substituting ethical with logical differentiations. If the texts of the prophets indicate conjugal fidelity and chastity as "truth," and adultery or harlotry, on the other hand, as "non-truth," as a falsity of the language of the body, this happens because in the first case the subject (that is, Israel as a spouse) is in accord with the spousal significance which corresponds to the human body (because of its masculinity or femininity) in the integral structure of the person. In the second case, however, the same subject contradicts and opposes this significance.

We can then say that the essential element for marriage as a sacrament is the language of the body in its aspects of truth. Precisely by means of that, the sacramental sign is constituted.

General audience of January 12, 1983

The Sacramental Covenant in the Dimension of Sign

The texts of the prophets have great importance for understanding marriage as a covenant of persons (in the likeness of the covenant of Yahweh with Israel) and, in particular, for understanding the sacramental covenant of man and woman in the dimension of sign. As already considered, the language of the body enters into the integral structure of the sacramental sign whose principal subject is man, male and female. The words of matrimonial consent constitute this sign, because the spousal significance of the body in its masculinity and femininity is found expressed in them. Such a significance is expressed especially by the words: "I take you as my wife...my husband." Moreover, the essential "truth" of the language of the body is confirmed with these words. The essential "non-truth," the falsity of the language of the body is also excluded (at least indirectly, implicitly). The body speaks the truth through conjugal love, fidelity and integrity, just as non-truth, that is, falsity, is expressed by all that is the negation of conjugal love, fidelity and integrity. It can then be said that in the moment of pronouncing the words of matrimonial consent, the newly-weds set themselves on the line of the same "prophetism of the body," of which the ancient prophets were the mouthpiece. Expressed by the ministers of marriage as a Sacrament of the Church, the language of the body institutes the visible sign itself of the covenant and of grace which, going back to its origin to the mystery of creation, is continually sustained by the power of the redemption of the body, offered by Christ to the Church.

According to the prophetic texts the human body speaks a language which it is not the author of. Its author is man who, as male and female, husband and wife, correctly rereads the significance of this language. He rereads that spousal significance of the body as integrally inscribed in the structure of the masculinity or femininity of the personal subject. A correct rereading "in truth" is an indispensable condition to proclaim this truth, that is, to institute the visible sign of marriage as a sacrament. The spouses proclaim precisely this language of the body, reread in truth, as the content and principle of their new life in Christ and in the Church. On the basis of the "prophetism of the body," the ministers of the sacrament of marriage perform an act of prophetic character. They confirm in this way their participation in the prophetic mission of the Church received from Christ. A prophet is one who expresses in human words the truth coming from God, who speaks this truth in the place of God, in his name and in a certain sense with his authority.

All this applies to the newlyweds who, as ministers of the sacrament of marriage, institute the visible sign by the words of matrimonial consent. They proclaim the language of the body, reread in truth, as content and principle of their new life in Christ and in the Church. This prophetic proclamation has a complex character. The matrimonial consent is at the same time the announcement and the cause of the fact that, from now on, both will be husband and wife before the Church and society. (We understand such an announcement as an indication in the ordinary sense of the term.) However, marriage consent has especially the character of a reciprocal profession of the newlyweds made before God. It is enough to examine the text attentively to be convinced that that prophetic proclamation of the language of the body, reread in truth, is immediately and directly addressed to the "I" and the "you"—by the man to the woman and by her to him. The central position in the matrimonial consent is held precisely by the words which indicate the personal subject, the pronouns "I" and "you." Reread in the truth of its spousal significance, the language of the body constitutes by means of the words of the newlyweds the union-communion of the persons. If the matrimonial consent has a prophetic character, if it is the proclamation of the truth coming from God and, in a certain sense, the statement of this truth in God's name, this is brought about especially in the dimension of the interpersonal communion, and only indirectly "before" others and "for" others.

The enduring language of the body stands against the background of the words spoken by the ministers of the sacrament of marriage. God originated this language by creating man as male and female—a language which has been renewed by Christ. This enduring language of the body carries within itself all the richness and depth of the mystery, first of creation and then of redemption. Bringing into being the visible sign of the sacrament by means of the words of their matrimonial consent, the spouses express therein the language of the body with all the profundity of the mystery of creation and of redemption. (The liturgy of the sacrament of marriage offers a rich context of it.) Rereading the language of the body in this way, the spouses enclose in the words of matrimonial consent the subjective fullness of the profession which is indispensable to bring about the sign proper to the sacrament. Not only this, they also arrive in a certain sense at the sources from which that sign on each occasion draws its prophetic eloquence and its sacramental power. One must not forget that before being spoken by the lips of the spouses, who are the ministers of marriage as a sacrament of the Church, the language of the body was spoken by the word of the living God, beginning from Genesis, through the prophets of the old covenant, until the author of the Letter to the Ephesians.

We use over and over again the expression "language of the body," harking back to the prophetic texts. As we have already said, in these texts the human body speaks a language which it is not the author of in the proper sense of the term. The author is man, male and female, who rereads the true sense of that language, bringing to light the spousal significance of the body as integrally inscribed in the very structure of the masculinity and femininity of the personal subject. This rereading "in truth" of the language of the body already confers, *per se,* a prophetic character on the words of the marriage consent, by means of which man and woman bring into being the visible sign of marriage as a sacrament of the Church. However, these words contain something more than a simple rereading in truth of that language spoken of by the femininity and masculinity of the newlyweds in their reciprocal relationships: "I take you as my wife...as my husband." The words of matrimonial consent contain the intention, the decision and the choice. Both of the spouses decide to act in conformity with the language of the body, reread in truth. If man, male and female, is the author of that language, he is so especially inasmuch as he wishes to confer, and does indeed confer, on his behavior and on his actions a significance in conformity with the reread eloquence of the truth of masculinity and femininity in the mutual conjugal relationship.

In this sphere man is the cause of the actions which have, *per se,* clear-cut meanings. He is then the cause of the actions and at the same time the author of their significance. The sum total of those meanings constitutes in a certain sense the ensemble of the language of the body, in which the spouses decide to speak to each other as ministers of the sacrament of marriage. The sign which they constitute by the words of matrimonial consent is not a mere immediate and passing sign, but a sign looking to the future which produces a lasting effect, namely, the marriage bond, one and indissoluble ("all the days of my life," that is, until death). In this perspective they should fulfill that sign of multiple content offered by the conjugal and family communion of the persons and also of that content which, originating from the language of the body, is continually reread in truth. In this way the essential "truth" of the sign will remain organically linked to the morality of matrimonial conduct. In this truth of the sign and, later, in the morality of matrimonial conduct, the procreative significance of the body is inserted with a view to the future—that is, paternity and maternity, which we have previously treated. To the question: "Are you willing to accept responsibly and with love the children that God may give you and to educate them according to the law of Christ and of the Church?"—the man and the woman reply: "Yes."

Now we postpone to later meetings further detailed examinations of the matter.

General audience of January 19, 1983

The Language of the Body
Strengthens the Marriage Covenant

The sign of marriage as a sacrament of the Church is constituted each time according to that dimension which is proper to it from the "beginning." At the same time it is constituted on the foundation of the spousal love of Christ and of the Church as the unique and unrepeatable expression of the covenant between "this" man and "this" woman. They are the ministers of marriage as a sacrament of their vocation and their life. In saying that the sign of marriage as a sacrament of the Church is constituted on the basis of the language of the body, we are using analogy (the analogy of attribution), which we have sought to clarify previously. It is obvious that the body as such does not "speak," but man speaks, rereading that which requires to be expressed precisely on the basis of the "body," of the masculinity and femininity of the personal subject, indeed, on the basis of what can be expressed by man only by means of the body.

In this sense man—male or female—does not merely speak with the language of the body. But in a certain sense he permits the body to speak "for him" and "on his behalf," I would say, in his name and with his personal authority. In this way even the concept of the "prophetism of the body" seems to be well founded. The prophet spoke "for" and "on behalf of"—in the name and with the authority of a person.

The newly wed spouses are aware of it when in contracting marriage they institute its visible sign. In the perspective of life in common and of the conjugal vocation, that initial sign, the original sign of marriage as a sacrament of the Church, will be continually completed by the "prophetism of the body." The spouses' bodies will speak "for" and "on behalf of" each of them. They will speak in the name of and with the authority of the person, of each of the persons, carrying out the conjugal dialogue proper to their vocation and based on the language of the body, reread in due course opportunely and continually—and it is necessary that it be reread in truth! The spouses are called to form their life and their living together as a communion of persons on the basis of that language. Granted that a complexus of meaning corresponds to the language, the spouses—by means of their conduct and comportment, by means of their actions and gestures ("gestures of tenderness"—cf. *GS* 49)—are called to become the authors of such meanings of the "language of the body." Consequently, love, fidelity, conjugal uprightness and that union which remains indissoluble until death are constructed and continually deepened.

The sign of marriage as a sacrament of the Church is formed precisely by those meanings which the spouses are the authors of. All these meanings are initiated and in a certain sense "programmed" in a synthetic manner in the conjugal consent for the purpose of constructing later—in a more analytical way, day by day—the same sign, identifying oneself with it in the dimension of the whole of life. There is an organic bond between rereading in truth the integral significance of the language of the body and the consequent use of that language in conjugal life. In this last sphere the human being—male and female—is the author of the meanings of the language of the body. This implies that this language which he is the author of corresponds to the truth which has been reread. On the basis of biblical tradition we speak here of the "prophetism of the body." If the human being—male and female—in marriage (and indirectly also in all the spheres of mutual life together) confers on his behavior a significance in conformity with the fundamental truth of the language of the body, then he also "is in the truth." In the contrary case he is guilty of a lie and falsifies the language of the body.

If we place ourselves on the perspective line of conjugal consent—which, as we have already said, offers the spouses a particular participation in the prophetic mission of the Church handed down from Christ himself—we can in this regard also use the biblical distinction between true and false prophets. By means of marriage as a sacrament of the Church, man and woman are called explicitly to bear witness—by using correctly the language of the body—to spousal and procreative love, a witness worthy of true prophets. The true significance and the grandeur of conjugal consent in the sacrament of the Church consists in this.

The problematic of the sacramental sign of marriage has a highly anthropological character. We construct it on the basis of theological anthropology and in particular on that which, from the beginning of the present considerations, we have defined as the theology of the body. Therefore, in continuing these analyses, we should always have before our minds the previous considerations which refer to the analysis of the key words of Christ. (We call them key words because they open up for us, like a key, the individual dimensions of theological anthropology, especially of the theology of the body.) Constructing on this basis the analysis of the sacramental sign of marriage in which the man and woman always participate, even after original sin, that is, man and woman as historical man, we must constantly bear in mind the fact that that historical man, male and female, is at the same time the man of concupiscence. As such, every man and every woman enter the history of salvation and they are involved in it through the sacrament which is the visible sign of the covenant and of grace.

Therefore, we bear this in mind in the context of the present reflections, on the sacramental structure of the sign of not only what Christ said on the unity and indissolubility of marriage by referring to the "beginning," but also (and still more) what he said in the Sermon on the Mount when he referred to the "human heart."

General audience of January 26, 1983

Man Is Called to Overcome Concupiscence

We said previously that in the context of the present reflections on the structure of marriage as a sacramental sign, we should bear in mind not only what Christ said about its unity and indissolubility in reference to the beginning, but also (and still more) what he said in the Sermon on the Mount when he referred to the human heart. Referring to the commandment, "You shall not commit adultery," Christ spoke of adultery in the heart. "Everyone who looks at a woman lustfully has already committed adultery with her in his heart" (Mt 5:28).

The sacramental sign of marriage—the sign of the conjugal covenant of a man and a woman—is formed on the basis of the language of the body reread in truth (and continuously reread). In stating this, we realize that he who rereads this language and then expresses it, not according to the requirements proper to marriage as a pact and a sacrament, is naturally and morally the man of concupiscence—male and female, both of them understood as the "man of concupiscence." The prophets of the Old Testament certainly have this man before their eyes when, using an analogy, they condemn the "adultery of Israel and Judah." The analysis of the words Christ spoke in the Sermon on the Mount lead us to understand more deeply "adultery" itself. At the same time it leads us to the conviction that the human heart is not so much accused and condemned by Christ because of concupiscence *(concupiscentia carnalis)*, as first of all called. Here there is a decisive difference between the anthropology (or the anthropological hermeneutics) of the Gospel and some influential representatives of the contemporary hermeneutics of man (the so-called masters of suspicion).

Continuing our present analysis we can observe that even though man, notwithstanding the sacramental sign of marriage, notwithstanding conjugal consent and its actuation, remains naturally the "man of concupiscence," he is at the same time *the man who has been "called."* He is called through the mystery of the redemption of the body, a divine mystery, which at the same time is—in Christ and through Christ in every man—a human reality. That mystery, besides, implies a determinate ethos which is essentially human, and which we have previously called the ethos of the redemption.

In the light of the words Christ spoke in the Sermon on the Mount, in the light of the whole Gospel and of the new covenant, the three-fold *concupiscence* (especially the concupiscence of the flesh) does not destroy the capacity to reread in truth the language of the body. It does not destroy the capacity to reread continually in an ever more mature and fuller way that language of the body, whereby the sacramental sign is constituted both in its first liturgical moment, and also later in the dimension of the whole of life. In this light one must note that concupiscence, *per se,* causes many errors in rereading the language of the body. Together with this it gave rise also to sin—moral evil, contrary to the virtue of chastity (whether conjugal or extra-conjugal). Nevertheless in the sphere of the ethos of redemption the possibility always remains of passing from error to the truth, as also the possibility of returning, that is, of conversion, from sin to chastity, as an expression of a life according to the Spirit (cf. Gal 5:16).

In this way, in the evangelical and Christian perspective of the problem, historical man (after original sin), on the basis of the language of the body reread in truth, is able—as male and female—to constitute the sacramental sign of love, of conjugal fidelity and integrity, and this as an *enduring sign:* "To be faithful to you always in joy and in sorrow, in sickness and in health, and to love and honor you all the days of my life." This signifies that man, in a real way, is the author of the meanings whereby, after having reread in truth the language of the body, he is also capable of forming in truth that language in the conjugal and family communion of the persons. He is capable of it also as the man of concupiscence, being at the same time called by the reality of the redemption of Christ *(simul lapsus et redemptus).*

By means of the dimension of the sign proper to marriage as a sacrament there is confirmed the specific theological anthropology, the specific hermeneutics of man. In this case it could also be called the hermeneutics of the sacrament, because it permits us to understand man on the basis of the analysis of the sacramental sign. Man—male and female—as the minister of the sacrament, the author (co-author) of the sacramental sign, is a conscious and capable subject of self-determination. Only on this basis can he be the author of the language of the body, the author (co-author) of marriage as a sign—a sign of the divine creation and redemption of the body. The fact that man (male and female) is the man of concupiscence does not prejudice his capacity to reread the language of the body in truth. He is the man of concupiscence. But at the same time he is capable of discerning truth from falsity in the language of the body. He can be the author of the meanings of that language, whether true or false.

He is the man of concupiscence, but he is not completely determined by libido (in the sense in which this term is often used). Such a determination would imply that the ensemble of man's behavior, even, for example, the choice of continence for religious motives, would be explained only by means of the specific transformations of this libido. In such a case—in the sphere of the language of the body—man would, in a certain sense, be condemned to essential falsifications. He would merely be one who expresses a specific determination on the part of the libido, but he would not express the truth or falsity of spousal love and of the communion of the persons, even though he might think to manifest it. Consequently, he would then be condemned to suspect himself and others in regard to the truth of the language of the body. Because of the concupiscence of the flesh he could only be accused, but he could not be really called.

The hermeneutics of the sacrament permits us to draw the conclusion that man is always essentially called and not merely accused, and this precisely inasmuch as he is the man of concupiscence.

General audience of February 9, 1983

Reflections on the Song of Songs

During the Holy Year I postponed the treatment of the theme of human love in the divine plan. I would now like to conclude that topic with some considerations especially about the teaching of *Humanae Vitae*, premising some reflections on the Song of Songs and the Book of Tobit. It seems to me that what I intend to explain in the coming weeks constitutes the crowning of what I have illustrated.

The theme of marital love which unites man and woman in a certain sense connects this part of the Bible with the whole tradition of the "great analogy." Through the writings of the prophets, this flows into the New Testament and especially into Ephesians (cf. Eph 5:21-33). I interrupted the explanation of this at the beginning of the Holy Year.

The Song of Songs has become the object of many exegetical studies, commentaries and hypotheses. With regard to its content, apparently "profane," the positions have varied. On the one hand its reading has often been discouraged, and on the other it has been the source from which the greatest mystical writers have drawn. The verses of the Song of Songs have been inserted into the Church's liturgy.[106] Although the analysis of the text of this book obliges us to situate its content outside the sphere of the great prophetic analogy, it is not possible to detach it from the reality of the original sacrament. It is not possible to reread it except along the lines of what is written in the first chapters of Genesis, as a testimony of the beginning—that beginning which Christ referred to in his decisive conversation with the Pharisees (cf. Mt 19:4).[107] The Song of Songs is certainly found in the wake of that sacrament in which, through the language of the body, the visible sign of man and woman's participation in the covenant of grace and love offered by God to man is constituted. The Song of Songs demonstrates the richness of this language, whose first expression is already found in Genesis 2:23-25.

Indeed, the first verses of the Song of Songs lead us immediately into the atmosphere of the whole poem, in which the groom and the bride seem to move in the circle traced by the irradiation of love. The words, movements and gestures of the spouses correspond to the interior movement of their hearts. It is possible to understand the language of the body only through the prism of this movement. In that language there comes to pass that discovery which the first man expressed in front of her who had been created as "a helper like himself" (cf. Gn 2:20, 23). As the biblical text reports, she had been taken from one of his ribs ("rib" seems to also indicate the heart).

This discovery—already analyzed on the basis of Genesis 2—in the Song of Songs is invested with all the richness of the language of human love. What was expressed in the second chapter of Genesis (vv. 23-25) in just a few simple and essential words, is developed here in a full dialogue, or rather in a duet, in which the groom's words are interwoven with the bride's and they complement each other. On seeing the woman created by God, man's first words express wonder and admiration, even more, the sense of fascination (cf. Gn 2:23). A similar fascination—which is wonder and admiration—runs in fuller form through the verses of the Song of Songs. It runs in a peaceful and homogeneous wave from the beginning to the end of the poem.

Even a summary analysis of the text of the Song of Songs allows the language of the body to be heard expressing itself in that mutual fascination. The point of departure as well as the point of arrival for this fascination—mutual wonder and admiration—are in fact the bride's femininity and the groom's masculinity, in the direct experience of their visibility. The words of love uttered by both of them are therefore concentrated on the body, not only because in itself it constitutes the source of the mutual fascination. But it is also, and above all, because on the body there lingers directly and immediately that attraction toward the other person, toward the other "I"—female or male—which in the interior impulse of the heart generates love.

In addition, love unleashes a special experience of the beautiful, which focuses on what is visible, but at the same time involves the entire person. The experience of beauty gave rise to mutual satisfaction.

"O most beautiful among women...." (Sg 1:8), the groom says, and the bride's words echo back to him: "I am dark—but lovely, O daughters of Jerusalem" (Sg 1:5). The words of the spellbound man are repeated continually. They return in all five stanzas of the poem, and they are echoed in similar expressions of the bride's.

It is a question here of metaphors that may surprise us today. Many of them were borrowed from the life of shepherds; others seem to indicate the royal status of the groom.[108] The analysis of that poetic language is left to the experts. The very fact of adopting the metaphor shows how much, in our case, the language of the body seeks support and corroboration in the whole visible world. This is without doubt a language that is reread at one and the same time with the heart and with the eyes of the groom, in the act of special concentration on the whole female "I" of the bride. This "I" speaks to him through every feminine trait, giving rise to that state of mind that can be defined as fascination, enchantment. This female "I" is expressed almost without words. Nevertheless, the language of the body, expressed wordlessly, finds a rich echo in the groom's words, in his speaking that is full of poetic transport and metaphors, which attest to the experience of beauty, a love of satisfaction. If the metaphors in the Song of Songs seek an analogy for this beauty in the various things of the visible world (in this world which is the groom's "own world"), at the same time they seem to indicate the insufficiency of each of these things in particular. "You are all-beautiful, my beloved, and there is no blemish in you" (Sg 4:7). The groom ends his song with this saying, leaving all the metaphors, in order to address himself to that sole one through which the language of the body seems to express what is more proper to femininity and the whole of the person.

We will continue the analysis of the Song of Songs at the next general audience.

General audience of May 23, 1984

Truth and Freedom—The Foundation of True Love

We resume our analysis of the Song of Songs with the purpose of understanding in a more adequate and exhaustive way the sacramental sign of marriage. This is manifested by the language of the body, a singular language of love originating in the heart.

At a certain point, expressing a particular experience of values that shines upon everything that relates to the person he loves, the groom says:

> You have ravished my heart, my sister, my bride;
> you have ravished my heart with one glance of your eyes,
> with one bead of your necklace.
> How sweet are your caresses, my sister, my bride... (Sg 4:9-10).

From these words emerges what is of essential importance for the theology of the body—and in this case for the theology of the sacramental sign of marriage—to know who the female "you" is for the male "I" and vice versa.

The groom in the Song of Songs exclaims: "You are all-beautiful, my beloved" (Sg 4:7) and calls her "my sister, my bride" (Sg 4:9). He does not call her by her name, but he uses expressions that say more.

Under a certain aspect, compared with the name "beloved," the name "sister" that is used for the bride seems to be more eloquent and rooted in the sum total of the Song of Songs, which illustrates how love reveals the other person.

The term "beloved" indicates what is always essential for love, which puts the second "I" beside one's own "I." Friendship—love of friendship *(amor amicitiae)*—signifies in the Song of Songs a particular approach felt and experienced as an interiorly unifying power. The fact that in this approach that female "I" is revealed for her groom as "sister" —and that precisely as both sister and bride—has a special eloquence. The expression "sister" speaks of the union in mankind and at the same time of her difference and feminine originality. This is not only with regard to sex, but to the very way of "being person," which means both "being subject" and "being in relationship." The term "sister" seems to express, in a more simple way, the subjectivity of the female "I" in personal relationship with the man, that is, in the openness of him toward others, who are understood and perceived as brothers. The sister in a certain sense helps man to identify himself and conceive of himself in this way, constituting for him a kind of challenge in this direction.

The groom in the Song of Songs accepts the challenge and seeks the common past, as though he and his woman were descended from the same family circle, as though from infancy they were united by memories of a common home. So they mutually feel as close as brother and sister who owe their existence to the same mother. From this a specific sense of common belonging follows. The fact that they feel like brother and sister allows them to live their mutual closeness in security and to manifest it, finding support in that, and not fearing the unfair judgment of other men.

Through the name "sister," the groom's words tend to reproduce, I would say, the history of the femininity of the person loved. They see her still in the time of girlhood and they embrace her entire "I," soul and body, with a disinterested tenderness. Hence that peace arises which the bride speaks of. This is the peace of the body, which in appearance resembles sleep ("Do not arouse, do not stir up love before its own time"). This is above all the peace of the encounter in mankind as the image of God—and the encounter by means of a reciprocal and disinterested gift. "So am I in your eyes, like one who has found peace" (Sg 8:10).

In relation to the preceding plot, which could be called a "fraternal" plot, another plot emerges in the loving duet of the Song of Songs, another substratum of the content. We can examine it by starting from certain sayings that seem to have a key significance in the poem. This plot never emerges explicitly, but through the whole composition, and is expressly manifested only in a few passages. So the groom says:

> You are an enclosed garden, my sister, my bride,
> an enclosed garden, a fountain sealed (Sg 4:12).

The metaphors just read, an "enclosed garden, a fountain sealed," reveal the presence of another vision of the same female "I," master of her own mystery. We can say that both metaphors express the personal dignity of the woman who as a spiritual subject is in possession and can decide not only on the metaphysical depth, but also on the essential truth and authenticity of the gift of herself, inclined to that union which Genesis speaks of.

The language of metaphors—poetic language—seems to be in this sphere especially appropriate and precise. The "sister bride" is for the man the master of her own mystery as a "garden enclosed" and a "fountain sealed." The language of the body reread in truth keeps pace with the discovery of the interior inviolability of the person. At the same time, this discovery expresses the authentic depth of the mutual belonging of the spouses who are aware of belonging to each other, of being destined for each other: "My lover belongs to me and I to him" (Sg 2:16; cf. 6:3).

This awareness of mutual belonging resounds especially on the lips of the bride. In a certain sense, with these words she responds to the groom's words with which he acknowledged her as the master of her own mystery. When the bride says, "My lover belongs to me," she means at the same time, "It is he to whom I entrust myself." Therefore she says, "and I to him" (Sg 2:16). The words "to me" and "to him" affirm here the whole depth of that entrustment, which corresponds to the interior truth of the person.

It likewise corresponds to the nuptial significance of femininity in relation to the male "I," that is, to the language of the body reread in the truth of personal dignity.

The groom states this truth with the metaphors of the "garden enclosed" and the "fountain sealed." The bride answers him with the words of the gift, that is, the entrustment of herself. As master of her own choice she says, "I belong to my lover." The Song of Songs subtly reveals the interior truth of this response. The freedom of the gift is the response to the deep awareness of the gift expressed by the groom's words. Through this truth and freedom that love is built up, which we must affirm is authentic love.

General audience of May 30, 1984

Love Is Ever Seeking and Never Satisfied

Today we will reflect again on the Song of Songs, with the aim of better understanding the sacramental sign of marriage. The truth about love, proclaimed by the Song of Songs, cannot be separated from the language of the body. The truth about love enables the same language of the body to be reread in truth. This is also the truth about the progressive approach of the spouses which increases through love. The nearness means also the initiation into the mystery of the person, without, however, implying its violation (cf. Sg 1:13-14, 16).

The truth about the increasing nearness of the spouses through love is developed in the subjective dimension "of the heart," of affection and sentiment. This dimension allows one to discover in itself the other as a gift and, in a certain sense, to "taste it" in itself (cf. Sg 2:3-6).

Through this nearness the groom more fully lives the experience of that gift which on the part of the female "I" is united with the spousal expression and meaning of the body. The man's words (cf. Sg 7:1-8) do not only contain a poetic description of his beloved, of her feminine beauty on which his senses dwell, but they speak of the gift and the self-giving of the person.

The bride knows that the groom's longing is for her and she goes to meet him with the quickness of the gift of herself (cf. Sg 7:9-13) because the love that unites them is at one and the same time of a spiritual and a sensual nature. It is also on the basis of this love that the rereading of the significance of the body in the truth comes to pass, since the man and woman must together constitute that sign of the mutual gift of self, which puts the seal on their whole life.

In the Song of Songs the language of the body becomes a part of the single process of the mutual attraction of the man and woman. This attraction is expressed in the frequent refrains that speak of the search that is full of nostalgia, of affectionate solicitude (cf. Sg 2:7) and of the spouses' mutual rediscovery (cf. Sg 5:2). This brings them joy and calm, and seems to lead them to a continual search. One has the impression that in meeting each other, in reaching each other, in experiencing one's nearness, they ceaselessly continued to tend toward something. They yield to the call of something that dominates the content of the moment and surpasses the limits of the eros, limits that are reread in the words of the mutual language of the body (cf. Sg 1:7-8; 2:17). This search has its interior dimension: "the heart is awake" even in sleep. This aspiration, born of love on the basis of the language of the body, is a search for integral beauty, for purity that is free of all stain. It is a search for perfection that contains, I would say, the synthesis of human beauty, beauty of soul and body.

In the Song of Songs the human eros reveals the countenance of love ever in search and, as it were, never satisfied. The echo of this restlessness runs through the strophes of the poem:

> I opened to my lover—but my lover had departed, gone.
> I sought him but I did not find him;
> I called to him but he did not answer me (Sg 5:6).
>
> I adjure you, daughters of Jerusalem, if you find my lover—
> What shall you tell him? That I am faint with love (Sg 5:8).

So then some strophes of the Song of Songs present the eros as the form of human love in which the energies of desire are at work. In them, the awareness or the subjective certainty of the mutual, faithful and exclusive belonging is rooted. At the same time, however, many other strophes of the poem lead us to reflect on the cause of the search and the restlessness that accompanies the awareness of belonging to each other. Is this restlessness also part of the nature of the eros? If it were, this restlessness would indicate also the need for self-control. The truth about love is expressed in the awareness of mutual belonging, the fruit of the aspiration and search for each other, and in the need for the aspiration and the search, the outcome of mutual belonging.

This interior necessity, this dynamic of love indirectly reveals the near impossibility of one person's being appropriated and mastered by the other. The person is someone who surpasses all measures of appropriation and domination, of possession and gratification, which emerge from the same language of the body. If the groom and the bride reread this language in the full truth about the person and about love, they arrive at the ever deeper conviction that the fullness of their belonging constitutes that mutual gift in which love is revealed as "stern as death," that is, it goes to the furthest limits of the language of the body in order to exceed them. The truth about interior love and the truth about the mutual gift in a certain sense continually call the groom and the bride—through the means of expressing the mutual belonging, and even by breaking away from those means—to arrive at what constitutes the very nucleus of the gift from person to person.

Following the paths of the words marked out by the strophes of the Song of Songs, it seems that we are therefore approaching the dimension in which the eros seeks to be integrated, through still another truth about love. Centuries later, in the light of the death and resurrection of Christ, Paul of Tarsus will proclaim this truth in the words of First Corinthians:

Love is patient; love is kind.
Love is not jealous; it does not put on airs; it is not snobbish.
Love is never rude; it is not self-seeking; it is not prone to anger;
    neither does it brood over injuries.
Love does not rejoice in what is wrong but rejoices with the truth.
There is no limit to love's forbearance, to its trust, its hope,
    its power to endure.
Love never fails (1 Cor 13:4-8).

Is the truth about love, expressed in the strophes of the Song of Songs, confirmed in the light of these words of Paul? In the Song of Songs we read, as an example of love, that its "jealousy" is "relentless as the nether world" (Sg 8:6). In the Pauline letter we read that "love is not jealous." What relationship do both of these expressions about love have? What relationship does the love that is "stern as death," according to the Song of Songs, have with the love that "never fails," according to the Pauline letter? We will not multiply these questions; we will not open the comparative analysis. Nevertheless, it seems that love opens up before us here in two perspectives. It is as though that in which the human eros closes its horizon is still opened, through Paul's words, to another horizon of love that speaks another language, the love that seems to emerge from another dimension of the person, and which calls, invites, to another communion. This love has been called *agape* and *agape* brings the eros to completion by purifying it.

So we have concluded these brief meditations on the Song of Songs, intended to further examine the theme of the language of the body. In this framework, the Song of Songs has a totally singular meaning.

General audience of June 6, 1984

Love Is Victorious in the Struggle between Good and Evil

During these past weeks, in commenting on the Song of Songs, I emphasized how the sacramental sign of matrimony is constituted on the basis of the language of the body, which man and woman express in the truth that is proper to it. Under this aspect, today I intend to analyze some passages from the Book of Tobit.

In the account of the wedding of Tobiah with Sarah, besides the expression "sister"—through which there seems to be a fraternal character rooted in spousal love—another expression is also found, likewise analogous to those in the Song of Songs.

As you will recall, in the spouses' duet, the love which they declare to each other is "stern as death" (Sg 8:6). In the Book of Tobit we find a phrase which, in saying that he fell deeply in love with Sarah and "his heart became set on her" (Tb 6:19), presents a situation confirming the truth of the words about love "stern as death."

For a better understanding, we must go back to some details that are explained against the background of the specific nature of the Book of Tobit. We read there that Sarah, daughter of Raguel, had "already been married seven times" (Tb 6:14), but all her husbands had died before having intercourse with her. This had happened through the work of a demon, and young Tobiah too had reason to fear a similar death.

So from the very first moment Tobiah's love had to face the test of life and death. The words about love "stern as death," spoken by the spouses in the Song of Songs in the transport of the heart, assume here the nature of a real test. If love is demonstrated as stern as death, this happens above all in the sense that Tobiah and, together with him, Sarah, unhesitatingly face this test. But in this test of life and death, life wins because, during the test on the wedding night, love, supported by prayer, is revealed as more stern than death.

This test of life and death also has another significance that enables us to understand the love and the marriage of the newlyweds. Becoming one as husband and wife, they find themselves in the situation in which the powers of good and evil fight and compete against each other. The spouses' duet in the Song of Songs seems not to perceive completely this dimension of reality. The spouses of the Song of Songs live and express themselves in an ideal or abstract world, in which it is as though the struggle of the objective forces between good and evil did not exist. Is it not precisely the power and the interior truth of love that subdues the struggle that goes on in man and around him?

The fullness of this truth and this power proper to love seems nevertheless to be different. It seems to tend rather to where the experience in the Book of Tobit leads us. The truth and the power of love are shown in the ability to place oneself between the forces of good and evil which are fighting in man and around him, because love is confident in the victory of good and is ready to do everything so that good may conquer. As a result, the love of the spouses in the Book of Tobit is not confirmed by the words expressed by the language of loving transport as in the Song of Songs, but by the choices and the actions that take on all the weight of human existence in the union of the two. The language of the body here seems to use the words of the choices and the acts stemming from the love that is victorious because it prays.

Tobiah's prayer (Tb 8:5-8), which is above all a prayer of praise and thanksgiving, then one of supplication, situates the language of the body on the level of the essential terms of the theology of the body. It is an "objectivized" language, pervaded not so much by the emotive power of the experience as by the depth and gravity of the truth of the experience.

The spouses profess this truth together, in unison before the God of the covenant: "God of our fathers." We can say that under this aspect the language of the body becomes the language of the ministers of the sacrament, aware that in the conjugal pact the mystery that has its origin in God himself is expressed and realized. Their conjugal pact is the image—and the original sacrament of the covenant of God with man, with the human race—of that covenant which took its origin from eternal Love.

Tobiah and Sarah end their prayer with the following words: "Call down your mercy on me and on her, and allow us to live together to a happy old age" (Tb 8:7).

We can admit (on the basis of the context) that they have before their eyes the prospect of persevering in their union to the end of their days—a prospect that opens up before them with the trial of life and death, already during their wedding night. At the same time, they see with the glance of faith the sanctity of this vocation in which—through the unity of the two, built upon the mutual truth of the language of the body—they must respond to the call of God himself which is contained in the mystery of the Beginning. This is why they ask: "Call down your mercy on me and on her."

With ardent words, the spouses in the Song of Songs declare to each other their human love. The newlyweds in the Book of Tobit ask God that they be able to respond to love. Both the one and the other find their place in what constitutes the sacramental sign of marriage. Both the one and the other share in forming this sign.

We can say that through the one and the other the "language of the body," reread in the subjective dimension of the truth of human hearts and in the "objective" dimension of the truth of living in union, becomes the language of the liturgy.

The prayer of the newlyweds in the Book of Tobit certainly seems to confirm this differently from the Song of Songs, and even in a way that is undoubtedly more deeply moving.

General audience of June 27, 1984

The Language of the Body and the Spirituality of Marriage

Today let us return to the classic text of the fifth chapter of Ephesians, which reveals the eternal sources of the covenant of the Father's love and at the same time the new and definitive institution of that covenant in Jesus Christ.

This text brings us to such a dimension of the language of the body that could be called mystical. It speaks of marriage as a great mystery—"This is a great mystery" (Eph 5:32). This mystery is fulfilled in the spousal union of Christ the Redeemer with the Church, and of the Church-Spouse with Christ ("I mean that it refers to Christ and the Church"—Eph 5:22), and it is definitively carried out in eschatological dimensions. Nevertheless the author of Ephesians does not hesitate to extend the analogy of Christ's union with the Church in spousal love, outlined in such an absolute and eschatological way, to the sacramental sign of the matrimonial pact between man and woman, who "defer to one another out of reverence for Christ" (Eph 5:21). He does not hesitate to extend that mystical analogy to the "language of the body," reread in the truth of the spousal love and the conjugal union of the two.

We must recognize the logic of this marvelous text which radically frees our way of thinking from elements of Manichaeism or from a nonpersonalistic consideration of the body. At the same time it brings the language of the body, contained in the sacramental sign of matrimony, nearer to the dimension of real sanctity.

The sacraments inject sanctity into the plan of man's humanity. They penetrate the soul and body, the femininity and the masculinity of the personal subject, with the power of sanctity. All of this is expressed in the language of the liturgy. It is expressed there and brought about there.

The liturgy, liturgical language, elevates the conjugal pact of man and woman, based on the language of the body reread in truth, to the dimensions of mystery. At the same time it enables that pact to be fulfilled in these dimensions through the language of the body.

Precisely the sign of the sacrament of marriage speaks of this. In liturgical language this sign expresses an interpersonal event, laden with intense personal content, assigned to the two "until death." The sacramental sign signifies not only the *fieri* (the "becoming")—the birth of the marriage—but builds its whole *esse* (its "being"), its duration. It signifies both the one and the other as a sacred and sacramental reality, rooted in the dimension of the covenant and grace in the dimension of creation and redemption. In this way, the liturgical language assigns to both, to the man and to the woman, love, fidelity and conjugal honesty through the language of the body. It assigns them the unity and the indissolubility of marriage in the language of the body. It assigns them as a duty all the *sacrum* (holy) of the person and of the communion of persons, and likewise their femininity and masculinity—precisely in this language.

In this sense we affirm that liturgical language becomes the language of the body. This signifies a series of acts and duties which form the spirituality of marriage, its ethos. In the daily life of the spouses these acts become duties, and the duties become acts. These acts—as also the commitments—are of a spiritual nature. Nevertheless, they are expressed at the same time with the language of the body.

The author of Ephesians writes in this regard: "Husbands should love their wives as they do their own bodies..." (Eph 5:28) ("as he loves himself"—Eph 5:33), and "the wife for her part showing respect for her husband" (Eph 5:33). Both, for that matter, are to "defer to one another out of reverence for Christ" (Eph 5:21).

The "language of the body," as an uninterrupted continuity of liturgical language, is expressed not only as the attraction and mutual pleasure of the Song of Songs, but also as a profound experience of the *sacrum* (the holy). This seems to be infused in the very masculinity and femininity through the dimension of the *mysterium* (mystery), the *mysterium magnum* of Ephesians. This mystery sinks its roots precisely in the beginning, that is, in the mystery of the creation of man, male and female, in the image of God, called from the beginning to be the visible sign of God's creative love.

So therefore that reverence for Christ and respect which the author of Ephesians speaks of, is none other than a spiritually mature form of that mutual attraction—man's attraction to femininity and woman's attraction to masculinity, which is revealed for the first time in Genesis (Gn 2:23-25). Consequently, the same attraction seems to flow like a wide stream through the verses of the Song of Songs to find, under entirely different circumstances, its concise and concentrated expression in the Book of Tobit.

The spiritual maturity of this attraction is none other than the blossoming of the gift of fear—one of the seven gifts of the Holy Spirit, which St. Paul speaks of in First Thessalonians (cf. 1 Thes 4:4-7).

On the other hand, Paul's doctrine on chastity as "life according to the Spirit" (cf. Rom 8:5) allows us (especially on the basis of First Corinthians, chapter 6) to interpret that respect in a charismatic sense, that is, as a gift of the Holy Spirit.

In exhorting spouses to defer to each other "out of reverence for Christ" (Eph 5:21), and in urging them, consequently, to show respect in their conjugal relationship, Ephesians seems to point out—in keeping with Pauline tradition—chastity as a virtue and as a gift.

In this way, through the virtue and still more through the gift ("life according to the Spirit") the mutual attraction of masculinity and femininity spiritually matures. Both the man and woman, getting away from concupiscence, find the proper dimension of the freedom of the gift, united to femininity and masculinity in the true spousal significance of the body.

Thus liturgical language, that is, the language of the sacrament and of the *mysterium,* becomes in their life and in their living together the language of the body in a depth, simplicity and beauty hitherto altogether unknown.

This seems to be the integral significance of the sacramental sign of marriage. In that sign, through the language of the body, man and woman encounter the great mystery. This is in order to transfer the light of that mystery—the light of truth and beauty, expressed in liturgical language—to the language of the body, that is, to the language of the practice of love, fidelity, and conjugal honesty, to the ethos rooted in the redemption of the body (cf. Rom 8:23). In this way, conjugal life becomes in a certain sense liturgical.

General audience of July 4, 1984

NOTES

General audience of July 28, 1982

[97] The question of Pauline authorship of Ephesians, acknowledged by some exegetes and denied by others, can be resolved by means of a median supposition which we accept here as a working hypothesis: namely, that St. Paul entrusted some concepts to his secretary, who then developed and refined them.

We have in mind this provisional solution of the question when we speak of "the author of the Letter to the Ephesians," the "Apostle," and "St. Paul."

General audience of September 8, 1982

[98] "Sacrament," a central concept for our reflections, has traveled a long way in the course of the centuries. The semantic history of the term "sacrament" must begin with the Greek term *mystérion* which, truth to tell, in the Book of Judith still means the king's military plans ("secret plan," cf. Jdt 2:2). But already in the Book of Wisdom (2:22) and in the prophecy of Daniel (2:27), the term signifies

the creative plans of God and the purpose which he assigns to the world, and which are revealed only to faithful confessors.

In this sense *mystérion* appears only once in the Gospels: "To you has been given the secret of the kingdom of God" (Mk 4:11 and par.). In the great letters of St. Paul, this term is found seven times, reaching its climax in the Letter to the Romans: "...according to my gospel and the preaching of Jesus Christ, according to the revelation of the mystery which was kept secret for long ages, but is now disclosed..." (Rom 16:25-26).

In the later letters we find the identification of *mystérion* with the Gospel (cf. Eph 6:19) and even with Jesus Christ himself (cf. Col 2:2; 4:3; Eph 3:4), which marks a turning point in the meaning of the term: *mystérion* is no longer merely God's eternal plan, but the accomplishment on earth of that plan revealed in Jesus Christ.

Therefore, in the Patristic period, the term *mystérion* begins to be applied also to the historical events by which the divine will to save man was manifested. Already in the second century in the writings of St. Ignatius of Antioch, Sts. Justin and Meliton, the mysteries of the life of Jesus, the prophecies and the symbolic figures of the Old Testament are defined with the term *mystérion*.

In the 3rd century the most ancient Latin versions of Sacred Scripture begin to appear, in which the Greek term is translated both by *mystérion* and by *sacramentum* (e.g., Wis 2:22; Eph 5:32). Perhaps this was to distance themselves explicitly from the pagan mystery rites and from the Neo-Platonic gnostic mystagogy.

However, *sacramentum* originally meant the military oath taken by the Roman legionaries. The aspects of "initiation to a new form of life," "commitment without reserve," "faithful service even at the risk of death" can be distinguished in it. Given this, Tertullian pointed out these dimensions in the Christian sacraments of Baptism, Confirmation and the Eucharist. In the third century, therefore, the term *sacramentum* was applied both to the mystery of God's salvific plan in Christ (cf., e.g., Eph 5:32), and to its concrete accomplishment by means of the seven sources of grace which are today called "sacraments of the Church."

Using various meanings of the term "sacrament," St. Augustine applied it to religious rites both of the old and the new covenant, to biblical symbols and figures as well as to the revealed Christian religion. All these "sacraments," according to St. Augustine, pertain to the great sacrament: the mystery of Christ and the Church. St. Augustine influenced the further clarification of the term "sacrament," emphasizing that the sacraments are sacred signs, that they contain in themselves a resemblance to what they signify and that they confer what they signify. By his analyses, he therefore contributed to the elaboration of the concise scholastic definition of sacrament: *signum efficax gratiae*.

St. Isidore of Seville (7th century) later stressed another aspect: the mysterious nature of the sacrament which, under the veils of material species, conceals the action of the Holy Spirit in the human soul.

The theological *summae* of the 12th and 13th centuries already formulate the systematic definitions of the sacraments, but a special signification belongs to the definition of St. Thomas: *"Non omne signum rei sacrae est sacramentum.... Sed solum ea quae significant perfectionem sanctitatis humanae."* "Not every sign of a sacred thing is a sacrament.... Only those are called sacraments which signify the perfection of holiness in man" (St. Thomas, *Summa Theol.*, III, q. 60, a. 2, ad 1, 3 [New York: Benziger, 1947]).

From then on, "sacrament" was understood exclusively as one of the seven sources of grace. Theological studies were directed to a deeper understanding of the essence and of the action of the seven sacraments, by elaborating in a systematic way the principal lines contained in the scholastic tradition.

Only in the last century was attention paid to the aspects of the sacrament which had been neglected in the course of the centuries, for example, to the ecclesial dimension and to the personal encounter with Christ, which have found expression in the *Constitution on the Sacred Liturgy* (no. 59). However, the Second Vatican Council returns above all to the original significance of *"sacramentum-mysterium,"* calling the Church "the universal sacrament of salvation" *(LG* 48), sacrament, or "sign and instrument of communion with God and of unity among all men" *(LG* 1).

Here sacrament is understood—in conformity with its original meaning—as the accomplishment of God's eternal plan in regard to the salvation of mankind.

General audience of September 22, 1982

[99] In the Hebrew text we have the words *hesed-rahamim,* which appear together on more than one occasion.

[100] Even though in the most ancient biblical books the word "redeemer" (Hebrew *Go'el)* signified the person bound by blood relationship to vindicate a relative who had been killed (cf. e.g., Nm 35:19), to help a relative who was unfortunate (e.g., Ru 4:6) and especially to ransom him from servitude (cf. e.g., Lv 25:48), with the passage of time this analogy was applied to Yahweh, "who redeemed Israel from the house of bondage, from the hand of Pharaoh, king of Egypt" (Dt 7:8). Especially in Deutero-Isaiah the accent changes from the act of redemption to the person of the Redeemer, who personally saves Israel as though merely by his very presence, "not for price or reward" (Is 45:13).

Therefore the passage from the "redeemer" of the prophecy of Isaiah chapter 54, to the Letter to the Ephesians, has the same motivation of the application, in the said letter, of the texts of the Canticle on the Servant of Yahweh (cf. Is 53:10-12; Eph 5:23, 25, 26).

[101] In place of the relationship "God-Israel," Paul introduces the relationship "Christ-Church," by applying to Christ everything in the Old Testament that refers to Yahweh *(Adonai-Kyrios).* Christ is God, but Paul also applies to him everything that refers to the Servant of Yahweh in the four canticles (Is 42:49; 50; 52-53) interpreted in a Messianic sense in the intertestimentary period.

The motif of "head" and of "body" is not of biblical derivation, but is probably Hellenistic (Stoic?). In Ephesians this theme is utilized in the context of marriage (while in First Corinthians the theme of the "body" serves to demonstrate the order which reigns in society).

From the biblical point of view the introduction of this motif is an absolute novelty.

General audience of September 29, 1982

[102] It is not merely a question of the personification of human society, which constitutes a fairly common phenomenon in world literature, but of a specific "corporate personality" of the Bible, marked by a continual reciprocal relationship of the individual to the group (cf. H. Wheeler Robinson, "The Hebrew Conception of Corporate Personality," *BZAW* 66 [1936], pp. 49-62; cf. also J. L. McKenzie, "Aspects of Old Testament Thought," *The Jerome Biblical Commentary,* Vol. 2 [London: 1970], p. 748).

General audience of October 20, 1982

[103] Cf. Leo XIII, *Acta,* Vol. II, 1881, p. 22.

[104] In this regard, cf. discourse at the general audience of September 8, 1982, note 1 (*L'Osservatore Romano,* English edition, September 13, 1982, p. 2).

General audience of November 24, 1982

[105] The text of St. Mark which speaks of the indissolubility of marriage clearly states that the woman also becomes a subject of adultery when she divorces her husband and marries another (cf. Mk 10:12).

General audience of May 23, 1984

[106] "The Song is therefore to be taken simply for what it manifestly is: a song of human love." This sentence of J. Winandy, O.S.B., expresses the conviction of growing numbers of exegetes (J. Winandy, *Le Cantique des Cantiques, Poém d'amour mué en écrit de Sagesse* [Maredsouse: 1960], p. 26).

M. Dubarle adds: "Catholic exegesis, which sometimes refers to the obvious meaning of biblical texts for passages of great dogmatic importance, should not lightly abandon it when it comes to Songs." Referring to the phrase of G. Gerleman, Dubarle continues: "Songs celebrates the love of man and woman without adding any mythological element, but considering it simply on its own level and in its specific nature. There is implicitly, without didactic insistence, the equivalent of the Yahwist faith (since sexual powers had not been placed under the patronage of foreign divinities and had not been attributed to Yahweh himself who appeared as transcending this sphere). The poem was therefore in tacit harmony with the fundamental convictions of the faith of Israel.

"The same open, objective, not expressly religious attitude with regard to physical beauty and sensual love is found in some collections of Yahwist documents. These various similarities show that the small book is not so isolated in the sum total of biblical literature as is sometimes stated" (A. M. Dubarle, "Le Cantique des Cantiques dans l'exégèse récente," *Aux grands carrefours de la*

Révélation et de l'exégèse de l'Ancien Testament, Recherches Bibliques VIII [Louvain: 1967], pp. 149, 151).

[107] This evidently does not exclude the possibility of speaking of a *sensus plenior* in the Song of Songs.

See, for example: "Lovers in the ecstasy of love seem to occupy and fill the whole book, as the only protagonists.... Therefore, Paul, in reading the words of Genesis, 'For this reason a man shall leave his father and mother, and shall cling to his wife, and the two shall be made into one' (Eph 5:31), does not deny the real and immediate meaning of the words that refer to human marriage. However, to this first meaning he adds another deeper one with an indirect reference: 'I mean that it refers to Christ and the Church,' confessing that 'this is a great fore-shadowing' (Eph 5:32)....

"Some readers of the Song of Songs rush to read immediately in its words a disembodied love. They have forgotten the lovers, or have petrified them in fictions, in an intellectual key.... They have multiplied the minute allegorical relations in every sentence, word or image....

"This is not the right way. Anyone who does not believe in the human love of the spouses, who must seek forgiveness for the body, does not have the right to be elevated.... With the affirmation of human love instead, it is possible to discover in it the revelation of God."

(L. Alonso-Schökel, "Cantico dei Cantici—Introduzione," *La Biblia, Parola di Dio scritti per noi.* Official text of the Italian Episcopal Conference, Vol. II [Torino: Marietti, 1980], pp. 425-427.)

[108] To explain the inclusion of a love song in the biblical canon, Jewish exegetes already in the first centuries after Christ saw in the Song of Songs an allegory of Yahweh's love for Israel, or an allegory of the history of the Chosen People, in which this love is manifested, and in the Middle Ages the allegory of divine Wisdom and of man who is in search of it.

Since the early Fathers, Christian exegesis extended such an idea to Christ and the Church (cf. Hippolytus and Origen), or to the individual soul of the Christian (cf. St. Gregory of Nyssa) or to Mary (cf. St. Ambrose) and also to her Immaculate Conception (cf. Richard of St. Victor). St. Bernard saw in the Song of Songs a dialogue of the Word of God with the soul, and this led to St. John of the Cross' concept about mystical marriage.

The only exception in this long tradition was Theodore of Mopsuestia, in the fourth century, who saw in the Song of Songs a poem that celebrated Solomon's human love for Pharaoh's daughter.

Luther, instead, referred the allegory to Solomon and his kingdom. In recent centuries new hypotheses have appeared. Some, for example, consider the Song of Songs as a drama of a bride's fidelity to a shepherd, despite all the temptations, or as a collection of songs used during the popular wedding rites or mythical rituals which reflected the Adonis-Tammuz worship. Finally, there is seen in the Song of Songs the description of a dream, recalling ancient ideas about the significance of dreams and also psychoanalysis.

In the 20th century there has been a return to the more ancient allegorical traditions (cf. Bea), seeing again in the Song of Songs the history of Israel (cf. Jouon, Ricciotte), and a developed midrash (as Robert calls it in his commentary, which constitutes a "summary" of the interpretation of Song of Songs).

Nevertheless, at the same time the book has begun to be read in its most evident significance as a poem exalting natural human love (cf. Rowley, Young, Laurin).

Karl Barth was the first to have demonstrated in what way this significance is linked with the biblical context of chapter two of Genesis. Dubarle begins with the premise that a faithful and happy human love reveals to man the attributes of divine love, and Van den Oudenrijn sees in the Song of Songs the antitype of that typical sense that appears in Ephesians 5:23. Excluding every allegorical and metaphorical explanation, Murphy stresses that human love, created and blessed by God, can be the theme of an inspired biblical book.

D. Lys notes that the content of the Song of Songs is at the same time sensual and sacred. When one prescinds from the second characteristic, the Song of Songs comes to be treated as a purely lay erotic composition, and when the first is ignored, one falls into allegorism. Only by putting these two aspects together is it possible to read the book in the right way.

Alongside the works of the above-mentioned authors, and especially with regard to an outline of the history of the exegesis of the Song of Songs, see H. H. Rowley, "The Interpretation of the Song of Songs," *The Servant of the Lord and Other Essays on the Old Testament* (London: Lutterworth, 1952), pp. 191-233; A. M. Dubarle, *Le Cantique des Cantiques dans l'exégèse de l'Ancien Testament,* Recherches Bibliques VIII (Louvain: Desclée de Brouwer, 1967), pp. 139-151; D. Lys, *Le plus beau chant de la création—Commentaire de Cantique des Cantiques. Lectio divina 51.* (Paris: Du Cerf, 1968), pp. 31-35; M. H. Pope, "Song of Songs," *Anchor Bible* (Garden City, NY: Doubleday, 1977), pp. 113-234.

Reflections on "Humanae Vitae"

The Morality of the Marriage Act Is Determined by the Nature of the Act and of the Subjects

The reflections we have thus far made on human love in the divine plan would be in some way incomplete if we did not try to see their concrete application in the sphere of marital and family morality. We want to take this further step that will bring us to the conclusion of our now long journey, under the guidance of an important recent pronouncement of the Magisterium, *Humanae Vitae,* which Pope Paul VI published in July 1968. We will reread this significant document in the light of the conclusions we have reached in examining the initial divine plan and the words of Christ which refer to it.

"The Church teaches as absolutely required that in any use whatever of marriage there must be no impairment of its natural capacity to procreate human life" *(HV* 11). "This particular doctrine, often expounded by the Magisterium of the Church, is based on the inseparable connection, established by God, which man on his own initiative may not break, between the unitive significance and the procreative significance which are both inherent to the marriage act" *(HV* 12).

The considerations I am about to make concern especially the passage of *Humanae Vitae* that deals with the "two significances of the marriage act" and their "inseparable connection." I do not intend to present a commentary on the whole encyclical, but rather to illustrate and examine one of its passages. From the point of view of the doctrine contained in the quoted document, that passage has a central significance. At the same time, that passage is closely connected with our previous reflections on marriage in its dimension as a (sacramental) sign.

As I said, since this is a central passage of the encyclical, it is obvious that it constitutes a very important part of its whole structure. Therefore, its analysis must direct us toward the various components of that structure, even if it is not our intention to comment on the entire text.

In the reflections on the sacramental sign, it has already been said several times that it is based on the language of the body reread in truth. It concerns a truth once affirmed at the beginning of the marriage when the newlyweds, promising each other "to be always faithful...and to love and honor each other all the days of their life," become ministers of marriage as a sacrament of the Church.

It concerns a truth that is always newly affirmed. In fact, the man and the woman, living in the marriage "until death," repropose uninterruptedly, in a certain sense, that sign that they made on their wedding day, through the liturgy of the sacrament.

The aforementioned words of Pope Paul VI's encyclical concern that moment in the common life of the spouses when both, joining each other in the marriage act, become, according to the biblical expression, "one flesh" (Gn 2:24). Precisely at such a moment so rich in significance, it is also especially important that the language of the body be reread in truth. This reading becomes the indispensable condition for acting in truth, that is, for behaving in accordance with the value and the moral norm.

The encyclical not only recalls this norm, but also seeks to give it adequate foundation. In order to clarify more completely that "inseparable connection, established by God...between the unitive significance and the procreative significance of the marriage act," Paul VI writes in the next sentence: "The reason is that the marriage act, because of its fundamental structure, while it unites husband and wife in the closest intimacy, also brings into operation laws written into the actual nature of man and of woman for the generation of new life" *(HV* 12).

We note that in the previous sentence, the text just quoted deals above all with the significance of marital relations. In the following sentence, it deals with the fundamental structure (that is, the nature) of marital relations. Defining that fundamental structure, the text refers to "laws written into the actual nature of man and of woman."

The passage from the sentence expressing the moral norm, to the sentence which explains and justifies it, is especially significant. The encyclical leads one to seek the foundation for the norm which determines the morality of the acts of the man and the woman in the marriage act, in the nature of this very act, and more deeply still, in the nature of the subjects themselves who are performing the act.

In this way, the fundamental structure (that is, the nature) of the marriage act constitutes the necessary basis for an adequate reading and discovery of the two significances that must be carried over into the conscience and the decisions of the acting parties. It also constitutes the necessary basis for establishing the adequate relationship of these significances, that is, their inseparable connection. "The marriage act..." at the same time "unites husband and wife in the closest intimacy" and together "makes them capable of generating new life." Both the one and the other happen "through the fundamental structure." Since this is so, then it follows that the human person (with the necessity proper to reason, logical necessity) must read at the same time the "twofold significance of the marriage act" and also the "inseparable connection between the unitive significance and the procreative significance of the marriage act."

Here we are dealing with nothing other than reading the language of the body in truth, as has been said many times in our previous biblical analyses. The moral norm, constantly taught by the Church in this sphere, and recalled and reconfirmed by Paul VI in his encyclical, arises from the reading of the language of the body in truth.

It is a question here of the truth first in the ontological dimension ("fundamental structure") and then—as a result—in the subjective and psychological dimension ("significance"). The text of the encyclical stresses that in the case in question we are dealing with a norm of the natural law.

General audience of July 11, 1984

The Norm of *Humanae Vitae* Arises from the Natural Law and the Revealed Order

In *Humanae Vitae* we read: "The Church, in urging men to the observance of the precepts of the natural law, which it interprets by its constant doctrine, teaches as absolutely required that in any use whatever of marriage there must be no impairment of its natural capacity to procreate human life" *(HV* 11).

At the same time this same text considers and even emphasizes the subjective and psychological dimension when it speaks of the significance, and precisely of the "two significances of the marital act."

The significance becomes known with the rereading of the (ontological) truth of the object. Through this rereading, the (ontological) truth enters, so to speak, into the cognitive dimension—subjective and psychological.

Humanae Vitae seems to draw our attention especially to this latter dimension. Among other ways, this is also indirectly confirmed by the following sentence: "We believe that our contemporaries are especially capable of seeing that this teaching is in harmony with human reason" *(HV* 12).

That reasonable character does not only concern the truth of the ontological dimension, namely, that which corresponds to the fundamental structure of the marital act. It also concerns the same truth in the subjective and psychological dimension, that is to say, it concerns the correct understanding of the intimate structure of the marital act. It concerns the adequate rereading of the significances corresponding to this structure and of their inseparable connection, in view of a morally right behavior. Herein lies precisely the moral norm and the corresponding regulation of human acts in the sphere of sexuality. In this sense we say that the moral norm is identified with the rereading, in truth, of the language of the body.

Therefore, *Humanae Vitae* contains the moral norm and its reason, or at least an examination of what constitutes the reason for the norm. Moreover, since in the norm the moral value is expressed in a binding way, it follows that acts in conformity with the norm are morally right, while acts contrary to it are intrinsically illicit. The author of the encyclical stresses that this norm belongs to the natural law, that is to say, it is in accordance with reason as such. The Church teaches this norm, although it is not formally (that is, literally) expressed in Sacred Scripture. It does this in the conviction that the interpretation of the precepts of natural law belongs to the competence of the Magisterium.

However, we can say more. Even if the moral law, formulated in this way in *Humanae Vitae,* is not found literally in Sacred Scripture, nonetheless, from the fact that it is contained in tradition and, as Pope Paul VI writes, has been "very often expounded by the Magisterium" *(HV* 12) to the faithful, it follows that this norm is in accordance with the sum total of revealed doctrine contained in biblical sources (cf. *HV* 4).

It is a question here not only of the sum total of the moral doctrine contained in Sacred Scripture, of its essential premises and the general character of its content. It is also a question of that fuller context to which we have previously dedicated many analyses when speaking about the theology of the body.

Precisely against the background of this full context it becomes evident that the above mentioned moral norm belongs not only to the natural moral law, but also to the *moral order revealed by God.* Also from this point of view, it could not be different, but solely what is handed down by Tradition and the Magisterium and, in our days, the encyclical *Humanae Vitae* as a modern document of this Magisterium.

Paul VI writes: "We believe that our contemporaries are especially capable of seeing that this teaching is in harmony with human reason" *(HV* 12). We can add that they are capable also of seeing its profound conformity with all that is transmitted by Tradition stemming from biblical sources. The bases of this conformity are to be sought especially in biblical anthropology. Moreover, we know the significance that anthropology has for ethics, that is, for moral doctrine. It seems to be totally reasonable to look precisely in the "theology of the body" for the foundation of the truth of the norms that concern the fundamental problematic of man as "body": "The two will become one flesh" (Gn 2:24).

The norm of *Humanae Vitae* concerns all men, insofar as it is a norm of the natural law and is based on conformity with human reason (when, it is understood, human reason is seeking truth). All the more does it concern all believers and members of the Church, since the reasonable character of this norm indirectly finds confirmation and solid support in the sum total of the theology of the body. From this point of view we have spoken in previous analyses about the ethos of the redemption of the body.

The norm of the natural law, based on this ethos, finds not only a new expression, but also a fuller anthropological and ethical foundation in the word of the Gospel and in the purifying and corroborating action of the Holy Spirit.

These are all reasons why every believer and especially every theologian should reread and ever more deeply understand the moral doctrine of the encyclical in this complete context. The reflections we have been making here for some time constitute precisely an attempt at this rereading.

General audience of July 18, 1984

The Importance of Harmonizing Human Love with Respect for Life

Today we continue our reflections which are directed toward linking *Humanae Vitae* to our whole treatment of the theology of the body. This encyclical is not limited to recalling the moral norm concerning conjugal life, reconfirming this norm in the face of new circumstances. In making a pronouncement with the authentic Magisterium through the encyclical (1968), Paul VI had before his eyes the authoritative statement of the Second Vatican Council contained in *Gaudium et Spes* (1965).

The encyclical is not only found to be along the lines of the Council's teaching. It also constitutes the development and completion of the questions contained there, especially regarding the question of the "harmony of human love with respect for life." On this point, we read the following words in *Gaudium et Spes:* "The Church issues the reminder that a true contradiction cannot exist between the divine laws pertaining to the transmission of life and those pertaining to the fostering of authentic conjugal love" *(GS* 51).

The pastoral constitution of Vatican II excludes any true contradiction whatsoever in the normative order. On his part Paul VI confirms this order by seeking at the same time to shed light on that "noncontradiction," and thus to justify the respective moral norm by demonstrating its conformity to reason.

Nevertheless, *Humanae Vitae* speaks not so much of the non-contradiction in the normative order as of the inseparable connection between the transmission of life and authentic marital love. It speaks from the point of view of the "two significances of the conjugal act: the unitive significance and the procreative significance" *(HV* 12), which we have already dealt with.

We could pause for some time here analyzing the norm itself, but the character of both documents leads rather to reflections that are at least indirectly pastoral. In fact, *Gaudium et Spes* is a pastoral constitution, and Paul VI's encyclical—with its doctrinal value—tends to have the same orientation. It is intended to be a response to the questions of modern man. These questions are of a demographic nature, and consequently of a socioeconomic and political nature, in relation to the population increase throughout the world. These questions begin from the field of particular sciences, and at the same rate are questions of modern moralists (theologians-moralists). They are above all questions of spouses which are already found at the center of attention in the conciliar constitution and are taken up again in the encyclical with all desirable precision. In fact, we read there: "Granted the conditions of life today and taking into account the relevance of married love to the harmony and mutual fidelity of husband and wife, would it not be right to review the moral norms in force till now, especially when it is felt that these can be observed only with the gravest difficulty, sometimes only by heroic effort?" *(HV* 3).

In the above text it is evident with what solicitude the encyclical's author tries to face the questions of modern man in all their import. The relevance of these questions presupposes a response that is proportionately thought out and profound. Therefore, if on the one hand it is right to expect a keenly sensitive treatment of the norm, on the other hand it can also be expected that no small weight be given to the pastoral arguments. These more directly concern the life of man in the concrete, of precisely those who are posing the questions mentioned in the beginning.

Paul VI always had these people before his eyes. The following passage of *Humanae Vitae* is evidence of this, among other things: "The teaching of the Church regarding the right ordering of the increase of a man's family is a promulgation of the law of God himself. And yet there is no doubt that to many it may appear not merely difficult but even impossible to observe. Now it is true that like all good things which are outstanding for their nobility and for the benefits which they confer on men, so this law demands from individual men and women, from families and from human society a resolute purpose and great endurance. Indeed it cannot be observed unless God comes to their help with that grace by which the good will of men is sustained and strengthened. But to those who consider this matter diligently it will indeed be evident that this endurance enhances man's dignity and confers benefits on human society" *(HV* 20).

At this point there is no more mention of the normative noncontradiction, but rather of the "possibility of observing the divine law," that is, of an argument that is at least indirectly pastoral. The fact that the law must be possible to observe belongs directly to the very nature of law and is therefore included in the framework of the normative noncontradiction. Nevertheless the possibility, understood as the feasibility of the norm, belongs also to the practical and pastoral sphere. In the text quoted, my predecessor speaks precisely from this point of view.

We can here arrive at a consideration. The whole biblical background, called the theology of the body, offers us, even though indirectly, the confirmation of the truth of the moral norm contained in *Humanae Vitae.* This fact prepares us to consider more deeply the practical and pastoral aspects of the problem in its entirety. Were not the principles and general presuppositions of the theology of the body all taken from the answers Christ gave to the questions of his actual audience? And are not Paul's texts—as, for example, in the Letter to the Corinthians—a small manual on the problems of the moral life of Christ's first followers? In these texts we certainly find that rule of understanding which seems so indispensable in the face of the problems treated in *Humanae Vitae* and which is present in this encyclical.

Whoever believes that the Council and the encyclical do not sufficiently take into account the difficulties present in concrete life does not understand the pastoral concern that was at the origin of those documents. Pastoral concern means the search for the true good of man, a promotion of the values engraved in his person by God. That is, it means observing that rule of understanding which is directed to the ever clearer discovery of God's plan for human love, in the certitude that the only true good of the human person consists in fulfilling this divine plan.

One could say that, precisely in the name of the aforementioned rule of understanding, the Council posed the question of the "harmony of human love with respect for life" *(GS* 51). *Humanae Vitae* then not only recalls the moral norms that are binding in this area, but is also fully concerned with the problem of the possibility of observing the divine law.

The present reflections on the nature of the document *Humanae Vitae* prepare us to deal then with the theme of responsible parenthood.

General audience of July 25, 1984

Responsible Parenthood

For today we have chosen the theme of responsible parenthood in the light of *Gaudium et Spes* and of *Humanae Vitae*. In treating of the subject, the Council document limits itself to recalling the basic premises. However, the papal document goes further, giving a more concrete content to these premises.

The Council text reads as follows: "When there is question of harmonizing conjugal love with the responsible transmission of life, the moral aspect of any procedure does not depend solely on sincere intentions or on an evaluation of motives, but must be determined by objective standards. These, based on the nature of the human person and his acts, preserve the full sense of mutual self-giving and human procreation in the context of true love. Such a goal cannot be achieved unless the virtue of conjugal chastity is sincerely practiced" *(GS 51)*.

The Council adds: "Relying on these principles, sons of the Church may not undertake methods of birth control which are found blameworthy by the teaching authority of the Church in its unfolding of the divine law" *(GS 51)*.

Before the passage quoted, the Council teaches that married couples "will fulfill their task with human and Christian responsibility, and, with docile reverence toward God, will make decisions by common counsel and effort" *(GS 50)*. This means they should "thoughtfully take into account both their own welfare and that of their children, those already born and those which the future may bring. For this accounting they need to reckon with both the material and the spiritual conditions of the times as well as of their state in life. Finally, they should consult the interests of the family group, of temporal society, and of the Church herself" *(GS 50)*.

At this point words of particular importance follow, to determine with greater precision the moral character of responsible parenthood. We read: "The parents themselves and no one else should ultimately make this judgment in the sight of God" *(GS 50)*.

It continues: "Spouses should be aware that they cannot proceed arbitrarily, but must always be governed according to a conscience dutifully conformed to the divine law itself, and should be submissive toward the Church's teaching office, which authentically interprets that law in the light of the Gospel. That divine law reveals and protects the integral meaning of conjugal love, and impels it toward a truly human fulfillment" *(GS 50)*.

In limiting itself to recalling the necessary premises for responsible parenthood, the Council document has set them out in a completely unambiguous manner. It clarifies the constitutive elements of such parenthood, that is, the mature judgment of the personal conscience in relationship to the divine law, authentically interpreted by the Magisterium of the Church.

Basing itself on the same premises, *Humanae Vitae* goes further and offers concrete indications. This is seen, first of all, in the way of defining responsible parenthood (cf. *HV* 10). Paul VI seeks to clarify this concept by considering its various aspects and excluding beforehand its reduction to one of the "partial aspects, as is done by those who speak exclusively of birth control." From the very beginning, Paul VI is guided in his reasoning by an integral concept of man (cf. *HV* 7) and of conjugal love (cf. *HV* 8, 9).

One can speak of responsibility in the exercise of the function of parenthood under different aspects. Thus he writes: "In relation to the biological processes involved, responsible parenthood is to be understood as the knowledge and observance of their specific functions. Human intelligence discovers in the faculty of procreating life, the biological laws which involve human personality" *(HV* 10). If, on the other hand, we examine "the innate drives and emotions of man, responsible parenthood expresses the domination which reason and will must exert over them" *(HV* 10).

Taking for granted the above-mentioned interpersonal aspects and adding to them the "economic and social conditions," those are considered "to exercise responsible parenthood who prudently and generously decide to have a large family, or who, for serious reasons and with due respect to the moral law, choose to have no more children for the time being or even for an indeterminate period" *(HV* 10).

From this it follows that the concept of responsible parenthood contains the disposition not merely to avoid a further birth but also to increase the family in accordance with the criteria of prudence. In this light in which the question of responsible parenthood must be examined and decided, there is always of paramount importance "the objective moral order instituted by God, the order of which a right conscience is the true interpreter" *(HV* 10).

The commitment to responsible parenthood requires that husband and wife, "keeping a right order of priorities, recognize their own duties toward God, themselves, their families and human society" *(HV* 10). One cannot therefore speak of acting arbitrarily. On the contrary the married couple "must act in conformity with God's creative intention" *(HV* 10). Beginning with this principle the encyclical bases its reasoning on the "intimate structure of the conjugal act" and on "the inseparable connection of the two significances of the conjugal act" (cf. *HV* 12), as was already stated. The relative principle of conjugal morality is, therefore, fidelity to the divine plan manifested in the "intimate structure of the conjugal act" and in the "inseparable connection of the two significances of the conjugal act."

General audience of August 1, 1984

Faithfulness to the Divine Plan in the Transmission of Life

We said previously that the principle of conjugal morality, taught by the Church (Second Vatican Council, Paul VI), is the criterion of faithfulness to the divine plan.

In conformity with this principle, *Humanae Vitae* clearly distinguishes between a morally illicit method of birth regulation or, more precisely, of the regulation of fertility, and one that is morally correct.

In the first place "the direct interruption of the generative process already begun [abortion]...is morally wrong" *(HV* 14), likewise "direct sterilization" and "any action, which either before, at the moment of, or after sexual intercourse, is specifically intended to prevent procreation" *(HV* 14)—therefore, all contraceptive means. It is however morally lawful to have "recourse to the infertile periods" *(HV* 16): "If therefore there are reasonable grounds for spacing births, arising from the physical or psychological conditions of husband or wife, or from external circumstances, the Church teaches that then married people may take advantage of the natural cycles immanent in the reproductive system and use their marriage at precisely those times that are infertile, and in this way control birth without offending moral principles..." *(HV* 16).

The encyclical emphasizes especially that "between the two cases there is an essential difference" *(HV* 16), and therefore a difference of an ethical nature: "In the first case married couples rightly use a facility provided them by nature; in the other case, they obstruct the natural development of the generative process" *(HV* 16).

Two actions that are ethically different, indeed, even opposed, derive from this: the natural regulation of fertility is morally correct; contraception is not morally correct. This essential difference between the two actions (modes of acting) concerns their intrinsic ethical character, even though my predecessor Paul VI states that "in each case married couples, for acceptable reasons, are both perfectly clear in their intention to avoid children." He even writes: "...that they mean to make sure that none will be born" *(HV* 16). In these words the document admits that even those who use contraceptive practices can be motivated by "acceptable reasons." However, this *does not change the moral character which is based on the very structure of the conjugal act as such.*

It might be observed at this point that married couples who have recourse to the natural regulation of fertility, might do so without the valid reasons spoken of above. However, this is a separate ethical problem, when one treats of the moral sense of responsible parenthood.

Supposing that the reasons for deciding not to procreate are morally correct, there remains the moral problem of the manner of acting in this case. This is expressed in an act which—according to the doctrine of the Church contained in the encyclical—possesses its own intrinsic moral qualification, either positive or negative. The first one, positive, corresponds to the "natural" regulation of fertility; the second, negative, corresponds to "artificial contraception." The entire previous discussion is summed up in the exposition of the doctrine contained in *Humanae Vitae,* by pointing out its normative and at the same time its pastoral character. In the normative dimension it is a question of making more precise and clear the moral principles of action; in the pastoral dimension it is a question especially of pointing out the possibility of acting in accordance with these principles ("the possibility of the observance of the divine law," *HV* 20).

We should dwell on the interpretation of the content of the encyclical. To this end one must view that content, that normative-pastoral ensemble, in the light of the theology of the body as it emerges from the analysis of the biblical texts.

The theology of the body is not merely a theory, but rather a specific, evangelical, Christian pedagogy of the body. This derives from the character of the Bible, and especially of the Gospel. As the message of salvation, it reveals man's true good, for the purpose of modeling—according to the measure of this good—man's earthly life in the perspective of the hope of the future world.

Following this line, *Humanae Vitae* responds to the question about the true good of man as a person, as male and female; about that which corresponds to the dignity of man and woman when one treats of the important problem of the transmission of life by married couples.

We shall devote further reflection to this.

General audience of August 8, 1984

The Church's Position on the Transmission of Life

What is the essence of the Church's doctrine concerning the transmission of life in the conjugal community, that doctrine which *Gaudium et Spes* and *Humanae Vitae* remind us of ?

The problem consists in maintaining an adequate relationship between what is defined as "domination...of the forces of nature" *(HV* 2), and the "mastery of self" *(HV* 21) which is indispensable for the human person. Modern man shows a tendency to transfer the methods proper to the former to those of the latter. "Man has made stupendous progress in the domination and rational organization of the forces of nature," we read in the encyclical, "to the point that he is endeavoring to extend this control over every aspect of his own life—over his body, over his mind and emotions, over his social life, and even over the laws that regulate the transmission of life" *(HV 2).*

This extension of the sphere of the means of "domination of the forces of nature" menaces the human person for whom the method of "self-mastery" is and remains specific. The mastery of self corresponds to the fundamental constitution of the person; it is indeed a "natural" method. On the contrary, the resort to artificial means destroys the constitutive dimension of the person. It deprives man of the subjectivity proper to him and makes him an object of manipulation.

The human body is not merely an organism of sexual reactions. But it is, at the same time, the means of expressing the entire man, the person, which reveals itself by means of the language of the body. This language has an important interpersonal meaning, especially in reciprocal relationships between man and woman. Moreover, our previous analyses show that in this case the language of the body should express, at a determinate level, the truth of the sacrament. Participating in the eternal plan of love ("sacrament hidden in God"), the language of the body becomes a kind of prophetism of the body.

It may be said that *Humanae Vitae* carries to the extreme consequences—not merely logical and moral, but also practical and pastoral—this truth concerning the human body in its masculinity and femininity.

The unity of the two aspects of the problem—the sacramental (or theological) dimension and the personalistic one—corresponds to the overall revelation of the body. From this derives also the connection of the strictly theological vision with the ethical one, which appeals to the natural law.

The subject of the natural law is man, not only in the "natural" aspect of his existence, but also in the integral truth of his personal subjectivity. He is shown to us, in revelation, as male and female, in his full temporal and eschatological vocation. He is called by God to be a witness and interpreter of the eternal plan of love, by becoming the minister of the sacrament which from the beginning was constituted by the sign of the union of flesh.

As ministers of a sacrament which is constituted by consent and perfected by conjugal union, man and woman are called to express that mysterious language of their bodies in all the truth which is proper to it. By means of gestures and reactions, by means of the whole dynamism, reciprocally conditioned, of tension and enjoyment—whose direct source is the body in its masculinity and its femininity, the body in its action and interaction—by means of all this, man, the person, "speaks."

Man and woman carry on in the language of the body that dialogue which, according to Genesis 2:24, 25, had its beginning on the day of creation. This language of the body is something more than mere sexual reaction. As authentic language of the persons, it is subject to the demands of truth, that is, to objective moral norms. Precisely on the level of this language, man and woman reciprocally express themselves in the fullest and most profound way possible to them by the corporeal dimension of masculinity and femininity. Man and woman express themselves in the measure of the whole truth of the human person.

Man is precisely a person because he is master of himself and has self-control. Indeed, insofar as he is master of himself he can give himself to the other. This dimension—the dimension of the liberty of the gift—becomes essential and decisive for that language of the body, in which man and woman reciprocally express themselves in the conjugal union. Granted that this is communion of persons, the language of the body should be judged according to the criterion of truth. *Humanae Vitae* recalls precisely this criterion, as the passages previously quoted confirm.

According to the criterion of this truth, which should be expressed in the language of the body, the conjugal act signifies not only love, but also potential fecundity. Therefore it cannot be deprived of its full and adequate significance by artificial means. In the conjugal act it is not licit to separate the unitive aspect from the procreative aspect, because both the one and the other pertain to the intimate truth of the conjugal act. The one is activated together with the other and in a certain sense the one by means of the other. This is what the encyclical teaches (cf. *HV* 12). Therefore, in such a case the conjugal act, deprived of its interior truth because it is artificially deprived of its procreative capacity, ceases also to be an act of love.

It can be said that in the case of an artificial separation of these two aspects, a real bodily union is carried out in the conjugal act, but it does not correspond to the interior truth and to the dignity of personal communion—communion of persons. This communion demands that the language of the body be expressed reciprocally in the integral truth of its meaning. If this truth be lacking, one cannot speak either of the truth of self-mastery, or of the truth of the reciprocal gift and of the reciprocal acceptance of self on the part of the person. Such a violation of the interior order of conjugal union, which is rooted in the very order of the person, constitutes the essential evil of the contraceptive act.

The above-given interpretation of moral doctrine expressed in *Humanae Vitae* is situated against the vast background of reflections connected with the theology of the body. The reflections on "sign" in connection with marriage understood as a sacrament are of special validity for this interpretation. The essence of the violation which upsets the interior order of the conjugal act cannot be understood in a theologically adequate way, without the reflections on the theme of the concupiscence of the flesh.

General audience of August 22, 1984

A Discipline that Ennobles Human Love

While demonstrating the moral evil of contraception, at the same time *Humanae Vitae* fully approves of the natural regulation of fertility and, in this sense, it approves of responsible parenthood. Here one must exclude the possibility of describing as "responsible" from the ethical point of view that procreation in which recourse is had to contraception in order to regulate fertility. On the contrary, the true concept of responsible parenthood is connected with the right and lawful regulation of fertility from the ethical viewpoint.

We read in this regard: "The right and lawful ordering of the births of children presupposes in husband and wife first and foremost that they fully recognize and value the true blessings of family life, and secondly, that they acquire complete mastery over themselves and their emotions. For if with the aid of reason and of free will they are to control their natural drives, there can be no doubt at all of the need for self-denial. Only then will the expression of love, particular to married life, conform to right order. And this is especially true as regards the practice of periodic continence. But self-discipline of this kind is a shining witness to the chastity of husband and wife and, so far from being a hindrance to their love of one another, transforms it by giving it a more truly human character. And if this self-discipline does demand that they persevere in their purpose and efforts, it has at the same time the salutary effect of enabling husband and wife to develop to the full their personalities and be enriched with spiritual blessings..." *(HV 21)*.

The encyclical then points out the consequences of such a line of conduct not merely for the couple themselves but also for the whole family understood as a community of persons. It will be necessary to treat this subject again. The encyclical underlines that a right and lawful regulation of fertility demands above all from husband and wife a definite family and procreative attitude. That is to say, it requires "that they acquire and possess solid convictions about the true values of life and of the family"

(HV 21). Beginning from this premise, it was necessary to proceed to an overall consideration of the question as the 1980 Synod of Bishops did (cf. *On the Role of the Christian Family).* Later, the doctrine concerning this particular problem of conjugal and family morality, treated in *Humanae Vitae,* found its proper place and fitting perspective in the comprehensive context of the Apostolic Exhortation *Familiaris Consortio.* In a certain sense, the theology of the body, especially as the pedagogy of the body, has its roots in the theology of the family and leads to it at the same time. This pedagogy of the body, whose key today is *Humanae Vitae,* is explained only in the full context of a correct vision of the values of life and of the family.

In the text quoted above, Pope Paul VI refers to conjugal chastity when he writes that the observance of periodic continence is the form of self-mastery in which conjugal chastity is manifested (cf. *HV* 21).

In undertaking now a deeper analysis of this problem, it is necessary to bear in mind the whole doctrine on chastity understood as the life of the Spirit (cf. Gal 5:25), already considered by us, in order to understand the respective statements of the encyclical on the theme of periodic continence. That doctrine remains indeed the real reason, beginning from which the teaching of Paul VI defines the regulation of births and responsible parenthood as ethically right and lawful.

Even though the periodicity of continence in this case is applied to the so-called "natural rhythms" *(HV* 16), the continence itself is a definite and permanent moral attitude. It is a virtue, and therefore the whole line of conduct guided by it acquires a virtuous character. The encyclical emphasizes clearly enough that here it is not merely a matter of a definite technique, but of ethics in the strict sense of the term as the morality of conduct.

Therefore, the encyclical opportunely sets out in relief, on the one hand, the necessity to respect in the above-mentioned line of conduct the order established by the Creator, and on the other hand, the necessity of an immediate motivation of an ethical character.

In regard to the first aspect we read: "To experience the gift of married love while respecting the laws of conception is to acknowledge that one is not the master of the sources of life, but rather the minister of the design established by the Creator" *(HV* 13). "Human life is sacred"—as our predecessor of holy memory, John XXIII, said in his encyclical *Mater et Magistra*—"from its very beginning it involves directly the creative action of God" *(AAS* 53, 1961; cf. *HV* 13). As regards the immediate motivation, *Humanae Vitae* requires that "there exist reasonable grounds for spacing births, arising from the physical or psychological condition of husband or wife, or from external circumstances..." *(HV* 16).

In the case of a morally upright regulation of fertility effected by means of periodic continence, one is clearly dealing with the practice of conjugal chastity, that is, of a definite ethical attitude. In biblical language we could say that it is a case of living by the Spirit (cf. Gal 5:25).

The morally correct regulation is also called "the *natural* regulation of fertility," which can be explained as conformity to the natural law. By natural law we mean that order of nature in the field of procreation, insofar as it is understood by right reason. This order is the expression of the Creator's plan for man. It is precisely this that the encyclical, together with the whole Tradition of Christian teaching and practice, stresses in a particular way: the virtuous character of the attitude which is expressed in the natural regulation of fertility is determined not so much by fidelity to an impersonal natural law as to the Creator-Person, the Source and Lord of the order which is manifested in such a law.

From this point of view, the reduction to a mere biological regularity, separated from the order of nature that is, from the Creator's plan, deforms the authentic thought of *Humanae Vitae* (cf. *HV* 14).

The document certainly presupposes that biological regularity. Indeed, it exhorts competent persons to study it and to apply it in a still deeper way. But it always understands this regularity as the expression of the order of nature, that is, of the providential plan of the Creator. The true good of the human person consists in the faithful execution of this plan.

General audience of August 28, 1984

Responsible Parenthood Is Linked to Moral Maturity

"The Lord was witness to the covenant between you and the wife of your youth.... Has not the one God made and sustained for us the spirit of life? What does he desire? Godly offspring. So take heed to yourselves and let none be faithless to the wife of his youth" (Mal 2:14-15).

We have previously spoken of the right and lawful regulation of fertility according to the doctrine contained in *Humanae Vitae (HV* 19), and in *Familiaris Consortio.* The description of "natural," attributed to the morally correct regulation of fertility (following the natural rhythms, cf. *HV* 16), is explained by the fact that that manner of conduct corresponds to the truth of the person and therefore to his dignity. This dignity by "nature" belongs to man as a rational and free being. As a rational free being, man can and must reread with discernment that biological rhythm which belongs to the natural order. He can and must conform to it so as to exercise that responsible parenthood, which, according to the Creator's design, is inscribed in the natural order of human fecundity. The concept of a morally correct regulation of fertility is nothing other than the rereading of the language of the body in truth. The "natural rhythms immanent in the generative functions" pertain to the objective truth of that language, which the persons concerned should reread in its full objective content. It is necessary to bear in mind that the body speaks not merely with the whole external expression of masculinity and femininity, but also with the internal structures of the organism, of the somatic and psychosomatic reaction. All this should find its appropriate place in that language in which husband and wife dialogue with each other, as persons called to the communion of the union of the body.

All efforts directed to an ever more precise knowledge of those natural rhythms which are manifested in relation to human procreation, all efforts of family counselors and indeed of the couple themselves, are not aimed at making the language of the body merely biological (at reducing ethics to biology, as some have mistakenly held). But they are aimed exclusively at ensuring the integral truth of that language of the body in which husband and wife should express themselves in a mature way before the demands of responsible parenthood.

Humanae Vitae stresses several times that responsible parenthood is connected with a continual effort and commitment, and that it is put into effect at the cost of a precise self-denial (cf. *HV* 21). All these and other similar expressions show that in the case of responsible parenthood, or of a morally correct regulation of fertility, it is a question of the real good of human persons and of what corresponds to the true dignity of the person.

The use of the infertile periods for conjugal union can be an abuse if the couple, for unworthy reasons, seeks in this way to avoid having children, thus lowering the number of births in their family below the morally correct level. This morally correct level must be established by taking into account not only the good of one's own family, and even the state of health and the means of the couple themselves, but also the good of the society to which they belong, of the Church, and even of all mankind.

Humanae Vitae presents responsible parenthood as an expression of a high ethical value. In no way is it exclusively directed to limiting, much less excluding, children. It means also the willingness to accept a larger family. Above all, according to *Humanae Vitae,* responsible parenthood implies "a deeper relationship with the objective moral order instituted by God—the order of which a right conscience is the true interpreter" *(HV* 10).

The truth of responsible parenthood and its implementation is linked with the moral maturity of the person. Here, the divergence is very frequently revealed between what the encyclical explicitly regards as of primary importance and the general viewpoint on the subject. The encyclical places in relief the ethical dimension of the problem, by underlining the role of the virtue of temperance correctly understood. Within the scope of this dimension there is also an adequate method for acting. In the common viewpoint it often happens that the method, separated from the ethical dimension proper to it, is put into effect in a merely functional and even utilitarian way. By separating the natural method from the ethical dimension, one no longer sees the difference between it and the other methods (artificial means). One comes to the point of speaking of it as if it were only a different form of contraception.

From the point of view of the true doctrine expressed by *Humanae Vitae,* it is therefore important to present this method correctly, and the encyclical refers to this (cf. *HV* 16). Above all it is important to examine in depth the ethical dimension. For it is in reference to this that the method, as natural, acquires its significance as a morally correct, upright method. Therefore within the framework of the present analysis, it is fitting that we should turn our attention principally to what the encyclical states on the subject of self-mastery and on continence. Without a searching interpretation of that subject we shall not arrive either at the heart of the moral truth, or at the heart of the anthropological truth of the problem. It was already pointed out that the roots of this problem lie deep in the theology of the body. When it becomes, as it ought to, the pedagogy of the body, this constitutes in reality the morally right and lawful method of the regulation of births, understood in its deepest and fullest sense.

Later when describing the specifically moral values of the natural regulation of fertility (that is, lawful or morally right), Paul VI writes as follows: "This self-discipline...brings to family life abundant fruits of tranquillity and peace. It helps in solving difficulties of other kinds. It fosters in husband and wife thoughtfulness and loving consideration for each other. It helps them to repel the excessive self-love which is the opposite of charity. It arouses in them a consciousness of their responsibilities. And finally, it confers upon parents a deeper and more effective influence in the education of their children. For these latter, both in childhood and in youth, as years go by, develop a right sense of values as regards the true blessings of life and achieve a serene and harmonious use of their mental and physical powers" *(HV* 21).

The passage cited completes the picture of what *Humanae Vitae* means by "the right and lawful ordering of the births of children" *(HV* 21). As can be seen, this is not merely a mode of behavior in a specific field. It is an attitude which is based on the integral moral maturity of the persons and at the same time completes it.

General audience of September 5, 1984

Prayer, Penance and the Eucharist Are the Principal Sources of Spirituality for Married Couples

Referring to the doctrine contained in *Humanae Vitae,* we will try to further outline the spiritual life of married couples. Here are the great words of this encyclical:

> While the Church does indeed hand on to her children the inviolable conditions laid down by God's law, she is also the herald of salvation. Through the sacraments she flings wide open the channels of grace through which man is made a new creature responding in charity and true freedom to the design of his Creator and Savior, experiencing too the sweetness of the yoke of Christ.
>
> In humble obedience then to her voice, let Christian husbands and wives be mindful of their vocation to the Christian life, a vocation which, deriving from their Baptism, has been confirmed anew and made more explicit by the sacrament of Matrimony. For by this sacrament they are strengthened and, one might also say, consecrated to the faithful fulfillment of their duties; to realizing to the full their vocation; and to bearing witness, as becomes them, to Christ before the world. For the Lord has entrusted to them the task of making visible to men and women the holiness, and the joy too, of the law which unites inseparably their love for one another and the cooperation they give to God's love, God who is the Author of human life *(HV* 25).

Humanae Vitae shows the moral evil of the contraceptive act and outlines at the same time a possibly integral framework for the honest practice of fertility regulation, that is, of responsible fatherhood and motherhood. By so doing, the encyclical creates the premises that allow us to draw the great lines of the Christian spirituality of the conjugal vocation and life, and likewise the spirituality of parents and of the family.

It can further be said that the encyclical presupposes the entire tradition of this spirituality, which is rooted in the biblical sources already analyzed, by offering the opportunity to reflect on them anew and to build an adequate synthesis.

It is well to recall here what was said about the organic relationship between the theology of the body and the pedagogy of the body. This "theology-pedagogy" already constitutes, *per se,* the essential nucleus of conjugal spirituality. This is indicated also by the above-quoted sentences from the encyclical.

Anyone who would only see in *Humanae Vitae* the reduction of responsible fatherhood and motherhood to mere biological rhythms of fertility would certainly read and interpret the encyclical erroneously. The author of the encyclical energetically disapproves of and contradicts any form of reductive interpretation (and in such a "partial" sense), and insistently reproposes the integral intention. Responsible fatherhood and motherhood, understood integrally, is none other than an important element of all conjugal and family spirituality—that is, of that vocation which the cited text of *Humanae Vitae* speaks about when it states that the married couple must "realize to the full their vocation" *(HV* 25). The sacrament of marriage strengthens them and, one would say, consecrates them to its fulfillment (cf. *HV* 25).

In the light of the doctrine expressed in the encyclical, it is well to become more aware of that strengthening power that is united to the *"sui generis* consecration" of the sacrament of marriage.

Since the analysis of the ethical problem of Paul VI's document was centered above all on the exactness of the respective norm, the sketch of conjugal spirituality which is found there intends to place in relief precisely those "powers" which make possible the authentic Christian witness of married life.

"We have no wish at all to pass over in silence the difficulties, at times very great, which beset the lives of Christian married couples. For them, as indeed for every one of us, the gate is narrow and the way is hard that leads to life (cf. Mt 7:14). Nevertheless, it is precisely the hope of that life which, like a brightly burning torch, lights up their journey, as, strong in spirit, they strive to live sober, upright and godly lives in this world (cf. Ti 2:12), knowing for sure that 'the form of this world is passing away'" (cf. 1 Cor 7:31) *(HV* 25).

In the encyclical, the view of married life is marked at every step by Christian realism. Precisely this helps more greatly to acquire those "powers" which allow the formation of the spirituality of married couples and parents in the spirit of an authentic pedagogy of heart and body.

The awareness of that future life opens up a broad horizon of those powers that must guide them through the hard way (cf. *HV* 25) and lead them through the narrow gate (cf. *HV* 25) of their evangelical vocation.

The encyclical says: "For this reason husbands and wives should take up the burden appointed to them, willingly, in the strength of faith and of that hope which does not disappoint us, because God's love has been poured out into our hearts through the Holy Spirit who has been given to us" (cf. Rom 5:5) *(HV* 25).

The essential and fundamental "power" is *the love planted in the heart* ("poured out into our hearts") *by the Holy Spirit.* Consequently, the encyclical points out how the married couple must implore this essential power and every other divine help by prayer; how they must draw grace and love from the ever-living fountain of the Eucharist; how "with humble perseverance" they must overcome their deficiencies and sins in the Sacrament of Penance.

These are the means—infallible and indispensable—for forming the Christian spirituality of married life and family life. With these, that essential and spiritual creative power of love reaches human hearts and, at the same time, human bodies in their subjective masculinity and femininity. This love allows the building of the whole life of the married couple according to that "truth of the sign," by means of which marriage is built up in its sacramental dignity, as the central point of the encyclical reveals (cf. *HV* 12).

General audience of October 3, 1984

The Power of Love Is Given to Man and Woman As a Share in God's Love

We are continuing to outline the spirituality of married life in the light of *Humanae Vitae*. According to the doctrine contained there, in conformity with biblical sources and all Tradition, love from the subjective viewpoint is a power, that is, a capacity of the human soul, of a theological nature. It is therefore the power given to man in order to participate in that love with which God himself loves in the mystery of creation and redemption. It is that love which "rejoices with the truth" (1 Cor 13:6). In it, the spiritual joy (Augustine's "enjoyment") of every authentic value is expressed. It is a joy like that of the Creator himself, who in the beginning saw that everything "was very good" (Gn 1:31).

If the powers of concupiscence try to detach the language of the body from the truth, that is, they try to falsify it, the power of love instead strengthens it ever anew in that truth, so that the mystery of the redemption of the body can bear fruit in it.

Love itself makes possible and brings about conjugal dialogue according to the full truth of the life of the spouses. At the same time love is a power or a capacity of a moral nature, actively oriented toward the fullness of good and for this reason toward every true good. Therefore its role consists in safeguarding the inseparable connection between the "two meanings of the conjugal act," which the encyclical deals with *(HV* 12). That is, it concerns protecting both the value of the true union of the couple (that is, the personal communion) and the value of responsible fatherhood and motherhood (in the form that is mature and worthy of man).

According to traditional language, love, as a higher power, coordinates the actions of the persons, the husband and the wife, in the sphere of the purposes of marriage. Although in dealing with the question neither the conciliar constitution nor the encyclical use the language at one time customary, they nonetheless deal with what the traditional expressions refer to.

As a higher power that the man and the woman receive from God along with the particular "consecration" of the sacrament of marriage, love involves a correct coordination of the purposes, according to which—in the traditional teaching of the Church—the moral (or rather "theological and moral") order of the life of the couple is constituted.

The doctrine of *Gaudium et Spes,* as well as that of *Humanae Vitae,* clarifies the same moral order in reference to love. Love is understood as a higher power that confers adequate content and value to conjugal acts according to the truth of the two meanings, the unitive and the procreative, with respect for their inseparability.

In this renewed formulation the traditional teaching on the purposes of marriage (and their hierarchy) is reaffirmed and at the same time deepened from the viewpoint of the interior life of the spouses, that is, of conjugal and family spirituality.

As was said, the role of love, which is "poured out into [the] hearts" (Rom 5:5) of the spouses as the fundamental spiritual power of their conjugal pact, consists in protecting both the value of the true communion of the spouses and the value of truly responsible fatherhood and motherhood. The power of love—authentic in the theological and ethical sense—is expressed in this, that love *correctly unites the two meanings of the conjugal act,* excluding not only in theory but above all in practice the contradiction that might be evidenced in this field. This contradiction is the most frequent reason for objecting to *Humanae Vitae* and the teaching of the Church. There must be a well-examined analysis, not only theological but also anthropological (we have tried to do this in the whole present reflection), to show that there is no need here to speak of contradiction, but only of difficulty. Well then, the encyclical itself stresses this difficulty in various passages.

This arises from the fact that the power of love is implanted in man lured by concupiscence. In human subjects love does battle with the threefold concupiscence (cf. 1 Jn 2:16), especially with the concupiscence of the flesh which distorts the truth of the language of the body. Therefore love too is not able to be realized in the truth of the language of the body except through overcoming concupiscence.

If the key element of the spirituality of spouses and parents—that essential power which spouses must continually draw from the sacramental consecration—is love, this love, as it is seen from the text of the encyclical (cf. *HV* 20), is by its nature linked with the chastity that is manifested as mastery over oneself, that is, continence, in particular, as periodic continence. In biblical language, the author of Ephesians seems to allude to this when in his classic text he exhorts spouses to "defer to one another out of reverence for Christ" (Eph 5:21).

We can say that *Humanae Vitae* constitutes precisely the development of this biblical truth about conjugal and family Christian spirituality. Nonetheless, to make it more manifest, there needs to be a deeper analysis of the virtue of continence and of its special significance for the truth of the mutual language of the body in married life and (indirectly) in the whole sphere of mutual relationships between man and woman.

General audience of October 10, 1984

Continence Protects the Dignity of the Conjugal Act

In keeping with what has already been said, today we will take up the analysis of the virtue of continence, which is part of the more general virtue of temperance. Continence consists in the capacity to dominate, control and direct drives of a sexual character (concupiscence of the flesh) and their consequences, in the psychosomatic subjectivity of man. Insofar as it is a constant disposition of the will, this capacity, merits being called a virtue.

We know from the previous analyses that concupiscence of the flesh, and the corresponding desire of a sexual character aroused by it, is expressed with a specific impulse in the sphere of somatic reaction and also with a psycho-emotive excitement of the sensual impulse. In order to succeed in mastering this impulse and excitement, the personal subject must be committed to a progressive education in self-control of the will, feelings and emotions. This education must develop beginning with the most simple acts in which it is relatively easy to put the interior decision into practice. As is obvious, this presupposes the clear perception of the values expressed in the law and the consequent formation of firm convictions. If accompanied by the respective disposition of the will, these convictions give rise to the corresponding virtue. This is precisely the virtue of continence (self-mastery). This virtue is seen to be the fundamental condition for the reciprocal language of the body to remain in the truth and for the couple to "defer to one another out of reverence for Christ," according to the words of Scripture (Eph 5:21). This "deferring to one another" means the common concern for the truth of the language of the body. Rather, deferring "out of reverence for Christ" indicates the gift of the fear of God (a gift of the Holy Spirit) which accompanies the virtue of continence.

This is very important for an adequate understanding of the virtue of continence and especially of the so-called "periodic continence" which *Humanae Vitae* deals with. The conviction that the virtue of continence is set against the concupiscence of the flesh is correct, but it is not altogether complete. It is not complete especially when we take into account the fact that this virtue does not appear and does not act abstractly and therefore in isolation. But it always appears and acts in connection with the other virtues *(nexus virtutum),* and therefore in connection with prudence, justice, fortitude and above all with charity.

In the light of these considerations it is easy to understand that continence is not limited to offering resistance to the concupiscence of the flesh. But through this resistance it is open likewise to those values, more profound and more mature, inherent in the spousal significance of the body in its femininity and masculinity, as well as in the authentic freedom of the gift in the reciprocal relations of the persons. Concupiscence of the flesh itself, insofar as it seeks above all carnal and sensual satisfaction, makes man in a certain sense blind and insensitive to the most profound values that spring from love and which at the same time constitute love in the interior truth that is proper to it.

In this way also the essential character of conjugal chastity is manifested in its organic link with the power of love, which is poured out into the hearts of the married couple along with the consecration of the sacrament of marriage. In addition, it becomes evident that the call directed to the couple that they "defer to one another out of reverence for Christ" (Eph 5:21) seems to open that interior space in which both become ever more sensitive to the most profound and most mature values that are connected with the spousal significance of the body and with the true freedom of the gift.

Conjugal chastity (and chastity in general) is manifested at first as the capacity to resist the concupiscence of the flesh. It later gradually reveals itself as a singular capacity to perceive, love and practice those meanings of the language of the body which remain altogether unknown to concupiscence itself. Those meanings progressively enrich the marital dialogue of the couple, purifying it, deepening it, and at the same time simplifying it.

Therefore, that asceticism of continence, which the encyclical speaks of (cf. *HV* 21), does not impoverish affective manifestations. But rather it makes them spiritually more intense and therefore enriches them.

Analyzing continence in this way, in the dynamics proper to this virtue (anthropological, ethical and theological), we see that that apparent contradiction disappears, which is often an objection to *Humanae Vitae* and to the doctrine of the Church on conjugal morality. That is, there would be a contradiction (according to those who offer this objection) between the two meanings of the conjugal act, the unitive meaning and the procreative meaning (cf. *HV* 12), so that if it were not licit to separate them, the couple would be deprived of the right to conjugal union when they could not responsibly be permitted to procreate.

Humanae Vitae answers this apparent contradiction, if one studies it in depth. Pope Paul VI confirms that there is no contradiction but only a difficulty connected with the whole interior situation of the "man of concupiscence." Rather, precisely by reason of this difficulty the true order of conjugal life is assigned to the interior and ascetical commitment of the couple. In view of this order, they become "strengthened and, one might say, consecrated" *(HV* 25) by the sacrament of marriage.

That order of conjugal life means in addition the subjective harmony between responsible parenthood and personal communion, a harmony created by conjugal chastity. The interior fruits of continence mature in it. Through this interior maturing, the conjugal act itself acquires the importance and dignity proper to it in its potentially procreative meaning. At the same time, all the affective manifestations acquire an adequate meaning (cf. *HV* 21). They serve to express the personal communion of the couple in proportion to the subjective richness of femininity and masculinity.

In keeping with experience and tradition, the encyclical reveals that the conjugal act is also a "manifestation of affection" *(HV* 16). But it is a "manifestation of particular affection" because at the same time it has a potentially procreative meaning. As a result, it is oriented to express personal union, but not only that. At the same time the encyclical indicates, although indirectly, many manifestations of affection, effective exclusively to express the personal union of the couple.

The role of conjugal chastity, and still more precisely that of continence, lies not only in protecting the importance and dignity of the conjugal act in relation to its procreative meaning. But it also lies in safeguarding the importance and the dignity proper to the conjugal act as expressive of interpersonal union, revealing to the awareness and the experience of the couple all the other possible manifestations of affection that can express this profound communion of theirs.

It is indeed a matter of not doing harm to the communion of the couple in the case where for just reasons they should abstain from the conjugal act. Still more, this communion—continually being built up, day by day, through suitable affective manifestations—may constitute a vast terrain on which, under suitable conditions, the decision for a morally right conjugal act matures.

General audience of October 24, 1984

Continence Frees One from Inner Tension

We are continuing the analysis of continence in the light of the teaching contained in *Humanae Vitae*. It is often thought that continence causes inner tensions which man must free himself from. In the light of the analyses we have done, continence, understood integrally, is rather the only way to free man from such tensions. It means nothing other than the spiritual effort aimed at expressing the "language of the body," not only in truth but also in the authentic richness of the manifestations of affection.

Is this effort possible? In other words (and under another aspect) the question returns here about the feasibility of the moral law, recalled and confirmed by *Humanae Vitae*. It constitutes one of the most essential questions (and currently also one of the most urgent ones) in the sphere of the spirituality of marriage.

The Church is totally convinced of the correctness of the principle that affirms responsible fatherhood and motherhood, in the sense explained in previous catecheses. This is not only for demographic reasons but for more essential reasons. We call that fatherhood and that motherhood responsible which correspond to the personal dignity of the couple as parents, to the truth of their person and of the conjugal act. Hence arises the close and direct relationship that links this dimension with the whole spirituality of marriage.

In *Humanae Vitae*, Pope Paul VI expressed what had been affirmed elsewhere by many authoritative moralists and scientists, even non-Catholics.[109] Namely, he affirmed that precisely in this field, so profoundly and essentially human and personal, it is necessary above all to refer to man as a person, the subject who decides by himself, and not to means which make him the object (of manipulations) and depersonalize him. It is therefore a question here of an authentically humanistic meaning of the development and progress of human civilization.

Is this effort possible? The whole question of *Humanae Vitae* is not reduced simply to the biological dimension of human fertility (the question of the "natural cycles of fertility"). But it goes back to the very subjectivity of man, to that personal "I" through which the person is man or woman.

Already during the discussion in the Second Vatican Council, in relation to the chapter of *Gaudium et Spes* on the "Dignity of Marriage and the Family and Its Promotion," the necessity was discussed for a deepened analysis of the reactions (and also of the emotions) connected with the mutual influence of masculinity and femininity on the human subject.[110] This question belongs not so much to biology as to psychology. From biology and psychology it then passes into the sphere of the spirituality of marriage and the family. Here this question is in close relationship with the way of understanding the virtue of continence, that is, self-mastery and especially of periodic continence.

A careful analysis of human psychology allows us to arrive at some other essential affirmations. (Psychology is at the same time a subjective self-analysis and then becomes an analysis of an "object" accessible to human knowledge.) In interpersonal relationships in which the mutual influence of masculinity and femininity is expressed, there is freed in the psycho-emotive subject in the human "I," alongside a reaction distinguishable as excitement, another reaction that can and must be called emotion. Although these two kinds of reaction appear joined, it is possible to distinguish them experimentally and to differentiate them with regard to their content or their object.[111]

The objective difference between the one and the other kind of reaction consists in the fact that the excitement is above all corporeal and in this sense sensual. On the other hand, even though aroused by the mutual reaction of masculinity and femininity, emotion refers above all to the other person understood in the person's integrality. We can say that this is an emotion caused by the person, in relation to the person's masculinity or femininity.

What we are stating here with regard to the psychology of the mutual reactions of masculinity and femininity helps in understanding the role of the virtue of continence, which we spoke about previously. Continence is not only, and not even principally, the ability to abstain, that is, mastery over the multiple reactions that are interwoven in the mutual influence of masculinity and femininity. Such a role would be defined as negative. But there is also another role (which we can call positive) of self-mastery. It is the ability to direct the respective reactions, both as to their content and their character.

It has already been said that in the field of the mutual reactions of masculinity and femininity, excitement and emotion appear not only as two distinct and different experiences of the human "I." But very often they appear joined in the sphere of the same experience as two different elements of that experience. The reciprocal degree to which these two elements appear in a given experience depends on various circumstances of an interior and an exterior nature. At times one of the elements is clearly prevalent; at other times there is rather a balance between them.

Continence has the ability to direct excitement and emotion in the sphere of the mutual influence of masculinity and femininity. Thus continence has the essential task of maintaining the balance between the comunion in which the couple wish to mutually express only their intimate union and that in which (at least implicitly) they accept responsible parenthood. In fact, on the part of the subject, excitement and emotion can jeopardize the orientation and the character of the mutual language of the body.

Excitement seeks above all to be expressed in the form of sensual and corporeal pleasure. That is, it tends toward the conjugal act which (depending on the natural cycles of fertility) includes the possibility of procreation. On the other hand, emotion, caused by another human being as a person, even if in its emotive content it is conditioned by the femininity or masculinity of the "other," does not *per se* tend toward the conjugal act. But it limits itself to other manifestations of affection, which express the spousal meaning of the body, and which nevertheless do not include its (potentially) procreative meaning.

It is easy to understand what conclusions arise from this with respect to the question of responsible fatherhood and motherhood. These conclusions are of a moral nature.

General audience of October 31, 1984

Continence Deepens Personal Communion

We are continuing the analysis of the virtue of continence in the light of the doctrine contained in *Humanae Vitae*. It is well to recall that the great classics of ethical (and anthropological) thought, both the pre-Christian ones and the Christian ones (St. Thomas Aquinas), see in the virtue of continence not only the capacity to contain bodily and sensual reactions, but even more the capacity to control and guide man's whole sensual and emotive sphere. In the case under discussion, it is a question of the capacity to direct the line of excitement toward its correct development and also the line of emotion itself, orienting it toward the deepening and interior intensification of its pure and, in a certain sense, disinterested character.

This differentiation between the line of excitement and the line of emotion is not an opposition. It does not mean that the conjugal act, as a result of excitement, does not at the same time involve the deep emotion of the other person. Certainly it does, or at any rate, it should not be otherwise.

In the conjugal act, the intimate union should involve a particular intensification of emotion, or rather the deep emotion, of the other person. This is also contained in Ephesians in the form of an exhortation directed to married couples: "Defer to one another out of reverence for Christ" (Eph 5:21).

The distinction between excitement and emotion, noted in this analysis, proves only the subjective reactive-emotive richness of the human "I." This richness excludes any unilateral reduction and enables the virtue of continence to be practiced as a capacity to direct the manifesting of both the excitement and the emotion, aroused by the reciprocal reacting of masculinity and femininity.

The virtue of continence, so understood, has an essential role in maintaining the interior balance between the two meanings of the conjugal act, the unitive and the procreative (cf. *HV* 12) in view of a truly responsible fatherhood and motherhood.

Humanae Vitae devotes due attention to the biological aspect of the question, that is to say, to the rhythmic character of human fertility. In the light of the encyclical, this "periodicalness" can be called a providential index for a responsible fatherhood and motherhood. Nevertheless a question such as this one, which has such a profoundly personalistic and sacramental (theological) meaning, is not resolved only on this level.

The encyclical teaches responsible fatherhood and motherhood "as a proof of a mature conjugal love." Therefore it contains not only the answer to the concrete question that is asked in the sphere of the ethics of married life but, as already has been stated—it also indicates a plan of conjugal spirituality, which we wish at least to outline.

The correct way of intending and practicing periodic continence as a virtue (that is, according to *Humanae Vitae* 21, the "mastery of self") also essentially determines the "naturalness" of the method, called also the "natural method." This is "naturalness" at the level of the person. Therefore there can be no thought of a mechanical application of biological laws. The knowledge itself of the rhythms of fertility, even though indispensable, still does not create that interior freedom of the gift, which is by its nature explicitly spiritual and depends on man's interior maturity. This freedom presupposes such a capacity to direct the sensual and emotive reactions as to make possible the giving of self to the other "I" on the grounds of the mature self-possession of one's own "I" in its corporeal and emotive subjectivity.

As we know from the biblical and theological analyses we have previously done, the human body in its masculinity and femininity is interiorly ordered to the communion of the persons *(communio personarum).* Its spousal meaning consists in this. The spousal meaning of the body has been distorted, almost at its roots, by concupiscence (especially by the concupiscence of the flesh in the sphere of the threefold concupiscence). The virtue of continence in its mature form gradually reveals the pure aspect of the spousal meaning of the body. In this way, continence develops the personal communion of the man and the woman, a communion that cannot be formed and developed in the full truth of its possibilities only on the level of concupiscence. This is precisely what *Humanae Vitae* affirms. This truth has two aspects: the personalistic and the theological.

General audience of November 7, 1984

Living according to the Spirit

In the light of *Humanae Vitae*, the fundamental element of the spirituality of married life is the love poured out into the hearts of the couple as a gift of the Holy Spirit (cf. Rom 5:5). In the sacrament the couple receive this gift along with a special consecration. Love is united to conjugal chastity, which, manifesting itself as continence, brings about the interior order of married life.

Chastity means to live in the order of the heart. This order permits the development of the manifestations of affection in their proper proportion and meaning. In this way conjugal chastity is also confirmed as "life by the Spirit" (cf. Gal 5:25), according to St. Paul's expression. The Apostle had in mind not only the immanent energies of the human spirit, but above all the sanctifying influence of the Holy Spirit and his special gifts.

Therefore, chastity lies at the center of the spirituality of marriage, not only as a moral virtue (formed by love), but likewise as a virtue connected with the gifts of the Holy Spirit—above all, the gift of respect for what comes from God *(donum pietatis)*. This gift is in the mind of the author of the Ephesians when he exhorts married couples to "defer to one another out of reverence for Christ" (Eph 5:21). So the interior order of married life, which enables the manifestations of affection to develop according to their right proportion and meaning, is a fruit not only of the virtue which the couple practice, but also of the gifts of the Holy Spirit which they cooperate with.

Dealing with the specific asceticism of married life, that is, the commitment to acquire the virtues of love, chastity, and continence, *Humanae Vitae* speaks indirectly of the gifts of the Holy Spirit in some passages of the text (especially 21 and 26). The couple acquire a sensitivity for these gifts in proportion to their development in virtue.

This corresponds to man's vocation to marriage. Those two who, according to the oldest expression in the Bible, "become one body" (Gn 2:24), cannot bring about this union on the proper level of persons *(communio personarum)* except through the powers coming from the spirit, and precisely from the Holy Spirit who purifies, enlivens, strengthens, and perfects the powers of the human spirit. "It is the Spirit that gives life; the flesh is useless" (Jn 6:63).

It follows from this that the essential lines of the spirituality of marriage are inscribed from the beginning in the biblical truth on marriage. This spirituality is also open from the beginning to the gifts of the Holy Spirit. If *Humanae Vitae* exhorts married couples to "unremitting prayer" and to the sacramental life (saying: "...let them drink deep of grace and charity from that unfailing fount which is the Eucharist"; "humble and persevering, they must have recourse to the mercy of God, abundantly bestowed in the Sacrament of Penance"—*HV* 25), it does so insofar as it is mindful of the Spirit who "gives life" (2 Cor 3:6).

The gifts of the Holy Spirit, and especially the gift of respect for what is sacred, seem to have a fundamental significance here. This gift sustains and develops in the married couple a particular sensitivity to everything in their vocation and life that bears the sign of the mystery of creation and redemption—a sensitivity to everything that is a created reflection of God's wisdom and love. Therefore that gift seems to introduce the man and woman to a specially profound respect for the two inseparable meanings of the conjugal act, which the encyclical speaks of in relation to the sacrament of marriage *(HV* 12). Respect for the two meanings of the conjugal act can develop fully only on the basis of a profound reference to the personal dignity of what in the human person is intrinsic to masculinity and femininity, and inseparably in reference to the personal dignity of the new life which can result from the conjugal union of the man and the woman. The gift of respect for what is created by God is expressed precisely in this reference.

Respect for the twofold meaning of the conjugal act in marriage, which results from the gift of respect for God's creation, is manifested also as a salvific fear. It is a fear of violating or degrading what bears in itself the sign of the divine mystery of creation and redemption. The author of the Ephesians speaks precisely of this fear: "Defer to one another out of reverence for Christ" (Eph 5:21).

This salvific fear is directly associated with the negative function of continence (that is, to resistance with regard to concupiscence of the flesh). It is also manifested—and to an ever greater degree as this virtue gradually matures—as sensitivity filled with veneration for the essential values of the conjugal union: for the two meanings of the conjugal act (or, to use the terminology of the previous analyses, veneration for the interior truth of the mutual language of the body).

On the basis of a profound reference to these two essential values, that which signifies union of the couple is harmonized in the subject with that which signifies responsible fatherhood and motherhood. The gift of respect for what is created by God enables the apparent contradiction in this area to disappear and the difficulty arising from concupiscence to be gradually overcome, thanks to the maturity of the virtue and the power of the Holy Spirit's gift.

If it is a question of the problem of so-called periodic continence (or recourse to natural methods), the gift of respect for the work of God helps, to the greatest extent, to reconcile human dignity with the natural cycles of fertility, that is, with the biological dimension of the femininity and masculinity of the couple. This dimension also has a significance of its own for the truth of the mutual language of the body in married life.

In this way, even what refers to conjugal union in the flesh—not so much in the biblical meaning as directly in the biological meaning—finds its humanly mature form thanks to the life in the Spirit.

The whole practice of the upright regulation of fertility, so closely linked to responsible fatherhood and motherhood, forms part of the Christian spirituality of married life and family life. Only by living "in the Spirit" can it become interiorly true and authentic.

General audience of November 14, 1984

Respect for the Work of God

On the basis of the doctrine contained in *Humanae Vitae*, we intend to trace an outline of conjugal spirituality. In the spiritual life of married couples the gifts of the Holy Spirit are at work, especially the gift of piety, that is, the gift of respect for what is a work of God.

Together with love and chastity, this gift helps to identify in the sum total of married life that act in which, at least potentially, the spousal meaning of the body is linked with the procreative meaning. It leads to understanding, among the possible manifestations of affection, the singular or rather the exceptional significance of that act—its dignity and the consequent serious responsibility connected with it. Therefore, the antithesis of conjugal spirituality is constituted, in a certain sense, by the subjective lack of this understanding which is linked to contraceptive practice and mentality. In addition to everything else, this does enormous harm from the point of view of man's interior culture. The virtue of conjugal chastity, and still more the gift of respect for what comes from God, mold the couple's spirituality to the purpose of protecting the particular dignity of this act, of this manifestation of affection. In it, the truth of the language of the body can be expressed only by safeguarding the procreative potential.

Responsible fatherhood and motherhood means the spiritual appraisal—conforming to truth—of the conjugal act in the knowledge and in the will of both spouses. In this manifestation of affection, after considering the interior and external circumstances, especially the biological ones, they express their mature readiness for fatherhood and motherhood.

Respect for the work of God contributes to seeing that the conjugal act does not become diminished and deprived of the interior meaning of married life as a whole, that it does not become a habit. It sees that it expresses a sufficient fullness of personal and ethical content, and also of religious content, that is, veneration for the majesty of the Creator, the only and the ultimate depository of the source of life, and for the spousal love of the Redeemer. All this creates and enlarges, so to speak, the interior space for the mutual freedom of the gift in which the spousal meaning of masculinity and femininity is fully manifested.

The obstacle to this freedom is presented by the interior constriction of concupiscence, directed to the other "I" as an object of pleasure. Respect for what God creates gives freedom from this constriction. It frees from all that reduces the other "I" to a mere object and it strengthens the interior freedom of the gift.

This can happen only through a profound appreciation of the personal dignity of both the feminine "I" and the masculine "I" in their shared life. This spiritual appreciation is the fundamental fruit of the gift of the Spirit, which urges the person to respect the work of God. From this appreciation, and therefore indirectly from that gift, all the affectionate manifestations which make up the fabric of remaining faithful to the union of marriage derive their true spousal meaning. This union is expressed through the conjugal act only in given circumstances. But it can and it must be manifested continually, every day, through various affectionate manifestations which are determined by the capacity of a disinterested emotion of the "I" in relation to femininity and, reciprocally, in relation to masculinity.

The attitude of respect for the work of God, which the Spirit stirs up in the couple, has an enormous significance for those affectionate manifestations. This is because side by side with it there is the capacity for deep satisfaction, admiration, disinterested attention to the visible and at the same time the invisible beauty of femininity and masculinity, and finally a deep appreciation of the disinterested gift of the other.

All this determines the spiritual identification of what is male or female, of what is corporeal and at the same time personal. From this spiritual identification the awareness emerges of the union through the body, in safeguarding the interior freedom of the gift. Through the affectionate manifestations the couple help each other remain faithful to the union. At the same time these manifestations protect in each of them that deep-rooted peace which is in a certain sense the interior resonance of chastity guided by the gift of respect for what God creates.

This gift involves a profound and universal attention to the person in one's masculinity and femininity, thus creating the interior climate suitable for personal communion. That procreation which we describe as responsible, rightly matures only in this climate of the personal communion of the couple.

Humanae Vitae enables us to trace an outline of conjugal spirituality. This is the human and supernatural climate which considers the "biological" order and, at the same time, is formed on the basis of chastity sustained by the gift of piety. The interior harmony of marriage is formed in this climate, in respect for what the encyclical calls "the twofold significance of the conjugal act" *(HV* 12). This harmony means that the couple live together in the interior truth of the language of the body. *Humanae Vitae* proclaims that the connection between this truth and love is inseparable.

General audience of November 21, 1984

The Redemption of the Body
and the Sacramentality of Marriage

As a whole, the catechesis which I began over four years ago and which I am concluding today can be summed up under the title: "Human love in the divine plan," or more precisely, "The redemption of the body and the sacramentality of marriage." The catechesis can be divided into two parts.

The first part was dedicated to a study of Christ's words, which prove to be suitable for opening the current theme. These words were analyzed at length in the totality of the Gospel text. Following the long-lasting reflection it was fitting to emphasize the three texts that were analyzed right in the first part of the catechesis.

First of all there is the text in which Christ referred to "the beginning" in his discussion with the Pharisees on the unity and indissolubility of marriage (cf. Mt 19:8; Mk 10:6-9). Next there are the words Christ spoke in the Sermon on the Mount concerning concupiscence as adultery committed in the heart (cf. Mt 5:28). Finally, there are the words reported by all the synoptic Gospels in which Christ referred to the resurrection of the body in the other world (cf. Mt 22:30; Mk 12:25; Lk 20:35).

The second part of the catechesis was dedicated to the analysis of the sacrament based on Ephesians (Eph 5:21-33). This goes back to the biblical beginning of marriage expressed in the words of Genesis: "A man leaves his father and mother and clings to his wife, and the two of them become one body" (Gn 2:24).

The catechesis of the first and second parts repeatedly used the term "theology of the body." In a certain sense, this is a "working" term. The introduction of the term and the concept of the theology of the body was necessary to establish the theme, "The redemption of the body and the sacramentality of marriage," on a wider base. We must immediately note that the term "theology of the body" goes far beyond the content of the reflections that were made. These reflections do not include multiple problems which, with regard to their object, belong to the theology of the body (as, for example, the problem of suffering and death, so important in the biblical message). We must state this clearly. Nonetheless, we must also recognize explicitly that the reflections on the theme, "The redemption of the body and the sacramentality of marriage," can be correctly carried out from the moment when the light of revelation touches the reality of the human body (that is, on the basis of the theology of the body). This is confirmed, among other ways, by the words of Genesis: "The two of them become one body." These words were originally and thematically at the basis of our argument.

The reflections on the sacrament of marriage were carried out by considering the two dimensions essential to this sacrament (as to every other sacrament), that is, the dimension of the covenant and grace, and the dimension of sign.

Throughout these two dimensions we continually went back to the reflections on the theology of the body, reflections linked to the key words of Christ. We went back to these reflections also when we took up, at the end of this whole series of catecheses, the analysis of *Humanae Vitae*.

The doctrine contained in this document of the Church's modern teaching is organically related to both the sacramentality of marriage and the whole biblical question of the theology of the body, centered on the key words of Christ. In a certain sense we can even say that all the reflections that deal with the redemption of the body and the sacramentality of marriage seem to constitute an ample commentary on the doctrine contained in *Humanae Vitae*.

This commentary seems quite necessary. In fact, in responding to some questions of today in the field of conjugal and family morality, at the same time the encyclical also raised other questions, as we know, of a biomedical nature. But also (and above all) they are of a theological nature.

They belong to that sphere of anthropology and theology that we have called the theology of the body.

The reflections we made consist in facing the questions raised with regard to *Humanae Vitae*. The reaction that the encyclical aroused confirms the importance and the difficulty of these questions. They are reaffirmed also by later pronouncements of Paul VI where he emphasized the possibility of examining the explanation of Christian truth in this area.

In addition, the Apostolic Exhortation *Familiaris Consortio,* fruit of the 1980 Synod of Bishops on "The Role of the Christian Family," confirms it. The document contains an appeal, directed especially to theologians, to elaborate more completely the biblical and personalistic aspects of the doctrine contained in *Humanae Vitae.*

To gather the questions raised by the encyclical means to formulate them and at the same time to search again for the answer to them. The doctrine contained in *Familiaris Consortio* requires that both the formulation of the questions and the search for an adequate answer focus on the biblical and personalistic aspects. This doctrine also points out the trend of development of the theology of the body, the direction of the development, and therefore also the direction of its progressive completion and deepening.

The analysis of the biblical aspects speaks of the way to place the doctrine of today's Church on the foundation of revelation. This is important for the development of theology. Development, that is, progress in theology, takes place through a continual restudying of the deposit of revelation.

The rooting of the doctrine proclaimed by the Church in all of Tradition and in divine revelation itself is always open to questions posed by man. It also uses the instruments most in keeping with modern science and today's culture. It seems that in this area the intense development of philosophical anthropology (especially the anthropology that rests on ethics) most closely faces the questions raised by *Humanae Vitae* regarding theology and especially theological ethics.

The analysis of the personalistic aspects of the doctrine contained in this document has an existential significance for establishing what true progress is, that is, the development of man. In fact, throughout all modern civilization, especially in Western civilization, there is an occult and at the same time an explicit enough tendency to measure this progress on the basis of "things," that is, material goods.

The analysis of the personalistic aspects of the Church's doctrine, contained in Paul VI's encyclical, emphasizes a determined appeal to measure man's progress on the basis of the person, that is, of what is good for man as man—what corresponds to his essential dignity. The analysis of the personalistic aspects leads to the conviction that the encyclical presents as a fundamental problem the viewpoint of man's authentic development. This development is measured to the greatest extent on the basis of ethics and not only on technology.

The catechesis dedicated to *Humanae Vitae* constitutes only one part, the final part, of those which dealt with the redemption of the body and the sacramentality of marriage.

If I draw your attention especially to this last catechesis, I do so not only because the subject dealt with is more closely connected to our contemporaneity. But I do so above all because of the fact that questions come from it which in a certain sense permeate the sum total of our reflections. It follows that this last part is not artificially added to the sum total but is organically and homogeneously united with it. In a certain sense, that part which in the complex arrangement is located at the end is at the same time found at the beginning of this sum total. This is important from the point of view of structure and method.

Even the historical moment seems to have its significance. The present catechesis was begun in the period of preparation for the 1980 Synod of Bishops on the theme of marriage and the family ("The role of the Christian family"), and ends after the publication of *Familiaris Consortio,* which is a result of the work of this Synod. Everyone knows that the 1980 Synod also referred to *Humanae Vitae* and fully reconfirmed its doctrine.

Nevertheless, the most important moment seems to be that essential moment when, in the sum total of the reflections carried out, we can precisely state the following: to face the questions raised by *Humanae Vitae,* especially in theology, to formulate these questions and seek their reply, it is necessary to find that biblical-theological sphere to which we allude when we speak of the redemption of the body and the sacramentality of marriage. In this sphere are found the answers to the perennial questions in the conscience of men and women, and also to the difficult questions of our modern world concerning marriage and procreation.

General audience of November 28, 1984

NOTES

General audience of October 31, 1984

[109] Cf., for example, the statements of the *Bund fur evangelisch-katholische Wiedervereinigung (L'Osservatore Romano,* September 19, 1968, p. 3); Dr. F. King, Anglican *(L'Osservatore Romano,* October 5, 1968, p. 3); and also the Muslim, Mr. Mohammed Cherif Zeghoudu (in the same issue). Especially significant is the letter written on November 28, 1968, to Cardinal Cicognani by Karl Barth, in which he praised the great courage of Paul VI.

[110] Cf. the interventions by Card. Leo Suenens at the 13th General Congregation on September 29, 1968: *Acta Synodalia S. Concilii Oecumenici Vaticani II,* vol. 4, part 3, p. 30.

[111] In this regard we should recall what St. Thomas says in a final analysis of human love in relation to the "concupiscible" and to the will (cf. *Summa Theol.,* I-II, q. 26, art. 2).

APPENDIX

Of Human Life

Encyclical Letter of His Holiness Pope Paul VI

To the venerable Patriarchs, Archbishops and Bishops and other local ordinaries in peace and communion with the Apostolic See, to priests, the faithful and to all men of good will.

Venerable brothers and beloved sons:

The Transmission of Life

1. The most serious duty of transmitting human life, for which married persons are the free and responsible collaborators of God the Creator, has always been a source of great joys to them, even if sometimes accompanied by not a few difficulties and by distress.

At all times the fulfillment of this duty has posed grave problems to the conscience of married persons, but, with the recent evolution of society, changes have taken place that give rise to new questions which the Church could not ignore, having to do with a matter which so closely touches upon the life and happiness of men.

I. NEW ASPECTS OF THE PROBLEM AND COMPETENCY OF THE MAGISTERIUM

New Formulation of the Problem

2. The changes which have taken place are in fact noteworthy and of varied kinds. In the first place, there is the rapid demographic development. Fear is shown by many that world population is growing more rapidly than the available resources, with growing distress to many families and developing countries, so that the temptation for authorities to counter this danger with radical measures is great. Moreover, working and lodging conditions, as well as increased exigencies

both in the economic field and in that of education, often make the proper education of an elevated number of children difficult today. A change is also seen both
in the manner of considering the person of woman and her place in society, and in
the value to be attributed to conjugal love in marriage, and also in the appreciation to be made of the meaning of conjugal acts in relation to that love.

Finally and above all, man has made stupendous progress in the domination
and rational organization of the forces of nature, such that he tends to extend this
domination to his own total being: to the body, to psychical life, to social life and
even to the laws which regulate the transmission of life.

3. This new state of things gives rise to new questions. Granted the conditions of life today, and granted the meaning which conjugal relations have with
respect to the harmony between husband and wife and to their mutual fidelity,
would not a revision of the ethical norms, in force up to now, seem to be advisable, especially when it is considered that they cannot be observed without sacrifices, sometimes heroic sacrifices?

And again: by extending to this field the application of the so-called "principle of totality," could it not be admitted that the intention of a less abundant but
more rationalized fecundity might transform a materially sterilizing intervention
into a licit and wise control of birth? Could it not be admitted, that is, that the
finality of procreation pertains to the ensemble of conjugal life, rather than to its
single acts? It is also asked whether, in view of the increased sense of responsibility of modern man, the moment has not come for him to entrust to his reason
and his will, rather than to the biological rhythms of his organism, the task of
regulating birth.

Competency of the Magisterium

4. Such questions required from the teaching authority of the Church a new
and deeper reflection upon the principles of the moral teaching on marriage:
a teaching founded on the natural law, illuminated and enriched by divine revelation.

No believer will wish to deny that the teaching authority of the Church is
competent to interpret even the natural moral law. It is, in fact, indisputable, as
our predecessors have many times declared,[1] that Jesus Christ, when communicating to Peter and to the apostles his divine authority and sending them to teach
all nations his commandments,[2] constituted them as guardians and authentic interpreters of all the moral law, not only, that is, of the law of the Gospel, but also
of the natural law, which is also an expression of the will of God, the faithful
fulfillment of which is equally necessary for salvation.[3]

Conformably to this mission of hers, the Church has always provided—and
even more amply in recent times—a coherent teaching concerning both the nature of marriage and the correct use of conjugal rights and the duties of husband
and wife.[4]

Special Studies

5. The consciousness of that same mission induced us to confirm and enlarge the study commission which our predecessor Pope John XXIII of happy memory had instituted in March 1963. That commission which included, besides several experts in the various pertinent disciplines, also married couples, had as its scope the gathering of opinions on the new questions regarding conjugal life, and in particular on the regulation of births, and of furnishing opportune elements of information so that the Magisterium could give an adequate reply to the expectation not only of the faithful, but also of world opinion.[5]

The work of these experts, as well as the successive judgments and counsels spontaneously forwarded by or expressly requested from a good number of our brothers in the episcopate, have permitted us to measure more exactly all the aspects of this complex matter. Hence with all our heart we express to each of them our lively gratitude.

Reply of the Magisterium

6. The conclusions at which the commission arrived could not, nevertheless, be considered by us as definitive, nor dispense us from a personal examination of this serious question; and this also because, within the commission itself, no full concordance of judgments concerning the moral norms to be proposed had been reached, and above all because certain criteria of solutions had emerged which departed from the moral teaching on marriage proposed with constant firmness by the teaching authority of the Church.

Therefore, having attentively sifted the documentation laid before us, after mature reflection and assiduous prayers, we now intend, by virtue of the mandate entrusted to us by Christ, to give our reply to these grave questions.

II. DOCTRINAL PRINCIPLES

A Total Vision of Man

7. The problem of birth, like every other problem regarding human life, is to be considered, beyond partial perspectives—whether of the biological or psychological, demographic or sociological orders—in the light of an integral vision of man and of his vocation, not only his natural and earthly, but also his supernatural and eternal vocation. And since, in the attempt to justify artificial methods of birth control, many have appealed to the demands both of conjugal love and of "responsible parenthood," it is good to state very precisely the true concept of these two great realities of married life, referring principally to what was recently set forth in this regard, and in a highly authoritative form, by the Second Vatican Council in its pastoral constitution *Gaudium et Spes* (Constitution on the Church in the Modern World).

8. Conjugal love reveals its true nature and nobility when it is considered in its supreme origin, God, who is love,[6] "the Father, from whom every family in heaven and on earth is named."[7]

Marriage is not, then, the effect of chance or the product of evolution of unconscious natural forces; it is the wise institution of the Creator to realize in mankind his design of love. By means of the reciprocal personal gift of self, proper and exclusive to them, husband and wife tend toward the communion of their beings in view of mutual personal perfection, to collaborate with God in the generation and education of new lives.

For baptized persons, moreover, marriage invests the dignity of a sacramental sign of grace, inasmuch as it represents the union of Christ and of the Church.

Its Characteristics

9. Under this light, there clearly appear the characteristic marks and demands of conjugal love, and it is of supreme importance to have an exact idea of these.

This love is first of all fully human, that is to say, of the senses and of the spirit at the same time. It is not, then, a simple transport of instinct and sentiment, but also, and principally, an act of the free will, intended to endure and to grow by means of the joys and sorrows of daily life, in such a way that husband and wife become one only heart and one only soul, and together attain their human perfection.

Then, this love is total, that is to say, it is a very special form of personal friendship, in which husband and wife generously share everything, without undue reservations or selfish calculations. Whoever truly loves his marriage partner loves not only for what he receives, but for the partner's self, rejoicing that he can enrich his partner with the gift of himself.

Again, this love is faithful and exclusive until death. Thus in fact do bride and groom conceive it to be on the day when they freely and in full awareness assume the duty of the marriage bond. This fidelity can sometimes be difficult, but is always possible, noble and meritorious, as no one can deny. The example of so many married persons down through the centuries shows, not only that fidelity is according to the nature of marriage, but also that it is a source of profound and lasting happiness and finally, this love is fecund, for it is not exhausted by the communion between husband and wife, but is destined to continue, raising up new lives. "Marriage and conjugal love are by their nature ordained toward the begetting and educating of children. Children are really the supreme gift of marriage and contribute very substantially to the welfare of their parents."[8]

Responsible Parenthood

10. Hence conjugal love requires in husband and wife an awareness of their mission of "responsible parenthood," which today is rightly much insisted upon,

and which also must be exactly understood. Consequently it is to be considered under different aspects which are legitimate and connected with one another.

In relation to the biological processes, responsible parenthood means the knowledge and respect of their functions; human intellect discovers in the power of giving life biological laws which are part of the human person.[9]

In relation to the tendencies of instinct or passion, responsible parenthood means that necessary dominion which reason and will must exercise over them.

In relation to physical, economic, psychological and social conditions, responsible parenthood is exercised, either by the deliberate and generous decision to raise a numerous family, or by the decision, made for grave motives and with due respect for the moral law, to avoid for the time being, or even for an indeterminate period, a new birth.

Responsible parenthood also and above all implies a more profound relationship to the objective moral order established by God, of which a right conscience is the faithful interpreter. The responsible exercise of parenthood implies, therefore, that husband and wife recognize fully their own duties toward God, toward themselves, toward the family and toward society, in a correct hierarchy of values.

In the task of transmitting life, therefore, they are not free to proceed completely at will, as if they could determine in a wholly autonomous way the honest path to follow; but they must conform their activity to the creative intention of God, expressed in the very nature of marriage and of its acts, and manifested by the constant teaching of the Church.[10]

Respect for the Nature and Purpose of the Marriage Act

11. These acts, by which husband and wife are united in chaste intimacy, and by means of which human life is transmitted, are, as the council recalled, "noble and worthy,"[11] and they do not cease to be lawful if, for causes independent of the will of husband and wife, they are foreseen to be infecund, since they always remain ordained toward expressing and consolidating their union. In fact, as experience bears witness, not every conjugal act is followed by a new life. God has wisely disposed natural laws and rhythms of fecundity which, of themselves, cause a separation in the succession of births. Nonetheless the Church, calling men back to the observance of the norms of the natural law, as interpreted by its constant doctrine, teaches that each and every marriage act *(quilibet matrimonii usus)* must remain open to the transmission of life.[12]

Two Inseparable Aspects: Union and Procreation

12. That teaching, often set forth by the Magisterium, is founded upon the inseparable connection, willed by God and unable to be broken by man on his own initiative, between the two meanings of the conjugal act: the unitive meaning and the procreative meaning. Indeed, by its intimate structure, the conjugal

act, while most closely uniting husband and wife, capacitates them for the generation of new lives, according to laws inscribed in the very being of man and of woman. By safeguarding both these essential aspects, the unitive and the procreative, the conjugal act preserves in its fullness the sense of true mutual love and its ordination toward man's most high calling to parenthood. We believe that the men of our day are particularly capable of seizing the deeply reasonable and human character of this fundamental principle.

Faithfulness to God's Design

13. It is in fact justly observed that a conjugal act imposed upon one's partner without regard for his or her condition and lawful desires is not a true act of love, and therefore denies an exigency of right moral order in the relationships between husband and wife. Hence, one who reflects well must also recognize that a reciprocal act of love, which jeopardizes the responsibility to transmit life which God the Creator, according to particular laws, inserted therein, is in contradiction with the design constitutive of marriage, and with the will of the Author of life. To use this divine gift destroying, even if only partially, its meaning and its purpose is to contradict the nature both of man and of woman and of their most intimate relationship, and therefore it is to contradict also the plan of God and his will. On the other hand, to make use of the gift of conjugal love while respecting the laws of the generative process means to acknowledge oneself not to be the arbiter of the sources of human life, but rather the minister of the design established by the Creator. In fact, just as man does not have unlimited dominion over his body in general, so also, with particular reason, he has no such dominion over his generative faculties as such, because of their intrinsic ordination toward raising up life, of which God is the principle. "Human life is sacred," Pope John XXIII recalled; "from its very inception it reveals the creating hand of God."[13]

Illicit Ways of Regulating Birth

14. In conformity with these landmarks in the human and Christian vision of marriage, we must once again declare that the direct interruption of the generative process already begun, and, above all, directly willed and procured abortion, even if for therapeutic reasons, are to be absolutely excluded as licit means of regulating birth.[14]

Equally to be excluded, as the teaching authority of the Church has frequently declared, is direct sterilization, whether perpetual or temporary, whether of the man or of the woman.[15] Similarly excluded is every action which, either in anticipation of the conjugal act, or in its accomplishment, or in the development of its natural consequences, proposes, whether as an end or as a means, to render procreation impossible.[16]

To justify conjugal acts made intentionally infecund, one cannot invoke as valid reasons the lesser evil, or the fact that such acts would constitute a whole together with the fecund acts already performed or to follow later, and hence would share in one and the same moral goodness. In truth, if it is sometimes licit to tolerate a lesser evil in order to avoid a greater evil or to promote a greater good,[17] it is not licit, even for the gravest reasons, to do evil so that good may follow therefrom,[18] that is, to make into the object of a positive act of the will something which is intrinsically disorder, and hence unworthy of the human person, even when the intention is to safeguard or promote individual, family or social well-being. Consequently it is an error to think that a conjugal act which is deliberately made infecund and so is intrinsically dishonest could be made honest and right by the ensemble of a fecund conjugal life.

Licitness of Therapeutic Means

15. The Church, on the contrary, does not at all consider illicit the use of those therapeutic means truly necessary to cure diseases of the organism, even if an impediment to procreation, which may be foreseen, should result therefrom, provided such impediment is not, for whatever motive, directly willed.[19]

Licitness of Recourse to Infecund Periods

16. To this teaching of the Church on conjugal morals, the objection is made today, as we observed earlier (no. 3), that it is the prerogative of the human intellect to dominate the energies offered by irrational nature and to orientate them toward an end conformable to the good of man. Now, some may ask: in the present case, is it not reasonable in many circumstances to have recourse to artificial birth control if, thereby, we secure the harmony and peace of the family, and better conditions for the education of the children already born? To this question it is necessary to reply with clarity: the Church is the first to praise and recommend the intervention of intelligence in a function which so closely associates the rational creature with his Creator; but she affirms that this must be done with respect for the order established by God.

If, then, there are serious motives to space out births, which derive from the physical or psychological conditions of husband and wife, or from external conditions, the Church teaches that it is then licit to take into account the natural rhythms immanent in the generative functions, for the use of marriage in the infecund periods only, and in this way to regulate birth without offending the moral principles which have been recalled earlier.[20]

The Church is coherent with herself when she considers recourse to the infecund periods to be licit, while at the same time condemning, as being always illicit, the use of means directly contrary to fecundation, even if such use is inspired by reasons which may appear honest and serious. In reality, there are essential differences between the two cases; in the former, the married couple make legitimate use of a natural disposition; in the latter, they impede the development of natural processes. It is true that, in the one and the other case, the married couple are concordant in the positive will of avoiding children for plausible reasons, seeking the certainty that offspring will not arrive; but it is also true that only in the former case are they able to renounce the use of marriage in the fecund periods when, for just motives, procreation is not desirable, while making use of it during infecund periods to manifest their affection and to safeguard their mutual fidelity. By so doing, they give proof of a truly and integrally honest love.

Grave Consequences of Methods of Artificial Birth Control

17. Upright men can even better convince themselves of the solid grounds on which the teaching of the Church in this field is based, if they care to reflect upon the consequences of methods of artificial birth control. Let them consider, first of all, how wide and easy a road would thus be opened up toward conjugal infidelity and the general lowering of morality. Not much experience is needed in order to know human weakness, and to understand that men—especially the young, who are so vulnerable on this point—have need of encouragement to be faithful to the moral law, so that they must not be offered some easy means of eluding its observance. It is also to be feared that the man, growing used to the employment of anticonceptive practices, may finally lose respect for the woman and, no longer caring for her physical and psychological equilibrium, may come to the point of considering her as a mere instrument of selfish enjoyment, and no longer as his respected and beloved companion.

Let it be considered also that a dangerous weapon would thus be placed in the hands of those public authorities who take no heed of moral exigencies. Who could blame a government for applying to the solution of the problems of the community those means acknowledged to be licit for married couples in the solution of a family problem? Who will stop rulers from favoring, from even imposing upon their peoples, if they were to consider it necessary, the method of contraception which they judge to be most efficacious? In such a way men, wishing to avoid individual, family, or social difficulties encountered in the observance of the divine law, would reach the point of placing at the mercy of the intervention of public authorities the most personal and most reserved sector of conjugal intimacy.

Consequently, if the mission of generating life is not to be exposed to the arbitrary will of men, one must necessarily recognize unsurmountable limits to the possibility of man's domination over his own body and its functions; limits which no man, whether a private individual or one invested with authority, may licitly surpass. And such limits cannot be determined otherwise than by the respect due to the integrity of the human organism and its functions, according to the principles recalled earlier, and also according to the correct understanding of the "principle of totality" illustrated by our predecessor Pope Pius XII.[21]

The Church, Guarantor of True Human Values

18. It can be foreseen that this teaching will perhaps not be easily received by all. Too numerous are those voices—amplified by the modern means of propaganda—which are contrary to the voice of the Church. To tell the truth, the Church is not surprised to be made, like her divine founder, a "sign of contradiction,"[22] yet she does not because of this cease to proclaim with humble firmness the entire moral law, both natural and evangelical. Of such laws the Church was not the author, nor consequently can she be their arbiter; she is only their depositary and their interpreter, without ever being able to declare to be licit that which is not so by reason of its intimate and unchangeable opposition to the true good of man.

In defending conjugal morals in their integral wholeness, the Church knows that she contributes toward the establishment of a truly human civilization; she engages man not to abdicate from his own responsibility in order to rely on technical means; by that very fact she defends the dignity of man and wife. Faithful to both the teaching and the example of the Savior, she shows herself to be the sincere and disinterested friend of men, whom she wishes to help, even during their earthly sojourn, "to share as sons in the life of the living God, the Father of all men."[23]

III. PASTORAL DIRECTIVES

The Church, Mater et Magistra

19. Our words would not be an adequate expression of the thought and solicitude of the Church, mother and teacher of all peoples, if, after having recalled men to the observance and respect of the divine law regarding matrimony, we did not strengthen them in the path of honest regulation of birth, even amid the difficult conditions which today afflict families and peoples. The Church, in fact, cannot have a different conduct toward men than that of the Redeemer. She knows their weaknesses, has compassion on the crowd, receives sinners; but she cannot renounce the teaching of the law which is, in reality, that law proper to a human life restored to its original truth and conducted by the spirit of God.[24]

Possibility of Observing the Divine Law

20. The teaching of the Church on the regulation of birth, which promulgates the divine law, will easily appear to many to be difficult or even impossible of actuation. And indeed, like all great beneficent realities, it demands serious engagement and much effort, individual, family and social effort. More than that, it would not be practicable without the help of God, who upholds and strengthens the good will of men. Yet, to anyone who reflects well, it cannot but be clear that such efforts ennoble man and are beneficial to the human community.

Mastery of Self

21. The honest practice of regulation of birth demands first of all that husband and wife acquire and possess solid convictions concerning the true values of life and of the family, and that they tend toward securing perfect self-mastery. To dominate instinct by means of one's reason and free will undoubtedly requires ascetical practices, so that the affective manifestations of conjugal life may observe the correct order, in particular with regard to the observance of periodic continence. Yet this discipline which is proper to the purity of married couples, far from harming conjugal love, rather confers on it a higher human value. It demands continual effort, yet thanks to its beneficent influence, husband and wife fully develop their personalities, being enriched with spiritual values. Such discipline bestows upon family life fruits of serenity and peace, and facilitates the solution of other problems; it favors attention for one's partner, helps both parties to drive out selfishness, the enemy of true love, and deepens their sense of responsibility. By its means, parents acquire the capacity of having a deeper and more efficacious influence in the education of their offspring; little children and youths grow up with a just appraisal of human values, and in the serene and harmonious development of their spiritual and sensitive faculties.

Creating an Atmosphere Favorable to Chastity

22. On this occasion, we wish to draw the attention of educators, and of all who perform duties of responsibility in regard to the common good of human society, to the need of creating an atmosphere favorable to education in chastity, that is, to the triumph of healthy liberty over license by means of respect for the moral order.

Everything in the modern media of social communications which leads to sense excitation and unbridled customs, as well as every form of pornography and licentious performances, must arouse the frank and unanimous reaction of all those who are solicitous for the progress of civilization and the defense of the common good of the human spirit. Vainly would one seek to justify such depravation with the pretext of artistic or scientific exigencies,[25] or to deduce an argument from the freedom allowed in this sector by the public authorities.

Appeal to Public Authorities

23. To rulers, who are those principally responsible for the common good, and who can do so much to safeguard moral customs, we say: do not allow the morality of your peoples to be degraded; do not permit that by legal means practices contrary to the natural and divine law be introduced into that fundamental cell, the family. Quite other is the way in which public authorities can and must contribute to the solution of the demographic problem: namely, the way of a provident policy for the family, of a wise education of peoples in respect of moral law and the liberty of citizens.

We are well aware of the serious difficulties experienced by public authorities in this regard, especially in the developing countries. To their legitimate preoccupations we devoted our encyclical letter *Populorum Progressio* (The Development of Peoples). But with our predecessor Pope John XXIII, we repeat: no solution to these difficulties is acceptable "which does violence to man's essential dignity" and is based only on an utterly materialistic conception of man himself and of his life. The only possible solution to this question is one which envisages the social and economic progress both of individuals and of the whole of human society, and which respects and promotes true human values.[26] Neither can one, without grave injustice, consider divine providence to be responsible for what depends, instead, on a lack of wisdom in government, on an insufficient sense of social justice, on selfish monopolization, or again on blameworthy indolence in confronting the efforts and the sacrifices necessary to ensure the raising of living standards of a people and of all its sons.[27]

May all responsible public authorities—as some are already doing so laudably—generously revive their efforts. And may mutual aid between all the members of the great human family never cease to grow. This is an almost limitless field which thus opens up to the activity of the great international organizations.

To Men of Science

24. We wish now to express our encouragement to men of science, who "can considerably advance the welfare of marriage and the family, along with peace of conscience, if by pooling their efforts they labor to explain more thoroughly the various conditions favoring a proper regulation of births.[28] It is particularly desirable that, according to the wish already expressed by Pope Pius XII, medical science succeed in providing a sufficiently secure basis for a regulation of birth, founded on the observance of natural rhythms.[29] In this way, scientists and especially Catholic scientists will contribute to demonstrate in actual fact that, as the Church teaches, "a true contradiction cannot exist between the divine laws pertaining to the transmission of life and those pertaining to the fostering of authentic conjugal love."[30]

To Christian Husbands and Wives

25. And now our words more directly address our own children, particularly those whom God calls to serve him in marriage. The Church, while teaching imprescriptible demands of the divine law, announces the tidings of salvation, and by means of the sacraments opens up the paths of grace, which makes man a new creature, capable of corresponding with love and true freedom to the design of his Creator and Savior, and of finding the yoke of Christ to be sweet.[31]

Christian married couples, then, docile to her voice, must remember that their Christian vocation, which began at baptism, is further specified and reinforced by the sacrament of matrimony. By it husband and wife are strengthened and as it were consecrated for the faithful accomplishment of their proper duties, for the carrying out of their proper vocation even to perfection, and the Christian witness which is proper to them before the whole world.[32]

To them the Lord entrusts the task of making visible to men the holiness and sweetness of the law which unites the mutual love of husband and wife with their cooperation with the love of God, the Author of human life.

We do not at all intend to hide the sometimes serious difficulties inherent in the life of Christian married persons; for them as for everyone else, "the gate is narrow and the way is hard, that leads to life."[33] But the hope of that life must illuminate their way, as with courage they strive to live with wisdom, justice and piety in this present time,[34] knowing that the figure of this world passes away.[35]

Let married couples, then, face up to the efforts needed, supported by the faith and hope which "do not disappoint...because God's love has been poured into our hearts through the Holy Spirit, who has been given to us."[36] Let them implore divine assistance by persevering prayer; above all, let them draw from the source of grace and charity in the Eucharist. And if sin should still keep its hold over them, let them not be discouraged, but rather have recourse with humble perseverance to the mercy of God, which is poured forth in the Sacrament of Penance. In this way they will be enabled to achieve the fullness of conjugal life described by the Apostle: "Husbands, love your wives, as Christ loved the Church...husbands should love their wives as their own bodies. He who loves his wife loves himself. For no man ever hates his own flesh, but nourishes and cherishes it, as Christ does the Church.... This is a great mystery, and I mean in reference to Christ and the Church. However, let each one of you love his wife as himself, and let the wife see that she respects her husband."[37]

Apostolate in Homes

26. Among the fruits which ripen forth from a generous effort of fidelity to the divine law, one of the most precious is that married couples themselves not infrequently feel the desire to communicate their experience to others. Thus there comes to be included in the vast pattern of the vocation of the laity a new and most noteworthy form of the apostolate of like to like; it is married couples themselves who become apostles and guides to other married couples. This is assuredly, among so many forms of apostolate, one of those which seem most opportune today.[38]

To Doctors and Medical Personnel

27. We hold those physicians and medical personnel in the highest esteem who, in the exercise of their profession, value above every human interest the superior demands of their Christian vocation. Let them persevere, therefore, in promoting on every occasion the discovery of solutions inspired by faith and right reason; let them strive to arouse this conviction and this respect in their

associates. Let them also consider as their proper professional duty the task of acquiring all the knowledge needed in this delicate sector, so as to be able to give to those married persons who consult them wise counsel and healthy direction, such as they have a right to expect.

To Priests

28. Beloved priest sons, by vocation you are the counselors and spiritual guides of individual persons and of families. We now turn to you with confidence. Your first task—especially in the case of those who teach moral theology—is to expound the Church's teaching on marriage without ambiguity. Be the first to give, in the exercise of your ministry, the example of loyal internal and external obedience to the teaching authority of the Church. That obedience, as you know well, obliges not only because of the reasons adduced, but rather because of the light of the Holy Spirit, which is given in a particular way to the pastors of the Church in order that they may illustrate the truth.[39]

You know, too, that it is of the utmost importance, for peace of consciences and for the unity of the Christian people, that in the field of morals as well as in that of dogma, all should attend to the magisterium of the Church, and all should speak the same language. Hence, with all our heart we renew to you the heartfelt plea of the great Apostle Paul: "I appeal to you, brethren, by the name of our Lord Jesus Christ, that all of you agree and that there be no dissensions among you, but that you be united in the same mind and the same judgment."[40]

29. To diminish in no way the saving teaching of Christ constitutes an eminent form of charity for souls. But this must ever be accompanied by patience and goodness, such as the Lord himself gave example of in dealing with men. Having come not to condemn but to save,[41] he was intransigent with evil, but merciful toward individuals. In their difficulties, may married couples always find, in the words and in the heart of a priest, the echo of the voice and the love of the Redeemer.

And then speak with confidence, beloved sons, fully convinced that the spirit of God, while he assists the Magisterium in proposing doctrine, illumines internally the hearts of the faithful inviting them to give their assent. Teach married couples the indispensable way of prayer; prepare them to have recourse often and with faith to the Sacraments of the Eucharist and of Penance, without ever allowing themselves to be discouraged by their own weakness.

To Bishops

30. Beloved and venerable brothers in the episcopate, with whom we most intimately share the solicitude of the spiritual good of the people of God, at the conclusion of this encyclical our reverent and affectionate thoughts turn to you. To all of you we extend an urgent invitation. At the head of the priests, your collaborators, and of your faithful, work ardently and incessantly for the safe-

guarding and the holiness of marriage, so that it may always be lived in its entire human and Christian fullness. Consider this mission as one of your most urgent responsibilities at the present time.

As you know, it implies concerted pastoral action in all the fields of human activity, economic, cultural and social; for, in fact, only a simultaneous improvement in these various sectors will make it possible to render the life of parents and of children within their families not only tolerable, but easier and more joyous, to render the living together in human society more fraternal and peaceful, in faithfulness to God's design for the world.

Final Appeal

31. Venerable brothers, most beloved sons, and all men of good will, great indeed is the work of education, of progress and of love to which we call you, upon the foundation of the Church's teaching, of which the successor of Peter is, together with his brothers in the episcopate, the depositary and interpreter. Truly a great work, as we are deeply convinced, both for the world and for the Church, since man cannot find true happiness—toward which he aspires with all his being-other than in respect of the laws written by God in his very nature, laws which he must observe with intelligence and love. Upon this work, and upon all of you, and especially upon married couples, we invoke the abundant graces of the God of holiness and mercy, and in pledge thereof we impart to you all our apostolic blessing.

Given at Rome, from St. Peter's, this 25th day of July, feast of St. James the Apostle, in the year 1968, the sixth of our pontificate.

PAULUS PP. VI

NOTES

[1] Cf. Pius IX, Encyclical Letter *Qui Pluribus* (Nov. 9, 1846): PII IX P.M. Acta, I, 9-10; St. Pius X, Encyclical Letter *Singulari Quadam* (Sept. 24, 1912): *AAS* 4 (1912), 658; Pius XI, Encyclical Letter *Casti Connubii* (Dec. 31, 1930): *AAS* 22 (1930), 579-581; Pius XII, Allocution *Magnificate Dominum* to the Episcopate of the Catholic World (Nov. 2, 1954): *AAS* 46 (1954), 671-672; John XXIII, Encyclical Letter *Mater et Magistra* (May 15, 1961): *AAS* 53 (1961), 457.

[2] Cf. Mt 28:18-19.

[3] Cf. Mt 7:21.

[4] Cf. *Catechismus Romanus Concilii Tridentini,* part II, Ch. VIII; Leo XII, Encyclical Letter *Arcanum* (Feb. 19, 1880): *Acta Leonis* XIII, II (1881), 26-29; Pius XI, Encyclical Letter *Divini Illius Magistri* (Dec. 31, 1929): *AAS* 22 (1930), 58-61; Encyclical Letter *Casti Connubii*: *AAS* 22 (1930), 545-546; Pius XII, Allocution to the Italian Medico-biological Union of St. Luke (Nov. 12, 1944): *Discorsi e Radiomessaggi,* VI,

191-192; To the Italian Catholic Union of Midwives (Oct. 29, 1951): *AAS* 43 (1951), 857-859; To the Seventh Congress of the International Society of Hematology (Sept. 12, 1958): *AAS* 50 (1958), 734-735; John XXIII, Encyclical Letter *Mater et Magistra: AAS* 53 (1961), 446-447; *Codex Iuris Canonici,* Canon 1067; Can. 1968, S1, Can. 1066 S1-2; Second Vatican Ecumenical Council, Pastoral Constitution on the Church in the Modern World *Gaudium et Spes,* 47-52.

⁵ Cf. Paul VI, Allocution to the Sacred College (June 23, 1964): *AAS* 56 (1964), 588; To the Commission for Study of Problems of Population, Family and Birth (March 27, 1965): *AAS* 57 (1965), 388; To the National Congress of the Italian Society of Obstetrics and Gynecology (Oct. 29, 1966): *AAS* 58 (1966), 1168.

⁶ Cf. 1 Jn 4:8.

⁷ Cf. Eph 3:15.

⁸ Cf. Second Vatican Ecumenical Council, Pastoral Constitution on the Church in the Modern World *Gaudium et Spes,* 50.

⁹ Cf. St. Thomas, *Summa Theologiae,* I-II, q. 94, art. 2.

¹⁰ Cf. Pastoral Constitution on the Church in the Modern World *Gaudium et Spes,* 50-51.

¹¹ *Ibid.,* 49.

¹² Cf. Pius XI, Encyclical Letter *Casti Connubii: AAS* 22 (1930), 560; Pius XII: *AAS* 43 (1951), 843.

¹³ Cf. John XXIII, Encyclical Letter *Mater et Magistra: AAS* 53 (1961), 447.

¹⁴ Cf. *Catechismus Romanus Concilii Tridentini,* part. II, Ch. VIII; Pius XI, Encyclical Letter *Casti Connubii: AAS* 22 (1930), 562-564; Pius XII, *Discorsi e Radiomessaggi,* VI (1944), 191-192; *AAS* 43 (1951), 842-843, 857-859; John XXIII, Encyclical Letter *Pacem in Terris* (Apr. 11, 1963): *AAS* 55 (1963), 259-260; *Gaudium et Spes,* 51.

¹⁵ Cf. Pius XI, Encyclical Letter *Casti Connubii: AAS* 22 (1930), 565; Decree of the Holy Office (Feb. 22, 1940): *AAS* 50 (1958), 734-735.

¹⁶ Cf. *Catechismus Romanus Concilii Tridentini,* part. II, Ch. VIII; Pius XI, Encyclical Letter *Casti Connubii: AAS* 22 (1930), 559-561; Pius XII, *AAS* 43 (1951), 843; *AAS* 50 (1958), 734-735; John XXIII, Encyclical Letter *Mater et Magistra: AAS* 53 (1961), 447.

¹⁷ Cf. Pius XII, Allocution to the National Congress of the Union of Catholic Jurists (Dec. 6, 1953): *AAS* 45 (1953), 798-799.

¹⁸ Cf. Rom 3:8.

¹⁹ Cf. Pius XII, Allocution to Congress of the Italian Association of Urology (October 8, 1953): *AAS* 45 (1953), 674-675; *AAS* 50 (1958), 734-735.

²⁰ Cf. Pius XII: *AAS* 43 (1951), 846.

²¹ Cf. *AAS* 45 (1953), 674-675; *AAS* 48 (1956), 461-462.

²² Cf. Lk 2:34.

²³ Cf. Paul VI, Encyclical Letter *Populorum Progressio* (March 26, 1967): 21.

²⁴ Cf. Rom 8.

²⁵ Cf. Second Vatican Ecumenical Council, Decree on the Media of Social Communications *Inter Mirifica,* 6-7.

[26] Cf. Encyclical Letter *Mater et Magistra: AAS* 53 (1961), 447.

[27] Cf. Encyclical Letter *Populorum Progressio,* 48-55.

[28] Cf. Pastoral Constitution on the Church in the Modern World *Gaudium et Spes,* 52.

[29] Cf. *AAS* 43 (1951), 859.

[30] Cf. Pastoral Constitution on the Church in the Modern World *Gaudium et Spes,* 51.

[31] Cf. Mt 11:30.

[32] Cf. Pastoral Constitution on the Church in the Modern World *Gaudium et Spes,* 48; Second Vatican Ecumenical Council, Dogmatic Constitution on the Church *Lumen Gentium,* 35.

[33] Mt 7:14; cf. Heb 11:12.

[34] Cf. Ti 2:12.

[35] Cf. 1 Cor 7:31.

[36] Cf. Rom 5:5.

[37] Eph 5:25, 28-29, 32-33.

[38] Cf. Dogmatic Constitution on the Church *Lumen Gentium,* 35 and 41; Pastoral Constitution on the Church in the Modern World *Gaudium et Spes,* 48-49; Decree on the Apostolate of the Laity *Apostolicam Actuositatem,* 11.

[39] Cf. Dogmatic Constitution on the Church *Lumen Gentium,* 25.

[40] Cf. 1 Cor 1:10.

[41] Cf. Jn 3:17.

On the Dignity and Vocation of Women on the Occasion of the Marian Year

Venerable Brothers and dear Sons and Daughters,
Health and the Apostolic Blessing.

I. INTRODUCTION

A Sign of the Times

1. The dignity and the vocation of women—a subject of constant human and Christian reflection—have gained exceptional prominence in recent years. This can be seen, for example, *in the statements of the Church's Magisterium* present in various documents of the *Second Vatican Council,* which declares in its Closing Message: "The hour is coming, in fact has come, when the vocation of women is being acknowledged in its fullness, the hour in which women acquire in the world an influence, an effect and a power never hitherto achieved. That is why, at this moment when the human race is undergoing so deep a transformation, women imbued with a spirit of the Gospel can do so much to aid humanity in not falling."[1] *This Message* sums up what had already been expressed in the Council's teaching, specifically in the Pastoral Constitution *Gaudium et Spes*[2] and in the Decree on the Apostolate of the Laity *Apostolicam Actuositatem.*[3]

Similar thinking had already been put forth in the period before the Council, as can be seen in a number of Pope *Pius XII's* Discourses[4] and in the Encyclical *Pacem in Terris* of Pope *John XXIII.*[5] After the Second Vatican Council, my predecessor *Paul VI* showed the relevance of this "sign of the times" when he conferred the title "Doctor of the Church" upon St. Teresa of Jesus and St. Catherine of Siena,[6] and likewise when, at the request of the 1971 Assembly of the Synod of Bishops, he set up *a special Commission* for the study of contemporary problems concerning the *"effective promotion of the dignity and the responsibility of women."*[7] In one of his Discourses Paul VI said: "Within Christianity, more than in any other religion, and since its very beginning, women have had a special dignity, of which the New Testament shows us many important aspects...; it is evident that women are meant to form part of the living and working structure of Christianity in so prominent a manner that perhaps not all their potentialities have yet been made clear."[8]

The Fathers of the recent Assembly of the Synod of Bishops (October 1987), which was devoted to "The Vocation and Mission of the Laity in the Church and in the World Twenty Years after the Second Vatican Council," once more dealt with the dignity and vocation of women. One of their recommendations was for a further study of the anthropological and theological bases that are needed in order to solve the problems connected with the meaning and dignity of being a woman and of being a man. It is a question of understanding the reason for and the consequences of the Creator's decision that the human being should always and only exist as a woman or a man. It is only by beginning from these bases, which make it possible to understand the greatness of the dignity and vocation of women, that one is able to speak of their active presence in the Church and in society.

This is what I intend to deal with in this document. The Post-Synodal Exhortation, which will be published later, will present proposals of a pastoral nature on the place of women in the Church and in society. On this subject the Fathers offered some important reflections, after they had taken into consideration the testimonies of the lay auditors—both women and men—from the particular Churches throughout the world.

The Marian Year

2. The last Synod took place *within the Marian Year,* which gives special thrust to the consideration of this theme, as the Encyclical *Redemptoris Mater* points out.[9] This Encyclical develops and updates the Second Vatican Council's teaching contained in Chapter VIII of the Dogmatic Constitution on the Church *Lumen Gentium.* The title of this chapter is significant: *"The Blessed Virgin Mary, the Mother of God, in the Mystery of Christ and of the Church."* Mary—the "woman" of the Bible (cf. Gn 3:15; Jn 2:4; 19:16)—intimately belongs to the salvific mystery of Christ, and is therefore also present in a special way in the mystery of the Church. Since "the Church is in Christ as a sacrament...of intimate union with God and of the unity of the whole human race,"[10] the special presence of the Mother of God in the mystery of the Church makes us think *of the exceptional link between this "woman" and the whole human family.* It is a question here of every man and woman, all the sons and daughters of the human race, in whom from generation to generation a *fundamental inheritance* is realized, the inheritance that belongs to all humanity and that is linked with the mystery of the biblical "beginning": "God created man in his own image, in the image of God he created him; male and female he created them" (Gn 1:27).[11]

This eternal *truth about the human being,*—man and woman—a truth which is immutably fixed in human experience—*at the same time constitutes the mys-*

tery which only in "the Incarnate Word takes on light...(since) Christ fully reveals man to himself and makes his supreme calling clear," as the Council teaches.[12] In this "revealing of man to himself," do we not need to find a special place for that "woman" who was the Mother of Christ? Cannot the *"message" of Christ,* contained in the Gospel, which has as its background the whole of Scripture, both the Old and the New Testament, say much to the Church and to humanity about the dignity of women and their vocation?

This is precisely what is meant to be the common thread running throughout the present document, which fits into the broader context of the Marian Year, as we approach the end of the second millennium after Christ's birth and the beginning of the third. And it seems to me that the best thing is to *give this text the style and character of a meditation.*

II. WOMAN—MOTHER OF GOD *(THEOTÓKOS)*

Union with God

3. "When the time had fully come, *God sent forth his son, born of woman."* With these words of his Letter to the Galatians (4:4), the Apostle Paul links together the principal moments which essentially determine the fulfillment of the mystery "predetermined in God" (cf. Eph 1:9). The Son, the Word, one in substance with the Father, becomes man, born of a woman, at "the fullness of time." This event leads *to the turning point* of man's history on earth, understood as salvation history. It is significant that St. Paul does not call the Mother of Christ by her own name "Mary," but calls her "woman": this coincides with the words of the Proto-evangelium in the Book of Genesis (cf. 3:15). She is that "woman" who is present in the central salvific event which marks the "fullness of time": this event is realized in her and through her.

Thus there begins *the central event, the key event in the history of salvation:* the Lord's Paschal Mystery. Perhaps it would be worthwhile to reconsider it from the point of view of man's spiritual history, understood in the widest possible sense, and as this history is expressed through the different world religions. Let us recall at this point the words of the Second Vatican Council: *"People look to the various religions for answers* to those profound mysteries of the human condition which, today, even as in olden times, deeply stir the human heart: What is a human being? What is the meaning and purpose of our life? What is goodness and what is sin? What gives rise to our sorrows, and to what intent? Where lies the path to true happiness? What is the truth about death, judgment and retribution beyond the grave? What, finally, is *that ultimate and unutterable mystery which engulfs our being,* and from which we take our origin and toward which we move?"[13] From ancient times down to the present, there has existed among different peoples a certain perception of that hidden power which is present in the course of things and in the events of human life; at times, indeed, recognition can be found of a Supreme Divinity or even a Supreme Father."[14]

Against the background of this broad panorama, which testifies to the aspirations of the human spirit in search of God—at times as it were "groping its way" (cf. Acts 17:27)—the "fullness of time" spoken of in Paul's Letter emphasizes *the response of God himself,* "in whom we live and move and have our being" (cf. Acts 17:28). This is the God who "in many and various ways spoke of old to our fathers by the prophets, but in these last days has spoken to us by a Son" (Heb 1:1-2). The sending of this Son, one in substance with the Father, as a man "born of woman," constitutes the culminating and *definitive point of God's self-revelation to humanity.* This self-revelation is *salvific in character,* as the Second Vatican Council teaches in another passage: "In his goodness and wisdom, God chose to reveal himself and to make known to us the hidden purpose of his will (cf. Eph 1:9) by which through Christ, the Word made flesh, man has access to the Father in the Holy Spirit and comes to share in the divine nature (cf. Eph 2:18; 2 Pt 1:4)."[15]

A woman is to be found at the *center of this salvific event.* The self-revelation of God, who is the inscrutable unity of the Trinity, is outlined *in the Annunciation at Nazareth.* "Behold, you will conceive in your womb and bear a son, and you shall call his name Jesus. He will be great, and will be called the Son of the Most High...." "How shall this be, since I have no husband?..." "The Holy Spirit will come upon you, and the power of the Most High will overshadow you; therefore the child to be born will be called holy, the Son of God.... For with God nothing will be impossible" (cf. Lk 1:31-37).[16]

It may be easy to think of this even *in the setting* of the *history of Israel,* the Chosen People of which Mary is a daughter, but it is also easy to think of it in the context of all the different ways in which humanity has always sought to answer the fundamental and definitive questions which most beset it. Do we not find in the Annunciation at Nazareth the beginning of that definitive answer by which God *himself "attempts to calm people's hearts"*?[17] It is not just a matter here of God's words revealed through the Prophets; rather with this response "the Word is truly made flesh" (cf. Jn 1:14). Hence *Mary* attains *a union with God that exceeds* all the expectations of the human spirit. It even exceeds the expectations of all Israel, in particular the daughters of this Chosen People, who, on the basis of the promise, could hope that one of their number would one day become the mother of the Messiah. Who among them, however, could have imagined that the promised Messiah would be "the Son of the Most High"? On the basis of the Old Testament's monotheistic faith such a thing was difficult to imagine. Only by the power of the Holy Spirit, who "overshadowed" her, was Mary able to accept what is "impossible with men, but not with God" (cf. Mk 10:27).

Theotókos

4. Thus the "fullness of time" manifests the extraordinary dignity of the "woman." On the one hand, this dignity consists *in the supernatural elevation to union with God* in Jesus Christ, which determines the ultimate finality of the

existence of every person both on earth and in eternity. From this point of view, the "woman" is the representative and the archetype of the whole human race: she *represents the humanity* which belongs to all human beings, both men and women. On the other hand, however, the event at Nazareth highlights a form of union with the living God which can *only belong to the "woman,"* Mary: *the union between mother and son.* The Virgin of Nazareth truly becomes the Mother of God.

This truth, which Christian faith has accepted from the beginning, was solemnly defined at the Council of Ephesus (431 A.D.).[18] In opposition to the opinion of Nestorius, who held that Mary was only the mother of the man Jesus, this Council emphasized the essential meaning of the motherhood of the Virgin Mary. At the moment of the Annunciation, by responding with her *"fiat,"* Mary conceived a man who was the Son of God, of one substance with the Father. Therefore *she is truly the Mother of God, because motherhood concerns the whole person,* not just the body, nor even just human "nature." In this way the name *"Theotókos"*—Mother of God—became the name proper to the union with God granted to the Virgin Mary.

The particular union of the "Theotókos" with God—which fulfills in the most eminent manner the supernatural predestination to union with the Father which is granted to every human being *(filii in Filio)*—is a pure grace and, as such, *a gift of the Spirit.* At the same time, however, through her response of faith Mary exercises her free will and thus fully shares with her personal and feminine "I" in the event of the Incarnation. With her *"fiat,"* Mary becomes the authentic subject of that union with God which was realized in the mystery of the Incarnation of the Word, who is of one substance with the Father. All of God's action in human history at all times respects the free will of the human "I." And such was the case with the Annunciation at Nazareth.

"To Serve Means to Reign"

5. This event is clearly *interpersonal in character:* it is a dialogue. We only understand it fully if we place the whole conversation between the Angel and Mary in the context of the words: "full of grace."[19] The whole Annunciation dialogue reveals the essential dimension of the event, namely, its *supernatural* dimension. Grace never casts nature aside or cancels it out, but rather perfects it and ennobles it *(kécharitôménê).* Therefore *the "fullness of grace"* that was granted to the Virgin of Nazareth, with a view to the fact that she would become *"Theotókos,"* also *signifies the fullness of the perfection of "what is characteristic of woman,"* of *"what is feminine."* Here we find ourselves, in a sense, at the culminating point, the archetype, of the personal dignity of women.

When Mary responds to the words of the heavenly messenger with her "fiat," she who is "full of grace" feels the need to express her personal relationship to the gift that has been revealed to her, saying: *"Behold, I am the handmaid of the Lord"* (Lk 1:38). This statement should not be deprived of its profound meaning, nor should it be diminished by artificially removing it from the overall context of the event and from the full content of the truth revealed about God and man. In the expression "handmaid of the Lord," one senses Mary's complete awareness of being a creature of God. The word "handmaid," near the end of the Annunciation dialogue, is inscribed throughout the whole history of the Mother and the Son. In fact, this *Son,* who is the true and consubstantial "Son of the Most High," will often say of himself, especially at the culminating moment of his mission: "The Son of Man came not to be served but to serve" (Mk 10:45).

At all times Christ is aware of being "the servant of the Lord" according to the prophecy of Isaiah (cf. Is 42:1; 49:3, 6; 52:13) which includes the essential content of his messianic mission, namely, his awareness of being the Redeemer of the world. From the first moment of her divine motherhood, of her union with the Son whom "the Father sent into the world, that the world might be saved through him" (cf. Jn 3:17), *Mary takes her place within Christ's messianic service.*[20] It is precisely this service which constitutes the very foundation of that Kingdom in which "to serve...means to reign."[21] Christ, the "Servant of the Lord," will show all people the royal dignity of service, the dignity which is joined in the closest possible way to the vocation of every person.

Thus, by considering the reality "Woman—Mother of God," we enter in a very appropriate way into this Marian Year meditation. *This reality* also *determines the essential horizon of reflection on the dignity and the vocation of women.* In anything we think, say or do concerning the dignity and the vocation of women, our thoughts, hearts and actions must not become detached from this horizon. The dignity of every human being and the vocation corresponding to that dignity find their definitive measure in *union with God.* Mary, the woman of the Bible, is the most complete expression of this dignity and vocation. For no human being, male or female, created in the image and likeness of God, can *in any* way attain fulfillment apart from this image and likeness.

III. THE IMAGE AND LIKENESS OF GOD

The Book of Genesis

6. Let us enter into the setting of the biblical "beginning." In it the revealed truth concerning man as "the image and likeness" of God constitutes the immutable *basis of all Christian anthropology.*[22] "God created man in his own image, in the image of God he created him; male and female he created them" (Gn 1:27). This concise passage contains the fundamental anthropological truths: man is the high point of the whole order of creation in the visible world; the human race, which takes its origin from the calling into existence of man and woman, crowns the whole work of creation; *both man and woman are human beings to an equal degree,* both are created *in God's image.* This image and like-

ness of God, which is essential for the human being, is passed on by the man and woman, as spouses and parents, to their descendants: "Be fruitful and multiply, and fill the earth and subdue it" (Gn 1:28). The Creator entrusts dominion over the earth to the human race, to all persons, to all men and women, who derive their dignity and vocation from the common "beginning."

In the Book of Genesis we find another description of the creation of man— man and woman (cf. 2:18-25)—to which we shall refer shortly. At this point, however, we can say that the biblical account puts forth the truth about the personal character of the human being. *Man is a person, man and woman equally so,* since both were created in the image and likeness of the personal God. What makes man like God is the fact that—unlike the whole world of other living creatures, including those endowed with senses *(animalia)*—man is also a rational being *(animal rationale).*[23] Thanks to this property, man and woman are able to "dominate" the other creatures of the visible world (cf. Gn 1:28).

The second description of the creation of man (cf. Gn 2:18-25) makes use of different language to express the truth about the creation of man, and especially of woman. In a sense the language is less precise, and, one might say, more descriptive and metaphorical—closer to the language of the myths known at the time. Nevertheless, we find no essential contradiction between the two texts. The text of Genesis 2:18-25 helps us to understand better what we find in the concise passage of Genesis 1:27-28. At the same time, if it is read together with the latter, it *helps us to understand even more profoundly* the fundamental *truth* which it contains *concerning man* created as man and woman in the image and likeness of God.

In the description found in Genesis 2:18-25, the woman is created by God "from the rib" of the man and is placed at his side as another "I"—as the companion of the man, who is alone in the surrounding world of living creatures and who finds in none of them a "helper" suitable for himself. Called into existence in this way, the woman is immediately recognized by the man as "flesh of his flesh and bone of his bones" (cf. Gn 2:23) and for this very reason she is called "woman." In biblical language this name indicates her essential identity with regard to man—*'is-'issah*—something which unfortunately modern languages in general are unable to express: "She shall be called woman *('issah)* because she was taken out of man *('is)*" (Gn 2:23).

The biblical text provides sufficient bases for recognizing the essential equality of man and woman from the point of view of their humanity.[24] From the very beginning, both are persons, unlike the other living beings in the world about them. *The woman* is *another "I" in a common humanity.* From the very beginning they appear as a "unity of the two": and this signifies that the original solitude is overcome, the solitude in which man does not find "a helper fit for him" (Gn 2:20). Is it only a question here of a "helper" in activity, in "subduing the earth" (cf. Gn 1:28)? Certainly it is a matter of a life's companion, with whom, as a wife, the man can unite himself, becoming with her "one flesh" and for this reason leaving "his father and his mother" (cf. Gn 2:24). Thus in the same context as the creation of man and woman, the biblical account speaks of God's *instituting marriage* as an indispensable condition for the transmission of life to new generations, the transmission of life to which marriage and conjugal love are by their nature ordered: "Be fruitful and multiply, and fill the earth and subdue it" (Gn 1:28).

Person-Communion-Gift

7. By reflecting on the whole account found in Genesis 2:18-25, and by interpreting it in light of the truth about the image and likeness of God (cf. Gn 1:26-27), we can *understand* even *more fully what constitutes the personal character* of the human being, thanks to which both man and woman are like God. For every individual is made in the image of God, insofar as he or she is a rational and free creature capable of knowing God and loving him. Moreover, we read that man cannot exist "alone" (cf. Gn 2:18); he can exist only as a "unity of the two," and therefore *in relation to another human person.* It is a question here of a mutual relationship: man to woman and woman to man. Being a person in the image and likeness of God thus also involves existing in a relationship, in relation to the other "I." This is a prelude to the definitive self-revelation of the Triune God: a living unity in the communion of the Father, Son and Holy Spirit.

At the beginning of the Bible this is not yet stated directly. The whole Old Testament is mainly concerned with revealing the truth about the oneness and unity of God. Within this fundamental truth about God the New Testament will reveal the inscrutable mystery of God's inner life. *God,* who allows himself to be known by human beings through Christ, is the *unity of the Trinity:* unity in communion. In this way new light is also thrown on man's image and likeness to God, spoken of in the Book of Genesis. The fact that man "created as man and woman" is the image of God means not only that each of them individually is like God, as a rational and free being. It also means that man and woman, created as a "unity of the two" in their common humanity, are called to live in a communion of love, and in this way to mirror in the world the communion of love that is in God, through which the Three Persons love each other in the intimate mystery of the one divine life. The Father, Son and Holy Spirit, one God through the unity of the divinity, exist as persons through the inscrutable divine relationship. Only in this way can we understand the truth that God in himself is love (cf. 1 Jn 4:16).

The image and likeness of God in man, created as man and woman (in the analogy that can be presumed between Creator and creature), thus also expresses the "unity of the two" in a common humanity. This "unity of the two," which is a sign of interpersonal communion, *shows that the creation of man* is also marked by a certain likeness to the divine communion *("communio").* This likeness is a quality of the personal being of both man and woman, and is also a call and a task. The foundation of the whole *human "ethos"* is rooted in the image and likeness of God which the human being bears within himself from the beginning. Both the Old and New Testament will develop that "ethos," which reaches its apex in the *commandment of love.*[25]

In the "unity of the two," man and woman are called from the beginning not only to exist "side by side" or "together," but they are also called *to exist mutually "one for the other."*

This also explains the meaning of the "help" spoken of in Genesis 2:18-25: "I will make him *a helper fit for him."* The biblical context enables us to understand this in the sense that the woman must "help" the man—and in his turn he must help her—first of all by the very fact of their "being human persons." In a certain sense this enables man and woman to discover their humanity ever anew and to confirm its whole meaning. We can easily understand that—on this fundamental level—it is *a question of a "help" on the part of both, and at the same time a mutual "help."* To be human means to be called to interpersonal communion. The text of Genesis 2:18-25 shows that marriage is the first and, in a sense, the fundamental dimension of this call. But it is not the only one. The whole of human history unfolds within the context of this call. In this history, on the basis of the principle of mutually being "for" the other, in interpersonal "communion," there develops in humanity itself, in accordance with God's will, the integration of *what is "masculine" and what is "feminine."* The biblical texts, from Genesis onward, constantly enable us to discover the ground in which the truth about man is rooted, the solid and inviolable ground amid the many changes of human existence.

This truth also has to do with *the history of salvation.* In this regard a statement of the Second Vatican Council is especially significant. In the chapter on "The Community of Mankind" in the Pastoral Constitution *Gaudium et Spes,* we read: "The Lord Jesus, when he prayed to the Father 'that all may be one...as we are one' (Jn 17:21-22), opened up vistas closed to human reason. For he implied *a certain likeness* between the union of the divine Persons and the union of God's children in truth and charity. This likeness reveals that man, who is the only creature on earth which God willed for its own sake, cannot fully find himself except through a sincere gift of self."[26]

With these words, the Council text presents a summary of the whole truth about man and woman—a truth which is already outlined in the first chapters of the Book of Genesis, and which is the structural basis of biblical and Christian anthropology. *Man*—whether man or woman—*is the only being among the creatures* of the visible world *that God the Creator "has willed for its own sake";* that creature is thus a person. Being a person means striving toward self-realization (the Council text speaks of self-discovery), which can only be achieved *"through a sincere gift of self."* The model for this interpretation of the person is God himself as Trinity, as a communion of Persons. To say that man is created in the image and likeness of God means that man is called to exist "for" others, to become a gift.

This applies to every human being, whether woman or man, who lives it out in accordance with the special qualities proper to each. Within the framework of the present meditation on the dignity and vocation of women, this truth about being human constitutes the *indispensable point of departure.* Already in the Book of Genesis we can discern, in preliminary outline, the spousal character of the relationship between persons, which will serve as the basis for the subsequent development of the truth about motherhood, and about virginity, as two particular dimensions of the vocation of women in the light of divine Revelation. These two dimensions will find their loftiest expression at the "fullness of time" (cf. Gal 4:4) in the "woman" of Nazareth: the Virgin-Mother.

The Anthropomorphism of Biblical Language

8. The presentation of man as "the image and likeness of God" at the very beginning of Sacred Scripture has *another significance too.* It is the key for understanding biblical Revelation as God's word about himself. Speaking about himself, whether through the prophets, or through the Son (cf. Heb 1:1, 2) who became man, *God speaks in human language,* using human concepts and images. If this manner of expressing himself is characterized by a certain anthropomorphism, the reason is that man is "like" God: created in his image and likeness. But then, *God too* is in some measure "like man," and precisely because of this likeness, he can be humanly known. At the same time, the language of the Bible is sufficiently precise to indicate the limits of the "likeness," the limits of the "analogy." For biblical Revelation says that, while man's "likeness" to God is true, the *"non-likeness"*[27] which separates the whole of creation from the Creator is *still more essentially true.* Although man is created in God's likeness, God does not cease to be for him the one "who dwells in unapproachable light" (1 Tim 6:16): he is the "Different One," by essence the "totally Other."

This observation on the limits of the analogy—the limits of man's likeness to God in biblical language—must also be kept in mind when, in different passages of Sacred Scripture (especially in the Old Testament), we find *comparisons that attribute to God "masculine" or "feminine" qualities.* We find in these passages an indirect confirmation of the truth that both man and woman were created in the image and likeness of God. If there is a likeness between Creator and creatures, it is understandable that the Bible would refer to God using expressions that attribute to him both "masculine" and "feminine" qualities.

We may quote here some characteristic passages from the prophet Isaiah: "But Zion said, 'The Lord has forsaken me, my Lord has forgotten me.' *Can a woman forget* her sucking child, that she should have no compassion on the son of her womb? Even these may forget, yet *I* will *not* forget you'" (49:14-15). And elsewhere: *"As one whom his mother comforts, so will I comfort you; you shall be comforted in Jerusalem"* (66:13). In the Psalms too God is compared to a caring mother: "Like a child quieted at its mother's breast; like a child that is quieted is my soul. O Israel, hope in the Lord" (Ps 131:2-3). In various passages the love of God who cares for his people is shown to be like that of a mother: thus, *like a mother God* "has carried" humanity, and in particular, his Chosen People, within his own womb; he has given birth to it in travail, has nourished and comforted it (cf. Is 42:14; 46:3-4). In many passages God's love is presented as the "masculine" love of the bridegroom and father (cf. Hos 11:1-4; Jer 3:4-19), but also sometimes as the "feminine" love of a mother.

This characteristic of biblical language—its anthropomorphic way of speaking about God—*points* indirectly *to the mystery of the eternal "generating"* which belongs to the inner life of God. Nevertheless, in itself this "generating" has neither "masculine" nor "feminine" qualities. It is by nature totally divine. It is spiritual in the most perfect way, since "God is Spirit" (Jn 4:24) and possesses no property typical of the body, neither "feminine" nor "masculine." Thus even *"fatherhood" in God is completely divine* and free of the "masculine" bodily characteristics proper to human fatherhood. In this sense the Old Testament spoke of God as a Father and turned to him as a Father. Jesus Christ—who called God "Abba-Father" (Mk 14:36), and who as the only-begotten and consubstantial Son placed this truth at the very center of his Gospel, thus establishing the norm of Christian prayer—referred to fatherhood in this ultra-corporeal, superhuman and completely divine sense. He spoke as the Son, joined to the Father by the eternal mystery of divine generation, and he did so while being at the same time the truly human Son of his Virgin Mother.

Although it is not possible to attribute human qualities to the eternal generation of the Word of God, and although the divine fatherhood does not possess "masculine" characteristics in a physical sense, we must nevertheless seek in God the absolute *model* of all *"generation"* among human beings. This would seem to be the sense of the Letter to the Ephesians: "I bow my knees before the Father, from whom every family in heaven and on earth is named" (3:14-15). All "generating" among creatures finds its primary model in that generating which in God is completely divine, that is, spiritual. All "generating" in the created world is to be likened to this absolute and uncreated model. Thus every element of human generation which is proper to man, and every element which is proper to woman, namely human *"fatherhood"* and *"motherhood,"* bears within itself a likeness to, or analogy with the divine "generating" and with that "fatherhood" which in God is "totally different"—that is, completely spiritual and divine in essence; whereas in the human order, generation is proper to the "unity of the two": both are "parents," the man and the woman alike.

IV. EVE—MARY

The "Beginning" and the Sin

9. "Although he was made by God in a state of justice, from the very dawn of history man abused his liberty, at the urging of the Evil One. Man set himself against God and sought to find fulfillment apart from God."[28] With these words the teaching of the last Council recalls the revealed doctrine about sin and in particular about that first sin, which is the "original" one. The biblical "beginning"—the creation of the world and of man in the world—*contains* in itself *the truth* about *this sin*, which can also be called the sin of man's "beginning" on the earth. Even though what is written in the Book of Genesis is expressed in the form of a symbolic narrative, as is the case in the description of the creation of man as male and female (cf. Gn 2:18-25), at the same time it reveals what should be called "the mystery of sin," and even more fully, "the mystery of evil" which exists in the world created by God.

It is not possible to read "the mystery of sin" without making reference to the whole truth about the "image and likeness" to God, which is the basis of biblical anthropology. This truth presents the creation of man as a special gift from the Creator, containing not only the foundation and source of the essential dignity of the human being—man and woman—in the created world, but also *the beginning of the call to both of them to share in the intimate life of God himself.* In the light of Revelation, *creation likewise means the beginning of salvation history.* It is precisely in this beginning that sin is situated and manifests itself as opposition and negation.

It can be said, paradoxically, that the sin presented in the third chapter of Genesis confirms the truth about the image and likeness of God in man, since this truth means freedom, that is, man's use of free will by choosing good or his abuse of it by choosing evil, against the will of God. In its essence, however, sin is a negation of God as Creator in his relationship to man, and of what God wills for man, from the beginning and for ever. Creating man and woman in his own image and likeness, God wills for them the fullness of good, or supernatural happiness, which flows from sharing in his own life. *By committing sin man rejects this gift* and at the same time wills to become "as God, knowing good and evil" (Gn 3:5), that is to say, deciding what is good and what is evil independently of God, his Creator. The sin of the first parents has its own human "measure": an interior standard of its own in man's free will, and it also has within itself a certain "diabolic" characteristic,[29] which is clearly shown in the Book of Genesis (3:15). Sin brings about a break in the original unity which man enjoyed in the state of original justice: union with God as the source of the unity within his own "I," in the mutual relationship between man and woman *("communio personarum")* as well as in regard to the external world, to nature.

The biblical description of original sin in the third chapter of Genesis in a certain way "distinguishes the roles" which the woman and the man had in it.

This is also referred to later in certain passages of the Bible, for example, Paul's Letter to Timothy: "For Adam was formed first, then Eve, and Adam was not deceived, but the woman was deceived and became a transgressor" (1 Tim 2:13-14). But there is no doubt that, independent of this "distinction of roles" in the biblical description, *that first sin is the sin of man,* created by God as male and female. It is also *the sin of the "first parents,"* to which is connected its hereditary character. In this sense we call it "original sin."

This sin, as already said, *cannot be properly understood without reference to the mystery of the creation* of the human being—man and woman—*in the image and likeness of God.* By means of this reference one can also understand the mystery of that "non-likeness" to God in which sin consists, and which manifests itself in the evil present in the history of the world. Similarly one can understand the mystery of that "non-likeness" to God, who "alone is good" (cf. Mt 19:17) and the fullness of good. If sin's "non-likeness" to God, who is Holiness itself, presupposes "likeness" in the sphere of freedom and free will, it can then be said that for this very reason *the "non-likeness" contained in sin* is all the more tragic and sad. It must be admitted that God, as Creator and Father, is here wounded, "offended"—obviously offended—in the very heart of that gift which belongs to God's eternal plan for man.

At the same time, however, as the author of the evil of sin, *the human being—man and woman—is affected by it.* The third chapter of Genesis shows this with the words which clearly describe the new situation of man in the created world. It shows the perspective of "toil," by which man will earn his living (cf. Gn 3:17-19) and likewise the great "pain" with which the woman will give birth to her children (cf. Gen. 3:16). And all this is marked by the necessity of death, which is the end of human life on earth. In this way man, as dust, will "return to the ground, for out of it he was taken": "you are dust, and to dust you shall return" (cf. Gn 3:19).

These words are confirmed generation after generation. They do not mean that *the image and the likeness of God in the human being,* whether woman or man, has been destroyed by sin; they mean rather that it has been *"obscured"*[30] and in a sense "diminished." Sin in fact "diminishes" man, as the Second Vatican Council also recalls.[31] If man is the image and likeness of God by his very nature as a person, then his greatness and his dignity are achieved in the covenant with God, in union with him, in striving toward that fundamental unity which belongs to the internal "logic" of the very mystery of creation. This unity corresponds to the profound truth concerning all intelligent creatures and in particular concerning man, who among all the creatures of the visible world was *elevated* from the beginning through the eternal choice of God in Jesus: "He chose us in [Christ] before the foundation of the world.... He destined us in love to be his sons through Jesus Christ, according to the purpose of his will" (Eph 1:4-6). The biblical teaching taken as a whole enables us to say that predestination concerns all human persons, men and women, each and every one without exception.

"He Shall Rule Over You"

10. The biblical description in the Book of Genesis outlines the truth about the consequences of man's sin, as it is shown by *the disturbance* of that original *relationship between man and woman* which corresponds to their individual dignity as persons. A human being, whether male or female, is a person, and therefore, "the only creature on earth which God willed for its own sake"; and at the same time this unique and unrepeatable creature "cannot fully find himself except through a sincere gift of self."[32] Here begins the relationship of "communion" in which the "unity of the two" and the personal dignity of both man and woman find expression. Therefore when we read in the biblical description the words addressed to the woman: *"Your desire shall be for your husband, and he shall rule over you"* (Gn 3:16), we discover a break and a constant threat precisely in regard to this "unity of the two" which corresponds to the dignity of the image and likeness of God in both of them. But this threat is more serious for the woman, since domination takes the place of "being a sincere gift" and therefore living "for" the other: "He shall rule over you." This "domination" indicates the disturbance and *loss of the stability* of that *fundamental equality* which the man and the woman possess in the "unity of the two": and this is especially to the disadvantage of the woman, whereas only the equality resulting from their dignity as persons can give to their mutual relationship the character of an authentic *"communio personarum."* While the violation of this equality, which is both a gift and a right deriving from God the Creator, involves an element to the disadvantage of the woman, at the same time it also diminishes the true dignity of the man. Here we touch upon *an extremely sensitive point in the dimension of that "ethos"* which was originally inscribed by the Creator in the very creation of both of them in his own image and likeness.

This statement in Genesis 3:16 is of great significance. It implies a reference to the mutual relationship of man and women *in marriage.* It refers to the desire born in the atmosphere of spousal love whereby the woman's "sincere gift of self" is responded to and matched by a corresponding "gift" on the part of the husband. Only on the basis of this principle can both of them, and in particular the woman, "discover themselves" as a true "unity of the two" according to the dignity of the person. The matrimonial union requires respect for and a perfecting of the true personal subjectivity of both of them. *The woman cannot become the "object" of "domination" and male "possession."* But the words of the biblical text directly concern original sin and its lasting consequences in man and woman. Burdened by hereditary sinfulness, they bear within themselves the constant *"inclination to sin,"* the tendency to go against the moral order which corresponds to the rational nature and dignity of man and woman as persons. This tendency is expressed in *a threefold concupiscence,* which St. John defines as the lust of the eyes, the lust of the flesh, and the pride of life (cf. 1 Jn 2:16). The words of the Book of Genesis quoted previously (3:16) show how this threefold concupiscence, the "inclination to sin," will burden the mutual relationship of man and woman.

These words of Genesis refer directly to marriage, but indirectly *they concern the different spheres of social life:* the situations in which the woman remains disadvantaged or discriminated against by the fact of being a woman. The revealed truth concerning the creation of the human being as male and female constitutes the principal argument against all the objectively injurious and unjust situations which contain and express the inheritance of the sin which all human beings bear within themselves. The books of Sacred Scripture confirm in various places *the actual existence of such situations* and at the same time proclaim the need for conversion, that is to say, for purification from evil and liberation from sin: from what offends neighbor, what "diminishes" man, not only the one who is offended but also the one who causes the offense. This is the unchangeable message of the Word revealed by God. In it is expressed the biblical "ethos" until the end of time.[33]

In our times the question of "women's rights" has taken on new significance in the broad context of the rights of the human person. *The biblical and evangelical message* sheds light on this cause, which is the subject of much attention today, *by safeguarding the truth about the "unity" of the "two,"* that is to say the truth about that dignity and vocation that result from the specific diversity and personal originality of man and woman. Consequently, even the rightful opposition of women to what is expressed in the biblical words, "He shall rule over you" (Gn 3:16) must not under any condition lead to the "masculinization" of women. In the name of liberation from male "domination," women must not appropriate to themselves male characteristics contrary to their own feminine "originality." There is a well founded fear that if they take this path, women will not "reach fulfillment," but instead will *deform and lose what constitutes their essential richness.* It is indeed an enormous richness. In the biblical description, the words of the first man at the sight of the woman who had been created are words of admiration and enchantment, words which fill the whole history of man on earth.

The personal resources of femininity are certainly no less than the resources of masculinity: they are merely different. Hence a woman, as well as a man, must understand her "fulfillment" as a person, her dignity and vocation, on the basis of these resources, according to the richness of the femininity which she received on the day of creation and which she inherits as an expression of the "image and likeness of God" that is specifically hers. *The inheritance of sin* suggested by the words of the Bible—"Your desire shall be for your husband, and he shall rule over you"—*can be conquered* only by following this path. The overcoming of this evil inheritance is, generation after generation, the task of every human being, whether woman or man. For whenever man is responsible for offending a woman's personal dignity and vocation, he acts contrary to his own personal dignity and his own vocation.

Proto-Evangelium

11. The Book of Genesis attests to the fact that sin is the evil at man's "beginning" and that since then its consequences weigh upon the whole human race. At the same time it contains *the first foretelling of victory* over evil, *over sin.* This is proved by the words which we read in Genesis 3:15, usually called the *"Proto-evangelium": "*I will put enmity between you and the woman, and between your seed and her seed; he shall bruise your head, and you shall bruise his heel." It is significant that the foretelling of the Redeemer contained in these words refers to "the woman." She is assigned the first place in the Proto-evangelium as the progenitrix of him who will be the Redeemer of man.[34] And since the redemption is to be accomplished through a struggle against evil—through the "enmity" between the offspring of the woman and the offspring of him who, as "the father of lies" (Jn 8:44), is the first author of sin in human history—it is also *an enmity between him and the woman.*

These words give us a comprehensive view of the whole of Revelation, first as a preparation for the Gospel and later as the Gospel itself. From this vantage point the two female figures, *Eve* and *Mary,* are joined under the *name of woman.*

The words of the Proto-evangelium, re-read in the light of the New Testament, express well the mission of woman in the Redeemer's salvific struggle against the author of evil in human history.

The comparison Eve-Mary constantly recurs in the course of reflection on the deposit of faith received from divine Revelation. It is one of the themes frequently taken up by the Fathers, ecclesiastical writers and theologians.[35] As a rule, from this comparison there emerges at first sight a difference, a contrast. *Eve,* as "the mother of all the living" (Gn 3:20), is *the witness to the biblical "beginning,"* which contains the truth about the creation of man made in the image and likeness of God and the truth about original sin. *Mary is the witness to the new "beginning"* and the "new creation" (cf. 2 Cor 5:17), since she herself, as the first of the redeemed in salvation history, is "a new creation": she is "full of grace." It is difficult to grasp why the words of the Proto-evangelium place such strong emphasis on the "woman," if it is not admitted that *in her the new and definitive Covenant* of God with humanity *has its beginning,* the *Covenant* in the redeeming blood of Christ. The Covenant begins with a woman, the "woman" of the Annunciation at Nazareth. Herein lies the absolute originality of the Gospel: many times in the Old Testament, in order to intervene in the history of his people, God addressed himself to women, as in the case of the mothers of Samuel and Samson. However, to make his Covenant with humanity, he addressed himself only to men: *Noah, Abraham, and Moses.* At the beginning of the New Covenant, which is to be eternal and irrevocable, there is a woman: the Virgin of Nazareth. It is a *sign* that points to the fact that "in Jesus Christ" *"there is neither male nor female"* (Gal 3:28). In Christ the mutual opposition between man and woman—which is the inheritance of original sin—is essentially over-come. "For you are all *one* in Jesus Christ," St. Paul will write (Gal 3:28).

These words concern that original "unity of the two" which is linked with the creation of the human being as male and female, made in the image and like-ness of God, and based on the model of that most perfect communion of Persons which is God himself. St. Paul states that the mystery of man's redemption in Jesus Christ, the son of Mary, resumes and renews that which in the mystery of creation corresponded to the eternal design of God the Creator. Precisely for this reason on the day of the creation of the human being as male and female "God saw everything that he had made, and behold, it was very good" (Gn 1:31). *The redemption restores,* in a sense, at its very root, *the good* that was essentially "diminished" by sin and its heritage in human history.

The "woman" of the Proto-evangelium fits into the perspective of the redemption. The comparison Eve-Mary can be understood also in the sense that *Mary assumes* in herself and embraces the *mystery of the "woman"* whose be-ginning is Eve, "the mother of all the living" (Gn 3:20). First of all she assumes and embraces it within the mystery of Christ, "the new and the last Adam" (cf. 1 Cor 15:45), who assumed in his own person the nature of the first Adam. The essence of the New Covenant consists in the fact that the Son of God, who is of one substance with the eternal Father, becomes man: he takes humanity into the unity of the divine Person of the Word. The one who accomplishes the redemp-tion is also a true man. The mystery of the world's redemption presupposes that *God the Son assumed humanity* as *the inheritance of Adam,* becoming like him and like every man in all things, "yet without sinning" (Heb 4:15). In this way he "fully reveals man to himself and makes man's supreme calling clear," as the Second Vatican Council teaches.[36] In a certain sense, he has helped man to dis-cover "who he is" (cf. Ps 8:5).

In the tradition of faith and of Christian reflection throughout the ages, *the coupling Adam-Christ* is often linked with that of *Eve-Mary.* If Mary is de-scribed also as the "new Eve," what are the meanings of this analogy? Certainly there are many. Particularly noteworthy is the meaning which sees Mary as the full revelation of all that is included in the biblical word "woman": a revelation commensurate with the mystery of the redemption. *Mary* means, in a sense, a going beyond the limit spoken of in the Book of Genesis (3:16) and a return to that "beginning" in which one finds the "woman" as she was intended to be in *creation,* and therefore in the eternal mind of God: in the bosom of the Most Holy Trinity. Mary *is* "the new beginning" of the *dignity and vocation of women,* of each and every woman.[37]

A particular key for understanding this can be found in the words which the Evangelist puts on Mary's lips after the Annunciation, during her visit to Eliza-beth: "He who is mighty has done great things for me" (Lk 1:49). These words certainly refer to the conception of her Son, who is the "Son of the Most High" (Lk 1:32), the "holy one" of God; but they can also signify *the discovery of her own feminine humanity. He "has done great things for me": this is the discovery of all the richness and personal resources of femininity,* all the eternal originality of the "woman," just as God wanted her to be, a person for her own sake, who discovers herself "by means of a sincere gift of self."

This discovery is connected with a clear awareness of God's gift, of his generosity. From the very "beginning" sin had obscured this awareness, in a sense had stifled it, as is shown in the words of the first temptation by the "father of lies" (cf. Gn 3:1-5). At the advent of the "fullness of time" (cf. Gal 4:4), when the mystery of redemption begins to be fulfilled in the history of humanity, this awareness bursts forth in all its power in the words of the biblical "woman" of Nazareth. *In Mary, Eve discovers* the nature of the true dignity of woman, of feminine humanity. This discovery must continually reach the heart of every woman and shape her vocation and her life.

V. JESUS CHRIST

"They Marveled That He Was Talking with a Woman"

12. The words of the Proto-evangelium in the Book of Genesis enable us to move into the context of the Gospel. Man's redemption, foretold in Genesis, now becomes a reality in the person and mission of Jesus Christ, in which we also recognize *what the reality of the redemption means* for the dignity and the vocation *of women.* This meaning becomes clearer for us from Christ's words and from his whole attitude toward women, an attitude which is extremely simple, and for this very reason extraordinary, if seen against the background of his time. It is an attitude marked by great clarity and depth. Various women appear along the path of the mission of Jesus of Nazareth, and his meeting with each of them is a confirmation of the evangelical "newness of life" already spoken of.

It is universally admitted—even by people with a critical attitude toward the Christian message—that *in the eyes of his contemporaries Christ became a promoter of women's true dignity* and of the *vocation* corresponding to this dignity. At times this caused wonder, surprise, often to the point of scandal. "They marveled that he was talking with a woman" (Jn 4:27), because this behavior differed from that of his contemporaries. Even Christ's own disciples "marveled." The Pharisee to whose house the sinful woman went to anoint Jesus' feet with perfumed oil "said to himself, 'If this man were a prophet, *he would have known who* and what sort of woman this is who is touching him, for she is a sinner'" (Lk 7:39). Even greater dismay, or even "holy indignation," must have filled the self-satisfied hearers of Christ's words. "The tax collectors and the harlots go into the Kingdom of God before you" (Mt 21:31).

By speaking and acting in this way, Jesus made it clear that "the mysteries of the Kingdom" were known to him in every detail. He also "knew what was in man" (Jn 2:25), in his innermost being, in his "heart." He was a witness of God's eternal plan for the human being, created in his own image and likeness as man and woman. He was also perfectly aware of the consequences of sin, of that "mystery of iniquity" working in human hearts as the bitter fruit of the obscuring of the divine image. It is truly significant that in his important discussion about marriage and its indissolubility, in the presence of "the Scribes," who by profession were experts in the Law, Jesus *makes reference to the "beginning."* The question asked concerns a man's right "to divorce one's wife for any cause" (Mt 19:3) and therefore also concerns the woman's right, her rightful position in marriage, her dignity. The questioners think they have on their side the Mosaic legislation then followed in Israel: "Why then did Moses command one to give a certificate of divorce, and to put her away?" (Mt 19:7) Jesus answers: "For your hardness of heart Moses allowed you to divorce your wives, but from the beginning it was not so" (Mt 19:8). Jesus appeals to the "beginning"—to the creation of man as male and female and their ordering by God himself, which is based upon the fact that *both were created "in his image and likeness."* Therefore, when "a man shall leave his father and mother and is joined to his wife, so that the two become one flesh," there remains in force the law which comes from God himself: "What therefore God has joined together, let no man put asunder" (Mt 19:6).

The principle of this "ethos," which from the beginning marks the reality of creation, is now confirmed by Christ in opposition to that tradition which discriminated against women. In this tradition the male "dominated," without having proper regard for woman and for her dignity, which *the "ethos"* of creation made the basis of the mutual relationships of two people united in marriage. This "ethos" is *recalled and confirmed by Christ's words;* it is the "ethos" of the Gospel and of redemption.

Women in the Gospel

13. As we scan the pages of the Gospel, *many women, of different ages and conditions,* pass before our eyes. We meet women with illnesses or physical sufferings, such as the one who had "a spirit of infirmity for eighteen years; she was bent over and could not fully straighten herself" (Lk 13:11); or Simon's mother-in-law, who "lay sick with a fever" (Mk 1:30); or the woman "who had a flow of blood" (cf. Mk 5:25-34)—who could not touch anyone because it was believed that her touch would make a person "impure." Each of them was healed, and the last-mentioned—the one with a flow of blood, who touched Jesus' garment "in the crowd" (Mk 5:27)—was praised by him for her great faith: "Your faith has made you well" (Mk 5:34). Then there is *the daughter of Jairus,* whom Jesus brings back to life, saying to her tenderly—"Little girl, I say to you, rise" (Mk 5:41). There is also *the widow of Naim,* whose only son Jesus brings back to life, accompanying his action by an expression of affectionate mercy—"He had compassion on her and said to her, 'Do not weep!'" (Lk 7:13). And finally there is the *Canaanite woman,* whom Christ extols for her faith, her humility and for that

greatness of spirit of which only a mother's heart is capable. "O woman, great is your faith! Be it done for you as you desire" (Mt 15:28). The Canaanite woman was asking for the healing of her daughter.

Sometimes the women whom Jesus met and who received so many graces from him, also accompanied him as he journeyed with the apostles through the towns and villages, proclaiming the Good News of the Kingdom of God; and they "provided for them out of their means." The Gospel names Joanna, who was the wife of Herod's steward, Susanna and "many others" (cf. Lk 8:1-3).

Sometimes *women* appear *in the parables* which Jesus of Nazareth used to illustrate for his listeners the truth about the Kingdom of God. This is the case in the parables of the lost coin (cf. Lk 15:8-10), the leaven (cf. Mt 13:33), and the wise and foolish virgins (cf. Mt 25:1-13). Particularly eloquent is the story of the widow's mite. While "the rich were putting their gifts into the treasury...a poor widow put in two copper coins." Then Jesus said: "This poor widow *has put in more than all of them*.... She out of her poverty put in all the living that she had" (Lk 21:1-4). In this way Jesus presents her as a model for everyone and defends her, for in the socio-juridical system of the time widows were totally defenseless people (cf. also Lk 18:1-7).

In all of Jesus' teaching, as well as in his behavior, one can find nothing which reflects the discrimination against women prevalent in his day. On the contrary, *his words and works always express the respect and honor due to women.* The woman with a stoop is called a "daughter of Abraham" (Lk 13:16), while in the whole Bible the title "son of Abraham" is used only of men. Walking the *Via Dolorosa* to Golgotha, Jesus will say to the women: "Daughters of Jerusalem, do not weep for me" (Lk 23:28). This way of speaking to and about women, as well as his manner of treating them, clearly constitutes an "innovation" with respect to the prevailing custom at that time.

This becomes even more explicit in regard to women whom popular opinion contemptuously labeled sinners, public sinners and adulteresses. There is the Samaritan woman, to whom Jesus himself says: "For you have had five husbands, and he whom you now have is not your husband." And she, realizing that he knows the secrets of her life, recognizes him as the Messiah and runs to tell her neighbors. The conversation leading up to this realization is one of the most beautiful in the Gospel (cf. Jn 4:7-27).

Then there is the public sinner who, in spite of her condemnation by common opinion, enters into the house of the Pharisee to anoint the feet of Jesus with perfumed oil. To his host, who is scandalized by this, he will say: "Her sins, which are many, are forgiven, for she loved much" (cf. Lk 7:37-47).

Finally, there is a situation which is perhaps the most eloquent: *a woman caught in adultery* is brought to Jesus. To the leading question: "In the law Moses commanded us to stone such. What do you say about her?" Jesus replies: "Let him who is without sin among you be the first to throw a stone at her." The power of truth contained in this answer is so great that "they went away, one by one, beginning with the eldest." Only Jesus and the woman remain. "Woman, where are they? Has no one condemned you?" "No one, Lord." "Neither do I condemn you; go, and do not sin again" (cf. Jn 8:3-11).

These episodes provide a very clear picture. Christ is the one who "knows what is in man" (cf. Jn 2:25)—in man and woman. He knows *the dignity of man, his worth in God's eyes.* He himself, the Christ, is the definitive confirmation of this worth. Everything he says and does is definitively fulfilled in the Paschal Mystery of the redemption. Jesus' attitude to the women whom he meets in the course of his Messianic service reflects the eternal plan of God, who, in creating each one of them, chooses her and loves her in Christ (cf. Eph 1:1-5). Each woman therefore is "the only creature on earth which God willed for its own sake." *Each of them from the "beginning" inherits as a women the dignity of personhood.* Jesus of Nazareth confirms this dignity, recalls it, renews it, and makes it a part of the Gospel of the redemption for which he is sent into the world. Every word and gesture of Christ about women must therefore he brought into the dimension of the Paschal Mystery. In this way everything is completely explained.

The Woman Caught in Adultery

14. Jesus enters *into the concrete and historical situation of women,* a situation which is *weighed down by the inheritance of sin.* One of the ways in which this inheritance is expressed is habitual discrimination against women in favor of men. This inheritance is rooted within women too. From this point of view the episode of the woman "caught in adultery" (cf. Jn 8:3-11) is particularly eloquent. In the end Jesus says to her*: "Do not sin again,"* but first he *evokes an awareness* of sin in the men who accuse her in order to stone her, thereby revealing his profound capacity to see human consciences and actions in their true light. Jesus seems to say to the accusers: Is not this woman, for all her sin, above all a confirmation of your own transgressions, of your "male" injustice, your misdeeds?

This truth is *valid for the whole human race.* The episode recorded in the Gospel of John is repeated in countless similar situations in every period of history. A woman is left alone, exposed to public opinion with "her sin," while behind "her" sin there lurks a man—a sinner, guilty "of the other's sin," indeed equally responsible for it. And yet his sin escapes notice, it is passed over in silence: he does not appear to be responsible for "the other's sin"! Sometimes, forgetting his own sin, he makes himself the accuser, as in the case described. How often, in a similar way, *the woman pays* for her own sin (maybe it is she, in some cases, who is guilty of the "other's sin"—the sin of the man), but she alone pays and she pays *all alone!* How often is she abandoned with her pregnancy, when the man, the child's father, is unwilling to accept responsibility for it? And besides the many "unwed mothers" in our society, we also might consider all those who as a result of various pressures, even on the part of the guilty man, very often "get rid of" the child before it is born. "They get rid of it": but at what price? Public opinion today tries in various ways to "abolish" the evil of this sin. Normally a *woman's conscience does not let her forget* that she has taken the life of her own child, for she cannot destroy that readiness to accept life which marks her "ethos" from the "beginning."

The attitude of Jesus in the episode described in John 8:3-11 is significant. This is one of the few instances in which his power—the power of truth—is so clearly manifested with regard to human consciences. Jesus is calm, collected and thoughtful. As in the conversation with the Pharisees (cf. Mt 19:3-9), is Jesus not aware of being in contact with the mystery of the "beginning," when man was created male and female, and the woman was entrusted to the man with her feminine distinctiveness, and with her potential for motherhood? The man was also entrusted by the Creator to the woman—they were *entrusted to each other as persons* made in the image and likeness of God himself. This entrusting is the test of love, spousal love. In order to become "a sincere gift" to one another, each of them has to feel responsible for the gift. This test is meant for both of them—man and woman—from the "beginning." After original sin, contrary forces are at work in man and woman as a result of the threefold concupiscence, the "stimulus of sin." They act from deep within the human being. Thus Jesus will say in the Sermon on the Mount: *"Every one who looks at a woman lustfully has already committed adultery with her in his heart"* (Mt 5:28). These words, addressed directly to man, show the fundamental truth of his responsibility vis-a-vis woman: her dignity, her motherhood, her vocation. But indirectly these words concern the woman. Christ did everything possible to ensure that—in the context of the customs and social relationships of that time—women would find in his teaching and actions their own subjectivity and dignity. On the basis of the eternal "unity of the two," *this dignity directly depends on woman herself, as a subject responsible for herself, and at the same time it is "given as a task" to man.* Christ logically appeals to man's responsibility. In the present meditation on women's dignity and vocation, it is necessary that we refer to the context which we find in the Gospel. The dignity and the vocation of women—as well as those of men—find their eternal source in the heart of God. And in the temporal conditions of human existence, they are closely connected with the "unity of the two." Consequently each man must look within himself to see whether she who was entrusted to him as a sister in humanity, as a spouse, has not become in his heart an object of adultery; to see whether she who, in different ways, is the co-subject of his existence in the world, has not become for him an "object": an object of pleasure, of exploitation.

Guardians of the Gospel Message

15. *Christ's way of acting, the Gospel of his words and deeds,* is a consistent *protest* against whatever offends the dignity of women. Consequently, the women who are close to Christ discover themselves in the truth which he

"teaches" and "does," even when this truth concerns their "sinfulness." They feel *"liberated" by this truth,* restored to themselves they feel loved with "eternal love," with a love which finds direct expression in Christ himself. In Christ's sphere of action their position is transformed. They feel that Jesus is speaking to them about matters which in those times one did not discuss with a woman. Perhaps the most significant example of this is the *Samaritan woman* at the well of Sychar. *Jesus*—who knows that she is a sinner and speaks to her about this—*discusses the most profound mysteries of God with her.* He speaks to her of God's infinite gift of love, which is like a "spring of water welling up to eternal life" (Jn 4:14). He speaks to her about God who is Spirit, and about the true adoration which the Father has a right to receive in spirit and truth (cf. Jn 4:24). Finally he reveals to her that he is the Messiah promised to Israel (cf. Jn 4:26).

This is an event without precedent: that a *woman,* and what is more a "sinful woman," becomes a "disciple" of Christ. Indeed, once taught, she proclaims Christ to the inhabitants of Samaria, so that they too receive him with faith (cf. Jn 4:39-42). This is an unprecedented event, if one remembers the usual way women were treated by those who were teachers in Israel; whereas in Jesus of Nazareth's way of acting such an event becomes normal. In this regard, the sisters of Lazarus also deserve special mention: "Jesus loved Martha and her sister [Mary] and Lazarus" (cf. Jn 11:5). Mary "listened to the teaching" of Jesus; when he pays them a visit, he calls Mary's behavior "the good portion" in contrast to Martha's preoccupation with domestic matters (cf. Lk 10:38-42). On another occasion—*after the death of Lazarus*—Martha is the one who talks to Christ, and the conversation concerns the most profound truths of revelation and faith: "Lord, if you had been here, my brother would not have died." "Your brother will rise again." "I know that he will rise again in the resurrection at the last day." Jesus said to her: "I am the resurrection and the life; he who believes in me, though he die, yet shall he live, and whoever lives and believes in me shall never die. Do you believe this?" "Yes, Lord; I believe that you are the Christ, the Son of God, he who is coming into the world" (Jn 11:21-27). After this profession of faith Jesus raises Lazarus. *This conversation with Martha is one of the most important in the Gospel.*

Christ speaks to women about the things of God, and they understand them; there is a true resonance of mind and heart, a response of faith. Jesus expresses appreciation and admiration for this distinctly "feminine" response, as in the case of the Canaanite woman (cf. Mt 15:28). Sometimes he presents this lively faith, filled with love, as an example. *He teaches,* therefore, taking as *his starting point this feminine response of mind and heart.* This is the case with the "sinful" woman in the Pharisee's house, whose way of acting is taken by Jesus as the starting point for explaining the truth about the forgiveness of sins: "Her sins, which are many, are forgiven, for she loved much, but he who is forgiven little, loves little" (Lk 7:47). On the occasion of another anointing, Jesus defends the woman and her action before the disciples, Judas in particular: "Why do you trouble this woman? *For she has done a beautiful thing to me....* In pouring this ointment on my body she has done it to prepare me for burial. Truly, I say to you, wherever this Gospel is preached in the whole world, what she has done will be told in memory of her" (Mt 26:6-13).

Indeed, the Gospels not only describe what that woman did at Bethany in the house of Simon the Leper; they also highlight the fact that *women were in the forefront at the foot of the cross,* at the decisive moment in Jesus of Nazareth's whole messianic mission. John was the only apostle who remained faithful, but there were many faithful women. Not only the Mother of Christ and "his mother's sister, Mary the wife of Clopas and Mary Magdalene" (Jn 19:25) were present, but "there were also many women there, looking on from afar, who had followed Jesus from Galilee, ministering to him" (Mt 27:55). As we see, in this most arduous test of faith and fidelity the women proved stronger than the apostles. In this moment of danger, those who love much succeed in overcoming their fear. Before this there were the *women on the Via Dolorosa,* "who bewailed and lamented him" (Lk 23:27). Earlier still, there was *Pilate's wife,* who had warned her husband: "Have nothing to do with that righteous man, for I have suffered much over him today in a dream" (Mt 27:19).

First Witnesses of the Resurrection

16. From the beginning of Christ's mission, women show to him and to his mystery a special *sensitivity which is characteristic* of their *femininity.* It must also be said that this is especially confirmed in the Paschal Mystery, not only at the cross but also at the dawn of the resurrection. The women *are the first at the tomb.* They are the first to find it empty. They are the first to hear: "He is not here. *He has risen,* as he said" (Mt 28:6). They are the first to embrace his feet (cf. Mt 28:9). They are also the first to be called to announce this truth to the apostles (cf. Mt 28:1-10; Lk 24:8-11). The Gospel of John (cf. also Mk 16:9) emphasizes *the special role of Mary Magdalene.* She is the first to meet the Risen Christ. At first she thinks he is the gardener; she recognizes him only when he calls her by name: "Jesus said to her, 'Mary.' She turned and said to him in Hebrew, 'Rabboni' (which means Teacher). Jesus said to her, 'Do not hold me, for I have not yet ascended to the Father, but go to my brethren and say to them, I am ascending to my Father and to your Father, to my God and your God.' Mary Magdalene went and said to the disciples, 'I have seen the Lord'; and she told them that he had said these things to her" (Jn 20:16-18).

Hence she came to be called "the apostle of the apostles."[38] Mary Magdalene was the first eyewitness of the Risen Christ, and for this reason she was also *the first to bear witness to him before the apostles.* This event, in a sense, crowns all that has been said previously about Christ entrusting divine truths to women as well as men. One can say that this fulfilled the words of the Prophet: *"I will pour out my spirit* on all flesh; your sons and *your daughters shall prophesy"* (Jl 3:1). On the fiftieth day after Christ's resurrection, these words are confirmed once more in the upper room in Jerusalem, at the descent of the Holy Spirit, the Paraclete (cf. Acts 2:17).

Everything that has been said so far about Christ's attitude to women confirms and clarifies, in the Holy Spirit, the truth about the equality of man and woman. One must speak of an essential "equality," since both of them—the woman as much as the man—are created in the image and likeness of God. Both of them are equally capable of receiving the outpouring of divine truth and love in the Holy Spirit. Both receive his salvific and sanctifying "visits."

The fact of being a man or a woman involves no limitation here, just as the salvific and sanctifying action of the Spirit in man is in no way limited by the fact that one is a Jew or a Greek, slave or free, according to the well-known words of St. Paul: "For you are all one in Christ Jesus" (Gal 3:28). *This unity does not cancel out diversity.* The Holy Spirit, who brings about this unity in the supernatural order of sanctifying grace, contributes in equal measure to the fact that "your sons will prophesy" and that "your daughters will prophesy." "To prophesy" means to express by one's words and one's life *"the mighty works of God"* (Acts 2:11), preserving the truth and originality of each person, whether woman or man. Gospel "equality," the "equality" of women and men in regard to the "mighty works of God"—manifested so clearly in the words and deeds of Jesus of Nazareth—constitutes the most obvious basis for the dignity and vocation of women in the Church and in the world. Every *vocation has* a profoundly *personal and prophetic meaning.* In "vocation" understood in this way, what is personally feminine reaches a new dimension: the dimension of the "mighty works of God," of which the woman becomes the living subject and an irreplaceable witness.

VI. MOTHERHOOD—VIRGINITY

Two Dimensions of Women's Vocation

17. We must now focus our meditation on virginity and motherhood as two particular dimensions of the fulfillment of the female personality. In the light of the Gospel, they acquire their full meaning and value in Mary, who as a Virgin became the Mother of the Son of God. These *two dimensions of the female vocation* were united in her in an exceptional manner, in such a way that one did not exclude the other but wonderfully complemented it. The description of the Annunciation in the Gospel of Luke clearly shows that this seemed impossible to the Virgin of Nazareth. When she hears the words: "You will conceive in your womb and bear a son, and you shall call his name Jesus," she immediately asks: "How can this be, since I have no husband?" (Lk 1:31, 34). In the usual order of things motherhood is the result of mutual "knowledge" between a man and woman in the marriage union. Mary, firm in her resolve to preserve her virginity, puts this question to the divine messenger, and obtains from him the explanation:

"The Holy Spirit will come upon you"—your motherhood will not be the consequence of matrimonial "knowledge," but will be the work of the Holy Spirit; the "power of the Most High" will "overshadow" the mystery of the Son's conception and birth; as the Son of the Most High, he is given to you exclusively by God, in a manner known to God. Mary, therefore, maintained her virginal "I have no husband" (cf. Lk 1:34) and at the same time became a Mother. *Virginity and motherhood co-exist in her:* they do not mutually exclude each other or place limits on each other. Indeed, the person of the Mother of God helps everyone—especially women—to see how these two dimensions, these two paths in the vocation of women as persons, explain and complete each other.

Motherhood

18. In order to share in this "vision," we must once again *seek a deeper understanding of the truth about the human person* recalled by the Second Vatican Council. The human being—both male and female—is the only being in the world which God willed for its own sake. The human being is a person, a subject who decides for himself. At the same time, man "cannot fully find himself except through a sincere gift of self."[39] It has already been said that this description, indeed this definition of the person, corresponds to the fundamental biblical truth about the creation of the human being—man and woman—in the image and likeness of God. This is not a purely theoretical interpretation, nor an abstract definition, for it *gives an essential indication of what it means to be human,* while emphasizing *the value of the gift of self, the gift of the person.* In this vision of the person we also find the essence of that "ethos" which, together with the truth of creation, will be fully developed by the books of Revelation, particularly the Gospels.

This truth about the person also opens up *the path to a full understanding of women's motherhood.* Motherhood is the fruit of the marriage union of a man and woman, of that biblical "knowledge" which corresponds to the "union of the two in one flesh" (cf. Gn 2:24). This brings about—on the woman's part—a special "gift of self" as an expression of that spousal love whereby the two are united to each other so closely that they become "one flesh." Biblical "knowledge" is achieved in accordance with the truth of the person only when the mutual self-giving is not distorted either by the desire of the man to become the "master" of his wife ("He shall rule over you") or by the woman remaining closed within her own instincts ("Your desire shall be for your husband," Gn 3:16).

This *mutual gift of the person in marriage* opens to the gift of a new life, *a new human being,* who is also a person in the likeness of his parents. Motherhood implies from the beginning a special openness to the new person: and this is precisely the woman's "part." In this openness, in conceiving and giving birth to a child, the woman "discovers herself through a sincere gift of self." The gift of interior readiness to accept the child and bring it into the world is linked to the marriage union, which—as mentioned earlier—should constitute a special moment in the mutual self-giving both by the woman and the man. According to the Bible, the conception and birth of a new human being are accompanied by the following words of the woman: *"I have brought a man into being with the help of the Lord"* (Gn 4:1). This exclamation of Eve, the "mother of all the living" is repeated every time a new human being comes into the world. It expresses the woman's joy and awareness that she is sharing in the great mystery of eternal generation. The spouses share in the creative power of God!

The woman's motherhood in the period between the baby's conception and birth is a biophysiological and psychological process which is better understood in our days than in the past, and is the subject of many detailed studies. Scientific analysis fully confirms that the very physical constitution of women is naturally disposed to motherhood—conception, pregnancy and giving birth—which is a consequence of the marriage union with the man. At the same time, this also corresponds to the psycho-physical structure of women. What the different branches of science have to say on this subject is important and useful, provided that it is not limited to an exclusively biophysiological interpretation of women and of motherhood. Such a *"restricted" picture* would go hand in hand with a materialistic concept of the human being and of the world. In such a case, what is truly essential would unfortunately be lost. Motherhood as a *human* fact and phenomenon is fully explained on the basis of the truth about the person. Motherhood *is linked to the personal structure of the woman and to the personal dimension of the gift:* "I have brought a man into being with the help of the Lord" (Gn 4:1). The Creator grants the parents the gift of a child. On the woman's part, this fact is linked in a special way to "a sincere gift of self." Mary's words at the Annunciation—"Let it be to me according to your word"—signify the woman's readiness for the gift of self and her readiness to accept a new life.

The eternal mystery of generation, which is in God himself, the one and Triune God (cf. Eph 3:14-15), is reflected in the woman's motherhood and in the man's fatherhood. Human parenthood is something shared by both the man and the woman. Even if the woman, out of love for her husband, says: "I have given you a child," her words also mean: "This is our child." Although both of them together are parents of their child, *the woman's motherhood constitutes a special "part" in this shared parenthood,* and the most demanding part. Parenthood—even though it belongs to both—is realized much more fully in the woman, especially in the prenatal period. It is the woman who "pays" directly for this shared generation, which literally absorbs the energies of her body and soul. It is therefore necessary that *the man* be fully aware that in their shared parenthood he *owes a special debt to the woman.* No program of "equal rights" between women and men is valid unless it takes this fact fully into account.

Motherhood involves a special communion with the mystery of life, as it develops in the woman's womb. The mother is filled with wonder at this mystery of life, and "understands" with unique intuition what is happening inside her. In the light of the "beginning," the mother accepts and loves as a person the child she is carrying in her womb. This unique contact with the new human being developing within her gives rise to an attitude toward human beings—not only toward her own child, but every human being—which profoundly marks the woman's personality. It is commonly thought that *women* are more capable than men of paying attention *to another person,* and that motherhood develops this predisposition even more. The man—even with all his sharing in parenthood—always remains "outside" the process of pregnancy and the baby's birth; in many ways he has to *learn* his own *"fatherhood" from the mother.* One can say that this is part of the normal human dimension of parenthood, including the stages that follow the birth of the baby, especially the initial period. The child's upbringing, taken as a whole, should include the contribution of both parents: the maternal and paternal contribution. In any event, the mother's contribution is decisive in laying the foundation for a new human personality.

Motherhood in Relation to the Covenant

19. Our reflection returns to *the biblical exemplar of the "woman"* in the Proto-evangelium. The "woman," as mother and first teacher of the human being (education being the spiritual dimension of parenthood), has a specific precedence over the man. Although motherhood, especially in the bio-physical sense, depends upon the man, it places an essential "mark" on the whole personal growth process of new children. Motherhood *in the bio-physical sense* appears to be passive: the formation process of a new life "takes place" in her, in her body, which is nevertheless profoundly involved in that process. At the same time, motherhood *in its personal-ethical sense* expresses a very important creativity on the part of the woman, upon whom the very humanity of the new human being mainly depends. In this sense too the woman's motherhood presents a special call and a special challenge to the man and to his fatherhood.

The biblical exemplar of the "woman" finds its culmination *in the motherhood of the Mother of God.* The words of the Proto-evangelium—"I will put enmity between you and the woman"—find here a fresh confirmation. We see that through Mary—through her maternal "fiat," ("Let it be done to me")—God *begins a New Covenant with humanity.* This is the eternal and definitive Covenant in Christ, in his body and blood, in his cross and resurrection. Precisely because this Covenant is to be fulfilled "in flesh and blood," its beginning is in the Mother. Thanks solely to her and to her virginal and maternal "fiat," the "Son of the Most High" can say to the Father: "A body you have prepared for me. Lo, I have come to do your will, O God" (cf. Heb 10:5, 7).

Motherhood has been introduced into the order of the Covenant that God made with humanity in Jesus Christ. Each and every time that *motherhood* is repeated in human history, it is always *related to the Covenant* which God established with the human race through the motherhood of the Mother of God.

Does not Jesus bear witness to this reality when he answers the exclamation of that woman in the crowd who blessed him for Mary's motherhood: "Blessed is the womb that bore you, and the breasts that you sucked!"? Jesus replies: "Blessed rather are those who hear the word of God and keep it" (Lk 11:27-28). Jesus confirms the meaning of motherhood in reference to the body, but at the same time he indicates an even deeper meaning, which is connected with the order of the spirit: it is a sign of the Covenant with God who "is spirit" (Jn 4:24). This is true above all for the motherhood of the Mother of God. The *motherhood* of every woman, understood in the light of the Gospel, is similarly not only "of flesh and blood": it expresses a profound *"listening to the word of the living God"* and a readiness to "safeguard" this Word, which is "the word of eternal life" (cf. Jn 6:68). For it is precisely those born of earthly mothers, the sons and daughters of the human race, who receive from the Son of God the power to become "children of God" (Jn 1:12). A dimension of the New Covenant in Christ's blood enters into human parenthood, making it a reality and a task for "new creatures" (cf. 2 Cor 5:17). The history of every human being passes through the threshold of a woman's motherhood; crossing it conditions "the revelation of the children of God" (cf. Rom 8:19).

"When a woman is in travail she has sorrow, because her hour has come; but when she is delivered of the child, *she no longer remembers the anguish,* for joy that a child is born into the world" (Jn 16:21). The first part of Christ's words refers to the "pangs of childbirth" which belong to the heritage of original sin; at the same time these words indicate *the link that exists between the woman's motherhood and the Paschal Mystery.* For this mystery also includes the Mother's sorrow at the foot of the cross—the Mother who through faith shares in the amazing mystery of her Son's "self-emptying": "This is perhaps the deepest 'kenosis' of faith in human history."[40]

As we contemplate this Mother, whose heart "a sword has pierced" (cf. Lk 2:35), our thoughts go to *all the suffering women in the world,* suffering either physically or morally. In this suffering a woman's sensitivity plays a role, even though she often succeeds in resisting suffering better than a man. It is difficult to enumerate these sufferings; it is difficult to call them all by name. We may recall her maternal care for her children, especially when they fall sick or fall into bad ways; the death of those most dear to her; the loneliness of mothers forgotten by their grown-up children; the loneliness of widows; the sufferings of women who struggle alone to make a living; and women who have been wronged or exploited. Then there are the sufferings of consciences as a result of sin, which has wounded the woman's human or maternal dignity: the wounds of consciences which do not heal easily. With these sufferings too we must place ourselves at the foot of the cross.

But the words of the Gospel about the woman who suffers when the time comes for her to give birth to her child, immediately afterward express *joy:* it is *"the joy that a child is born into the world."* This joy too is referred to the Paschal Mystery, to the joy which is communicated to the apostles *on the day of Christ's resurrection:* "So you have sorrow now" (these words were said the day before the Passion); "but I will see you again and your hearts will rejoice, and no one will take your joy from you" (Jn 16:22-23).

Virginity for the Sake of the Kingdom

20. In the teaching of Christ, *motherhood is connected with virginity*, but also *distinct from it*. Fundamental to this is Jesus' statement in the conversation on the indissolubility of marriage. Having heard the answer given to the Pharisees, the disciples say to Christ: "If such is the case of a man with his wife, it is not expedient to marry" (Mt 19:10). Independently of the meaning which "it is not expedient" had at that time in the mind of the disciples, *Christ* takes their mistaken opinion as a starting point for instructing them *on the value of celibacy*. He distinguishes celibacy which results from natural defects—even though they may have been caused by man—from *"celibacy for the sake of the Kingdom of heaven."* Christ says, "and there are eunuchs who have made themselves eunuchs for the sake of the Kingdom of heaven" (Mt 19:12). It is, then, a voluntary celibacy, chosen for the sake of the Kingdom of heaven, in view of man's eschatological vocation to union with God. He then adds: "He who is able to receive this, let him receive it." These words repeat what he had said at the beginning of the discourse on celibacy (cf. Mt 19:11). Consequently, *celibacy for the Kingdom of heaven* results not only from a free *choice* on the part of man, but also from a special *grace* on the part of God, who calls a particular person to live celibacy. While this is a special sign of the Kingdom of God to come, it also serves as a way to devote all the energies of soul and body during one's earthly life exclusively for the sake of the eschatological kingdom.

Jesus' words are the answer to the disciples' question. They are addressed directly to those who put the question: in this case they were men. Nevertheless, Christ's answer, in itself, has a *value for men and for women*. In this context it indicates the evangelical ideal of virginity, an ideal which constitutes a clear "innovation" with respect to the tradition of the Old Testament. Certainly that tradition was connected in some way with Israel's expectation of the Messiah's coming, especially among the women of Israel from whom he was to be born. In fact, the ideal of celibacy and virginity for the sake of greater closeness to God was not entirely foreign to certain Jewish circles, especially in the period immediately preceding the coming of Jesus. Nevertheless, celibacy for the sake of the Kingdom, or rather virginity, is undeniably an innovation connected with the incarnation of God.

From the moment of Christ's coming, the expectation of the People of God has to be directed to the eschatological Kingdom which is coming and to which he must lead "the new Israel." A new awareness of faith is essential for such a turnabout and change of values. Christ emphasizes this twice: "He who is able to receive this, let him receive it." Only "those to whom it is given" understand it (Mt 19:11). *Mary* is the first person in whom this *new awareness* is manifested, for she asks the angel: "How can this be, since I have no husband?" (Lk 1:34).

Even though she is "betrothed to a man whose name was Joseph" (cf. Lk 1:27) she is firm in her resolve to remain a virgin. The motherhood which is accomplished in her comes exclusively from the "power of the Most High," and is the result of the Holy Spirit's coming down upon her (cf. Lk 1:35). This divine motherhood, therefore, is an altogether unforeseen response to the human expectation of women in Israel; it comes to Mary as a gift from God himself. This gift is the beginning and the prototype of a new expectation on the part of all. It measures up to the Eternal Covenant, to God's new and definitive promise: it is *a sign of eschatological hope.*

On the basis of the Gospel, the meaning of virginity was developed and better understood as a vocation for women too, one in which their dignity, like that of the Virgin of Nazareth, finds confirmation. The Gospel puts forward *the ideal of the consecration of the person,* that is, the person's exclusive dedication to God by virtue of the evangelical counsels: in particular, chastity, poverty and obedience. Their perfect incarnation is Jesus Christ himself. Whoever wishes to follow him in a radical way chooses to live according to these counsels. They are distinct from the commandments and show the Christian the radical way of the Gospel. From the very beginning of Christianity men and women have set out on this path, since the evangelical ideal is addressed to human beings without any distinction of sex.

In this wider context, *virginity* has to be considered *also as a path for women,* a path on which they realize their womanhood in a way different from marriage. In order to understand this path, it is necessary to refer once more to the fundamental idea of Christian anthropology. By freely choosing virginity, women confirm themselves as persons, as beings whom the Creator from the beginning has willed for their own sake.[41] At the same time they realize the personal value of their own femininity by becoming "a sincere gift" for God who has revealed himself in Christ, a gift for Christ, the Redeemer of humanity and the spouse of souls: a "spousal" gift. *One cannot correctly understand virginity*—a woman's consecration in virginity—*without referring to spousal love.* It is through this kind of love that a person becomes a gift for the other.[42] Moreover, a man's consecration in priestly celibacy or in the religious state is to be understood analogously.

The naturally spousal predisposition of the feminine personality finds a response in virginity understood in this way. Women, called from the very "beginning" to be loved and to love, in a vocation to virginity *find Christ* first of all as the Redeemer who "loved until the end" through his total gift of self; and *they respond to this gift with a "sincere gift"* of their whole lives. They thus give themselves to the divine Spouse, and this personal gift tends to union, which is properly spiritual in character. Through the Holy Spirit's action a woman becomes "one spirit" with Christ the Spouse (cf. 1 Cor 6:17).

This is the evangelical ideal of virginity, in which both the dignity and the vocation of women are realized in a special way. In virginity thus understood the so-called *radicalism of the Gospel* finds expression: "Leave everything and follow Christ" (cf. Mt 19:27). This cannot be compared to remaining simply unmarried or single, because virginity is not restricted to a mere "no," but contains a profound "yes" in the spousal order: the gift of self for love in a total and undivided manner.

Motherhood According to the Spirit

21. Virginity according to the Gospel means *renouncing marriage and thus physical motherhood.* Nevertheless, the renunciation of this kind of motherhood, a renunciation that can involve great sacrifice for a woman, makes possible a different kind of motherhood: motherhood *"according to the Spirit"* (cf. Rom 8:4). For virginity does not deprive a woman of her prerogatives. Spiritual motherhood takes on many different forms. In the life of consecrated women, for example, who live according to the charism and the rules of the various apostolic institutes, it can express itself as concern for people, especially the most needy: the sick, the handicapped, the abandoned, orphans, the elderly, children, young people, the imprisoned and, in general, people on the margins of society. *In this way a consecrated woman finds her Spouse,* different and the same in each and every person, according to his very words: "As you did it to one of the least of these my brethren, you did it to me" (Mt 25:40). Spousal love always involves a special readiness to be poured out for the sake of those who come within one's range of activity. In marriage this readiness, even though open to all, consists mainly in the love that parents give to their children. In virginity this readiness is open *to all people, who are embraced by the love of Christ the Spouse.*

Spousal love—with its maternal potential hidden in the heart of the woman as a virginal bride—when joined to Christ, the Redeemer of each and every person, is also predisposed to being open to each and every person. This is confirmed in the religious communities of apostolic life, and in a different way in communities of contemplative life, or the cloister. There exist still other forms of vocation to virginity for the sake of the Kingdom; for example, the secular institutes, or the communities of consecrated persons which flourish within movements, groups and associations. In all of these *the same truth about the spiritual motherhood* of virgins is confirmed in various ways. However, it is not only a matter of communal forms but also of non-communal forms. In brief, virginity as a woman's vocation is always the vocation of a person—of a unique, individual person. Therefore the spiritual motherhood which makes itself felt in this vocation is also profoundly personal.

This is also the basis of a specific *convergence between the virginity* of the unmarried woman and *the motherhood* of the married woman. This convergence moves not only from motherhood toward virginity, as emphasized above; it also moves from virginity toward marriage, the form of woman's vocation in which she becomes a mother by giving birth to her children. The starting point of this second analogy is *the meaning of marriage.* A woman is "married" either through the sacrament of marriage or spiritually through marriage to Christ. *In both cases marriage* signifies the "sincere gift of the person" of the bride to the groom. In this way, one can say that the profile of marriage is found spiritually in virginity. And does not physical motherhood also have to be a spiritual motherhood, in order to respond to the whole truth about the human being who is a unity of body and spirit? Thus there exist many reasons for discerning in these two different paths—the two different vocations of women—a profound complementarity, and even a profound union within a person's being.

"My Little Children with Whom I Am Again in Travail"

22. The Gospel reveals and enables us to understand precisely this *mode of being of the human person.* The Gospel helps every woman and every man to live it and thus attain fulfillment. There exists a total equality with respect to the gifts of the Holy Spirit, with respect to the "mighty works of God" (Acts 2:11). Moreover, it is precisely in the face of the "mighty works of God" that St. Paul, as a man, feels the need to refer to what is essentially feminine in order to express the truth about his own apostolic service. This is exactly what Paul of Tarsus does when he addresses the Galatians with the words: *"My little children, with whom I am again in travail"* (Gal 4:19). In the First Letter to the Corinthians (7:38), St. Paul proclaims the superiority of virginity over marriage, which is a constant teaching of the Church in accordance with the spirit of Christ's words recorded in the Gospel of Matthew (19:10-12); he does so without in any way obscuring the importance of physical and spiritual motherhood. Indeed in order to illustrate the Church's fundamental mission, he finds nothing better than the reference to motherhood.

The same analogy—and the same truth—are present in the *Dogmatic Constitution on the Church. Mary is the "figure" of the Church:*[43] "For in the mystery of the Church, herself rightly called mother and virgin, the Blessed Virgin came first as an eminent and singular exemplar of both virginity and motherhood.... The Son whom she brought forth is he whom God placed as the firstborn among many brethren (cf. Rom 8:29), namely, among the faithful. In their birth and development she cooperates with a maternal love."[44] "Moreover, contemplating Mary's mysterious sanctity, imitating her charity, and faithfully fulfilling the Father's will, the Church *herself becomes a mother* by accepting God's word in faith. For by her preaching and by baptism she brings forth to a new and immortal life children who are conceived by the Holy Spirit and born of God."[45] This is motherhood "according to the Spirit" with regard to the sons and daughters of the human race. And this motherhood—is already mentioned—becomes the woman's "role" also in virginity. "The Church *herself is a virgin*, who keeps whole and pure the fidelity she has pledged to her Spouse."[46] This is most perfectly fulfilled in Mary. The Church, therefore, "imitating the Mother of her Lord, and by the power of the Holy Spirit...preserves with virginal purity an integral faith, a firm hope, and a sincere charity."[47]

The Council has confirmed that, unless one looks to the Mother of God, it is impossible to understand the mystery of the Church, her reality, her essential vitality. *Indirectly* we find here *a reference to the biblical exemplar of the "woman"* which is already clearly outlined in the description of the "beginning" (cf. Gn 3:15) and which proceeds from creation, through sin to the redemption. In this way there is a conformation of the profound union between what is human and what constitutes the divine economy of salvation in human history. The Bible convinces us of the fact that one can have no adequate hermeneutic of man, or of what is "human," without appropriate reference to what is "feminine." There is an analogy in God's salvific economy: if we wish to understand it fully in relation to the whole of human history, we cannot omit, in the perspective of our faith, the mystery of "woman": virgin-mother-spouse.

VII. THE CHURCH—THE BRIDE OF CHRIST

The "Great Mystery"

23. Of fundamental importance here are the words of the Letter to the Ephesians: "Husbands, love your wives, as Christ loved the Church and gave himself up for her, that he might sanctify her, having cleansed her by the washing of water with the word, that he might present the Church to himself in splendor, without spot or wrinkle or any such thing, that she might be holy and without blemish. Even so husbands should love their wives as their own bodies. He who loves his wife loves himself. For no man ever hates his own flesh, but nourishes and cherishes it, as Christ does the Church, because we are members of his body. 'For this reason a man shall leave his father and mother and be joined to his wife, and the two shall become one flesh.' *This mystery is a profound one,* and I am saying that *it refers to Christ and the Church"* (5:25-32).

In this letter the author expresses the truth about the Church as the bride of Christ, and also indicates how this truth *is rooted in the biblical reality of the creation of the human being as male and female.* Created in the image and likeness of God as a "unity of the two," both have been called to a spousal love. Following the description of creation in the Book of Genesis (2:18-25), one can also say that this fundamental call appears in the creation of woman, and is inscribed by the Creator in the institution of marriage, which, according to Genesis 2:24, has the character of a union of persons *("communio personarum")* from the very beginning. Although not directly, the very description of the "beginning" (cf. Gn 1:27; 2:24) shows that the whole "ethos" of mutual relations between men and women has to correspond to the personal truth of their being.

All this has already been considered. The Letter to the Ephesians once again confirms this truth, while at the same time comparing the spousal character of the love between man and woman to the mystery of Christ and of the Church.

Christ is the Bridegroom of the Church—the Church is the Bride of Christ. This analogy is not without precedent; it transfers to the New Testament what was already contained *in the Old Testament,* especially in the prophets Hosea, Jeremiah, Ezekiel and Isaiah.[48] The respective passages deserve a separate analysis. Here we will cite only one text. This is how God speaks to his Chosen People through the Prophet: "Fear not, for you will not be ashamed; be not confounded, for you will not be put to shame; for you will forget the shame of your youth, and the reproach of your widowhood you will remember no more. *For your Maker is your husband,* the Lord of hosts is his name; and the Holy One of Israel is *your Redeemer,* the God of the whole earth he is called. For the Lord has called you like a wife forsaken and grieved in spirit, like a wife of youth when she is cast off, says your God. For a brief moment I forsook you, but with great compassion I will gather you. In overflowing wrath for a moment I hid my face from you, but with everlasting love I will have compassion on you, says the Lord, your Redeemer.... For the mountains may depart and the hills be removed, *but my steadfast love shall not depart from you,* and my covenant of peace shall not be removed says the Lord, who has compassion on you" (Is 54:4-8, 10).

Since the human being—man and woman—has been created in God's image and likeness, God can speak about himself through the lips of the Prophet using language which is essentially human. In the text of Isaiah quoted above, the expression of God's love is *"human,"* but the *love* itself *is divine.* Since it is God's love, its spousal character is properly divine, even though it is expressed by the analogy of a man's love for a woman. The woman-bride is Israel, God's Chosen People, and this choice originates exclusively in God's gratuitous love. It is precisely this love which explains the Covenant, a Covenant often presented as a marriage covenant which God always renews with his Chosen People. On the part of God the Covenant is a lasting "commitment"; he remains faithful to his spousal love even if the bride often shows herself to be unfaithful.

This *image of spousal love,* together with the figure of the divine Bridegroom—a very clear image in the texts of the Prophets—finds crowning confirmation in the Letter to the Ephesians (5:23-8:32). *Christ* is greeted as the bridegroom by John the Baptist (cf. Jn 3:27-29). Indeed Christ applies to himself this comparison drawn from the Prophets (cf. Mk 2:19-20). The Apostle Paul, who is a bearer of the Old Testament heritage, writes to the Corinthians: "I feel a divine jealousy for you, for I betrothed you to Christ to present you as a pure bride to her one husband" (2 Cor 11:2). But the fullest expression of the truth about Christ the Redeemer's love, according to the analogy of spousal love in marriage, is found in the Letter to the Ephesians: *"Christ loved the Church and gave himself up for her"* (5:25), thereby fully confirming the fact that the Church is the bride of Christ: "The Holy One of Israel is your Redeemer" (Is 54:5). In St. Paul's text the analogy of the spousal relationship moves simultaneously in two directions which make up the whole of the "great mystery" *("sacramentum magnum").* The covenant proper to spouses "explains" the spousal character of the union of Christ with the Church, and in its turn this union, as a "great sacrament," determines the sacramentality of marriage as a holy covenant between the two spouses, man and woman. Reading this rich and complex passage, which *taken as a whole is a great analogy,* we must *distinguish* that element which expresses the human reality of interpersonal relations from that which expresses in symbolic language the "great mystery" which is divine.

The Gospel "Innovation"

24. The text is addressed to the spouses as real women and men. It reminds them of the "ethos" of spousal love which goes back to the divine institution of marriage from the "beginning." Corresponding to the truth of this institution is the exhortation: *"Husbands, love your wives,"* love them because of that special and unique bond whereby in marriage a man and a woman become "one flesh" (Gn 2:24; Eph 5:31). In this love there is a fundamental *affirmation of the woman* as a person. This affirmation makes it possible for the female personality to develop fully and be enriched. This is precisely the way Christ acts as the bridegroom of the Church; he desires that she be "in splendor, without spot or wrinkle" (Eph 5:27). One can say that this fully captures the whole "style" of Christ in dealing with women. Husbands should make their own the elements of this style in regard to their wives; analogously, all men should do the same in regard to women in every situation. In this way both men and women bring about "the sincere gift of self."

The author of the Letter to the Ephesians sees no contradiction between an exhortation formulated in this way and the words: "Wives, be subject to your husbands, as to the Lord. For the husband is the head of the wife" (5:22-23). The author knows that this way of speaking, so profoundly rooted in the customs and religious tradition of the time, is to be understood and carried out in a new way: as *a "mutual subjection out of reverence for Christ"* (cf. Eph 5:21). This is especially true because the husband is called the "head" of the wife *as* Christ is the head of the Church; he is so in order to give "himself up for her" (Eph 5:25), and giving himself up for her means giving up even his own life. However, whereas in the relationship between Christ and the Church the subjection is only on the part of the Church, in the relationship between husband and wife the "subjection" is not one-sided but mutual.

In relation to the "old" this is evidently something "new": it is an innovation of the Gospel. We find various passages in which the apostolic writings express this innovation, even though they also communicate what is "old": what is rooted in the religious tradition of Israel, in its way of understanding and explaining the sacred texts, as for example the second chapter of the Book of Genesis.[49]

The apostolic letters are addressed to people living in an environment marked by that same traditional way of thinking and acting. The "innovation" of Christ is a fact: it constitutes the unambiguous content of the evangelical message and is the result of the redemption. However, the awareness that in marriage there is mutual "subjection of the spouses out of reverence for Christ," and not just that of the wife to the husband, must gradually establish itself in hearts, consciences, behavior and customs. This is a call which from that time onwards does not cease to challenge succeeding generations; it is a call which people have to accept ever anew. St. Paul not only wrote: "In Christ Jesus...there is no more man or woman," but also wrote: "There is no more slave or freeman." Yet how many generations were needed for such a principle to be realized in the history of humanity through the abolition of slavery! And what is one to say of the many forms of slavery to which individuals and peoples are subjected, which have not yet disappeared from history?

But *the challenge presented by the "ethos" of the redemption* is clear and definitive. All the reasons in favor of the "subjection" of woman to man in marriage must be understood in the sense of a "mutual subjection" of both "out of reverence for Christ." The measure of true spousal love finds its deepest source in Christ, who is the Bridegroom of the Church, his Bride.

The Symbolic Dimension of the "Great Mystery"

25. In the Letter to the Ephesians we encounter *a second dimension* of the analogy which, taken as a whole, serves to reveal the "great mystery." This is *a symbolic dimension.* If God's love for the human person, for the Chosen People of Israel, is presented by the Prophets as the love of the bridegroom for the bride, such an analogy expresses the "spousal" quality and the divine and nonhuman character of God's love: "For your Maker is your husband...the God of the whole earth he is called" (Is 54:5). The same can also be said of the spousal love of Christ the Redeemer: "For God so loved the world that he gave his only son" (Jn 3:16). It is a matter, therefore, of God's love expressed by means of the redemption accomplished by Christ. According to St. Paul's letter, this love is "like" the spousal love of human spouses, but naturally it is not "the same." For the analogy implies a likeness, while at the same time leaving ample room for non-likeness.

This is easily seen in regard to the person of the "bride." According to the Letter to the Ephesians, the bride *is the Church,* just as for the Prophets the bride was Israel. She is therefore *a collective subject* and not *an individual person.* This collective subject is the People of God, a community made up of many persons, both women and men. "Christ has loved the Church" precisely as a community, as the People of God. At the same time, in this Church, which in the same passage is also called his "body" (cf. Eph 5:23), he has loved every individual person. For Christ has redeemed all without exception, every man and woman. It is precisely this love of God which is expressed in the redemption; the spousal character of this love reaches completion in the history of humanity and of the world.

Christ has entered this history and remains in it as the Bridegroom who "has given himself." "To give" means "to become a sincere gift" in the most complete and radical way: "Greater love has no man than this" (Jn 15:13). According to this conception, *all human beings—both women and men—are called* through the Church, *to be the "Bride" of Christ, the Redeemer of the world.* In this way "being the bride," and thus the "feminine" element, becomes a symbol of all that is "human," according to the words of Paul: "There is neither male nor female; for you are all *one* in Christ Jesus" (Gal 3:28).

From a linguistic viewpoint we can say that the analogy of spousal love found in the Letter to the Ephesians links what is "masculine" to what is "feminine," since, as members of the Church, men too are included in the concept of "Bride." This should not surprise us, for St. Paul, in order to express his mission in Christ and in the Church, speaks of the "little children with whom he is again in travail" (cf. Gal 4:19). In the sphere of what is "human"—of what is humanly personal—*"masculinity" and "femininity" are distinct,* yet at the same time they *complete and explain each other.* This is also present in the great analogy of the "Bride" in the Letter to the Ephesians. In the Church every human being—male and female—is the "Bride," in that he or she accepts the gift of the love of Christ the Redeemer, and seeks to respond to it with the gift of his or her own person.

Christ is the Bridegroom. This expresses the truth about the love of God who "first loved us" (cf. 1 Jn 4:19) and who, with the gift generated by this spousal love for man, has exceeded all human expectations: "He loved them to the end" (Jn 13:1). The Bridegroom—the Son consubstantial with the Father as God—became the Son of Mary; he became the "son of man," true man, a male. *The symbol of the Bridegroom is masculine.* This masculine symbol represents the human aspect of the divine love which God has for Israel, for the Church, and for all people. Meditating on what the Gospels say about Christ's attitude toward women, we can conclude that *as a man,* a son of Israel, he *revealed* the dignity of the "daughters of Abraham" (cf. Lk 13:16), *the dignity belonging to women* from the very "beginning" on an equal footing with men. At the same time Christ emphasized the originality which distinguishes women from men, all the richness lavished upon women in the mystery of creation. Christ's attitude toward women serves as a model of what the Letter to the Ephesians expresses with the concept of "bridegroom." Precisely because Christ's divine love is the love of a Bridegroom, it is the model and pattern of all human love, men's love in particular.

The Eucharist

26. Against the broad background of the "great mystery" expressed in the spousal relationship between Christ and the Church, it is possible to understand adequately the calling of the "Twelve." *In calling only men as his apostles,* Christ *acted in a completely free and sovereign manner.* In doing so, he exercised the same freedom with which, in all his behavior, he emphasized the dignity and the vocation of women, without conforming to the prevailing customs and to the traditions sanctioned by the legislation of the time. Consequently, the

assumption that he called men to be apostles in order to conform with the widespread mentality of his times, does not at all correspond to Christ's way of acting. "Teacher, we know that you are true, and teach the way of God truthfully, and care for no man; for *you do not regard the position of men*" (Mt 22:16). These words fully characterize *Jesus of Nazareth's behavior.* Here one also finds an explanation for the calling of the "Twelve." They are with Christ at the Last Supper. They alone receive the sacramental charge, "Do this in remembrance of me" (Lk 22:19; 1 Cor 11:24), which is joined to the institution of the Eucharist. On Easter Sunday night they receive the Holy Spirit for the forgiveness of sins: "Whose sins you forgive are forgiven them, and whose sins you retain are retained" (Jn 20:23).

We find ourselves at the very heart of the Paschal Mystery, which completely reveals the spousal love of God. Christ is the Bridegroom because "he has given himself": his body has been "given," his blood has been "poured out" (cf. Lk 22:19-20). In this way "he loved them to the end" (Jn 13:1). The "sincere gift" contained in the sacrifice of the cross gives definitive prominence to the spousal meaning of God's love. As the Redeemer of the world, Christ is the Bridegroom of the Church. *The Eucharist* is *the Sacrament of our redemption.* It is *the Sacrament of the Bridegroom and of the Bride.* The Eucharist makes present and realizes anew in a sacramental manner the redemptive act of Christ, who "creates" the Church, his body. Christ is united with this "body" as the bridegroom with the bride. All this is contained in the Letter to the Ephesians. The perennial "unity of the two" that exists between man and woman from the very "beginning" is introduced into this "great mystery" of Christ and of the Church.

Since Christ, in instituting the Eucharist, linked it in such an explicit way to the priestly service of the apostles, it is legitimate to conclude that he thereby wished to express the relationship between man and woman, between what is "feminine" and what is "masculine." It is a relationship willed by God both in the mystery of creation and in the mystery of redemption. It is *the Eucharist* above all that expresses *the redemptive act of Christ the Bridegroom toward the Church the Bride.* This is clear and unambiguous when the sacramental ministry of the Eucharist, in which the priest *acts "in persona Christi,"* is performed by a man. This explanation confirms the teaching of the Declaration *Inter Insigniores,* published at the behest of Paul VI in response to the question concerning the admission of women to the ministerial priesthood.[50]

The Gift of the Bride

27. The Second Vatican Council renewed the Church's awareness of the universality of the priesthood. In the New Covenant there is only one sacrifice and only one priest: Christ. *All the baptized share in the one priesthood of Christ,* both men and women, inasmuch as they must present their bodies as a living sacrifice, holy and acceptable to God (cf. Rom 12:1), give witness to

Christ in every place, and give an explanation to anyone who asks the reason for the hope in eternal life that is in them (cf. 1 Pt 3:15).[51] Universal participation in Christ's sacrifice, in which the Redeemer has offered to the Father the whole world and humanity in particular, brings it about that all in the Church are "a kingdom of priests" (Rv 5:10; cf. 1 Pt 2:9), who not only share in the priestly mission but also in the prophetic and kingly mission of Christ the Messiah. Furthermore, this participation determines the organic unity of the Church, the People of God, with Christ. It expresses at the same time the "great mystery" described in the Letter to the Ephesians: *the Bride united to her Bridegroom;* united, because she lives his life; united, because she shares in his threefold mission *(tria munera Christi);* united *in such a manner as to respond* with a "sincere gift" of *self to the inexpressible gift of the love of the Bridegroom,* the Redeemer of the world. This concerns everyone in the Church, women as well as men. It obviously concerns those who share in the "ministerial priesthood,"[52] which is characterized by service. In the context of the "great mystery" of Christ and of the Church, all are called to respond—as a bride—with the gift of their lives to the inexpressible gift of the love of Christ, who alone, as the Redeemer of the world, is the Church's Bridegroom. The "royal priesthood," which is universal, at the same time expresses the gift of the Bride.

This is of *fundamental importance for understanding the Church in her own essence,* so as to avoid applying to the Church—even in her dimension as an "institution" made up of human beings and forming part of history—criteria of understanding and judgment which do not pertain to her nature. Although the Church possesses a "hierarchical" structure,[53] nevertheless this structure is totally ordered to the holiness of Christ's members. And holiness is measured according to the "great mystery" in which the Bride responds with the gift of love to the gift of the Bridegroom. She does this "in the Holy Spirit," since "God's love has been poured into our hearts through the Holy Spirit who has been given to us" (Rom 5:5). The Second Vatican Council, confirming the teaching of the whole of tradition, recalled that in the hierarchy of holiness it is *precisely the "woman,"* Mary of Nazareth, who is the "figure" of the Church. She "precedes" everyone on the path to holiness; in her person "the Church has already reached that perfection whereby she exists without spot or wrinkle" (cf. Eph 5: 27).[54] In this sense, one can say that the Church is *both* "Marian" and "Apostolic-Petrine."[55]

In the history of the Church, even from earliest times, there were side-by-side with men *a number of women,* for whom the response of the Bride to the Bridegroom's redemptive love acquired full expressive force. First we see those women who had personally encountered Christ and followed him. After his departure, together with the apostles, they "devoted themselves to prayer" in the upper room in Jerusalem until the day of Pentecost. On that day the Holy Spirit spoke through "the sons and daughters" of the People of God, thus fulfilling the words of the prophet Joel (cf. Acts 2:17). These women, and others afterwards, played *an active and important role in the life of the early Church,* in building up from its foundations the first Christian community—and subsequent communities—*through their own charisms and their varied service.* The apostolic writings note their names, such as Phoebe, "a deaconess of the Church at Cenchreae" (cf. Rom 16:1), Prisca with her husband Aquila (cf. 2 Tm 4:19), Evodia and Syntyche (cf. Phil 4:2), Mary, Tryphaena, Persis, and Tryphosa (cf. Rom 16:6, 12). St. Paul speaks of their "hard work" for Christ, and this hard work indicates the various fields of the Church's apostolic service, beginning with the "domestic Church." For in the latter, "sincere faith" passes from the mother to her children and grandchildren, as was the case in the house of Timothy (cf. 2 Tm 1:5).

The same thing is repeated down the centuries, from one generation to the next, as *the history of the Church* demonstrates. By defending the dignity of women and their vocation, the Church has shown honor and gratitude for those women who—faithful to the Gospel—have shared in every age in the apostolic mission of the whole People of God. They are the holy martyrs, virgins, and mothers of families, who bravely bore witness to their faith and passed on the Church's faith and tradition by bringing up their children in the spirit of the Gospel.

In every age and in every country we find many "perfect" women (cf. Prv 31:10) who, despite persecution, difficulties and discrimination, have shared in the Church's mission. It suffices to mention: Monica, the mother of Augustine, Macrina, Olga of Kiev, Matilda of Tuscany, Hedwig of Silesia, Jadwiga of Cracow, Elizabeth of Thuringia, Birgitta of Sweden, Joan of Arc, Rose of Lima, Elizabeth Ann Seton and Mary Ward.

The witness and the achievements of Christian women have had a significant impact on the life of the Church as well as of society. Even in the face of serious social discrimination, holy women have acted "freely," strengthened by their union with Christ. Such union and freedom rooted in God explain, for example, the great work of St. Catherine of Siena in the life of the Church, and the work of St. Teresa of Jesus in the monastic life.

In our own days too the Church is constantly enriched by the witness of the many women who fulfill their vocation to holiness. Holy women are an incarnation of the feminine ideal; they are also a model for all Christians, a model of the *"sequela Christi,"* an example of how the Bride must respond with love to the love of the Bridegroom.

VIII. "THE GREATEST OF THESE IS LOVE"

In the Face of Changes

28. "The Church believes that Christ, who died and was raised up for all, can through his Spirit offer man the light and the strength to respond to his supreme destiny."[56] We can apply these words of the Conciliar Constitution *Gaudium et Spes* to the present reflections. The particular reference to the

dignity of women and their vocation, precisely in our time, can and must be received in the "light and power" which the Spirit grants to human beings, including the people of our own age, which is marked by so many different transformations. The Church "holds that in her Lord and Master can be found the key, the focal point, and the goal" of man and "of all human history," and she "maintains *that beneath all changes there are many realities which do not change and which have their ultimate foundation in Christ,* who is the same yesterday and today, yes and forever."[57]

These words of the *Constitution on the Church in the Modern World* show the path to be followed in undertaking the tasks connected with the dignity and vocation of women, against the background of the significant changes of our times. We can face these changes correctly and adequately only *if we go back* to the foundations which are to be found in Christ, to those *"immutable" truths and values* of which he himself remains the "faithful witness" (cf. Rv 1:5) and Teacher. A different way of acting would lead to doubtful, if not actually erroneous and deceptive results.

The Dignity of Women and the Order of Love

29. The passage from the Letter to the Ephesians already quoted (5:21-33), in which the relationship between Christ and the Church is presented as the link between the Bridegroom and the Bride, also makes reference to the institution of marriage as recorded in the Book of Genesis (cf. 2:24). This passage connects the truth about marriage as a primordial sacrament with the creation of man and woman in the image and likeness of God (cf. Gn 1:27; 5:1). The significant comparison in the Letter to the Ephesians gives perfect clarity to *what is decisive for the dignity of women both in the eyes of God*—the Creator and Redeemer—*and in the eyes of human beings*—men and women. In God's eternal plan, woman is the one in whom the order of love in the created world of persons takes first root. The order of love belongs to the intimate life of God himself, the life of the Trinity. In the intimate life of God, the Holy Spirit is the personal hypostasis of love. Through the spirit, Uncreated Gift, love becomes a gift for created persons. *Love, which is of God, communicates itself to creatures:* "God's love has been poured into our hearts through the Holy Spirit who has been given to us" (Rom 5:5).

The calling of women into existence at man's side as "a helper fit for him" (Gn 2:18) in the "unity of the two," provides the visible world of creatures with particular conditions so that "the love of God may be poured into the hearts" of the beings created in his image. When the author of the Letter to the Ephesians calls Christ "the Bridegroom" and the Church "the Bride," he indirectly confirms through this analogy *the truth about woman as bride.* The Bridegroom is the one who loves. The Bride is loved: *it is she who receives love, in order to love in return.*

Rereading Genesis in light of the spousal symbol in the Letter to the Ephesians enables us to grasp a truth which seems to determine in an essential manner the question of women's dignity, and, subsequently, also the question of their vocation: *the dignity of women is measured by the order of love,* which is essentially the order of justice and charity.[58]

Only a person can love and only a person can be loved. This statement is primarily ontological in nature, and it gives rise to an ethical affirmation. Love is an ontological and ethical requirement of the person. The person must be loved, since love alone corresponds to what the person is. This explains *the commandment of love,* known already in the Old Testament (cf. Dt 6:5; Lv 19:18) and placed by Christ at the very center of the Gospel *"ethos"* (cf. Mt 22:36-40, Mk 12:28-34). This also explains the *primacy of love* expressed by St. Paul in the First Letter to the Corinthians: "The greatest of these is love" (cf. 13:13).

Unless we refer to this order and primacy we cannot give a complete and adequate answer to the question about women's dignity and vocation. When we say that the woman is the one who receives love in order to love in return, this refers not only or above all to the specific spousal relationship of marriage. It means something more universal, based on the very fact of her being a woman within all the interpersonal relationships which, in the most varied ways, shape society and structure the interaction between all persons—men and women. In this broad and diversified context, a *woman represents a particular value by the fact that she is a human person,* and, at the same time, this particular person, *by the fact of her femininity.* This concerns each and every woman, independently of the cultural context in which she lives, and independently of her spiritual, psychological and physical characteristics, as for example, age, education, health, work, and whether she is married or single.

The passage from the Letter to the Ephesians which we have been considering enables us to think of a special kind of "prophetism" that belongs to women in their femininity. The analogy of the Bridegroom and the Bride speaks of the love with which every human being—man and woman—is loved by God in Christ. But in the context of the biblical analogy and the text's interior logic, it is precisely the woman—the bride—who manifests this truth to everyone. This *"prophetic" character of women in their femininity* finds its highest expression in the Virgin Mother of God. She emphasizes, in the fullest and most direct way, the intimate linking of the order of love—which enters the world of human persons through a woman—with the Holy Spirit. At the Annunciation Mary hears the words: "The Holy Spirit will come upon you" (Lk 1:35).

Awareness of a Mission

30. A woman's dignity is closely connected with the love which she receives by the very reason of her femininity; it is likewise connected *with the love which she gives in return.* The truth about the person and about love is thus confirmed. With regard to the truth about the person, we must turn again to the Second Vatican Council: "Man, who is the only creature on earth that God willed for its own sake, cannot fully find himself except through a sincere gift of self."[59] This

applies to every human being, as a person created in God's image, whether man or woman. This ontological affirmation also indicates the ethical dimension of a person's vocation. *Woman can only find herself by giving love to others.*

From the "beginning," woman—like man—was created and "placed" by God in this order of love. The sin of the first parents did not destroy this order, nor irreversibly cancel it out. This is proved by the words of the Proto-evangelium (cf. Gn 3:15). Our reflections have focused on *the particular place occupied by the "woman"* in this key text of revelation. It is also to be noted how the same Woman, who attains the position of a biblical "exemplar," also appears within the eschatological perspective of the world and of humanity given in the Book of Revelation.[60] She is *"a woman clothed with the sun,"* with the moon under her feet, and on her head a crown of stars (cf. Rv 12:1). One can say she is a Woman of cosmic scale, on a scale with the whole work of creation. At the same time she is "suffering the pangs and anguish of childbirth" (Rv 12:2) like Eve "the mother of all the living" (Gn 3:20). She also suffers because "before the woman who is about to give birth" (cf. Rv 12:4) there stands "the great dragon...that ancient serpent" (Rv 12:9), already known from the Proto-evangelium: the Evil One, the "father of lies" and of sin (cf. Jn 8:44). The "ancient serpent" wishes to devour "the child." While we see in this text an echo of the infancy narrative (cf. Mt 2:13, 16), we can also see that the struggle with evil and the Evil One marks the biblical exemplar of the "woman" from the beginning to the end of history. It is also *a struggle for man, for his true good, for his salvation.* Is not the Bible trying to tell us that it is precisely in the "woman"—Eve-Mary—that history witnesses a dramatic struggle for every human being, the struggle for his or her fundamental "yes" or "no" to God and God's eternal plan for humanity?

While the dignity of woman witnesses to the love which she receives in order to love in return, the biblical "exemplar" of the Woman also seems to reveal *the true order of love which constitutes woman's own vocation.* Vocation is meant here in its fundamental, and one may say universal significance, a significance which is then actualized and expressed in women's many different "vocations" in the Church and the world.

The moral and spiritual strength of a woman is joined to her awareness that *God entrusts the human being to her in a special way.* Of course, God entrusts every human being to each and every other human being. But this entrusting concerns women in a special way—precisely by reason of their femininity—and this in a particular way determines their vocation.

The moral force of women, which draws strength from this awareness and this entrusting, expresses itself in a great number of figures of the Old Testament, of the time of Christ, and of later ages right up to our own day.

A woman is strong because of her awareness of this entrusting, strong because of the fact that God "entrusts the human being to her," always and in every way, even in the situations of social discrimination in which she may find herself. This awareness and this fundamental vocation speak to women of the dignity which they receive from God himself, and this makes them "strong" and strengthens their vocation. Thus the "perfect woman" (cf. Prv 31:10) becomes an irreplaceable support and source of spiritual strength for other people, who perceive the great energies of her spirit. These "perfect women" are owed much by their families, and sometimes by whole nations.

In our own time, the successes of science and technology make it possible to attain material well being to a degree hitherto unknown. While this favors some, it pushes others to the margins of society. In this way, unilateral progress can also lead to a gradual *loss of sensitivity for man, that is, for what is essentially human.* In this sense, our time in particular *awaits the manifestation* of that "genius" which belongs to women, and which can ensure sensitivity for human beings in every circumstance: because they are human!—and because "the greatest of these is love" (cf. 1 Cor 13:13).

Thus a careful reading of the biblical exemplar of the Woman—from the Book of Genesis to the Book of Revelation—confirms that which constitutes woman's dignity and vocation, as well as that which is unchangeable and ever relevant in them, because it has its "ultimate foundation in Christ, who is the same yesterday and today, yes and forever."[61] If the human being is entrusted by God to women in a particular way, does not this mean that *Christ looks to them for the accomplishment of the "royal priesthood"* (1 Pt 2:9), which is the treasure he has given to every individual? Christ, as the supreme and only priest of the New and Eternal Covenant, and as the Bridegroom of the Church, does not cease to submit this same inheritance to the Father through the Spirit, so that God may be "everything to everyone" (1 Cor 15:28).[62]

Then the truth that "the greatest of these is love" (cf. 1 Cor 13:13) will have its definitive fulfillment.

IX. CONCLUSION

"If You Knew the Gift of God"

31. "If you knew the gift of God" (Jn 4:10), Jesus says to the Samaritan woman during one of those remarkable conversations which show his great esteem for the dignity of women and for the vocation which enables them to share in his messianic mission.

The present reflections, now at an end, have sought to recognize, within the "gift of God," what he, as Creator and Redeemer, entrusts to women, to every woman. In the Spirit of Christ, in fact, women can discover the entire meaning of their femininity and thus be disposed to making a "sincere gift of self" to others, thereby finding themselves.

During the Marian Year *the Church desires to give thanks to the Most Holy Trinity* for the "mystery of woman" and for every woman—for that which constitutes the eternal measure of her feminine dignity, for the "great works of God," which throughout human history have been accomplished in and through her. After all, was it not in and through her that the greatest event in human history—the incarnation of God himself—was accomplished?

Therefore *the Church gives thanks for each and every woman:* for mothers, for sisters, for wives; for women consecrated to God in virginity; for women dedicated to the many human beings who await the gratuitous love of another person; for women who watch over the human persons in the family, which is the fundamental sign of the human community; for women who work professionally, and who at times are burdened by a great social responsibility; for *"perfect"* women and for "weak" women—for all women as they have come forth from the heart of God in all the beauty and richness of their femininity; as they have been embraced by his eternal love; as, together with men, they are pilgrims on this earth, which is the temporal "homeland" of all people and is transformed sometimes into a "valley of tears"; as they assume, together with men, *a common responsibility for the destiny of humanity* according to daily necessities and according to that definitive destiny which the human family has in God himself, in the bosom of the ineffable Trinity.

The Church gives thanks *for all the manifestations of the feminine "genius"* which have appeared in the course of history, in the midst of all peoples and nations, she gives thanks for all the charisms which the Holy Spirit distributes to women in the history of the People of God, for all the victories which she owes to their faith, hope and charity: she gives thanks for all *the fruits of feminine holiness.*

The Church asks at the same time that these invaluable "manifestations of the Spirit" (cf. 1 Cor 12:4ff.), which with great generosity are poured forth upon the "daughters" of the eternal Jerusalem, may be attentively recognized and appreciated so that they may return for the common good of the Church and of humanity, especially in our times. Meditating on the biblical mystery of the "woman," the Church prays that in this mystery all women may discover themselves and their "supreme vocation."

May *Mary,* who "is a model of the Church in the matter of faith, charity, and perfect union with Christ,"[63] obtain for all of us *this same "grace,"* in the year which we have dedicated to her as we approach the third millennium from the coming of Christ.

With these sentiments, I impart the Apostolic Blessing to all the faithful, and in a special way to women, my sisters in Christ.

Given in Rome, at St. Peter's, on August 15, the Solemnity of the Assumption of the Blessed Virgin Mary, in the year 1988, the tenth of my Pontificate.

JOHN PAUL II

NOTES

[1] The Council's Message to Women (December 8, 1965): *AAS* 58 (1966), 13-14.

[2] Cf. Second Vatican Ecumenical Council, Pastoral Constitution on the Church in the Modern World *Gaudium et Spes,* 8, 9, 60.

[3] Cf. Second Vatican Ecumenical Council, Decree on the Apostolate of the Laity *Apostolicam Actuositatem,* 9.

[4] Cf. Pius XII, Address to Italian Women (October 21, 1945): *AAS* 37 (1945), 284-295; Address to the World Union of Catholic Women's Organizations (April 24, 1952): *AAS* 44 (1952), 420-424; Address to the participants in the XIV International Meeting of the World Union of Catholic Women's Organizations (September 29,1957): *AAS* 49 (1957), 906-922.

[5] Cf. John XXIII, Encyclical Letter *Pacem in Terris* (April 11, 1963): *AAS* 55 (1963), 267-268.

[6] Proclamation of St. Teresa of Jesus as a "Doctor of the Universal Church" (September 27, 1970): *AAS* 62 (1970), 590-596; Proclamation of St. Catherine of Siena as a "Doctor of the Universal Church" (October 4, 1970): *AAS* 62 (1970), 673-678.

[7] Cf. *AAS* 65 (1973), 284f.

[8] Paul VI, Address to participants at the National Meeting of the Centro Italiano Femminile (December 6, 1976): *Insegnamenti de Paolo VI,* XIV (1976), 1017.

[9] Cf. Encyclical Letter *Redemptoris Mater* (March 25, 1987), 46: *AAS* 79 (1987), 424f.

[10] Second Vatican Ecumenical Council, Dogmatic Constitution on the Church *Lumen Gentium,* 1.

[11] An illustration of the anthropological and theological significance of the "beginning" can be seen in the first part of the Wednesday General Audience Addresses dedicated to the "Theology of the Body," beginning September 5, 1979: *Insegnamenti* II, 2 (1979), 234-236.

[12] Second Vatican Ecumenical Council, Pastoral Constitution on the Church in the Modern World *Gaudium et Spes,* 22.

[13] Second Vatican Ecumenical Council, Declaration on the Relation of the Church to Non-Christian Religions *Nostra Aetate,* 1.

[14] *Ibid.,* 2.

[15] Second Vatican Ecumenical Council, Dogmatic Constitution on Divine Revelation *Dei Verbum,* 2.

[16] Already according to the Fathers of the Church the first revelation of the Trinity in the New Testament took place in the Annunciation. One reads in a homily attributed to St. Gregory Thaumaturgus: "You, O Mary, are resplendent with light in the sublime spiritual kingdom! In you the Father, who is without beginning and whose power has covered you, is glorified. In you the Son, whom you bore in the flesh, is adored. In you the Holy Spirit, who has brought about in your womb the birth of the great King, is celebrated. And it is thanks to you, O Full of grace, that the holy and consubstantial Trinity has been able to be known in the world" *(Hom. 2 in Annuntiat. Virg. Mariae: PG* 10, 1169). Cf. also St. Andrew of Crete, *In Annuntiat. B. Mariae: PG* 97, 909.

[17] Cf. Second Vatican Ecumenical Council, Declaration on the Relation of the Church to Non-Christian Religions *Nostra Aetate, 2.*

[18] The theological doctrine on the Mother of God (Theotókos), held by many Fathers of the Church, and clarified and defined at the Council of Ephesus *(DS* 251) and at the Council of Chalcedon *(DS* 301), has been stated again by the Second Vatican Council in Chapter VIII of the Dogmatic Constitution on the Church *Lumen Gentium,* 52-69. Cf. Encyclical Letter *Redemptoris Mater,* 4, 31-32 and the Notes 9, 78-83: *loc. cit.,* 365, 402-404.

[19] Cf. Encyclical Letter *Redemptoris Mater,* 7-11 and the texts of the Fathers cited in Note 21: *loc. cit.,* 367-373.

[20] Cf. *ibid.,* 39-41: *loc. cit.,* 412-418.

[21] Cf. Second Vatican Ecumenical Council, Dogmatic Constitution on the Church *Lumen Gentium,* 36.

[22] Cf. St. Irenaeus, *Adv. haer;* V, 6, 1; V, 16, 2-3: *S. Ch.* 153, 72-81 and 216-221; St. Gregory of Nyssa, *De hom. op.* 16: *PG* 44, 180; *In Cant. Cant. Hom.* 2: *PG* 44, 805-808; St. Augustine, *In Ps.* 4, 8: *CCL* 38, 17.

[23] "Persona est naturae rationalis individua substantia": Manlius Severinus Boethius, *Liber de persona et duabus naturis,* III: *PL* 64, 1343; cf. St. Thomas Aquinas, *Summa Theologiae,* Ia, q. 29, art. 1.

[24] Among the Fathers of the Church who affirm the fundamental equality of man and woman before God cf. Origen, *In Iesu nave* IX, 9: *PG* 12, 878; Clement of Alexandria, *Paed.* 1, 4: *S. Ch.* 70, 128-131; St. Augustine, *Sermo* 51, II, 3: *PL* 38, 334-335.

[25] St. Gregory of Nyssa states: "God is above all love and the fount of love. The great John says this: 'Love is of God' and 'God is love' (1 Jn 4:7-8). The Creator has impressed this character also on us. 'By this all men will know that you are my disciples, if you have love for one another' (Jn 13:35). Therefore, if this is not present, all the image becomes disfigured" *(De hom. op.* 5: *PG* 44, 137).

[26] Second Vatican Ecumenical Council, Pastoral Constitution on the Church in the Modern World *Gaudium et Spes,* 24.

[27] Cf. Nm 23:19; Hos 11:9; Is 40:18; 46:5; cf. also Fourth Lateran Council *(DS* 806).

[28] Second Vatican Ecumenical Council, Pastoral Constitution on the Church in the Modern World *Gaudium et Spes,* 13.

[29] "Diabolic" from the Greek "dia-ballo" = "I divide, separate, slander."

[30] Cf. Origen, *In Gen. hom.* 13, 4: *PG* 12, 234; St. Gregory of Nyssa, *De virg.* 12: *S. Ch.* 119, 404-419; *De beat.* VI: *PG* 44, 1272.

[31] Cf. Second Vatican Ecumenical Council, Pastoral Constitution on the Church in the Modern World *Gaudium et Spes,* 13.

[32] Cf. *ibid.,* 24.

[33] It is precisely by appealing to the divine law that the Fathers of the fourth century strongly react against the discrimination still in effect with regard to women in the customs and the civil legislation of their time. Cf. St. Gregory of Nazianzus, *Or.* 37, 6: *PG* 36, 290; St. Jerome, *Ad Oceanum ep.* 77, 3: *PL* 22, 691; St. Ambrose, *De instit. virg.* III, 16: *PL* 16, 309; St. Augustine, *Sermo* 132, 2: *PL* 38, 735; *Sermo* 392, 4: *PL* 39, 1711.

[34] Cf. St. Irenaeus, *Adv. haer.* III, 23, 7: *S. Ch.* 211, 462-465; V, 21, 1: *S. Ch.* 153, 260-265; St. Epiphanius, *Panar.* III, 2, 78: *PG* 42, 728-729; St. Augustine, *Enarr. in Ps.* 103, S. 4, 6: *CCL* 40, 1525.

[35] Cf. St. Justin, *Dial. cum Tryph.* 100: *PG* 6, 709-712; St. Irenaeus, *Adv. haer.* III, 22, 4: *S. Ch.* 211, 438-445; V, 19, 1: *S. Ch.* 153, 248-251; St. Cyril of Jerusalem, *Catech.* 12, 15: *PG* 33, 741; St. John Chrysostom, *In Ps.* 44, 7: *PG* 55, 193; St. John Damascene, *Hom. 2 in dorm. B.V.M.* 3: *S. Ch.* 80, 130-135; Hesychius, *Sermo 5 in Deiparam; PG* 93, 1464f.; Tertullian, *De carne Christi* 17: *CCL* 2, 904f.; St. Jerome, *Epist.* 22, 21: *PL* 22, 408; St. Augustine, *Sermo* 51, 2-3: *PL* 38, 335; *Sermo* 232, 2: *PL* 38, 1108; J. H. Newman, *A Letter to the Rev. E. B. Pusey,* Longmans, London 1865; M. J. Scheeben, *Handbuch der Katholischen Dogmatik,* V/1 (Freiburg 1954), 243-266; V/2 (Freiburg 306-499).

[36] Second Vatican Ecumenical Council, Pastoral Constitution on the Church in the Modern World *Gaudium et Spes,* 22.

[37] Cf. St. Ambrose, *De instit. virg.* V, 33: *PL* 16, 313.

[38] Cf. Rabanus Maurus, *De vita beatae Mariae Magdalenae,* XXVII: "Salvator... ascensionis suae eam (=Mariam Magdalenam) ad apostolos instituit apostolam" *(PL* 112, 1474). "Facta est Apostolorum Apostola per hoc quod ei committitur ut resurrectionem dominicam discipulis annuntiet": St. Thomas Aquinas, *In Ioannem Evangelistam Expositio,* c. XX, 11. III, 6 *(Sancti Thomae Aquinatis Comment in Matthaeum et Ioannem Evangelistas),* Ed. Parmen. X, 629.

[39] Second Vatican Ecumenical Council, Pastoral Constitution on the Church in the Modern World *Gaudium et Spes,* 24.

[40] Encyclical Letter *Redemptoris Mater,* 18: *loc. cit.,* 383.

[41] Cf. Second Vatican Ecumenical Council, Pastoral Constitution on the Church in the Modern World *Gaudium et Spes,* 24.

[42] Cf. John Paul II, Wednesday General Audience Addresses, April 7 and 21, 1982: *Insegnamenti* V, 1, (1982), 1126-1131 and 1175-1179.

[43] Cf. Second Vatican Ecumenical Council, Dogmatic Constitution on the Church *Lumen Gentium,* 63; St. Ambrose, *In Lc* II, 7: *S. Ch.* 45, 74; *De instit. virg.* XIV, 87-89: *PL* 16, 326-327; St. Cyril of Alexandria, *Hom.* 4: *PG* 77, 996; St. Isidore of Seville, *Allegoriae* 139: *PL* 83, 117.

[44] Second Vatican Ecumenical Council, Dogmatic Constitution on the Church *Lumen Gentium,* 63.

[45] *Ibid.,* 64.

[46] *Ibid.,* 64.

[47] *Ibid.,* 64. Concerning the relation Mary-Church which continuously recurs in the reflection of the Fathers of the Church and of the entire Christian Tradition, cf. Encyclical Letter *Redemptoris Mater,* 42-44 and Notes 117-127: *loc. cit.,* 418-422. Cf. also: Clement of Alexandria, *Paed.* 1, 6: *S. Ch.* 70, 186f.; St. Ambrose, *In Lc* II, 7: *S. Ch.* 45, 74; St. Augustine, *Sermo* 192, 2: *PL* 38, 1012; *Sermo* 195, 2: *PL* 38, 1018; *Sermo* 25, 8: *PL* 46, 938; St. Leo the Great, *Sermo* 25, 5: *PL* 54, 211; *Sermo* 26, 2: *PL* 54, 213; St. Bede the Venerable, *In Lc* I, 2: *PL* 92, 330. "Both mothers—writes Isaac of Stella, disciple of St. Bernard—both virgins, both conceive through the work of the Holy Spirit...Mary...has given birth in body to her Head; the Church...gives to this Head her

body. The one and the other are mothers of Christ: but neither of the two begets him entirely without the other. Properly for that reason...that which is said in general of the virgin mother Church is understood especially of the virgin mother Mary; and that which is said in a special way of the virgin mother Mary must be attributed in general to the virgin mother Church; and all that is said about one of the two can be understood without distinction of one from the other" *(Sermo* 51, 7-8: *S. Ch.* 339, 202-205).

[48] Cf. for example, Hos 1:2; 2:16-18; Jer 2:2; Ez 16:8; Is 50:1; 54:5-8.

[49] Cf. Col 3:18; 1 Pt 3:1-6; Ti 2:4-5; Eph 5:22-24; 1 Cor 11:3-16; 14:33-35; 1 Tm 2:11-15.

[50] Cf. Congregation for the Doctrine of the Faith, Declaration Concerning the Question of the Admission of Women to the Ministerial Priesthood *Inter Insigniores* (October 15, 1976): *AAS* 69 (1977), 98-116.

[51]. Cf. Second Vatican Ecumenical Council, Dogmatic Constitution on the Church *Lumen Gentium,* 10.

[52] Cf. *ibid.,* 10.

[53] Cf. *ibid.,* 18-29.

[54] *Ibid.,* 65; cf. also 63; cf. Encyclical Letter *Redemptoris Mater,* 2-6; *loc. cit.,* 362-367.

[55] "This *Marian profile* is also—even perhaps more so—fundamental and characteristic for the Church as is the *apostolic* and *Petrine* profile to which it is profoundly united.... The Marian dimension of the Church is antecedent to that of the Petrine, without being in any way divided from it or being less complementary. Mary Immaculate precedes all others, including obviously Peter himself and the apostles. This is so, not only because Peter and the apostles, being born of the human race under the burden of sin, form part of the Church which is 'holy from out of sinners,' but also because their triple *function* has no other purpose except to form the Church in line with the ideal of sanctity already programmed and prefigured in Mary. A contemporary theologian has rightly stated that Mary is 'Queen of the Apostles without any pretensions to apostolic powers: she has other and greater powers' (H. U. von Balthasar, *Neue Klarstellungen)."* Address to the Cardinal and Prelates of the Roman Curia (December 22, 1987); *L'Osservatore Romano,* December 23, 1987.

[56] Cf. Second Vatican Ecumenical Council, Pastoral Constitution on the Church in the Modern World *Gaudium et Spes,* 10.

[57] *Ibid.,* 10.

[58] Cf. St. Augustine, *De Trinitate,* L. VIII, VII, 10-X, 14: *CCL* 50, 284-291.

[59] Second Vatican Ecumenical Council, Pastoral Constitution on the Church in the Modern World *Gaudium et Spes,* 24.

[60] Cf. in the Appendix to the works of St. Ambrose, *In Apoc.* IV, 3-4: *PL* 17, 876; St. Augustine, *De symb. ad. catech. sermo* IV: *PL* 40, 661.

[61] Second Vatican Ecumenical Council, Pastoral Constitution on the Church in the Modern World *Gaudium et Spes,* 10.

[62] Second Vatican Ecumenical Council, Dogmatic Constitution on the Church *Lumen Gentium,* 36.

[63] Cf. *ibid.,* 63.

The Gospel of Life

John Paul II

Encyclical Letter To the Bishops, Priests and Deacons, Men and Women Religious, Lay Faithful and All People of Good Will on the Value and Inviolability of Human Life.

Introduction

1. The Gospel of life is at the heart of Jesus' message. Lovingly received day after day by the Church, it is to be preached with dauntless fidelity as "good news" to the people of every age and culture.

At the dawn of salvation, it is the birth of a child which is proclaimed as joyful news: "I bring you good news of a great joy which will come to all the people; for to you is born this day in the city of David a Savior, who is Christ the Lord" (Lk 2:10-11). The source of this "great joy" is the birth of the Savior; but Christmas also reveals the full meaning of every human birth, and the joy which accompanies the birth of the Messiah is thus seen to be the foundation and fulfillment of joy at every child born into the world (cf. Jn 16:21).

When he presents the heart of his redemptive mission, Jesus says: "I came that they may have life, and have it abundantly" (Jn 10:10). In truth, he is referring to that "new" and "eternal" life which consists in communion with the Father, to which every person is freely called in the Son by the power of the Sanctifying Spirit. It is precisely in this "life" that all the aspects and stages of human life achieve their full significance.

The incomparable worth of the human person

2. Man is called to a fullness of life which far exceeds the dimensions of his earthly existence, because it consists in sharing the very life of God. The loftiness of this supernatural vocation reveals the *greatness and the inestimable value* of human life even in its temporal phase. Life in time, in fact, is the fundamental condition, the initial stage and an integral part of the entire unified pro-

cess of human existence. It is a process which, unexpectedly and undeservedly, is enlightened by the promise and renewed by the gift of divine life, which will reach its full realization in eternity (cf. 1 Jn 3:1-2). At the same time, it is precisely this supernatural calling which highlights the *relative character* of each individual's earthly life. After all, life on earth is not an "ultimate" but a "penultimate" reality; even so, it remains *a sacred reality* entrusted to us, to be preserved with a sense of responsibility and brought to perfection in love and in the gift of ourselves to God and to our brothers and sisters.

The Church knows that this *Gospel of life,* which she has received from her Lord,[1] has a profound and persuasive echo in the heart of every person—believer and non-believer alike—because it marvelously fulfills all the heart's expectations while infinitely surpassing them. Even in the midst of difficulties and uncertainties, every person sincerely open to truth and goodness can, by the light of reason and the hidden action of grace, come to recognize in the natural law written in the heart (cf. Rom 2:14-15) the sacred value of human life from its very beginning until its end, and can affirm the right of every human being to have this primary good respected to the highest degree. Upon the recognition of this right, every human community and the political community itself are founded.

In a special way, believers in Christ must defend and promote this right, aware as they are of the wonderful truth recalled by the Second Vatican Council: "By his incarnation the Son of God has united himself in some fashion with every human being."[2] This saving event reveals to humanity not only the boundless love of God who "so loved the world that he gave his only Son" (Jn 3:16), but also *the incomparable value of every human person.*

The Church, faithfully contemplating the mystery of the Redemption, acknowledges this value with ever new wonder.[3] She feels called to proclaim to the people of all times this "Gospel," the source of invincible hope and true joy for every period of history. *The Gospel of God's love for man, the Gospel of the dignity of the person and the Gospel of life are a single and indivisible Gospel.*

For this reason, man—living man—represents the primary and fundamental way for the Church.[4]

New threats to human life

3. Every individual, precisely by reason of the mystery of the Word of God who was made flesh (cf. Jn 1:14), is entrusted to the maternal care of the Church. Therefore every threat to human dignity and life must necessarily be felt in the Church's very heart; it cannot but affect her at the core of her faith in the Redemptive Incarnation of the Son of God, and engage her in her mission of proclaiming the Gospel of life in all the world and to every creature (cf. Mk 16:15).

Today this proclamation is especially pressing because of the extraordinary increase and gravity of threats to the life of individuals and peoples, especially where life is weak and defenseless. In addition to the ancient scourges of poverty, hunger, endemic diseases, violence and war, new threats are emerging on an alarmingly vast scale.

The Second Vatican Council, in a passage which retains all its relevance today, forcefully condemned a number of crimes and attacks against human life. Thirty years later, taking up the words of the Council and with the same forcefulness I repeat that condemnation in the name of the whole Church, certain that I am interpreting the genuine sentiment of every upright conscience: "Whatever is opposed to life itself, such as any type of murder, genocide, abortion, euthanasia, or willful self-destruction, whatever violates the integrity of the human person, such as mutilation, torments inflicted on body or mind, attempts to coerce the will itself; whatever insults human dignity, such as sub-human living conditions, arbitrary imprisonment, deportation, slavery, prostitution, the selling of women and children; as well as disgraceful working conditions, where people are treated as mere instruments of gain rather than as free and responsible persons; all these things and others like them are infamies indeed. They poison human society, and they do more harm to those who practice them than to those who suffer from the injury. Moreover, they are a supreme dishonor to the Creator."[5]

4. Unfortunately, this disturbing state of affairs, far from decreasing, is expanding: with the new prospects opened up by scientific and technological progress there arise new forms of attacks on the dignity of the human being. At the same time a new cultural climate is developing and taking hold, which gives crimes against life *a new and—if possible—even more sinister character,* giving rise to further grave concern: broad sectors of public opinion justify certain crimes against life in the name of the rights of individual freedom, and on this basis they claim not only exemption from punishment but even authorization by the state, so that these things can be done with total freedom and indeed with the free assistance of health-care systems.

All this is causing a profound change in the way in which life and relationships between people are considered. The fact that legislation in many countries, perhaps even departing from basic principles of their Constitutions, has determined not to punish these practices against life, and even to make them altogether legal, is both a disturbing symptom and a significant cause of grave moral decline. Choices once unanimously considered criminal and rejected by the common moral sense are gradually becoming socially acceptable. Even certain sectors of the medical profession, which by its calling is directed to the defense and care of human life, are increasingly willing to carry out these acts against the person. In this way the very nature of the medical profession is distorted and contradicted, and the dignity of those who practice it is degraded. In such a cultural and legislative situation, the serious demographic, social and family problems which weigh upon many of the world's peoples and which require responsible and effective attention from national and international bodies, are left open to false and deceptive solutions, opposed to the truth and the good of persons and nations.

The end result of this is tragic: not only is the fact of the destruction of so many human lives still to be born or in their final stage extremely grave and disturbing, but no less grave and disturbing is the fact that conscience itself, darkened as it were by such widespread conditioning, is finding it increasingly difficult to distinguish between good and evil in what concerns the basic value of human life.

In communion with all the bishops of the world

5. *The Extraordinary Consistory* of Cardinals held in Rome on April 4-7, 1991 was devoted to the problem of the threats to human life in our day. After a thorough and detailed discussion of the problem and of the challenges it poses to the entire human family and in particular to the Christian community, the Cardinals unanimously asked me to reaffirm with the authority of the Successor of Peter the value of human life and its inviolability, in the light of present circumstances and attacks threatening it today.

In response to this request, at Pentecost in 1991, I wrote a *personal letter* to each of my brother bishops asking them, in the spirit of episcopal collegiality, to offer me their cooperation in drawing up a specific document.[6] I am deeply grateful to all the bishops who replied and provided me with valuable facts, suggestions and proposals. In so doing they bore witness to their unanimous desire to share in the doctrinal and pastoral mission of the Church with regard to the *Gospel of life.*

In that same letter, written shortly after the celebration of the centenary of the Encyclical *Rerum Novarum,* I drew everyone's attention to this striking analogy: "Just as a century ago it was the working classes which were oppressed in their fundamental rights, and the Church very courageously came to their defense by proclaiming the sacrosanct rights of the worker as a person, so now, when another category of persons is being oppressed in the fundamental right to life, the Church feels in duty bound to speak out with the same courage on behalf of those who have no voice. Hers is always the evangelical cry in defense of the world's poor, those who are threatened and despised and whose human rights are violated."[7] Today there exists a great multitude of weak and defenseless human beings, unborn children in particular, whose fundamental right to life is being trampled upon. If, at the end of the last century, the Church could not be silent about the injustices of those times, still less can she be silent today, when the social injustices of the past, unfortunately not yet overcome, are being compounded in many regions of the world by still more grievous forms of injustice and oppression, even if these are being presented as elements of progress in view of a new world order.

The present encyclical, the fruit of the cooperation of the episcopate of every country of the world, is therefore meant to be a *precise and vigorous reaffirmation of the value of human life and its inviolability,* and at the same time a pressing appeal addressed to each and every person, in the name of God:

respect, protect, love and serve life, every human life! Only in this direction will you find justice, development, true freedom, peace and happiness!

May these words reach all the sons and daughters of the Church! May they reach all people of good will who are concerned for the good of every man and woman and for the destiny of the whole of society!

6. In profound communion with all my brothers and sisters in the faith, and inspired by genuine friendship toward all, I wish to *meditate upon once more and proclaim the Gospel of life,* the splendor of truth which enlightens consciences, the clear light which corrects the darkened gaze, and the unfailing source of faithfulness and steadfastness in facing the ever new challenges which we meet along our path.

As I recall the powerful experience of the Year of the Family, as if to complete the *Letter* which I wrote "to every particular family in every part of the world,"[8] I look with renewed confidence to every household and I pray that at every level a general commitment to support the family will reappear and be strengthened, so that today too—even amid so many difficulties and serious threats—the family will always remain, in accordance with God's plan, the "sanctuary of life."[9] To all the members of the Church, *the people of life and for life,* I make this most urgent appeal, that together we may offer this world of ours new signs of hope, and work to ensure that justice and solidarity will increase and that a new culture of human life will be affirmed, for the building of an authentic civilization of truth and love.

CHAPTER I

The Voice of Your Brother's Blood Cries to Me from the Ground

Present-Day Threats to Human Life

"Cain rose up against his brother Abel, and killed him" (Gn 4:8):
The roots of violence against life

7. "God did not make death, and he does not delight in the death of the living. For he has created all things that they might exist.... *God created man for incorruption,* and made him in the image of his own eternity, but through the devil's *envy death entered the world,* and those who belong to his party experience it" (Wis 1:13-14; 2:23-24).

The Gospel of life, proclaimed in the beginning when man was created in the image of God for a destiny of full and perfect life (cf. Gn 2:7; Wis 9:2-3), is contradicted by the painful experience of *death which enters the world* and casts its shadow of meaninglessness over man's entire existence. Death came into the world as a result of the devil's envy (cf. Gn 3:1, 4-5) and the sin of our first parents (cf. Gn 2:17, 3:17-19). And death entered it in a violent way, *through the killing of Abel by his brother Cain:* "And when they were in the field, Cain rose up against his brother Abel, and killed him" (Gn 4:8).

This first murder is presented with singular eloquence in a page of the Book of Genesis which has universal significance: it is a page rewritten daily, with inexorable and degrading frequency, in the book of human history.

Let us reread together this biblical account which, despite its archaic structure and its extreme simplicity, has much to teach us.

> Now Abel was a keeper of sheep, and Cain a tiller of the ground. In the course of time Cain brought to the Lord an offering of the fruit of the ground, and Abel brought of the firstlings of his flock and of their fat portions. And the Lord had regard for Abel and his offering, but for Cain and his offering he had not regard. So Cain was very angry, and his countenance fell. The Lord said to Cain, "Why are you angry and why has your countenance fallen? If you do well, will you not be accepted? And if you do not do well, sin is crouching at the door; its desire is for you, but you must master it."
>
> Cain said to Abel his brother, "Let us go out to the field." And when they were in the field, Cain rose up against his brother Abel, and killed him. Then the Lord said to Cain, "Where is Abel your brother?" He said, "I do not know; am I my brother's keeper?" And the Lord said, "What have you done? The voice of your brother's blood is crying to me from the ground. And now you are cursed from the ground, which has opened its mouth to receive your brother's blood from your hand. When you till the ground, it shall no longer yield to you its strength; you shall be a fugitive and a wanderer on the earth." Cain said to the Lord, "My punishment is greater than I can bear. Behold, you have driven me this day away from the ground; and from your face I shall be hidden; and I shall be a fugitive and a wanderer on the earth, and whoever finds me will slay me." Then the Lord said to him, "Not so! If any one slays Cain, vengeance shall be taken on him sevenfold." And the Lord put a mark on Cain, lest any who came upon him should kill him. Then Cain went away from the presence of the Lord, and dwelt in the land of Nod, east of Eden (Gn 4:2-16).

8. Cain was "very angry" and his countenance "fell" because "the Lord had regard for Abel and his offering" (Gn 4:4-5). The biblical text does not reveal the reason why God prefers Abel's sacrifice to Cain's. It clearly shows however that God, although preferring Abel's gift, *does not interrupt his dialogue with Cain.* He admonishes him, *reminding him of his freedom in the face of evil* man is in no way predestined to evil. Certainly, like Adam, he is tempted by the malevolent force of sin which, like a wild beast, lies in wait at the door of his heart, ready to leap on its prey. But Cain remains free in the face of sin. He can and must overcome it: "Its desire is for you, but you must master it" (Gn 4:7).

Envy and anger have the upper hand over the Lord's warning, and so Cain attacks his own brother and kills him. As we read in the *Catechism of the Catholic Church:* "In the account of Abel's murder by his brother Cain, Scripture reveals the presence of anger and envy in man, consequences of original sin, from the beginning of human history. Man has become the enemy of his fellow man."[10]

Brother kills brother. Like the first fratricide, every murder is a violation of the *"spiritual" kinship* uniting mankind in one great family,[11] in which all share the same fundamental good: equal personal dignity. Not infrequently the *kinship "of flesh and blood"* is also violated; for example when threats to life arise within the relationship between parents and children, such as happens in abortion or when, in the wider context of family or kinship, euthanasia is encouraged or practiced.

At the root of every act of violence against one's neighbor there is *a concession to the "thinking of the evil one,"* the one who "was a murderer from the beginning" (Jn 8:44). As the Apostle John reminds us: "For this is the message which you have heard from the beginning, that we should love one another, and not be like Cain who was of the evil one and murdered his brother" (1 Jn 3:11-12). Cain's killing of his brother at the very dawn of history is thus a sad witness of how evil spreads with amazing speed: man's revolt against God in the earthly paradise is followed by the deadly combat of man against man.

After the crime, *God intervenes to avenge the one killed.* Before God, who asks him about the fate of Abel, Cain, instead of showing remorse and apologizing, arrogantly eludes the question: "I do not know; am I my brother's keeper?" (Gn 4:9). *"I do not know":* Cain tries to cover up his crime with a lie. This was and still is the case, when all kinds of ideologies try to justify and disguise the most atrocious crimes against human beings. *"Am I my brother's keeper?":* Cain does not wish to think about his brother and refuses to accept the responsibility which every person has toward others. We cannot but think of today's tendency for people to refuse to accept responsibility for their brothers and sisters. Symptoms of this trend include the lack of solidarity toward society's weakest members—such as the elderly, the infirm, immigrants, children—and the indifference frequently found in relations between the world's peoples even when basic values such as survival, freedom and peace are involved.

9. But God *cannot leave the crime unpunished,* from the ground on which it has been spilt, the blood of the one murdered demands that God should render justice (cf. Gn 37:26; Is 26:21; Ez 24:7-8). From this text the Church has taken the name of the "sins which cry to God for justice," and, first among them, she has included willful murder.[12] For the Jewish people, as for many peoples of antiquity, blood is the source of life. Indeed "the blood is the life" (Dt 12:23), and life, especially human life, belongs only to God: for this reason *whoever attacks human life, in some way attacks God himself.*

Cain is cursed by God and also by the earth, which will deny him its fruit (cf. Gn 4:11-12). *He is punished:* he will live in the wilderness and the desert. Murderous violence profoundly changes man's environment. From being the "garden of Eden" (Gn 2:15), a place of plenty, of harmonious interpersonal relationships and of friendship with God, the earth becomes "the land of Nod"

(Gn 4:16), a place of scarcity, loneliness and separation from God. Cain will be "a fugitive and a wanderer on the earth" (Gn 4:14): uncertainty and restlessness will follow him forever.

And yet God, who is always merciful even when he punishes, *"put a mark on Cain,* lest any who came upon him should kill him" (Gn 4:15). He thus gave him a distinctive sign, not to condemn him to the hatred of others, but to protect and defend him from those wishing to kill him, even out of a desire to avenge Abel's death. *Not even a murderer loses his personal dignity,* and God himself pledges to guarantee this. And it is precisely here that the *paradoxical mystery of the merciful justice of God* is shown forth. As Saint Ambrose writes: "Once the crime is admitted at the very inception of this sinful act of parricide, then the divine law of God's mercy should be immediately extended. If punishment is forthwith inflicted on the accused, then men in the exercise of justice would in no way observe patience and moderation, but would straightaway condemn the defendant to punishment.... God drove Cain out of his presence and sent him into exile far away from his native land, so that he passed from a life of human kindness to one which was more akin to the rude existence of a wild beast. God, who preferred the correction rather than the death of a sinner, did not desire that a homicide be punished by the exaction of another act of homicide."[13]

"What have you done?" (Gn 4:10): The eclipse of the value of life

10. The Lord said to Cain: "What have you done? The voice of your brother's blood is crying to me from the ground" (Gn 4:10). *The voice of the blood shed by men continues to cry* out, from generation to generation, in ever new and different ways. The Lord's question: "What have you done?", which Cain cannot escape, is addressed also to the people of today, to make them realize the extent and gravity of the attacks against life which continue to mark human history; to make them discover what causes these attacks and feeds them; and to make them ponder seriously the consequences which derive from these attacks for the existence of individuals and peoples.

Some threats come from nature itself, but they are made worse by the culpable indifference and negligence of those who could in some cases remedy them. Others are the result of situations of violence, hatred and conflicting interests, which lead people to attack others through murder, war, slaughter and genocide.

And how can we fail to consider the violence against life done to millions of human beings, especially children, who are forced into poverty, malnutrition and hunger because of an unjust distribution of resources between peoples and between social classes? And what of the violence inherent not only in wars as such but in the scandalous arms trade, which spawns the many armed conflicts which stain our world with blood? What of the spreading of death caused by reckless tampering with the world's ecological balance, by the criminal spread of drugs, or by the promotion of certain kinds of sexual activity which, besides being morally unacceptable, also involve grave risks to life? It is impossible to catalogue completely the vast array of threats to human life, so many are the forms, whether explicit or hidden, in which they appear today!

11. Here though we shall concentrate particular attention on *another category of attacks*, affecting life in its earliest and in its final stages, attacks which present *new characteristics with respect to the past and which raise questions of extraordinary seriousness.* It is not only that in generalized opinion these attacks tend no longer to be considered as "crimes"; paradoxically they assume the nature of "rights," to the point that the state is called upon to give them *legal recognition and to make them available through the free services of health-care personnel.* Such attacks strike human life at the time of its greatest frailty, when it lacks any means of self-defense. Even more serious is the fact that, most often, those attacks are carried out in the very heart of and with the complicity of the family—the family which by its nature is called to be the "sanctuary of life."

How did such a situation come about? Many different factors have to be taken into account. In the background there is the profound crisis of culture, which generates skepticism in relation to the very foundations of knowledge and ethics, and which makes it increasingly difficult to grasp clearly the meaning of what man is, the meaning of his rights and his duties. Then there are all kinds of existential and interpersonal difficulties, made worse by the complexity of a society in which individuals, couples and families are often left alone with their problems. There are situations of acute poverty, anxiety or frustration in which the struggle to make ends meet, the presence of unbearable pain, or instances of violence, especially against women, make the choice to defend and promote life so demanding as sometimes to reach the point of heroism.

All this explains, at least in part, how the value of life can today undergo a kind of "eclipse," even though conscience does not cease to point to it as a sacred and inviolable value, as is evident in the tendency to disguise certain crimes against life in its early or final stages by using innocuous medical terms which distract attention from the fact that what is involved is the right to life of an actual human person.

12. In fact, while the climate of widespread moral uncertainty can in some way be explained by the multiplicity and gravity of today's social problems, and these can sometimes mitigate the subjective responsibility of individuals, it is no less true that we are confronted by an even larger reality, which can be described as a veritable *structure of sin.* This reality is characterized by the emergence of a culture which denies solidarity and in many cases takes the form of a veritable "culture of death." This culture is actively fostered by powerful cultural, economic and political currents which encourage an idea of society excessively concerned with efficiency. Looking at the situation from this point of view, it is possible to speak in a certain sense of a *war of the powerful against the weak:* a life which would require greater acceptance, love and care is considered useless, or held to be an intolerable burden, and is therefore rejected in one way or

another. A person who, because of illness, handicap or, more simply, just by existing, compromises the well-being or life-style of those who are more favored tends to be looked upon as an enemy to be resisted or eliminated. In this way a kind of *"conspiracy against life"* is unleashed. This conspiracy involves not only individuals in their personal, family or group relationships, but goes far beyond, to the point of damaging and distorting, at the international level, relations between peoples and states.

13. In order to facilitate the spread of *abortion,* enormous sums of money have been invested and continue to be invested in the production of pharmaceutical products which make it possible to kill the fetus in the mother's womb without recourse to medical assistance. On this point, scientific research itself seems to be almost exclusively preoccupied with developing products which are ever more simple and effective in suppressing life and which at the same time are capable of removing abortion from any kind of control or social responsibility.

It is frequently asserted that *contraception,* if made safe and available to all, is the most effective remedy against abortion. The Catholic Church is then accused of actually promoting abortion, because she obstinately continues to teach the moral unlawfulness of contraception. When looked at carefully, this objection is clearly unfounded. It may be that many people use contraception with a view to excluding the subsequent temptation of abortion. But the negative values inherent in the "contraceptive mentality"—which is very different from responsible parenthood, lived in respect for the full truth of the conjugal act— are such that they in fact strengthen this temptation when an unwanted life is conceived. Indeed, the pro-abortion culture is especially strong precisely where the Church's teaching on contraception is rejected. Certainly, from the moral point of view contraception and abortion are *specifically different* evils: the former contradicts the full truth of the sexual act as the proper expression of conjugal love, while the latter destroys the life of a human being; the former is opposed to the virtue of chastity in marriage, the latter is opposed to the virtue of justice and directly violates the divine commandment "You shall not kill."

But despite their differences of nature and moral gravity, contraception and abortion are often closely connected, as fruits of the same tree. It is true that in many cases contraception and even abortion are practiced under the pressure of real life difficulties, which nonetheless can never exonerate from striving to observe God's law fully. Still, in very many other instances such practices are rooted in a hedonistic mentality unwilling to accept responsibility in matters of sexuality, and they imply a self-centered concept of freedom, which regards procreation as an obstacle to personal fulfillment. The life which could result from a sexual encounter thus becomes an enemy to be avoided at all costs, and abortion becomes the only possible decisive response to failed contraception.

The close connection which exists, in mentality, between the practice of contraception and that of abortion is becoming increasingly obvious. It is being demonstrated in an alarming way by the development of chemical products, intrauterine devices and vaccines which, distributed with the same ease as contraceptives, really act as abortifacients in the very early stages of the development of the life of the new human being.

14. The various *techniques of artificial reproduction,* which would seem to be at the service of life and which are frequently used with this intention, actually open the door to new threats against life. Apart from the fact that they are morally unacceptable, since they separate procreation from the fully human context of the conjugal act,[14] these techniques have a high rate of failure: not just failure in relation to fertilization but with regard to the subsequent development of the embryo, which is exposed to the risk of death, generally within a very short space of time. Furthermore, the number of embryos produced is often greater than that needed for implantation in the woman's womb, and these so-called "spare embryos" are then destroyed or used for research which, under the pretext of scientific or medical progress, in fact reduces human life to the level of simple "biological material" to be freely disposed of.

Prenatal diagnosis, which presents no moral objections if carried out in order to identify the medical treatment which may be needed by the child in the womb, all too often becomes an opportunity for proposing and procuring an abortion. This is eugenic abortion, justified in public opinion on the basis of a mentality—mistakenly held to be consistent with the demands of "therapeutic interventions"—which accepts life only under certain conditions and rejects it when it is affected by any limitation, handicap or illness.

Following this same logic, the point has been reached where the most basic care, even nourishment, is denied to babies born with serious handicaps or illnesses. The contemporary scene, moreover, is becoming even more alarming by reason of the proposals, advanced here and there, to justify even *infanticide,* following the same arguments used to justify the right to abortion. In this way, we revert to a state of barbarism which one hoped had been left behind forever.

15. Threats which are no less serious hang over the *incurably ill* and the *dying.* In a social and cultural context which makes it more difficult to face and accept suffering, the *temptation* becomes all the greater *to resolve the problem of suffering by eliminating it at the root,* by hastening death so that it occurs at the moment considered most suitable.

Various considerations usually contribute to such a decision, all of which converge in the same terrible outcome. In the sick person the sense of anguish, of severe discomfort, and even of desperation brought on by intense and prolonged suffering can be a decisive factor. Such a situation can threaten the already fragile equilibrium of an individual's personal and family life, with the result that, on the one hand, the sick person, despite the help of increasingly effective medical and social assistance, risks feeling overwhelmed by his or her own frailty; and on the other hand, those close to the sick person can be moved by an understandable even if misplaced compassion. All this is aggravated by a cultural climate which fails to perceive any meaning or value in suffering, but rather considers suffering the epitome of evil, to be eliminated at all costs. This is especially the case in the absence of a religious outlook which could help to provide a positive understanding of the mystery of suffering.

On a more general level, there exists in contemporary culture a certain Promethean attitude which leads people to think that they can control life and death by taking the decisions about them into their own hands. What really happens in this case is that the individual is overcome and crushed by a death deprived of any prospect of meaning or hope. We see a tragic expression of all this in the spread of *euthanasia—disguised* and surreptitious, or practiced openly and even legally. As well as for reasons of a misguided pity at the sight of the patient's suffering, euthanasia is sometimes justified by the utilitarian motive of avoiding costs which bring no return and which weigh heavily on society. Thus it is proposed to eliminate malformed babies, the severely handicapped, the disabled, the elderly, especially when they are not self-sufficient, and the terminally ill. Nor can we remain silent in the face of other more furtive, but no less serious and real, forms of euthanasia. These could occur for example when, in order to increase the availability of organs for transplants, organs are removed without respecting objective and adequate criteria which verify the death of the donor.

16. Another present-day *phenomenon,* frequently used to justify threats and attacks against life, is the *demographic* question. This question arises in different ways in different parts of the world. In the rich and developed countries there is a disturbing decline or collapse of the birthrate. The poorer countries, on the other hand, generally have a high rate of population growth, difficult to sustain in the context of low economic and social development, and especially where there is extreme underdevelopment. In the face of overpopulation in the poorer countries, instead of forms of global intervention at the international level—serious family and social policies, programs of cultural development and of fair production and distribution of resources—anti-birth policies continue to be enacted.

Contraception, sterilization and abortion are certainly part of the reason why in some cases there is a sharp decline in the birthrate. It is not difficult to be tempted to use the same methods and attacks against life also where there is a situation of "demographic explosion."

The Pharaoh of old, haunted by the presence and increase of the children of Israel, submitted them to every kind of oppression and ordered that every male child born of the Hebrew women was to be killed (cf. Ex 1:7-22). Today not a few of the powerful of the earth act in the same way. They too are haunted by the current demographic growth, and fear that the most prolific and poorest peoples represent a threat for the well-being and peace of their own countries. Consequently, rather than wishing to face and solve these serious problems with respect for the dignity of individuals and families and for every person's inviolable right to life, they prefer to promote and impose by whatever means a massive program of birth control. Even the economic help which they would be ready to give is unjustly made conditional on the acceptance of an anti-birth policy.

17. Humanity today offers us a truly alarming spectacle, if we consider not

only how extensively attacks on life are spreading but also their unheard-of numerical proportion, and the fact that they receive widespread and powerful support from a broad consensus on the part of society, from widespread legal approval and the involvement of certain sectors of health-care personnel.

As I emphatically stated at Denver, on the occasion of the Eighth World Youth Day, "with time the threats against life have not grown weaker. They are taking on vast proportions. They are not only threats coming from the outside, from the forces of nature or the 'Cains' who kill the 'Abels'; no, they are scientifically and *systematically programmed threats*. The twentieth century will have been an era of massive attacks on life, an endless series of wars and a continual taking of innocent human life. False prophets and false teachers have had the greatest success."[15] Aside from intentions, which can be varied and perhaps can seem convincing at times, especially if presented in the name of solidarity, we are in fact faced by an objective *"conspiracy against life,"* involving even international institutions, engaged in encouraging and carrying out actual campaigns to make contraception, sterilization and abortion widely available. Nor can it be denied that the mass media are often implicated in this conspiracy, by lending credit to that culture which presents recourse to contraception, sterilization, abortion and even euthanasia as a mark of progress and a victory of freedom, while depicting as enemies of freedom and progress those positions which are unreservedly pro-life.

"Am I my brother's keeper?" (Gn 4:9): A perverse idea of freedom

18. The panorama described needs to be understood not only in terms of the phenomena of death which characterize it but also in the *variety of causes* which determine it. The Lord's question: "What have you done?" (Gn 4:10), seems almost like an invitation addressed to Cain to go beyond the material dimension of his murderous gesture, in order to recognize in it all the gravity of the *motives* which occasioned it and the *consequences* which result from it.

Decisions that go against life sometimes arise from difficult or even tragic situations of profound suffering, loneliness, a total lack of economic prospects, depression and anxiety about the future. Such circumstances can mitigate even to a notable degree subjective responsibility and the consequent culpability of those who make these choices which in themselves are evil. But today the problem goes far beyond the necessary recognition of these personal situations. It is a problem which exists at the cultural, social and political level, where it reveals its more sinister and disturbing aspect in the tendency, ever more widely shared, to interpret the above crimes against life as *legitimate expressions of individual freedom, to be acknowledged and protected as actual rights.*

In this way, and with tragic consequences, a long historical process is reaching a turning-point. The process which once led to discovering the idea of "human rights"—rights inherent in every person and prior to any Constitution and state legislation—is today marked by a *surprising contradiction*. Precisely in

an age when the inviolable rights of the person are solemnly proclaimed and
the value of life is publicly affirmed, the very right to life is being denied or
trampled upon, especially at the more significant moments of existence: the
moment of birth and the moment of death.

On the one hand, the various declarations of human rights and the many initiatives inspired by these declarations show that at the global level there is a
growing moral sensitivity, more alert to acknowledging the value and dignity of
every individual as a human being, without any distinction of race, nationality,
religion, political opinion or social class.

On the other hand, these noble proclamations are unfortunately contradicted
by a tragic repudiation of them in practice. This denial is still more distressing,
indeed more scandalous, precisely because it is occurring in a society which
makes the affirmation and protection of human rights its primary objective and
its boast. How can these repeated affirmations of principle be reconciled with the
continual increase and widespread justification of attacks on human life? How
can we reconcile these declarations with the refusal to accept those who are
weak and needy, or elderly, or those who have just been conceived? These attacks go directly against respect for life and they represent a *direct threat to the
entire culture of human rights.* It is a threat capable, in the end, of jeopardizing
the very meaning of democratic coexistence: *rather than societies of "people
living together," our cities risk becoming societies of people who are rejected,*
marginalized, uprooted and oppressed. If we then look at the wider worldwide
perspective, how can we fail to think that the very affirmation of the rights of
individuals and peoples made in distinguished international assemblies is a
merely futile exercise of rhetoric, if we fail to unmask the selfishness of the rich
countries which exclude poorer countries from access to development or make
such access dependent on arbitrary prohibitions against procreation, setting up
an opposition between development and man himself? Should we not question
the very economic models often adopted by states which, also as a result of in-
ter-national pressures and forms of conditioning, cause and aggravate situations
of injustice and violence in which the life of whole peoples is degraded and
trampled upon?

19. What are *the roots of this remarkable contradiction?* We can find them
in an overall assessment of a cultural and moral nature, beginning with the mentality which *carries the concept of subjectivity to an extreme* and even distorts it,
and recognizes as a subject of rights only the person who enjoys full or at least
incipient autonomy and who emerges from a state of total dependence on others.
But how can we reconcile this approach with *the exaltation of man as a being
who is "not to be used"?* The theory of human rights is based precisely on the
affirmation that the human person, unlike animals and things, cannot be subjected to domination by others. We must also mention the mentality which tends
to *equate personal dignity with the capacity for verbal and explicit,* or at least
perceptible, *communication.* It is clear that on the basis of these presuppositions

there is no place in the world for anyone who, like the unborn or the dying, is a weak element in the social structure, or for anyone who appears completely at the mercy of others and radically dependent on them, and can only communicate through the silent language of a profound sharing of affection. In this case it is force which becomes the criterion for choice and action in interpersonal relations and in social life. But this is the exact opposite of what a state ruled by law, as a community in which the "reasons of force" are replaced by the "force of reason," historically intended to affirm.

At another level, the roots of the contradiction between the solemn affirmation of human rights and their tragic denial in practice lies in a *notion of freedom* which exalts the isolated individual in an absolute way, and gives no place to solidarity, to openness to others and service of them. While it is true that the taking of life not yet born or in its final stages is sometimes marked by a mistaken sense of altruism and human compassion, it cannot be denied that such a culture of death, taken as a whole, betrays a completely individualistic concept of freedom, which ends up by becoming the freedom of "the strong" against the weak who have no choice but to submit.

It is precisely in this sense that Cain's answer to the Lord's question: "Where is Abel your brother?" can be interpreted: "I do not know; *am I my brother's keeper?*" (Gn 4:9). Yes, every man is his "brother's keeper," because God entrusts us to one another. And it is also in view of this entrusting that God gives everyone freedom, a freedom which possesses an *inherently relational dimension*. This is a great gift of the Creator, placed as it is at the service of the person and of his fulfillment through the gift of self and openness to others; but when freedom is made absolute in an individualistic way, it is emptied of its original content, and its very meaning and dignity are contradicted.

There is an even more profound aspect which needs to be emphasized: freedom negates and destroys itself, and becomes a factor leading to the destruction of others, when it no longer recognizes and respects its *essential link with the truth*. When freedom, out of a desire to emancipate itself from all forms of tradition and authority, shuts out even the most obvious evidence of an objective and universal truth, which is the foundation of personal and social life, then the person ends up by no longer taking as the sole and indisputable point of reference for his own choices the truth about good and evil, but only his subjective and changeable opinion or, indeed, his selfish interest and whim.

20. This view of freedom *leads to a serious distortion of life in society*. If the promotion of the self is understood in terms of absolute autonomy, people inevitably reach the point of rejecting one another. Everyone else is considered an enemy from whom one has to defend oneself. Thus society becomes a mass of individuals placed side by side, but without any mutual bonds. Each one wishes to assert himself independently of the other and in fact intends to make his own interests prevail. Still, in the face of other people's analogous interests, some kind of compromise must be found, if one wants a society in which the maximum

possible freedom is guaranteed to each individual. In this way, any reference to common values and to a truth absolutely binding on everyone is lost, and social life ventures on to the shifting sands of complete relativism. At that point, *everything is negotiable, everything is open to bargaining:* even the first of the fundamental rights, the right to life.

This is what is happening also at the level of politics and government: the original and inalienable right to life is questioned or denied on the basis of a parliamentary vote or the will of one part of the people—even if it is the majority. This is the sinister result of a relativism which reigns unopposed: the "right" ceases to be such, because it is no longer firmly founded on the inviolable dignity of the person, but is made subject to the will of the stronger part. In this way democracy, contradicting its own principles, effectively moves toward a form of totalitarianism. The state is no longer the "common home" where all can live together on the basis of principles of fundamental equality, but is transformed into a *tyrant state,* which arrogates to itself the right to dispose of the life of the weakest and most defenseless members, from the unborn child to the elderly, in the name of a public interest which is really nothing but the interest of one part. The appearance of the strictest respect for legality is maintained, at least when the laws permitting abortion and euthanasia are the result of a ballot in accordance with what are generally seen as the rules of democracy. Really, what we have here is only the tragic caricature of legality; the democratic ideal, which is only truly such when it acknowledges and safeguards the dignity of every human person, *is betrayed in its very foundations:* "How is it still possible to speak of the dignity of every human person when the killing of the weakest and most innocent is permitted? In the name of what justice is the most unjust of discriminations practiced: some individuals are held to be deserving of defense and others are denied that dignity?"[16] When this happens, the process leading to the breakdown of a genuinely human co-existence and the disintegration of the state itself has already begun.

To claim the right to abortion, infanticide and euthanasia, and to recognize that right in law, means to attribute to human freedom a *perverse and evil significance:* that of an *absolute power over others and against others.* This is the death of true freedom: "Truly, truly, I say to you, every one who commits sin is a slave to sin" (Jn 8:34).

"And from your face I shall be hidden" (Gn 4:14):
The eclipse of the sense of God and of man

21. In seeking the deepest roots of the struggle between the "culture of life" and the "culture of death," we cannot restrict ourselves to the perverse idea of freedom mentioned above. We have to go to the heart of the tragedy being experienced by modern man: *the eclipse of the sense of God and of man,* typical of a social and cultural climate dominated by secularism, which, with its ubiquitous tentacles, succeeds at times in putting Christian communities themselves to the

test. Those who allow themselves to be influenced by this climate easily fall into a sad vicious circle: *when the sense of God is lost, there is also a tendency to lose the sense of man,* of his dignity and his life; in turn, the systematic violation of the moral law, especially in the serious matter of respect for human life and its dignity, produces a kind of progressive darkening of the capacity to discern God's living and saving presence.

Once again we can gain insight from the story of Abel's murder by his brother. After the curse imposed on him by God, Cain thus addresses the Lord: "My punishment is greater than I can bear. Behold, you have driven me this day away from the ground; and *from your face I shall be hidden,* and I shall be a fugitive and wanderer on the earth, and whoever finds me will slay me" (Gn 4:13-14). Cain is convinced that his sin will not obtain pardon from the Lord and that his inescapable destiny will be to have to "hide his face" from him. If Cain is capable of confessing that his fault is "greater than he can bear," it is because he is conscious of being in the presence of God and before God's just judgment. It is really only before the Lord that man can admit his sin and recognize its full seriousness. Such was the experience of David who, after "having committed evil in the sight of the Lord," and being rebuked by the Prophet Nathan, exclaimed: "My offenses truly I know them; my sin is always before me. Against you, you alone, have I sinned; what is evil in your sight I have done" (Ps 51:5-6).

22. Consequently, when the sense of God is lost, the sense of man is also threatened and poisoned, as the Second Vatican Council concisely states: "Without the Creator the creature would disappear.... But when God is forgotten the creature itself grows unintelligible."[17] Man is no longer able to see himself as "mysteriously different" from other earthly creatures; he regards himself merely as one more living being, as an organism which, at most, has reached a very high stage of perfection. Enclosed in the narrow horizon of his physical nature, he is somehow reduced to being "a thing," and no longer grasps the "transcendent" character of his "existence as man." He no longer considers life as a splendid gift of God, something "sacred" entrusted to his responsibility and thus also to his loving care and "veneration." Life itself becomes a mere "thing," which man claims as his exclusive property, completely subject to his control and manipulation.

Thus, in relation to life at birth or at death, man is no longer capable of posing the question of the truest meaning of his own existence, nor can he assimilate with genuine freedom these crucial moments of his own history. He is concerned only with "doing," and, using all kinds of technology, he busies himself with programming, controlling and dominating birth and death. Birth and death, instead of being primary experiences demanding to be "lived," become things to be merely "possessed" or "rejected."

Moreover, once all reference to God has been removed, it is not surprising that the meaning of everything else becomes profoundly distorted. Nature itself, from being *"mater"* (mother), is now reduced to being "matter," and is subjected to every kind of manipulation. This is the direction in which a certain technical and scientific way of thinking, prevalent in present-day culture, appears to be leading when it rejects the very idea that there is a truth of creation which must be acknowledged, or a plan of God for life which must be respected. Something similar happens when concern about the consequences of such a "freedom without law" leads some people to the opposite position of a "law without freedom," as for example in ideologies which consider it unlawful to interfere in any way with nature, practically "divinizing" it. Again, this is a misunderstanding of nature's dependence on the plan of the Creator. Thus it is clear that the loss of contact with God's wise design is the deepest root of modern man's confusion, both when this loss leads to a freedom without rules and when it leaves man in "fear" of his freedom.

By living "as if God did not exist," man not only loses sight of the mystery of God, but also of the mystery of the world and the mystery of his own being.

23. The eclipse of the sense of God and of man inevitably leads to a *practical materialism,* which breeds individualism, utilitarianism and hedonism. Here too we see the permanent validity of the words of the Apostle: "And since they did not see fit to acknowledge God, God gave them up to a base mind and to improper conduct" (Rom 1:28). The values of *being* are replaced by those of *having.* The only goal which counts is the pursuit of one's own material well-being. The so-called "quality of life" is interpreted primarily or exclusively as economic efficiency, inordinate consumerism, physical beauty and pleasure, to the neglect of the more profound dimensions—interpersonal, spiritual and religious—of existence.

In such a context *suffering,* an inescapable burden of human existence but also a factor of possible personal growth, is "censored," rejected as useless, indeed opposed as an evil, always and in every way to be avoided. When it cannot be avoided and the prospect of even some future well-being vanishes, then life appears to have lost all meaning and the temptation grows in man to claim the right to suppress it.

Within this same cultural climate, the *body* is no longer perceived as a properly personal reality, a sign and place of relations with others, with God and with the world. It is reduced to pure materiality: it is simply a complex of organs, functions and energies to be used according to the sole criteria of pleasure and efficiency. Consequently, *sexuality* too is depersonalized and exploited: from being the sign, place and language of love, that is, of the gift of self and acceptance of another, in all the other's richness as a person, it increasingly becomes the occasion and instrument for self-assertion and the selfish satisfaction of personal desires and instincts. Thus the original import of human sexuality is distorted and falsified, and the two meanings, unitive and procreative, inherent in the very nature of the conjugal act, are artificially separated: in this way the marriage union is betrayed and its fruitfulness is subjected to the caprice of the couple. *Procreation* then becomes the "enemy" to be avoided in sexual activity: if it is welcomed, this is only because it expresses a desire, or indeed the intention, to have a child "at all costs," and not because it signifies the complete acceptance of the other and therefore an openness to the richness of life which the child represents.

In the materialistic perspective described so far, *interpersonal relations are seriously impoverished.* The first to be harmed are women, children, the sick or suffering, and the elderly. The criterion of personal dignity—which demands respect, generosity and service—is replaced by the criterion of efficiency, functionality and usefulness: others are considered not for what they "are," but for what they "have, do and produce." This is the supremacy of the strong over the weak.

24. *It is at the heart of the moral conscience* that the eclipse of the sense of God and of man, with all its various and deadly consequences for life, is taking place. It is a question, above all, of the *individual* conscience, as it stands before God in its singleness and uniqueness.[18] But it is also a question, in a certain sense, of the "moral conscience" *of society:* in a way it too is responsible, not only because it tolerates or fosters behavior contrary to life, but also because it encourages the "culture of death," creating and consolidating actual "structures of sin" which go against life. The moral conscience, both individual and social, is today subjected, also as a result of the penetrating influence of the media, to an *extremely serious and mortal danger:* that of *confusion between good and evil,* precisely in relation to the fundamental right to life. A large part of contemporary society looks sadly like that humanity which Paul describes in his Letter to the Romans. It is composed "of men who by their wickedness suppress the truth" (1:18): having denied God and believing that they can build the earthly city without him, "they became futile in their thinking" so that "their senseless minds were darkened" (1:21); "claiming to be wise, they became fools" (1:22), carrying out works deserving of death, and "they not only do them but approve those who practice them" (1:32). When conscience, this bright lamp of the soul (cf. Mt 6:22-23), calls "evil good and good evil" (Is 5:20), it is already on the path to the most alarming corruption and the darkest moral blindness.

And yet all the conditioning and efforts to enforce silence fail to stifle the voice of the Lord echoing in the conscience of every individual: it is always from this intimate sanctuary of the conscience that a new journey of love, openness and service to human life can begin.

"You have come to the sprinkled blood" (cf. Heb 12:22, 24): *Signs of hope and invitation to commitment*

25. "The voice of your brother's blood is crying to me from the ground" (Gn 4:10). It is not only the voice of the blood of Abel, the first innocent man to be murdered, which cries to God, the source and defender of life. The blood of every other human being who has been killed since Abel is also a voice raised to the Lord. In an absolutely singular way, as the author of the Letter to the Hebrews reminds us, *the voice of the blood of Christ,* of whom Abel in his

innocence is a prophetic figure, cries out to God: "You have come to Mount Zion and to the city of the living God...to the mediator of a new covenant, and to the sprinkled blood that speaks more graciously than the blood of Abel" (12:22, 24).

It is *the sprinkled blood.* A symbol and prophetic sign of it had been the blood of the sacrifices of the Old Covenant, whereby God expressed his will to communicate his own life to men, purifying and consecrating them (cf. Ex 24:8; Lv 17:11). Now all of this is fulfilled and comes true in Christ: his is the sprinkled blood which redeems, purifies and saves; it is the blood of the Mediator of the New Covenant "poured out for many for the forgiveness of sins" (Mt 26:28). This blood, which flows from the pierced side of Christ on the Cross (cf. Jn 19:34), "speaks more graciously" than the blood of Abel; indeed, it expresses and requires a more radical "justice," and above all it implores mercy,[19] it makes intercession for the brethren before the Father (cf. Heb 7:25), and it is the source of perfect redemption and the gift of new life.

The blood of Christ, while it reveals the grandeur of the Father's love, *shows how precious man is in God's eyes and how priceless the value of his life.* The Apostle Peter reminds us of this: "You know that you were ransomed from the futile ways inherited from your fathers, not with perishable things such as silver or gold, but with the precious blood of Christ, like that of a lamb without blemish or spot" (1 Pt 1:18-19). Precisely by contemplating the precious blood of Christ, the sign of his self-giving love (cf. Jn 13:1), the believer learns to recognize and appreciate the almost divine dignity of every human being and can exclaim with ever renewed and grateful wonder: "How precious must man be in the eyes of the Creator, if he 'gained so great a Redeemer' *(Exsultet* of the Easter Vigil), and if God 'gave his only Son' in order that man 'should not perish but have eternal life!'" (cf. Jn 3:16).[20]

Furthermore, Christ's blood reveals to man that his greatness, and therefore his vocation, consists in *the sincere gift of self.* Precisely because it is poured out as the gift of life, the blood of Christ is no longer a sign of death, of definitive separation from the brethren, but the instrument of a communion which is richness of life for all. Whoever in the Sacrament of the Eucharist drinks this blood and abides in Jesus (cf. Jn 6:56) is drawn into the dynamism of his love and gift of life, in order to bring to its fullness the original vocation to love which belongs to everyone (cf. Gn 1:27; 2:18-24).

It is from the blood of Christ that all draw *the strength to commit themselves to promoting life.* It is precisely this blood that is *the most powerful source of hope, indeed it is the foundation of the absolute certitude that in God's plan life will be victorious.* "And death shall be no more," exclaims the powerful voice which comes from the throne of God in the Heavenly Jerusalem (Rv 21:4). And St. Paul assures us that the present victory over sin is a sign and anticipation of the definitive victory over death, when there "shall come to pass the saying that is written: 'Death is swallowed up in victory.' 'O death, where is your victory? O death, where is your sting?'" (1 Cor 15:54-55).

26. In effect, signs which point to this victory are not lacking in our societies and cultures, strongly marked though they are by the "culture of death." It would therefore be to give a one-sided picture, which could lead to sterile discouragement, if the condemnation of the threats to life were not accompanied by the presentation of the *positive signs* at work in humanity's present situation.

Unfortunately it is often hard to see and recognize these positive signs, perhaps also because they do not receive sufficient attention in the communications media. Yet, how many initiatives of help and support for people who are weak and defenseless have sprung up and continue to spring up in the Christian community and in civil society, at the local, national and international level, through the efforts of individuals, groups, movements and organizations of various kinds!

There are still many *married couples* who, with a generous sense of responsibility, are ready to accept children as "the supreme gift of marriage."[21] Nor is there a lack of *families* which, over and above their everyday service to life, are willing to accept abandoned children, boys and girls and teenagers in difficulty, handicapped persons, elderly men and women who have been left alone. Many *centers in support of life,* or similar institutions, are sponsored by individuals and groups which, with admirable dedication and sacrifice, offer moral and material support to mothers who are in difficulty and are tempted to have recourse to abortion. Increasingly, there are appearing in many places *groups of volunteers* prepared to offer hospitality to persons without a family, who find themselves in conditions of particular distress or who need a supportive environment to help them to overcome destructive habits and discover anew the meaning of life.

Medical science, thanks to the committed efforts of researchers and practitioners, continues in its efforts to discover ever more effective remedies: treatments which were once inconceivable but which now offer much promise for the future are today being developed for the unborn, the suffering and those in an acute or terminal stage of sickness. Various agencies and organizations are mobilizing their efforts to bring the benefits of the most advanced medicine to countries most afflicted by poverty and endemic diseases. In a similar way national and international associations of physicians are being organized to bring quick relief to peoples affected by natural disasters, epidemics or wars. Even if a just international distribution of medical resources is still far from being a reality, how can we not recognize in the steps taken so far the sign of a growing solidarity among peoples, a praiseworthy human and moral sensitivity and a greater respect for life?

27. In view of laws which permit abortion and in view of efforts, which here and there have been successful, to legalize euthanasia, *movements and initiatives to raise social awareness in defense of life* have sprung up in many parts of the world. When, in accordance with their principles, such movements act resolutely, but without resorting to violence, they promote a wider and more profound consciousness of the value of life, and evoke and bring about a more determined commitment to its defense.

Furthermore, how can we fail to mention *all those daily gestures of openness, sacrifice and unselfish care* which countless people lovingly make in families, hospitals, orphanages, homes for the elderly and other centers or communities which defend life? Allowing herself to be guided by the example of Jesus the "Good Samaritan" (cf. Lk 10:29-37) and upheld by his strength, the Church has always been in the front line in providing charitable help: so many of her sons and daughters, especially men and women religious, in traditional and ever new forms, have consecrated and continue to consecrate their lives to God, freely giving of themselves out of love for their neighbor, especially for the weak and needy. These deeds strengthen the bases of the "civilization of love and life," without which the life of individuals and of society itself loses its most genuinely human quality. Even if they go unnoticed and remain hidden to most people, faith assures us that the Father "who sees in secret" (Mt 6:6) not only will reward these actions but already here and now makes them produce lasting fruit for the good of all.

Among the signs of hope we should also count the spread, at many levels of public opinion, of a *new sensitivity ever more opposed to war* as an instrument for the resolution of conflicts between peoples, and increasingly oriented to finding effective but "non-violent" means to counter the armed aggressor. In the same perspective there is evidence of a *growing public opposition to the death penalty,* even when such a penalty is seen as a kind of "legitimate defense" on the part of society. Modern society in fact has the means of effectively suppressing crime by rendering criminals harmless without definitively denying them the chance to reform.

Another welcome sign is the growing attention being paid to the *quality of life* and to *ecology,* especially in more developed societies, where people's expectations are no longer concentrated so much on problems of survival as on the search for an overall improvement of living conditions. Especially significant is the reawakening of an ethical reflection on issues affecting life. The emergence and ever more widespread development of *bioethics* is promoting more reflection and dialogue—between believers and non-believers, as well as between followers of different religions—on ethical problems, including fundamental issues pertaining to human life.

28. This situation, with its lights and shadows, ought to make us all fully aware that we are facing an enormous and dramatic clash between good and evil, death and life, the "culture of death" and the "culture of life." We find ourselves not only "faced with" but necessarily "in the midst of" this conflict: we are all involved and we all share in it, with the inescapable responsibility of *choosing to be unconditionally pro-life.*

For us too Moses' invitation rings out loud and clear: "See, I have set before you this day life and good, death and evil.... I have set before you life and death, blessing and curse; *therefore choose life, that you and your descendants may live"* (Dt 30:15, 19). This invitation is very appropriate for us who are called day by day to the duty of choosing between the "culture of life" and the "culture of death." But the call of Deuteronomy goes even deeper, for it urges us to make a choice which is properly religious and moral. It is a question of giving our own existence a basic orientation and living the law of the Lord faithfully and consistently: "If you obey the commandments of the Lord your God which I command you this day, by *loving the Lord your God,* by *walking in his ways,* and by *keeping his commandments* and his statutes and his ordinances, then you shall live...therefore choose life, that you and your descendants may live, loving the Lord your God, obeying his voice, and cleaving to him; *for that means life to you and length of days"* (30:16,19-20).

The unconditional choice for life reaches its full religious and moral meaning when it flows from, is formed by and nourished by *faith in Christ.* Nothing helps us so much to face positively the conflict between death and life in which we are engaged as faith in the Son of God who became man and dwelt among men so "that they may have life, and have it abundantly" (Jn 10:10). It is a matter of *faith in the Risen Lord, who has conquered death;* faith in the blood of Christ "that speaks more graciously than the blood of Abel" (Heb 12:24).

With the light and strength of this faith, therefore, in facing the challenges of the present situation, the Church is becoming more aware of the grace and responsibility which come to her from her Lord of proclaiming, celebrating and serving *the Gospel of life.*

CHAPTER II

I Came That They May Have Life

The Christian Message Concerning Life

"The life was made manifest, and we saw it" (1 Jn 1:2):
With our gaze fixed on Christ, "the Word of life"

29. Faced with the countless grave threats to life present in the modern world, one could feel overwhelmed by sheer powerlessness: good can never be powerful enough to triumph over evil!

At such times the People of God, and this includes every believer, is called to profess with humility and courage its faith in Jesus Christ, "the Word of life" (1 Jn 1:1). *The Gospel of life* is not simply a reflection, however new and profound, on human life. Nor is it merely a commandment aimed at raising awareness and bringing about significant changes in society. Still less is it an illusory promise of a better future. The *Gospel of life* is something concrete and personal, for it consists in the proclamation of *the very person of Jesus.* Jesus made himself known to the Apostle Thomas, and in him to every person, with the words: "I am the way, and the truth, and the life" (Jn 14:6). This is also how he spoke of himself to Martha, the sister of Lazarus: "I am the resurrection and the life; he who believes in me, though he die, yet shall he live, and whoever lives and believes in me shall never die" (Jn 11:25-26). Jesus is the Son who from all eternity receives life from the Father (cf. Jn 5:26), and who has come among men to make them sharers in this gift: "I came that they may have life, and have it abundantly" (Jn 10:10).

Through the words, the actions and the very person of Jesus, man is given the possibility of "knowing" *the complete truth* concerning the value of human life. From this "source" he receives, in particular, the capacity to "accomplish" this truth perfectly (cf. Jn 3:21), that is, to accept and fulfill completely the responsibility of loving and serving, of defending and promoting human life. In Christ, *the Gospel of life* is definitively proclaimed and fully given. This is the Gospel which, already present in the Revelation of the Old Testament, and indeed written in the heart of every man and woman, has echoed in every conscience "from the beginning," from the time of creation itself, in such a way that, despite the negative consequences of sin, *it can also be known in its essential traits by human reason.* As the Second Vatican Council teaches, Christ "perfected revelation by fulfilling it through his whole work of making himself present and manifesting himself; through his words and deeds, his signs and wonders, but especially through his death and glorious Resurrection from the dead and final sending of the Spirit of truth. Moreover, he confirmed with divine testimony what revelation proclaimed: that God is with us to free us from the darkness of sin and death, and to raise us up to life eternal."[22]

30. Hence, with our attention fixed on the Lord Jesus, we wish to hear from him once again "the words of God" (Jn 3:34) and meditate anew on *the Gospel of life.* The deepest and most original meaning of this meditation on what revelation tells us about human life was taken up by the Apostle John in the opening words of his First Letter: "That which was from the beginning, which we have heard, which we have seen with our eyes, which we have looked upon and touched with our hands, concerning the word of life—the life was made manifest, and we saw it, and testify to it, and proclaim to you the eternal life which was with the Father and was made manifest to us—that which we have seen and heard we proclaim also to you, so that you may have fellowship with us" (1:1-3).

In Jesus, the "Word of life," God's eternal life is thus proclaimed and given. Thanks to this proclamation and gift, our physical and spiritual life, also in its earthly phase, acquires its full value and meaning, for God's eternal life is in fact the end to which our living in this world is directed and called. In this way *the Gospel of life* includes everything that human experience and reason tell us about the value of human life, accepting it, purifying it, exalting it and bringing it to fulfillment.

"The Lord is my strength and my song, and he has become my salvation" (Ex 15:2): Life is always a good

31. The fullness of the Gospel message about life was prepared for in the Old Testament. Especially in the events of the Exodus, the center of the Old Testament faith experience, Israel discovered the preciousness of its life in the eyes of

God. When it seemed doomed to extermination because of the threat of death hanging over all its newborn males (cf. Ex 1:15-22), the Lord revealed himself to Israel as *its* Savior, with the power to ensure a future to those without hope. Israel thus comes to know clearly that its existence is not at the mercy of a Pharaoh who can exploit it at his despotic whim. On the contrary, Israel's life is *the object of God's gentle and intense love.*

Freedom from slavery meant the gift of an identity, the recognition of an indestructible dignity and *the beginning of a new history* in which the discovery of God and discovery of self go hand in hand. The Exodus was a foundational experience and a model for the future. Through it, Israel comes to learn that whenever its existence is threatened it need only turn to God with renewed trust in order to find in him effective help: "I formed you, you are my servant; O Israel, you will not be forgotten by me" (Is 44:21).

Thus, in coming to know the value of its own existence as a people, Israel also grows in its *perception of the meaning and value of life itself.* This reflection is developed more specifically in the Wisdom Literature, on the basis of daily experience of the precariousness of life and awareness of the threats which assail it. Faced with the contradictions of life, faith is challenged to respond.

More than anything else, it is the problem of suffering which challenges faith and puts it to the test. How can we fail to appreciate the universal anguish of man when we meditate on the Book of Job? The innocent man overwhelmed by suffering is understandably led to wonder: "Why is light given to him that is in misery, and life to the bitter in soul, who long for death, but it comes not, and dig for it more than for hid treasures?" (3:20-21). But even when the darkness is deepest, faith points to a trusting and adoring acknowledgment of the "mystery": "I know that you can do all things, and that no purpose of yours can be thwarted" (Job 42:2).

Revelation progressively allows the first notion of immortal life planted by the Creator in the human heart to be grasped with ever greater clarity: "He has made everything beautiful in its time; also he has put eternity into man's mind" (Eccl 3:11). This *first notion of totality and fullness* is waiting to be manifested in love and brought to perfection, by God's free gift, through sharing in his eternal life.

"The name of Jesus...has made this man strong" (Acts 3:16): In the uncertainties of human life, Jesus brings life's meaning to fulfillment

32. The experience of the people of the Covenant is renewed in the experience of all the "poor" who meet Jesus of Nazareth. Just as God who "loves the living" (cf. Wis 11:26) had reassured Israel in the midst of danger, so now the Son of God proclaims to all who feel threatened and hindered that their lives too are a good to which the Father's love gives meaning and value.

"The blind receive their sight, the lame walk, lepers are cleansed, and the deaf hear, the dead are raised up, the poor have good news preached to them"

(Lk 7:22). With these words of the Prophet Isaiah (35:5-6, 61:1), Jesus sets forth the meaning of his own mission: all who suffer because their lives are in some way "diminished" thus hear from him the "good news" of God's concern for them, and they know for certain that their lives too are a gift carefully guarded in the hands of the Father (cf. Mt 6:25-34).

It is above all the "poor" to whom Jesus speaks in his preaching and actions. The crowds of the sick and the outcasts who follow him and seek him out (cf. Mt 4:23-25) find in his words and actions a revelation of the great value of their lives and of how their hope of salvation is well-founded.

The same thing has taken place in the Church's mission from the beginning. When the Church proclaims Christ as the one who "went about doing good and healing all that were oppressed by the devil, for God was with him" (Acts 10:38), she is conscious of being the bearer of a message of salvation which re-sounds in all its newness precisely amid the hardships and poverty of human life. Peter cured the cripple who daily sought alms at the "Beautiful Gate" of the Temple in Jerusalem, saying: "I have no silver and gold, but I give you what I have; in the name of Jesus Christ of Nazareth, walk" (Acts 3:6). By faith in Jesus, "the Author of life" (Acts 3:15), life which lies abandoned and cries out for help regains self-esteem and full dignity.

The words and deeds of Jesus and those of his Church are not meant only for those who are sick or suffering or in some way neglected by society. On a deeper level they affect *the very meaning of every person's life in its moral and spiritual dimensions.* Only those who recognize that their life is marked by the evil of sin can discover in an encounter with Jesus the Savior the truth and the authenticity of their own existence. Jesus himself says as much: "Those who are well have no need of a physician, but those who are sick; I have not come to call the righteous, but sinners to repentance" (Lk 5:31-32).

But the person who, like the rich landowner in the Gospel parable, thinks that he can make his life secure by the possession of material goods alone, is deluding himself. Life is slipping away from him, and very soon he will find himself bereft of it without ever having appreciated its real meaning: "Fool! This night your soul is required of you; and the things you have prepared, whose will they be?" (Lk 12:20).

33. In Jesus' own life, from beginning to end, we find a singular "dialectic" between the experience of the uncertainty of human life and the affirmation of its value. Jesus' life is marked by uncertainty from the very moment of his birth. He is certainly *accepted* by the righteous, who echo Mary's immediate and joyful "yes" (cf. Lk 1:38). But there is also, from the start, *rejection* on the part of a world which grows hostile and looks for the child in order "to destroy him" (Mt 2:13); a world which remains indifferent and unconcerned about the fulfillment of the mystery of this life entering the world: "there was no place for them in the inn" (Lk 2:7). In this contrast between threats and insecurity on the one hand and the power of God's gift on the other, there shines forth all the more clearly the

glory which radiates from the house at Nazareth and from the manger at Bethlehem: this life which is born is salvation for all humanity (cf. Lk 2:11).

Life's contradictions and risks were fully accepted by Jesus: "though he was rich, yet for your sake he became poor, so that by his poverty you might become rich" (2 Cor 8:9). The poverty of which Paul speaks is not only a stripping of divine privileges, but also a sharing in the lowliest and most vulnerable conditions of human life (cf. Phil 2:6-7). Jesus lived this poverty throughout his life, until the culminating moment of the Cross: "he humbled himself and became obedient unto death, even death on a cross. Therefore God has highly exalted him and bestowed on him the name which is above every name" (Phil 2:8-9). It is precisely *by his death* that *Jesus reveals all the splendor and value of life,* inasmuch as his self-oblation on the cross becomes the source of new life for all people (cf. Jn 12:32). In his journeying amid contradictions and in the very loss of his life, Jesus is guided by the certainty that his life is in the hands of the Father. Consequently, on the Cross, he can say to him: "Father, into your hands I commend my spirit!" (Lk 23:46), that is, my life. Truly great must be the value of human life if the Son of God has taken it up and made it the instrument of the salvation of all humanity!

"Called...to be conformed to the image of his Son" (Rom 8:28-29): God's glory shines on the face of man

34. Life is always a good. This is an instinctive perception and a fact of experience, and man is called to grasp the profound reason why this is so.

Why is life a good? This question is found everywhere in the Bible, and from the very first pages it receives a powerful and amazing answer. The life which God gives man is quite different from the life of all other living creatures, inasmuch as man, although formed from the dust of the earth (cf. Gn 2:7, 3:19; Job 34:15; Ps 103:14; 104:29), *is a manifestation of God in the world, a sign of his presence, a trace of his glory* (cf. Gn 1:26-27; Ps 8:6). This is what St. Irenaeus of Lyons wanted to emphasize in his celebrated definition: "Man, living man, is the glory of God."[23] Man has been given *a sublime dignity,* based on the intimate bond which unites him to his Creator: in man there shines forth a reflection of God himself.

The Book of Genesis affirms this when, in the first account of creation, it places man at the summit of God's creative activity, as its crown, at the culmination of a process which leads from indistinct chaos to the most perfect of creatures. *Everything in creation is ordered to man and everything is made subject to him:* "Fill the earth and subdue it; and have dominion over...every living thing" (1:28); this is God's command to the man and the woman. A similar message is found also in the other account of creation: "The Lord God took the man and put him in the garden of Eden to till it and keep it" (Gn 2:15). We see here a clear affirmation of the primacy of man over things; these are made subject to him and entrusted to his responsible care, whereas for no reason can he be made subject to other men and almost reduced to the level of a thing.

In the biblical narrative, the difference between man and other creatures is shown above all by the fact that only the creation of man is presented as the result of a special decision on the part of God, a deliberation to establish a *particular and specific bond with the Creator:* "Let us make man in our image, after our likeness" (Gn 1:26). *The life* which God offers to man *is a gift by which God shares something of himself with his creature.*

Israel would ponder at length the meaning of this particular bond between man and God. The Book of Sirach too recognizes that God, in creating human beings, "endowed them with strength like his own, and made them in his own image" (17:3). The biblical author sees as part of this image not only man's dominion over the world but also *those spiritual faculties which are distinctively human,* such as reason, discernment between good and evil, and free will: "He filled them with knowledge and understanding, and showed them good and evil" (Sir 17:7). *The ability to attain truth and freedom are human prerogatives* inasmuch as man is created in the image of his Creator, God who is true and just (cf. Dt 32:4). Man alone, among all visible creatures, is "capable of knowing and loving his Creator,"[24] The life which God bestows upon man is much more than mere existence in time. It is a drive toward fullness of life; *it is the seed of an existence which transcends the very limits of time:* "For God created man for incorruption, and made him in the image of his own eternity" (Wis 2:23).

35. The Yahwist account of creation expresses the same conviction. This ancient narrative speaks of *a divine breath* which *is breathed into man* so that he may come to life: "The Lord God formed man of dust from the ground, and breathed into his nostrils the breath of life; and man became a living being" (Gn 2:7).

The divine origin of this spirit of life explains the perennial dissatisfaction which man feels throughout his days on earth. Because he is made by God and bears within himself an indelible imprint of God, man is naturally drawn to God. When he heeds the deepest yearnings of the heart, every man must make his own the words of truth expressed by St. Augustine: "You have made us for yourself, O Lord, and our hearts are restless until they rest in you."[25]

How very significant is the dissatisfaction which marks man's life in Eden as long as his sole point of reference is the world of plants and animals (cf. Gn 2:20). Only the appearance of the woman, a being who is flesh of his flesh and bone of his bones (cf. Gn 2:23), and in whom the spirit of God the Creator is also alive, can satisfy the need for interpersonal dialogue, so vital for human existence. In the other, whether man or woman, there is a reflection of God himself, the definitive goal and fulfillment of every person.

"What is man that you are mindful of him, and the son of man that you care for him?" the Psalmist wonders (Ps 8:4). Compared to the immensity of the universe, man is very small, and yet this very contrast reveals his greatness: "You have made him little less than a god, and crown him with glory and honor" (Ps 8:5). *The glory of God shines on the face of man.* In man the Creator finds his rest, as St. Ambrose comments with a sense of awe: "The sixth day is finished and the creation of the world ends with the formation of that masterpiece which is man, who exercises dominion over all living creatures and is as it were the crown of the universe and the supreme beauty of every created being. Truly we should maintain a reverential silence, since the Lord rested from every work he had undertaken in the world. He rested then in the depths of man, he rested in man's mind and in his thought; after all, he had created man endowed with reason, capable of imitating him, of emulating his virtue, of hungering for heavenly graces. In these his gifts God reposes, who has said: 'Upon whom shall I rest, if not upon the one who is humble, contrite in spirit and trembles at my word?' (Is 66:1-2). I thank the Lord our God who has created so wonderful a work in which to take his rest."[26]

36. Unfortunately, God's marvelous plan was marred by the appearance of sin in history. Through sin, man rebels against his Creator and ends up by *worshipping creatures:* "They exchanged the truth about God for a lie and worshipped and served the creature rather than the Creator" (Rom 1:25). As a result man not only deforms the image of God in his own person, but is tempted to offenses against it in others as well, replacing relationships of communion by attitudes of distrust, indifference, hostility and even murderous hatred. When *God* is not acknowledged *as God,* the profound meaning of man is betrayed and communion between people is compromised.

In the life of man, God's image shines forth anew and is again revealed in all its fullness at the coming of the Son of God in human flesh. "Christ is the image of the invisible God" (Col 1:15), he "reflects the glory of God and bears the very stamp of his nature" (Heb 1:3). He is the perfect image of the Father.

The plan of life given to the first Adam finds at last its fulfillment in Christ. Whereas the disobedience of Adam had ruined and marred God's plan for human life and introduced death into the world, the redemptive obedience of Christ is the source of grace poured out upon the human race, opening wide to everyone the gates of the kingdom of life (cf. Rom 5:12-21). As the Apostle Paul states: "The first man Adam became a living being; the last Adam became a life-giving spirit" (1 Cor 15:45).

All who commit themselves to following Christ are given the fullness of life: the divine image is restored, renewed and brought to perfection in them. God's plan for human beings is this, that they should "be conformed to the image of his Son" (Rom 8:29). Only thus, in the splendor of this image, can man be freed from the slavery of idolatry, rebuild lost fellowship and rediscover his true identity.

"Whoever lives and believes in me shall never die" (Jn 11:26):
The gift of eternal life

37. The life which the Son of God came to give to human beings cannot be reduced to mere existence in time. The life which was always "in him" and which is the "light of men" (Jn 1:4) *consists in being begotten of God and sharing in the fullness of his love:* "To all who received him, who believed in his name, he gave power to become children of God; who were born, not of blood nor of the will of the flesh nor of the will of man, but of God" (Jn 1:12-13).

Sometimes Jesus refers to this life which he came to give simply as "life," and he presents being born of God as a necessary condition if man is to attain the end for which God has created him: "Unless one is born anew, he cannot see the kingdom of God" (Jn 3:3). To give this life is the real object of Jesus' mission: he is the one who "comes down from heaven, and gives life to the world" (Jn 6:33). Thus can he truly say: "He who follows me...will have the light of life" (Jn 8:12).

At other times, Jesus speaks of "eternal life." Here the adjective does more than merely evoke a perspective which is beyond time. The life which Jesus promises and gives is "eternal" because it is a full participation in the life of the "Eternal One." Whoever believes in Jesus and enters into communion with him has eternal life (cf. Jn 3:15; 6:40) because he hears from Jesus the only words which reveal and communicate to his existence the fullness of life. These are the "words of eternal life" which Peter acknowledges in his confession of faith: "Lord, to whom shall we go? You have the words of eternal life; and we have believed, and have come to know, that you are the Holy One of God" (Jn 6:68-69). Jesus himself, addressing the Father in the great priestly prayer, declares what eternal life consists in: "This is eternal life, that they may know you the only true God, and Jesus Christ whom you have sent" (Jn 17:3). To know God and his Son is to accept the mystery of the loving communion of the Father, the Son and the Holy Spirit into one's own life, which even now is open to eternal life because it *shares in the life of God.*

38. Eternal life is therefore the life of God himself and at the same time the *life of the children of God.* As they ponder this unexpected and inexpressible truth which comes to us from God in Christ, believers cannot fail to be filled with ever new wonder and unbounded gratitude. They can say in the words of the Apostle John: "See what love the Father has given us, that we should be called children of God; and so we are.... Beloved, we are God's children now; it does not yet appear what we shall be, but we know that when he appears we shall be like him, for we shall see him as he is" (1 Jn 3:1-2).

Here the Christian truth about life becomes most sublime. The dignity of this life is linked not only to its beginning, to the fact that it comes from God, but also to its final end, to its destiny of fellowship with God in knowledge and love of him.

In the light of this truth St. Irenaeus qualifies and completes his praise of man: "the glory of God" is indeed, "man, living man," but "the life of man consists in the vision of God."[27]

Immediate consequences arise from this for human life in *its earthly state,* in which, for that matter, eternal life already springs forth and begins to grow. Although man instinctively loves life because it is a good, this love will find further inspiration and strength, and new breadth and depth, in the divine dimensions of this good. Similarly, the love which every human being has for life cannot be reduced simply to a desire to have sufficient space for self-expression and for entering into relationships with others; rather, it develops in a joyous awareness that life can become the "place" where God manifests himself, where we meet him and enter into communion with him. The life which Jesus gives in no way lessens the value of our existence in time; it takes it and directs it to its final destiny: "I am the resurrection and the life...whoever lives and believes in me shall never die" (Jn 11:25-26).

"From man in regard to his fellow man I will demand an accounting" (Gn 9:5): Reverence and love for every human life

39. Man's life comes from God; it is his gift, his image and imprint, a sharing in his breath of life. God therefore *is the sole Lord of this life:* man cannot do with it as he wills. God himself makes this clear to Noah after the flood: "For your own lifeblood, too, I will demand an accounting...and from man in regard to his fellow man I will demand an accounting for human life" (Gn 9:5). The biblical text is concerned to emphasize how the sacredness of life has its foundation in God and in his creative activity: "For God made man in his own image" (Gn 9:6).

Human life and death are thus in the hands of God, in his power: "In his hand is the life of every living thing and the breath of all mankind," exclaims Job (12:10). "The Lord brings to death and brings to life; he brings down to Sheol and raises up" (1 Sam 2:6). He alone can say: "It is I who bring both death and life" (Dt 32:39).

But God does not exercise this power in an arbitrary and threatening way, but rather as part of his *care and loving concern for his creatures.* If it is true that human life is in the hands of God, it is no less true that these are loving hands, like those of a mother who accepts, nurtures and takes care of her child: "I have calmed and quieted my soul, like a child quieted at its mother's breast; like a child that is quieted is my soul" (Ps 131:2; cf. Is 49:15; 66:12-13; Hos 11:4). Thus Israel does not see in the history of peoples and in the destiny of individuals the outcome of mere chance or of blind fate, but rather the results of a loving plan by which God brings together all the possibilities of life and opposes the powers of death arising from sin: "God did not make death, and he does not delight in the death of the living. For he created all things that they might exist" (Wis 1:13-14).

40. The sacredness of life gives rise to its *inviolability, written from the beginning in man's heart,* in his conscience. The question: "What have you done?" (Gn 4:10), which God addresses to Cain after he has killed his brother

Abel, interprets the experience of every person: in the depths of his conscience, man is always reminded of the inviolability of life—his own life and that of others—as something which does not belong to him, because it is the property and gift of God the Creator and Father.

The commandment regarding the inviolability of human life reverberates *at the heart of the "ten words" in the covenant of Sinai* (cf. Ex 34:28). In the first place that commandment prohibits murder: "You shall not kill" (Ex 20:13); "do not slay the innocent and righteous" (Ex 23:7). But, as is brought out in Israel's later legislation, it also prohibits all personal injury inflicted on another (cf. Ex 21:12-27). Of course we must recognize that in the Old Testament this sense of the value of life, though already quite marked, does not yet reach the refinement found in the Sermon on the Mount. This is apparent in some aspects of the current penal legislation, which provided for severe forms of corporal punishment and even the death penalty. But the overall message, which the New Testament will bring to perfection, is a forceful appeal for respect for the inviolability of physical life and the integrity of the person. It culminates in the positive commandment which obliges us to be responsible for our neighbor as for ourselves: "You shall love your neighbor as yourself" (Lv 19:18).

41. The commandment "You shall not kill," included and more fully expressed in the positive command of love for one's neighbor, is *reaffirmed in all its force by the Lord Jesus*. To the rich young man who asks him: "Teacher, what good deed must I do, to have eternal life?" Jesus replies: "If you would enter life, keep the commandments" (Mt 19:16, 17). And he quotes, as the first of these: "You shall not kill" (Mt 19:18). In the Sermon on the Mount, Jesus demands from his disciples a *righteousness which surpasses* that of the Scribes and Pharisees, also with regard to respect for life: "You have heard that it was said to the men of old, 'You shall not kill; and whoever kills shall be liable to judgment.' But I say to you that every one who is angry with his brother shall be liable to judgment" (Mt 5:21-22).

By his words and actions Jesus further unveils the positive requirements of the commandment regarding the inviolability of life. These requirements were already present in the Old Testament, where legislation dealt with protecting and defending life when it was weak and threatened: in the case of foreigners, widows, orphans, the sick and the poor in general, including children in the womb (cf. Ex 21:22; 22:20-26). With Jesus these positive requirements assume new force and urgency, and are revealed in all their breadth and depth: they range from caring for the life of one's *brother* (whether a blood brother, someone belonging to the same people, or a foreigner living in the land of Israel) to showing concern for the *stranger,* even to the point of loving one's *enemy.*

A stranger is no longer a stranger for the person who must *become a neighbor* to someone in need, to the point of accepting responsibility for his life, as the parable of the Good Samaritan shows so clearly (cf. Lk 10:25-37). Even an enemy ceases to be an enemy for the person who is obliged to love him (cf. Mt

5:38-48; Lk 6:27-35), to "do good" to him (cf. Lk 6:27, 33, 35) and to respond
to his immediate needs promptly and with no expectation of repayment (cf. Lk
6:34-35). The height of this love is to pray for one's enemy. By so doing we
achieve harmony with the providential love of God: "But I say to you, love your
enemies and pray for those who persecute you, so that you may be children of
your Father who is in heaven; for he makes his sun rise on the evil and on the
good and sends rain on the just and on the unjust" (Mt 5:44-45; cf. Lk 6:28, 35).

Thus the deepest element of God's commandment to protect human life is
the *requirement to show reverence and love* for every person and the life of every person. This is the teaching which the Apostle Paul, echoing the words of
Jesus, addresses to the Christians in Rome: "The commandments, 'You shall not
commit adultery, You shall not kill, You shall not steal, You shall not covet,' and
any other commandment, are summed up in this sentence, *'You shall love your
neighbor as yourself.'* Love does no wrong to a neighbor; therefore love is the
fulfilling of the law" (Rom 13:9-10).

"Be fruitful and multiply, and fill the earth and subdue it" (Gn 1:28): Man's responsibility for life

42. To defend and promote life, to show reverence and love for it, is a task
which God entrusts to every man, calling him as his living image to share in his
own lordship over the world: "God blessed them, and God said to them, 'Be
fruitful and multiply, and fill the earth and subdue it; and have dominion over the
fish of the sea and over the birds of the air and over every living thing that moves
upon the earth'" (Gn 1:28).

The biblical text clearly shows the breadth and depth of the lordship which
God bestows on man. It is a matter first of all of *dominion over the earth and
over every living creature,* as the Book of Wisdom makes clear: "O God of my
fathers and Lord of mercy...by your wisdom you have formed man, to have
dominion over the creatures you have made, and rule the world in holiness and
righteousness" (Wis 9:1, 2-3). The Psalmist too extols the dominion given to
man as a sign of glory and honor from his Creator: "You have given him dominion over the works of your hands; you have put all things under his feet, all sheep
and oxen, and also the beasts of the field, the birds of the air, and the fish of the
sea, whatever passes along the paths of the sea" (Ps 8:6-8).

As one called to till and look after the garden of the world (cf. Gn 2:15),
man has a specific responsibility toward *the environment in which he lives,* toward the creation which God has put at the service of his personal dignity, of his
life, not only for the present but also for future generations. It is the *ecological
question*—ranging from the preservation of the natural habitats of the different
species of animals and of other forms of life to "human ecology" properly speaking[28] —which finds in the Bible clear and strong ethical direction, leading to a
solution which respects the great good of life, of every life. In fact, "the dominion granted to man by the Creator is not an absolute power, nor can one speak of

a freedom to 'use and misuse,' or to dispose of things as one pleases. The limitation imposed from the beginning by the Creator himself and expressed symbolically by the prohibition not to 'eat of the fruit of the tree' (cf. Gn 2:16-17) shows clearly enough that, when it comes to the natural world, we are subject not only to biological laws but also to moral ones, which cannot be violated with impunity."[29]

43. A certain sharing by man in God's lordship is also evident in the *specific responsibility* which he is given *for human life as such.* It is a responsibility which reaches its highest point in the giving of life *through procreation* by man and woman in marriage. As the Second Vatican Council teaches: "God himself who said, 'It is not good for man to be alone' (Gn 2:18) and 'who made man from the beginning male and female' (Mt 19:4), wished to share with man a certain special participation in his own creative work. Thus he blessed male and female saying: 'Increase and multiply'" (Gn 1:28).[30]

By speaking of "a certain special participation" of man and woman in the "creative work" of God, the Council wishes to point out that having a child is an event which is deeply human and full of religious meaning, insofar as it involves both the spouses, who form "one flesh" (Gn 2:24), and God who makes himself present. As I wrote in my *Letter to Families:* "When a new person is born of the conjugal union of the two, he brings with him into the world a particular image and likeness of God himself: *the genealogy of the person is inscribed in the very biology of generation.* In affirming that the spouses, as parents, cooperate with God the Creator in conceiving and giving birth to a new human being, we are not speaking merely with reference to the laws of biology. Instead, we wish to emphasize that *God himself is present in human fatherhood and motherhood* quite differently than he is present in all other instances of begetting 'on earth.' Indeed, God alone is the source of that 'image and likeness' which is proper to the human being, as it was received at Creation. Begetting is the continuation of Creation."[31]

This is what the Bible teaches in direct and eloquent language when it reports the joyful cry of the first woman, "the mother of all the living" (Gn 3:20). Aware that God has intervened, Eve exclaims: "I have begotten a man with the help of the Lord" (Gn 4:1). In procreation therefore, through the communication of life from parents to child, God's own image and likeness is transmitted, thanks to the creation of the immortal soul.[32] The beginning of the "book of the genealogy of Adam" expresses it in this way: "When God created man, he made him in the likeness of God. Male and female he created them, and he blessed them and called them man when they were created. When Adam had lived a hundred and thirty years, he became the father of a son in his own likeness, after his image, and named him Seth" (Gn 5:1-3). It is precisely in their role as co-workers with God *who transmits his image to the new creature* that we see the greatness of couples who are ready "to cooperate with the love of the Creator and the Savior, who through them will enlarge and enrich his own family day by day."[33] This is why the Bishop Amphilochius extolled "holy matrimony, chosen and elevated above all other earthly gifts" as "the begetter of humanity, the creator of images of God."[34]

Thus, a man and woman joined in matrimony become partners in a divine undertaking: through the act of procreation, God's gift is accepted and a new life opens to the future.

But over and above the specific mission of parents, *the task of accepting and serving life involves everyone; and this task must be fulfilled above all toward life when it is at its weakest.* It is Christ himself who reminds us of this when he asks to be loved and served in his brothers and sisters who are suffering in any way: the hungry, the thirsty, the foreigner, the naked, the sick, the imprisoned.... Whatever is done to each of them is done to Christ himself (cf. Mt 25:31-46).

"For you formed my inmost being" (Ps 139:13):
The dignity of the unborn child

44. Human life finds itself most vulnerable when it enters the world and when it leaves the realm of time to embark upon eternity. The word of God frequently repeats the call to show care and respect, above all where life is undermined by sickness and old age. Although there are no direct and explicit calls to protect human life at its very beginning, specifically life not yet born, and life nearing its end, this can easily be explained by the fact that the mere possibility of harming, attacking, or actually denying life in these circumstances is completely foreign to the religious and cultural way of thinking of the People of God.

In the Old Testament, sterility is dreaded as a curse, while numerous offspring are viewed as a blessing: "Sons are a heritage from the Lord, the fruit of the womb a reward" (Ps 127:3; cf. Ps 128:3-4). This belief is also based on Israel's awareness of being the people of the Covenant, called to increase in accordance with the promise made to Abraham: "Look toward heaven, and number the stars, if you are able to number them...so shall your descendants be" (Gn 15:5). But more than anything else, at work here is the certainty that the life which parents transmit has its origins in God. We see this attested in the many biblical passages which respectfully and lovingly speak of conception, of the forming of life in the mother's womb, of giving birth and of the intimate connection between the initial moment of life and the action of God the Creator.

"Before I formed you in the womb I knew you, and before you were born I consecrated you" (Jer 1:5): *the life of every individual, from its very beginning, is part of God's plan.* Job, from the depth of his pain, stops to contemplate the work of God who miraculously formed his body in his mother's womb. Here he finds reason for trust, and he expresses his belief that there is a divine plan for his life: "You have fashioned and made me; will you then turn and destroy me? Remember that you have made me of clay; and will you turn me to dust again? Did you not pour me out like milk and curdle me like cheese? You clothed me with skin and flesh, and knit me together with bones and sinews. You have granted me life and steadfast love; and your care has preserved my spirit" (Job 10:8-12). Expressions of awe and wonder at God's intervention in the life of a child in its mother's womb occur again and again in the Psalms.[35]

How can anyone think that even a single moment of this marvelous process of the unfolding of life could be separated from the wise and loving work of the Creator, and left prey to human caprice? Certainly the mother of the seven brothers did not think so; she professes her faith in God, both the source and guarantee of life from its very conception, and the foundation of the hope of new life beyond death: "I do not know how you came into being in my womb. It was not I who gave you life and breath, nor I who set in order the elements within each of you. Therefore the Creator of the world, who shaped the beginning of man and devised the origin of all things, will in his mercy give life and breath back to you again, since you now forget yourselves for the sake of his laws" (2 Mc 7:22-23).

45. The New Testament revelation confirms *the indisputable recognition of the value of life from its very beginning.* The exaltation of fruitfulness and the eager expectation of life resound in the words with which Elizabeth rejoices in her pregnancy: "The Lord has looked on me...to take away my reproach among men" (Lk 1:25). And even more so, the value of the person from the moment of conception is celebrated in the meeting between the Virgin Mary and Elizabeth, and between the two children whom they are carrying in the womb. It is precisely the children who reveal the advent of the Messianic age: in their meeting, the redemptive power of the presence of the Son of God among men first becomes operative. As Saint Ambrose writes: "The arrival of Mary and the blessings of the Lord's presence are also speedily declared.... Elizabeth was the first to hear the voice; but John was the first to experience grace. She heard according to the order of nature; he leaped because of the mystery. She recognized the arrival of Mary; he the arrival of the Lord. The woman recognized the woman's arrival; the child, that of the child. The women speak of grace; the babies make it effective from within to the advantage of their mothers who, by a double miracle, prophesy under the inspiration of their children. The infant leaped, the mother was filled with the Spirit. The mother was not filled before the son, but after the son was filled with the Holy Spirit, he filled his mother too."[36]

"I kept my faith even when I said, 'I am greatly afflicted'"
(Ps 116:10): Life in old age and at times of suffering

46. With regard to the last moments of life too, it would be anachronistic to expect biblical revelation to make express reference to present-day issues concerning respect for elderly and sick persons, or to condemn explicitly attempts to hasten their end by force. The cultural and religious context of the Bible is in no way touched by such temptations; indeed, in that context the wisdom and experience of the elderly are recognized as a unique source of enrichment for the family and for society.

Old age is characterized by dignity and surrounded with reverence (cf. 2 Mc 6:23). The just man does not seek to be delivered from old age and its burden; on the contrary his prayer is this: "You, O Lord, are my hope, my trust, O Lord, from my youth...so even to old age and grey hairs, O God, do not forsake me, till I proclaim your might to all the generations to come" (Ps 71:5, 18). The ideal of the Messianic age is presented as a time when "no more shall there be...an old man who does not fill out his days" (Is 65:20).

In old age, how should one face the inevitable decline of life? *How should one act in the face of death? The believer knows that his life is in the hands of God:* "You, O Lord, hold my lot" (cf. Ps 16:5), and he accepts from God the need to die: "This is the decree from the Lord for all flesh, and how can you reject the good pleasure of the Most High?" (Sir 41:3-4). Man is not the master of life, nor is he the master of death. In life and in death, he has to entrust himself completely to the "good pleasure of the Most High," to his loving plan.

In moments of *sickness* too, man is called to have the same trust in the Lord and to renew his fundamental faith in the One who "heals all your diseases" (cf. Ps 103:3). When every hope of good health seems to fade before a person's eyes—so as to make him cry out: "My days are like an evening shadow; I wither away like grass" (Ps 102:11)—even then the believer is sustained by an unshakable faith in God's life-giving power. Illness does not drive such a person to despair and to seek death, but makes him cry out in hope: "I kept my faith, even when I said, 'I am greatly afflicted'" (Ps 116:10); "O Lord my God, I cried to you for help, and you have healed me. O Lord, you have brought up my soul from Sheol, restored me to life from among those gone down to the pit" (Ps 30:2-3).

47. The mission of Jesus, with the many healings he performed, *shows God's great concern even for man's bodily life.* Jesus, as "the physician of the body and of the spirit,"[37] was sent by the Father to proclaim the good news to the poor and to heal the brokenhearted (cf. Lk 4:18; Is 61:1). Later, when he sends his disciples into the world, he gives them a mission, a mission in which healing the sick goes hand in hand with the proclamation of the Gospel: "And preach as you go, saying, 'The kingdom of heaven is at hand.' Heal the sick, raise the dead, cleanse lepers, cast out demons" (Mt 10:7-8; cf. Mk 6:13; 16:18).

Certainly *the life of the body in its earthly state is not an absolute good for the believer,* especially as he may be asked to give up his life for a greater good. As Jesus says: "Whoever would save his life will lose it; and whoever loses his life for my sake and the gospel's will save it" (Mk 8:35). The New Testament gives many different examples of this. Jesus does not hesitate to sacrifice himself and he freely makes of his life an offering to the Father (cf. Jn 10:17) and to those who belong to him (cf. Jn 10:15). The death of John the Baptist, precursor of the Savior, also testifies that earthly existence is not an absolute good; what is more important is remaining faithful to the word of the Lord even at the risk of one's life (cf. Mk 6:17-29). Stephen, losing his earthly life because of his faithful witness to the Lord's Resurrection, follows in the Master's footsteps and meets those who are stoning him with words of forgiveness (cf. Acts 7:59-60), thus becoming the first of a countless host of martyrs whom the Church has venerated since the very beginning.

No one, however, can arbitrarily choose whether to live or die; the absolute master of such a decision is the Creator alone, in whom "we live and move and have our being" (Acts 17:28).

"All who hold her fast will live" (Bar 4:1):
From the law of Sinai to the gift of the Spirit

48. Life is indelibly marked by *a truth of its own.* By accepting God's gift, man is obliged to *maintain life in this truth* which is essential to it. To detach oneself from this truth is to condemn oneself to meaninglessness and unhappiness, and possibly to become a threat to the existence of others, since the barriers guaranteeing respect for life and the defense of life, in every circumstance, have been broken down.

The truth of life is revealed by God's commandment. The word of the Lord shows concretely the course which life must follow if it is to respect its own truth and to preserve its own dignity. The protection of life is not only ensured by the specific commandment "You shall not kill" (Ex 20:13; Dt 5:17); *the entire Law of the Lord* serves to protect life, because it reveals that truth in which life finds its full meaning.

It is not surprising, therefore, that God's Covenant with his people is so closely linked to the perspective of life, also in its body dimension. In that Covenant, God's *commandment* is offered as *the path of life:* "I have set before you this day life and good, death and evil. If you obey the commandments of the Lord your God which I command you this day, by loving the Lord your God, by walking in his ways, and by keeping his commandments and his statutes and his ordinances, then you shall live and multiply, and the Lord your God will bless you in the land which you are entering to take possession of" (Dt 30:15-16). What is at stake is not only the land of Canaan and the existence of the people of Israel, but also the world of today and of the future, and the existence of all humanity. In fact, it is altogether impossible for life to remain authentic and complete once it is detached from the good; and the good, in its turn, is essentially bound to the commandments of the Lord, that is, to the "law of life" (Sir 17:11). The good to be done is not added to life as a burden which weighs on it, since the very purpose of life is that good and only by doing it can life be built up.

It is thus *the Law as a whole* which fully protects human life. This explains why it is so hard to remain faithful to the commandment "You shall not kill" when the other "words of life" (cf. Acts 7:38) with which this commandment is bound up are not observed. Detached from this wider framework, the commandment is destined to become nothing more than an obligation imposed from without, and very soon we begin to look for its limits and try to find mitigating factors and exceptions. Only when people are open to the fullness of the truth about God, man and history will the words "You shall not kill" shine forth once more as a good for man in himself and in his relations with others. In such a perspective we can grasp the full truth of the passage of the Book of Deuteronomy which Jesus repeats in reply to the first temptation: "Man does not live by bread alone, but...by everything that proceeds out of the mouth of the Lord" (Dt 8:3; cf. Mt 4:4).

It is by listening to the word of the Lord that we are able to live in dignity and justice. It is by observing the Law of God that we are able to bring forth fruits of life and happiness: "All who hold her fast will live, and those who forsake her will die" (Bar 4:1).

49. The history of Israel shows how *difficult it is to remain faithful to the Law of life* which God has inscribed in human hearts and which he gave on Sinai to the people of the Covenant. When the people look for ways of living which ignore God's plan, it is the Prophets in particular who forcefully remind them that the Lord alone is the authentic source of life. Thus Jeremiah writes: "My people have committed two evils: they have forsaken me, the fountain of living waters, and hewed out cisterns for themselves, broken cisterns, that can hold no water" (2:13). The Prophets point an accusing finger at those who show contempt for life and violate people's rights: "They trample the head of the poor into the dust of the earth" (Amos 2:7); "they have filled this place with the blood of innocents" (Jer 19:4). Among them, the Prophet Ezekiel frequently condemns the city of Jerusalem, calling it "the bloody city" (22:2; 24:6, 9), the city that sheds blood in her own midst" (22:3).

But while the Prophets condemn offenses against life, they are concerned above all to awaken *hope for a new principle of life,* capable of bringing about a renewed relationship with God and with others, and of opening up new and extraordinary possibilities for understanding and carrying out all the demands inherent in the *Gospel of life.* This will only be possible thanks to the gift of God who purifies and renews: "I will sprinkle clean water upon you, and you shall be clean from all your uncleannesses, and from all your idols I will cleanse you. A new heart I will give you, and a new spirit I will put within you" (Ez 36:25-26; cf. Jer 31:34). This "new heart" will make it possible to appreciate and achieve the deepest and most authentic meaning of life: namely, that of being *a gift which is fully realized in the giving of self.* This is the splendid message about the value of life which comes to us from the figure of the Servant of the Lord: "When he makes himself an offering for sin, he shall see his offspring, he shall prolong his life...he shall see the fruit of the travail of his soul and be satisfied" (Is 53:10, 11).

It is in the coming of Jesus of Nazareth that the Law is fulfilled and that a new heart is given through his Spirit. Jesus does not deny the Law but brings it to fulfillment (cf. Mt 5:17): the Law and the Prophets are summed up in the golden rule of mutual love (cf. Mt 7:12). In Jesus the Law becomes once and for all the "Gospel," the good news of God's lordship over the world, which brings all life back to its roots and its original purpose. This is *the New Law,* "the law of the

Spirit of life in Christ Jesus" (Rom 8:2), and its fundamental expression, following the example of the Lord who gave his life for his friends (cf. Jn 15:13), is *the
gift of self in love for one's brothers and sisters:* "We know that we have passed
out of death into life, because we love the brethren" (1 Jn 3:14). This is the law
of freedom, joy and blessedness.

"They shall look on him whom they have pierced" (Jn 19:37):
The Gospel of life is brought to fulfillment on the tree of the Cross

50. At the end of this chapter, in which we have reflected on the Christian
message about life, I would like to pause with each one of you to *contemplate
the One who was pierced* and who draws all people to himself (cf. Jn 19:37;
12:32). Looking at "the spectacle" of the Cross (cf. Lk 23:48) we shall discover
in this glorious tree the fulfillment and the complete revelation of the whole *Gospel of life.*

In the early afternoon of Good Friday, "there was darkness over the whole
land...while the sun's light failed; and the curtain of the temple was torn in two"
(Lk 23:44, 45). This is the symbol of a great cosmic disturbance and a massive
conflict between the forces of good and the forces of evil, between life and
death. Today we too find ourselves in the midst of a dramatic conflict between
the "culture of death" and the "culture of life." But the glory of the Cross is not
overcome by this darkness; rather, it shines forth ever more radiantly and
brightly, and is revealed as the center, meaning and goal of all history and of
every human life.

Jesus is nailed to the Cross and is lifted up from the earth. He experiences
the moment of his greatest "powerlessness," and his life seems completely delivered to the derision of his adversaries and into the hands of his executioners:
he is mocked, jeered at, insulted (cf. Mk 15:24-36). And yet, precisely amid all
this, having seen him breathe his last, the Roman centurion exclaims: "Truly this
man was the Son of God!" (Mk 15:39). It is thus, at the moment of his greatest
weakness, that the Son of God is revealed for who he is: *on the Cross his glory is
made manifest.*

By his death, Jesus sheds light on the meaning of the life and death of every
human being. Before he dies, Jesus prays to the Father, asking forgiveness for his
persecutors (cf. Lk 23:34), and to the criminal who asks him to remember him in
his Kingdom he replies: "Truly, I say to you, today you will be with me in Paradise" (Lk 23:43). After his death "the tombs also were opened, and many bodies
of the saints who had fallen asleep were raised" (Mt 27:52). The salvation
wrought by Jesus is the bestowal of life and resurrection. Throughout his earthly
life, Jesus had indeed bestowed salvation by healing and doing good to all (cf.
Acts 10:38). But his miracles, healings and even his raising of the dead were
signs of another salvation, a salvation which consists in the forgiveness of sins,
that is, in setting man free from his greatest sickness and in raising him to the
very life of God.

On the Cross, the miracle of the serpent lifted up by Moses in the desert (Jn 3:14-15; cf. Num 21:8-9) is renewed and brought to full and definitive perfection. Today too, by looking upon the one who was pierced, every person whose life is threatened encounters the sure hope of finding freedom and redemption.

51. But there is yet another particular event which moves me deeply when I consider it. "When Jesus had received the vinegar, he said, 'It is finished'; and he bowed his head and gave up his spirit" (Jn 19:30). Afterward, the Roman soldier "pierced his side with a spear, and at once there came out blood and water" (Jn 19:34).

Everything has now reached its complete fulfillment. The "giving up" of the spirit describes Jesus' death, a death like that of every other human being, but it also seems to allude to the "gift of the Spirit," by which Jesus ransoms us from death and opens before us a new life.

It is the very life of God which is now shared with man. It is the life which through the Sacraments of the Church—symbolized by the blood and water flowing from Christ's side—is continually given to God's children, making them the people of the New Covenant. *From the Cross, the source of life, the "people of life" is born and increases.*

The contemplation of the Cross thus brings us to the very heart of all that has taken place. Jesus, who upon entering into the world said: "I have come, O God, to do your will" (cf. Heb 10:9), made himself obedient to the Father in everything and, "having loved his own who were in the world, he loved them to the end" (Jn 13:1), giving himself completely for them.

He who had come "not to be served but to serve, and to give his life as a ransom for many" (Mk 10:45), attains on the Cross the heights of love: "Greater love has no man than this, that a man lay down his life for his friends" (Jn 15:13). And he died for us while we were yet sinners (cf. Rom 5:8).

In this way Jesus proclaims that *life finds its center, its meaning and its fulfillment when it is given up.*

At this point our meditation becomes praise and thanksgiving, and at the same time urges us to imitate Christ and follow in his footsteps (cf. 1 Pt 2:21).

We too are called to give our lives for our brothers and sisters, and thus to realize in the fullness of truth the meaning and destiny of our existence.

We shall be able to do this because you, O Lord, have given us the example and have bestowed on us the power of your Spirit. We shall be able to do this if every day, with you and like you, we are obedient to the Father and do his will.

Grant, therefore, that we may listen with open and generous hearts to every word which proceeds from the mouth of God. Thus we shall learn not only to obey the commandment not to kill human life, but also to revere life, to love it and to foster it.

CHAPTER III

You Shall Not Kill

God's Holy Law

"If you would enter life, keep the commandments" (Mt 19:17):
Gospel and commandment

52. "And behold, one came up to him, saying, 'Teacher, what good deed must I do, to have eternal life?'" (Mt 19:6). Jesus replied, "If you would enter life, keep the commandments" (Mt 19:17). The Teacher is speaking about eternal life, that is, a sharing in the life of God himself. This life is attained through the observance of the Lord's commandments, including the commandment "You shall not kill." This is the first precept from the Decalogue which Jesus quotes to the young man who asks him what commandments he should observe: "Jesus said, 'You shall not kill, you shall not commit adultery, you shall not steal...'" (Mt 19:18).

God's commandment is never detached from his love: it is always a gift meant for man's growth and joy. As such, it represents an essential and indispensable aspect of the Gospel, actually becoming "gospel" itself: joyful good news. The *Gospel of life* is both a great gift of God and an exacting task for humanity. It gives rise to amazement and gratitude in the person graced with freedom, and it asks to be welcomed, preserved and esteemed, with a deep sense of responsibility. In giving life to man, God *demands* that he love, respect and promote life. *The gift* thus *becomes a commandment,* and *the commandment is itself a gift.*

Man, as the living image of God, is willed by his Creator to be ruler and lord. St. Gregory of Nyssa writes that "God made man capable of carrying out his role as king of the earth.... Man was created in the image of the One who governs the universe. Everything demonstrates that from the beginning man's nature was marked by royalty.... Man is a king. Created to exercise dominion over the world, he was given a likeness to the king of the universe; he is the living image who participates by his dignity in the perfection of the divine archetype."[38] Called to be fruitful and multiply, to subdue the earth and to exercise dominion over other lesser creatures (cf. Gn 1:28), man is ruler and lord not only over things but especially over himself,[39] and in a certain sense, over the life which he has received and which he is able to transmit through procreation, carried out with love and respect for God's plan. Man's *lordship* however is not absolute, but *ministerial:* it is a real reflection of the unique and infinite lordship of God. Hence man must exercise it with *wisdom and love,* sharing in the boundless wisdom and love of God. And this comes about through obedience to God's holy Law: a free and joyful obedience (cf. Ps 119), born of and fostered by an awareness that the precepts of the Lord are a gift of grace entrusted to man always and solely for his good, for the preservation of his personal dignity and the pursuit of his happiness.

With regard to things, but even more with regard to life, man is not the absolute master and final judge, but rather—and this is where his incomparable greatness lies—he is the "minister of God's plan."[40]

Life is entrusted to man as a treasure which must not be squandered, as a talent which must be used well. Man must render an account of it to his Master (cf. Mt 25:14-30; Lk 19:12-27).

"From man in regard to his fellow man I will demand an accounting for human life" (Gn 9:5): Human life is sacred and inviolable

53. "Human life is sacred because from its beginning it involves 'the creative action of God,' and it remains forever in a special relationship with the Creator, who is its sole end. God alone is the Lord of life from its beginning until its end: no one can, in any circumstance, claim for himself the right to destroy directly an innocent human being."[41] With these words the Instruction *Donum Vitae* sets forth the central content of God's revelation on the sacredness and inviolability of human life.

Sacred Scripture in fact presents the precept "You shall not kill" as a divine commandment (Ex 20:13; Dt 5:17). As I have already emphasized, this commandment is found in the Decalogue, at the heart of the Covenant which the Lord makes with his chosen people; but it was already contained in the original covenant between God and humanity after the purifying punishment of the Flood, caused by the spread of sin and violence (cf. Gn 9:5-6).

God proclaims that he is absolute Lord of the life of man, who is formed in his image and likeness (cf. Gn 1:26-28). Human life is thus given a sacred and inviolable character, which reflects the inviolability of the Creator himself. Precisely for this reason God will severely judge every violation of the commandment "You shall not kill," the commandment which is at the basis of all life together in society. He is the *"goel,"* the defender of the innocent (cf. Gn 4:9-15; Is 41:14; Jer 50:34; Ps 19:14). God thus shows that he does not delight in the death of the living (cf. Wis 1:13). Only Satan can delight therein: for through his envy death entered the world (cf. Wis 2:24). He who is "a murderer from the beginning," is also "a liar and the father of lies" (Jn 8:44). By deceiving man he leads him to projects of sin and death, making them appear as goals and fruits of life.

54. As explicitly formulated, the precept "You shall not kill" is strongly negative: it indicates the extreme limit which can never be exceeded. Implicitly, however, it encourages a positive attitude of absolute respect for life; it leads to the promotion of life and to progress along the way of a love which gives, receives and serves. The people of the Covenant, although slowly and with some contradictions, progressively matured in this way of thinking, and thus prepared

for the great proclamation of Jesus that the commandment to love one's neighbor is like the commandment to love God; "on these two commandments depend all the law and the prophets" (cf. Mt 22:36-40). St. Paul emphasizes that "the commandment...you shall not kill...and any other commandment, are summed up in this phrase: 'You shall love your neighbor as yourself'" (Rom 13:9; cf. Gal 5:14). Taken up and brought to fulfillment in the New Law, the commandment "You shall not kill" stands as an indispensable condition for being able "to enter life" (cf. Mt 19:16-19). In this same perspective, the words of the Apostle John have a categorical ring: "Anyone who hates his brother is a murderer, and you know that no murderer has eternal life abiding in him" (1 Jn 3:15).

From the beginning, the *living Tradition of the Church*—as shown by the *Didache,* the most ancient non-biblical Christian writing—categorically re-peated the commandment "You shall not kill": "There are two ways, a way of life and a way of death; there is a great difference between them.... In accordance with the precept of the teaching: you shall not kill...you shall not put a child to death by abortion nor kill it once it is born.... The way of death is this: ...they show no compassion for the poor, they do not suffer with the suffering, they do not acknowledge their Creator, they kill their children and by abortion cause God's creatures to perish; they drive away the needy, oppress the suffering, they are advocates of the rich and unjust judges of the poor; they are filled with every sin. May you be able to stay ever apart, O children, from all these sins!"[42]

As time passed, the Church's Tradition has always consistently taught the absolute and unchanging value of the commandment "You shall not kill." It is a known fact that in the first centuries, murder was put among the three most seri-ous sins—along with apostasy and adultery—and required a particularly heavy and lengthy public penance before the repentant murderer could be granted forgiveness and readmission to the ecclesial community.

55. This should not cause surprise: to kill a human being, in whom the im-age of God is present, is a particularly serious sin. *Only God is the master of life!* Yet from the beginning, faced with the many and often tragic cases which occur in the life of individuals and society, Christian reflection has sought a fuller and deeper understanding of what God's commandment prohibits and prescribes.[43] There are in fact situations in which values proposed by God's Law seem to in-volve a genuine paradox. This happens for example in the case of *legitimate defense,* in which the right to protect one's own life and the duty not to harm someone else's life are difficult to reconcile in practice. Certainly, the intrinsic value of life and the duty to love oneself no less than others are the basis of *a true right to self-defense.* The demanding commandment of love of neighbor, set forth in the Old Testament and confirmed by Jesus, itself presupposes love of oneself as the basis of comparison: "You shall love your neighbor *as yourself*" (Mk 12:31). Consequently, no one can renounce the right to self-defense out of lack of love for life or for self. This can only be done in virtue of a heroic love which deepens and transfigures the love of self into a radical self-offering,

according to the spirit of the Gospel Beatitudes (cf. Mt 5:38-40). The sublime example of this self-offering is the Lord Jesus himself.

Moreover, "legitimate defense can be not only a right but a grave duty for someone responsible for another's life, the common good of the family or of the state."[44] Unfortunately it happens that the need to render the aggressor incapable of causing harm sometimes involves taking his life. In this case, the fatal outcome is attributable to the aggressor whose action brought it about, even though he may not be morally responsible because of a lack of the use of reason.[45]

56. This is the context in which to place the problem of *the death penalty*. On this matter there is a growing tendency, both in the Church and in civil society, to demand that it be applied in a very limited way or even that it be abolished completely. The problem must be viewed in the context of a system of penal justice ever more in line with human dignity and thus, in the end, with God's plan for man and society. The primary purpose of the punishment which society inflicts is "to redress the disorder caused by the offense."[46] Public authority must redress the violation of personal and social rights by imposing on the offender an adequate punishment for the crime, as a condition for the offender to regain the exercise of his or her freedom. In this way authority also fulfills the purpose of defending public order and ensuring people's safety, while at the same time offering the offender an incentive and help to change his or her behavior and be rehabilitated.[47]

It is clear that, for these purposes to be achieved, *the nature and extent of the punishment* must be carefully evaluated and decided upon, and ought not go to the extreme of executing the offender except in cases of absolute necessity: in other words, when it would not be possible otherwise to defend society. Today however, as a result of steady improvements in the organization of the penal system, such cases are very rare, if not practically non-existent.

In any event, the principle set forth in the new *Catechism of the Catholic Church* remains valid: "If bloodless means are sufficient to defend human lives against an aggressor and to protect public order and the safety of persons, public authority must limit itself to such means, because they better correspond to the concrete conditions of the common good and are more in conformity to the dignity of the human person."[48]

57. If such great care must be taken to respect every life, even that of criminals and unjust aggressors, the commandment "You shall not kill" has absolute value when it refers to the *innocent person*. And all the more so in the case of weak and defenseless human beings, who find their ultimate defense against the arrogance and caprice of others only in the absolute binding force of God's commandment.

In effect, the absolute inviolability of innocent human life is a moral truth clearly taught by Sacred Scripture, constantly upheld in the Church's Tradition and consistently proposed by her Magisterium. This consistent teaching is the evident result of that "supernatural sense of the faith" which, inspired and sustained by the Holy Spirit, safeguards the People of God from error when "it shows universal agreement in matters of faith and morals."[49]

Faced with the progressive weakening in individual consciences and in society of the sense of the absolute and grave moral illicitness of the direct taking of all innocent human life, especially at its beginning and at its end, *the Church's Magisterium* has spoken out with increasing frequency in defense of the sacredness and inviolability of human life. The Papal Magisterium, particularly insistent in this regard, has always been seconded by that of the bishops, with numerous and comprehensive doctrinal and pastoral documents issued either by Episcopal Conferences or by individual bishops. The Second Vatican Council also addressed the matter forcefully, in a brief but incisive passage.[50]

Therefore, by the authority which Christ conferred upon Peter and his Successors, and in communion with the bishops of the Catholic Church, *I confirm that the direct and voluntary killing of an innocent human being is always gravely immoral.* This doctrine, based upon that unwritten law which man, in the light of reason, finds in his own heart (cf. Rom 2:14-15), is reaffirmed by Sacred Scripture, transmitted by the Tradition of the Church and taught by the ordinary and universal Magisterium.[51]

The deliberate decision to deprive an innocent human being of his life is always morally evil and can never be licit either as an end in itself or as a means to a good end. It is in fact a grave act of disobedience to the moral law, and indeed to God himself, the author and guarantor of that law; it contradicts the fundamental virtues of justice and charity. "Nothing and no one can in any way permit the killing of an innocent human being, whether a fetus or an embryo, an infant or an adult, an old person, or one suffering from an incurable disease, or a person who is dying. Furthermore, no one is permitted to ask for this act of killing, either for himself or herself or for another person entrusted to his or her care, nor can he or she consent to it, either explicitly or implicitly. Nor can any authority legitimately recommend or permit such an action."[52]

As far as the right to life is concerned, every innocent human being is ab-solutely equal to all others. This equality is the basis of all authentic social re-lationships which, to be truly such, can only be founded on truth and justice, recognizing and protecting every man and woman as a person and not as an object to be used. Before the moral norm which prohibits the direct taking of the life of an innocent human being "there are no privileges or exceptions for anyone. It makes no difference whether one is the master of the world or the 'poorest of the poor' on the face of the earth. Before the demands of morality we are all absolutely equal."[53]

"Your eyes beheld my unformed substance" (Ps 139:16): The unspeakable crime of abortion

58. Among all the crimes which can be committed against life, procured abortion has characteristics making it particularly serious and deplorable. The

Second Vatican Council defines abortion, together with infanticide, as an "unspeakable crime."[54]

But today, in many people's consciences, the perception of its gravity has become progressively obscured. The acceptance of abortion in the popular mind, in behavior and even in law itself, is a telling sign of an extremely dangerous crisis of the moral sense, which is becoming more and more incapable of distinguishing between good and evil, even when the fundamental right to life is at stake. Given such a grave situation, we need now more than ever to have the courage to look the truth in the eye and to *call things by their proper name,* without yielding to convenient compromises or to the temptation of self-deception. In this regard the reproach of the Prophet is extremely straightforward: "Woe to those who call evil good and good evil, who put darkness for light and light for darkness" (Is 5:20). Especially in the case of abortion there is a widespread use of ambiguous terminology, such as "interruption of pregnancy," which tends to hide abortion's true nature and to attenuate its seriousness in public opinion. Perhaps this linguistic phenomenon is itself a symptom of an uneasiness of conscience. But no word has the power to change the reality of things: procured abortion is *the deliberate and direct killing, by whatever means it is carried out, of a human being in the initial phase of his or her existence, extending from conception to birth.*

The moral gravity of procured abortion is apparent in all its truth if we recognize that we are dealing with murder and, in particular, when we consider the specific elements involved. The one eliminated is a human being at the very beginning of life. No one more absolutely *innocent* could be imagined. In no way could this human being ever be considered an aggressor, much less an unjust aggressor! He or she is *weak,* defenseless, even to the point of lacking that minimal form of defense consisting in the poignant power of a newborn baby's cries and tears. The unborn child is *totally entrusted* to the protection and care of the woman carrying him or her in the womb. And yet sometimes it is precisely the mother herself who makes the decision and asks for the child to be eliminated, and who then goes about having it done.

It is true that the decision to have an abortion is often tragic and painful for the mother, insofar as the decision to rid herself of the fruit of conception is not made for purely selfish reasons or out of convenience, but out of a desire to protect certain important values such as her own health or a decent standard of living for the other members of the family. Sometimes it is feared that the child to be born would live in such conditions that it would be better if the birth did not take place. Nevertheless, these reasons and others like them, however serious and tragic, *can never justify the deliberate killing of an innocent human being.*

59. As well as the mother, there are often other people too who decide upon the death of the child in the womb. In the first place, the father of the child may be to blame, not only when he directly pressures the woman to have an abortion, but also when he indirectly encourages such a decision on her part by leaving her

alone to face the problems of pregnancy:[55] in this way the family is thus mortally wounded and profaned in its nature as a community of love and in its vocation to be the "sanctuary of life." Nor can one overlook the pressures which sometimes come from the wider family circle and from friends. Sometimes the woman is subjected to such strong pressure that she feels psychologically forced to have an abortion: certainly in this case moral responsibility lies particularly with those who have directly or indirectly obliged her to have an abortion. Doctors and nurses are also responsible, when they place at the service of death skills which were acquired for promoting life.

But responsibility likewise falls on the legislators who have promoted and approved abortion laws, and, to the extent that they have a say in the matter, on the administrators of the health-care centers where abortions are performed. A general and no less serious responsibility lies with those who have encouraged the spread of an attitude of sexual permissiveness and a lack of esteem for motherhood, and with those who should have ensured—but did not—effective family and social policies in support of families, especially larger families and those with particular financial and educational needs. Finally, one cannot overlook the network of complicity which reaches out to include international institutions, foundations and associations which systematically campaign for the legalization and spread of abortion in the world. In this sense abortion goes beyond the responsibility of individuals and beyond the harm done to them, and takes on a distinctly social dimension. It is a most serious *wound* inflicted on society and its culture by the very people who ought to be society's promoters and defenders. As I wrote in my *Letter to Families,* "we are facing an immense threat to life: not only to the life of individuals but also to that of civilization itself."[56] We are facing what can be called *a "structure of sin" which opposes human life not yet born.*

60. Some people try to justify abortion by claiming that the result of conception, at least up to a certain number of days, cannot yet be considered a personal human life. But in fact, "from the time that the ovum is fertilized, a life is begun which is neither that of the father nor the mother; it is rather the life of a new human being with his own growth. It would never be made human if it were not human already. This has always been clear, and...modern genetic science offers clear confirmation. It has demonstrated that from the first instant there is established the program of what this living being will be: a person, this individual person with his characteristic aspects already well determined. Right from fertilization the adventure of a human life begins, and each of its capacities requires time—a rather lengthy time—to find its place and to be in a position to act."[57] Even if the presence of a spiritual soul cannot be ascertained by empirical data, the results themselves of scientific research on the human embryo provide "a valuable indication for discerning by the use of reason a personal presence at the moment of the first appearance of a human life: how could a human individual not be a human person?"[58]

Furthermore, what is at stake is so important that, from the standpoint of moral obligation, the mere probability that a human person is involved would suffice to justify an absolutely clear prohibition of any intervention aimed at killing a human embryo. Precisely for this reason, over and above all scientific debates and those philosophical affirmations to which the Magisterium has not expressly committed itself, the Church has always taught and continues to teach that the result of human procreation, from the first moment of its existence, must be guaranteed that unconditional respect which is morally due to the human being in his or her totality and unity as body and spirit: *"The human being is to be respected and treated as a person from the moment of conception;* and therefore from that same moment his rights as a person must be recognized, among which in the first place is the inviolable right of every innocent human being to life."[59]

61. The texts of *Sacred Scripture* never address the question of deliberate abortion and so do not directly and specifically condemn it. But they show such great respect for the human being in the mother's womb that they require as a logical consequence that God's commandment "You shall not kill" be extended to the unborn child as well.

Human life is sacred and inviolable at every moment of existence, including the initial phase which precedes birth. All human beings, from their mothers' womb, belong to God who searches them and knows them, who forms them and knits them together with his own hands, who gazes on them when they are tiny shapeless embryos and already sees in them the adults of tomorrow whose days are numbered and whose vocation is even now written in the "book of life" (cf. Ps 139:1, 13-16). There too, when they are still in their mothers' womb—as many passages of the Bible bear witness[60]—they are the personal objects of God's loving and fatherly providence.

Christian Tradition—as the *Declaration* issued by the Congregation for the Doctrine of the Faith points out so well[61]—is clear and unanimous, from the beginning up to our own day, in describing abortion as a particularly grave moral disorder. From its first contacts with the Greco-Roman world, where abortion and infanticide were widely practiced, the first Christian community, by its teaching and practice, radically opposed the customs rampant in that society, as is clearly shown by the *Didache* mentioned earlier.[62] Among the Greek ecclesiastical writers, Athenagoras records that Christians consider as murderesses women who have recourse to abortifacient medicines, because children, even if they are still in their mother's womb, "are already under the protection of Divine Providence."[63] Among the Latin authors Tertullian affirms: "It is anticipated murder to prevent someone from being born; it makes little difference whether one kills a soul already born or puts it to death at birth. He who will one day be a man is a man already."[64]

Throughout Christianity's two thousand year history, this same doctrine has been constantly taught by the Fathers of the Church and by her Pastors and Doctors. Even scientific and philosophical discussions about the precise moment of the infusion of the spiritual soul have never given rise to any hesitation about the moral condemnation of abortion.

62. The more recent *Papal Magisterium* has vigorously reaffirmed this common doctrine. Pius XI in particular, in his Encyclical *Casti Connubii,* rejected the specious justifications of abortion.[65] Pius XII excluded all direct abortion, i.e., every act tending directly to destroy human life in the womb "whether such destruction is intended as an end or only as a means to an end."[66] John XXIII reaffirmed that human life is sacred because "from its very beginning it directly involves God's creative activity."[67] The Second Vatican Council, as mentioned earlier, sternly condemned abortion: "From the moment of its conception life must be guarded with the greatest care, while abortion and infanticide are unspeakable crimes."[68]

The *Church's canonical discipline,* from the earliest centuries, has inflicted penal sanctions on those guilty of abortion. This practice, with more or less severe penalties, has been confirmed in various periods of history. The 1917 *Code of Canon Law* punished abortion with excommunication.[69] The revised canonical legislation continues this tradition when it decrees that "a person who actually procures an abortion incurs automatic *(latae sententiae)* excommunication."[70] The excommunication affects all those who commit this crime with knowledge of the penalty attached, and thus includes those accomplices without whose help the crime would not have been committed.[71] By this reiterated sanction, the Church makes clear that abortion is a most serious and dangerous crime, thereby encouraging those who commit it to seek without delay the path of conversion. In the Church the purpose of the penalty of excommunication is to make an individual fully aware of the gravity of a certain sin and then to foster genuine conversion and repentance.

Given such unanimity in the doctrinal and disciplinary tradition of the Church, Paul VI was able to declare that this tradition is unchanged and unchangeable.[72] Therefore, by the authority which Christ conferred upon Peter and his Successors, in communion with the bishops—who on various occasions have condemned abortion and who in the aforementioned consultation, albeit dispersed throughout the world, have shown unanimous agreement concerning this doctrine *declare that direct abortion, that is, abortion willed as an end or as a means, always constitutes a grave moral disorder,* since it is the deliberate killing of an innocent human being. This doctrine is based upon the natural law and upon the written Word of God, is transmitted by the Church's Tradition and taught by the ordinary and universal Magisterium.[73]

No circumstance, no purpose, no law whatsoever can ever make licit an act which is intrinsically illicit, since it is contrary to the Law of God which is written in every human heart, knowable by reason itself, and proclaimed by the Church.

63. This evaluation of the morality of abortion is to be applied also to the recent forms of *intervention on human embryos* which, although carried out for purposes legitimate in themselves, inevitably involve the killing of those

embryos. This is the case with *experimentation on embryos,* which is becoming increasingly widespread in the field of biomedical research and is legally permitted in some countries. Although "one must uphold as licit procedures carried out on the human embryo which respect the life and integrity of the embryo and do not involve disproportionate risks for it, but rather are directed to its healing, the improvement of its condition of health, or its individual survival,"[74] it must nonetheless be stated that the use of human embryos or fetuses as an object of experimentation constitutes a crime against their dignity as human beings who have a right to the same respect owed to a child once born, just as to every person.[75]

This moral condemnation also regards procedures that exploit living human embryos and fetuses—sometimes specifically "produced" for this purpose by *in vitro* fertilization—either to be used as "biological material" or as *providers of organs or tissue for transplants* in the treatment of certain diseases. The killing of innocent human creatures, even if carried out to help others, constitutes an absolutely unacceptable act.

Special attention must be given to evaluating the morality of *prenatal diagnostic techniques* which enable the early detection of possible anomalies in the unborn child. In view of the complexity of these techniques, an accurate and systematic moral judgment is necessary. When they do not involve disproportionate risks for the child and the mother, and are meant to make possible early therapy or even to favor a serene and informed acceptance of the child not yet born, these techniques are morally licit. But since the possibilities of prenatal therapy are today still limited, it not infrequently happens that these techniques are used with a eugenic intention which accepts selective abortion in order to prevent the birth of children affected by various types of anomalies. Such an attitude is shameful and utterly reprehensible, since it presumes to measure the value of a human life only within the parameters of "normality" and physical well-being, thus opening the way to legitimizing infanticide·and euthanasia as well.

And yet the courage and the serenity with which so many of our brothers and sisters suffering from serious disabilities lead their lives when they are shown acceptance and love bears eloquent witness to what gives authentic value to life, and makes it, even in difficult conditions, something precious for them and for others. The Church is close to those married couples who, with great anguish and suffering, willingly accept gravely handicapped children. She is also grateful to all those families which, through adoption, welcome children abandoned by their parents because of disabilities or illnesses.

"It is I who bring both death and life" (Dt 32:39): The tragedy of euthanasia

64. At the other end of life's spectrum, men and women find themselves facing the mystery of death. Today, as a result of advances in medicine and in a cultural context frequently closed to the transcendent, the experience of dying is marked by new features. When the prevailing tendency is to value life only to the extent that it brings pleasure and well-being, suffering seems like an unbearable

setback, something from which one must be freed at all costs. Death is considered "senseless" if it suddenly interrupts a life still open to a future of new and interesting experiences. But it becomes a "rightful liberation" once life is held to be no longer meaningful because it is filled with pain and inexorably doomed to even greater suffering.

Furthermore, when he denies or neglects his fundamental relationship to God, man thinks he is his own rule and measure, with the right to demand that society should guarantee him the ways and means of deciding what to do with his life in full and complete autonomy. It is especially people in the developed countries who act in this way: they feel encouraged to do so also by the constant progress of medicine and its ever more advanced techniques. By using highly sophisticated systems and equipment, science and medical practice today are able not only to attend to cases formerly considered untreatable and to reduce or eliminate pain, but also to sustain and prolong life even in situations of extreme frailty, to resuscitate artificially patients whose basic biological functions have undergone sudden collapse, and to use special procedures to make organs available for transplanting.

In this context the temptation grows to have recourse to euthanasia, that is, *to take control of death and bring it about before its time, "gently"* ending one's own life or the life of others. In reality, what might seem logical and humane, when looked at more closely is seen to be *senseless and inhumane.* Here we are faced with one of the more alarming symptoms of the "culture of death," which is advancing above all in prosperous societies, marked by an attitude of excessive preoccupation with efficiency and which sees the growing number of elderly and disabled people as intolerable and too burdensome. These people are very often isolated by their families and by society, which are organized almost exclusively on the basis of criteria of productive efficiency, according to which a hopelessly impaired life no longer has any value.

65. For a correct moral judgment on euthanasia, in the first place a clear definition is required. *Euthanasia in the strict sense* is understood to be an action or omission which of itself and by intention causes death, with the purpose of eliminating all suffering. "Euthanasia's terms of reference, therefore, are to be found in the intention of the will and in the methods used."[76]

Euthanasia must be distinguished from the decision to forego so-called "aggressive medical treatment," in other words, medical procedures which no longer correspond to the real situation of the patient, either because they are by now disproportionate to any expected results or because they impose an excessive burden on the patient and his family. In such situations, when death is clearly imminent and inevitable, one can in conscience "refuse forms of treatment that would only secure a precarious and burdensome prolongation of life, so long as the normal care due to the sick person in similar cases is not interrupted."[77] Certainly there is a moral obligation to care for oneself and to allow oneself to be cared for, but this duty must take account of concrete circumstances. It needs to be determined whether the means of treatment available are objectively proportionate to the prospects for improvement. To forego extraordinary or disproportionate means is not the equivalent of suicide or euthanasia; it rather expresses acceptance of the human condition in the face of death.[78]

In modern medicine, increased attention is being given to what are called "methods of palliative care," which seek to make suffering more bearable in the final stages of illness and to ensure that the patient is supported and accompanied in his or her ordeal. Among the questions which arise in this context is that of the licitness of using various types of painkillers and sedatives for relieving the patient's pain when this involves the risk of shortening life. While praise may be due to the person who voluntarily accepts suffering by forgoing treatment with painkillers in order to remain fully lucid and, if a believer, to share consciously in the Lord's Passion, such "heroic" behavior cannot be considered the duty of everyone. Pius XII affirmed that it is licit to relieve pain by narcotics, even when the result is decreased consciousness and a shortening of life, "if no other means exist, and if, in the given circumstances, this does not prevent the carrying out of other religious and moral duties."[79] In such a case, death is not willed or sought, even though for reasonable motives one runs the risk of it: there is simply a desire to ease pain effectively by using the analgesics which medicine provides. All the same, "it is not right to deprive the dying person of consciousness without a serious reason"[80]: as they approach death people ought to be able to satisfy their moral and family duties, and above all they ought to be able to prepare in a fully conscious way for their definitive meeting with God.

Taking into account these distinctions, in harmony with the Magisterium of my Predecessors[81] and in communion with the bishops of the Catholic Church, *I confirm that euthanasia is a grave violation of the law of God,* since it is the deliberate and morally unacceptable killing of a human person. This doctrine is based upon the natural law and upon the written Word of God, is transmitted by the Church's Tradition and taught by the ordinary and universal Magisterium.[82]

Depending on the circumstances, this practice involves the malice proper to suicide or murder.

66. Suicide is always as morally objectionable as murder. The Church's tradition has always rejected it as a gravely evil choice.[83] Even though a certain psychological, cultural and social conditioning may induce a person to carry out an action which so radically contradicts the innate inclination to life, thus lessening or removing subjective responsibility, *suicide,* when viewed objectively, is a gravely immoral act. In fact, it involves the rejection of love of self and the renunciation of the obligation of justice and charity toward one's neighbor, toward the communities to which one belongs, and toward society as a whole.[84] In its deepest reality, suicide represents a rejection of God's absolute sovereignty over life and death, as proclaimed in the prayer of the ancient sage of Israel: "You have power over life and death; you lead men down to the gates of Hades and back again" (Wis 16:13; cf. Tb 13:2).

To concur with the intention of another person to commit suicide and to help in carrying it out through so-called "assisted suicide" means to cooperate in, and at times to be the actual perpetrator of, an injustice which can never be excused, even if it is requested. In a remarkably relevant passage St. Augustine writes that "it is never licit to kill another: even if he should wish it, indeed if he request it because, hanging between life and death, he begs for help in freeing the soul struggling against the bonds of the body and longing to be released; nor is it licit even when a sick person is no longer able to live."[85] Even when not motivated by a selfish refusal to be burdened with the life of someone who is suffering, euthanasia must be called a *false mercy,* and indeed a disturbing "perversion" of mercy. True "compassion" leads to sharing another's pain; it does not kill the person whose suffering we cannot bear. Moreover, the act of euthanasia appears all the more perverse if it is carried out by those, like relatives, who are supposed to treat a family member with patience and love, or by those, such as doctors, who by virtue of their specific profession are supposed to care for the sick person even in the most painful terminal stages.

The choice of euthanasia becomes more serious when it takes the form of a *murder* committed by others on a person who has in no way requested it and who has never consented to it. The height of arbitrariness and injustice is reached when certain people, such as physicians or legislators, arrogate to themselves the power to decide who ought to live and who ought to die. Once again we find ourselves before the temptation of Eden: to become like God who "knows good and evil" (cf. Gn 3:5). God alone has the power over life and death: "It is I who bring both death and life" (Dt 32:39; cf. 2 Kg 5:7; 1 Sam 2:6). But he only exercises this power in accordance with a plan of wisdom and love. When man usurps this power, being enslaved by a foolish and selfish way of thinking, he inevitably uses it for injustice and death. Thus the life of the person who is weak is put into the hands of the one who is strong; in society the sense of justice is lost, and mutual trust, the basis of every authentic interpersonal relationship, is undermined at its root.

67. Quite different from this is the *way of love and true mercy,* which our common humanity calls for, and upon which faith in Christ the Redeemer, who died and rose again, sheds ever new light. The request which arises from the human heart in the supreme confrontation with suffering and death, especially when faced with the temptation to give up in utter desperation, is above all a request for companionship, sympathy and support in the time of trial. It is a plea for help to keep on hoping when all human hopes fail. As the Second Vatican Council reminds us: "It is in the face of death that the riddle of human existence becomes most acute" and yet "man rightly follows the intuition of his heart when he abhors and repudiates the absolute ruin and total disappearance of his own person. Man rebels against death because he bears in himself an eternal seed which cannot be reduced to mere matter."[86]

This natural aversion to death and this incipient hope of immortality are illumined and brought to fulfillment by Christian faith, which both promises and offers a share in the victory of the Risen Christ: it is the victory of the One who, by his redemptive death, has set man free from death, "the wages of sin" (Rom 6:23), and has given him the Spirit, the pledge of resurrection and of life (cf. Rom 8:11). The certainty of future immortality and *hope in the promised resurrection* cast new light on the mystery of suffering and death, and fill the believer with an extraordinary capacity to trust fully in the plan of God.

The Apostle Paul expressed this newness in terms of belonging completely to the Lord who embraces every human condition: "None of us lives to himself, and none of us dies to himself. If we live, we live to the Lord, and if we die, we die to the Lord; so then, whether we live or whether we die, we are the Lord's" (Rom 14:7-8). *Dying to the Lord* means experiencing one's death as the supreme act of obedience to the Father (cf. Phil 2:8), being ready to meet death at the "hour" willed and chosen by him (cf. Jn 13:1), which can only mean when one's earthly pilgrimage is completed. *Living to the Lord* also means recognizing that suffering, while still an evil and a trial in itself, can always become a source of good. It becomes such if it is experienced for love and with love through sharing, by God's gracious gift and one's own personal and free choice, in the suffering of Christ Crucified. In this way, the person who lives his suffering in the Lord grows more fully conformed to him (cf. Phil 3:10; 1 Pt 2:21) and more closely associated with his redemptive work on behalf of the Church and humanity.[87] This was the experience of St. Paul, which every person who suffers is called to relive: "I rejoice in my sufferings for your sake, and in my flesh I complete what is lacking in Christ's afflictions for the sake of his Body, that is, the Church" (Col 1:24).

"We must obey God rather than men" (Acts 5:29): *Civil law and the moral law*

68. One of the specific characteristics of present-day attacks on human life —as has already been said several times—consists in the trend to demand a *legal justification* for them, as if they were rights which the state, at least under certain conditions, must acknowledge as belonging to citizens. Consequently, there is a tendency to claim that it should be possible to exercise these rights with the safe and free assistance of doctors and medical personnel.

It is often claimed that the life of an unborn child or a seriously disabled person is only a relative good: according to a proportionalist approach, or one of sheer calculation, this good should be compared with and balanced against other goods. It is even maintained that only someone present and personally involved in a concrete situation can correctly judge the goods at stake: consequently, only that person would be able to decide on the morality of his choice. The state therefore, in the interest of civil coexistence and social harmony, should respect this choice, even to the point of permitting abortion and euthanasia.

At other times, it is claimed that civil law cannot demand that all citizens should live according to moral standards higher than what all citizens themselves acknowledge and share. Hence the law should always express the opinion and will of the majority of citizens and recognize that they have, at least in certain extreme cases, the right even to abortion and euthanasia. Moreover the prohibition and the punishment of abortion and euthanasia in these cases would inevitably lead—so it is said—to an increase of illegal practices: and these would not be subject to necessary control by society and would be carried out in a medically unsafe way. The question is also raised whether supporting a law which in practice cannot be enforced would not ultimately undermine the authority of all laws.

Finally, the more radical views go so far as to maintain that in a modern and pluralistic society people should be allowed complete freedom to dispose of their own lives as well as of the lives of the unborn: it is asserted that it is not the task of the law to choose between different moral opinions, and still less can the law claim to impose one particular opinion to the detriment of others.

69. In any case, in the democratic culture of our time it is commonly held that the legal system of any society should limit itself to taking account of and accepting the convictions of the majority. It should therefore be based solely upon what the majority itself considers moral and actually practices. Furthermore, if it is believed that an objective truth shared by all is *de facto* unattainable, then respect for the freedom of the citizens—who in a democratic system are considered the true rulers—would require that on the legislative level the autonomy of individual consciences be acknowledged. Consequently, when establishing those norms which are absolutely necessary for social coexistence, the only determining factor should be the will of the majority, whatever this may be. Hence every politician, in his or her activity, should clearly separate the realm of private conscience from that of public conduct.

As a result we have what appear to be two diametrically opposed tendencies. On the one hand, individuals claim for themselves in the moral sphere the most complete freedom of choice and demand that the state should not adopt or impose any ethical position but limit itself to guaranteeing maximum space for the freedom of each individual, with the sole limitation of not infringing on the freedom and rights of any other citizen. On the other hand, it is held that, in the exercise of public and professional duties, respect for other people's freedom of choice requires that each one should set aside his or her own convictions in order to satisfy every demand of the citizens which is recognized and guaranteed by law; in carrying out one's duties the only moral criterion should be what is laid down by the law itself. Individual responsibility is thus turned over to the civil law, with a renouncing of personal conscience, at least in the public sphere.

70. At the basis of all these tendencies lies the *ethical relativism* which characterizes much of present-day culture. There are those who consider such relativism an essential condition of democracy, inasmuch as it alone is held to guarantee tolerance, mutual respect between people and acceptance of the decisions of the majority, whereas moral norms considered to be objective and binding are held to lead to authoritarianism and intolerance.

But it is precisely the issue of respect for life which shows what misunderstandings and contradictions, accompanied by terrible practical consequences, are concealed in this position.

It is true that history has known cases where crimes have been committed in the name of "truth." But equally grave crimes and radical denials of freedom have also been committed and are still being committed in the name of "ethical relativism." When a parliamentary or social majority decrees that it is legal, at least under certain conditions, to kill unborn human life, is it not really making a "tyrannical" decision with regard to the weakest and most defenseless of human beings? Everyone's conscience rightly rejects those crimes against humanity of which our century has had such sad experience. But would these crimes cease to be crimes if, instead of being committed by unscrupulous tyrants, they were legitimated by popular consensus?

Democracy cannot be idolized to the point of making it a substitute for morality or a panacea for immorality. Fundamentally, democracy is a "system" and as such is a means and not an end. Its "moral" value is not automatic, but depends on conformity to the moral law to which it, like every other form of human behavior, must be subject: in other words, its morality depends on the morality of the ends which it pursues and of the means which it employs. If today we see an almost universal consensus with regard to the value of democracy, this is to be considered a positive "sign of the times," as the Church's Magisterium has frequently noted.[88] But the value of democracy stands or falls with the values which it embodies and promotes. Of course, values such as the dignity of every human person, respect for inviolable and inalienable human rights, and the adoption of the "common good" as the end and criterion regulating political life are certainly fundamental and not to be ignored.

The basis of these values cannot be provisional and changeable "majority" opinions, but only the acknowledgment of an objective moral law which, as the "natural law" written in the human heart, is the obligatory point of reference for civil law itself. If, as a result of a tragic obscuring of the collective conscience, an attitude of skepticism were to succeed in bringing into question even the fundamental principles of the moral law, the democratic system itself would be shaken in its foundations, and would be reduced to a mere mechanism for regulating different and opposing interests on a purely empirical basis.[89]

Some might think that even this function, in the absence of anything better, should be valued for the sake of peace in society. While one acknowledges some element of truth in this point of view, it is easy to see that without an objective moral grounding not even democracy is capable of ensuring a stable peace, especially since peace which is not built upon the values of the dignity of every individual and of solidarity between all people frequently proves to be illusory. Even in participatory systems of government, the regulation of interests often occurs to the advantage of the most powerful, since they are the ones most capable of maneuvering not only the levers of power but also of shaping the formation of consensus. In such a situation, democracy easily becomes an empty word.

71. It is therefore urgently necessary, for the future of society and the development of a sound democracy, to rediscover those essential and innate human and moral values which flow from the very truth of the human being and express and safeguard the dignity of the person: values which no individual, no majority and no state can ever create, modify or destroy, but must only acknowledge, respect and promote.

Consequently there is a need to recover the *basic elements of a vision of the relationship between civil law and moral law,* which are put forward by the Church, but which are also part of the patrimony of the great juridical traditions of humanity.

Certainly the *purpose of civil law* is different and more limited in scope than that of the moral law. But "in no sphere of life can the civil law take the place of conscience or dictate norms concerning things which are outside its competence,"[90] which is that of ensuring the common good of people through the recognition and defense of their fundamental rights, and the promotion of peace and of public morality.[91] The real purpose of civil law is to guarantee an ordered social coexistence in true justice, so that all may "lead a quiet and peaceable life, godly and respectful in every way" (1 Tm 2:2). Precisely for this reason, civil law must ensure that all members of society enjoy respect for certain fundamental rights which innately belong to the person, rights which every positive law must recognize and guarantee. First and fundamental among these is the inviolable right to life of every innocent human being. While public authority can sometimes choose not to put a stop to something which—were it prohibited—would cause more serious harm,[92] it can never presume to legitimize as a right of individuals—even if they are the majority of the members of society—an offense against other persons caused by the disregard of so fundamental a right as the right to life. The legal toleration of abortion or of euthanasia can in no way claim to be based on respect for the conscience of others, precisely because society has the right and the duty to protect itself against the abuses which can occur in the name of conscience and under the pretext of freedom.[93]

In the Encyclical *Pacem in Terris,* John XXIII pointed out that "it is generally accepted today that the common good is best safeguarded when personal rights and duties are guaranteed. The chief concern of civil authorities must therefore be to ensure that these rights are recognized, respected, coordinated, defended and promoted, and that each individual is enabled to perform his duties more easily. For 'to safeguard the inviolable rights of the human person, and to facilitate the performance of his duties, is the principal duty of every public authority.' Thus any government which refused to recognize human rights or acted in violation of them would not only fail in its duty; its decrees would be wholly lacking in binding force."[94]

72. The doctrine on the necessary *conformity of civil law with the moral law* is in continuity with the whole tradition of the Church. This is clear once more from John XXIII's Encyclical: "Authority is a postulate of the moral order and

derives from God. Consequently, laws and decrees enacted in contravention of the moral order, and hence of the divine will, can have no binding force in conscience...; indeed, the passing of such laws undermines the very nature of authority and results in shameful abuse."[95] This is the clear teaching of St. Thomas Aquinas, who writes that "human law is law inasmuch as it is in conformity with right reason and thus derives from the eternal law. But when a law is contrary to reason, it is called an unjust law; but in this case it ceases to be a law and becomes instead an act of violence."[96] And again: "Every law made by man can be called a law insofar as it derives from the natural law. But if it is somehow opposed to the natural law, then it is not really a law but rather a corruption of the law."[97]

Now the first and most immediate application of this teaching concerns a human law which disregards the fundamental right and source of all other rights which is the right to life, a right belonging to every individual. Consequently, laws which legitimize the direct killing of innocent human beings through abortion or euthanasia are in complete opposition to the inviolable right to life proper to every individual; they thus deny the equality of everyone before the law. It might be objected that such is not the case in euthanasia, when it is requested with full awareness by the person involved. But any state which made such a request legitimate and authorized it to be carried out would be legalizing a case of suicide-murder, contrary to the fundamental principles of absolute respect for life and of the protection of every innocent life. In this way the state contributes to lessening respect for life and opens the door to ways of acting which are destructive of trust in relations between people. Laws which authorize and promote abortion and euthanasia are therefore radically opposed not only to the good of the individual but also to the common good; as such they are completely lacking in authentic juridical validity. Disregard for the right to life, precisely because it leads to the killing of the person whom society exists to serve, is what most directly conflicts with the possibility of achieving the common good. Consequently, a civil law authorizing abortion or euthanasia ceases by that very fact to be a true, morally binding civil law.

73. Abortion and euthanasia are thus crimes which no human law can claim to legitimize. There is no obligation in conscience to obey such laws; instead there is a *grave and clear obligation to oppose them by conscientious objection.* From the very beginnings of the Church, the apostolic preaching reminded Christians of their duty to obey legitimately constituted public authorities (cf. Rom 13:7; 1 Pt 2:13-14), but at the same time it firmly warned that "we must obey God rather than men" (Acts 5:29). In the Old Testament, precisely in regard to threats against life, we find a significant example of resistance to the unjust command of those in authority. After Pharaoh ordered the killing of all newborn males, the Hebrew midwives refused, "They did not do as the king of Egypt commanded them, but let the male children live" (Ex 1:17). But the ultimate reason for their action should be noted: *"The midwives feared God"* (Ex 1:17). It is precisely from obedience to God—to whom alone is due that fear

which is acknowledgment of his absolute sovereignty—that the strength and the courage to resist unjust human laws are born. It is the strength and the courage of those prepared even to be imprisoned or put to the sword, in the certainty that this is what makes for "the endurance and faith of the saints" (Rv 13:10).

In the case of an intrinsically unjust law, such as a law permitting abortion or euthanasia, it is therefore never licit to obey it, or to "take part in a propaganda campaign in favor of such a law, or vote for it."[98]

A particular problem of conscience can arise in cases where a legislative vote would be decisive for the passage of a more restrictive law, aimed at limiting the number of authorized abortions, in place of a more permissive law already passed or ready to be voted on. Such cases are not infrequent. It is a fact that while in some parts of the world there continue to be campaigns to introduce laws favoring abortion, often supported by powerful international organizations, in other nations—particularly those which have already experienced the bitter fruits of such permissive legislation—there are growing signs of a rethinking in this matter. In a case like the one just mentioned, when it is not possible to overturn or completely abrogate a pro-abortion law, an elected official, whose absolute personal opposition to procured abortion was well known, could licitly support proposals aimed at *limiting the harm* done by such a law and at lessening its negative consequences at the level of general opinion and public morality. This does not in fact represent an illicit cooperation with an unjust law, but rather a legitimate and proper attempt to limit its evil aspects.

74. The passing of unjust laws often raises difficult problems of conscience for morally upright people with regard to the issue of cooperation, since they have a right to demand not to be forced to take part in morally evil actions. Sometimes the choices which have to be made are difficult; they may require the sacrifice of prestigious professional positions or the relinquishing of reasonable hopes of career advancement. In other cases, it can happen that carrying out certain actions, which are provided for by legislation that overall is unjust, but which in themselves are indifferent, or even positive, can serve to protect human lives under threat. There may be reason to fear, however, that willingness to carry out such actions will not only cause scandal and weaken the necessary opposition to attacks on life, but will gradually lead to further capitulation to a mentality of permissiveness.

In order to shed light on this difficult question, it is necessary to recall the general principles concerning *cooperation in evil actions.* Christians, like all people of good will, are called upon under grave obligation of conscience not to cooperate formally in practices which, even if permitted by civil legislation, are contrary to God's law. Indeed, from the moral standpoint, it is never licit to cooperate formally in evil. Such cooperation occurs when an action, either by its very nature or by the form it takes in a concrete situation, can be defined as a direct participation in an act against innocent human life or a sharing in the immoral intention of the person committing it. This cooperation can never be justified either by invoking respect for the freedom of others or by appealing to the fact that civil law permits it or requires it. Each individual in fact has moral responsibility for the acts which he personally performs; no one can be exempted from this responsibility, and on the basis of it everyone will be judged by God himself (cf. Rom 2:6; 14:12).

To refuse to take part in committing an injustice is not only a moral duty; it is also a basic human right. Were this not so, the human person would be forced to perform an action intrinsically incompatible with human dignity, and in this way human freedom itself, the authentic meaning and purpose of which are found in its orientation to the true and the good, would be radically compromised. What is at stake therefore is an essential right which, precisely as such, should be acknowledged and protected by civil law. In this sense, the opportunity to refuse to take part in the phases of consultation, preparation and execution of these acts against life should be guaranteed to physicians, health-care personnel, and directors of hospitals, clinics and convalescent facilities. Those who have recourse to conscientious objection must be protected not only from legal penalties but also from any negative effects on the legal, disciplinary, financial and professional plane.

"You shall love your neighbor as yourself" (Lk 10:27): "Promote" life

75. God's commandments teach us the way of life. *The negative moral precepts,* which declare that the choice of certain actions is morally unacceptable, have an absolute value for human freedom: they are valid always and everywhere, without exception. They make it clear that the choice of certain ways of acting is radically incompatible with the love of God and with the dignity of the person created in his image. Such choices cannot be redeemed by the goodness of any intention or of any consequence; they are irrevocably opposed to the bond between persons; they contradict the fundamental decision to direct one's life to God.[99]

In this sense, the negative moral precepts have an extremely important positive function. The "no" which they unconditionally require makes clear the absolute limit beneath which free individuals cannot lower themselves. At the same time they indicate the minimum which they must respect and from which they must start out in order to say "yes" over and over again, a "yes" which will gradually embrace the *entire horizon of the good* (cf. Mt 5:48). The commandments, in particular the negative moral precepts, are the beginning and the first necessary stage of the journey toward freedom. As St. Augustine writes, "the beginning of freedom is to be free from crimes...like murder, adultery, fornication, theft, fraud, sacrilege and so forth. Only when one stops committing these crimes (and no Christian should commit them), one begins to lift up one's head toward freedom. But this is only the beginning of freedom, not perfect freedom."[100]

76. The commandment "You shall not kill" thus establishes the point of departure for the start of true freedom. It leads us to promote life actively, and to

develop particular ways of thinking and acting which serve life. In this way we exercise our responsibility toward the persons entrusted to us and we show, in deeds and in truth, our gratitude to God for the great gift of life (cf. Ps 139:13-14).

The Creator has entrusted man's life to his responsible concern, not to make arbitrary use of it, but to preserve it with wisdom and to care for it with loving fidelity. The God of the Covenant has entrusted the life of every individual to his or her fellow human beings, brothers and sisters, according to the law of reciprocity in giving and receiving, of self-giving and of the acceptance of others. In the fullness of time, by taking flesh and giving his life for us, the Son of God showed what heights and depths this law of reciprocity can reach. With the gift of his Spirit, Christ gives new content and meaning to the law of reciprocity, to our being entrusted to one another. The Spirit who builds up communion in love creates between us a new fraternity and solidarity, a true reflection of the mystery of mutual self-giving and receiving proper to the Most Holy Trinity. The Spirit becomes the new law which gives strength to believers and awakens in them a responsibility for sharing the gift of self and for accepting others, as a sharing in the boundless love of Jesus Christ himself.

77. This new law also gives spirit and shape to the commandment "You shall not kill." For the Christian it involves an absolute imperative to respect, love and promote the life of every brother and sister, in accordance with the requirements of God's bountiful love in Jesus Christ. "He laid down his life for us; and we ought to lay down our lives for the brethren" (1 Jn 3:16).

The commandment "You shall not kill," even in its more positive aspects of respecting, loving and promoting human life, is binding on every individual human being. It resounds in the moral conscience of everyone as an irrepressible echo of the original covenant of God the Creator with mankind. It can be recognized by everyone through the light of reason and it can be observed thanks to the mysterious working of the Spirit who, blowing where he wills (cf. Jn 3:8), comes to and involves every person living in this world.

It is therefore a service of love which we are all committed to ensure to our neighbor, that his or her life may be always defended and promoted, especially when it is weak or threatened. It is not only a personal but a social concern which we must all foster: a concern to make unconditional respect for human life the foundation of a renewed society.

We are asked to love and honor the life of every man and woman and to work with perseverance and courage so that our time, marked by all too many signs of death, may at last witness the establishment of a new culture of life, the fruit of the culture of truth and of love.

CHAPTER IV

You Did It to Me

For a New Culture of Human Life

"You are God's own people, that you may declare the wonderful deeds
of him who called you out of darkness into his marvelous light" (1 Pt 2:9):
A people of life and for life

78. The Church has received the Gospel as a proclamation and a source of joy and salvation. She has received it as a gift from Jesus, sent by the Father "to preach good news to the poor" (Lk 4:18). She has received it through the Apostles, sent by Christ to the whole world (cf. Mk 16:15; Mt 28:19-20). Born from this evangelizing activity, the Church hears every day the echo of St. Paul's words of warning: "Woe to me if I do not preach the Gospel!" (1 Cor 9:16). As Paul VI wrote, *"evangelization is the grace and vocation proper to the Church, her deepest identity. She exists in order to evangelize."*[101]

Evangelization is an all-embracing, progressive activity through which the Church participates in the prophetic, priestly and royal mission of the Lord Jesus. It is therefore inextricably linked to *preaching, celebration and the service of charity.* Evangelization is a *profoundly ecclesial act,* which calls all the various workers of the Gospel to action, according to their individual charisms and ministry.

This is also the case with regard to the proclamation of the *Gospel of life,* an integral part of that Gospel which is Jesus Christ himself. We are at the service of this Gospel, sustained by the awareness that we have received it as a gift and are sent to preach it to all humanity, "to the ends of the earth" (Acts 1:8). With humility and gratitude we know that we are the *people of life and for life,* and this is how we present ourselves to everyone.

79. We are the *people of life* because God, in his unconditional love, has given us the *Gospel of life* and by this same Gospel we have been transformed and saved. We have been ransomed by the "Author of life" (Acts 3:15) at the price of his precious blood (cf. 1 Cor 6:20, 7:23; 1 Pt 1:19). Through the waters of Baptism we have been made a part of him (cf. Rom 6:4-5; Col 2:12), as branches which draw nourishment and fruitfulness from the one tree (cf. Jn 15:5). Interiorly renewed by the grace of the Spirit, "who is the Lord and giver of life," we have become a *people for life* and we are called to act accordingly.

We have been sent. For us, being at the service of *life* is not a boast but rather a duty, born of our awareness of being "God's own people, that we may declare the wonderful deeds of him who called us out of darkness into his marvelous light" (cf. 1 Pt 2-9). On our journey we are guided and sustained by the law of love: a love which has as its source and model the Son of God made man, who "by dying gave life to the world."[102]

We have been sent as a people. Everyone has an obligation to be at the service of life. This is a properly "ecclesial" responsibility, which requires concerted and generous action by all the members and by all sectors of the Christian community. This community commitment does not however eliminate or lessen the responsibility of each *individual,* called by the Lord to "become the neighbor" of everyone: "Go and do likewise" (Lk 10:37).

Together we all sense our duty to *preach the Gospel of life,* to *celebrate it* in the Liturgy and in our whole existence, and to *serve it* with the various programs and structures which support and promote life.

"That which we have seen and heard we proclaim also to you" (1 Jn 1:3): Proclaiming the Gospel of life

80. "That which was from the beginning, which we have heard, which we have seen with our eyes, which we have looked upon and touched with our hands, concerning the word of life...we proclaim also to you, so that you may have fellowship with us" (1 Jn 1:1, 3). *Jesus is the only Gospel:* we have nothing further to say or any other witness to bear.

To proclaim Jesus is itself to proclaim life. For Jesus is "the word of life" (1 Jn 1:1). In him "life was made manifest" (1 Jn 1:2); he himself is "the eternal life which was with the Father and was made manifest to us" (1 Jn 1:2). By the gift of the Spirit, this same life has been bestowed on us. It is in being destined to life in its fullness, to "eternal life," that every person's earthly life acquires its full meaning.

Enlightened by this *Gospel of life,* we feel a need to proclaim it and to bear witness to it in all its *marvelous newness.* Since it is one with Jesus himself, who makes all things new[103] and conquers the "oldness" which comes from sin and leads to death,[104] this Gospel exceeds every human expectation and reveals the sublime heights to which the dignity of the human person is raised through grace. This is how St. Gregory of Nyssa understands it: "Man, as a being, is of no account; he is dust, grass, vanity. But once he is adopted by the God of the universe as a son, he becomes part of the family of that Being, whose excellence and greatness no one can see, hear or understand. What words, thoughts or flight of the spirit can praise the superabundance of this grace? Man surpasses his nature: mortal, he becomes immortal; perishable, he becomes imperishable; fleeting, he becomes eternal; human, he becomes divine."[105]

Gratitude and joy at the incomparable dignity of man impel us to share this message with everyone: "that which we have seen and heard we proclaim also to you, so that you may have fellowship with us" (1 Jn 1:3). We need to bring the *Gospel of life* to the heart of every man and woman and to make it penetrate every part of society.

81. This involves above all proclaiming *the core* of this Gospel. It is the proclamation of a living God who is close to us, who calls us to profound communion with himself and awakens in us the certain hope of eternal life. It is the

affirmation of the inseparable connection between the person, his life and his bodiliness. It is the presentation of human life as a life of relationship, a gift of God, the fruit and sign of his love. It is the proclamation that Jesus has a unique relationship with every person, which enables us to see in every human face the face of Christ. It is the call for a "sincere gift of self" as the fullest way to realize our personal freedom.

It also involves making clear all *the consequences* of this Gospel. These can be summed up as follows: human life, as a gift of God, is sacred and inviolable. For this reason procured abortion and euthanasia are absolutely unacceptable. Not only must human life not be taken, but it must be protected with loving concern. The meaning of life is found in giving and receiving love, and in this light human sexuality and procreation reach their true and full significance. Love also gives meaning to suffering and death; despite the mystery which surrounds them, they can become saving events. Respect for life requires that science and technology should always be at the service of man and his integral development. Society as a whole must respect, defend and promote the dignity of every human person, at every moment and in every condition of that person's life.

82. To be truly a people at the service of life we must propose these truths constantly and courageously from the very first proclamation of the Gospel, and thereafter *in catechesis, in the various forms of preaching, in personal dialogue and in all educational activity.* Teachers, catechists and theologians have the task of emphasizing the *anthropological reasons* upon which respect for every human life is based. In this way, by making the newness of *the Gospel of life* shine forth, we can also help everyone discover in the light of reason and of personal experience how the Christian message fully reveals what man is and the meaning of his being and existence. We shall find important points of contact and dialogue also with nonbelievers, in our common commitment to the establishment of a new culture of life.

Faced with so many opposing points of view, and a widespread rejection of sound doctrine concerning human life, we can feel that Paul's entreaty to Timothy is also addressed to us: "Preach the word, be urgent in season and out of season, convince, rebuke, and exhort, be unfailing in patience and in teaching" (2 Tm 4:2). This exhortation should resound with special force in the hearts of those members of the Church who directly share, in different ways, in her mission as "teacher" of the truth. May it resound above all for us who are *bishops:* we are the first ones called to be untiring preachers of the *Gospel of life.* We are also entrusted with the task of ensuring that the doctrine which is once again being set forth in this Encyclical is faithfully handed on in its integrity. We must use appropriate means to defend the faithful from all teaching which is contrary to it. We need to make sure that in theological faculties, seminaries and Catholic institutions sound doctrine is taught, explained and more fully investigated.[106] May Paul's exhortation strike a chord in *all theologians, pastors, teachers* and in all those responsible for *catechesis and the formation of consciences.* Aware of their specific role, may they never be so grievously irresponsible as to betray the truth and their own mission by proposing personal ideas contrary to the *Gospel of life* as faithfully presented and interpreted by the Magisterium.

In the proclamation of this Gospel, we must not fear hostility or unpopularity, and we must refuse any compromise or ambiguity which might conform us to the world's way of thinking (cf. Rom 12:2). We must be *in the world but not of the world* (cf. Jn 15:19; 17:16), drawing our strength from Christ, who by his death and resurrection has overcome the world (cf. Jn 16:33).

"I give you thanks that I am fearfully, wonderfully made" (Ps 139:14): Celebrating the Gospel of life

83. Because we have been sent into the world as a "people for life," our proclamation must also become *a genuine celebration of the Gospel of life.* This celebration, with the evocative power of its gestures, symbols and rites, should become a precious and significant setting in which the beauty and grandeur of this Gospel is handed on.

For this to happen, we need first of all to *foster,* in ourselves and in others, *a contemplative outlook.*[107] Such an outlook arises from faith in the God of life, who has created every individual as a "wonder" (cf. Ps 139:14). It is the outlook of those who see life in its deeper meaning, who grasp its utter gratuitousness, its beauty and its invitation to freedom and responsibility. It is the outlook of those who do not presume to take possession of reality but instead accept it as a gift, discovering in all things the reflection of the Creator and seeing in every person his living image (cf. Gn 1:27; Ps 8:5). This outlook does not give in to discouragement when confronted by those who are sick, suffering, outcast or at death's door. Instead, in all these situations it feels challenged to find meaning, and precisely in these circumstances it is open to perceiving in the face of every person a call to encounter, dialogue and solidarity.

It is time for all of us to adopt this outlook, and with deep religious awe to rediscover the ability to *revere and honor every person,* as Paul VI invited us to do in one of his first Christmas messages.[108] Inspired by this contemplative outlook, the new people of the redeemed cannot but respond with *songs of joy, praise and thanksgiving for the priceless gift of life,* for the mystery of every individual's call to share through Christ in the life of grace and in an existence of unending communion with God our Creator and Father.

84. *To celebrate the Gospel of life means to celebrate the God of life, the God who gives life:* "We must celebrate Eternal Life, from which every other life proceeds. From this, in proportion to its capacities, every being which in any way participates in life, receives life. This Divine Life, which is above every other life, gives and preserves life. Every life and every living movement proceed from this Life which transcends all life and every principle of life. It is to this that souls owe their incorruptibility and because of this all animals and plants live, which receive only the faintest glimmer of life. To men, beings made

of spirit and matter, Life grants life. Even if we should abandon Life, because of its overflowing love for man, it converts us and calls us back to itself. Not only this: it promises to bring us, soul and body, to perfect life, to immortality. It is too little to say that this Life is alive: it is the Principle of life, the Cause and sole Wellspring of life. Every living thing must contemplate it and give it praise: it is Life which overflows with life."[109]

Like the Psalmist, we too, in our *daily prayer* as individuals and as a community, praise and bless God our Father, who knitted us together in our mother's womb, and saw and loved us while we were still without form (cf. Ps 139:13, 15-16). We exclaim with overwhelming joy: "I give you thanks that I am fearfully, wonderfully made; wonderful are your works. You know me through and through" (Ps 139:14). Indeed, "despite its hardships, its hidden mysteries, its suffering and its inevitable frailty, this mortal life is a most beautiful thing, a marvel ever new and moving, an event worthy of being exalted in joy and glory."[110] Moreover, man and his life appear to us not only as one of the greatest marvels of creation: for God has granted to man a dignity which is near to divine (Ps 8:5-6). In every child which is born and in every person who lives or dies we see the image of God's glory. We celebrate this glory in every human being, a sign of the living God, an icon of Jesus Christ.

We are called to express wonder and gratitude for the gift of life and to welcome, savor and share the *Gospel of life* not only in our personal and community prayer, but above all in the *celebrations of the liturgical year.* Particularly important in this regard are the *Sacraments,* the efficacious signs of the presence and saving action of the Lord Jesus in Christian life. The Sacraments make us sharers in divine life, and provide the spiritual strength necessary to experience life, suffering and death in their fullest meaning. Thanks to a genuine rediscovery and a better appreciation of the significance of these rites, our liturgical celebrations, especially celebrations of the Sacraments, will be ever more capable of expressing the full truth about birth, life, suffering and death, and will help us to live these moments as a participation in the Paschal Mystery of the Crucified and Risen Christ.

85. In celebrating the *Gospel of life* we also need to *appreciate and make good use of the wealth of gestures and symbols present in the traditions and customs of different cultures and peoples.* There are special times and ways in which the peoples of different nations and cultures express joy for a newborn life, respect for and protection of individual human lives, care for the suffering or needy, closeness to the elderly and the dying, participation in the sorrow of those who mourn, and hope and desire for immortality.

In view of this and following the suggestion made by the Cardinals in the Consistory of 1991, I propose that a *Day for Life* be celebrated each year in every country, as already established by some Episcopal Conferences. The celebration of this Day should be planned and carried out with the active participation of all sectors of the local Church. Its primary purpose should be to foster in individual consciences, in families, in the Church and in civil society a recognition of the meaning and value of human life at every stage and in every condition. Particular attention should be drawn to the seriousness of abortion and euthanasia, without neglecting other aspects of life which from time to time deserve to be given careful consideration, as occasion and circumstances demand.

86. As part of the spiritual worship acceptable to God (cf. Rom 12:1), *the Gospel of life* is to be celebrated above all in *daily living,* which should be filled with self-giving love for others. In this way, our lives will become a genuine and responsible acceptance of the gift of life and a heartfelt song of praise and gratitude to God who has given us this gift. This is already happening in the many different acts of selfless generosity, often humble and hidden, carried out by men and women, children and adults, the young and the old, the healthy and the sick.

It is in this context, so humanly rich and filled with love, that *heroic actions* too are born. These are *the most solemn celebration of the Gospel of life,* for they proclaim it *by the total gift of self.* They are the radiant manifestation of the highest degree of love, which is to give one's life for the person loved (cf. Jn 15:13). They are a sharing in the mystery of the Cross, in which Jesus reveals the value of every person, and how life attains its fullness in the sincere gift of self. Over and above such outstanding moments, there is an everyday heroism, made up of gestures of sharing, big or small, which build up an authentic culture of life. A particularly praiseworthy example of such gestures is the donation of organs, performed in an ethically acceptable manner, with a view to offering a chance of health and even of life itself to the sick who sometimes have no other hope.

Part of this daily heroism is also the silent but effective and eloquent witness of all those "brave mothers who devote themselves to their own family without reserve, who suffer in giving birth to their children and who are ready to make any effort, to face any sacrifice, in order to pass on to them the best of themselves."[111] In living out their mission "these heroic women do not always find support in the world around them. On the contrary, the cultural models frequently promoted and broadcast by the media do not encourage motherhood. In the name of progress and modernity the values of fidelity, chastity, sacrifice, to which a host of Christian wives and mothers have borne and continue to bear outstanding witness, are presented as obsolete.... We thank you, heroic mothers, for your invincible love! We thank you for your intrepid trust in God and in his love. We thank you for the sacrifice of your life.... In the Paschal Mystery, Christ restores to you the gift you gave him. Indeed, he has the power to give you back the life you gave him as an offering."[112]

"What does it profit, my brethren, if a man says he has faith but has not works?" (Jas 2:14): Serving the Gospel of life

87. By virtue of our sharing in Christ's royal mission, our support and promotion of human life must be accomplished through the *service of charity,* which finds expression in personal witness, various forms of volunteer work, social

activity and political commitment. This is a *particularly pressing need at the present time,* when the "culture of death" so forcefully opposes the "culture of life" and often seems to have the upper hand. But even before that it is a need which springs from "faith working through love" (Gal 5:6). As the Letter of James admonishes us: "What does it profit, my brethren, if a man says he has faith but has not works? Can his faith save him? If a brother or sister is ill-clad and in lack of daily food, and one of you says to them, 'Go in peace, be warmed and filled,' without giving them the things needed for the body, what does it profit? So faith by itself, if it has no works, is dead" (2:14-17).

In our service of charity, *we must be inspired and distinguished by a specific attitude:* we must care for the other as a person for whom God has made us responsible. As disciples of Jesus, we are called to become neighbors to everyone (cf. Lk 10:29-37), and to show special favor to those who are poorest, most alone and most in need. In helping the hungry, the thirsty, the foreigner, the naked, the sick, the imprisoned—as well as the child in the womb and the old person who is suffering or near death—we have the opportunity to serve Jesus. He himself said: "As you did it to one of the least of these my brethren, you did it to me" (Mt 25:40). Hence we cannot but feel called to account and judged by the ever relevant words of St. John Chrysostom: "Do you wish to honor the body of Christ? Do not neglect it when you find it naked. Do not do it homage here in the church with silk fabrics only to neglect it outside where it suffers cold and nakedness."[113]

Where life is involved, the service of charity must be profoundly consistent. It cannot tolerate bias and discrimination, for human life is sacred and inviolable at every stage and in every situation; it is an indivisible good. We need then to "show care" *for all life and for the life of everyone.* Indeed, at an even deeper level, we need to go to the very roots of life and love.

It is this deep love for every man and woman which has given rise down the centuries to an *outstanding history of charity,* a history which has brought into being in the Church and society many forms of service to life which evoke admiration from all unbiased observers. Every Christian community, with a renewed sense of responsibility, must continue to write this history through various kinds of pastoral and social activity. To this end, appropriate and effective programs of *support for new life* must be implemented, with special closeness to mothers who, even without the help of the father, are not afraid to bring their child into the world and to raise it. Similar care must be shown for the life of the marginalized or suffering, especially in its final phases.

88. All of this involves a patient and fearless *work of education* aimed at encouraging one and all to bear each other's burdens (cf. Gal 6:2). It requires a continuous promotion of *vocations to service,* particularly among the young. It involves the implementation of long-term practical *projects and initiatives* inspired by the Gospel.

Many are the *means* toward this end which *need to be developed* with skill and serious commitment. At the first stage of life, *centers for natural methods of regulating fertility* should be promoted as a valuable help to responsible parenthood, in which all individuals, and in the first place the child, are recognized and respected in their own right, and where every decision is guided by the ideal of the sincere gift of self. *Marriage and family counseling agencies* by their specific work of guidance and prevention, carried out in accordance with an anthropology consistent with the Christian vision of the person, of the couple and of sexuality, also offer valuable help in rediscovering the meaning of love and life, and in supporting and accompanying every family in its mission as the "sanctuary of life." Newborn life is also served by *centers of assistance and homes or centers where new life receives a welcome.* Thanks to the work of such centers, many unmarried mothers and couples in difficulty discover new hope and find assistance and support in overcoming hardship and the fear of accepting a newly conceived life or life which has just come into the world.

When life is challenged by conditions of hardship, maladjustment, sickness or rejection, other programs—such as *communities for treating drug addiction, residential communities for minors or the mentally ill, care and relief centers for AIDS patients, associations for solidarity especially toward the disabled*—are eloquent expressions of what charity is able to devise in order to give everyone new reasons for hope and practical possibilities for life.

And when earthly existence draws to a close, it is again charity which finds the most appropriate means for enabling the *elderly,* especially those who can no longer look after themselves, and the *terminally ill* to enjoy genuinely humane assistance and to receive an adequate response to their needs, in particular their anxiety and their loneliness. In these cases the role of families is indispensable; yet families can receive much help from social welfare agencies and, if necessary, from recourse to *palliative care,* taking advantage of suitable medical and social services available in public institutions or in the home.

In particular, the role of *hospitals, clinics and convalescent homes* needs to be reconsidered. These should not merely be institutions where care is provided for the sick or the dying. Above all they should be places where suffering, pain and death are acknowledged and understood in their human and specifically Christian meaning. This must be especially evident and effective in *institutes staffed by religious or in any way connected with the Church.*

89. Agencies and centers of service to life, and all other initiatives of support and solidarity which circumstances may from time to time suggest, need to be directed by *people who are generous in their involvement and fully aware* of the importance of the *Gospel of life* for the good of individuals and society.

A unique responsibility belongs to health-care personnel: doctors, pharmacists, nurses, chaplains, men and women religious, administrators and volunteers. Their profession calls for them to be guardians and servants of human life. In today's cultural and social context, in which science and the practice of medicine risk losing sight of their inherent ethical dimension, health-care professionals can be strongly tempted at times to become manipulators of life, or even agents of death. In the face of this temptation their responsibility today is greatly increased. Its deepest inspiration and strongest support lie in the intrinsic and undeniable ethical dimension of the health-care profession, something already recognized by the ancient and still relevant *Hippocratic Oath,* which requires every doctor to commit himself to absolute respect for human life and its sacredness.

Absolute respect for every innocent human life also requires the *exercise of conscientious objection* in relation to procured abortion and euthanasia. "Causing death" can never be considered a form of medical treatment, even when the intention is solely to comply with the patient's request. Rather, it runs completely counter to the health-care profession, which is meant to be an impassioned and unflinching affirmation of life. Biomedical research too, a field which promises great benefits for humanity, must always reject experimentation, research or applications which disregard the inviolable dignity of the human being, and thus cease to be at the service of people and become instead means which, under the guise of helping people, actually harm them.

90. *Volunteer workers* have a specific role to play: they make a valuable contribution to the service of life when they combine professional ability and generous, selfless love. The *Gospel of life* inspires them to lift their feelings of good will toward others to the heights of Christ's charity; to renew every day, amid hard work and weariness, their awareness of the dignity of every person; to search out people's needs and, when necessary, to set out on new paths where needs are greater but care and support weaker.

If charity is to be realistic and effective, it demands that the *Gospel of life* be implemented also by means of certain *forms of social activity and commitment in the political field,* as a way of defending and promoting the value of life in our ever more complex and pluralistic societies. *Individuals, families, groups and associations,* albeit for different reasons and in different ways, all have a responsibility for shaping society and developing cultural, economic, political and legislative projects which, with respect for all and in keeping with democratic principles, will contribute to the building of a society in which the dignity of each person is recognized and protected and the lives of all are defended and enhanced.

This task is the particular responsibility of *civil leaders.* Called to serve the people and the common good, they have a duty to make courageous choices in support of life, especially through *legislative measures.* In a democratic system, where laws and decisions are made on the basis of the consensus of many, the sense of personal responsibility in the consciences of individuals invested with authority may be weakened. But no one can ever renounce this responsibility, especially when he or she has a legislative or decision-making mandate, which calls that person to answer to God, to his or her own conscience and to the whole of society for choices which may be contrary to the common good. Although laws are not the only means of protecting human life, nevertheless they do play a very important and sometimes decisive role in influencing patterns of thought and behavior. I repeat once more that a law which violates an innocent person's natural right to life is unjust and, as such, is not valid as a law. For this reason I urgently appeal once more to all political leaders not to pass laws which, by disregarding the dignity of the person, undermine the very fabric of society.

The Church well knows that it is difficult to mount an effective legal defense of life in pluralistic democracies, because of the presence of strong cultural currents with differing outlooks. At the same time, certain that moral truth cannot fail to make its presence deeply felt in every conscience, the Church encourages political leaders, starting with those who are Christians, not to give in, but to make those choices which, taking into account what is realistically attainable, will lead to the re-establishment of a just order in the defense and promotion of the value of life. Here it must be noted that it is not enough to remove unjust laws. The underlying causes of attacks on life have to be eliminated, especially by ensuring proper support for families and motherhood. *A family policy must be the basis and driving force of all social policies.* For this reason there need to be set in place social and political initiatives capable of guaranteeing conditions of true freedom of choice in matters of parenthood. It is also necessary to rethink labor, urban, residential and social service policies so as to harmonize working schedules with time available for the family, so that it becomes effectively possible to take care of children and the elderly.

91. Today an important part of policies which favor life is the *issue of population growth.* Certainly public authorities have a responsibility to "intervene to orient the demography of the population."[114] But such interventions must always take into account and respect the primary and inalienable responsibility of married couples and families, and cannot employ methods which fail to respect the person and fundamental human rights, beginning with the right to life of every innocent human being. It is therefore morally unacceptable to encourage, let alone impose, the use of methods such as contraception, sterilization and abortion in order to regulate births. The ways of solving the population problem are quite different. Governments and the various international agencies must above all strive to create economic, social, public health and cultural conditions which will enable married couples to make their choices about procreation in full freedom and with genuine responsibility. They must then make efforts to ensure "greater opportunities and a fairer distribution of wealth so that everyone can share equitably in the goods of creation. Solutions must be sought on the global level by establishing a *true economy of communion and sharing of goods,* in both the national and international order."[115] This is the only way to respect the dignity of persons and families, as well as the authentic cultural patrimony of peoples.

Service of the *Gospel of life* is thus an immense and complex task. This service increasingly appears as a valuable and fruitful area for positive cooperation with our brothers and sisters of other Churches and ecclesial communities, in accordance with the *practical ecumenism* which the Second Vatican Council authoritatively encouraged.[116] It also appears as a providential area for dialogue and joint efforts with the followers of other religions and with all people of good will. *No single person or group has a monopoly on the defense and promotion of life. These are everyone's task and responsibility.* On the eve of the Third Millennium, the challenge facing us is an arduous one: only the concerted efforts of all those who believe in the value of life can prevent a setback of unforeseeable consequences for civilization.

"Your children will be like olive shoots around your table" (Ps 128:3): The family as the "sanctuary of life"

92. Within the "people of life and the people for life," *the family has a decisive responsibility.* This responsibility flows from its very nature as a community of life and love, founded upon marriage, and from its mission to "guard, reveal and communicate love."[117] Here it is a matter of God's own love, of which parents are co-workers and as it were interpreters when they transmit life and raise it according to his fatherly plan.[118] This is the love that becomes selflessness, receptiveness and gift. Within the family each member is accepted, respected and honored precisely because he or she is a person; and if any family member is in greater need, the care which he or she receives is all the more intense and attentive.

The family has a special role to play throughout the life of its members, from birth to death. It is truly *"the sanctuary of life:* the place in which life—the gift of God—can be properly welcomed and protected against the many attacks to which it is exposed, and can develop in accordance with what constitutes authentic human growth."[119] Consequently the role of the family in building a culture of life is *decisive and irreplaceable.*

As the *domestic church,* the family is summoned to proclaim, celebrate and serve the *Gospel of life.* This is a responsibility which first concerns married couples, called to be givers of life, on the basis of an ever greater *awareness of the meaning of procreation* as a unique event which clearly reveals that *human life is a gift received in order then to be given as a gift.* In giving origin to a new life, parents recognize that the child, "as the fruit of their mutual gift of love, is, in turn, a gift for both of them, a gift which flows from them."[120]

It is above all in *raising children* that the family fulfills its mission to proclaim the *Gospel of life.* By word and example, in the daily round of relations and choices, and through concrete actions and signs, parents lead their children to authentic freedom, actualized in the sincere gift of self, and they cultivate in them respect for others, a sense of justice, cordial openness, dialogue, generous service, solidarity and all the other values which help people to live life as a gift. In raising children Christian parents must be concerned about their children's faith and help them to fulfill the vocation God has given them. The parents' mission as educators also includes teaching and giving their children an example of the true meaning of suffering and death. They will be able to do this if they are sensitive to all kinds of suffering around them and, even more, if they succeed in fostering attitudes of closeness, assistance and sharing toward sick or elderly members of the family.

93. The family *celebrates the Gospel of life* through *daily prayer,* both individual prayer and family prayer. The family prays in order to glorify and give thanks to God for the gift of life, and implores his light and strength in order to face times of difficulty and suffering without losing hope. But the celebration which gives meaning to every other form of prayer and worship is found in *the family's actual daily life together,* if it is a life of love and self-giving.

This celebration thus becomes a *service to the Gospel of life,* expressed through *solidarity* as experienced within and around the family in the form of concerned, attentive and loving care shown in the humble, ordinary events of each day. A particularly significant expression of solidarity between families is a willingness to *adopt or take* in children abandoned by their parents or in situations of serious hardship. True parental love is ready to go beyond the bonds of flesh and blood in order to accept children from other families, offering them whatever is necessary for their well-being and full development. Among the various forms of adoption, consideration should be given to *adoption-at-a-distance,* preferable in cases where the only reason for giving up the child is the extreme poverty of the child's family. Through this type of adoption, parents are given the help needed to support and raise their children, without their being uprooted from their natural environment.

As "a firm and persevering determination to commit oneself to the common good,"[121] solidarity also needs to be practiced through *participation in social and political life.* Serving the *Gospel of life* thus means that the family, particularly through its membership of family associations, works to ensure that the laws and institutions of the State in no way violate the right to life, from conception to natural death, but rather protect and promote it.

94. Special attention must be given to the *elderly.* While in some cultures older people remain a part of the family with an important and active role, in others the elderly are regarded as a useless burden and are left to themselves. Here the temptation to resort to euthanasia can more easily arise.

Neglect of the elderly or their outright rejection are intolerable. Their presence in the family, or at least their closeness to the family in cases where limited living space or other reasons make this impossible, is of fundamental importance in creating a climate of mutual interaction and enriching communication between the different age-groups. It is therefore important to preserve, or to re-establish where it has been lost, a sort of "covenant" between generations. In this way parents, in their later years, can receive from their children the acceptance and solidarity which they themselves gave to their children when they brought them into the world. This is required by obedience to the divine commandment to honor one's father and mother (cf. Ex 20:12; Lv 19:3). But there is more. The elderly are not only to be considered the object of our concern, closeness and service.

They themselves have a valuable contribution to make to the *Gospel of life*. Thanks to the rich treasury of experiences they have acquired through the years, the elderly can and must *be sources of wisdom and witnesses of hope and love.*

Although it is true that "the future of humanity passes by way of the family,"[122] it must be admitted that modern social, economic and cultural conditions make the family's task of serving life more difficult and demanding. In order to fulfill its vocation as the "sanctuary of life," as the cell of a society which loves and welcomes life, *the family urgently needs to be helped and supported.* Communities and states must guarantee all the support, including economic support, which families need in order to meet their problems in a truly human way. For her part, the Church must untiringly promote a plan of pastoral care for families, capable of making every family rediscover and live with joy and courage its mission to further the *Gospel of life*.

"Walk as children of light" (Eph 5:8): *Bringing about a transformation of culture*

95. "Walk as children of light...and try to learn what is pleasing to the Lord. Take no part in the unfruitful works of darkness" (Eph 5:8, 10-11). In our present social context, marked by a dramatic struggle between the "culture of life" and the "culture of death," there is need to develop a *deep critical sense,* capable of discerning true values and authentic needs.

What is urgently called for is a *general mobilization of consciences* and *a united ethical effort* to activate *a great campaign in support of life. All together, we must build a new culture of life:* new, because it will be able to confront and solve today's unprecedented problems affecting human life; new, because it will be adopted with deeper and more dynamic conviction by all Christians; new, because it will be capable of bringing about a serious and courageous cultural dialogue among all parties. While the urgent need for such a cultural transformation is linked to the present historical situation, it is also rooted in the Church's mission of evangelization. The purpose of the Gospel, in fact, is "to transform humanity from within and to make it new."[123] Like the yeast which leavens the whole measure of dough (cf. Mt 13:33), the Gospel is meant to permeate all cultures and give them life from within,[124] so that they may express the full truth about the human person and about human life.

We need to begin with *the renewal of a culture of life within Christian communities themselves.* Too often it happens that believers, even those who take an active part in the life of the Church, end up by separating their Christian faith from its ethical requirements concerning life, and thus fall into moral subjectivism and certain objectionable ways of acting. With great openness and courage, we need to question how widespread is the culture of life today among individual Christians, families, groups and communities in our dioceses. With equal clarity and determination we must identify the steps we are called to take in order to serve life in all its truth. At the same time, we need to promote a serious and in-depth exchange about basic issues of human life with everyone, including non-believers, in intellectual circles, in the various professional spheres and at the level of people's everyday life.

96. The first and fundamental step toward this cultural transformation consists in *forming consciences* with regard to the incomparable and inviolable worth of every human life. It is of the greatest importance *to re-establish the essential connection between life and freedom.* These are inseparable goods: where one is violated, the other also ends up being violated. There is no true freedom where life is not welcomed and loved; and there is no fullness of life except in freedom. Both realities have something inherent and specific which links them inextricably: the vocation to love. Love, as a sincere gift of self,[125] is what gives the life and freedom of the person their truest meaning.

No less critical in the formation of conscience is *the recovery of the necessary link between freedom and truth.* As I have frequently stated, when freedom is detached from objective truth it becomes impossible to establish personal rights on a firm rational basis; and the ground is laid for society to be at the mercy of the unrestrained will of individuals or the oppressive totalitarianism of public authority.[126]

It is therefore essential that man should acknowledge his inherent condition as a creature to whom God has granted being and life as a gift and a duty. Only by admitting his innate dependence can man live and use his freedom to the full, and at the same time respect the life and freedom of every other person. Here especially one sees that "at the heart of every culture lies the attitude man takes to the greatest mystery: the mystery of God."[127] Where God is denied and people live as though he did not exist, or his commandments are not taken into account, the dignity of the human person and the inviolability of human life also end up being rejected or compromised.

97. Closely connected with the formation of conscience is the *work of education,* which helps individuals to be ever more human, leads them ever more fully to the truth, instills in them growing respect for life, and trains them in right interpersonal relationships.

In particular, there is a need for education about the value of life *from its very origins.* It is an illusion to think that we can build a true culture of human life if we do not help the young to accept and experience sexuality and love and the whole of life according to their true meaning and in their close interconnection. Sexuality, which enriches the whole person, "manifests its inmost meaning in leading the person to the gift of self in love."[128] The trivialization of sexuality is among the principal factors which have led to contempt for new life. Only a true love is able to protect life. There can be no avoiding the duty to offer, especially to adolescents and young adults, an authentic *education in sexuality and in love,* an education which involves *training in chastity* as a virtue which fosters personal maturity and makes one capable of respecting the "spousal" meaning of the body.

The work of educating in the service of life involves the *training of married couples in responsible procreation*. In its true meaning, responsible procreation requires couples to be obedient to the Lord's call and to act as faithful interpreters of his plan. This happens when the family is generously open to new lives, and when couples maintain an attitude of openness and service to life, even if, for serious reasons and in respect for the moral law, they choose to avoid a new birth for the time being or indefinitely. The moral law obliges them in every case to control the impulse of instinct and passion, and to respect the biological laws inscribed in their person. It is precisely this respect which makes legitimate, at the service of responsible procreation, the *use of natural methods of regulating fertility*. From the scientific point of view, these methods are becoming more and more accurate and make it possible in practice to make choices in harmony with moral values. An honest appraisal of their effectiveness should dispel certain prejudices which are still widely held, and should convince married couples, as well as health-care and social workers, of the importance of proper training in this area. The Church is grateful to those who, with personal sacrifice and often unacknowledged dedication, devote themselves to the study and spread of these methods, as well to the promotion of education in the moral values which they presuppose.

The work of education cannot avoid a consideration of suffering and death. These are a part of human existence, and it is futile, not to say misleading, to try to hide them or ignore them. On the contrary, people must be helped to understand their profound mystery in all its harsh reality. Even pain and suffering have meaning and value when they are experienced in close connection with love received and given. In this regard, I have called for the yearly celebration of the *World Day of the Sick,* emphasizing "the salvific nature of the offering up of suffering which, experienced in communion with Christ, belongs to the very essence of the Redemption."[129] Death itself is anything but an event without hope. It is the door which opens wide on eternity and, for those who live in Christ, an experience of participation in the mystery of his death and resurrection.

98. In a word, we can say that the cultural change which we are calling for demands from everyone the courage to *adopt a new lifestyle,* consisting in making practical choices—at the personal, family, social and international level—on the basis of a correct scale of values: *the primacy of being over having,*[130] *of the person over things.*[131] This renewed lifestyle involves a passing from *indifference to concern for others, from rejection to acceptance of them.* Other people are not rivals from whom we must defend ourselves, but brothers and sisters to be supported. They are to be loved for their own sakes, and they enrich us by their very presence.

In this mobilization for a new culture of life no one must feel excluded: *everyone has an important role to play.* Together with the family, *teachers and educators* have a particularly valuable contribution to make. Much will depend on them if young people, trained in true freedom, are to be able to preserve for themselves and make known to others new, authentic ideals of life, and if they are to grow in respect for and service to every other person, in the family and in society.

Intellectuals can also do much to build a new culture of human life. A special task falls to *Catholic* intellectuals, who are called to be present and active in the leading centers where culture is formed, in schools and universities, in places of scientific and technological research, of artistic creativity and of the study of man. Allowing their talents and activity to be nourished by the living force of the Gospel, they ought to place themselves at the service of a new culture of life by offering serious and well documented contributions, capable of commanding general respect and interest by reason of their merit. It was precisely for this purpose that I established the *Pontifical Academy for Life,* assigning it the task of "studying and providing information and training about the principal problems of law and biomedicine pertaining to the promotion of life, especially in the direct relationship they have with Christian morality and the directives of the Church's Magisterium."[132] A specific contribution will also have to come from *universities,* particularly from *Catholic* universities, and from *centers, institutes and committees of bioethics.*

An important and serious responsibility belongs to *those involved in the mass media,* who are called to ensure that the messages which they so effectively transmit will support the culture of life. They need to present noble models of life and make room for instances of people's positive and sometimes heroic love for others. With great respect they should also present the positive values of sexuality and human love, and not insist on what defiles and cheapens human dignity. In their interpretation of things, they should refrain from emphasizing anything that suggests or fosters feelings or attitudes of indifference, contempt or rejection in relation to life. With scrupulous concern for factual truth, they are called to combine freedom of information with respect for every person and a profound sense of humanity.

99. In transforming culture so that it supports life, *women* occupy a place, in thought and action, which is unique and decisive. It depends on them to promote a "new feminism" which rejects the temptation of imitating models of "male domination," in order to acknowledge and affirm the true genius of women in every aspect of the life of society, and overcome all discrimination, violence and exploitation.

Making my own the words of the concluding message of the Second Vatican Council, I address to women this urgent appeal: *"Reconcile people with life."*[133] You are called to *bear witness to the meaning of genuine love,* of that gift of self and of that acceptance of others which are present in a special way in the relationship of husband and wife, but which ought also to be at the heart of every other interpersonal relationship. The experience of motherhood makes you acutely aware of the other person and, at the same time, confers on you a particular task: "Motherhood involves a special communion with the mystery of life, as it develops in the woman's womb.... This unique contact with the new human being developing within her gives rise to an attitude toward human beings not only toward her own child, but every human being, which profoundly marks the woman's personality."[134] A mother welcomes and carries in herself another human being, enabling it to grow inside her, giving it room, respecting it in its otherness. Women first learn and then teach others that human relations are authentic if they are open to accepting the other person: a person who is recognized and loved because of the dignity which comes from being a person and not from other considerations, such as usefulness, strength, intelligence, beauty or health. This is the fundamental contribution which the Church and humanity expect from women. And it is the indispensable prerequisite for an authentic cultural change.

I would now like to say a special word to *women who have had an abortion.* The Church is aware of the many factors which may have influenced your decision, and she does not doubt that in many cases it was a painful and even shattering decision. The wound in your heart may not yet have healed. Certainly what happened was and remains terribly wrong. But do not give in to discouragement and do not lose hope. Try rather to understand what happened and face it honestly. If you have not already done so, give yourselves over with humility and trust to repentance. The Father of mercies is ready to give you his forgiveness and his peace in the Sacrament of Reconciliation. You will come to understand that nothing is definitively lost and you will also be able to ask forgiveness from your child, who is now living in the Lord. With the friendly and expert help and advice of other people, and as a result of your own painful experience, you can be among the most eloquent defenders of everyone's right to life. Through your commitment to life, whether by accepting the birth of other children or by welcoming and caring for those most in need of someone to be close to them, you will become promoters of a new way of looking at human life.

100. In this great endeavor to create a new culture of life we are *inspired and sustained by the confidence* that comes from knowing that the *Gospel of life,* like the Kingdom of God itself, is growing and producing abundant fruit (cf. Mk 4:26-29). There is certainly an enormous disparity between the powerful resources available to the forces promoting the "culture of death" and the means at the disposal of those working for a "culture of life and love." But we know that we can rely on the help of God, for whom nothing is impossible (cf. Mt 19:26).

Filled with this certainty, and moved by profound concern for the destiny of every man and woman, I repeat what I said to those families who carry out their challenging mission amid so many difficulties:[135] *a great prayer for life is urgently needed,* a prayer which will rise up throughout the world. Through special initiatives and in daily prayer, may an impassioned plea rise to God, the Creator and lover of life, from every Christian community, from every group and association, from every family and from the heart of every believer. Jesus himself has shown us by his own example that prayer and fasting are the first and most effective weapons against the forces of evil (cf. Mt 4:1-11). As he taught his disciples, some demons cannot be driven out except in this way (cf. Mk 9:29). Let us therefore discover anew the humility and the courage to *pray and fast* so that power from on high will break down the walls of lies and deceit: the walls which conceal from the sight of so many of our brothers and sisters the evil of practices and laws which are hostile to life. May this same power turn their hearts to resolutions and goals inspired by the civilization of life and love.

"We are writing this that our joy may be complete" (1 Jn 1:4): The Gospel of life is for the whole of human society

101. "We are writing you this that our joy may be complete" (1 Jn 1:4). The revelation of the *Gospel of life* is given to us as a good to be shared with all people: so that all men and women may have fellowship with us and with the Trinity (cf. 1 Jn 1:3). Our own joy would not be complete if we failed to share this Gospel with others but kept it only for ourselves.

The *Gospel of life* is not for believers alone: *it is for everyone.* The issue of life and its defense and promotion is not a concern of Christians alone. Although faith provides special light and strength, this question arises in every human conscience which seeks the truth and which cares about the future of humanity. Life certainly has a sacred and religious value, but in no way is that value a concern only of believers. The value at stake is one which every human being can grasp by the light of reason; thus it necessarily concerns everyone.

Consequently, all that we do as the "people of life and for life" should be interpreted correctly and welcomed with favor. When the Church declares that unconditional respect for the right to life of every innocent person—from conception to natural death—is one of the pillars on which every civil society stands, she "wants simply to *promote a human state.* A state which recognizes the defense of the fundamental rights of the human person, especially of the weakest, as its primary duty."[136]

The *Gospel of life* is for the whole of human society. To be actively pro-life is to contribute to the *renewal of society* through the promotion of the common good. It is impossible to further the common good without acknowledging and defending the right to life, upon which all the other inalienable rights of individuals are founded and from which they develop. A society lacks solid foundations when, on the one hand, it asserts values such as the dignity of the person, justice and peace, but then, on the other hand, radically acts to the contrary by allowing or tolerating a variety of ways in which human life is devalued and violated, especially where it is weak or marginalized. Only respect for life can be the foundation and guarantee of the most precious and essential goods of society, such as democracy and peace.

There can be no *true democracy* without a recognition of every person's dignity and without respect for his or her rights.

Nor can there be *true peace* unless *life is defended and promoted.* As Paul VI pointed out: "Every crime against life is an attack on peace, especially if it strikes at the moral conduct of people.... But where human rights are truly professed and publicly recognized and defended, peace becomes the joyful and operative climate of life in society."[137]

The "people of life" rejoices in being able to share its commitment with so many others. Thus may the "people for life" constantly grow in number and may a new culture of love and solidarity develop for the true good of the whole of human society.

Conclusion

102. At the end of this Encyclical, we naturally look again to the Lord Jesus, "the Child born for us" (cf. Is 9:6), that in him we may contemplate "the Life" which "was made manifest" (1 Jn 1:2). In the mystery of Christ's birth the encounter of God with man takes place and the earthly journey of the Son of God begins, a journey which will culminate in the gift of his life on the Cross. By his death Christ will conquer death and become for all humanity the source of new life.

The one who accepted "Life" in the name of all and for the sake of all was Mary, the Virgin Mother; she is thus most closely and personally associated with the *Gospel of life.* Mary's consent at the Annunciation and her motherhood stand at the very beginning of the mystery of life which Christ came to bestow on humanity (cf. Jn 10:10). Through her acceptance and loving care for the life of the Incarnate Word, human life has been rescued from condemnation to final and eternal death.

For this reason, Mary, "like the Church of which she is the type, is a mother of all who are reborn to life. She is in fact the mother of the Life by which everyone lives, and when she brought it forth from herself she in some way brought to rebirth all those who were to live by that Life."[138]

As the Church contemplates Mary's motherhood, she discovers the meaning of her own motherhood and the way in which she is called to express it. At the same time, the Church's experience of motherhood leads to a most profound understanding of Mary's experience as the *incomparable model of how life should be welcomed and cared for.*

"A great portent appeared in heaven, a woman clothed with the sun" (Rv 12:1): The motherhood of Mary and of the Church

103. The mutual relationship between the mystery of the Church and Mary appears clearly in the "great portent" described in the Book of Revelation: "A great portent appeared in heaven, a woman clothed with the sun, with the moon

under her feet, and on her head a crown of twelve stars" (12:1). In this sign the Church recognizes an image of her own mystery: present in history, she knows that she transcends history, inasmuch as she constitutes on earth the "seed and beginning" of the Kingdom of God.[139] The Church sees this mystery fulfilled in complete and exemplary fashion in Mary. She is the woman of glory in whom God's plan could be carried out with supreme perfection.

The "woman clothed with the sun"—the Book of Revelation tells us—"was with child" (12:2). The Church is fully aware that she bears within herself the Savior of the world, Christ the Lord. She is aware that she is called to offer Christ to the world, giving men and women new birth into God's own life. But the Church cannot forget that her mission was made possible by the motherhood of Mary, who conceived and bore the One who is "God from God," "true God from true God." Mary is truly the Mother of God, the *Theotókos,* in whose motherhood the vocation to motherhood bestowed by God on every woman is raised to its highest level. Thus Mary becomes the model of the Church, called to be the "new Eve," the mother of believers, the mother of the "living" (cf. Gn 3:20).

The Church's spiritual motherhood is only achieved—the Church knows this too—through the pangs and "the labor" of childbirth (cf. Rv 12:2), that is to say, in constant tension with the forces of evil which still roam the world and affect human hearts, offering resistance to Christ: "In him was life, and the life was the light of men. The light shines in the darkness, and the darkness has not overcome it" (Jn 1:4-5).

Like the Church, Mary too had to live her motherhood amid suffering: "This child is set...for a sign that is spoken against—and a sword will pierce through your own soul also—that thoughts out of many hearts may be revealed" (Lk 2:34-35). The words which Simeon addresses to Mary at the very beginning of the Savior's earthly life sum up and prefigure the rejection of Jesus, and with him of Mary, a rejection which will reach its culmination on Calvary. "Standing by the cross of Jesus" (Jn 19:25), Mary shares in the gift which the Son makes of himself: she offers Jesus, gives him over, and begets him to the end for our sake. The "yes" spoken on the day of the Annunciation reaches full maturity on the day of the Cross, when the time comes for Mary to receive and beget as her children all those who become disciples, pouring out upon them the saving love of her Son: "When Jesus saw his mother, and the disciple whom he loved standing near, he said to his mother, 'Woman, behold, your son!'" (Jn 19:26).

"And the dragon stood before the woman...that he might devour her child when she brought it forth" (Rv 12:4): Life menaced by the forces of evil

104. In the Book of Revelation, the "great portent" of the "woman" (12:1) is accompanied by "another portent which appeared in heaven": "a great red dragon" (Rv 12:3), which represents Satan, the personal power of evil, as well as all the powers of evil at work in history and opposing the Church's mission.

Here too Mary sheds light on the community of believers. The hostility of the powers of evil is, in fact, an insidious opposition which, before affecting the disciples of Jesus, is directed against his mother. To save the life of her Son from those who fear him as a dangerous threat, Mary has to flee with Joseph and the Child into Egypt (cf. Mt 2:13-15).

Mary thus helps the Church to *realize that life is always at the center of a great struggle* between good and evil, between light and darkness. The dragon wishes to devour "the child brought forth" (cf. Rv 12:4), a figure of Christ, whom Mary brought forth "in the fullness of time" (Gal 4:4) and whom the Church must unceasingly offer to people in every age. But in a way that child is also a figure of every person, every child, especially every helpless baby whose life is threatened, because as the Council reminds us—"by his Incarnation the Son of God has united himself in some fashion with every person."[140] It is precisely in the "flesh" of every person that Christ continues to reveal himself and to enter into fellowship with us, so that *rejection of human life,* in whatever form that rejection takes, is *really a rejection of Christ.* This is the fascinating but also demanding truth which Christ reveals to us and which his Church continues untiringly to proclaim: "Whoever receives one such child in my name receives me" (Mt 18:5); "Truly, I say to you, as you did it to one of the least of these my brethren, you did it to me" (Mt 25:40).

"Death shall be no more" (Rv 21:4):
The splendor of the Resurrection

105. The angel's Annunciation to Mary is framed by these reassuring words: "Do not be afraid, Mary" and "with God nothing will be impossible" (Lk 1:30, 37). The whole of the Virgin Mother's life is in fact pervaded by the certainty that God is near to her and that he accompanies her with his providential care. The same is true of the Church, which finds "a place prepared by God" (Rv 12:6) in the desert, the place of trial but also of the manifestation of God's love for his people (cf. Hos 2:16). Mary is a living word of comfort for the Church in her struggle against death. Showing us the Son, the Church assures us that in him the forces of death have already been defeated: "Death with life contended: combat strangely ended! Life's own Champion, slain, yet lives to reign."[141]

The Lamb who was slain is alive, bearing the marks of his passion in the splendor of the Resurrection. He alone is master of all the events of history: he opens its "seals" (cf. Rv 5:1-10) and proclaims, in time and beyond, *the power of life over death.* In the "new Jerusalem," that new world toward which human history is traveling, *"death shall be no more,* neither shall there be mourning nor crying nor pain any more, for the former things have passed away" (Rv 21:4).

And as we, the pilgrim people, the people of life and for life, make our way in confidence toward "a new heaven and a new earth" (Rv 21:1), we look to her who is for us "a sign of sure hope and solace."[142]

O Mary,
bright dawn of the new world,
Mother of the living,
to you do we entrust the *cause of life:*
Look down, O Mother,
upon the vast numbers of babies not allowed to be born,
of the poor whose lives are made difficult,
of men and women who are victims of brutal violence,
of the elderly and the sick killed
by indifference or out of misguided mercy.
Grant that all who believe in your Son
may *proclaim the Gospel of life*
with honesty and love to the people of our time.
Obtain for them the grace
to *accept that Gospel* as a gift ever new,
the joy *of celebrating* it with gratitude
throughout their lives and the courage to *bear witness to it* resolutely,
in order to build,
together with all people of good will,
the civilization of truth and love,
to the praise and glory of God,
the Creator and lover of life.

Given in Rome, at Saint Peter's, on March 25, the Solemnity of the Annunciation of the Lord, in the year 1995, the seventeenth of my Pontificate.

JOHN PAUL II

NOTES

[1] The expression "Gopel of life" is not found as such in Sacred Scripture. But it does correspond to an essential dimension of the biblical message.

[2] Pastoral Constitution on the Church in the Modern World *Gaudium et Spes,* 22.

[3] Cf. John Paul II, Encyclical Letter *Redemptor Hominis* (March 4, 1979), 10: *AAS* 71 (1979), 275.

[4] Cf. *ibid.,* 14: *loc. cit.,* 285.

[5] Pastoral Constitution on the Church in the Modern World *Gaudium et Spes,* 27.

[6] Cf. Letter to all my Brothers in the Episcopate regarding the "Gospel of Life" (May 19, 1991): *Insegnamenti* IV, 1 (1991), 1293-1296.

[7] *Ibid., loc. cit.,* p. 1294.

[8] Letter to Families *Gratissimam Sane* (February 2, 1994), 4: *AAS* 86 (1994), 871.

[9] John Paul II, Encyclical Letter *Centesimus Annus* (May 1, 1991), 39: *AAS* 83 (1991), 842.

[10] No. 2259.

[11] Cf. St. Ambrose, *De Noe,* 26:94-96: *CSEL* 32, 480-481.

[12] Cf. *Catechism of the Catholic Church,* nos. 1867 and 2268.

[13] *De Cain et Abel,* II, 10, 38: *CSEL* 32, 408.

[14] Cf. Congregation for the Doctrine of the Faith, Instruction on Respect for Human Life in Its Origin and on the Dignity of Procreation *Donum Vitae: AAS* 80 (1988), 70-102.

[15] Address during the Prayer Vigil for the Eighth World Youth Day, Denver, August 14, 1993, 11, 3: *AAS* 86 (1994), 419.

[16] John Paul II, Address to the Participants at the Study Conference on "The Right to Life and Europe," December 18, 1987: *Insegnamenti,* X, 3 (1987), 1446-1447.

[17] Pastoral Constitution on the Church in the Modern World *Gaudium et Spes,* 36.

[18] Cf. *ibid.,* 16.

[19] Cf. St. Gregory the Great, *Moralia in Job,* 13, 23: *CCL* 143A, 683.

[20] John Paul II, Encyclical Letter *Redemptor Hominis* (March 4, 1979), 10: *AAS* 71 (1979), 274.

[21] Second Vatican Ecumenical Council, Pastoral Constitution on the Church in the Modern World *Gaudium et Spes,* 50.

[22] Dogmatic Constitution on Divine Revelation *Dei Verbum,* 4.

[23] "Gloria Dei vivens homo": *Adversus Haereses,* IV, 20, 7: S. Ch. 100/2, 648-649.

[24] Second Vatican Ecumenical Council, Pastoral Constitution on the Church in the Modern World *Gaudium et Spes,* 12.

[25] *Confessions,* I, 1: *CCL* 27, 1.

[26] *Exameron,* VI, 75-76: *CSEL* 32, 260-261.

[27] "Vita autem hominis visio Dei": *Adversus Haereses,* IV, 20, 7: S. Ch. 100/12, 648-649.

[28] Cf. John Paul II, Encyclical Letter *Centesimus Annus* (May 1, 1991), 38: *AAS* 83 (1991), 840-841.

[29] John Paul II, Encyclical Letter *Sollicitudo Rei Socialis* (December 30, 1987), 34: *AAS* 80 (1988), 560.

[30] Pastoral Constitution on the Church in the Modern World *Gaudium et Spes,* 50.

[31] Letter to Families *Gratissimam Sane* (February 2, 1994), 9: *AAS* 86 (1994), 878; cf. Pius XII, Encyclical Letter *Humani Generis* (August 12, 1950): *AAS* 42 (1950), 574.

[32] "Animas enim a Deo immediate creari catholica fides nos retinere iubet": Pius XII, Encyclical Letter *Humani Generis* (August 12, 1950): *AAS* 42 (1950), 575.

[33] Second Vatican Ecumenical Council, Pastoral Constitution on the Church in the Modern World *Gaudium et Spes,* 50; cf. John Paul II, Post-Synodal Apostolic Exhortation *Familiaris Consortio* (November 22, 1981), 28: *AAS* 74 (1982), 114.

[34] *Homilies,* 11, 1; *CCSG* 3, 39.

[35] See, for example, Psalms 22:10-11; 71:6; 139:13-14.

[36] *Expositio Evangelii secundum Lucam,* II, 22-23: *CCL* 14, 40-41.

[37] St. Ignatius of Antioch, *Letter to the Ephesians,* 7, 2: *Patres Apostolici,* ed. F. X. Funk, II, 82.

[38] *De Hominis Opificio,* 4: *PG* 44, 136.

[39] Cf. St. John Damascene, *De Fide Orthodoxa,* 2, 12: *PG* 94, 920.922, quoted in St. Thomas Aquinas, *Summa Theologiae,* I-II, *Prologue.*

[40] Paul VI, Encyclical Letter *Humanae Vitae* (July 25, 1968), 13: *AAS* 60 (1968), 489.

[41] Congregation for the Doctrine of the Faith, Instruction on Respect for Human Life in Its Origin and on the Dignity of Procreation *Donum Vitae* (February 22, 1987), Introduction, no. 5: *AAS* 80 (1988), 76-77; cf. *Catechism of the Catholic Church,* no. 2258.

[42] *Didache,* I, 1; II, 1-2; V, 1 and 3: *Patres Apostolici,* ed. F. X. Funk, I, 2-3, 6-9, 14-17; cf. *Letter of Pseudo-Barnabas,* XI, 5: *loc. cit.,* 90-93.

[43] Cf. *Catechism of the Catholic Church,* nos. 2263-2269; cf. also *Catechism of the Council of Trent* III, 327-332.

[44] *Catechism of the Catholic Church,* no. 2265.

[45] Cf. St. Thomas Aquinas, *Summa Theologiae,* II-II, q. 64, a. 7; St. Alphonsus De' Liguori, *Theologia Moralis,* I. III, tr. 4, c. 1, dub. 3.

[46] *Catechism of the Catholic Church,* no. 2266.

[47] Cf. *ibid.*

[48] No. 2267.

[49] Second Vatican Ecumenical Council, Dogmatic Constitution on the Church *Lumen Gentium,* 12.

[50] Cf. Second Vatican Ecumenical Council, Pastoral Constitution on the Church in the Modern World *Gaudium et Spes,* 27.

[51] Cf. Second Vatican Ecumenical Council, Dogmatic Constitution on the Church *Lumen Gentium,* 25.

[52] Congregation for the Doctrine of the Faith, Declaration on Euthanasia *Iura et Bona* (May 5, 1980), II: *AAS* 72 (1980), 546.

[53] John Paul II, Encyclical Letter *Veritatis Splendor* (August 6, 1993), 96: *AAS* 85 (1993), 1209.

[54] Pastoral Constitution on the Church in the Modern World *Gaudium et Spes,* 51: "Abortus necnon infanticidium nefanda sunt crimina."

[55] Cf. John Paul II, Apostolic Letter *Mulieris Dignitatem* (August 15, 1988), 14: *AAS* 80 (1988), 1686.

[56] No. 21: *AAS* 86 (1994), 920.

[57] Congregation for the Doctrine of the Faith, *Declaration on Procured Abortion* (November 18, 1974), nos. 12-13: *AAS* 66 (1974), 738.

[58] Congregation for the Doctrine of the Faith, Instruction on Respect for Human Life in Its Origin and on the Dignity of Procreation *Donum Vitae* (February 22, 1987), I, no. 1: *AAS* 80 (1988), 78-79.

[59] *Ibid., loc. cit.,* 79.

[60] Hence the Prophet Jeremiah: "The word of the Lord came to me saying: 'Before I formed you in the womb I knew you, and before you were born I consecrated you; I appointed you a prophet to the nations'" (1:4-5). The Psalmist, for his part, addresses

the Lord in these words: "Upon you I have leaned from my birth; you are he who took me from my mother's womb" (Ps 71:6; cf. Is 46:3; Job 10:8-12; Ps 22:10-11). So too the Evangelist Luke in the magnificent episode of the meeting of the two mothers, Elizabeth and Mary, and their two sons, John the Baptist and Jesus, still hidden in their mothers' wombs (cf. 1:39-45) emphasizes how even before their birth the two little ones are able to communicate: the child recognizes the coming of the Child and leaps for joy.

[61] Cf. *Declaration on Procured Abortion* (November 18, 1974), no. 7: *AAS* 66 (1974), 740-747.

[62] "You shall not kill a child by abortion nor shall you kill it once it is born": V, 2: *Patres Apostolici,* ed. F. X. Funk, I, 17.

[63] *Apologia on behalf of the Christians,* 35: *PG* 6, 969.

[64] *Apologeticum,* IX, 8: *CSEL* 69, 24.

[65] Cf. Encyclical Letter *Casti Connubii* (December 31, 1930), II: *AAS* 22 (1930), 562-592.

[66] Address to the Biomedical Association "San Luca" (November 12, 1944): *Discorsi e Radiomessaggi,* VI (1944-1945), 191; cf. Address to the Italian Catholic Union of Midwives (October 29, 1951), no. 2: *AAS* 43 (1951), 838.

[67] Encyclical Letter *Mater et Magistra* (May 15, 1961), 3: *AAS* 53 (1961), 447.

[68] Pastoral Constitution on the Church in the Modern World *Gaudium et Spes,* 51.

[69] Canon 2350, §1.

[70] *Code of Canon Law,* canon 1398; cf. *Code of Canons of the Eastern Churches,* canon 1450, § 2.

[71] Cf. *ibid.,* canon 1329; also *Code of Canons of the Eastern Churches,* canon 1417.

[72] Cf. Address to the National Congress of Italian Jurists (December 9, 1972): *AAS* 64 (1972), 777; Encyclical Letter *Humanae Vitae* (July 25, 1968), 14: *AAS* 60 (1968), 490.

[73] Cf. Second Vatican Ecumenical Council, Dogmatic Constitution on the Church *Lumen Gentium,* 25.

[74] Congregation for the Doctrine of the Faith, Instruction on Respect for Human Life in Its Origin and on the Dignity of Procreation *Donum Vitae* (February 22, 1987) I, 3: *AAS* 80 (1988), 80.

[75] *Charter of the Rights of the Family* (October 22, 1983), article 4b: Vatican Polyglot Press, 1983.

[76] Congregation for the Doctrine of the Faith, Declaration on Euthanasia *Iura et Bona* (May 5, 1980), II: *AAS* 72 (1980), 546.

[77] *Ibid.,* IV: *loc. cit.,* 551.

[78] Cf. *ibid.*

[79] Pius XII, Address to an International Group of Physicians (February 24, 1957), III: *AAS* 49 (1957), 147; cf. Congregation for the Doctrine of the Faith, Declaration on Euthanasia *Iura et Bona,* III: *AAS* 72 (1980), 547-548.

[80] Pius XII, Address to an International Group of Physicians (February 24, 1957), III: *AAS* 49 (1957), 1´45.

[81] Cf. Pius XII, Address to an International Group of Physicians, (February 24, 1957): *loc. cit.,* 129-147; Congregation of the Holy Office, *Decretum de directa*

insontium occisione (December 2, 1940): *AAS* 32 (1940), 553-554; Paul VI, Message to French Television: "Every life is sacred" (January 27, 1971): *Insegnamenti* IX (1971), 57-58; Address to the International College of Surgeons (June 1, 1972): *AAS* 64 (1972), 432-436; Second Vatican Ecumenical Council, Pastoral Constitution on the Church in the Modern World *Gaudium et Spes,* 27.

[82] Cf. Second Vatican Ecumenical Council, Dogmatic Constitution on the Church *Lumen Gentium,* 25.

[83] Cf. St. Augustine, *De Civitate Dei* I, 20: *CCL* 47, 22; St. Thomas Aquinas, *Summa Theologiae,* II-II, q. 6, a. 5.

[84] Congregation for the Doctrine of the Faith, Declaration on Euthanasia *Iura et Bona* (May 5, 1980), I: *AAS* 72 (1980), 545; *Catechism of the Catholic Church,* nos. 2281-2283.

[85] *Ep.* 204, 5: *CSEL* 57, 320.

[86] Pastoral Constitution on the Church in the Modern World *Gaudium et Spes,* 18.

[87] Cf. John Paul II, Apostolic Letter *Salvifici Doloris* (February 11, 1984), 14-24: *AAS* 76 (1984), 214-234.

[88] Cf. John Paul II, Encyclical Letter *Centesimus Annus* (May 1, 1991), 46: *AAS* 83 (1991), 850; Pius XII, Christmas Radio Message (December 24, 1944): *AAS* 37 (1945), 10-20.

[89] Cf. John Paul II, Encyclical Letter *Veritatis Splendor* (August 6, 1993), 97 and 99: *AAS* 85 (1993), 1209-1211.

[90] Congregation for the Doctrine of the Faith, Instruction on Respect for Life in Its Origin and on the Dignity of Procreation *Donum Vitae* (February 22, 1987), III: *AAS* 80 (1988), 98.

[91] Cf. Second Vatican Ecumenical Council, Declaration on Religious Freedom *Dignitatis Humanae,* 7.

[92] Cf. St. Thomas Aquinas, *Summa Theologiae* I-II, q. 96, a. 2.

[93] Cf. Second Vatican Ecumenical Council, Declaration on Religious Freedom *Dignitatis Humanae,* 7.

[94] Encyclical Letter *Pacem in Terris* (April 11, 1963), II: *AAS* 55 (1963), 273-274. The internal quote is from Pius XII, Radio Message of Pentecost 1941 (June 1, 1941): *AAS* 33 (1941), 200. On this topic, the Encyclical cites: Pius XI, Encyclical Letter *Mit Brennender Sorge* (March 14, 1937): *AAS* 29 (1937), 159; Encyclical Letter *Divini Redemptoris* (March 19, 1937), III: *AAS* 29 (1937), 79; Pius XII, Christmas Radio Message (December 24, 1942): *AAS* 35 (1943), 9-24.

[95] Encyclical Letter *Pacem in Terris* (April 11, 1963), II: *loc. cit.,* 271.

[96] *Summa Theologiae,* I-II, q. 93, a. 3, ad 2um.

[97] *Ibid.,* I-II, q. 95, a. 2. Aquinas quotes St. Augustine: "Non videtur esse lex, quae iusta non fuerit," *De Libero Arbitrio,* I, 5, 11: *PL* 32, 1227.

[98] Congregation for the Doctrine of the Faith, *Declaration on Procured Abortion* (November 18, 1974), no. 22: *AAS* 66 (1974), 744.

[99] Cf. *Catechism of the Catholic Church,* nos. 1753-1755; John Paul II, Encyclical Letter *Veritatis Splendor* (August 6, 1993), 81-82: *AAS* 85 (1993), 1198-1199.

[100] *In Iohannis Evangelium Tractatus,* 41, 10: *CCL* 36, 3 63; cf. John Paul II, Encyclical Letter *Veritatis Splendor* (August 6, 1993), 13: *AAS* 85 (1993), 1144.

[101] Apostolic Exhortation *Evangelii Nuntiandi* (December 8, 1975), 14: *AAS* 68 (1976), 13.

[102] Cf. *Roman Missal,* prayer of the celebrant before communion.

[103] Cf. St. Irenaeus: "Omnem novitatem attulit, semetipsum afferens, qui fuerat annuntiatus," *Adversus Haereses,* IV, 34, 1: S. Ch 100/12, 846-847.

[104] Cf. St. Thomas Aquinas, "Peccator inveterascit, recedens a novitate Christi," *In Psalmos Davidis Lectura:* 6, 5.

[105] *De Beatitudinibus,* Oratio VII: *PG* 44, 1280.

[106] Cf. John Paul II, Encyclical Letter *Veritatis Splendor* (August 6, 1993), 116: *AAS* 85 (1993), 1224.

[107] Cf. John Paul II, Encyclical Letter *Centesimus Annus* (May 1, 1991), 37: *AAS* 83 (1991), 840.

[108] Cf. Message for Christmas 1967: *AAS* 60 (1968), 40.

[109] Pseudo-Dionysius the Areopagite, *On the Divine Names,* 6, 1-3: *PG* 3, 856-857.

[110] Paul VI, *Pensiero alla Morte,* Instituto Paolo VI, Brescia 1988, 24.

[111] John Paul II, Homily for the Beatification of Isidore Bakanja, Elisabetta Canori Mora and Gianna Beretta Molla (April 24, 1994): *L'Osservatore Romano,* April 25-26, 1994, 5.

[112] *Ibid.*

[113] *In Matthaeum, Hom.* L, 3: *PG* 58, 508.

[114] *Catechism of the Catholic Church,* no. 2372.

[115] John Paul II, Address to the Fourth General Conference of Latin American Bishops in Santo Domingo (October 12, 1992), no. 15: *AAS* 85 (1993), 819.

[116] Cf. Decree on Ecumenism *Unitatis Redintegratio,* 12; Pastoral Constitution on the Church in the Modern World *Gaudium et Spes,* 90.

[117] John Paul II, Post-Synodal Apostolic Exhortation *Familiaris Consortio* (November 22, 1981), 17: *AAS* 74 (1982), 100.

[118] Cf. Second Vatican Ecumenical Council, Pastoral Constitution on the Church in the Modern World *Gaudium et Spes,* 50.

[119] John Paul II, Encyclical Letter *Centesimus Annus* (May 1, 1991), 39: *AAS* 83 (1991), 842.

[120] John Paul II, Address to Participants in the Seventh Symposium of European Bishops, on the theme of "Contemporary Attitudes toward Life and Death: a Challenge for Evangelization" (October 17, 1989), no. 5: *Insegnamenti* XII, 2 (1989), 945. Children are presented in the biblical tradition precisely as God's gift (cf. Ps 127:3) and as a sign of his blessing on those who walk in his ways (cf. Ps 128:3-4).

[121] John Paul II, Encyclical Letter *Sollicitudo Rei Socialis* (December 30, 1987), 38: *AAS* 80 (1988), 565-566.

[122] John Paul II, Post-Synodal Apostolic Exhortation *Familiaris Consortio* (November 22, 1981), 86: *AAS* 74 (1982), 188.

[123] Paul VI, Apostolic Exhortation *Evangelii Nuntiandi* (December 8, 1975), 18: *AAS* 68 (1976), 17.

[124] Cf. *ibid.,* 20: *loc. cit.,* 18.

[125] Cf. Second Vatican Ecumenical Council, Pastoral Constitution on the Church in the Modern World *Gaudium et Spes,* 24.

[126] Cf. John Paul II, Encyclical Letter *Centesimus Annus* (May 1, 1991), 17: *AAS* 83 (1991), 814; Encyclical Letter *Veritatis Splendor* (August 6, 1993), 95-101: *AAS* 85 (1993), 1208-1213.

[127] John Paul II, Encyclical Letter *Centesimus Annus* (May 1, 1991), 24: *AAS* 83 (1991), 822.

[128] John Paul II, Post-Synodal Apostolic Exhortation *Familiaris Consortio* (November 22, 1981), 37: *AAS* 74 (1982), 128.

[129] Letter establishing the World Day of the Sick (May 13, 1992), no. 2: *Insegnamenti* XV, 1 (1992), 1410.

[130] Cf. Second Vatican Ecumenical Council, Pastoral Constitution on the Church in the Modern World *Gaudium et Spes,* 35; Paul VI, Encyclical Letter *Populorum Progressio* (March 26, 1967), 15: *AAS* 59 (1967), 265.

[131] Cf. John Paul II, Letter to Families *Gratissimam Sane* (February 2, 1994), 13: *AAS* 86 (1994), 892.

[132] John Paul II, Motu Proprio *Vitae Mysterium* (February 11, 1994), 4: *AAS* 86 (1994), 386-387.

[133] Closing Messages of the Council (December 8, 1965): *To Women.*

[134] John Paul II, Apostolic Letter *Mulieris Dignitatem* (August 15, 1988), 18: *AAS* 80 (1988), 1696.

[135] Cf. John Paul II, Letter to Families *Gratissimam Sane* (February 2, 1994), 5: *AAS* 86 (1994), 872.

[136] John Paul II, Address to Participants in the Study Conference on "The Right to Life in Europe" (December 18, 1987): *Insegnamenti* X, 3 (1987), 1446.

[137] *Message for the 1977 World Day of Peace: AAS* 68 (1976), 711-712.

[138] Blessed Guerric of Igny, *In Assumptione B. Mariae,* Sermo I, 2: *PL* 185, 188.

[139] Second Vatican Ecumenical Council, Dogmatic Constitution on the Church *Lumen Gentium,* 5.

[140] Pastoral Constitution on the Church in the Modern World *Gaudium et Spes,* 22.

[141] *Roman Missal,* Sequence for Easter Sunday.

[142] Second Vatican Ecumenical Council, Dogmatic Constitution on the Church *Lumen Gentium,* 68.

INDEX

A

Abel, murder of, 497-500
  Cain's punishment, 509

abortion, 432, 464, 502-503, 538-543
  conscientious objection to, 551-553, 563
  dignity of life of unborn child, 527-528
  forgiveness for, 571
  responsibility for, 539-540

Abraham, covenant with, 265

absence of shame, 55-57

abstinence, periodic in marriage, 298, 399-401, 436

adoption, 566

adultery
  avoiding by purity of heart, 158
  body in art, ethical issues, 226
  Christ's teaching on, 103-105, 133, 152-156
  of David, 134
  definition of, 106-108
  ethos of redemption, 346
  in the heart, 142-144
  idolatry analogy, 139-140
  of Israel, 359
  language of the body, 366
  lust, 108-111
    Christ's teaching on, 156-159
    mutual attraction, compared to, 147-150
    passion of, 145-147
    relationship to, 154

marriage
  compared to, 107-108
  effect on, 140-141, 158
  Old Testament laws, 133-138
  prophets, teaching on, 137-142
  purity of heart, contrasted with, 212-213
  sinfulness of, 141-142
  woman caught in, Christ's attitude toward, 463-464

affirmation of life in Christ, 517-519

affirmation of marriage by continence for the kingdom of heaven, 285-287

agape, 320, 375

alone. *See* original solitude of man

angels, compared to resurrection of the body, 239-240

anger, 498-499

animals, sexual instinct of, 62-63, 282

Annunciation at Nazareth, 446-447, 467-468
  anointing of Christ by sinful woman, Christ's attitude toward, 465-466
  anonymity of body in art, 220
  anthropological content, definition of adultery, 106-108
  anthropomorphism of God, 452-453
  appropriation. *See* possession

Aquinas, Thomas
  purity, teaching on, 200
  resurrection of the body, teaching on, 240

Pauline
BOOKS & MEDIA

The Daughters of St. Paul operate book and media centers at the following addresses. Visit, call or write the one nearest you today, or find us on the World Wide Web, www.pauline.org

CALIFORNIA
 3908 Sepulveda Blvd, Culver City, CA 90230 310-397-8676
 5945 Balboa Avenue, San Diego, CA 92111 858-565-9181
 46 Geary Street, San Francisco, CA 94108 415-781-5180

FLORIDA
 145 S.W. 107th Avenue, Miami, FL 33174 305-559-6715

HAWAII
 1143 Bishop Street, Honolulu, HI 96813 808-521-2731
 Neighbor Islands call: 800-259-8463

ILLINOIS
 172 North Michigan Avenue, Chicago, IL 60601 312-346-4228

LOUISIANA
 4403 Veterans Memorial Blvd, Metairie, LA 70006 504-887-7631

MASSACHUSETTS
 Rte. 1, 885 Providence Hwy, Dedham, MA 02026 781-326-5385

MISSOURI
 9804 Watson Road, St. Louis, MO 63126 314-965-3512

NEW JERSEY
 561 U.S. Route 1, Wick Plaza, Edison, NJ 08817 732-572-1200

NEW YORK
 150 East 52nd Street, New York, NY 10022 212-754-1110
 78 Fort Place, Staten Island, NY 10301 718-447-5071

OHIO
 2105 Ontario Street, Cleveland, OH 44115 216-621-9427

PENNSYLVANIA
 9171-A Roosevelt Blvd, Philadelphia, PA 19114 215-676-9494

SOUTH CAROLINA
 243 King Street, Charleston, SC 29401 843-577-0175

TENNESSEE
 4811 Poplar Avenue, Memphis, TN 38117 901-761-2987

TEXAS
 114 Main Plaza, San Antonio, TX 78205 210-224-8101

VIRGINIA
 1025 King Street, Alexandria, VA 22314 703-549-3806

CANADA
 3022 Dufferin Street, Toronto, Ontario, Canada M6B 3T5 416-781-9131
 1155 Yonge Street, Toronto, Ontario, Canada M4T 1W2 416-934-3440

¡También somos su fuente para libros, videos y música en español!

ISBN 1-55586-344-2

Pub# 344-2

NCCB

Retreats for Diocesan Priest